SEVEN SONS
Millionaires and Vagabonds

Gift of Ruth Hultgren

Theodore A. Webb
February 2,000

Canadian Cataloguing in Publication Data

Webb, Theodore A.
  Seven sons, millionaires and vagabonds

  Includes bibliographical references and index.
  ISBN 1-55212-255-7

  1. Washburn family. 2. Maine--Biography. 3.
Politicians--Maine--Biography. 4. United States--Politics and
government--19th century. I. Title.
CT274.W373W42 1999 929'.2'0973 C99-910704-6

TRAFFORD

This book is published *on-demand* in cooperation with Trafford Publishing.
On-demand publishing is a unique process and service of making a book available for retail
sale to the public taking advantage of on-demand manufacturing and Internet marketing.
On-demand publishing includes promotions, retail sales, manufacturing, order fulfilment,
accounting and collecting royalties on behalf of the author.

Suite 2, 3050 Nanaimo St., Victoria, B.C. V8T 4Z1, CANADA

Phone	250-383-6864	Toll-free	1-888-232-4444 (Canada & US)
Fax	250-383-6804	E-mail	sales@trafford.com
Web site	www.trafford.com	TRAFFORD PUBLISHING IS A DIVISION OF TRAFFORD HOLDINGS LTD.	
Trafford Catalogue #99-0024		www.trafford.com/robots/99-0024.html	

10   9   8   7   6   5

SEVEN SONS
Millionaires and Vagabonds

Theodore A. Webb

Book of Contents

Chapters

Preface

There were Washburn warriors. There were non-combatant fighters as well: profiteers certainly, two millionaires, and two plenipotentiaries among seven. One brother, Elihu Washburne, "fought" for the re-election to the presidency of his friend, Abraham Lincoln; and though a civilian he befriended the warrior, Ulysses S. Grant, and guided him through his career in the military into the office of president. There were contemporaries who considered some of those "fighters" to be geniuses. Elihu, Cadwallader, Charles and William at different times in their careers were judged geniuses.

How these extraordinary men, their three sisters, father and mother, related to each other, to themselves and to society is part of this story. Thinking of the males in the family, each of the seven brothers was "his own man," to use a colloquialism. They were strongly-motivated individuals, each possessing his own distinctive talents and traits, with the range represented from genius to ordinary. When failures are included, as failures there were, these brothers are seen as Representative Men on the American scene.

The "Washburn phenomenon" antedates by 183 years the birth of the first of the children. In other words, what precedes Israel, Jr's., birth in 1813 was the landing of the first Washburn on the western edge of the Atlantic in 1630. Part of this book is an exposé of the now aged Washburn clan, but concentrating in one century a startling segment of this country's history. The book is about history as R.W. Emerson's described it. He saw "history as biography."

The story is about more in the American experience than the lives of the brothers and sisters. An attempt is made to reconstruct the context which was real to all of them, their growing up in poverty and reaching highly desirable positions as when one of them became a power next greatest to that of president of the country. Among other things, It is a story about Elihu Washburne and three presidents, one of whom, Abraham Lincoln, was rebuked to his face by Elihu; about a man who was supported by Washburne through the War and then catapulted into office; and about a third President, Rutherford B. Hayes, who declared that he wished to be associated with men like E.B. Washburne. Washburne was himself a reluctant nominee for the office of President in 1880.

History carried by the written word plays tricks in fortuitous ways so that some who deserve the plaudits of the masses remain for long unknown. There are not so many *greats* in any country's history that the people can afford to drop from the chronicles of the past those interesting imaginative citizens who helped make America what it is. Though the Washburns are not widely known, those seen to be the *greats* in the 19th century and who are known to every schoolchild were in most cases friends of the Washburns. Few whose names are remembered over the generations lived a life more to be appreciated and emulated than the lives of brothers Israel, Jr., Elihu, Cadwallader, Charles and William. Furthermore, familiar personages who associated with the Washburns and who are known to history buffs are not just Americans. E.B. Washburne's name was closely associated with leading French and German leaders in the tumultuous period of the Franco-Prussian war and communist uprising in Paris.

❖

The nature of regional and national politics was radically altered during the lifetime of the Washburns. They played a part in altering the power balance between the states and federal government. They were involved in bringing about some of the changes. William Hesseltine illustrates the transformation noting that at the ceremony surrounding the death of President Lincoln, "officers of the nation, senators and representatives, bore the pall between ranks of the nation's generals and admirals. They were followed by cabinet members and bureau chiefs. Far back in the teeming crowd, hardly more than spectators themselves, were the governors of the *once important states*."[i] In the way of example, at the start of the Civil War, Elihu's elder brother, Governor Israel Washburn, Jr., symbolized the power and leverage held by the heads of states. He was governor of the State of Maine. At that time, Elihu, serving in the House of Representatives, was a lesser figure in the political arena. He, however, lived to see his brother's Maine office become symbolic of the power shift, for in the funeral procession following President Lincoln's cortege, Governor Washburn trailed far behind those who now had status, as noted by historian Hesseltine. E.B. Washburne, on the other hand, symbolically signified the radical nature of the change. He was at the front of the great march. Indeed, he was co-leader of the procession which took to its final resting place the body of his friend, Abraham Lincoln.

This is a kind of parable then, introducing the reader to the complex lives of the Washburns, their significant roles in the arenas of politics, religion, economics--an American family which in modest ways shaped the United States during their century.

It has been my hope that the work produced with the seven Washburn brothers as central can provide a broad picture of what a somewhat typical American family, ambitious to achieve, was able to do in the America of the 19th and early 20th century. The thought which has been with me from the beginning is that students of American Studies, as well as of American history, will benefit from the resource offered.

❖

The making of this book has taken from the busy life of a minister 25 years of research and writing. The final production finds one appreciating what George Orwell once said, that "writing a book is like having a long and serious illness." Part of the research used up an entire sabbatical spent at the Library of Congress; and there were trips around the country where time was spent in historical societies in Maine, Illinois, Wisconsin, and California as well as Washington, D.C., and some of the southern states. Acquiring a more extensive awareness of our history and people has made this protracted venture rewarding. Rewarding and appreciated also has been assistance provided by many friends. My wife has been a patient critic, my daughter, Christine has done duty as editor, enriching the written words, and my son, Noel, has been a source of inspiration in ways I cannot number. Edmund Sherman of the University of New York at Albany, has given me encouragement over the years, as has James Hulse of the University of Nevada. Thomas Whigham, the University of Georgia, has been enormously helpful as I studied and wrote about Charles Ames Washburn, the enigma among the brothers. I will always be grateful for the attention given to my work by the late Dr. Betty Chmaj of Sacramento, American Studies scholar and teacher. Billie Gammon of Livermore, Maine, with her extensive knowledge of Maine, of Livermore history and of the Washburns, should in my estimation be joining those helpful

---

[i] Emphasis added.

scholars with their Ph.D's, she also deserving to be Dr. Gammon. Finally, many of those at work in historical societies in Maine, Illinois, Wisconsin, Minnesota and California have my profound gratitude.

❖

A title discarded as seeming too facetious for a serious work was *My mother made me do it, my father told me how.* The title was intended to suggest--and I believe it does suggest--what all the Washburn children might wish to assert that their mother in important ways remained a vital part of their lives from birth to the end of their time, and that their father instructed and prepared them for the work they undertook. Nurture more than nature guided the mother's offspring and in such forceful ways that the more contemporary language could have seemed useful. While it will appear to be true, as has been said, that one mother is every mother, there are different degrees of influence rendered by different matriarchs. The results of some efforts is magnificent and warrants tributes which the Washburns over the generations have continued to pay to Martha.

Chapter One

A FAMILY WITHOUT EQUAL

This saga of a down-east Yankee family's successes and failures began in an obscure village in the State of Maine. The Town of Livermore, settled on a plateau, was a village of a dozen farm families strewn over the tableland. Across the plateau ran a country road. Ascending from the south it lifted up from the plateau to the town's cemetery at the north of town. At the edge of their world villagers could look west and watch the changing skies playing over a dark silhouette of mountains.

Farm buildings were at the center of the tableland, home to the family of Israel and Martha Washburn. A stone's throw from the farm was a one-room schoolhouse marking the edge of the level area on the north. The farmhouse was centered between the schoolhouse on the north and a church immediately to the south of the Washburn home.

Israel Washburn

In this out-of-the way community lived the Washburns parents and their ten children, three daughters and seven sons. The children of the family of Israel and Martha, living intense ambitious lives, furnish material for an American romance possessing stuff of stark reality. Myth or fiction is hardly required to embellish the tale of the brothers Israel, Jr., Algernon Sidney, Elihu Benjamin, Cadwallader Colden, Charles Ames, Samuel Benjamin, and William Drew. The daughters were Martha Benjamin, Mary Benjamin, and Caroline Ann. Given repetitive use of "Banjamin" we are not surprised to learn that mother Martha -- sometimes called Patty -- was a Benjamin, daughter of Lieut. Samuel Benjamin who was at the battles of Lexington on April 19, 1775, Bunker Hill, Monmouth, Yorktown and other battles of the Revolutionary War.

❖

Patty Washburn

In his Introduction to *James and John Stuart Mill,* Bruce Mazlish reflected views the young Mill expressed on the theme of "generations and their importance." "Mill," wrote Mazlish, " . . . linked his belief in progress with the change of generations. He thought of such change as occurring in intervals of one generation."(1) With generation after generation of Washburns, the Mill's thesis is demonstrated. Local fame of the several brothers of Livermore increased following which they acquired national and then international renown, exceeding the fame of the generation of father and mother Washburn. The apex was reached by Elihu Benjamin Washburne(2), celebrity known and admired in France and Germany as well as his native country, state and town.

Forebears of Israel Washburn, Sr., were among the earliest settlers on the continental shelf. Father Israel's lineage trailed back to England and the founder of the tribe where a Washbourne was knighted on the field of battle by William the Conqueror.(3)

Elihu was the third son born to Israel and Martha. The name *Elihu* does not say who this boy and man was and tells nothing of his lineage. The *Book of Job* depicts an Elihu as one of Job's irritants with his long speeches and his self-importance. Elihu's middle name, Benamin, however, tells a story important to the Washburn chronicle. Leon Edel writes,

C.C. Washburn

> When certain children, possessed of a strong will and drive, bear a proud name, they acquire a sense of their own significance; the name carries an emanation of grandeur or greatness; represents on occasion a kind of consecration and gives a sense of vocation, purpose, status, responsibility.(4)

This was the case with Elihu as well as other of the Washburn brothers. Elihu's grandfather, Lieutenant Samuel Benjamin, entered the U.S. Army when the war with England began and he saw it through to the end. He was the fourth settler in the town of Livermore. Early settlers were important among citizens of the town for the generations immediately following the Revolutionary War. Elihu's grandfather on his mother's side lent the Washburn children a sense of their importance, and perhaps played a part in the choice of two of the brothers' attending the military academy at Annapolis. One, Cadwallader, without schooling at Annapolis, became a Major General and served during the Civil War. A third brother, Samuel, became commander of ships in the War. The name, *Benjamin*, given in turn to four of the Washburn offspring tells about mother Martha's importance also as a decision-maker in the family. She bestowed her maiden name upon Elihu, Samuel, Martha, and Mary.

❖

The making of Elihu Benjamin can be attributed to place as well as to people. Livermore citizens had a hardy history. Stories were told in downeast families about contests between the Indian and white man to control the territory where the town was located. Elihu knew that his town was the tribal home of the Androscoggin Indians, then considered the most hostile of all the tribes of the region.(5) He learned about atrocities committed by Indians and whites alike. Citizens in the area knew about the decision of the General Court of Massachusetts to make war on the Androscoggins at the time Maine was a district of the Commonwealth. They knew that Major Church and his company of soldiers hunted down enemy Indians, putting whole villages to the tomahawk or sword. They knew how Indians retaliated, capturing whites and selling them to the French in Canada. One story is told of a woman carrying a child who could not keep up with the Indians. An Indian took the child from the mother's arms and crushed its skull with a tomahawk. The English likewise, hating Indians, took vengeance upon captured tribal members. Captain James Cargill's company, meeting a band of friendly Indians, shot 12 of them and took their scalps. One of the soldiers in Cargill's company saw an Indian woman with a child, shot her, and as the woman in her last throes pleaded with the soldier to protect her child, the soldier killed the baby before the mother's dimming eyes. So it was that when Elihu's brother, Charles, wrote a novel, he created as villains, "Indians, gamblers and cut-throats."(6)

Men alive in Livermore during Elihu's growing up were becoming characters for the history books. Elijah Fisher of Livermore was George Washington's body-guard. Thomas Chase served with John Paul Jones. Lieut. Samuel Benjamin, Elihu's grandfather, as noted, fought in the entire War. Some of these men, together with Daniel Holman, John Walker and Josiah Wyer, may have traded at Israel Washburn, Sr.'s, country store in Livermore. Holman was one of the minutemen at Concord, Massachusetts. John Walker was with Arnold's expedition to Quebec, and Josiah Wyer was at the battle of Bunker Hill, as was grandfather Benjamin. Elihu probably felt he was on the fringes of living history, both because he knew, or knew about, citizens with the dust of battle powdering uniforms tucked away in attic trunks.

Elihu knew about the Washburn family's part played in settling America. As children of the family grew up in Livermore they heard their father and mother relate anecdotes revealing the personality and character of figures familiar in the early

Martha Stevenson   **Mary Buffum**   **Caroline Washburn**

history of the country. On one occasion, Israel, Jr., was reading aloud to his father who had lost his sight in old age. Junior read about Miles Standish and John Alden. When he finished, father Israel said the Aldens who descended from John settled in Middleboro, Massachusetts.

> It was always their custom to pack their poorest beef at the bottom of the barrel so that if they should not live to reach it, they would have made sure of the best.(7)

Israel, Jr.'s, commentary was, "canny people, those descendants of 'Puritan Priscilla'."

❖

There is an American counterpart to Jewish tradition in which a mother with child prayed that her offspring would be a son and "savior of the nation." In early America, a mother feeling movement in the womb expressed the hope that her child might be a son and "President of the United States." A more modest dream was that the son might become a governor, a leader of industry, or a great warrior. Mother Martha had some of those expectations when her children began to arrive. She demonstrated her hope for his greatness when her first son was born. Mother instructed father to "take Israel, Jr., upstairs 'so he may rise,'" invoking a popular superstition of the day, but more importantly illustrating an attitude which induced mother Martha to embrace the superstition. Martha's words have been remembered and several generations of descendants have invoked her words to explain in part why her sons "rose." It was as though she anticipated what Algie M. Simons, in *Class Struggles in America*, noted, that the capitalist mind would make possible an "infinite opportunity to 'rise' --the highest ideal of the bourgeois mind." Her lively ambition was demonstrated in her prediction. She said confidently that her firstborn son would be governor of Maine, as indeed he was. Mother Martha, ambitious for her sons, instructed them to "aim at the stars," assuring them that if they did not hit anything they would have the satisfaction of seeing their arrow go up and come back again.

❖

Struggle against poverty was part of the story of the Washburn family and why they succeeded. In the 1830s, the Great Depression found Americans having to leave their homes. Children's schooling was interrupted, Many ill-educated youth went to work in factories, stores, or did a man's job on the family farm. Teen-age youths found work in the cities. Washburns like thousands of others went west. Father Israel owned a country store and during the depression saw his store closed. Farmers who traded there were given groceries on credit and the time came when Farmer Brown could not pay his bills. Inability to pay bills was a mark of shame for the penurious Israel and Martha. The pain of poverty therefore sent Washburn sons spilling forth from their happy home in the village. Israel, Jr., went to live with an uncle, Attorney Reuel Washburn. Sidney went to Boston, a ragamuffin of 14 on the streets looking for work. Elihu at 13 did a man's work for five months to pay off a 25-dollar debt. Cadwallader clerked in a store at Hallowell, 20 miles from home. Samuel went to sea. Brother number five, Charles Ames Washburn, was young enough to benefit from early successes of older brothers. Arrangements were made for Charles to be educated at Bowdoin College in Brunswick, Maine. The youngest son, William, was also sent to Bowdoin.

Sadly, seeing the family break up, one-time teacher, father Israel, had a lesson to teach the children before they scattered. In hidden places of memory the Washburn boys and girls heard their father's voice and saw him again teaching his lesson. He held a bundle of sticks in his hands. With the sticks their father illustrated graphically the impossibility of breaking the bundle he held. But with a flair for the dramatic he announced that each stick taken separately could be broken, and he set about breaking them one by one. The lesson represented for children the importance of mutual dependence. As they moved into their teens and twenties, the brothers grew apart geographically as residents of Massachusetts, Illinois, Wisconsin, Minnesota, California and Maine, but when any of them needed help, one or more of the wealthier brothers obliged. Throughout their lives, for example, Charles and Samuel needed assistance. Israel, Sidney, Elihu, Cadwallader, and William, though not always generous, became their benefactors.

In later life the eldest sister, Martha, needed help. Elihu was at hand to improve the lot of her husband, Charles Stephenson. Elihu lived protectively in the block adjacent to his sister, Martha, and her family. In La Crosse, Cadwallader took Caroline into his home. Later she became dependent upon her brother, William, who helped provide a home for her in Minneapolis. Sister Mary's husband was given a substantial position working for Cadwallader.

Samuel Washburn

Most of the seven Washburn brothers fared well. Four of the seven were numbered among the first families in cities where they settled, adding luster to their names as they became U.S. Representatives, a Senator, diplomats, a Major General, a commander, governors, authors, business tycoons and banker. The depression experience then drove family members to become ambitious and industrious. Each became an achiever. Israel, Jr., the eldest among the brothers, became a model encouraging the others to strive. Israel, Jr., intelligent and a natural leader, became an example when he left home.(8) He settled down to study in his uncle's home and became a lawyer, the first of five attorneys among the seven brothers. Israel, Sidney, Elihu, Cadwallader, and William were unusual in the intensity with which they aspired to achieve goals they set for themselves. Charles and Samuel, while eager to succeed, stumbled and blundered in ways to be explored in this book. Stumble though Charles did, he led a remarkable life as gold miner, newspaper man, duelist, author of fiction and non-fiction books, and United States Minister to Paraguay where he became infamous in that country but famous elsewhere for his exploits.

Struggles experienced by the brothers did not have to be repeated by the sisters. Martha, a good student, was not unattractive, possessing bright, piercing eyes, a Roman nose, and a prominent chin like her father's. She graduated from the

C.A. Washburn

one-room school a few steps removed from the farm at Livermore and attended the Liberal Institute in Waterville, Maine. She became a teacher and as teacher was paid $5.50 a month for services -- "exclusive of board."(9) Despite discouraging ordeals in teaching she remained in the profession until she married, fearful that she would otherwise have to work in a factory. Yet this Washburn, Martha, was optimistic and cheerful, "enjoy[ing] everything," she allowed, "that is at all enjoyable" grateful she did not have to experience privation.

Mary's anxieties revolved around her love life. This Washburn was a long-faced, thin-lipped, stern, mannish-looking woman, austere with a hair style like her mother's, parted in the middle and pulled severely around the head and over her ears. Middle sister Mary feared she would never find a mate. Matchmaker Israel, Jr., introduced her to a carpenter in the town of Orono where Israel practiced law. The carpenter's name was Gustavus Buffum. Gustavus put an engagement ring on Mary's finger, promised to marry her, and then headed west to the gold country. He returned eight years later, joining Mary at Livermore, and the two were married.

Caroline was a gentle, pleasant sister with an open face and kind eyes. She did not know poverty but, of course, heard about it from her mother, father and older brothers. Caroline attracted the interest of a young man, Freeland, about whom a Bowdoin classmate, General O.O. Howard of Civil War fame, wrote, "[Freeland,] you have a fondness for the [opposite] sex." Freeland Holmes found in Caroline the "pretty wife and all else which [was] essential to [his] happiness." Caroline Washburn's hardship came after her young husband, a medical doctor, went off to war. Holmes died leaving her and two children to fend for themselves. Carrie, as Caroline was called by the family, returned to Livermore and later went to live, first with Cadwallader and finally to Minneapolis where she ended her days, dying in 1920.

One hundred and seven years after the birth of Israel, Jr., in 1813, Caroline closed the final chapter of the Washburn saga, the last of the generation to die.

❖

MACROCOSMIC AND MICROCOSMIC VIEWS

Washburn siblings lived in a time of momentous change. Even family structures were being transformed. Class structure was undergoing innovation. The Puritan community of the previous century had produced a number of classes building strong, stable, extended-families in the face of poverty. Depressions, however, brought a fragmentation of households. Typically, artisan families imparted values and skills needed by children which would lead to upward mobility. "Few boys escaped being told that they might become President."(10) According to Max Weber, values provided an ethic promoting "the development of capitalistic enterprise in America." The Washburn children were authentic archetypes, Representative of the artisan class evolving from the Puritan ethos with distinct emphasis upon capitalistic ventures.

A child's values derive from experiences with the family. Who Elihu became can be gauged by the social, political and religious ideas preached and practiced by Israel and Martha Washburn. It has been said that "habit, conditioning, and family relations account for almost all human behavior . . . "(11) In a cultivated, democratic setting, the Washburn children saw their mother and father sharing the tasks of maintaining the home where there was a minimum of the traditional, patriarchal customs practiced by the father.(12) Children pursued their careers in homemaking, politics and industry, and their parents, observing them in their respective careers, recognized important values they had attempted to transmit validated in the persons of Elihu and his brothers and sisters, more particularly in the realm of politics which was of extreme interest to father Israel.

Like their parents, Washburn children championed Whig political views.(13) They adopted the Whig emphasis on material wealth and cognitive abilities. A Whig principle which impressed itself upon the children was the importance of public speaking. They would have agreed with George Santayana who said that "eloquence is a republican art."(14) While they were not known for their eloquence when later in life they served in Congress, there were times when Israel, Jr., excelled in the art. Prominent constituents wrote telling the Maine legislator he was another Daniel Webster.(15) Of Elihu it was said his style of oratory was easy, off-hand and more convincing than that of any other member of the House.

Whigs had strong feelings about family and home. During their lives, the brothers centered their attention on the homes they constructed in Galena, La Crosse, Orono, Hallowell, and Minneapolis. When the house in Livermore burned in 1867, the brothers cooperated in rebuilding. The house they built still stands, a testimony to the children's acceptance of values emphasized by Israel and Martha. Another pronounced Whig value was education and the cultivation of the mind. A family tale has it that mother Martha rebuked one of her children, saying it was better to have brains in one's head than tails to one's coat. While Israel, Jr., lacked a formal education, he was an avid reader and scholar as is evidenced in his congressional addresses and published essays. His understanding of the writings of Jefferson, Madison, Rush, John Adams, and a host of other early American political essayists were often mentioned in speeches. In an interview published in a

Charles Sumner

Boston newspaper, Charles Sumner spoke of "the remarkable oration of Hon. Israel Washburn, Jr.," after Washburn delivered a Fourth of July address in Maine. The Massachusetts Senator, himself counted among America's great orators, mentioned Israel's style, his logic in argument, and his eloquence. "Such a voice from Maine ought to be a key-note." Sumner wrote Israel to congratulate him for one of his essays, saying "we are all under obligation to you who has put [your argument] so clearly . . . and persuasively."(16) These complimentary words from Sumner were in writing to Washburn despite the fact that Israel disagreed with some of the Senator's views expressed in an *Atlantic Monthly* article published following the Civil War in which Sumner asserted that the rebel states had ceased to be states and were territories.(17) Israel contended in a letter to Sumner that the southern states were states having no administration and no government.

A treatise by Israel was carried in an issue of the *Universalist Quarterly*.(18) What becomes clear upon reading his essay is that Israel, Jr., studied the masters in English and American literature and held in high regard Walter Savage Landor and Charles Lamb. That Washburn could be loyal in his devotion to these two whose views of life were antipodal reveals in the scholar, Israel, a depth he was able to plumb to find affinities.

Charles and William Washburn were graduates of Bowdoin College in Maine and their writings, particularly Charles', show the two to be well educated. A few years after graduation Charles adopted the writing profession as a newsman, composing editorials for his San Francisco newspaper, publishing fiction and non-fiction works. Washburn's daughter, Lilian, said of her father that he was witty and sarcastic with the pen; "each [word was] barbed and aimed at a spot where he knew it would hurt the most."(19) After graduating from Bowdoin William studied law and was a practicing attorney.

Elihu felt comfortable as a student without the formality of undergraduate university training. He read widely, not only in law, including in his study prominent authors of English and American letters. His choice of poetry, and quotations pasted in his scrap book, however, reveal pedestrian taste. A collection of Washburne clippings from books, magazines and newspapers indicate his greatest interest, not in literary matters, critical or otherwise, but in politics and business topics. Elihu took from newspapers poems about mother, comical matters, human interest stories, such as the observation made by an Arab chief who visited Paris and when asked what impressed him said, "The stars that you put inside the lamps every evening."

"An Extraordinary Revelation," gained the attention of the Ambassador, as well as articles about "Boiling Eggs," and "The Ideal Lovers." Many of the choices of scrap book material are indicative of Elihu's interest in humor which reveals frailties in the human species about which he could laugh. Washburne's published writings, including a two-volume work on France, were read by thousands, many of whom appreciated his style and stimulating content about France during the Franco-Prussian war and the communist uprising in Paris.(20)

MATTERS WHICH INFLUENCE IN SUBSTANTIAL WAYS

The front porch is an American invention.(21) The Washburns made the most of the invention. The large frame building constructed by the family in 1867 has a deep porch with a railing built the correct height for feet to rest upon. The porch provided a view to the west where foul weather could be seen gathering to descend upon onlookers from miles away. At night family members looked out on the sky sparkling with stars to the delight of adult and child. Sidney waxed poetic, writing from the porch,

> Contrary to the surmises of the crowd last night sitting on the pizarro [sic] till 11 o'clock, watching the clouds zig zag over the cold watery moon, passing on in meditation fancy free, that we should have a heyday, or hayday.[sic]

Visitors joining the Washburns on the porch, sat in their ladder-back rockers, and there, guests and children had what father Israel referred to as his "pulls." Each of the boys, except William who was almost of another generation, had such porches at the fronts of their homes. Israel in Orono, Maine, was able to sit outside and look up and down the Main Street, the best way to know what was happening in town. Elihu's porch was just off a principal road leading in and out of Galena. The Washburne

Adele Washburne

family members knew who came into town, who left and when. Cadwallader's home in La Crosse, Wisconsin, stood at the center of an entire city block with a piazza enabling family and visiting friends to rock in their chairs watching neighborhood children at play. For the Washburn family convened on the porch of the Livermore home became a visual experience that remained vivid in Elihu's memory. He felt the presence of the place of his birth while living in far away

Paris. There he recalled picturesque Livermore scenes, the changing weather patterns about which members of the family wrote lyrically, and about the nearby hills where children and parents slid on the slopes in winter and farmed in summer. In the middle of Paris as the Franco-Prussian war raged around him, Elihu thought of the hill which rose from the plateau to the north of the farm. A few hundred yards up that hill, Washburn and Benjamin ancestors lay in their graves. From the porch was a view of a pond down the hill where children went swimming in summer and skating in winter. All the scenes were imprinted indelibly, as sharply etched as Currier and Ives paintings, recalled on the instant and keeping Elihu loyally devoted to his childhood home.

In old age, when his wife Adele died, Elihu returned home to Livermore where he wallowed in despair at his loss. It was exactly the place he wanted to be, surrounded by memories of childhood times. When he was to leave the Livermore home after one of his visits, he revealed his emotional attachment writing in the *Family Journal*,

> Goodbye Norlands. Goodbye the pleasant, blazing wood fire in the sunny south west room. Goodbye pleasant, genial, cheerful old Gramps (his aged father,) and goodbye Sam and Addie and little Ben.(22)

THE CULTIVATED SOULS
"The Religious Equation"

Universalist Church - Norlands

A hearty laugh was heard all the way down the aisle and up on the platform by the Reverend in his pulpit. Something struck youthful Elihu and Cadwallader as funny and church members were shocked when shrill laughter interrupted the sermon. There was an informality about Universalist church services, however, and laughter in church was not considered sacrilegious. However, the boy's laughter intruded upon the attention of listeners and was, it was thought, an affront to the preacher. The boys felt the lash of their mother's tongue as they left the service walking across the lawn to the farmhouse. It was an experience they did not forget. It was said by Elihu that he and Cadwallader never again laughed in services.

The Universalist church attended by the Washburns was half on Washburn land, and suitably--given the name--half on Pray property. Located in a village with a population of fewer than 200 families, still there were times when the country church was filled. Distinguished ministers sometimes occupied the village pulpit. When a popular preacher spoke, he had difficulty getting through the audience to the pulpit. On one occasion, the crowd was so dense that the Governor of the State who was the speaker had to be lifted through a window. A world renowned diva, Anna Louise Cary, sang at the church, filling the pews as well as chairs very likely placed on the stage behind the pulpit.

❖

An American historian concludes that Universalism in the United States, along with the Unitarian and Quaker movements, commanded "the allegiance of a distinguished if not a numerous body."(23) The Universalist movement included among other well-known persons, Benjamin Rush, signer of the Declaration of Independence, and Clara Barton, founder of the American Red Cross. The religion taught by ministers and lay members was appealing in a country where success and happiness in this life were likely prospects. With their optimism, there was a carryover into the concept of future. The future in an afterlife was not a dreaded likelihood for people like the Washburns. While the belief in future life was feared in the religion of Calvinism which had been brought over the waters from Geneva, Universalism stressed belief in the possibility of success in this life and salvation in an afterlife. Universalism was part of the optimistic approach engendered in the secular life of the century. The movement was advantaged in its rivalry with forbidding, gloomy Calvinism.

In the pulpit, Universalist preachers emphasized this life, discussing problems which face people in their daily existence. The religion sought to instill values of honesty, hard work, loyalty, individualism, and regard for community. Some adherents in the religious movement formed communal groups. The Reverend Adin Ballou(24) at Hopedale, Massachusetts, organized such a group. William S. Balch expressed a view which prompted Universalist historian Russell Miller to write that it was Adin Ballou who attempted to make the following words of Balch an actuality. Said Balch," . . . [T]he countervailing and overpowering influence of evil shall be taken away, and the great and positive ends of human life pursued in concert."(25) The religion's appeal grew out of Universalism's reaction to pervasive Calvinism which taught a dreaded orthodoxy foretelling a time of eternal punishment, disheartening to Universalists and Unitarians alike. For the orthodox, eternal damnation was reserved to be endured not only by those who performed heinous deeds, but for those who were not elected by God, irrespective of the laudable tenor of their lives.

The Reverend D.T. Stevens, occasional preacher at Livermore, said that Universalism "delivers those who all their lifetime have been subject to bondage through fear of death," saying that the religion "makes man feel that he belongs to a universal brotherhood." A preacher at the Livermore church was G.W. Quinby. Quinby said, perhaps in the presence of Elihu, that "a purgatory, and an endless hell of fire and flames, peopled with devils and damned spirits, suffering tortures inconceivable and eternal, these horrid dogmas were all taught by the Romish church." Anti-Roman Catholic statements such as those pronounced by Quinby could not have prejudiced Elihu. When Elihu was Ambassador to France he was praised by French and American Catholics for his effort to save Archbishop Darboy from execution, and for his success in rescuing nuns from the hands of Parisian revolutionaries during the communist uprising.

Many religious views considered of vital importance to the orthodox were either derided by Universalists, or Universalists emphasized contrary convictions. The Arian-Athanasian dispute over the question of Jesus as created being or part of a godhead continued into the 19th century. Universalists were Arian, believing Jesus to have been a man, the son of Mary and Joseph. Origen, one of the early Church Fathers and a Universalist, was anathematized in the 7th century by the Catholic denomination for dismissing the idea of hell. Universalists of Washburn's time considered Origen's notion of universal salvation, deemed heretical by Roman Catholics, a central issue of their faith.(26)

Leadership in the denomination broke from the practice of orthodox churches wherein members were expected to agree unanimously on creedal statements devised by the clergy. Ministers and laity continued to write and re-write statements of faith. They made it a practice to append a sentence to adopted affirmations making it clear that statements adopted at conclaves should not be taken as creedal tests.

Members of the movement invoke a 15th-century Universalist, Caspar Schwenkfeld, who said,

> In Christianity there can be no standing still;
> there must be progress and growth. Let no one
> allow his mind to be found by creeds and articles
> of faith so that he may not accept something
> better.(27)

Notable in Universalism also, preparing the politically astute Washburns for the abolition movements of the 1840s, '50s and '60s, was a 1790 Universalist Article of Faith calling for the abolition of slavery. The story of Washburns which follows relates the tale of their involvement in that central issue of 19th century, slavery.

❖

Some of the humor enjoyed by Elihu and the Washburns was a by-product of religious exchanges. The family chuckled when they heard what Uncle Jack said to Baptist Elder Norton. Uncle Jack said, "he'd be d---d [sic] if he'd belong to a church that wouldn't allow him to swear when his oxen corked themselves." The Washburns chortled over the story of a reverend, certainly not one of their own preachers, who visited a poor but saintly woman on her deathbed. The clergyman wanting to try her faith said, "Janet, what would you say if after all he has done for you, God should let you drop into hell?" She answered, "E'en as He likes. He'll lose more than I do."(28) Someone asked a stern Baptist what he thought of the spire on the Universalist church in Livermore. The Baptist said in droning tones that it would be a good place for the devil to light when he flew from Farmington to Buckfield. This bit of humor was repeated by the Washburns whose church's spire was located between the two towns.

Chapter Two

FATHER ISRAEL AND MOTHER MARTHA

Farmer, teacher, raconteur Israel Washburn, father of a brood of ten, was to his children "the ultimate optimist." When their father was blind and in his 90s there was laughter in his voice and he continued to tell his hopeful, often humorous stories. One morning, the eighty-four year old father came from his bedroom into the kitchen where Israel, Jr., was writing in the Washburn Journal. Israel, Jr., kept writing as his father entered:

> The Autocrat of the Breakfast Table comes in *and* his genial voice. He sings a Hymn of Trust, bringing pleasantness to the Senior's face.(1)

He looked up to see father. Yes, his father was old. His coarse, wrinkled features looked like a dried catalpa leaf. However, Israel, Jr., knew that even at his age, people effect him the way the sun makes the rose to bloom. Whoever came into father's presence turned those crinkled lines into the arc of a smile.

A cynic might say, a reason for Israel's optimism was his wife, Martha. Martha kept Israel alive and fed, watching over her blind, easy-going husband, from the time he lost his eyesight three years before Martha's death. He was tended after that by his generous and thoughtful sons and daughters, and by Samuel in particular.

Israel, Sr. had a large head and a high forehead. His eyes were alive and as ready to smile as his mouth. Dressed in his Sunday, go-to-meeting clothes, his great head was sunk into a wing collar which gathered around his chin like a suit of mail on a medieval warrior. Father Israel, called the Venerable, was as said a raconteur, known throughout the district as a man of cheerful disposition. Horatio Livermore in distant California once told one of Israel's sons he remembered his father "as a man of humor and dry wit."(2) It was said by those who knew Abraham Lincoln that father Washburn rivaled Lincoln as a story-teller. One of the boys recalled that "Father makes it light within, dark as it is outside." As the children grew older and learned about the dark side of life, some of them may have thought of their father as Pollyanish, having what G.K. Chesterton called "a mania for declaring when things are going badly that all is well."

Father Israel taught school as a young man. Later as teacher-father he adopted entertaining methods of conveying ideas and instilling attitudes in the youthful members of his family, like the able teacher he was. His stories, while often amusing, taught lessons in history, psychology, and character. A story which had a lasting affect upon the children was told by father Israel about Joseph Coolidge of Livermore. The children knew the Coolidges. Lieutenant Daniel Coolidge was a member of their church. That made the story more interesting and their listening more intense. The Washburns were sitting around the table with father at the head. The story told by the Venerable father was about the time Coolidge came to Livermore.

There was, father explained, a great scarcity of provisions in the town at that time. Coolidge's family had no food. Mr. Coolidge went to Deacon Livermore and asked for a loan of corn. The Deacon had no corn but he gave money to Coolidge and said he must go to a town on the Kennebec River and buy food. Off went Coolidge on his horse, said father swinging his fork in an arc. The children brightened, listening more attentively. Coolidge, said Israel, was successful in his quest for provisions. He made his purchases and started the journey back to Livermore. It was late at night when he reached the Androscoggin river. The ferry was on the other side of the river, and the ferryman lived so far away that he could not be roused to come for his customer. How would Coolidge get home to feed the family? Mr. Coolidge, said Israel, Sr., plunged into the river, swam to the other side, took the boat and crossed back to where the horse was tethered. He then re-crossed to the west side of the Androscoggin.

Father said that when Mr. Coolidge reached his home at two o'clock in the morning he woke his wife and she made him a Johnny cake. "That Johnny cake," said Coolidge, "was the sweetest bread I ever ate." And Father Israel then made an observation which he hung onto the end of the tale. Conscious of the importance of history, he added, "Mr. Coolidge's father 'was the first man killed in the battle of Lexington.'"

In this story told by the teacher-father were classic themes of literature and theology. There was suffering, redemption, private initiative, generosity, application of talents, heroic identification, and a denouement of humor. The effect of his addendum, calling attention to Joseph Coolidge's father, implies that Joseph was part of a continuing history. It might have been in father Israel's mind that a son carries the genes of his father, the hero who died in Concord at the hands of the British. Joseph Coolidge was the son of a revolutionary, and that was important. Father wished that to be remembered. Since Joseph's father was who he was, it was not the son's personal achievements but the fact of his inheritance from his honored father that gave young Coolidge dignity and identity. Father Washburn felt it helped to be a Coolidge. And, of course, by implication, it helped to be a Washburn.

The story-telling father impressed the children with his exceptional memory. When he was eighty-four years old, father Israel could stretch a still vital memory to bring into consciousness incidents he had learned about people who lived in 1690! What the father said to Israel, Jr. on one occasion was convoluted but illustrated what the children came to realize, that memory for their father was tied to the fact that people were central in their father's life. The incident which tested father's memory came about when Hannibal Hamlin and Israel, Jr. were riding together on the lecture circuit during an election campaign. Senator Hamlin asked who was living on the old Deacon Livermore farm. Israel, Jr., one of Livermore's historians, was unable to provide the answer. The next day, when the eldest son told his father about Hannibal Hamlin's question, it evoked a lengthy response from the old man. Father Israel said that the person living at the Livermore place was a Mr. Cummings:

> Millet Cummings son of Jonathan Millet
> Cummings of Paris, [Maine]. His mother was
> a Rumford woman, grand daughter of the Rev.
> Dr. Hemminway of Old Wells. Cummings
> (sic) wife is a daughter of Eunice Merrill, nee
> Livermore, Da.. of Uncle Amos who was
> related to Dea. Livermore. The common
> ancestor was Samuel Livermore who died Dec.

5, 1690. He had sons -- inter alies [sic] --Thomas and Jonathan. Thomas was a Deacon and had Nathaniel, b. April 13, 1713 d. 1783, this Nathaniel had *Amos* father of Eunice b. June 3, 1765. Jonathan b. 1678 d. 1705, had Samuel b. Mar. 14, 1701 d. Aug. 7, 1773, had *Elijah* b. Mar. 4, 1730-1. d. Aug. 5, 1808.(3)

Israel, Jr., said that his father remembered that when he was a child five years old he advocated the adoption of the federal constitution!

When father Israel was critical of others, as he sometimes was, his criticisms were tinged with whimsy. His stories sometimes required reflection before an intended meaning became clear. The classic "put down," for example, is seen in a story told by father Washburn as he regaled his small audience of wife, sons and daughters. To appreciate the thrust of the tale it must be remembered that the essential democrat disdains rank or any display of superiority. This was an attitude familiar to Maineites a century ago, and continues to the present day. If a person, such as the medical doctor in a story told by father Washburn, were to pull rank, then the story was to be told with an overlay of downeast humor.

"Old Sam Johnson," said Israel, "was given hodge-podge for supper by the lady of the house entertaining him. She said to Sam Johnson,

'This is very good, Dr. Johnson.'

'Yes, for hogs,' replied the doctor.

'Pray let me give you some more of it,' said Madam."(4)

The telling of the story helped the Washburn clan members to retain their essentially democratic disposition, such as is implicit in the father's tale. Whether or not the subtility was conveyed for all members of his small audience, as when the madam slipped in an insult, calling the doctor a "hog," remains a question. There are downeasterners who refuse to see intended humor.

Virtue and vice are two sides of Puritan thrift. On an occasion when Israel, Jr., finished reading to his blind father about Miles Standish his father said about the Aldens that they settled in Middleboro, [Massachusetts]. It was always their custom, explained the father, to pack their poorest beef at the bottom of the barrel so that "if they should not live to reach it, they would have made sure of [having] the best."(5)

The values were imperative to the father and were cherished by his children when they were grown men, --the virtues of honesty, justice, generosity, hard work, responsibility, and patriotism. With exceptions yet to be noted, the brothers' lives bore out those virtues with distinction in the fields of law, politics, business enterprise, government, and religion.

The father of the family was a walking encyclopedia of facts concerning the perennially interesting subjects of religion and politics. A New England newspaper, the *Galaxy*, brought political news to the Washburn household, along with the *Advocate* published in Hallowell, Maine. The Lewiston *Journal* and the Portland *Advertiser*, together with a Universalist newspaper edited by the Reverend William Drew, were delivered regularly to the home. Books published in England as well as the United States lined the parlor shelves. The father of the hilltop farmhouse could speak the name of every member of Congress and he knew the districts from which each member came. "He was always *au courant* with our public affairs and

[with] the principle events of the world," wrote the Galena, Illinois, son, Elihu.(6)

❖

There is above all for these pages mother Martha of the blue eyes and brown hair, --stern, determined and forceful. Martha's eyes were bright as a bird's, her mouth was soft. She had open, oval features and a ready smile, possessed a strong survival instinct, perhaps influenced by her father's Revolutionary War stories. She possessed an excess of energy and ambition which were transferred to each of her sons.

Martha Benjamin married Israel at age nineteen. The marriage ceremony received the benediction of the minister; the young husband saddled his horse and Martha, taking his hand, stepped on his extended foot, rose up onto the pillion behind the saddle, and said, "Go ahead, Israel. I'm with you." In her eyes, the commitment was for life in all untoward circumstances, in good times and bad. She turned out to be self-assertive as wife and mother of the small band of Washburns. She was supportive of Israel, a husband who was a great talker, and a student of the political scene in America. To this day, looking upon likenesses of Martha is to be held hypnotically by a woman who is saying, as she doubtless said to her husband and children, "Make something of yourself. Do not delay. This life is yours in this country which is yours. Make the most of it. Succeed!" Mother Martha had unswerving faith in the ability of her children "to rise." In their childhood and youth Martha fixed upon them her assurance that they would succeed. Israel, Jr. knew that in accordance with his mother's expectations he was to be governor of Maine. Her ambition for the children is illustrated in a superstitious sentiment expressed by Martha. When Israel, Jr. was born she instructed his father to "take Israel upstairs so he may rise."(7)

A bonnet pulled her hair close and straight around her long cherubic face. Her square jaw, much like a man's, was inherited by two of her male children, Elihu and Cadwallader. Their set, thin, unsmiling mouths depicted in paintings and photographs are a mirror image of the determined Martha.(8)

Algernon Sidney developed a trait characteristic of his mother, a determination not to look back on what cannot be helped, but to press on "to see what might be done in going forward."(9) William, brother number seven, illustrates the same trait. Major W.D. Hale, William's agent in Minneapolis, wrote the him detailing serious financial problems facing Senator Washburn's in 1889. What came back to Hale was a letter from William saying, "I do not know of anything to do but to go forward..."(10) This attitude impressed itself upon succeeding generations of Washburns. Martha's grandson, Cadwallader Lincoln Washburn, a deaf mute, as he lay dying, made his last gesture in life, raising his arm, pushing it forward, signing to his wife at the bedside, saying, "Forward, always forward, never backward."(11)

"Aim at the stars," was Martha's advice to the children. "If you don't hit them," she declared, "you will have the fun of watching your arrows go up."(12) Martha possessed energy and courage that did not waver.(13) That was the tribute paid by an acquaintance who added, "these qualities she transmitted to her sons."(14) One of Martha's ministers claimed she had few superiors in the land. While the

15

observation may have been hyperbole, it doubtless tells a kind of truth about mother Martha. Elihu, in his unfinished autobiography written in 1874, summed up his feeling about his mother, and expressed sentiments shared by his brothers and sisters. Writing from France, Elihu explained Martha's qualities of courage in the presence of adversity: "When I think of her labors, her anxieties, her watchfulness, her good and wise counsels and her attention to all our wants[,] my heart swells with emotions of gratitude towards her which no language can express."(15) E.B. Washburne was no sentimentalist, even where his own mother was concerned. The expression of sentiment in his autobiography was genuine, not eulogistic.

While Mother Martha's counsel and advice were sought by many, her educated children took note of grammatical errors in her letters. For "hope" Martha spelled "hop." For "better," she wrote "beter." "Home" was "holm." She misspelled the name of her brother-in-law, kind Reuel.

The daughters referred to their mother as "the old woman." If Mother Martha felt there was greatness possible in her three daughters, Martha, Mary and Caroline, she did not succeed in pushing them forward to success as she did the boys.

The sisters were intelligent and educated. Not having become public figures, however, they did not gain the notoriety of their brothers. Mother Martha could not boast of the girls, saying about them what she said about her sons, that they needed a State apiece for their exploits.

Chapter Three

"RELIGION AND THE WASHBURNS"

"The foundations of a later America were laid in vigorous polemics, and the rough stone was plentifully mortared with idealism. To enter once more into the spirit of those fine old idealisms, and to learn that the promise of the future has always lain in the keeping of liberal minds that never were discouraged from their dreams, is scarcely a profitless undertaking." --Vernon Louis Parrington.

❖

The romance of religion, the pervasive values unique to each family, and thirdly, community standards are influences which have a bearing on the Washburn children., their growth and development. The factor of religion must be taken as of particular significance. Growing up a Washburn in Livermore was not unlike developing and maturing in the context of a minister's family. The home was like a parsonage. Father and mother, devout in their alligiance to Universalism, were prepared to instruct any who came by inquiring about religion. At least two of the seven brothers were of such a nature that they were thought to be potential ministers, Sidney and Charles. The Israels, father and son, knew theology as well as the clergy.

Universalism in 19th century America was a doctrinaire notion assuring all individuals that they were to experience final holiness and happiness. Holiness and happiness were interpreted as personal equations. Success in achieving happiness was by many people to be judged not by what might happen in an after life, as much as by this life's experience. The experience was to be realized in this America, a young country with a promising future. There was the West waiting to be conquered. Mineral deposits were held in escrow by Nature, to be developed by enterprising Americans. Everybody was expected to have a chance to catch the proverbial ring. The promising note had been sounded in the Declaration of Independence: All are created equal. All are endowed with unalienable rights, including the pursuit of happiness available to every person. The French Encyclopaedists' view of progress was pervasive on the American scene in the nineteenth century. Americans considered themselves to have left on the other side of the Atlantic ancient theories of religion and politics which had enthralled humans for centuries. A new day was at hand. To that end, new religious formulas were sought. While Universalism was an ancient religion, it was a religion whose time had come in the new, burgeoning culture in America. It matched the ideals of Americans bent upon being successful.

As noted, Universalism, an ancient religion had been driven underground as a heresy in the fifth century A.D. During the first few centuries after Jesus' death, however, this religious outlook was the orthodoxy of the day. It was the dominant Christian belief system. Believers then were called "Origenists" or "The Merciful Doctors." Believing in free will, Origen, for whom the Origenist movement was named, adopted Universalism expecting punishment would remedy sinfulness. His theory was that anguish follows the discovery of sin, so that eventually there would be repentence and harmony of the soul with God. Another early Church Father,

Clement Alexandrinus, advocated Universalism, also believing in the remedial character of punishment. The Bishop of Jerusalem, Diodorus, was a Universalist. He believed in God's mercy which exceeds the effects of sin.

When it was thriving as an idea, Universalism appeared in a variety of forms. At one time and place, Universalism might mean only the *possibility* of universal salvation. At another, it might represent protest against the melancholy theories of Calvinism and Augustinianism. Wherever it flourished, Universalism introduced optimism and hope. Proclamations about deity's goodness and forgiveness brought confidence and fresh idealism to the people of both ancient and modern times.

In America, Universalism had prominent antecedents in the persons of Sir Henry Vane, George De Benneville, Samuel Gorton, Joseph Gatchell, and others. Sir Henry Vane was "a man of rare scholarly attainments, a radical thinker, and a fearless exponent of his convictions;"(1) Dr. George De Benneville came to America in 1741, having been sentenced to death in France because of his Universalist views, and was given last minute reprieve by Louis XV.

John Murray, an Englishman who migrated to America in 1770, became the leading exponent of Universalism, centering his activities in the environs of Boston, Massachusetts. Simply expounded, his belief was that Jesus died sacrificially so that all would be saved. "No one can be eternally lost for whom the Redeemer shed his precious blood."(2) Universalism succeeded in transforming the theology of redemption on the American religious scene. One American historian stated that "except in the Unitarian and Universalist churches there was little effort to accomodate inherited theology to the realities of American experience..."(3) Universalism did, and for a time was effective in its efforts.

With few exceptions, the names of early Universalist thinkers and theologians are lost for contemporaries. Exceptions may be Elhanan Winchester, Dr. Benjamin Rush, signer of the Declaration of Independence, and George Washington. Washington, though a member of the Episcopal faith, was Universalist in his sentiment.(4) A convert to Universalism, the Reverend Elhanan Winchester, gathered around him followers which included Benjamin Rush. Rush was one of the outstanding radical thinkers of his day, a pioneer in the field of temperance, a man who helped organize the first anti-slavery society, and was one of the first advocates of a public school system in America.

Israel Washburn, Jr. and the Reverend A. St. John Chambre, the latter having strayed from the Universalist into the Episcopal fold, once had an exchange of letters. Israel informed Chambre that he regretted his loss to Universalism, and in his letter gave what, at that time was the indispensable Universalist argument. The highest truth is the best, Israel wrote to Chambre. God, the infinite love and power, is the highest truth, and the "descent under His rule of any one of His children . . . into eternal ruin denies His infinite love or His sufficient power."(5) Washburn noted that the Episcopal church did not affirm, or it avoided, stating a position on the subject of endless suffering. Israel granted that ritual services such as Chambre felt was inspiring might be appropriate, but that it must not be placed before that truth which Washburn felt was the highest form of religion.

❖

There was a decided emphasis upon ethical norms in the religion of the

Washburns. Of their religious movement it has been said that "from the beginnings Universalism was a theological *and* ethical revolt."(6) A friend of the Washburns, and a powerful Universalist leader, Sylvanus Cobb, believed in the abolition of slavery, in total abstinence from alcoholic drinks, in prison reform, and was a pioneer in religious education. Charles Spear, Universalist minister and editor of the *Prisoner's Friend*, pioneered among humanitarians and sociologists in trying to do away with punitive penal practices. He sought to substitute intelligent rehabilitation methods. Adin Ballou, another minister in the Universalist movement, called for non-resistance, and a love which is "not mere natural affection, nor sentimantal passion, but a pure, enlightened, conscientious principle."(7) His principles had more influence in other lands than America since Mohandas Gandhi and Leo Tolstoy were persuaded of its effectiveness.

Liberal thinker and popular minister and lecturer, Edwin H. Chapin, found followers and admirers in the Washburn family. On special occasions, Chapin occupied the pulpit of the Livermore Universalist church. On the lecture circuit, Chapin spoke in Mineral Point, Wisconsin, where Cadwallader lived. Samuel Washburn attended services to hear the eminent divine whenever he was in New York and wrote in his diary about how grand Chapin's talks were. William D. Washburn named one of his sons after the minister.

In his lectures, Chapin was given to extending reason into the realm of faith, asserting that though faith leads to "an Infinite Father and an Immortal Life,"(8) yet "faith is not the surrendering of our minds to that which is irrational and inconsistent."(9) The appeal of Chapin was to Universalists and non-Universalists who were beginning to struggle with science's challenge to religion. The Washburn's Universalism began early to wrestle with the meaning of Darwin's findings.

Universalist ministers, in sermons clarifying their understanding of the faith, were effected by Ralph Waldo Emerson's transcendentalist views. L.P. Rand, one of Israel, Jr's., ministers in Orono, Maine, talked about people achieving the "divine image in which God dwells in us, and we in God."(10) Little thought was given by the ministers to its Neo-Platonism since Emerson's poetry suited the Universalist treatises on God's "all conquering love." Philosophy which inspired the works of Mary Baker Eddy played a part in the thinking of some Universalists. The Reverend William Drew after whom two boys in the Washburn family were named, spoke about the soul of man being "a child of the Immortal mind," a sentence reminiscent of Mrs. Eddy's musings, though Mrs. Eddy's writings came after Mr. Drew's proclamations. Emerson wrote of "Divine mind," Frederick Henry Hedge of "the free self-movement of the eternal mind."(11) In addition, Mr. Drew's canons of belief were prescient of a movement which prevailed a century later in the American "Me Decade." The beginning of love is self love, minister-editor Drew wrote.

Emphasis upon self and individuality was sometimes obscured beneath arguments sustaining notions about immortality. "Personal identity is not destroyed [at the time of death]," Mr. Drew asserted, and accused "semi-Sadducean theology [with] obliterat[ing]...individuality." He preached that there is a spirit in man which exists independently of the body; that that spirit "preserves its individuality."(12) *Individualisme* was "in the air" and infused the thinking of Universalist spokesmen, and was a distinctive part of R.W. Emerson's philosophy.

George Bates was a Livermore minister listened to by the Washburn families in Livermore. Sixteen Washburns, including father Israel's and his brother Reuel's family members occupied the pews when Bates and other Universalist leaders spoke. Bates' sermons bore signs of an essentially democratic thesis endemic to the Universalist faith. With a thrust at the sister Unitarian movement, Bates in a sermon on experimental religion insisted that religion should be regarded not merely as intellectual in its character, and therefore attainable by the learned only; it should...be...within the reach of all, without distinction of nation, color, caste, or grade." Reiterating the theme, he reminded his readers that "it is to be feared that many become flushed with spiritual pride, by supposing themselves the favored objects of God's love..."(13) Bates, together with all ministers of the faith, denied the putative aristocratic argument of Calvinists with their belief in salvation for some with the expectation of eternal flames to be suffered by others. Bates denied the Augustinian notion of man's innate sinfulness. Invoking the New Testament, Bates explained that he did not understand the Apostle to be speaking of the hereditary corruption of human nature, but to the *habits of life* which had been formed while in a state of unbelief and sin.(14)

D.T. Stevens, another Livermore minister, defined Christianity for his congregation, illustrating puissant Universalist ideas. Christianity, he said, makes man feel he belongs to a universal brotherhood, makes the follower a philanthropist, knows no denominational distinctions, loves the Jew, not because he is a Jew, and the Gentile, not simply as a Gentile. Stevens praised republican institutions, applauded Christianity for abolishing slavery, and for tearing down "thrones . . . of . . . tyranny."(15) Stressing the republican form of government, which Universalist preachers were wont to do,(16) relayed an important political philosophy to the Washburns which was manifested dramatically in the performance of Elihu B. Washburne. When Washburne was Ambassador to France in 1871, he extended United States recognition promptly to the new republican government. Washburne was kissed on both cheeks and Frenchmen in throngs gathered outside the embassy shouting *"Vive l'Amerique!"*(17)

The notion of progress was also integral to the tenets of the Universalist faith. William Drew Washburn's ministers in Minneapolis, Minnesota, James Harvey Tuttle and Marion Daniel Shutter were classic examples of teacher/preachers conveying the import of the concept. Tuttle reminded his congregation that we are "impelled onward and upward by internal forces." His optimism concerning human nature and its possibilities for growth and reformation was reinforced by a hardy belief in "divine influences."(18) Shutter's preaching was consistent with his work in the community. He established Unity House Social Settlement, was instrumental in organizing public playgrounds for the city, and created the Minneapolis Kindergarten Association, explaining that he thought it "better to be with the constructive forces in a city than to indulge in denunciation of evil from the pulpit."(19)

❖

With the advent of Civil War, Universalists, including the Washburns, notwithstanding their professed love of God and God's children, became minions of the war machine. George H. Emerson, editor of the *Universalist Quarterly* and a friend of Israel's, produced a treatise on *Christianity and the War*.(20) Departing from the non-resistence views of Universalist Adin Ballou, Emerson in his essay pronounced the enemy "insane," and then proceeded to regard as Heaven's will the obligation to "strike our brother." He wrote, "Rendering unto Caesar the things that are Caesar's should mean that citizens should submit to every ordinance of man, for that is the will of God." He reminded his readers that the essence of government is force. The closing argument of an Emerson's essay was that "the soldier . . . may consistently carry the New Testament . . . have the spirit of the New Testament in his heart . . . and in the deadly onset lift a prayer to the Father and Friend of all, that the fearful missile may go straight to the mark!"(21)

The Reverend Elbridge Gerry Brooks, one-time congressman and friend of the Washburns, published an article on *Our Civil War*.(22) It also was a call to arms in which Universalist Brooks invited the citizens to "make history fragrant with the aroma of sacrifice."(23) These two tracts by leading Universalist preachers were carefully thought out. Should congressional representatives, Israel, Elihu or Cadwallader, have needed a kind of canon law to justify their actions in giving total support to the war, the Emerson-Brooks forty page works could have sufficed.

Israel was seen as favoring a symbiotic relationship between the Universalist movement and the American Republic. Speaking to twelve thousand Universalists at the 1870 Centennial Celebration of the landing of John Murray on American soil, Governor Washburn insisted that "Strictly speaking, the Universalist is not a Protestant Church."(24) He felt it to be a Church of the Republic. Another Universalist minister insisted that the Universalist "has a right to be called the Church of America."(25) That these views could be expressed and accepted demonstrates why Universalist audiences were sympathetic to a statement made by the Reverend L.C. Todd as early as 1844, that "every Universalist is a Republican, and every Republican should be a Universalist."(26)

The religion of Universalism and his devotion to it had a pronounced effect upon William Drew Washburn. In Minneapolis, two years after arriving in the little village on the Mississippi, he assembled a group of men and women for the purpose of organizing a Universalist church. William was a faithful attendant and supporter for fifty three years of the church he was instrumental in establishing. He was President of the national body of Universalists in 1903-04. In 1909, speaking on the occasion of the Fiftieth Anniversary of the founding of the Minneapolis church, he expressed satisfaction that the Universalist emphases had been adopted by the major denominations in America. That fact, he added, explains why the church, which, incidentally his brother had thought would become the Church of the American Republic, was still small and inconsequential among the several Christian movements of the country.(27) That is, many other churches had become Universalist in their essential tenets.(28)

❖

Who could say how thoroughly each of the Washburns was imbued with the tenets of Universalism, effecting thought and action as their careers unfolded? It is of dubious merit to attempt to make a correlation between religious belief and an individual's social, ethical or political outlook. Some things are clear, however. Israel and William were motivated in their work, and some of their social and political views were shaped, by beliefs peculiar to their Universalism.

As for Sidney, it can only be said that he was a regular attendant at services, and his philosophical outlook on life was fashioned by liberal religion.

Elihu was said to have "wandered far from the stern old faith of the forefathers,"(29) which suggests he was perceived by the Galena Presbyterian clergy as outside mainstream religion because of his Universalism. Elihu made no effort in his resettlement in Galena, however, to establish or support a Universalist church, as Israel had in Orono, Maine, and as William did in Minneapolis, Minnesota. There were a small number of Universalists in Galena with their own minister. There is , however, no evidence of the Washburne family attending or supporting the church. A Unitarian minister also held forth in his Illinois hometown. Elihu was aware of his presence. He gave no encouragement to the minister, except to recommend him as a speaker to his brother, Cadwallader, in Mineral Point.(30) Washburne noted that members of two denominations in town were persecuted, namely Catholics and Universalists. Dr. Smith of Galena said that Washburne "was still a typical Puritan," despite his having "wandered."(31) The extent to which what the Galena Presbyterian called Puritanism in Elihu was residual Universalism must be decided as we deepen our knowledge of the Galena Washburne. Whatever the conclusion, Israel at least insisted that his brother remained loyal to the faith of his father and mother. Elihu gave generously in support of the Livermore church, and he presented to the church beside the Livermore home a Memorial Window in remembrance of his wife, Adele.

Cadwallader was active in the LaCrosse Universalist church and attended services faithfully in LaCrosse as well as in Minneapolis when he was in the city. Some of the ablest and most scholarly Universalist ministers served the church in LaCrosse. It is more than likely that Washburn had a hand in their selection.

Charles, while thought to be the logical Washburn brother to become a Universalist minister, yet wrote little about religion, and virtually nothing about Universalism. There is evidence only that he attended the Unitarian church in San Francisco where the family's friend, Thomas Starr King, was minister. He announced the hours for King's services in the newspaper he edited.(32) The puritanism of Charles, like Elihu, can be attributed to his upbringing in the faith of his fathers. His interest in the subject of poverty and re-distribution of wealth can be said to have stemmed in part from his religio-ethical bent, but is also related to his own impecunious condition for much of his own life.(33)

Samuel was seldom located where there was a Universalist church. When he settled in Owatonna, Minnesota, he was a party to constructing the church of the Washburns. In the absence of the church of his choice he attended other services. He was sharply critical of orthodox ministers, making comparisons between those he had known growing up in Livermore, and those he heard in Eau Galle, or Pepin, or Durand. He attended the Universalist church in New York before shipping out on the Galena to do battle on the James River.

The Washburn Journals are replete with references to church life and to "pulls," as religious and political discussions were called. General O.O. Howard and his brothers, General Charles Howard, with his wife, and the Reverend Roland Howard, visited the Washburns in their home. "[Father] had a brief theological 'pull' with [O.O. Howard]." There were references frequently in the Journals to sermons and preachers, but the longest accounts related to humorous incidents connected to religion or the church. Israel, Jr. copied into the Journal an amusing tale from a book by Dr. John Brown about a poor old woman who was on her death bed. The orthodox minister, wishing to try her faith, said to her,

"Janet, what would you say if after all he has done for you, God should let you drop into Hell?"

"E'n as He likes," she said. "He'll lose more than I do"

This was the type of humor which tickled Universalists; anything that referred in a witty manner to hell.(34)

One of the reinforcements of religious commitment was the kind of incident which Israel recorded on November 5, 1867. "Aunt Andrews at Raynham--she is 94 years old and remarkably, wonderfully bright and active--is in full possession of her faculties, goes to church, keeps up with the busy world, talks theology like Theo. Parker."(36)

❖

The Universalist movement bore the seeds of its own death. It was a theological concept gradually adopted by the major denominations, displacing Calvinistic views. What transpired in the city where William was influential in organizing a church around Universalist ideas illustrates the melding more generally into other churches. The minister serving the historic Plymouth Congregational church in that city announced publically that he was a Universalist. He did not join with the Universalist movement to minister in a Universalist church, which is what Marion Shutter, the church's minister for forty years, had done. Shutter left the Baptists and became a Universalist minister. Israel also, like William, serves as an example of what many loyal Universalists did which made predictable the demise of the movement. In 1881 when Universalists had reached the pinnacle of their success as an American religious movement, foreign missions were discussed. The General Convention wanted to send a missionary to Scotland. Washburn, Jr. was critical of the idea. It was Israel's assumption that the essential truths of Universalism were being taught in many other denominations. As historian Russell Miller notes, raising money for the purpose of sending missionaries "was an unnecessary diversion of effort and resources."(37)

❖

The Universalist movement lost its separate identity in a consolidation of the Unitarian and Universalist churches in 1961. No descendants of the prolific Washburn family were present.

Chapter Four

A FORWARD LOOK

"Jefferson's warning bell in the night"

John Holmes, U.S. Senator from Maine, anxiously awaited a letter from ex-

President Thomas Jefferson. Senator Holmes had presented a petition to Congress seeking his state's admission to the Union. He now wanted to know what the retired sage of Monticello thought of the Missouri Compromise of 1820, which had been written to make possible Maine's and Missouri's admission. In point of fact, the measure had been reported out of a Conference Committee Holmes co-chaired. The subject of the measure was a touchy one. If passed it would give licit recognition to differences existing between North and South on the subject of slavery. Holmes wrote Jefferson on April 12. It did not take the ex-President long to respond. Ten days later he penned his answer to the Maine Senator. His reply was historic. It has been used to illustrate Jefferson's prescient grasp of an issue which, 41 years later,

Sen. John Holmes

broke into War. As he expressed it, the 1820 Compromise measure was a

firebell in the night. I considered it at once as the knell of the Union. It is hushed, indeed, for the moment. But this is a reprieve only, not a final sentence. A geographical line, coinciding with a marked principle, moral and political, once conceived and held up to the angry passions of men, will never be obliterated; and every new irritation will mark it deeper and deeper.(1)

Jefferson's weighty words were a source of disquiet, but represented gratification for Holmes. The Compromise measure, wrote the oracle of Monticello, is about *"justice.. .in one scale, and self-preservation in the other."** Reflecting the mood of his fellow citizens in the district of Maine, the Senator must have been pleased to realize that the moral aspect relating to justice was part of the ex-President's view. As for the subject of self-preservation, it may not have been clear to Holmes that that aspect of the measure would become the shocking *cause celebre* of the Civil War.

The Missouri Compromise of 1820, the first warning as Jefferson saw it, was succeeded 30 years hence by the ringing of a more intrusive alarm bell, namely the Compromise of 1850, alerting the country more exactly to the coming of war. The yet more distinctive clanging of the bell was the Kansas-Nebraska Act four years later. Stephen A. Douglas of Illinois was to submit the Act, having as its purpose to make room for slavery expansion. Given Douglas' plan, "mutual and moral hatred [would] render separation preferable to eternal discord." Separation, however, was

---

* Emphasis added.

not going to be an option. War was to be the option. It would not be justice, but preservation of a Way of Life that would make the threat of separation seem worth a war. Separation such as was foreshadowed by Jefferson in 1820 was going to be brought about by the machinations of the Washburns of Maine, Illinois and Wisconsin among others

The decade of the '50s during which three Washburn brothers brought to Congress their father's anti-slavery sentiments was a period of unparalleled danger in the history of the country. That decade verged upon the war and promised turbulence which Congressmen Elihu, Israel or Cadwallader could not have imagined or anticipated. During those anxious years, the most innocuous legislative business submitted to the House created a tempest between North-South sections. The publication of a book, *The Impending Crisis of the South*, "fed the fires of sectional controversy leading up to the Civil War," and was the only tome in U.S. history "to become the center of bitter and prolonged Congressional debate." Elihu and Israel endorsed and gave their blessing to the book and its author, Hinton Rowan Helper, later a personal friend of their brother Charles.(2) Physical violence erupted in the tumultuous House and in the sedate Senate. Such violence was invariably related to the issue which finally brought on the bloody conflict where state versus federal power was tested.(3) One of those acts of violence involved a friend of the Washburns, Senator Charles Sumner of Massachusetts. Sumner delivered a provocative oration in the Senate, *The Crime Against Kansas*. He spoke specifically of Mr. Butler of South Carolina, referring to him as having "chosen a mistress to whom he has made his vows, and who, though ugly to others, is always lovely to him . . . the harlot, Slavery."(4) When Sumner used the harlot analogy, Stephen A. Douglas was overheard saying about the Massachusetts Senator, "That damned fool will get himself killed by some other damned fool."(5) Douglas was correct. Butler's nephew Preston Brooks chose to defend the honor of his uncle. He waited for the right moment, approached Sumner sitting at his desk and beat the Senator senseless. On another occasion, violence bubbled into a mix-up on the floor of the House involving the three Washburn Congressmen. Israel was presiding, but unable to quell a fracas with the use of his gavel. Elihu rushed from the Whig to the Democratic side of the House to defend Congressman Grow who had been attacked by Lawrence M. Keitt of South Carolina. Next, Cadwallader hastened to the defense of his brother Elihu. The melee ended when Cadwallader grabbed Representative Barksdale by the hair of his head, under the impression that Barksdale had struck Elihu. Barksdale's hair came off in Cadwallader's hand, causing laughter throughout the House. The brawl was aborted then and there by the humor of the situation.

These acts of violence were a prelude to the open wound of war in the American body politic. Issues having a bearing upon the uneasy Union during the fractious '50s comprise a list including:

--The Compromise of 1850,
--Internal improvements such as the construction of
   railroads and the building of canals,
--The tariff,
--The Dred Scott decision by the Supreme Court,
--The Kansas-Nebraska bill,
--The creation of the Republican party,
--The opening up of the intractable problem of States Rights.

Of these, the most consequential was the Kansas-Nebraska decision resulting in the organization of a new, sectional political party.

The Washburn brothers were particularly sensitive about Henry Clay's 1850 Compromise. The earlier, 1820 Compromise, gave to Maine the status of statehood. The 1850 Compromise was used to justify abolishing the 1820 measure. Among other things, the 1850 Act established territorial governments without restricting slavery, and agreed that slavery in the District of Columbia would not be abolished. It enacted a stringent fugitive slave law, and asserted that Congress has no power to interfere with the slave trade between the states. Israel, Sr., was an elected member of the Commonwealth government in Massachusetts when statehood for Maine was favorably voted, resulting of course from Clay's handling of the sensitive issue of voting balance between North and South. "Equilibrium between the two sections" must be maintained, warned Senator John C. Calhoun in his famous speech on *Slavery*.(6) Bitterness on the part of southern Representatives therefore made it necessary for Missouri to be voted statehood before Maine could be admitted into the Union. With Missouri in the Union along with the Pine Tree State, Maine, an equal number of Representatives were added to South and North. The balance arranged with Clay's astute politicking had worked satisfactorily for 30 years, until

John C. Calhoun

in 1850 the issue of territorial recognition exploded into a debate in house and senate, a debate unequaled in the annals of American legislative history. On that occasion, Senator Calhoun composed a speech which, though entitled *Slavery*, was a disquisition on the subject of secession. His talk, provoked by the introduction of Clay's Compromise bill of 1850, was read by another Senator since Calhoun was too ill to stand or speak. Calhoun's sallow cheeks, his great head of hair flowing like a lion's mane, arms folded, the dying Senator followed every word as it was read by a colleague. His words unabashedly declared, ". . . The agitation of the subject of slavery would, if not prevented by some timely and effective measure, end in disunion."(7)

The gauntlet had been thrown down. The threat had now been stated boldly, and one might almost say officially, by the South's chief nullification spokesperson. It remained only to fix the time and await the precipitating events which were to bring a 19th century cold war to a fierce boil. As it was, it took two years of pressure from southern exponents in face of agitation from Whigs and the death of the President, Zachary Taylor, to pass the Compromise of 1850. The Compromise once passed, however, did not satisfy the people, North or South. As soon as the vote was taken in Congress, the governors of Arkansas, Carolina and Texas plotted together to defy the United States government, seeking political means by which southern states could secede from the Union. In addition, the Whigs were unhappy with the proviso in the Fugitive Slave Act requiring runaway slaves to be returned to their owners [sic] in the South. In Boston, two ministers, Theodore Parker and Thomas Wentworth Higginson, led resisters in a failed attempt to maintain the freedom of the runaway slave, Anthony Burns. Many communities in the North refused to cooperate with the federal government's newest mandate. Congressman Israel Washburn, Jr., received a letter dipped in vitriol from a Bowdoin professor, R.D.

Hitchcock. In his letter, the professor reacted angrily to Anthony Burns' imprisonment. He wrote, "The Anthony Burns outrage in Boston. . .is putting fire into the bones of the most conservative amongst us."(8)

In this internecine struggle, Representative Washburn of Maine came to be seen as a leader among radical, anti-slavery members of the House. As he put it, he was so fiercely liberal as a "conscience Whig" that there was even "a gulf fixed between [me] and Daniel Webster;"(9) this, even though Webster was one of Washburn's clients. Junior's stance as a conscience Whig brought mother Washburn into the picture. She with her husband kept informed of agitated political issues, and she had opinions she tried to put into intelligible and legible English. Israel, Jr., was a conscience Whig, yet it struck Martha as "laughibel to see these conshens Whigs that coled not vote for that nobel hero. . .(10)

Israel, different from Elihu who had no clergy to motivate him, knew Universalist ministers who were summoning Americans to disobey the Fugitive Slave laws. Wrote one minister, "The law is a sin; is despotic." Sure of himself, the Reverend Elbridge Gerry Brooks said, "[Slavery] arrays itself against the instincts of our nature and *the law of God*."(11) Israel took a vital and leading part in the debate which raged between Whigs and Democrats at this critical moment in American history.

In the 1852 argument over the Clay Compromise, Whigs in the southern section of the country involved themselves for the last time speaking disparagingly of their fellow northern Whigs. They simply switched. Southern Whigs began to side with southern Democrats; northern Democrats began to express unhappiness with Fugitive Slave laws, and many even left the party later to join with Republicans.

On May 24 bright, eager Washburn standing, his upper body hardly lifted above the height of his desk, raised his voice to bring fellow Congressmen to attention. In a stern resonating tone of voice that did not match his slight stature, he led off with his opening sentences, ". . . A question of vital interest to the Whig party is now claiming the consideration of its members."(12)

Southern Democrats aroused the ire of Whigs, said Israel, in demanding that fugitive slave laws be instituted *in perpetuity*.** The unkindest cut of all, he said, was for southerners to claim Whigs were denying the Constitution. Equally offensive was their insistence that the idea of permanence or finality be made "a test of party loyalty." This accusation struck home inasmuch as Israel and his Illinois brother, Elihu, were champions of General Winfield Scott; and the loyalty test, were it to be required, would be a threat to the electability of Scott as President. Since a southern Whig had judged the position of northern Whigs to be derelict, Israel,

Winfield S. Scott

with a touch of sarcasm, said that if tests were to be imposed, loyal, faithful Whigs would accept judgments by "new light" southern Whigs only after they had passed through "purgatorial flame in which political sinners bleach like linen."(13)

Israel turned to the left to address the other side of the House.

** Emphasis added.

"Your law may be constitutional but another might be quite as clearly so."
The fugitive laws, he fumed, cannot be final and unchangeable, to be changed only
by the South. A Whig nominee, Washburn complained, would be bound to veto laws
inconsistent with the Compromise. As President, the nominee would have to be loyal
not to the Constitution, but to the Baltimore Convention where Whigs would be
expected to put their nominees for President to the acid southern test, asking,
"Would the nominees accept the Fugitive Slave laws in perpetuity?"

Israel declared the requirement would lead to the formation of a sectional party.
Ironically, against Israel's own wishes and contrary to the advice of his old friend,
ex-Governor Kent, it was to be Maine's Representative Washburn who would give
corporeality to the new, sectional party two years hence in 1854.

After the Baltimore Convention, with the nomination by Whigs of Winfield
Scott, voters were given a choice between Franklin Pierce and the Compromise, *or*
General Scott and uncertainty. In Scott's case, he would not declare on the
Compromise measure. Finally, there was an understanding among Whig party
leaders that the northern Whigs would select the candidate, and southern Whigs
would have the last word on the platform. In the end, therefore, the platform
included the finality of the Fugitive Slave codes, resulting in the election of Franklin
Pierce. The defeat of Scott brought the party, claimed to be "an 'organized
incompatibility'," to a virtual end.(14)

The choice of Pierce, a northerner, a graduate of Bowdoin College in Maine and
a Democrat, seemed for a time to mollify citizens of both sections. His election was
approved by the South because as President he sided with the slavery contingent. As
for voters in the North, they were tired of squabbling and were willing to trust a man
from New Hampshire to quell the bellicosity. The new President therefore brought
on an "era of good feelings."

Notwithstanding, the so-called era of good feelings was deceptive, since the
Baltimore Convention, and subsequently the election, readied the country for
another, and a winning, political party.

While it was thought by many that the slavery question was laid to rest with the
election of Franklin Pierce, Elihu Washburne did not think so. He was a 36-year-old
determined Whig bent upon winning a seat in the U.S. House of Representatives as
an anti-slavery candidate. Expecting to win his bid for a seat in the House in 1852,
Elihu kept the slavery question alive in his district of Illinois by turning for support
to the South's nemesis, the Free-soil party. The Free-soil faction, intending to see the
territories enter the Union with slavery exterpated, exasperated southerners. Free-
soilers approved of opening territories to free white men only. Elihu told his father
there was a powerful effort under way to defeat him, supposedly because of his
support of Free-soilers. "There is work to be done and I am just the boy to do it," he
wrote.(15) In his district, the Galena candidate spoke once or twice a day for ten
weeks in support of the Free-soil position. With Free-soil, Whig and Abolitionist
support, the candidate won by a slim margin of two hundred and eighty-six votes
more than his Galena opponent's total won him his seat in Congress.(16)

"An understanding of temperament is indispensable for our understanding of
the past," Philip Greven has remarked.(17) For the reader, it will be helpful to know
about the personality of this 36-year-old "boy" in order fully to appreciate the
dedication displayed for 26 years following his appearance in the political arena in
1852. Elihu is a stamped-out version personifying the Whig. A Whig, said R.

McKinley Ormsby, is a person who

> has not the gratification of a present passion in
> view; but crushes out and sacrifices private
> feelings and interests, and compromises with
> antagonistic views, to secure the stability of the
> country, develop its resources, and place its
> future on a safe and enduring basis. His ideas
> are not formed on partial views, nor inspired
> by local interests; but are liberal, enlarged,
> comprehensive, and are the growth of long-
> continued and mature reflection.(18)

This classic definition of the 18th century Whig fits Elihu, Israel and Cadwallader, proper sons of their political father. Each frequently used the word "duty" indicating loyalty to principles learned at mother's knee and father's tutoring. With Elihu, duty was given as a reason for his decision later to remain in Paris when all other consuls and Ambassadors representing their governments left the city as Paris was being bombarded. Elihu insisted on remaining, writing Adele to say, "This is my place where duty calls me and here I must remain."(19) He wrote that it would be cowardly to run when there is danger. Israel Washburn, Jr., preferred to remain in the House of Representatives when urgent calls came from Maine leaders insisting he be the Republican nominee for governor. It was his private wish to remain in the House, expecting Congress would be a springboard into the Senate. Israel gave in to the appeals of Maine leaders out of a sense of duty.

Implicit in the Ormsby definition of the prototypical Whig was a troublesome ambiguity which characterized party members, including Elihu and his brothers. While they were referred to as radicals or "conscience Whigs" in the 1850s, Whigs had a deeply-dyed conservative tinge. They opposed slavery, but were fearful of the emigration of blacks from the South into Western Territories. While in favor of Clay's Missouri Compromise of 1820, as noted, they were disturbed by his second Compromise plan since the 1850 measure resolved that Negroes could be taken into Territories. For Whigs, that was impermissible, because, as Israel pointed out,

> If the Constitution of the United States
> declares that a man held as a slave is property,
> he may be so held, treated, and regarded, *in all*
> *places**** where that fundamental and supreme
> law is in operation.(20)

Israel saw clearly that the 1850 measure opened the door to slavery's being sanctioned by law throughout the United States. He gave voice to the sentiment when speaking to a Fourth of July audience in Cherryfield, Maine. "Chattel slavery," he said, "demanded the possession of the government."(21)

Approximating the Whig ideal, the Reverend Horace Bushnell of Connecticut was anti-Southern, but he was not an abolitionist. Negroes, he asserted, were created as inferior beings. Another of the Whig types was Harvard professor Charles Eliot Norton, an anti-Negro anti-egalitarian. He thought there should be no expansion of slavery and believed the Negro must be confined within the South. He therefore

----

*** Emphasis added.

found himself comfortable with Free-soil doctrine. With his likeness to Whig types, Elihu bore out the imprint in his failure to display a lucid, consistent philosophy. Daniel Walker Howe, as though he had Elihu Washburne in mind, explained that Whigs "built up their world view and put it to work . . . by interacting with the world."(22) Washburne's method of developing his theories, if they can be dignified by the use of the term, was by way of interacting with the "world" to which Howe was alluding. The Illinoisan reacted to events and individuals, exploding exclamatory judgments in the manner of a termagant. What he felt strongly about was "the worst" or "the best," "the most" or "the cruelest and most thoughtless." A speech of Stephen A. Douglas' was deemed "utterly infamous and damnable, the crowning atrocity of his life." Referring to railroad legislation, Elihu believed it was the most criminal legislation ever recorded in the annals of any country. A riot in

Memphis during the Reconstruction period was said by Elihu to be "one of the most bloody recorded in the annals of history." Referring to Andrew Johnson's Union party, Washburne proclaimed that that "history had no parallel. ..." During the Franco-American war Elihu wrote, "I have been in the midst of the greatest event of the century." These views are almost the harridan's bullying. They do not suggest a cool appraisal of events. A newspaper described Elihu as possessing an impulsive manner and a look of fanaticism. His typical reactions support the evaluation made by Howe who noted that "values must often have

President Andrew Johnson been implicit in [Whigs'] lives rather than the product of . . . self-conscious reflection."(23) An outlook rooted more thoroughly in his own native religion of Universalism might have moderated his exaggerated opinions. His Universalism did not do for Elihu what it did for Israel whose attention to religion provided him a deeper understanding of human nature and behavior.

The metaphor of the Jeremiad, faded with the passage of time from 17th century Puritan New England reappeared in prophetic pronouncements defining typical Whig responses to events of the 1850s. Francis Lieber prophesied, "God in his mercy has sometimes condescended to smite [nations], and to smite them hard, in order to bring them to their senses. .."(24) Ralph Waldo Emerson also believed the war was "God's doing."(25)

Lieber, Norton, Bushnell, Emerson, like the Washburns, were conservative intellectuals, predicting in prophetic tones blood sacrifice in an approaching God-imposed national calamity. The Washburns' clergy were Whig-Jeremiads using pulpits to predict the coming of redemptive blood-letting in war.

The contradictions found in early Whig-Republican philosophy are illustrated by Israel, if not always by Elihu. Whigs, for example, were inheritors of the Jeffersonian view of government, yet they favored centralism. They wanted government to assist in the internal development of the country calling for government planning and did not care to rely on market forces. This ambiguity is seen in a speech by Israel in 1874. Drawing upon his experience with government, he declared that "centralization, with its hundreds of millions for yearly disbursement, must breed carelessness and prodigality, while vast and loose expenditures feed and strengthen centralization."(26) This critical view of government "intervention" came naturally to Whig Washburn. He was operating with party values learned in his youth and practiced for 61 years as Congressman, Governor, and director of the Custom House at Portland, Maine, intending to be a responsible *individual*. Nonetheless, in Congress he sought federal aid for the Androscoggin Railroad Company in Maine, as well as for the European and North American Railway, which was to traverse the State for the purpose of shortening the delivery of goods to England and the continent.(27)

The brothers Washburn with their brilliant careers are parodies of Republicanism which, in Norman Graebner's words, "gave expression to certain powerful forces and aspirations in American life which were probably irrepressible."(28) These brothers were involved at the heart of political maneuvering, doing their part to create a government to accommodate emerging capitalism and an expanding frontier. The brothers profited personally, harnessing those "powerful forces," thereby achieving wealth and power. There were discouraging moments with recurring depressions when it seemed hopes for wealth and power must be dashed. On the economic side, the re-run of depressions in the '30s, '50s, and '80s took the heart out of Cadwallader and William who were the millionaires. "I shall not live to go through another such year, --and would not," wrote the Washburn with the deepest pockets, Cadwallader, during the decade of the 1850s.(29) The consequence of politics pursued in Washington by the Washburns, as the new Republican party they had launched helped solidify North and South politically, accounted in great part for the coming terrors of Civil War.(30)

In September 1862, Elihu Washburne stayed the night at General Winfield Scott's home where the two men talked about war and the future. The next day, Elihu wrote Adele, "I have never before had such feelings of despondency as now. . ." He continued, "I fear there is no more happiness or prosperity for us or our dear, dear children. The future has an awful look."(31)

The classic Whig, with the Washburn brothers as archetypes, was a capitalist. The brothers were inheritors of the post-feudal era, and as traders were ambitious to make their fortunes as they traveled west where they assisted in the building of cities and industries. Corresponding to the definition of the Whig, the Washburns displayed a fervent ambition to "rise." Elihu, like Cadwallader and William, starting poor, ascended, acquiring large business interests. Elihu was part owner with Cadwallader and Samuel of the Town of Waubec with extensive woodlands in Wisconsin. The Galenean was part owner of a local flour mill, a Plank Road Company in Mineral Point, a bank in Hallowell, Maine, operated by his Whig brother, Sidney. Over the years in capitalist fashion, Washburne invested in promising enterprises including a horse-rail system in Chicago. He invested judiciously in his brother Cadwallader's numerous ventures. Never seeking to benefit illegally from privileged positions he held in Congress or when he was Ambassador to France, still Washburne died a wealthy man, having risen, as did Cadwallader and William, from "rags to riches." Ironically, the Civil War was a contributing factor for the Washburns as for the capitalist North in general. William reaped a fortune from railroading, and Cadwallader, investing in the flour industry, acquired millions, expanding his business by selling abroad.

Chapter Five

THE CHILD, FATHER TO THE MAN

Elihu Washburne commanded a tribe of ten Washburn brothers and sisters. He behaved as though he were master of the ten, including six brothers, some older, some younger. Elihu's childhood exploits as commander over his small army of siblings suggests the time when this tyke would be a principal sachem. He would be advising, ordering, and surveillant of congressmen, businessmen, politicians, statesmen, governors, emperors, and presidents of the United States and France. His sisters and brothers at first dubbed him Gentle Elihu. The nickname was soon abandoned since gentle was not precisely synonymous with Elihu's temperament as chief. The name *Cibber* became the life-time *nom de plume* for the youth born to wield the scepter. Cibber did not bully his way to positions of domination, either with his siblings when they were youngsters, or with some of the country's major political figures as he reached his majority. His overriding emotions found him on many occasions using fiery language. A reporter noted his nervous waving of arms and "gestures . . . wild in the extreme" when speaking to the public. There were times when the impression was of a man at the edge of neurosis. His overbearing manner tried presidents, cabinet members and fellow legislators. On one occasion Elihu overrode President Lincoln's advice to his general of the army, Grant. Gideon Welles, the eternal curmudgeon of Lincoln's cabinet, had his own reasons for calling Elihu "a demagogue without statesmanship . . . " Representative Ignatius Donnelly, feeling Washburne displayed an "air of superior virtue" delivered a vituperative attack on the Illinois congressman standing on the floor of the house. Nonetheless, there were respects in which it must be said of Washburne that he was like those who are always listened to, whether they speak with soft voice or strident bellow. In Congress he expressed himself in stentorian tones and could be heard above the din. When he spoke people listened and heeded. As a social being Elihu "was a delightful person, intelligent, informed and cultured . . ." He filled the room he entered evoking thoughts of Daniel Webster who elicited the same magical effect among people.

ELIHU THE DESTINED BROTHER

Elihu was brother number three and yet it was he, not the older boys, Israel, Jr., or Sidney, who was removed from the happy family in the happy village. For a year Elihu was forced to live with grandfather and grandmother Washburn in Massachusetts. His dad doubtless anticipated unhappiness for Elihu or any other of his children who must be left at his old Raynham home. Israel, Sr., had left home in Raynham at the earliest opportunity. It was apparently believed that Elihu, better than Israel, Jr., or Algernon Sidney, could best endure the no-nonsense Puritan grandfather, "stern and severe, talking but little, abrupt and . . . vehement in speech."

A miserable year in Raynham and Elihu was home again in Livermore, where he became a hero in the village. He had seen Boston. Few youths in town had been so privileged. The experience of living under the austere regime of grandfather Washburn turned Gentle Elihu into a studious child and reader. He borrowed books from the minister on the subjects of history, biography and romance. He began to learn about adult affairs. At the age of eight, this Washburn child was watching and listening to the villagers who sat around the wood stove in his father's store. Customers included soldiers who fought in the American for the trip Elihu was to take to the West. Washburne wanted it known that he paid Otis with interest shortly after he settled in Galena. He wrote, "I was [Otis'] friend till his death." The Livermore farm boy made important friends and when he was ready to turn his face to the west he was able to turn for financial aid to his uncle, David Benjamin, and to Colonel Dumont, in addition to John Otis. All were promptly paid with interest.

Elihu thought he was to become an invalid when one day when walking to his grandfather Washburn's, he felt a severe pain in his right hip. The pain did not pass and he learned he had "hip disease." A doctor friend introduced a seton on Elihu's hip. Later as patient he learned to replace the seton by himself.

DECISIONS, DECISIONS

Elihu tried out a number of career choices until he found his niche in the political arena. It could be said that when he chose politics he was carrying out his father's hopes for him. Unquestionably, Israel, Sr., had aspired to enter that arena. In fact, he did serve his district in the Massachusetts legislature, but stopped short of trying for the greater goal, representing his state in Congress. Despite the Oedipal contest that goes on between fathers and sons, Elihu did not "fight" his father. He established goals he knew were dear to his dad's heart. He moved into political circles, and together with Israel, Cadwallader, William, Charles and Samuel, Elihu strove to be like Israel, Sr., as an elective officer. Several of the Washburn boys were notable in the political sphere.

Restless and ambitious, Washburne at age 22 was still not ready to launch his career. First, Harvard must have him. He went to Cambridge where he attended Dane School of Law, dividing his time between school and work at the Derby-Andrews law firm in Boston. At Harvard, his classmates included Richard Henry Dana, Jr., James Russell Lowell, Charles A. Peabody, and one of America's distinguished lawyers, lecturers and statesmen, William M. Evarts. Elihu did not excel in his studies, and when he attempted to pass the bar, Justice Wilde, "an able and upright judge," found Elihu wanting. Wilde expected three years of college training or seven years of rigorous study before he would issue a license to practice. It was not sufficiently convincing for Justice Wilde to have been provided with good reports from Judge Story and Dr. Greenleaf, Washburne's faculty members, both of whom attested to Elihu's scholastic standing. A few months later Elihu appeared before another examiner, Judge Strong, whose "heart and sympathy had not been frozen by the east winds of Boston." Strong ordered the clerk of the court to make out a license for Washburne to practice law in all the courts of Massachusetts.

William Evarts

THE CRITICAL DECISION

"Cadr. popped along yesterday and brought me from you the drawers and shirt." Elihu in a letter to his mother. Elihu depended on his mother to make his clothes and sew his socks. She provided modest amounts of money for his schooling at Harvard. He was emotional when he thought of her doing these things for him. He wrote to her, "God grant the time may come ere long when there will be no necessity for you . . . to labor. My hands are now tied and I can do nothing, but I will get them loose one of these days."

Feelings of gratitude induced Elihu to study harder so as to free himself from obligations to his mother and others who championed his cause. He worked from 5:30 a.m. until 10 at night, taking time to work for Derby and Andrews in Boston. As a part-time worker, he impressed the head of the firm, E.H. Derby. When President Grant appointed Washburne secretary of state, Derby wrote a letter of congratulation confessing he felt in the old days Elihu would achieve cabinet status, but he did not expect him to achieve such distinction as comes with the office of secretary of state.

Money from his mother and friends kept Washburne at Dane School for two years, writing long letters to his friends as a kind of compensation. Letters served the purpose of assuring father, mother, and others that he was working diligently and deserved assistance, for all of which he was, he said, "under a thousand obligations." A 1500 word letter was dropped in the mail to "my dear father" two weeks after Elihu settled on the campus at Cambridge. It was mid-April 1839. Elihu wanted it known as a matter of fact, not boastfully, that in two weeks since his arrival he had formed his opinion of Dane and the faculty. Judge Story, he said, was a great man and scholar, and yet, "one of the most commonplace, easy, frank, familiar and kind men that ever lived." Judge Story became an example to Elihu. Washburne always appreciated the common touch, and was happy later to find it in his friends Lincoln and Grant. Elihu did not put on airs. Not infrequently he spoke humbly of his own mediocre intelligence, insisting he was but a poor farmer. He was, of course, neither a farmer nor lacking in intelligence.

Richard Henry Dana, Jr.

Humble or not, Elihu was judgmental, delivering severe verdicts about vice, whether smoking, drinking, carousing or lying. He roundly damned a classmate, John Nourse, when Nourse accused Alexander Hamilton Bullock of being a thief. Elihu declared he would never again speak to Nourse. He drew a distasteful portrait of Richard Henry Dana, Jr., saying he was haughty, supercilious, and mean. That student, rejected by Washburne, left Harvard to become a voyager, after which he wrote *Two Years Before the Mast*, became a celebrated lawyer and was active as a Free-soil party member.

Conclusions reached about school mates display not mere gossip on Elihu's part, but insights, some of which were clearly mistaken. His judgments displayed a democratic, down-to-earth attitude. His attitude colored his analysis of fellow students and faculty members. Nathan Hale, Jr., son of the editor of the *Boston Patriot*, "feigns aristocracy," Elihu wrote, and is a rowdy. Hale "feels [he is] too much above the people to succeed . . . as a lawyer." William Wetmore Story was the son of Judge Story whom Elihu admired. William, Elihu confided to his diary, was an example of how the sons of great men "generally 'turn out' miserably." He was disposed to say that Story's son was a contemptible being. As described by Washburne, young Story curled his hair with exquisite care, and had a silly, foolish-looking face. Rufus King, later a notable lawyer and philanthropist, if he could have read what Elihu said of him as a student would likely have smiled. King, said Washburne, is "self-conceited, profane and a little rowdish." But Washburne granted he was a good, fair fellow. Withal, there were fellow students Elihu admired. One of his cronies was from Louisiana, a tall, rough, green gawkish fellow who, Elihu boasted, had fought two duels. When mother Martha or the girls in the family used to say that young Elihu or his brothers were rowdy, their mother's opinion was received pridefully. To the boys it was a mark of their maleness to be thought rowdy by their sisters. Elihu's stern judgment of the rowdy at age 23 had in it a touch of envy as is noticed in his judgment of James Russell Lowell, "talented to be sure," Elihu allowed, but "rowdish." It can be said that Elihu in training at Harvard acquired a vocabulary of colorful adjectives to be used for descriptive purposes. He made fluent use of such descriptive terms when in contests with political foes.

Martha "Patty" Washburn

Drawing word pictures of his contemporaries illustrates a tendency Elihu had to record, either in writing or by carving in his retentive memory, the names of associates with their positive and negative traits. In this respect, the farmer's son from Livermore inherited a strength of his father whose memory was remarkable.

❖

The end of Washburne's college career was near in December of 1839. He wrote the school's Dr. Lemuel Shaw explaining that Judge Story had advised him to submit to examination for entrance to the bar. Elihu had studied two years and a half, and during that time, he explained, he had "labored under many disadvantages." Elihu did not explain that it was lack of money which had put him at a disadvantage. It was time also for Washburne to make a decision about locating himself where he might "hang out his shingle." He had told his mother he might go to the West, but that he was bent upon going South. He wrote his mother saying "I cannot believe you will press any objection to my going south . . . I feel that it is the best thing I can possibly do." However, he was still indecisive about which of several places he might go. He would go South, or, he added, to the far West, "leaving circumstances to determine which way." He even asked if his mother would prefer that he go to Detroit. His sponsor, Col. Otis, advised him to go South. But once he had his diploma, more than circumstances determined where Elihu would go. Cadwallader was the determining factor.

When Elihu was settled on the campus at Cambridge, Cad and Sidney visited him. Sidney came out from Boston, and Cadwallader stopped by on his way west. In the evening, Elihu sent Sid back to Boston and kept his younger brother overnight. He explained in a letter that he "fed [Cad] with milk and honey" and at night let him have one half of his little straw bed, "which is just about as soft as a fine board." The next day, Cad was taken by Elihu to Boston where he saw Cad off for the then Northwest. Mixing metaphors in a letter to their mother, the brother saying goodbye, reported that Cad was "in high glee, kicking up his heels like a house on fire." It was in this same letter that Elihu rebuked his mother for complaining about Cadwallader's wish to go west, telling her she viewed his departure in the wrong light. He wrote, "The western country presents a wide field for enterprise, determination and perseverance . . . " Elihu thought his mother ought to be thankful she had a son of sufficient energy, enterprise and determination to pioneer his way into that great opening. To assure Martha that it was what was being done those days he pointed out that, "Dan'l Webster's son is in Michigan; Buckingham, of the *Courier*, has a son in the same State; Ex-Gov. Lincoln has a son in Illinois, and Judge Thatcher has a son in Natchez, Miss. --all of them lawyers. And he added that "Emerson Coolidge, (a local Livermore boy) is going out there in the spring of 1840." Elihu closed his letter with what may not have been comforting to Martha. It was that he too, Elihu, "may possibly turn footsteps that way . . . "

❖

In the month of March, 1840, Elihu left Massachusetts for the wilds of the West. He had made up his mind. He traveled first to the heartland of political America, Washington, D.C. In Washington, he went to the office of Maine's Senator George Evans, asking Evans to introduce him to the President of the United States, Martin Van Buren. The President and Elihu met. Van Buren was the first of a number of highly placed individuals Elihu would come to know as he made his way West. In Cincinnati, a merchant took Elihu to meet General Harrison, future President of the United States. After a lengthy visit with Harrison, Elihu scribbled a note describing the general, saying he found Harrison "a hard-faced, keen, eagle-eyed, grey headed old gentleman--frank, plain, simple, cordial, ingenuous." Once again, Washburne was attracted to "the plain man," as he had been charmed by humble Judge Story. Elihu's model was his own father, a simple man. Unlike the persons Elihu was meeting as he went west, Israel, Sr., was not powerful politically. George Alfred Townsend once reported that Washburne admired Ulysses Grant because of the general's "simplicity, introspection, sincerity . . . " Elihu referred to Harrison as the man he would strive to elect President, as "chaste and pure . . . a man of the people." Farther along in his journey, Elihu met James W. Grimes of Burlington, Iowa, a person destined to be governor of his State and a United States senator. Another man Elihu met on his journey west was a Maine acquaintance, Joseph B. Wells, later lieutenant governor of Illinois. The opportunity to meet so many people who either were already notable or gave promise of being successful in American political and economic spheres reveals that there was a relatively small elite in the America of the last century and most came to know each other. The experience Elihu had in meeting notables also tells something about Washburne as himself assertive and outgoing, a man who did not hesitate to intrude himself into the lives of other aspiring and active men. In this, Washburne was part of a growing section of the American population feeling "new winds" that had begun to blow in the country.

From 1830 to 1850 new concepts began to dominate American life. Americans became "hustlers." The "new winds" of democracy meant that the *parvenu* were instantly singled out, evaluated and shunned. The democratic spirit manifested itself among politicians as is illustrated in a letter A.C. Buffum of Orono, Maine, wrote to Elihu's brother Israel in 1854. Buffum assumed, as he said in his letter that Congressman Washburn smoked a pipe, adding, "A great many . . . politicians at Augusta ignore cigars because it is not democratic."

Elihu and General Harrison talked beyond the time when Washburne had to leave. The steamboat *Reporter* left Cincinnati without the traveler from Maine. Elihu, however, got aboard a steam packet and caught up with the larger, slowly moving *Reporter*. A few miles down the Ohio river, the *Reporter's* main shaft hoved through the floor of the cabin, and the traveler from Maine was told days were to be added to his journey. Impatient Elihu caught another boat passing down the river to Cairo. Landing at Cairo, Elihu went ashore, saw the community, noting its primitive conditions and said he wanted promptly to shake the dust of Cairo from his feet, to leave the "river thieves, gamblers and cut throats." The ruffians were too much for the village-taught young man whose home was in the shadow of a church.

He boarded the first boat out of port, the *Otter*. The *Otter*  was a new and unfinished boat, and Elihu had to sleep on the floor for the three days and two nights it took to make it to St. Louis. At St. Louis, Elihu went ashore and found himself intrigued with the French character of the city. He remained three days, walking the streets, without knowing, of course, that the family of the woman he was to marry was living in St. Louis; not realizing his future wife had been educated there. Adele Gratiot, as a young girl lived with an aunt, Marie Antoinette de Perdreauville. Marie's mother had been lady-in-waiting to Queen Marie Antoinette. Traveling north on the Mississippi, Elihu landed next at Keokuk, and at this strangely-named community, he experienced something of the past of his

Marie Antoinette

own native State, Maine, with its Indian population. On the shore of the Mississippi at Keokuk he observed the half-breed population with drunken squaws yelling and hooting. He felt fortunate when the *Amaranth* pulled into shore taking on passengers going to Galena. The *Amaranth* made its way north, stopping at every town along the way, and at last arrived in Stephenson, Iowa. The arduous and eventful trip would be finished if, as the boat slipped slowly into shore, Elihu could see his brother waiting. As the boat eased up onto the shore, he strained his eyes, anxious to see the familiar face of his Cadwallader. Sure enough, there on shore stood his brother, "a tall, spare green-looking young man with [a] gray plush cap."

Cad was eagerly waiting the arrival of his big brother. From the time the two men rejoined in Stephenson, Iowa, in 1840, they became inseparable, two loving brothers often separated but always in intimate communication until Cadwallader died 42 years later.

The wide-open mouth of the Fever river seemed to suck ships out of the Mississippi. With Elihu Washburne aboard, the Fever river took the steamboat *Pike* moving slowly up stream until, rounding a bend, there, spread before the curious on board, was a small surprise of the town of Galena. Captain Powers' boat turned perpendicular to the bank and moved cautiously until the lip of the *Pike* was hanging over the sandy shore and a plank connected ship with shore.

April 1, 1840, was a beautiful day for meeting the town and its citizens. Elihu could have been picked out by a native Galenean as a visitor, for in his curiosity Elihu was awestruck looking up to the top of the hill towering far above business road. Elihu walked down the plank. It was early morning. He knew he must make an acquaintance or two and find lodgings. He made it to the Main street from the shore pulling his boots, one after the other, out of knee-deep mud. It was spring. He struggled up to the wooden sidewalk and his life in Galena began. Washburne dated the beginning of his career and his new life from that first day of April in 1840. Thirty-one years later to the day, he sat in the legation in Paris, France, reminding himself that he arrived at Galena before dawn in the stern-wheel steamboat. Reminiscing as he wrote he recalled the spring season with its freshets overflowing the banks of the Fever river. He remembered the precipitous hillside rising from a setback thoroughfare, subjecting businesses along the street with the annual spring floods from the river with water pouring into the principal artery.

Chapter Six

COSMOPOLITAN GALENA

With his cravat appearing to hold up his head, E.B. Washburne's thin-lined  mouth and heavy lines curving from his nose to the sides of his unsmiling mouth, posed for his first portrait. In Galena, as in rural Maine, a portrait was a symbol of success. The photograph captured feelings the subject had about himself, thus the portrait transmitted a message. For one thing, it said the re-settled easterner was Victorian, judgmental, self-composed and determined, a man who was "going places." With the impression Elihu communicated by being entirely himself, he had no difficulty making connections with leading figures in town before the sun set on April 1, 1840. Leaving the steamboat and struggling through the mud to the boardwalk, Elihu met and became friendly with H.H. Houghton, editor of the Whig paper in Galena. Learning that

E.B. Washburne

Washburne was also a Whig, editor Houghton made arrangements for him to deliver a speech to party faithfuls. Four months from that April fateful first day when Elihu made his entrance into the city, he was invited to join Galena's leading attorney, Charles Hempstead. With Houghton and Hempstead looking after the enterprising lawyer's social and political affairs, Elihu had entrée to the gentry of the city, Henry and Nathan Corwin, bankers; Frederick Stahl, insurance broker; John Potts and J.R. Jones, businessmen; and Augustus Chetlain.

Elihu Washburne had chosen the most prosperous community in the northwest for his new home. Galena, Illinois, was the leading commercial town on the Upper Mississippi. In 1840, inhabitants referred to the bustling community as "The Metropolis of the Northwest."(1) It was a pioneer settlement 20 years before Washburne arrived. In Washburne's time, Galena was a river port and mercantile center. Its chief source of wealth was lead. High grade surface ore made mining easy and attracted easterners, as a decade later California gold mines were to lure transient miners. Keelboats laden with lead chugged their way six miles down the Fever River to the Mississippi and then drifted down river to St. Louis. Fifty-four million pounds of ore were shipped from Galena during the year 1845.

Galena was a primitive settlement less than a decade before the New Englander set foot on its shore. His wife-to-be, Adele Gratiot, was the first white child born in the community 14 years prior to his arrival. Among the first white settlers in town was Elihu's father-in-law, Henry Gratiot. Adele told her children that her father, Henry, was in Galena in 1824 when "there were but five log cabins" strung out far up on the shore of the river in the shadow of the cliff rising above. "Those were days," she wrote, "that try men's souls and proved what metal [sic] they were made of." When Henry's wife landed at Galena in 1825 she expected to see a town. There were those few crudely-built cabins. Seventeen people, including Henry's wife Susan, slept in a small cabin until he was able to build a hut with a "clapboard door . . . wooden window, [and] a sod roof," with Buffalo robes spread on the clay floor. There was suffering and hunger, but Adele said her mother told her "she was never so happy as [when] she lived in that rude hut."

Adele Washburne told her children that she weighed three pounds when she was born. To keep her from freezing her father laid her in a cigar box cradle and placed the cradle and baby on the mantlepiece. The woman watching over Adele and mother when Susan was near death was the mother of Augustus Chetlain. Augustus was later to become a strong supporter of Congressman Elihu Wasburne and was one of the nine Civil War Galena Generals.

In the shadow of the past, recovered by Adele Washburne for her children, were stories so dramatic as to appear to be fictional accounts of pioneer life, stories lived by Adele who grew up in Indian territory. When she was six years old, the Black Hawk War broke out. The Sauk and Fox Indians were departing the region too slowly for frontiersmen. White men forced Indians to move west across the nearby Mississippi. The natives were given $1,000 compensation for the rich territory they left under duress. Adele's town was in the war zone where white settlers had usurped territory belonging to tribes. Crops which had been sown in the spring by Indians induced Chief Black Hawk to re-cross the Mississippi with his tribe.

American Indian

In a skirmish, a white man shot and killed an Indian who was carrying a flag of truce. That deed initiated one of the many horrible White-Indian wars in America. Outnumbered and out-gunned, Indians were vanquished. Despite Indians' pleas for mercy at Bad Axe, a volunteer army of white men massacred old men, little children and women. Chief Black Hawk was captured and like a circus animal was put on display in eastern cities. In spite of hardships and adversity she endured growing up, Elihu's wife was known as kind, intelligent, guileless Adele, embraced by the Queens of France and Belgium, and loved by many for her unpretentious ways.

❖

It was said of Washburne's newly-chosen settlement that it had "cosmopolitan grace." Ralph Waldo Emerson, traveling in the west and visiting Galena, noted that northern Illinois communities were culturally "only ten years old." Regardless of Emerson's less than glowing account, Galena actually gave the appearance of being typical of long-settled eastern towns. Like eastern communities, Galena had its levels of rich and poor, professionals and day laborers. Fourteen years after the town was planned in 1826, there was an influx of population amounting to a virtual boom, with a large contingent arriving from the east. The town prospered. As many as 11 steamboats sometimes lined up like pigs at a trough on the shore of the Feve River.

Elihu Washburne added to the attractiveness of the thriving metropolitan center when, three years after he strode up the main street of the town, he constructed a two-floor brick house for his home.(2) When his house was completed and furnished, he married the lovely young Adele. He was ten years her senior. Adele Washburne, née Gratiot, slick black hair parted in the middle, a dusky skin, and entrancing oval brown eyes, captivated Elihu when he first saw her. He drew a word picture of the scene saying Adele leaned into the attorneys' office where he was at work to call her uncle and him to dinner. That glimpse of the pleasant, French-American teenager was enough to entice Elihu. He determined then-and-there she was to be a Washburne.

❖

THE AMBASSADOR'S WIFE KISSED BY THE QUEEN

When Elihu's mother died, Elihu wrote the then-ancient father of the Washburn clan, Israel, Sr., "How terrible must be the deprivation . . . to be left alone in your old age." In 1887 when Elihu's wife died, the despair Washburne felt authenticated for him what he supposed must have been his father's pain. Adele's death in Elihu's old age devastated him. What happened to him and his state of mind is illustrated in an altered writing style. Washburne's thousands of letters, written with lines hastily scribbled across the page always swung upward like a smile. The penned lines of letters written at Livermore where he had gone to die angled sharply, downward a clear sign of loss of fortitude.

Adele Washburne

Who was this maiden Elihu married when she was a teenager and he was in his late 20s, this "Ma Chere Petit"? Who was this woman kissed by Queens om Europe, the woman Elihu said he was going to steal out of Paris to visit, she who was escorted at a banquet by Emperor Napoleon III? The German army surrounding Paris made it necessary for Parisians to eat rats to stay alive. But the Rothschilds sent this woman a delicacy of turtle soup, expensive in the best of times. Bismarck took time to write a personal letter to her while a war raged, assuring her he would forward her letters to her husband in Paris even if the letters were sealed! That letter and promise from the German Chancellor was sent to her when her husband, Elihu, was within enemy lines during the Franco-Prussian war.

Elihu's brother referred to his new "sister," Adele, as the bright-eyed daughter of *La belle France*, descendant of French Huguenots who played with Indian children in her childhood. In fact, Adele owed her life to Josette, an Indian woman who saved Adele's mother's life. Had her mother died, Adele would have followed her to the grave. Susan Gratiot née Hempstead, like Washburne's mother, was the daughter of a Revolutionary soldier. Her family emigrated west from Connecticut, settling in St. Louis where teenager Susan met and married Henry when he was 24 years of age.

Elihu and Adele were married in 1845. Elihu's semi-literate mother wrote him, saying, "I feel from my heart as if you had got a kind and good wife. What she sent us," she assured her son, "it shew a kind and tender heart." Elihu and Adele were apart much of the time during his long career, first when he was a lawyer traveling in the district for the team of Hempstead and Washburne. As Congressman he spent time in Washington, often without his wife who remained at home to raise their seven children. As Ambassador in the 1870s and living in Paris, Elihu was again *sans* wife. Adele had to leave the city during the Franco-Prussian war and communist uprising. Letters passed back and forth constantly, however, between husband and wife. The language of the letters was restrained and always in keeping with the Puritan attitude of New Englander Washburne, yet it is clear there was deep affection and physical attraction which the two felt toward each other. Elihu always confided in Adele, relating sensitive political, economic, and foreign affairs, as well as sharing with her his inner feelings, of delight and despair. His affection for Adele is seen in terms he used in his letters. "My heart is always with you, my happiness would be . . . complete if you could only be here with me. . . pressing you . . . to my heart of hearts . . . glad you are so happy and well." Once when Elihu traveled to Brussels from Paris, he wrote, "I felt that every day I was there [in Brussels] was a day taken from you." Elihu pleaded, "[w]rite me a long letter *three* times a week," "write a little tiny word every day . . . "(3) In her letters to him, Adele expressed the need to have her husband keep messages coming. "I feel very anxious to hear from you," she wrote from Gratiot's Grove. Elihu had gone down to St. Louis from Galena and she wrote, "you scarcely have time to bestow a wandering thought on your little one in Wisconsin." Her more romantic turn of a phrase warmed the heart of her absent husband as she sent, "a thousand messages of love . . . for yourself." A young bride still, she penned a note saying, "write me oftener . . . " and with a practical turn of mind reminded Elihu not to forget "to buy yourself a pair of buffalo overshoes."(4)

Washburne revered Adele's virtue, he said, by which he could have meant her faithfulness to a husband unable to satisfy her desires because of absences. More likely when he used the word to describe Adele, Elihu intended merely to compliment her with the use of that sacred word, virtue. But his choice of words sometimes throws into question his respect for her as a grown woman, referring to her as "a noble little girl," and telling her he would "issue some orders" for her as though she were a child. *She* addressed *him* by telegram on one occasion, asking, childlike, "Can I come[?] Am perfectly able to stand the journey." The custom of the times was for women as wives to be quiet and pleasing to their domineering husbands. Adele appreciated those qualities in herself and, intentionally or otherwise, attempted to teach those virtues to her daughters. As an adult she retained childlike characteristics. It was her ingenuous manner which prompted Napoleon's wife to embrace her.

As a young bride, Adele's interest was in partying, sleighing in winter, attending fairs, suppers and balls. But others had to be depended upon to accompany her in the absence of her husband. Cadwallader, who lived 20 miles away in Mineral Point, sometimes came to Galena to take her to affairs, or Adele traveled to Mineral Point and was shepherded there by Cadwallader. Charles Stephenson and Martha, Elihu's brother-in-law and sister who lived next door in Galena, also tended to her desire to socialize.

A portrait enlivens Adele, creating an impression of a woman at peace. She had a ready smile, and her brown eyes smiled engagingly. The portrait shows dark eyebrows and coal black hair parted in the middle, a custom of the times. The right side of Adele's face hints of gaiety and pleasure-loving. The left reveals the maternal side.

Adele was a small woman. As someone wrote, she was "piquant, pretty and petite." One reporter who knew her said she was Elihu's social equal and equal to any rank to which her husband might ascend. The exception to the beguiling affection which so many had of Adele was a snide remark made by Mary Todd Lincoln. Writing to Sally Orne, she said about Adele, she said she was sure she was a very good little woman, "but scarcely fitted for a *French* Court--All of which manner of confidential expression on *my part--* you will never whisper--I am sure . . . " During the Civil War, Elihu sent letters to Adele daily describing events in Washington and on the war front. He shared with her his thoughts about personalities: Lincolns, Generals McClellan and McDowell, Scott and Ulysses S. Grant, the last, of course,, being the Washburne family friend. There was irony in the letter Elihu mailed off to Adele in March 1861. He wrote that he would be home by April Fool's Day "so as to plant the garden." It was upon the turn of that new month of April that the Civil War began.

Adele Washburne

When Elihu was seven years from retirement, he wrote Adele saying he had no other ambition than to "make you and the children happy," adding, "my heart yearns more than ever for repose and for the happiness of the domestic circle." It may have been one of those times when he was, as he explained, "oppressed with anxiety and sadness." The one person in the world in addition to his brother Cadwallader whom he trusted absolutely was Adele. He was able to share himself with her, able to confess feelings, something the New England male type of the time did not do with ease. He confessed to his wife, "I sometimes get quite discouraged and I dare not tell of the extent of the oppression I . . . experience." At those times, he admitted, he sighed for her presence and her sympathy. Still, Elihu continued to remain away from Adele and home, for he must do his duty, accomplish much, he said to her, "in the face of obloquy and abuse." What he shared with her, his feelings of persecution, was not exaggerated. Adele knew Elihu was the reputed Watchdog of the Treasury. She knew he consistently opposed tendencies by Congressmen to spend money, often unlawfully.

All the while, Washburne thought of himself as a simple, plain man with no pretensions, and he continued to assure Adele that he wanted to retire like a village character. He and Adele, he declared, were old fogy country people. "Old fogy" Elihu may have been in his 70s, but Adele, a spirited, vivacious French-American damoiselle when young, was a mature woman of warmth and without guile in her 60s when she died.

WASHBURNE'S METEORIC RISE TO POWER

"The Immediate Politician"

The New England immigrant had 12 years before he reached the starting line as a political professional on the ladder upward to Congress. When the Maine farmer's son made his way up the shore in Galena in the month of April 1840, he began immediately to feel the tug of career politics. Before April turned into May, he had spoken three times at political assemblies. He was so much into politics, committed to the Whig party, that he brazenly attempted to have himself appointed governor of the Minnesota Territory. He was unsuccessful in the attempt, and was equally unsuccessful in an effort to have himself appointed judge of the Territory. He was successful, however, and sufficiently well- connected politically to receive an appointment from the Governor of Illinois who made Elihu prosecuting attorney for Jo Daviess County.

❖

Truman Smith, the "master spirit of General Taylor's administration," met the ambitious Galenean attorney in Washington, D.C.(5) Smith promptly recognized the political aptitude of the westerner from northern Illinois, and wanted him on his and the President's team. This encounter between Smith and Washburne occurred before Elihu had attained a place of importance, and before he had proven himself on the national level. Nonetheless, the "master spirit," as Elihu called him, came right out and asked, "Do you want anything for yourself or for some of your friends?" The President's man said Elihu could command his influence for anything reasonable. The Galenean's response to Smith was that his proposition was a "matter for future consideration."(6)

Washburne's duties as a lawyer took the aspiring political neophyte to district court sessions where he became acquainted with another ambitious political careerist, Abraham Lincoln. The two attorneys, Washburne and Lincoln, teamed up to work for General Zachary Taylor's nomination for President on the Whig ticket. "Send us a good Taylor delegate from your circuit,"(7) Lincoln wrote Elihu. The prominence of Washburne in ever larger political circles explains his appointment as a delegate to the national Whig convention in 1844. At the Baltimore convention he helped nominate Henry Clay for the office of President.(8) Much later, he said proudly in a floor debate in Congress that he had been at that convention and "helped to nominate Clay." Following the assembly in Maryland, Elihu traveled down to Washington to do more politicking, visiting Senator Evans of Maine to discuss legislation.

Elihu was a natural in the role of politician. He took pleasure in attending Whig conventions. There were consequential matters discussed at those gatherings. In 1848, he was at Washington on behalf of his father-in-law, Henry Gratiot, sponsoring a bill. Washburne was on the floor of the Senate and noticed that when Senator Dodge made a motion to pass the bill, the chairman in the confusion did not put the motion. "Mr. Washburne, however, saw this instantly and as instantly and as dexterously had the motion renewed, and the bill passed."(9) Conventions and court sessions brought him into touch with Lincoln whose humor he enjoyed. He told his Wisconsin brother Cad about an incident which occurred at one gathering. A delegate said he overheard another delegate attack his political opponent, insisting, said the delegate, that he had the same objection to his adversary as he had to the coon. The higher the coon climbed the plainer he showed his asse [sic].

In 1848 Washburne, along with Abraham Lincoln, settled on General Zachary Taylor as the preferred Whig nominee for President. If Lincoln and Washburne were in agreement on Taylor, Elihu and his father were not. Israel, Sr., complained, saying he was sure General Taylor did not know whether he was, or was not, a Whig.(10) Not to be a Whig and yet to let himself be run for high office was shameful. The General, Israel, complained, had never voted in his life, and paid no attention to issues before the country. Father Israel complained further that Elihu's preferred candidate had failed to cultivate statesmanship. Statesmanship was one of the fixed principles in the Whig handbook. All Taylor had done was fight Seminole Indians and poor degraded Mexicans. These deficiencies irked Elihu's father. He wanted Taylor to "go to school."(11) With a touch of humor, the senior Washburn asked who would be chosen to be Taylor's schoolmaster, hinting that it would be a good job for his son.

Like his father, Elihu actually preferred Henry Clay to Taylor or Lewis Cass. He agreed with his critical father, particularly in regard to what he had to say about Cass. President James Polk's Secretary of War, Cass, was held responsible for atrocities in the treatment of Indians on the Trail of Tears. Israel, Sr., wrote of Cass, "he is the meanest of all and would descend to do things for the Slave and war Power which they would not think of asking Taylor to do."(12) Showing his concern for his son as well as for the country, Israel, Sr., ended his letter by assuring himself and Elihu that Elihu would never become a demagogue.

A week after receiving his father's letter Washburne wrote his brother in Mineral Point. Clay, he said to Cad, was his first choice as nominee on the Whig ticket, as it was their father's, but (and this was his reason for disagreeing with his well-informed father), Elihu wanted "a man who can win, and that man," he wrote, "is Taylor."(13) Thinking of his father's criticism he said to Cad, "there is no further dispute about [Taylor's] being a good Whig," and he underscored this contention, adding, "[Taylor] will run with a Whig and act as a Whig after he shall be elected. He will prove omnipotent with the *people*."(14) Elihu felt he knew this for certain having talked confidentially with Taylor's aide and advisor, Truman Smith. In his letter, Elihu instructed Cadwallader in Wisconsin to see that good Taylor men were appointed to attend the national convention, advising Cad to become a delegate, and further, to organize a *Rough and Ready Club* at Mineral Point.

Polk's war with Mexico had provided a reason why Washburne's party made the effort to elect General Taylor. President Polk had pushed hard to provoke the war with Mexico after Texas was annexed. Polk's first message as President intended to arouse ire on the part of the public. In the manner of Presidents before and after Polk, Polk incited the people with propaganda, reporting that "Mexico had been marshaling . . . armies, issuing proclamations, and avowing the intention to make war on the United States, either by open declaration, or by invading Texas."(15) Elihu, a good Whig, explained that while Democratic party's President Polk wanted to send more troops to the conquered country, Elihu, along with Whigs in General, wanted no more men sent out of the country. He felt Polk wanted some 500 officers scattered over the country to electioneer "under the pretense of recruiting."(16) Taylor was, of course, the Whigs' choice, and according to what Cadwallader reported he had read in the papers, Elihu was about the first to put the General's name in nomination at the convention.

❖

In 1848 Washburne reported to his brother that "there is a movement on foot

. . . to bring me out for Congress,"(17) explaining that a move was undertaken without his knowledge and that "it [was] backed by the right people." He was to run against Tom Campbell, four-year veteran of the House of Representatives, a popular public speaker and a dissolute Galena lawyer. According to Elihu, Campbell was a bully. But the Whig candidate, Elihu, would stand for no tormenting from his opponent or anyone else. Washburne proved he was not going to let anyone bully him when a certain client threatened him. The client was thrown down the stairs by the farmer's muscular son. A lesser competitor was another Campbell, Newman, an abolitionist candidate. Elihu wrote years afterward to a Free-soil leader,(18) Zebina Eastman, about his abolitionist opponent, Newman Campbell. Eastman's newspaper, Elihu recalled, "induced many old abolitionists to vote for me, instead of Newman . . . their own candidate." Sitting in Paris writing to Eastman in 1874, Elihu expressed gratitude for those citizens. "My respect for that class of men increases."(19)

Washburne campaigned for Congress aided by a number of prominent Galena citizens, including Augustus Chetlain, S.W. McMaster and R.H. McClellan among many others. These supporters were ranked among leading businessmen, most of whom lived in the elegant houses of Galena overlooking poorer sections of the city from their hilltop homes. In this first attempt to win an office, Washburne was unsuccessful. But in 1852 he was elected and joined his brother, Israel, in Washington. Soon a third Washburn, Cadwallader, was elected and was in the capitol working alongside Israel and Elihu.

❖

There was something irresistible in the person of Elihu Washburne which persuaded people in political circles to recognize the significance and to appreciate the stature of the Galena Whig. The appraisal by highly-placed Truman Smith, in itself, was palpable proof of Elihu's brilliance and promise as a political boss. Indeed, as early as 1855, an opponent of Washburne's was calling him a genius;(20) and at the end of Elihu's life, William H. Bradley who had known the politician for 48 years classed him a genius with his "habits of self-control and mental discipline."

Thus Elihu began his career as a professional politician, 12 years after stepping on the shore at Galena. In the decades following, he would be found, if not a heart-beat from the presidency, at least a nominee for that high office in 1872 and 1880, a man who made unique and exceptional contributions as Father of the House, Watchdog of the Treasury, author of historic legislation, confidant of two Presidents, Abraham Lincoln and Ulysses S. Grant, and Ambassador to France.

Chapter Seven

THE END AND BEGINNING

No period in American history dramatizes the genesis of a new political party as do circumstances surrounding the birth of the Republican coalition of 1854, and the development of that party in 1856 and 1860. Washburns from Maine, Illinois, and Wisconsin were mid-wives as the party came into being. Since the means by which the coalition was formed have not been glamorized, however, the public knows little of the Washburns involvement in the unfolding drama. That is as it should be, given the outlook of the family of brothers. They emphasized the importance of the individual and what the individual could accomplish for larger purposes. Few attempts therefore were made by the Washburns to advertise their wares or publicize their achievements. At most, there were reporters and authors who singled them out and wrote of their triumphs. What has not been documented is the suspense and excitement of the party's birth including the Washburns as among key players.

Algernon Sidney Washburn

The story of a 19th century political party's birth does not begin with its full-blown delivery in 1854. Since the Republican party had many progenitors, it can be said it had its beginning in the 1840s when Whigs were giving expression to the same thoughts Sidney Washburn in Boston had when he wrote to Israel in 1842. Devoted Whig though he was, Sid expressed doubts about his party. They "diddled" in Massachusetts, he said, and in his estimation, "the Whigs never profit from experience and never can remain long in power."(1)
Later, with the benefit of hindsight, Israel referred to the demise of his party as "a kind of euthanasia."(2)

Elihu Washburne's march to power, matching Israel's, outlines the course followed by many loyal Whigs during the '40s into the mid-'50s. Elihu got himself elected by fostering relations with the Free-soil and Liberty parties as well as with abolitionist movements in Illinois. That signified a movement away from the conservative wing of the Whig party. Israel made clear his stand on the divisive slavery issue from the moment he appeared in the capital in 1850, and as expected, he found himself at odds with the party's leading New England Whig, Daniel Webster.

Weeks before a critical Whig convention of 1852 in Baltimore, Israel was heard by an attentive audience which included old-time New England Whigs along with Union Whigs of the South. In anticipation of the Baltimore convention, he spoke on May 24 about *The Compromise as a National Party Test*. As indicated earlier, in his speech Israel predicted that the battle for power by the political parties would be won or lost "on the question of finality resolutions."(3) With a Whig defeat, he said, there would be consequences "we should all deplore." With a succession of defeats, including the Baltimore vote on the finality issue, Israel, as early as 1850, was having doubts about his father's and his own loyalty to the Whigs. The consequences of the "national party test" would be felt, said Israel, not merely by political parties, but by the nation as a whole. The crease in the political fabric, obvious in 1854, would, he believed, become a nation torn and bleeding.

The divergence between northern and southern Whigs occurred when the remnants of the southern Whig party in attendance at a pre-Baltimore caucus lost 11 of 24 delegates. A resolution favoring what was touted as a compromise measure, but a measure distasteful to northern Congressmen, was submitted by a southern Whig. The measure was voted as a result of which 11 southern Whigs withdrew leaving 13 bitter but loyal Whigs from the same bloc. When that occurred, some among northern Whigs felt the way Elihu's friend Truman Smith of Connecticut felt, that "losing the 'ultra mad-cap Southern Whigs' would be beneficial for it would enhance the party's appeal in the North."(4) The Washburns were substantially implicated in a series of unfolding events of monumental importance, events which accounted for the division of sentiments by people across the nation. Three Washburn votes among so many Congressmen would seem inconsequential, though in jest, Thomas Starr King wrote Israel suggesting that Israel "call a caucus of the Washburns" to get through legislation. It was said that the Washburns "at one time were spoken of as one might speak of a distinct party, so great were their influence and fame."(5) Elihu gave teasing credence to that idea, saying to Israel and Cadwallader, that among them they could make Congress listen. To loyal followers and admirers there were times when gargantuan feats could be performed by the three.

The country was settling into a comfortable assurance that with Pierce's election, the sympathy for disunion was dwindling. To be sure, the electoral vote for Pierce had been impressive, 254 for Pierce, 42 two for Scott. Shrewd politicians such as Elihu, however, were searching beneath those misleading electoral numbers, taking note of the popular vote. The President received 1,601,274 votes. Scott had 1,386,580. John B. Hale, Free-soil candidate, received 155,825 votes. Interpretation of the popular vote gave northern analysts courage. They noted that Pierce's majority added up to 58,896 out of a total vote count of 3,143,679.

Once in office, President Pierce said he would do all in his power to resist agitation on the slavery question. While the President was hoping to silence agitators, Senator Douglas of Illinois was laying plans to repeal the Missouri Compromise. The dismayed President was sure the plans of Douglas would prove to be a volatile act provoking strife. It was true, the Little Giant's plan was bound to lead to agitation, certainly agitation for Elihu, Israel, Cadwallader, the Whigs, American party members, Free-soilers, and northern Democrats. The Douglas bill aimed "to legislate slavery into any Territory or State . . . [leaving] people perfectly free to regulate their domestic institutions in their own way." Nebraska and Kansas, Territories seeking recognition, became the subject of heated debate. These were new states north of previously agreed-upon latitude and longitude where slavery was supposed never to be permitted. If Douglas's Compromise bill passed, slaves would be allowed *as property** to be taken into the new states, contrary to the 1820 Compromise agreement. Douglas's legislation was submitted in January 1854. An ally of the Illinois Senator, Dixon of Kentucky, immediately misinterpreted the

---

* Emphasis added.

intent of the measure. The Illinoisan, softly rebuking Dixon, said the bill stands for what (Dixon) "did not intend it should mean." Later, Israel demonstrated clearly that the bill meant exactly what Senator Dixon said it meant, that if passed it would legalize in all States of the Union ownership of human beings.

Benjamin Wade

Senator Douglas had seen to it as early as 1845 that territory south of 36°30' latitude would be open to slavery. Wanting to be assured that slavery could exist north of the line as well as south, Douglas invoked a law passed in 1812 allowing citizens in Missouri to do as they pleased on the subject of slavery. He reminded Congressmen that the 1850 Compromise measure established territorial governments without restrictions as to slavery. Douglas aggravated northern Senators who accused him of undermining the Compromise of 1820 by claiming northerners, not southern Democrats, were the first to abandon the 1820 measure. Northerners, he maintained, voted against extending the line to the Pacific coast. The 1850 bill therefore did what it should, Douglas thought, by doing away with the line altogether and replacing it with the principle of choice to be made by the citizens of new states. Douglas finished his lengthy address in the Senate chambers. Salmon Chase rose to refute the Illinoisan. Chase disputed claims made by Douglas that he, Chase, along with others who opposed the Nebraska bill, had attacked the Little Giant personally. There was, said Chase, only a brief note at the end of the message identifying Douglas as the author. Chase effectively disproved the Illinoisan's assertion that the statement as published was concocted at a caucus of abolitionists. Ohio Senator Chase pointed out that the message critical of Douglas' plan was written by independent Democrats. Senator Wade followed Chase and made bold to say in the course of his remarks that "the slave . . . is equal to anybody else . . . " indicating that the Constitution speaks of blacks as persons. Senator Douglas, on the other hand, made no references in a human vein to those who were being victimized, the blacks. There was only one sentence near the end of his speech in which he referred to "a few miserable negroes." Douglas argued about institutions, concepts, law and the Constitution, as though none of those could be in error. The Illinois Senator, said Wade, was not interested in inquiring of blacks if they wanted to be free. Instead, he relied upon the votes of white majorities in southern states to determine the destiny of a minority of the American population. In following this course, Douglas in effect nullified Constitutional guarantees to minorities. So also did the Supreme Court in the Dred Scott decision. Chief Justice Taney and his court, thinking to reinforce their interpretation of the United States Constitution, asserted that the Missouri Compromise itself was unconstitutional. If the Court were correct, the Nebraska bill and the bill to declare the Missouri Compromise null and void, and the explosive agitation and break-up of Whig party, none of these were necessary and would not have been endured. When the decision was handed down in 1860, though, the furor was once again activated.

Congressman Israel Washburn was floor manager for Whig, Democratic, American, and Free-soiler legislators who opposed the Nebraska-Kansas bill. That meant a four-month stint for the floor manager, Washburn, lining up speakers, watching for openings to take advantage of parliamentary rules which could assist in defeating the bill. As a leading parliamentarian, Israel knew the rules thoroughly.(6) Elihu also had full knowledge of rules and invoked them frequently during the several weeks of debate.

In his lengthy statement of April 4, 1854, Elihu referred not only to blacks as persons but to Indians who were to be compelled to abandon their homes if the Nebraska bill passed. Thinking of the Winnebago who had been befriended by his wife's father, Henry Gratiot, Elihu said Douglas' bill would mean the government "must violate solemn treaty stipulations."(7) Washburne wanted a territorial government organized to preserve the rights of Indians. He did not want to soil Nebraska territory with slavery. Elihu complained of what happened after the Jeffersonian ordinance of 1787 when the Northwest Territory was consecrated to freedom. Despite the ordinance, Kentucky, he said, was admitted into the Union as a slave State in 1791. Several states followed Kentucky's lead to become slave states. Now in 1854, he declared, it was being proposed that even the Missouri Compromise, nearly as inviolable as the Constitution itself, be set aside so slavery might spread over the vast new empire.

Since Douglas and his bill called for non-intervention in the new states, Elihu sought clarification of the meanings of intervention and non-intervention. He wanted to know what privileges the federal government has in states and territories. House members, including Israel, went into detail speaking to this question raised by Elihu. Another unhappy part of the Nebraska plan, Elihu pointed out, would deny unnaturalized citizens "the right of sufferance and of holding office . . . for five years."(8) He pointed out that in the old Northwest Territories there were no such restrictions. The Galena legislator then spent his last few minutes warning Congressmen that the consequences of the repeal of the Missouri measure could not be foretold, though one result would likely be the formation of sectional political parties. He declared in defiance of the President that he would himself become an agitator. He named other agitators: Galileo, Columbus, the Pilgrim Fathers, the Revolutionary men of the previous century, meaning for Elihu his own forebears who fought beside George Washington.

While the Douglas bill was being discussed in the Senate, Israel became concerned upon learning that there was apathy among the New England populace. He therefore wrote letters to newspapers and strategic Whigs in the region, including editor Brewer of the *Boston Atlas*. In response to one of Washburn's letters, Brewer explained he had written an editorial, making good use of the letter from the Maine Congressman. Amos Tuck of New Hampshire reported to Washburn that righteous anger was growing in his state of New Hampshire. The Nebraska bill, he said, was being condemned, and President Pierce was discarded. (New Hampshire was, of course, Pierce's native state.) April 7, three days after Elihu addressed the Legislature, Israel delivered his oration, the finest of his career. As some claim, his April 7 speech was the most vital of all those made in Congress on the subjects of the Nebraska-Kansas and Missouri bills.(9)

Whether intending to or not, Israel evoked laughter at the moment the Nebraska-Kansas bill number 236 was put before the House. Israel moved to lay aside the bill. To the southern delegation that seemed like making a motion to lay aside a tornado. After laughter subsided, the chair called for the vote. Eighty-five voted "yes," 105 voted "no," indicating on the first day how demanding a job the northern contingent had on its hands. Israel's motion was intended to sharpen an awareness of the numerical differences, giving hope, to be sure, to the southern bloc, providing hardly more than a deepening and dutiful determination to northern members to fight vigorously.

The Maine Representative began his April 7th address, noting that in earlier times, even southern leaders saw slavery as an evil. They believed, he said, that slavery would and should be abolished. Rehearsing historical events, Israel explained that a convention in Williamsburg, Virginia, in 1774 resolved that slaves would no longer be imported. In the district of Darien, Georgia, in 1775 a resolution passed with members declaring their abhorrence of "the unnatural practice of slavery . . . " Washington, Madison, Jefferson, Patrick Henry, each southerners, Israel reminded legislators, thought slavery an evil.

The North, he continued, to be sure had submitted to the Compromise of 1850. He assured the audience, however, that there would be no acceptance of a decision to eliminate the Missouri Compromise.

Henry Wilson

Previously, northerners "had been influenced by abstractions and sentiment . . . "(11) He wanted southern delegates to understand clearly that there would be a more direct interest on the part of northerners, should the Douglas bill pass, for free labor would be competing with unsalaried slaves. There was nothing abstract in that instance.

Before Israel finished his hour-long speech, he addressed directly his southern Whig colleagues, some of them warm friends, warning them, if a sectional party were formed there would no longer be a national Whig party to be dissolved. In that case, he said sadly, northern Whigs must bid their fellow southern friends a "long good night."(12) He wished them to realize, too, that as southern Whigs, they would be assisting in "creating a North"(13) if the Nebraska bill were passed.

Senator Henry Wilson of Massachusetts wrote Israel on May 28, 1854. In strong terms he goaded Washburn to "act boldly" to "make a North." Washburn, when he received the letter, realized more fully than ever that the creation of a new party would mean separation from southern Whigs as he had said in his House address, and as Wilson put it, "crush[ing] the National Whig party."(14)

The Maine Congressman had acted boldly several weeks before receiving Wilson's letter. Barbara Dunn Hitchner, historian in Israel Washburn, Jr's., home town of Orono, declared that Israel and her father, Maine Supreme Court Judge Dunn, sat in the living room of the Congressman's house on Main Street where they planned the sequence to be followed in creating the Republican party.(15)

The bill repealing the Missouri compromise passed in the House on May 8. On that May day, Israel set about alerting Conscience Whigs, northern

James Pike

Democratic, Free-soil, and American party members, of a meeting he was organizing. On May 9, 31 House members met with Congressman Washburn and Gamaliel Bailey, editor of the newspaper the *National Era*. Members of the group concluded that the time had come for a new party to be created. This decision-making clique decided expressly to use the name Israel recommended for the new fusion group, the Jeffersonian epithet, Republican.

An interesting comparison can be made of the two Washburns, Israel and Elihu, as a result of the course of events leading to the crucial, history-making vote on the Nebraska bill. The day before the vote in the House, Elihu wrote his Maine friend, James Pike, reporter working for Horace Greeley's New York *Tribune*. Elihu was so angry he swore in writing. Cursing northern legislators who had failed to speak against the bill, he said, "there was no heart, no concert, no courage exhibited by the opponents of the bill." He closed his letters with the words, "I am too d---[sic] mad to write any more."(16)

A few days later Israel wrote Pike. The Congressman from Maine began his letter, "Alive, hearty, and indomitable." He had worked, he said, for 36 hours to hold the enemy at bay. Still, his attitude was one of confidence.(17) He had "done his duty," Israel felt, by organizing what would be permanent opposition to pro-slavery legislation.

In a word, Israel Washburn, Jr., had launched the Republican party.

The Maine Congressman's more jubilant manner, in comparison with his brother, Elihu, elicited letters from constituents showing a similar jollity. A.C. Buffum wrote about the Nebraska bill while the vote was still pending, saying he was of the opinion that all who supported the bill, not excepting the President "ought to go to h--l"[sic].(18) He said in his letter to Washburn that he had told the Orono parson he would be sent to Washington to use the rifle "as he is the best shot among us."(19)

In early June 1854 Israel returned to Maine and spoke at the City Hall in Bangor. He talked to his fellow citizens about the historic meeting organized at Washington, and spoke favorably of a new national party, referring to the use of the name Republican to identify the party. In July a convention was held in his native state, and on the 27th of the month the Republican party of Maine was created.(20)

A few days before making another speech dealing with Kansas, Israel received a letter from a leading political figure in Maine, Isaac Reed. Whig Reed was running for the office of governor of the state. Reed asked Washburn if he would consider accepting a place on the Maine Supreme Court. The letter may have seemed gratuitous to Washburn, knowing he had a fight on his hands with Maine Whig conservatives, Reed being counted among the conservatives. Whigs wrapped their robes close around themselves refusing to unite behind the new party composed of Free-soilers, Know Nothings, Conscience Whigs and Liberty Party members who were to endorse Lot Morrill, a former Democrat. Israel had no interest in the position offered by Isaac Reed. He was hoping rather that there would be an opening for him in the U.S. Senate.

Two years later on the 14th of March, the Maine Congressman rose to speak about the contested elections in the Territory of Kansas.(21) The cogency of his arguments impressed listeners, including southern Representatives who challenged Israel in vain as he made his presentation. The subject matter called forth Washburn's clearest thinking concerning charges of irregularity in the election process in Kansas. Allegations of corruption in the election of Kansas legislators was what prompted Washburn's speech. A pro-slavery Lecompton Constitution had been passed by a fraudulent legislature. The question was then, who has jurisdiction, the Kansas Legislature or Congress? Once again, it was the states' rights issue being brought into focus. The infamous Lecompton Constitution had been forwarded to Congress with a message from President Buchanan recommending its acceptance.

David Broderick

It can only be surmised that the formidable arguments put forth by the Maine Congressman influenced Senator Douglas. Israel's reasoning could have made clear to the Little Giant that he would lose his seat in the senate in the next Illinois election if he favored the Lecompton Constitution. Being made to realize as much, Douglas broke with the Democratic administration.

Douglas was assisted in his effort to transform the party by California Senator David Broderick. Like Douglas, Democrat Broderick opposed the Lecompton Constitution. His endorsement of Douglas' position resulted in his death in a duel. Judge Terry, a southern Democrat living in California, killed Broderick. Another Broderick-inspired duel had been fought five years earlier involving Elihu's brother, Charles. Charles, editor of the San Francisco *Alta California*, was promoting Broderick for governor.

What happened in Elihu's State of Illinois is part of the story of the beginnings of the new party. Slavery was a sectional issue in Washburne's State. In Elihu's Northwest Territory there were many who favored fusion, and who were greatly exercised over the Nebraska bill. A Free Democratic party, with Washburne's friend Zebina Eastman taking the initiative, organized an anti-Nebraska coalition. Eastman sat down with Whig Lincoln and tried in vain to convert him to the movement. Cassius Clay also talked with Lincoln while, said he, Old Abe lay on the grass whittling a stick, but again in vain. Ichabod Codding and a number of other prominent leaders, along with Clay and Senator Salmon Chase, collaborated in an effort to abolitionize the State of Illinois. In late August, Codding, speaking at Peoria, made the claim that Free-soil and Liberty parties were finished. He invited his audience to join him in forming another party.

Washburne returned to Galena from Washington prepared to campaign for his re-election. In July, he and Zebina Eastman worked to establish a base of support for a fusion party. Eastman wanted to see a party organized based on the Declaration of Independence. He knew Washburne of Galena would be nominated at a September convention of Whigs and was confident of where Elihu's loyalties were. The Galenean had let it be known that he was interested in the platforms of the Liberty and Free-soil parties. The Free soil party had been formed by "Conscience Whigs," one of whom was his brother, Israel. A classmate of Elihu's, Richard Henry Dana, Jr., with a few others, had already broken with the Whigs, coalescing with other antislavery men to form the Free soil party. Eastman knew Elihu was seeing signs of dissolution in his own Whig party, but he knew he was not ready to give up and join another party, even while he was impressed by the vitality and efficiency of the Liberty and Free-soil parties. Eastman concluded that a member of either of those two parties could not be elected, but that if people voted for principles, ignoring party ties, a good man could be chosen. He turned to Washburne who was willing that his Whig party should die when it had outlived its usefulness. The two men adopted a strategy. For Elihu it meant he would run as a Whig accepting the anti-slavery principles of the Liberty party. Washburne found new strength with the shift. Constituents wrote to congratulate him. C.G. Holbrook of Buffalo, Illinois, reported to the Congressman that "[h]undreds in our county have been wanting an opportunity to leave the insolent democratic and the narrow-minded 'one idee' parties . . . "(22) Abolitionist William B. Dodge wrote, "You have nothing to fear, dear sir, from your constituency in following out the high moral course of legislation which you have adopted."(23)

Washburne joined Eastman in planning an anti-Nebraska convention. It was to take place in Rockford, Illinois, on August 30, 1844. There were Whigs present, some who were aspirants working to take Washburne's place in Congress, who refused to endorse the Rockford gathering because they considered the convention to be a Washburne undertaking. Elihu spoke at the gathering resulting in his re-nomination by acclamation as candidate for the house seat. The Fusion party at its Rockford meeting adopted the designation "Republican" as its official name.(24)

Whigs disappointed in Washburne's new loyalty called for a second and strictly Whig convention. Partisans of Elihu's attended the Rockford Whig assembly to make certain a third ticket was not nominated. They were successful and Washburne went on to victory, winning with a plurality of 5905 votes, compared with only 286 two years earlier.

❖

As noted, the Republican party became official in Maine in July 1854. In the same month the party became official in Wisconsin. One month later, the party name was adopted in Illinois.

A meeting had been called in Madison, Wisconsin, after a dramatic Paul Revere-type horseback ride made in Milwaukee by black-bearded, six-foot tall Sherman Booth. Booth learned that a runaway slave, Joshua Glover, had been

Sherman Booth

bloodied and bruised by a southern agent. Glover had been taken from his home to be returned to his southern master. Outraged by the incident, Booth "mounted a dark, blazed-face horse, and full-bearded, bald-headed, and in trumpet tones, [rode] through the principal streets,"(25) of the city, shouting that a meeting was to be held in the courthouse square. This sensational event was a further illustration of what Israel predicted would occur. He had declared that the "finality" principle--referring to the Fugitive Slave law--would be responsible for the destruction of the Whig movement. It was that finality law which lead to the arrest of Whig Booth for obstructing justice. The result of Booth's arrest was that he was made a martyr. Anti-Nebraska Whigs and Democrats alike responded heartily to the martyr's invitation to anti-Nebraska folks for a follow-up meeting in Madison on the 13th of July. Martyr Booth's wish was for the Whigs to extend the call of the Madison convention. They hesitated. Booth acted resulting in the official establishment of the Republican party at the Madison gathering.

The following month self-selected leaders in the 2nd district of Wisconsin wrote Cadwallader Washburn asking him to run for Congress on the Republican ticket. Like his brothers, Cadwallader modestly confessed surprise upon being invited to stand, stating in his letter of response that he doubted if his business affairs would permit him to campaign. On August 9 Washburn responded to J.A. Sleeper, Representative of the Republican State Convention, expressing surprise that his name was mentioned for Congress. He could not promise to accept the nomination for Congress on account of business engagements but if the tender came with entire unanimity on the part of the Convention, he would consider the propriety of accepting. As he undertook this career change, Washburn's self-confidence was to be seen in his unwillingness to go out of his way to cultivate a speaking style to correspond with the politician's typical stump mannerisms. The Crawford County *Courier* reported that, "without attempting any unnecessary flourish at oratory [Washburn] gave an unsophisticated exposition of his view . . . in such a manner as to be . . . understood by all."(26) The final count gave Washburn 8136 votes, and his opponent, Dr. Hoyt, 4708. He took his place beside his brothers in December 1855.

On the west coast another brother became a promoter of the cause of Republicanism. Charles Ames Washburn intended to do his part in making the party a reality in California.

As with thousands of others in 1849, Charles, sometimes called (and he called himself) the vagabond of the family, went to the land's end, California, and to Mariposa to mine gold. Tiring of the occupation he turned reporter and editor. His first position was as a member of the newspaper staff in "violence-torn" Sonora.(27) In San Francisco in 1853-4 Charles became editor of the "monument among our political institutions," the *Alta California*. Charles used his historically neutral newspaper for political purposes to advance the Republican cause, and yet at the same time, he was supportive of a leading Democratic political leader, David Broderick. It is possible Charles had received encouragement from Elihu in Illinois to promote the idea of anti-Lecompton people's coming into the party under the umbrella of the fusion party. Elihu, it seems, had given the appearance of welcoming Stephen A. Douglas into the party.(28) Horace Greeley, editor of the New York *Tribune*, fellow Universalist and friend of the Washburns, was said to have persuaded Elihu to adopt this posture vis-à-vis anti-Nebraska Democrats.(29) Having taken that position, Elihu found himself at odds with Lincoln. Lincoln did not want to see the powerful and popular Douglas coming into the party as a competitor for high office. But correspondence made it clear that a letter Washburne wrote was misconstrued, upsetting a number of politicians, including Mr. Lincoln. Lincoln, however, straightened out the matter to his own satisfaction and wrote Washburne on April 26 saying in the sensitive way the future President had of making persons feel agreeable, "I am satisfied you have done no wrong, and nobody has intended any wrong to you."(30)

If Elihu aroused the ire of Lincoln, mistakenly giving the impression that he was attempting to lure Democrat Douglas into the Republican fold in Illinois, Charles in

San Francisco, also misconstruing Greeley's and his brother's intent, stirred up a hornet's nest with editor Pixley of the *Daily Whig and Commercial Advertiser.* Charles, Whig Pixley thought, was trying to entice Democrat Broderick. Charles was clearly "his own man." As a result, when patronage plums were handed out after the election of Mr. Lincoln, Charles did not receive the appointment he desired, which was to head the U.S. mint in the city. The post did not go to Charles, even though one of Lincoln's closest friends, Edward Baker, recommended Charles. Lincoln was instead impressed with arguments from Republicans of California who knew Charles and who insisted he was unreliable--this, despite the fact that Charles left Chicago in 1859 to return to San Francisco to team up with Alvan Flanders for the purpose of establishing a Republican newspaper.(31) Charles' paper gave strong support to Lincoln. J.F. Hoyt, in a letter to Elihu, reported that Charles was one of the pioneer Republicans in the state party and said, "he has made more sacrifices for the party than most any other man here." Hoyt added, "old Wheel Horses of the Party ought not to receive the go-by in favor of new-born Republicans."(32) Still, Lincoln balked and only after making Charles wait five months did he appoint him Washburn Commissioner to Paraguay.

Thomas Jefferson

❖

Four Washburns were "winners" in the effort made to organize a second major party in the United States in 1854. Elihu and his Mineral Point brother, Cad, together with Charles in San Francisco had accepted the challenge resulting from Israel's launching of the party. The Maine Washburn had seen fit to take seriously the warning mailed off to Maine's Senator John Holmes 34 years before. The letter to Holmes from the Sage of Monticello reverberated in the elder Washburn brother's head. Jefferson had said he considered the Clay Compromise of 1820 to foretell "the knell of the Union."

Winner Israel, fighter Elihu, ambitious Cad, and western warrior Charles agreed that the time was at hand when a new politics was called for in America. They felt that only a new politics could create a party able to counter the weight and strength of Democrats whose influence was pervasive in the North as well as in the South.

Chapter Eight

THE NEW ADMINISTRATION AND WAR

The Republican party's first great victory came in 1860 when Illinoisan, Abraham Lincoln, ran for the office of President and won. It represented triumph for the coalition of former Whigs, Northern Democrats, Free-soilers, and the American party. The victor, Abe Lincoln, was elected at a crucial nexus in the history of the Republic, with people thereafter thinking in terms of the *before* and *after* of his election and as a consequence the preservation of the union.

The nominee chosen at the Republican convention in Chicago on May 17, 1860 had enjoyed the assistance of Galena politician, Elihu Washburne. Advice given by the Galena Congressman as he surveyed constituents was that Abe Lincoln must take an *ultra* stand on the slave question. While his attitude toward blacks and slaves became clear to Lincoln's advisors, he was nonetheless advised to refrain from making public statements between the time of his election and inauguration. He wrote Washburne's old friend, Truman Smith, to that effect, saying he felt "constrained, for the present at least, to make no declarations for the public."(1) The President-elect wanted to make it clear, however, that there must be no compromise on the issue of slavery extension. He wrote Washburne saying,

> Prevent, as far as possible, any of our friends from demoralizing
> themselves and our cause by entertaining propositions for
> compromise of any sort on 'slavery extension.'(2)

As it became apparent that the candidate was "right" on the slave question, Washburne began to work with Free-soilers on behalf of his Springfield friend. The Galenean contacted Salmon Chase and Joshua Giddings seeking their help in electing Lincoln. Giddings expressed his delight in the nomination of Old Abe, saying he would walk from Ohio to Illinois to elect Lincoln.

At the convention in Chicago, Israel and Cadwallader, different from Elihu, supported the candidacy of William Seward. Editor Charles Ames Washburn in San Francisco also favored Seward, declaring in an editorial that there had been but one

man in the country comparable to the aspiring Republican candidate, Seward; and that man, wrote Charles, was Thomas Jefferson.(3) Actually, Elihu, like his brothers, favored Seward, but after the *Irrepressible Conflict* speech, he turned to Lincoln with his more moderate views on the subject of slavery. The brothers laughed at Elihu for thinking Lincoln might win. Joining with Charles Ray, formerly of Galena, friend and supporter of Elihu, were Leonard Swett from Maine, also a Washburne friend, and Judge David Davis, Richard Oglesby, and Norman Judd.

Salmon P. Chase

These saw to it that Lincoln was elected on the fourth ballot. During the campaign that followed, the Galena Representative delivered a speech in Congress entitled *Abraham Lincoln, His Personal History and Public Record*.(4) The Republican Congressional Committee printed Elihu's biography of Lincoln, which was said to be one of "the most meritorious of the campaign of 1860."

As for Seward, after the defeat he planned to drop out of politics, disillusioned with what had transpired at Chicago. Israel, joined by Charles Francis Adams, visited the disappointed candidate in his home in Washington. They talked Seward out of returning upstate to his home and retirement.

. . . Two prominent members of the House, Charles Francis Adams and Israel Washburn, called at [Seward's] home. The  *Tribune* was industriously circulating reports of his resignation from the Senate, and there were other rumors of his retirement from public life. The two men urged him to remain an active Republican leader, for they were alarmed lest, with Lincoln at the helm, the party might lose direction. Seward listened to them and, much to their relief, appeared to be receptive.(5)

William Pitt Fessenden

Shortly thereafter, the President-elect sent a letter to the disappointed candidate, Seward, telling him that, "at the proper time [I shall] nominate you to the Senate for confirmation as Secretary of State . . . ."(6) During the campaign, Seward went to Maine to visit his champion, Israel, who was in the running for Governor of the State. At Bangor, Seward was introduced by the Mayor of the city who embarrassed the visitor by expressing regret that Seward had not been nominated Republican contender. Seward, who was not temperamentally cordial, responded politely urging the people of Bangor to vote for Lincoln.

Elihu was looked upon as an advisor to candidate Lincoln. When the President arrived in the capital for the inauguration, Washburne was regarded as his spokesman. The candidate was scheduled to speak in Pennsylvania. Washburne advised him not to address the subject of the party's plank relating to the rights of immigrants. Proponents of the American party position regarding immigrants were numerous in the Keystone State and Elihu did not want Lincoln to lose the election in Pennsylvania, one of the important states. Elihu reminded Lincoln that the Republicans must have the American party's support. Advisor Washburne opposed the appointment to the Cabinet by Lincoln of Simon Cameron of Pennsylvania. Washburne felt confident Lincoln would not appoint Cameron. He was so confident that he wrote Salmon Chase saying Cameron would not have a place in the Cabinet, adding that it was necessary that Chase should go into the Cabinet "if Lincoln has tended you a place." Elihu had written to Lincoln December 10, "If it were understood today that Chase would take the Treasury, the country would draw a long and easy breath." Washburne, known as the Watchdog of the Treasury, was in a position to know the exacting demands made of the Treasurer and felt certain Chase was the man the President needed to accede to that Cabinet position. When Elihu learned that Lincoln had chosen Cameron as Secretary of War, he wrote a letter to the President-elect, saying bitterly, "The report which has reached here this morning, that Cameron is going into your cabinet has created intensive excitement and consternation among *all* of our friends here. I trust in God, it is not so."

Washburne advised Lincoln that it was absolutely necessary for Salmon Chase to be Secretary of the Treasury. Lincoln listened to the Congressman's advice with regard to Chase and promptly appointed him Treasury Secretary. But he also appointed Cameron. Cameron came into the Department "under the imputation of corruption, and he lived up to the worst expectations."(7) Lincoln had cause to regret not listening to Washburne's advice about the Pennsylvanian given Cameron's record. When later Chase resigned from the Treasury, Washburne once again advised Lincoln, this time to appoint William P. Fessenden of Maine to succeed Chase. Lincoln complied and his advisor from Illinois happily reported to John Hay that "the appointment of Fessenden [was] received with great eclat." Skillfully gauging the interests of congressmen, and knowing about the growing discontent of the Southern delegation, Washburne advised "masterly inactivity" as the proper stance for candidate Lincoln to assume during the campaign. Vengefully, Elihu helped to frustrate Edward Bakers attempt to have Lincoln place him in his Cabinet. Washburne was successful in blocking the Bakers appointment. He assisted Caleb Smith in Smith's efforts to obtain the position.(8) In the early fifties, Baker had moved into Washburne's area, ran for a seat sought by Elihu and won. For that and other reasons, the Galena candidate wrote critically of him saying that as he moved through the area he heard bitter denunciations of Baker, and referring to his nemesis as "traitor-in-chief" of a cabal which had succeeded in weakening the Whigs.(9)

Another example of the leverage Washburne possessed took place when the President said he was going to appoint David Davis to a judgeship in Illinois. Washburne protested. Davis, he said, might remove his friend, William H. Bradley, Clerk of the U.S. Court in Chicago. The President in his letter to Davis said he was anxious that Mr. Bradley be retained, and asked Davis to tell him that he would not remove Bradley. Davis obliged.

The obligation Lincoln felt toward Elihu resulted in numerous appointments of Washburne's relatives and friends. Such favors as Lincoln granted to the Northern Illinois Congressman prompted one House member to elicit laughter as he said of the Washburns,

[E]very young male of the gentleman's family is born into the
world with 'M.C,' franked across his broadest part.(10)

Washburne spoke at important meetings on behalf of Lincoln. At a Republican Ratification meeting in New York, Washburne and Vice President Hannibal Hamlin, a Washburne relative, spoke to a large public which included Douglas supporters. When Elihu began to speak, gangs of rowdies threw brickbats, attempting to break up the assemblage. When Elihu began to speak about Lincoln, saying, "a nobler man . . . combining more fully all the characteristics which challenge . . .," the disruption began a second time. Elihu, "[u]nmoved amidst the excitement and confusion" was heard proclaiming in stentorian tones to the audience made up largely of Republicans, "Stand your ground; are you cowards? . . . [M]aintain your rights, or die." What Congressman Washburne shouted intimidated the mob and strengthened the backbone of the Republican audience. The meeting continued.

A President-elect cannot perform necessary duties in the months leading up to his inauguration. Lincoln was not yet in office and could not plan for contingencies. He realized "war talk" was everywhere and was concerned. His Washburn friends were among those making threatening sounds as they held forth in the House and talked about disunion. Were there to be disunion, Cadwallader Washburn declared, there would be war. He said he preferred disunion to having to pass "obedient necks beneath the southern yoke."(11) Under the circumstances, the President-elect needed to know the position of the Commander-in-Chief of the army, Winfield Scott.(12) Lincoln knew his friend Elihu had worked for Whig nominee Scott when the General sought the presidency in 1852.(13) Perhaps Lincoln had somehow learned also of the gracious letter Scott had written in 1856, telling Elihu of his affection for "my three friends, the Washburns." A letter went to the Galenean from the anxious President-elect, asking Elihu to visit the General and to tell him that he, Lincoln, would be obliged if the Commander-in-Chief of the army would be "as well prepared as he [could be] to either *hold* or retake the forts, as the case may require, at and after the inauguration."(14) Washburne met with the general and reported back to Lincoln that Scott was prepared to either hold or retake the forts.

In the Scrapbook of Washburne's Illinois friend, Russell Jones, is a newspaper

clipping in which it is written that "Nobody enjoys the confidence of the President in a higher degree than Mr. Washburne . . .," In their book on Lincoln, Nicolay and Hay indicated that after the election in '64 the Galena politician "was in constant touch with Lincoln," and that Lincoln consulted Elihu about persons in Illinois who should be considered for the Cabinet. In 1861, the Administration began with Washburne representing the President's views to committees of the House. Years later Isaac Arnold, biographer of the assassinated President, wrote a letter to Elihu's daughter, Susan, saying he could with truth report that "the strong arm of Lincoln did lean on [your father] for support and that [he, your father] yielded that support with unwavering loyalty and vigor."(15)

Abraham Lincoln

Not a congressman's, but a farmer's hours, found E.B. Washburne walking up and down the railroad platform in the still dark morning hours awaiting the arrival of the President-elect. Washburne expected William Seward to accompany him as he paced the platform. Seward and Washburne were the only two men in Washington who knew when Abraham Lincoln would arrive. It was kept mysterious because threats had been made against the life of the President-elect; and, in fact, while Lincoln was still in Springfield, Washburne had received word that there was a plot to assassinate him. Washburne saw to it that General Stone was put in charge of detectives who were to guard Lincoln. Elihu wrote to Springfield, saying he and three others had procured the services of detectives who were looking into the conspiracy. Elihu wrote a second letter to Springfield to say he was being posted every day with regard to the alleged plot, and that he, Washburne, was *"satisfied there does not NOW exist any organization . . .* to prevent your inauguration." The Congressman said he did not want Mrs. Lincoln to "entertain any fears."(16) Routes and times of arrival had been changed to foil the assassins.

Since Seward failed to appear, the sole Washington host, Elihu, stood by a post watching the train enter the station. The hiss of steam and the clanging bell aroused Elihu and he looked back down the line of cars to see passengers alighting. No Old Abe appeared until the cars had emptied their Washington bound commuters. The long legs of Lincoln emerged, his feet dropping upon the filigreed iron step and down onto the platform. There was no mistaking Elihu's Illinois friend. Accompanying him were two Pinkerton guards, E.J. Allen and Ward Hill Lamon. The latter was no friend of Washburne's and was about to take action against a possible threat to the President when Lincoln identified the Congressman. "That's old Washburne," said the Old Abe. The two high-hatted Illinois old friends, Lincoln and Washburne, exited the station and entered the carriage Elihu had arranged to have wait.

When the President-elect entered the capital, Washburne advised him to move into a private house. In fact, Elihu rented a residence and chose a private secretary who was to help Lincoln as a new-comer, and, one supposes, help Washburne himself to whom the secretary would be indebted. Instead, Lincoln, after having asked Washburne to consult with the Illinois delegation about living quarters, settled in at Willard's Hotel upon the advice of Norman B. Judd, Chairman of the State Central Committee of Illinois. Abraham Lincoln's reign was about to begin.

❖

A bitterly cold wind from the northwest discouraged applause as President Lincoln delivered his first inaugural speech. Hands pushed deep into coat pockets could not have made General Scott's soldiers happy, or Pinkerton's men as they circulated in the crowd watching for possible assassins. It was feared that the cold day in March might be a fated "ides of March" for the ungainly man standing outside the capitol *sans* overcoat, ready to place his heavy hand upon the pages of the bible to be made President of the United States of America.

Recalling the occasion, Senator William D. Washburn of Minnesota told a journalist that on that fated day, "the national capital was . . . a veritable volcano."(17) With the forbidding weather, the metaphor was not exactly fitting. It was germane nonetheless, given the circumstances of "a southern city . . . filled with southern sympathizers [and] men bitterly hostile to the new President."(18) The Minnesota Washburn told the journalist, "every second that Lincoln stood out upon the portico of the capital . . . his friends expected him to be shot . . . "(19)

Six Washburn were at the inauguration. Not all of them had patronage on their minds. Charles and William did, however. Elihu, Israel and Cadwallader were present as members of Congress. Sidney was present, sure to have some comical observations to make when it was over. Samuel was in Wisconsin where he wrote plaintively in his diary,

"I would be glad if it were so I could go to Washington," adding wryly, "it is no difficult matter to get money enough to stay at home."

Following the installation ceremony, William was taken by Elihu to meet Mr. Lincoln. His recollection of the meeting was recounted by him for the journalist:
No man could have posed less than Lincoln. The consciousness that he had been suddenly advanced into the most absolute power, perhaps, that any American has ever held was never suggested by a word or a look. He knew how to discipline with a phrase, the most masterful general, Cabinet Minister, or foreign diplomat. His manner always enforced respect. Yet it was the manner of an 'every-day' man. On being presented to him, you soon began to think that you were meeting once more some old and intimate friend.

RESPONSE TO FORT SUMTER IN A NORTHERN VILLAGE

In the beginning war is a national not a provincial phenomenon. While historians report findings which account for the initiation of combat begun at the national level, they are well advised to report steps explaining the means by which cooperation with the federal government arises in neighborhoods, hamlets, villages, and cities. In fact, when the "God of Battles" is invoked on the national level summoning people to engage an enemy, the call evokes a response on the local level. Often, reports from the proverbial grass roots demonstrate coercive tactics used by a patriotic populace and those who are acknowledged community leaders. Accounts indicate that the law operates against dissidents. What transpires demonstrates the appeal to primitive instincts, the allure of adventure, the creation of a nationalistic spirit, and the process by which community leaders are substituted for those who are out of step with the patriotic mood. Dissidents are removed from the political arena and returned to the routine of mundane life, if not ostracized or jailed.

In March 1861 elections were held in Galena. Democrats won eight out of ten seats, and Democrat Mayor Robert Brand was re-elected. However, the Democratic victory was not complete in Washburne's town. Republicans had worked vigorously to line up votes for Abraham Lincoln. Democrats were attracted to the Republican candidate and the Free-soil, Free Men Republican platform. Democrats were impressed by the unofficial Republican position expressed in the *Gazette* written by Washburne's friend, H.H. Houghton. Houghton declared that, "Any sensible man cannot fail to know that . . . the negro [sic] is regarded mentally, socially, and politically beneath the whites . . . " but "the Republican party holds that [Negroes] . . . are persons, and, as human beings, are entitled to rational treatment . . . "(20)

Lincoln loyalists outvoted Douglas in East and West Galena, indicating allegiance, not only to the Republican party but to the Union. To be sure, in the election of local leaders, Democrat Robert Brand was elected Mayor along with eight of ten Democratic City Council members. But a month after the election, the first challenge to Democratic Mayor Brand was made by a respected Republican leader in town, Elihu B. Washburne.

❖

On April 12, 1861 Major Robert Anderson and his company came under the siege of guns fired from Charleston, South Carolina, at Fort Sumter. Edmund Ruffin, a fanatical old man who later committed suicide rather than live under the American flag, pulled the trigger which activated the bombardment of the fort. The Civil War had begun. The response in Galena, Illinois, illustrates what happened across the northern part of the country. As word of the unprovoked attack on a Federal fort raced over the wires to communities, there was swift response. In Galena, the anger of bulldog Washburne prompted action. The people of the city were called together at the courthouse. Washburne and other leading citizens intended there would be a thorough airing of the unprovoked attack in South Carolina. Among the decision-makers in Galena who took the reins in response to the shelling of the fort was no-nonsense Washburne with vitriolic tongue ready to target dissenters. Frederick Stahl was another, monk-like in his business suit, a merchant looking for all the world like a sharp-nosed Savanarola. There also was kindly-looking Henry Corwith, bald, round-headed with heavy dark eyebrows, a shrewd banker sitting like an icon behind a desk doling out money at generous interest rates. Other leading characters in the Galena drama were businessmen, lawyers, professionals, teachers, bankers, and politicians.

At the meeting in the city courthouse was another--a complete nonentity lost in the crowd--a short, chunky, full-bearded, quiet man, obscure even to the handshaking politician, Washburne. This was a leather salesman named Ulysses Grant who worked out of a shop on the Main street of the town. John Rawlins was there, black-bearded Democratic lawyer ready with a speech to thrill the patriots. On that April night Rawlins tried to "avoid forcing the issue between the slave and free states."(21) Listening to the half-hearted Democrat Rawlins was the Congressman, Washburne, whose brother had launched the sectional party responsible in part for the crisis being addressed at the courthouse. Before Rawlins finished speaking, his tone changed and he completed his remarks with a rousing call for loyalty to the federal government, arousing the fervor of the ex-Captain of the United States Army and leather salesman, Grant. For years, the General remembered the Rawlins speech and his own emotional reaction on that historic occasion.

Washburne's law partner, Charles Hempstead, had called to order the April 16th courthouse session. Mayor Brand was elected by the audience to preside. He took the podium addressing the assembly in a halting voice. Virginia was Brand's native State and he must have asked himself what war would mean for relatives and friends. He was now a northerner, but ambiguity clearly burdened the chairman of the conclave. As Mayor and chairman, he declared that he favored a compromise. He was opposed to making war on any portion of the country.

Brand's hesitancy to declare his loyalty to the government was unacceptable to the fiery Congressman, Washburne. Washburne came to his feet looking fierce, and casting his eyes over the crowd of neighbors, friends and Democratic loyalists. He exploded his disapproval of Brand's opening remarks. Gesticulating wildly, Elihu submitted a motion that Brand vacate the chair. His motion was seconded, and as chairman the Mayor called for the "yes" votes and was ready to withdraw. He neglected to call for the negative until he was urged to complete the vote. It became clear that the majority wished the Mayor to continue in the chair. There was confusion until the monk-like Stahl, himself a Democrat, stood to deplore partisan feelings, urging harmony. Elihu saw the wisdom of Stahl's remarks, withdrew his motion, and submitted a resolution. It called for the formation of two military companies, and urged the Illinois legislature to respond to Lincoln's summons for troops. A vote on the resolution followed and Galena townsmen agreed they would support the government of the United States; "having lived under the stars and stripes, by the blessing of God, we propose to die under them."

One meeting was not sufficient to work up the war spirit in Galena. Two days later another rally was held and at the second gathering Washburne submitted the name of ex-Captain Ulysses Grant as presiding officer. The modest, reluctant, Democratic salesman was surprised that a Republican, Elihu, would nominate a Democrat to a place of leadership. Democrat Rawlins, "who electrified the audience with [his] stirring war speech,"(22) also won the applause of Washburne. Washburne had no trouble with bi-partisanship and recognition of lawyer Rawlins. Elihu not only encouraged the formation of a company of soldiers invited to drill on his spacious lawn, he saw to it that Democrat Grant headed the company. Washburne encouraged businesses to provide uniforms. He persuaded women to solicit subscriptions to procure a flag for the Galena company. The Congressman's heavy hand brought about a turn-around on the part of the Mayor. When the company was to leave for Camp Washburne, Brand announced to the soldiers, "We have nothing now left but to unfurl the star spangled banner, and to defend it with our lives. Soldiers! Our Union is in danger. Let no one falter now--that the 'star spangled banner' must wave in triumph over the whole Union as long as there is one drop of blood in our veins to protect it . . .. The Union, the whole Union, now and forever!"

❖

Kenneth Owens writes that meetings similar to the courthouse gatherings in Galena "were taking place in a hundred towns through the Northwest that week . . .."(23) Ministers in their sermons called for the sacrifice of lives for principles of right and godliness. Political parsons in New England, including Universalist ministers who preached to Governor Washburn, spoke in the vein of George Emerson who declared "it is God's war." Emerson, editor of the *Universalist Quarterly*, wrote, "we, the subjects of his government, have but to obey his will."(24) Unlike Israel, Elihu depended for inspiration upon fellow politicians such as William B. Dodge, who wrote,

> The storm has come and God will direct to his glory and the confusion of his enemies. . . . For myself, I will never cease to plead the cause of God's downtrodden poor. The slave is my brother suffering cruel bondage; and I pray for his deliverance by any means which divine providence shall direct.(25)

❖

While Elihu whipped up war fever in Galena, Governor Washburn took action in Maine. He called together a special session of legislators. On April 22nd, the Governor as Commander-in-Chief published General Order No. 6. Ten thousand volunteers were to be organized into ten regiments. Prompt action resulted in Maine's soldiers' being the first from any State offered to the federal government. 15,767 volunteers and 16,345 were mustered. To Maine legislators Washburn said the request had come for

> Gentlemen of the Senate and the House of Representatives: All of us, even the wisest and farseeing, have failed to perceive the intentions, or to understand fully the movements of the malign spirits who have dominated the policy of a large number of the Southern States for many years. For years, as recent developments have shown, they have been laboring with one object and plotting to one end, the subversion of the government.

❖

A few months earlier during the winter of 1860-61, slavery had been officially adopted by a majority of Congressmen in Washington. Members of the House conceded, Congress could not interfere with slavery in the District of Columbia, "except with the consent of Virginia and Maryland." Representatives with a healthy-sized vote provided for the "perpetual existence" of slavery, denying citizens the means of revising slavery amendments. Francis Adams, descendant of two Presidents, insisted that fugitive slaves be tried, not in the free state, but in the slave state from which they escaped. Adams submitted to the Committee of Thirty-three a proposal stating that no person, "unless he was of the Caucasian race and of pure and unmixed blood, should ever be allowed to vote for any officer of the National Government." House members John Sherman of Ohio, brother of General William Tecumseh Sherman; and Schuyler Colfax, later Vice President under Ulysses Grant, favored these offensive measures. In the Senate, 24 members voted for the continuation of slavery "in perpetuity." Twelve members voted against it. Among those in favor were Gwin of California, Baker of Oregon, Harlan of Iowa, and Morrill of Maine.

Three men serving on the recreant Committee of Thirty-three, towers of strength possessing the courage of their conviction, submitted a minority report. They were Cadwallader C. Washburn of Wisconsin, Mason W. Tappan of New Hampshire, and William Kellogg of Illinois. When the report with recommendations was submitted to Congress, Washburn, Tappan and Kellogg were joined in sentiment and vote by E.B. Washburne. Cadwallader and Elihu would have had Israel's support as well, but the elder Washburn had left the House to become Governor of Maine. Only a modest number of Representatives on the Committee refused to vote for the continuation of slavery "in perpetuity." The report was submitted to the House. Following several days of angry debate, the telling vote was cast, 133 to 65. Some among those 65 in opposition to the Committee's repulsive recommendations were Thaddeus Stevens of Pennsylvania, John A. Bingham of Ohio, Roscoe Conkling of New York, Anson Burlingame of Massachusetts, Owen Lovejoy of Illinois, Gilman Marston and Mason W. Tappan of New Hampshire, Cadwallader Washburn, Wisconsin, Galusha Grow of Pennsylvania, and Reuben E. Fenton of New York. The Committee's report, now an Act of Congress, was not submitted to the states because of the outbreak of war. James G. Blaine of Maine writing about the low point reached by members of the August bodies, House and Senate, wrote,

The only words spoken [in disagreement with the Committee of Thirty-three] were in the able report by . . . Washburn . . . and Mason W. Tappan . . . They made an exhaustive analysis of the situation in plain language. . . .. They vindicated the conduct of the General Government, and showed that the Union was not to be preserved by compromises nor by sacrifice of principle.(26)

Roscoe Conkling

Blaine ended his encomium indicating that Washburn and Tappan maintained that the provisions of the Constitution were ample for the preservation of the Union; that the Constitution needed to be obeyed rather than amended . . ..(27) In an hour-long speech Washburn claimed that the resolutions submitted by the Committee of Thirty-three were "powerless for good, even if they were all to be adopted," saying that the adoption would subject the people of the North to derision and contempt. He argued that the South had controlled the Legislative, Executive and Judicial Departments of Government for so long--seventy-two years--that "they have forgotten how to obey . . . .." With Abraham Lincoln in mind, the Wisconsin Congressman maintained that southerners could not brook the idea that a man who is peculiarly "the representative of the great laboring classes should be at the head of the Executive Department of the Government." He quoted an Alabama member of the House who referred to people of the North as the South's bitter, relentless, vindictive enemies. Alabama's Congressman declared that, "We [in the South] cannot live under the same Government with these people, unless we [can] control it."

Washburn explained that he had submitted an amendment to the Committee of Thirty-three's Resolution, "so as to give the fugitive a trial by jury in the state where he was seized." Sadly, he reported, his amendment was voted down. Cadwallader also took note of the fact that the South now desired to bring to Congress two more pro-slavery senators from New Mexico. He was therefore against the proposal that New Mexico be made a state.

Before closing, Washburn invoked a religious belief, to the effect that he had "an abiding faith in a kind Providence that has ever watched over us, that passing events will be all overruled for good and for the welfare of mankind . . .." He expressed the hope that people of the North would not "pass their too obedient necks beneath the southern yoke," adding that there should be disunion and civil war rather than dishonor. These strong words were sincere.

The Wisconsin Congressman did not intend that others should fight his battles. Shortly after the war began, he declined renomination to Congress, returned to Wisconsin, organized a regiment of cavalry, and went off to war. Washburn doubtless knew the Welsh meaning of the name, Cadwallader, which was "battle arranger."

❖

Elihu remained in Congress, his health preventing his being accepted, even if he had chosen to join the federal forces. Samuel Washburn was another story. Sam wrote in his diary on April 22 that "Fort Sumpter [sic] has been surrendered to the traitors, d--n 'em." Weeks passed. Reports from the front intensified Sam's feelings of patriotism. He wrote in his diary that 1,400 rebels had been captured. He hoped it was true, "but they had better have killed them and saved paying their keep." This Washburn among the seven wrote easily of death. "'War to the knife' is my doctrine," wrote Sam, "and death to all traitors, whether North or South." Still later he scrawled a sentence in his journal which appeared to be his way of encouraging himself to join the fray. "A person might almost as well be out of the world as up here [in Waubec, Wisconsin]." At last, in August 1861, he wrote he had "a great mind to go to the war," and in November he received his commission from the Navy with the rank of Acting Master. Reporting to Admiral Pauling, brother number six responded to what Israel imagined his mother would say to her children in times like these, " . . . the country needs you."

Seaworthy Sam was assigned to the *USS Galena*, one of three experimental iron-belted vessels. The other two iron ships were the *New Ironsides* and the *Monitor*.

Charles went off to what turned out to be worse than war, eight years representing the United States in Paraguay, barely getting out of the country alive.

William, as Surveyor General in Minnesota had a sinecure, thanks to Elihu and President Lincoln. He faced few dangers during the time battles raged in the South.

Chapter Nine

THE COUNTDOWN TO APRIL 1861

There were times in the busy life of Congressman Washburne when he felt he was neglecting duties at home. By the mid-50s, Elihu had fathered three children, and Adele was feeling burdened. Father Elihu was beginning to feel guilty. Adele stopped writing to him about their youngest child, William Pitt, and Elihu surmised something was not healthy at home. He wrote his wife in February 1855 declaring he would come home and look out for the children. He probably did, but it was like him to forget the promise and run off to Europe with friends including Galusha Grow. Grow, opponent of slavery from Pennsylvania who was to be Speaker of the House during the coming war, was the person Elihu and Cad fought for in the House when Grow was threatened physically by a southern Representative. In April and May 1855 Elihu was in Paris attending the World Fair, and went to Italy where he bought artifacts, including "an old thing," a Roman lamp found in Caesar's tomb.

When father Washburne returned to Galena he brought with him a Virginia architect and made arrangements for carpenters to begin work enlarging his little brick matchbox house. The house on the will was too small to accommodate his growing family. He added a story and a half and a cantilevered roof extending from the unadorned face of his dwelling. His modest house was made over into an impressive Greek temple. Six enormous pillars held up the new roof fronting the house, giving the appearance of a southern, not a New England, structure. On the southern side of the imposing mansion like an after-thought, a homely wooden porch was added, destroying the aesthetics of the otherwise grand design.

An exciting part of 1855 in Galena came in the announcement of another construction, a Marine hospital Elihu had succeeded in obtaining for Galena. He was effective in arranging for new post offices and post roads in his district. The year 1855 was also when Washburne came to Lincoln's assistance as he was seeking a place in the U.S. Senate. In the decade of the '50s, Elihu was a more powerful politician than the Springfield lawyer. The previous year, Lincoln, listening to the advice of his manager, William Herndon, did not join the Republican party with which Washburne was associated. Lincoln did, however, deliver a speech at a Republican assembly in Springfield in 1854, hoping his talk would bring support in his bid for the Senate. Completing his oration on that occasion, the aspirant left the assemblage the moment he climbed down from the speaker's platform. Manager Herndon felt that in their enthusiasm the zealous Republicans would try to persuade Lincoln to change his party affiliation. Lincoln was not persuaded to change, despite the claim made by the newspaper *Free West* in November that the old Whig party was dead. Attorney General Usher F. Linder announced that with the demise of the Whig party he was left a widower. For Lincoln, an announcement of the Whig party's death was premature. Failing to choose an alliance with the Republicans meant that the newspaper, the *Free West,* and its editor, Zabina Eastman, would not endorse Lincoln as a candidate. Editor Eastman was not alone in feeling lukewarm about the tall, lanky lawyer. Dr. Charles Ray, confidante of Washburne's, was suspicious of Lincoln. Neither Ray nor Eastman could, as Dr. Ray said, "go for Lincoln or anyone of his tribe."(1) Washburne had success in modifying the views of the former Galena Democrat, Ray, who later became an ardent fighter for the

Republican cause, and a warm and loyal proponent of the Lincoln crusade. Elihu did not have immediate success with the *Free West* editor, Eastman. Neither was he effective in moving Old Abe into the circle of Republican leaders. The aspiring candidate had depended upon Elihu to help him in northern Illinois when he entered the fray in Springfield, hoping to be elected Senator. Lincoln telegraphed Washburne to report what was taking place in the two Houses. He explained that there were 26 men committed to him. Shortly thereafter, Lincoln sent a telegram to Elihu explaining that he lost the election. A long letter from the loser followed the telegram to Elihu, giving a complete account of what had occurred. Lincoln began his letter to his friend in Galena, saying, "The agony is over at last . . . " When the voting began, Lincoln explained that he had 44 votes. Lyman Trumbull had five. Lincoln said that Governor Matteson, Democrat who favored the Lecompton constitution, had been a secret candidate all along. Planning by the Governor had been carried out with such skill that he was about to be elected United States Senator from Illinois. At that point, Lincoln directed 15 of his supporters to switch to Trumbull. Those 15 votes clinched the election for Trumbull, who, though a Democrat, was anti-Nebraska. In his letter to Elihu, the disappointed candidate stated that he thought Washburne "would have done the same under the circumstances . . .. " Abe's cause having been served loyally by Elihu, the Springfield lawyer closed his letter with an especially affectionate note, saying, "[W]ith . . . grateful acknowledgment for the kind, active, and continued interest you have taken for me in this matter, allow me to subscribe, myself [y]ours forever, A. Lincoln."(2)

❖

Defeat for Mr. Lincoln turned into a victory for the burgeoning of Washburne's newly-chosen Republican party. Since the time of the convention held in Rockford, those thought to be radicals and abolitionists had been in control of the Fusionists, the result of which was that Lincoln remained with a company of hard-line conservative Whig editors who declared that they were unwilling to use their influence to benefit "mere sectional parties."(3) It was true; the new party was sectional. It had been sectional since Israel launched the movement in May, taking on that appearance when the southern wing of the Whigs dropped away. The editors were correct, however. The Republicans constituted a sectional party, but in the final analysis, the fear expressed by die-hard Whigs was a rationalization. Whig editors and Lincoln were actually fearful of men like Codding, Lovejoy and Joshua Giddings of Ohio, who, they believed, were "abolitionizing" the Republicans. Before the reluctant Whigs would join with Republicans for the purpose of calling a convention, conservatives had to be mollified and given power and place within the movement.

Two key figures attempting to save the Republican party from radicals were Abraham Lincoln and Lyman Trumbull. These two were willing to join the fusionists for the purpose of halting the spread of slavery, but not with the intention of eradicating the iniquitous practice itself.

Editor Paul Silby of the *Morgan Journal* of Jacksonville, Illinois, misled historians into believing the Republican movement in his state collapsed after the November elections in 1854. Elihu Washburne, who had "placed himself at the head of an anti-Nebraska movement in his 1854 fight for reelection,"(4) knew that the party was taking on the character of a permanent organization.(5) A Republican committee was continuing in an attempt to fuse members of several parties, including Whigs, Free-soilers, Liberty party constituents, as well as anti-Nebraska Democrats. At one point, these were joined by leaders of a new "Know-something Order" who attended a meeting called by radical editor, Zabina Eastman. At the Eastman-called meeting it was decided to bring into Illinois a New England abolitionist, the Reverend Ichabod Codding.

Arriving in Illinois, Codding spoke to audiences throughout the state, always urging that a state convention be called before the year (1855) was out. Washburne's paper in Galena, the *Advertiser*, proposed that such a convention be held at the state fair in Chicago. Cyrus Woodman wrote Elihu on his and Cadwallader's behalf, saying the two of them thought it was "of vast importance to have a meeting held on the fair grounds at Chicago."(6) A Whig leader in attendance at a public meeting in Quincy was intent upon organizing the Illinois Republican party. He submitted resolutions adopted by the conclave. Significantly, resolutions prompted Abraham Lincoln to express his willingness to join with the Fusionists on the basis of those and other Whig-inspired resolutions. Lincoln's response was significant because he had consistently supported Whigs who refused to participate in the calling of a convention for the purpose of developing a new party in Illinois. Joshua Giddings of Ohio joined Codding in lecturing audiences throughout Illinois at county meetings. Conservative Whig editor Paul Silby, dominating a hard core of Whig editors, declared that Codding and Giddings did not represent the views of Whigs such as himself. Some Whig editors even called for the formation of a Conservative party. County meetings were held as they had been during the time radicals were moderating their demands to accommodate conservatives. Washburne supporters attended county meetings keeping Elihu informed. John A. Clark wrote the Galenean from Freeport(7) explaining that at the Freeport meeting, resolutions forwarded from the New York Republican convention had been adopted.

Owen Lovejoy

Republican committee members realized that Fusionists would not be successful in consolidating for the purpose of creating a state party to include Whigs and anti-Nebraska Democrats unless conservative spokesmen were brought into the circle of leaders on their terms. In a word, proto Republican party members must convince Lincoln and Trumbull. An attempt to do so was made by Owen Lovejoy. Lovejoy was not successful. Those who were thought to be radicals, consisting among others of Lovejoy, Codding, Eastman and Washburne, let it be known that their interest was in forming a party standing for Free-soil. That single issue as a platform at last drew a positive response.

At the turn of the year, Republicans convened in Pittsburgh from all over the nation. Abolitionist Codding was there and took the floor after several radicals had called for yet more militancy on the slavery issue. With his credentials Codding was able to convince delegates that moderation and compromise were necessary. The spirit of the convention at Pittsburgh was said to be radical, but "its address was conservative."(8) While radicals were hard at work at the Pittsburgh Republican convention, conservatives in Illinois gathered at Decatur for the purpose of establishing a permanent state organization acceptable to the moderates. Lincoln had been appointed a delegate to the Pittsburgh convention but chose to forgo attendance to attend the meeting at Decatur. There were only a dozen men present including Washburne's warm friend, Dr. Ray. At the meeting, the Whigs were prepared to stand on the constitutional existence of slavery and the constitutionality of the Fugitive Slave Law,(9) and were ready on that basis to recommend the calling of a state convention for the month of May 1856 in Bloomington. Lincoln headed a list of signers calling for an anti-Nebraska convention. Trumbull agreed to the meeting provided the fusionists would stand solely in opposition to the spread of slavery into Kansas. He was willing also, he said, to accept the label "Republican." Orville Hickman Browning, whose name

Charles Ray

and influence were to have a telling effect as Lincoln acceded to positions of power, joined the conservative forces, working to keep the new Republican party under the control of moderation. Lincoln, as he made his way to Bloomington, expressed the hope that conservative southern Illinois delegates would attend in force at Bloomington. One of the delegates from southern Illinois, Jesse Dubois, when he arrived at the convention and saw Owen Lovejoy with Ichabod Codding, wanted to turn around and go home. He would have done so but for the urging of Lincoln.

Paul Silby had been responsible for planning the Bloomington meeting and was brutally beaten by slavery sympathizers. In his absence, the reins fell into the hands of conservative Browning. He called a meeting of Fusion leaders, and together they set the agenda, adopting resolutions which were to be submitted to delegates with the understanding that resolutions could not be amended. Historian Victor B. Howard, in his account of happenings at Bloomington, reported that a committee was selected and charged with choosing permanent officers of the convention, and that the committee was "composed of safe conservative men."(10) The committee included Charles H. Ray. Ray was no conservative. He had written to Washburne saying, "I must confess I am afraid of 'Abe'. He is Southern by birth and . . . associations, and Southern, if I am not mistaken, in his sympathy."(11)

More radical men who were present at the convention, such as Lovejoy and Codding, were sensitive to the politics of the occasion. They accommodated to conservatives, eager to leave Bloomington having organized the Illinois Republican party. A good description of what transpired at Bloomington was written by the brother of William Cullen Bryant who said to his editor brother in New York,

[T]he movement represented old Democrats, old Whigs, and old Liberty men who had never acted shoulder to shoulder before but had united to 'save the heritage of liberty from destruction, and to drive back the all-grasping power of slavery to its acknowledged bounds.(12)

The strongest anti-Nebraska speech at the convention was delivered by Abraham Lincoln. From his oration came the familiar line addressed to the South, "We won't go out of the union, and you shant!"

In the elections of 1856, radical Owen Lovejoy was elected in his district in preference to a conservative friend of Lincoln's, Leonard Swett.(13) When the radical, Lovejoy, defeated Swett, Lincoln was so disappointed that he said "it turned me blind."(14) At the Bloomington Convention, there was discussion of possible Republican Presidential candidates. While radicals favored Salmon Chase, moderate "new" Republicans preferred John Charles Fremont. Radicals "watched helplessly as the party they had done so much to nurture and cultivate was taken over by Lincoln and the conservatives."(15)

Fremont was not the first choice of Congressman Washburne. Loyal to the party, he supported the candidate once selected. In time to come, Elihu would have reason to confirm his opinions about Fremont. During the Civil War, the Congressman ran into inefficiency on the part of the 1856 Republican candidate. Fremont was Commander in the West and Washburne chaired a Congressional committee investigating charges of fraud in his division. Still later, when Elihu was Ambassador to France, Fremont was thought to be scheming to swindle the French. Washburne dealt with the problem when it arose by asking the State Department in Washington to research the matter. It embittered Fremont back in the States. Charles knew Fremont in San Francisco; and as early as 1856 expressed doubt about his honesty and reliability, Charles referring to him with his favorite pejorative word, ass.(16) Elihu's brother's views may have colored Washburne's opinions of Fremont. The negative view of Pathfinder Fremont may have been widespread as is illustrated by the comparative voting strength in Jo Daviess County for Fremont and Washburne, Fremont received 2110 votes and Washburne, 18,399.

The national Republican party had existed for less than one year. The Presidential and vice-Presidential candidates, Fremont and Dayton, ran on an anti-slavery platform. Partisans thought their cause a holy one. That sentiment accounts in part for the Republicans winning in all but five of the free states, with the Republican majority in those states 100,000 votes over the Democratic candidate, James Buchanan. Even though a Democrat occupied the office of President, the election results prompted the hearty Senator Hale to predict that in 1860 the Republican party, not the Democrats, would "wind up this dynasty."(17)

❖

The single most significant national issue in 1857 was a countrywide panic or depression related to growing divergence between issues marking north-south positions. Differences had been escalating between sections as Democrats continued to foster free trade, and northern states followed a protectionist economic philosophy as a means of protecting industry. The slavery issue, like bread rising, was heated up in March 1857 when President Buchanan announced in his inaugural address that the Supreme Court was about to solve the slavery controversy. The Court, made up of seven Democrats and two Republicans, handed down the Dred Scott decision on March 6. Besides giving the black man chattel status, as though he were a wheelbarrow or a mule, the Court decided that the Missouri Compromise of 1820 was unconstitutional. A third issue aggravated the sectional quarrel. Pro-slavery Missourians crossed the border into Kansas and at Lecompton established a government, writing a constitution and denying even Stephen A. Douglas' popular sovereignty--a constitution which would not permit slavery to be eliminated.

The Taney Court was going to be appraised by Maine's Representative from Orono, Israel Washburn, who was to pass harsh judgment on the court's decisions. The Maine Congressman would have severe words also for the pernicious decree which made brother human beings into *things*.

Otherwise, life ran on as usual for most Americans in that crucial year of 1857. Some took note of the founding of the *Atlantic Monthly*. In England Charles Darwin outlined his theories of evolution and natural selection. A Mormon fanatic massacred about 140 non-Mormon emigrants in Utah. Japan opened the port of Nagasaki to U.S. trade. Incidental matters kept the Washburns in elevator moods, up and down. In 1857, Elihu, Cadwallader, and Sam became proprietors of a town in Wisconsin, which they named Waubec. From Reed's Landing, 25 miles from Waubec, Elihu wrote Adele to explain that he was getting to be a philosopher in the wilds of Wisconsin. He was doing a good deal of reading and thinking of Adele and the children(18) and that he would return to Galena in June. He had been home in April and petitioned the Committee on Streets to lay a sidewalk on Decatur Street. This was also a year in which the Washburnes celebrated the birth of Elihu's namesake, Elihu Benjamin.

During the panic period of 1857, a practice was adopted by an enterprising Cadwallader and La Crosse businessmen. With the depression losing pioneers their farms and their savings, and with railroad companies going bankrupt, merchants in La Crosse dressed in Prince Albert suits and high silk hats. When steamboat passengers disembarked, the men of the city "sauntered around hotels and the waterfront, hoping their conversation and opulent appearance" would induce strangers to want to settle in their [city].(19)

In 1852 Israel Washburn had predicted the coming catastrophe. He did not give the year of the dread depression, but the panic, as it was called, occurred in the fateful year 1857. As mentioned, it was brought about in part by divergences based on northern and southern economic systems. In Congress, the sharp little man from Orono moved an amendment permitting him to speak about the need to revise revenue laws. There was, he said, a large surplus in the Treasury amounting to $15,000,000. Wanting to play down political differences, Washburn said urgently, "[a] question so important, so widely affecting the interests, the comforts, and the happiness of the whole people, ought not to be dependent upon the shifting fortunes of our political parties."(20) He conceded that no party wanted high protective duties. In his speech in the house Washburn made reference to Mr. Woodward of South Carolina who had maintained that a permanent system was impossible. "It strikes me," said Israel, "that a permanent system is not only possible, but very necessary . . . "(21) He granted, however, that changes can and should be made on rates within the system. Israel took a hit at the free traders, remarking upon the fact that

Israel Washburn, Jr.

inventions had been encouraged ("for which we owe nothing to free trade"), which made available products the country no longer needed to protect. He assured southerners that a duty on cotton would neither help nor hinder South Carolina, but that years earlier protection had helped raw cotton to compete with the world.

Representative Washburn mentioned auxiliary benefits such as work for the laboring class, and a reduction in trade balances in our favor.

What . . . we ought to do is to reduce or abolish the duties on those necessaries of life for which we are wholly dependent on other countries than our own, and on such raw materials as enter into our manufactures, and are not the product or growth of this country; and to have such legislation in regard to imported articles which come in competition with articles of our own production as will restrain their importation, and thereby decrease the revenues.(22)

He reminded legislators and the audience in the galleries that European wars in the late 1840s provided a lush market for American goods; that European money had been invested, the U.S. being the safest place for such venture capital. However, stocks would soon cease to be in demand in foreign markets, and Israel wanted to know how to prevent catastrophe likely to follow. For him, the answer, he stated,

Orestes Brownson

was to stop the enormous importation of foreign goods. Without protection in the past, we should not have become the producers that we are; without it in the future, we shall not produce as much as we might.(23)

In his book, *The Panic of 1857 and the Coming of the Civil War*,(24) James Huston writes that, "The Panic . . . reawakened the economic question of free trade or protectionism at a time when furor over the extension of slavery was reaching its climax." The moral question was introduced, not necessarily favoring the side of the North with its argument against slavery, but giving credence to southerners who pointed out that "free white worker[s] in the North" were in such miserable straits that they had to initiate bread riots. "How eagerly would these poor wretches [free laborers] devour what our well fed slaves waste!"[1] A Universalist minister-editor, Orestes A. Brownson of Boston, who had once spoken in Washburn's town of Orono, asked, "[I]s the condition of a laborer at wages the best that the great mass of the working people ought to be able to aspire to?" In a vigorous attack upon the northern system of were he referred to as serfdom, Brownson attacked mercantilism, saying in substance what the abolitionists had been saying about the South with its system. "Put your best men, your wisest, most moral, and most religious men, at the head of your paper money banks," Brownson wrote, "and the evils of the present banking system will remain scarcely diminished. The only way to get rid of its evils is to change the system, not its managers."(25)

Little attention was paid outside Boston's clergy, merchants and bankers, with Brownson's protestations about the system. Northerners preferred to believe that the free trade practices were responsible for the Panic of '57, so the slave system continued to be railed against as another reason for the depression. A friend of the Washburns, Hinton Rowan Helper, intensified anxieties North and South when he published what has been referred to as "the most important single book, in terms of its political impact, that has ever been published in the United States . . .." The Helper book, *The Impending Crisis of the South*, became the center of bitter and prolonged Congressional debate.(26) Elihu, Israel and Cadwallader permitted the use of their names in support of Helper and his book. Charles was a friend of Helper's. The two probably knew each other in San Francisco, and Washburn became better acquainted when Helper was Consul in Buenos Aires and Charles was Commissioner to Paraguay. In later years, the two were engaged in business in the United States. The chapters of the Helper book illustrate the manner in which published writings aggravated southerners and confirmed some of the prejudices of northerners. Chapter I is entitled, *Comparison Between the Free and the Slave States*. The substance of Helper's argument was that "slavery was totally incompatible with economic progress and individual opportunity, and should be abolished in the interest of the oppressed non-slaveholding majority of the South."(28)

Dred Scott

Another of the strident voices of 1857 was that of Chief Justice Taney of the Supreme Court. More than the timbre or tone of his voice, what Taney reported dismayed the listening audience in the North; for as Washburn said, "Dred Scott was turned out of court."(29) What disturbed the Maine Congressman in particular was a decision which stated that "this kind of property [indicating that Dred Scott, a Negro, was declared by the court to be property] may be taken, held, used, bought and sold, in each and all of the States of the Union."(30) Interpreted, this meant to Israel that "every State in the Union shall be a slave State." " . . . [I]f the Dred Scott decision is good law, and it shall be acquiesced in as such, the question of freedom or slavery in this country is irrevocably sesettled . . . ."(31) Israel asked, "Had the Chief Justice never heard that in his native State of Maryland there were very decided opinions in regard to the wrongfulness and inexpediency of slavery, at and before the formation of the Constitution? . . . Under what hallucination was he suffering . . . ?"(32)

When Congressman Washburn delivered his analysis of the Supreme Court's 1857 decision, he was mindful of the fact that an election was imminent. As he drew to a close, Israel said,

> [I]t is in this unprecedented and alarming condition of the country, and against combinations and purposes such as I have described, that the Republican party enters upon the campaign of 1860.(33)

Washburn had in mind the long list of issues which, preceding the decision of Taney's court, added up to awareness on his part that there was what Russel B. Nye identified as "the great slave power conspiracy."(34) The listing of divisive issues amounts to Ossa piled on Pelion to reach at last the Dred Scott case,(35) the most egregious.

The election, which placed Abraham Lincoln at the head of the government and caused the withdrawal of states with the formation of the Confederacy, brought to a head a problem which was to be solved by Civil War. The Washburns were involved as decision-makers with at least half the issues which led to the War, including the election of Lincoln, the President-designate. Washburne, considered by some to be "the compeer of Lincoln...,"(36) was said to have enjoyed the confidence of the President more than any other person. The influence of the

Congressman was demonstrated in appointments he made favoring members of the family. After Israel served the State of Maine as Civil War Governor, Lincoln selected him Collector of the Custom House in Portland, Maine. He appointed Elihu's brother, William, Surveyor General of Minnesota, and his brother, Charles, the first Diplomatic Agent accredited from the United States to Paraguay. Charles Stephenson, Elihu's brother-in-law, was appointed by the President Supervising Inspector of Steamboats for the District. Amos Tuck of Exeter, New Hampshire, struck a chord which must have resonated among Washburne's countless friends. Tuck wrote, expressing his wishes for an office, adding, "I open my mind knowing I am safe with you."(37)

Chapter Ten

THE WASHBURN BROTHERS WHEN WAR BEGAN

Senator William Drew Washburn

In the period In before the War, the Washburn brothers had become substantial citizens, each in his newly-chosen community. Israel, Elihu, Cadwallader, and William were looked upon as young lords in their new-found homes and hamlets-- Israel in Orono, Maine; Elihu in Galena, Illinois; Cadwallader in La Crosse, Wisconsin. When he settled in 1857 William's Minneapolis had a population of 2,500. It was easy for him to follow the techniques observed in his older brothers. Within a year he was in the running for a seat in the Minnesota House of Representatives. He ran and won. Fellow townsmen regarded each of these Washburns as men of promise. It was said that they were destined for greatness. A prominent Minnesotan said of William that he was born for greatness, and he "measured up to his capabilities." Likewise, William Bradley who had known Elihu for forty-eight years said of him that Elihu was a genius. Despite an enormous outpouring of adulation for these four brothers, none thought or acted as though he were conscious of being distinctive. There was an occasion when Elihu acknowledged he had devoted friends who would fight and die for him. He was amazed, he said, since he knew himself to be but a simple, plain man with no pretensions. That observation was written, not for the benefit of his public, nor to impress his wife but out of modesty. When the Civil War began, fourteen children had been born to the ten Washburn brothers and sisters. The presence of progeny settled some of the brothers who up to that time had been wanderers still uncertain of their future. In the year 1861 their lives had been made more solemn, not alone by the War's commencement and the arrival of children, but by the death of their mother. Martha died two days after the birth of William's first-born son, Franklin, and three weeks after the war's starting gun was fired from Charleston. In her final days she delivered a message to her brood, saying, "I have done what I could. It is now for my children to keep the faith, to follow on in the path that I have shown."(1) A grandchild reported that the daughter of Lieutenant Benjamin who had fought to cut the chord holding the United States to the bosom of Mother England, Martha, said Lilian Washburn, could be heard saying, "Up, my children. The country calls."(2) She had not been anxious for her boys to prepare for war as soldiers, however. Cadwallader and Charles tried to enter West Point. Fortunately, Martha felt, they did not succeed. The '60s, then, as hard, rough, cruel, threatening months and years was a time of total commitment to the spirit of achievement inspired by the now dead mother of the children. Some of the children may have said to themselves, her sacrifice was for us, bearing out the Christological myth familiar to Americans of the period.

So, in the 1860s, Israel, Elihu and Cadwallader were as solidly-established as high-strung Washburns could ever be. As for Charles, when the war came he was not yet a father. Charles, though 39, was not married. He was still the self-described vagabond. His ambition to achieve was not motivated by a sense of loyalty, either to his parents or the government. Charles strove to serve in an appointed position, which position he believed he deserved because of what he had done for the party in California. The youngest brother, William, when he graduated from Bowdoin College, moved into circumstances which assured his future. Until he was appointed Surveyor General by President Lincoln, W.D., as he was called, worked as agent for Cadwallader in Minneapolis, renting water rights and providing access to the Mississippi at St. Anthony Falls. Samuel was settled in Wisconsin but unsettled in himself. Sam was lonely. The anger and resentment he felt for his older and successful brother, Cadwallader, was disguised as plain failure to perform. Sitting in his lonely refuge in Waubec, Sam wanted a change and for months contemplated going to the war. It was not that he heard the voice of his mother, "Up my sons . . . " As with Charles and William, his was a more secular response, tinged with a large personal need to benefit. In 1860 at age 36 his friendship for Lorette May Thompson kept him in Waubec living on his brother's paycheck without satisfying Cad that he was earning his keep. In November 1861, Sam received a commission in the Navy, still "lone and wan," as he put it in his diary.(3)

❖

One reality had borne in upon the brothers early in their careers--an awareness that the United States was growing up out of the immense wilderness of the West. They knew in their pocketbooks that there were houses to be built, roads to be scratched out of the forests, schools and churches to be erected, rules yet to be devised for a people who were to live together as citizens of one country. They knew that the people of the nation, including themselves, must transform into bank balances the natural resources: timber, gold, iron ore, water, and fields which must be plowed and planted. In a word, there were fortunes to be made. William was only 15 when he began to think of what the future held for him. His school teacher asked students to write a composition. Willie turned in a paper describing a village he wanted to live in. He wrote that the place where he wanted to live must have a "good large river . . . [with] its banks covered with factories and mills . . . " As a teenager, this Washburn sensed the challenge of growth and development taking place in the country. He anticipated the city he was to have a hand in developing beginning a dozen years after he drew his word picture of Minneapolis, Minnesota, sitting in a schoolroom in secluded Livermore, Maine.

Knowledge of history played a part in creating character and demeanor in the brothers who were to play a part in the growth of burgeoning America. The brothers were proud of the fact that six generations of Washburns had been on these shores beginning in 1631, and were conscious of blood relatives having been engaged in "making America." In the two families there were eminent ministers, teachers, attorneys, farmers, members of the notorious Committee of Correspondence, and revolutionary soldiers who bore arms against the British.(4) One ancestor served in the General Court of Massachusetts when Maine was part of the Commonwealth, and when the Constitution of the State was adopted.

Israel, Jr., had left Livermore with his capacious knowledge of history, learned in the law, possessing an appreciation of literature, and with confidence in himself and his evolving career. By the 1860s, his settlement in Orono in 1834 was itself history. When he arrived in Orono, it was as though he had found a place and status waiting for him. There was a noticeable similarity between his and his father's experience in settling in Orono and Livermore, respectively. When his father settled in Livermore, it was natural for him to move into political and religious circles, Whig and Universalist. The Orono Washburn, like his father, moved promptly into Whig and Universalist circles. Unlike his father, however, Israel, Jr., moved into a group of monied families with influence reaching beyond Orono. He was associated with middle-and-upper-middle-class people and in 1841 married a Universalist, Mary Maud Webster. Maud's family once owned their own town of Webster, by then incorporated into the town of Orono. Young lawyer Washburn constructed a beautiful home in his new village, conspicuously located at the center of the community, and in sight of the church he helped establish. His home in Orono, like the family home in Livermore, was in the shadow of the family church and beside the road leading through town. A Maine Supreme Court Justice Dunn was associated with Israel. In fact, the judge and Israel sat together to plan the launching of the Republican party in 1854 as Dunn's daughter reported.(5)

❖

Within the family, senior brother, Israel, was like a second father to some of the younger siblings. He was 18 when William was born, and 20 when Caroline came into the world. His role as a kind of surrogate father led to his defending Charles who was plagued by his playmates and sometimes irritated by his brothers.(6) The precedent for marriageable age was established by Israel, Jr. He watched and waited seven years before taking Mary Maud to the altar at age 28. None of the brothers or sisters married before they were in their late twenties, except the baby of the family, Caroline, who was overly anxious for wedded bliss. She was 24 when she married Charles' Bowdoin classmate, Dr. Freeland Holmes. More than half Sidney's life flitted away before he and Sarah joined in marriage when he was 40 years old. William Drew's attitude toward this most intimate of relationships in life had a quality of disinterest. William and Elizabeth Muzzy made plans for their wedding, and the prospective groom sent a letter off to his brother, Sidney. Willie wrote in a casual manner that a wedding was

Caroline Washburn

to take place "about a week from tonight . . . " He referred to it as a 'shindig'." The one-sentence invitation summoning Sid and Sarah was set in the letter as a diamond set in cold metal. He began his dispatch, not with a joyous exclamation, but by writing, "I enclose you my note for $400 on three months which you must give the money for." William wrote half a page about financial affairs before he penned the invitation, "I think you and Sally must come . . . " giving no indication of the exact day or precise time for what William declared was to be "the programme."(7) Three days into the marriage state, with the blossoming bliss of the honeymoon behind him, William wrote again to Sid, coolly excusing himself for mentioning the pleasures of marriage. At most, he let Sid know he was happy and that he regarded any man as stupid "who does not have enough *sense** to get married." In Willie's estimation, it made *good sense* to take a maid.(8) It was *sensible* for a man to choose a mate, but, like Israel, William had waited a few years to test the prospective bride who was to be the mother of a new generation of Washburns.

❖

    The depth of feeling and passion about people and political events were acknowledge by the "two peas in a pod" brothers, as Adele expressed it. Elihu and Charles were members of the family who exhibited emotional highs and lows, exposing their feelings in the choice of colorful, pejorative words, and with excited flaying of arms as they spoke. Their eyes deepened into wells of glittering anger and listeners drew in their breath as they anticipated judgmental utterances from the lips of Elihu or Charles.

    In the literature of the family, words Elihu addressed to Adele in letters to her were like hearing his voice reciting endearing words. "My heart is always with you," the lover wrote Adele. In a different period of American history, poetry would fill the pages of letters to one's love, but not Elihu's love for Adele. It was not to be a public matter. The generation of males following these two lovers did not hesitate to write lyrics. Their son, William Pitt, wrote mediocre lines of poetry to his loves, which his father, Elihu, a man of another age and from New England, would not have composed. Neither Elihu nor William would write in the vein of William Pitt who spoke of,

        Love . . .
        It makes the bravest heart to quake
        And turns the coward brave.
        It can the miser generous make
        The spendthrift try to save.

Elihu allowed himself to be sentimental about his mother. In that genre, it was acceptable to breathe lyricisms. Elihu pasted poems in his scrapbook about mother. One was by Louise Billings Spaulding, in which it was written,

        In all the wide world there is none like unto her,
        There's none half so tender, there's none half so wise . . . (9)

    It is too late by a hundred years, of course, for us to find out if big, blustering Elihu, at one point the most powerful figure in the House of Representatives, when

---

    * Emphasis added

79

he was home from Washington, would go into the kitchen, playfully pull the knot to untie Adele's apron, turn her around and embrace her; too late to ask Elihu about lifting his children above his head, their stomachs tightening as they shouted with delight; too late to do more than guess that Elihu, like many another wore messy clothes on a Saturday morning, with an old, wrinkled fishing hat askew on his head, prompting Adele to complain, "O, Elihu, what shall I do with you? You look like a tramp."

It is not too late, however, to report that Washburne was the kind of man who did ordinary things around the house when he was in Galena. He worked in the garden, did the dishes, went on errands for Adele, and looked after the children. He was not, however, the kind of man to write in his letters about common things. He said of himself that he "never wasted an hour." That at least was when he was a young man anticipating a life of achievement. It was the schedule for the Washington Washburne, but not for the Galena Washburne. In Galena, it was quite like Elihu to sit around with friends reminiscing, though not to have a beer, or smoke a cheroot. In leisurely fashion, Elihu drew from memory events from the past with exact dates and details. That talent made him his father's son. Israel, Sr., could recall minutiae from 60 years back. Elihu remembered details from his childhood. He remembered the brutal beating he received from a teacher when he was nine years old. When he was in his

Daniel Webster

twenties, he saw and heard many of the great men who then served in Congress, and he wrote about them. "I can distinctly call to mind," he said, "the personal appearance of [Clay, Webster, Calhoun, Benton, etc.]." For an illustration of detail, in an 1870 letter to Mrs. Charles Hempstead, Elihu wrote,

It was at your house that I first became acquainted with Adele, who has been to me a wife so faithful, so devoted, so affectionate, and the mother of our children, the pride and the hope of our lives.

Washburne remembered his knotted stomach when his father told him that the sheriff was after him to pay his bills, and that the store had to be sold. Actually, everything in the home had to be sold "except what the charity of the law exempted." The little home where the ten children were born was mortgaged. Father's brother, Reuel, took the mortgage and the family remained on the farm. Uncle Reuel, Elihu would say in a reminiscing mood, said he was one of the noblest men he ever knew.

❖

Elihu read carefully a long letter from his father. His father was writing about Cad. "Cadwallader . . . seemed to be more delinquent in spirits than I have ever known," he wrote.(10) Their father's analysis was sound in that he recognized Cadwallader as reproaching himself for failing to achieve. "He must go ahead with confidence," said Israel, Sr., who then added that Elihu should go to him. Elihu did what his father suggested, visiting Cad in Mineral Point, taking with him a "home remedy" for men who were discouraged. The panacea for Cad was Elihu's unremitting, contagious self-confidence. His beneficial attitude had the effect of renewing strength *in others, including his brother. It is reminiscent of what critic John Bayley said of William James and James' effectiveness in enlivening his brother, Henry. " . . . William, the medically-trained elder brother, had verbal resources equal to the case, probably a great deal more effective than the actual practical remedies . . .."(11) A few days later, Elihu wrote his father from Mineral Point. He reported that he found Cadwallader in a depressed state of mind, but added, "[Cad] is now cheerful and himself again." In the war years when the younger brother depleted his strength, overburden with responsibilities and battle fatigue, he invariably called on Elihu to come to him.

A FAMILY MAN WHO COULDN'T STAY HOME

Adele's mother, writing to Eliza, Adele's sister, allowed that "Elihu is delighted to be at home." Washburne was, however, away from Galena frequently. When he was an attorney, he was chasing off on behalf of the Hempstead-Washburne partnership, and trying cases in state and federal courts. Later, Elihu made his home in Washington and saw Galena but occasionally. The impression is that Elihu was nearly the kind of person Charles said of himself, a vagabond.

In 1853 Elihu and Adele had hard thinking to do about the demands of home. On the one hand, there was Adele with children coming at biennial intervals, and on the
other there were extraordinary demands made of the conscientious Congressman. He said to Adele that the subject about which she had written him in despair and hope, namely the possibility of his coming home to live, was to him a source of anxiety. In his letter, Washburne thought through options as he wrote. Should Adele spend the winter in dull Washington, or remain where she was, visiting the Washburns in Livermore?(12) Should the children be in the capital, or should they go to the little one-room schoolhouse where their father, uncles and aunts had attended? Should Adele come to Washington and be there with him, or could she come to the capital and then return to Maine? Elihu said, "If you come I shall not let you go back." He wrote his letter during his first year in Congress. Already, he scribbled, he wanted desperately to see "Grats" and "Hempins."**

THE MAN IN WASHINGTON

Washburne's bills were often said to fit the term "radical," as in "radical Republican." He sought to have Congress investigate the railroads because, as he said to his father, "Father, those men who are doing so much to open up the [N]orthwest and the far [W]est with their railroad tracks are not all doing it for public benefit."(13) The capitalist enterprise soured both Elihu and Israel at times when selfish entrepreneurs were out "to get all sorts of privileges for themselves and their stockholders." The avarice of the money-lender, with his prejudices against the immigrant and blacks, prompted Washburne to pound his fist on his House desk, shouting his insistence that, "every citizen [should] . . . have the benefit of [the act

---

** "Grats" is Gratiot. "Hemps" is Hempstead.

before the House] without regard to the color of his skin."(14) He wanted no discrimination made against any class of persons. His home town of Galena was peopled by immigrants from many countries. His religious upbringing trained him to think in terms of *individuals*. His home base, together with people he knew throughout his district, continued to shape much of his thinking about legislation. What kinds of corporations and institutions, he asked, were meeting the needs of *persons*? Some of the answers to that rhetorical question made him feel completely disgusted with public life. As he began his service in Congress, his disgust induced him to stay in his room at the capitol where he found his pleasure in reading and studying French. While in Washington, his thoughts remained with those at home. "What I would not give to be with you . . . " he wrote. "Only two short months more and I am off for home, sweet home." Elihu maintained a high interest in the person, the individual, the citizen. He amended a territorial bill charging that "[e]very citizen of the United States, or every person who shall have declared his intention to become a citizen of the States, should be given one quarter section, or 160 acres . . .."

One wonders about values cherished by Elihu and about what were the sources of this thinking and actions. When Israel, Sr., died, Elihu hastily penned a message to Adele in which he said memories were awakened of all his [father's] virtues, all his kindness, all his devotion to his family . . . "his honesty, nobility, humor, his rare intelligence, his genial disposition." Those words begin to indicate what were Elihu's ideals and to suggest the source of his defining ethic. The strengths of his father were reinforced in Elihu as the son read his dad's Whig journals, such as the *American Whig Review* and the *North American Review*. As historian Howe has noted concerning Whigs, "ethical norms were considered objective, immutable principles."(15) Whig ethics were replicated in the performance of Washburne's daily assignments. Ideas couched in party publications had the effect of moving the Congressman nearer in sympathy and in his activity to that exceptional period in American history when the first Republican President was to be chosen, and to the time when war would break upon the nation. Whig-Republican Washburne further reinforced values displayed by Israel, Sr., as Washburne played a part in the election of Abraham Lincoln, and as he joined in the maneuvers which brought about the War.

Chapter Eleven

WASHBURNS AT WAR

Wars are not brought about by any one person. We do well, however, to contemplate the part single persons play in bringing wars to pass. Abraham Lincoln will not be found to have started the Civil War. Indeed, he once said to a newspaper editor that he, Lincoln, though President and powerful in his position, claimed "not to have controlled events, but, " confessing plainly " that events have controlled me."(1)

If the war were not activated by the President, then it cannot have been started by the Washburns, singly or collectively. In the sense in which all can be held responsible to different degrees, however, Elihu B. Washburne, Israel and Cadwallader Washburn, are among those who, like Lincoln, must be judged. Elihu, in his own way, displayed persistence and doggedness in contending against Fugitive Slave laws. He voted against plans such as Stephen A. Douglas' Nebraska Compromise, and worked to persuade Congress to pass the Homestead bill--in these ways Elihu numbers among the initiators of war. Likewise, Israel, for having launched the sectional Republican party, thereby intensifying antagonism, can be counted among those who began the conflict. Cadwallader as a member of the Committee of Thirty-three, had it as an option to support the Committee's recommendations in order to mollify an antagonistic South. Instead of agreeing with the substantial majority he virtually declared himself ready for war.

Ulysses S. Grant

Samuel, lonely in the far reaches of Wisconsin's woodlands, revealed his deep hatred for southerners, calling them traitors worthy of death, wishing to sight them down a gun barrel. In his malignity, Sam also became a maker-of-war. His attitude affected his fellowmen, making killing more acceptable.

War and death laid heavily on the minds of southerners who persisted in believing a geographic area--the South--could fragment the Union to satisfy the needs of an economic and elite sectional class. War and its dismal consequences for people of the South arose out of sheer prejudice, which kept fellow Americans in thralldom despite the logic and ethics promulgated by abolitionists in both sections of the country. Southerners also in a personal way must feel the weight of war-making.

The War came, and before War's end, a half million men lost their lives. Wives were robbed of husbands and children of fathers. The country suffered immeasurable losses as the work force was depleted. The United States continues into the 20th century to suffer consequences of the War, North and South. To this day, meanings in life are no more ample or enriching for the descendants of those who endured the carnage of Civil War. Even the encumbered blacks have continued to suffer the cost of the War, having had to fight a nonviolent battle in this century to realize some of the benefits of living in a democracy where there still exists the identical prejudices which brought on the costly civil strife.

In the midst of the slaughter were the Washburns. Because of the nature of their responsibilities, they lived their lives close to the burden of war. Elihu, having played his part in commencing the conflict at both the local and federal levels, turned his efforts toward the successful prosecution of war. One of his first moves was to take the man he located in his hometown of Galena and launch him on his career as the war's great hero. Elihu Washburne perceived his fellow Galenean , U.S. Grant, to be a man with peculiar talents, including an aptitude for managing men to equip them for the making of war. (The Congressman, incidentally had not read the *Panama Herald*, in which it was written of Grant, "[This man is] unfitted by either natural ability or education for the post he occupied, he evinced his incapacity at every movement.")(2) In fact, over the years there was to be a succession of incidents involving Grant which were judged by some to be indictable. Washburne, however, stood behind his choice from first to last, without fear or flinching.

First, he took Captain Grant to see the Governor of Illinois. The two men, Washburne and Grant, made the trip to Springfield; and Grant was introduced to Governor Richard Yates. Elihu advised Yates to find a suitable place for Grant. Even though Yates and Washburne had traveled and partied together, at the time Washburne took Grant to see him, the Governor was unhappy with the powerful Galenean and was doing him no favors. At first, Yates put the Captain to work at a desk, which was discouraging to Grant. Grant wrote Washington asking for a commission, and when there was no reply, he went directly to the capital and tried to see General McClellan. He was not successful in talking with the General of the Army. When he returned to Springfield, Yates commissioned him Colonel and

Julia Grant

placed him at the head of a regiment difficult to discipline. His new career began with his success in handling unruly men. Feeling confident about the course the federal government must take to defeat the Confederacy, Grant returned to Galena and had a long talk with his benefactor, Elihu. Washburne became even more convinced that the Captain had workable plans for achieving victory for the Union. Elihu therefore set about making plans a reality. Since he was entitled to patronage, he saw to it that the President advance Grant to the rank of Brigadier General. Still later, and at Elihu's urging, the leather merchant was made Major General. As that was taking place, Ulysses told his wife, Julia, that since his fellow townsman had been urging him for the place of Major General, she should forget protocol and visit Adele. Commander Grant realized he was indebted to Washburne, and upon being told he had been made General, he said it was "some of Washburne's work." The next step taken by actionist Elihu was to arrange for Grant's Galena friends to be added to the General's staff.

John Rawlins, who impressed Grant at the Galena courthouse in April of 1861, was one of the nine men from Galena who were made Generals upon recommendation by the Congressman. It all went in Grant's favor, so that it has been recited since then that, "Without Washburne, there might have been nothing [for

Grant]." Grant wrote his sponsor, promising in his letter that the Congressman would "never have cause to regret the part [he had] taken." That promise would turn sour near the end of the lives of the two men, Grant and Washburne, but that story has yet to be told.

❖

Grant was ordered to report to Cairo, Illinois, in August to take command of the District of Southwest Missouri. He did not own a uniform and had to borrow money to purchase a horse and equipment. Even then, as Brigadier General, he was so much a nonentity that photographers mistakenly chose a bearded beef contractor, thinking it was Grant. If Elihu's brother, Charles, had been in the region he may well have been mistaken for the General.

In September, Union forces under Grant seized Paducah, Kentucky, thus gaining control of the Tennessee and Cumberland rivers. At the beginning of the year he captured Fort Henry and then set about taking the Confederate fort at Donelson, where Grant first felt the sting of Nathan Bedford Forrest's cavalry. As General Simon Bolivar Buckner prepared to surrender the fort to Grant, Forrest, who said he did not come to Donelson "for the purpose of surrendering [his] command," left in the night with his 700 men. He would continue to bedevil federal forces until Grant placed the responsibility of chasing Forrest from Western Tennessee in the hands of a Washburn General, Cadwallader.

Grant's first victory at Donelson turned into a bitter and humiliating personal defeat. General Halleck, western theater commander, was jealous of Grant, and complained to General McClellan that his field commander failed to report to him. Halleck complained that Grant had disobeyed orders. The victorious General was deposed and McClellan expressed a willingness that Ulysses be arrested. Fortunately, Cadwallader Washburn had by then been appointed to serve with Grant at the request of Elihu. Grant shared his problem with staff members, and copies of exchanges which took place between Grant and Halleck were sent to Elihu. Congressman Washburne visited Lincoln, and the two, Congressman and President, reviewed the Halleck-Grant problem. Elihu told Lincoln that his brother, General Washburn, believed charges against Grant were "frivolous and contemptible" and "destitute of truth." Perhaps Elihu passed along to Lincoln a remark made to him by Cadwallader, that the victory at Fort Donelson "makes Grant the man of the war," declaring, said Washburn, " . . . [that Grant] will put out Halleck's pipe." Cad had asked, "why in the h--l[sic] they don't send an army . . . down the Mississippi . . .." That, too, may have been passed along to the President. Grant had said to Elihu that he believed he had won a great victory at Donelson, and that the battle he had supervised "would figure well with many of those fought in Europe . . .. " The whole matter of the Halleck-Grant dispute was settled at the insistence of Galena's - and Grant's - Representative, E.B. Washburne.

❖

April, "the cruellest month" proved the accuracy of Thomas Eliot's axiom when federal forces were almost backed into the Tennessee River by the Confederate Army. Despite the heralded victory at Donelson two months earlier during that "cruel" spring month, Grant's army fought at Shiloh. The battle was called the greatest ever fought on the American continent. On that April Sunday, the rebels were said to be thicker than fleas on a dog's back. They pounded away at Union forces at the Shiloh church, the Peach Orchard, the Hornet's Nest, and Pittsburgh Landing. A mile of wavering lines of Union soldiers bulged in the middle, pushed back against the enemy at the Landing. The officer in charge had instructions from Grant that the protective Pittsburgh Landing line must hold. It was only the day's end, plus the arrival of federal reinforcements under Don Carlos Buell, that saved the cause for Union forces.

So it was a Sabbath-day defeat. On Monday, however, a hard-fought battle was victorious. Victory came at terrible expense. It had its dark side, for 13,000 young lives were snuffed out.

In Washington President Lincoln was besieged with demands that the "General who fights, Grant," must be dismissed. The driving demands of the populace and politicians induced Lincoln to call on Washburne whom he told sadly, "Grant will have to go." The President said he could not stand it any longer. "I am," he said, "annoyed to death by the demands for his removal."

Grant at Cold Harbor

That must not be done, the irritated Galena Congressman declared. Washburne reminded Lincoln that Grant was an able and successful commander. He impressed upon the President that the General had won more important battles than any other officer.

"His removal," Elihu maintained, "would be an act of injustice to a deserving officer." Commander-in-Chief Lincoln relented.

"Well," he said, "if you insist upon it, I will retain him, but it is . . . hard on me."

It comes as no surprise to learn that Gustav Koerner, a Supreme Court Justice in Illinois, believed people were beginning to realize that, "had it not been for the most strenuous efforts of Washburne, who stood very high at Washington, . . . there is no doubt but Grant would have been deprived of his command."

This is illustrative of the part E.B. Washburne played, not fighting on the front but in the corridors of the capitol, using his not inconsiderable influence with the President and with the heads of Departments in government.

A number of the Washburns wanted to be "where the action [was]." Cadwallader demonstrated that need in a letter, saying, "This holiday soldiering I do not fancy." More than once, another Washburn, Charles, put himself in a position to be killed. As for Sam, he wanted "war to the knife." Elihu was unable to keep himself away from the fighting. He left Washington several times to join warriors on the battlefield, and was present both at the first great contest at Manassas, as well as at the end of the War when he joined Grant, living with him in his tent during the hard fought Battle of the Wilderness.

In mid-July 1861 Washburne left the capital with three other men, all of whom intended to watch the opening phase of the War which was to be fought on the low hills and in the valleys near Centerville, Virginia. "Forward to Richmond," was the cry of the day with the expectation that, as Horace Greeley demanded, "the rebel Congress . . . not be allowed to meet . . . on the 20th of July." Washburne was accompanied by Schuyler Colfax of Indiana, later to be Grant's Vice-President during his first term. Accompanying Elihu also were Governor Lane, newly-elected Senator from Indiana; and Adams Sherman Hill of the *New York Tribune* who was on his first assignment as a war correspondent. The men rose before the sun peeped through the haze, took a carriage, and made their way toward "the sacred soil of Virginia," as Elihu put it. What excited Washburne that day was witnessing the movement onto the battlefield of a great army. The quartet passed immense guns being pulled over the road by eight horses. Making the journey to Centerville, the horse and carriage and its passengers exceeded the speed limit set by the marching masses of soldiers. The carriage was ordered out of the column. Washburne, Colfax, Lane and Hill continued on foot, still outdistancing the marching units. A colonel who knew Elihu lent his horse to the Congressman and Washburne was able to ride within 100 yards of the advance column. His horse loped around Germantown and Fairfax, and Elihu had the opportunity to look over the handsome homes. He was unhappy to learn that Union soldiers had been pillaging and robbing.

Since no fighting was to take place on that day, the adventurers turned their faces toward Washington in the late afternoon, traveling 18 miles and arriving home after dark. Two days later, Saturday the 20th of July, the bug bit Elihu again; and he and Senator Henry Wilson made the journey west out of Washington, this time expecting to see action. Arriving on the battleground, the two made their way to General McDowell's headquarters. McDowell was a general who had never impressed Washburne; and so, even though the General shared with Elihu his entire plans, the Congressmen left his headquarters feeling discouraged, feeling that sheer politics had forced McDowell to move to battle when the Army was not properly trained. Washburne sensed defeat.

The two found housing for the night in a Centreville home. While they slept, troops were moved into position for a fight in the morning. During the night, 30,000 men poured onto the Gainesville Road and on the road to Manassas Junction. In the morning, Washburne and Wilson took their wagon to the top of a hill where they could see the action. They wanted to be closer to the fighting so went back to Centreville and out the Gainesville Road. General McDowell sent a message to them saying that the enemy was retreating, but the message was premature. The two Washingtonians were close enough to see the enemy, though they supposed they were safe, given McDowell's ill-founded message. Bullets and balls were whistling over their heads. The Congressmen were thirsty and found it necessary to return to town for water. They found the wounded filling the highway. Stopping their wagon, Washburne gave his seat to a wounded soldier and continued on his journey walking to Centreville. He did not realize rebel soldiers were chasing the federal soldiers passing him. Washburne stopped, turned and tried to turn the soldiers back. They overwhelmed him, leaving him vainly trying to stop the avalanche. Wilson delivered the wounded and returned for Elihu. The two made their way straight to the capital, arriving in Washington at midnight. Washburne went immediately to the headquarters of General Scott where he found Lincoln and his Cabinet in session.

Elihu was soon made to realize that he and Wilson had been but three minutes ahead of the enemy's cavalry when they were on the Gainsville Road approaching Centreville--and a drink of cold water. Elihu told Lincoln that in his judgment, rebel forces with reinforcements could move in and take Washington. In his apartment again, he finished his lengthy report to Adele, ending, "I was on the spot. Goodbye for to-night."

Governor Israel Washburn in Maine began to pressure the Administration "to put blacks in uniform and on the payroll." The Governor wrote his cousin, Hannibal Hamlin, declaring in no uncertain terms that the armies should be recruited from the South and not the North.(3) He buttressed his argument in a reminder to Hamlin (and to Lincoln, since Israel expected the Vice-President to share the substance of his letter with the President), that the North cannot hold the southern country without the cooperation of people living there, shrewdly pointing out that blacks live there. He was implying that among the leaders of the future in towns, cities and states of the Confederacy will be loyal Americans who fought and bled for the Union. The country, wrote Washburn, is going to be unified with the aid of loyal people--white and black.

The Governor of Maine had other reasons for urging black recruitment. Brave white men of the North were being sacrificed. Washburn had in mind that the record, which continued to the War's end, was set by Maine men, many of whom were dying in battles in the South. He could have included in his letter a reminder that the First Maine Heavy Artillery had more men killed and mortally wounded than any other regiment in the Union Army. In fact, the first Maine Cavalry had more men killed in battle than any other cavalry regiment. At Fredericksburg, Union forces had been repulsed with fearful loss, but the flag of the Sixth Maine was the first to be planted on the redoubt at the top of Marye's Heights. The Maine regiment did not fire a shot during the charge, but "carried the works with the bayonet."(4) Blacks, too, the Governor insisted, must be ready to die for the cause. In his Hamlin letter Israel used an unfortunate term revealing a lapse into racism. In itself, that was surprising in a Governor who had stood steadfastly for legislation to free the blacks. In 1859 he even antagonized Abraham Lincoln at the time Congressman Washburn objected to the Oregon constitution because it excluded free Negroes.(5) The Governor asked Hamlin in his letter,

Hannibal Hamlin

"Why are our leaders unwilling that Sambo should save white boys?"(6)

And why, Israel wanted to know, why doesn't Lincoln act? Hamlin appreciated Washburn's disgust with the want of action. He said he wished the President had "more of energy in his character, a little of Henry Clay or Andrew Jackson."(7) In the following month, Negro regiments were organized.

In Washington Elihu was supportive of the President, perhaps accounting for Lincoln's choice of Elihu wishing out loud that he were to be Speaker of the House "above all others." It seemed like a plot to Democrats. A speech delivered in Galena contained the exaggerated claim that Washburne controlled the Cabinet, and that Mr. Lincoln was "a mere cipher compared with [Elihu]." Like Israel, however,

Washburne crowded the President. By way of illustration, the Congressman expected, or at least hoped, Lincoln would learn about the speech he delivered in New York. Elihu and said to a large and attentive audience that the Administration should have less strategy and more fighting.

Making the journey to Centreville to witness what was featured as the first great battle of the War; getting enmeshed in it, returning hastily to Washington; going directly to General Scott's headquarters at a late hour where the President was present, and expecting to provide a first-hand account of the battle illustrates loyalty to the Administration. But more than that, it can be seen as a first attempt to goad Lincoln's Administration.

❖

As a student of history, Washburne realized he was part of the unfolding history and of the story of a government which had been around only a few years more than Elihu was old. When he corresponded with Adele, he therefore wrote with more than Adele in mind. She probably realized and perhaps lamented that Elihu was using her as a medium. He wrote pages of script about what was happening around him with little or no mention of how much he missed her, as doubtless he did. His memoranda written when he accompanied General Grant during the most momentous battles of the General's career illustrate Elihu's devotion to the history yet to be written. He kept careful notes, sometimes registering events taking place at 15-minute intervals. In addition, he was always on the look-out for collectable memorabilia, even the bark of a tree in whose shade General Lee sat with Grant when Lee surrendered.

On May 3, 1864, Congressman Washburne left the capital to join the Army of the Potomac. Washington inhabitants, including a worried President, realized Elihu would not have far to go to reach the edge of the battle zone. Everyone was keenly aware that Lee's Confederate Army continued to be a threat to the capital. Given the slow pace of travel for the period, it yet took the Congressman less than six hours to arrive at the headquarters of his Galena constituent, Grant, at Culpepper. He had been met at Brandy Station by the General's brother-in-law, Colonel Dent, and taken directly to Grant. William Swinton of the *New York Times* accompanied Elihu on the trip to the front, and the two of them, entering Grant's unimposing cottage headquarters, interrupted the general reading his newspaper. He turned his attention to Washburne and in the next hour the two went over Grant's entire plans for the march to Richmond. Elihu, having reached Grant's headquarters in mid-afternoon, learned before the sun had drifted behind the distant Alleghenies, that he was to be part of a midnight operation, the end result of which would be the slaughter of 54,000 men. Also, as a result of what was to unfold, Grant would earn the moniker, "the Butcher." The commanding General selected an old house atop a hill "affording a splendid view of the troops as they passed in one continued stream all

General George Meade

afternoon." In photographs taken in the morning, the blurred Grand Army of the Potomac could be seen drifting back from the Rapidan River, wandering over hill and valley like the Great Wall of China. On the eastern side of the Rapidan, 60,000 confederates wait in a thicket called the Wilderness. On the morning and afternoon of May 4, the Army, Grant, Washburne and Swinton traveled over land where skulls of thousands of soldiers were either lying atop the ground or lightly covered with earth. There had been a battle at Chancellorville a year before to the day , and the Union Army had been defeated with tremendous losses. Fighting on the following day began with an announcement made to Grant by a member of General Meade's staff who said the enemy was forcing the fight. Meade ordered General Warren to attack. Musketry firing heralded a beginning; but cannon shot, when heard at noontime, suggested the armies were now fixed to fight for several days to come. The fighting continued unabated for a month. The sound of battle moved Elihu and Grant to the front; but they soon turned back, galloping their horses to headquarters where Grant began giving orders in his inimitable, unperturbed manner.

What happened in the following days was characterized by observers, not as a battle, but as murder--a "bloody hunt to the death." With death in their nostrils, it was not to be wondered that some wit, seeing black-suited Congressman Washburne with the General, asked if Grant had brought his undertaker along.

At headquarters on Friday, May 7, news was brought by the son of General James Wadsworth of his father's death when a bullet entered Wadsworth's brain. That day ended with a failure for federal forces with the enemy having broken through the lines of General Hancock's divisions. But Elihu talked with Hancock the next afternoon who reported that the enemy had left his front. General Meade heartened the soldiers at this low point in the fighting, saying that "the hopes of the world rest upon . . . success and that he (Meade) will fight so long as there is a man to stand up." The battle grew increasingly fierce with rebels flanking the forces by "Uncle John" Sedgwick. On Monday as reported by Washburne, the dead body of that fine General, Sedgwick, was taken to the rear--"a sad sight. His loss . . . irreparable . . . possessing the entire confidence of his troops."

On the 9th, Elihu sat down to write Adele. He underplayed the tragedies of the previous four days, even as he reported in typical fashion, exaggerating to the point of caricaturing happenings. It was, he wrote, "war on the greatest scale the world has ever seen;" yet with an offhand sentence he passed over the one battle of all battles which Grant himself most regretted having commanded--namely, the Bloody Angle at Spotsylvania. A Union officer more intimately involved than Washburne wrote that he never expected to be fully believed when he told what he had seen of the horrors of Spotsylvania, "because I should be loathe to believe it myself were the case reversed." One wounded man was seen slitting his own throat. But Elihu wrote almost casually to Adele, "It was a hard fight all day . . . " He had written in his own notes that day, "He who talks lightly of war, knows little of war."

Adele read that the great day of battle was Friday. In his memorandum Elihu said the day started on a "clear and beautiful morng."[sic] total of 17,500 men lost their lives that Friday. As fire raced through the Wilderness woods, 200 men were burned to death, not knowing which way was out, if indeed they were not wounded and unable to move and were therefore burned alive. On the sixth day of fighting, reporter Washburne noted that at sundown, the enemy was advancing to within three- fourths of a mile of headquarters. This announcement sent Washburne, Meade and Grant to the front to a ridge where they watched the battle raging, and Elihu wrote that before nightfall the federals had "gained a decided advantage."

Wednesday morning, May 11, Washburne was to return to Washington with a cavalry escort. He said to the General he would like to take a message to the President. Grant felt it would be more appropriate to send a message to Chief-of-Staff Henry Wager Halleck. His brief message has endured beyond the life of the General himself. Grant wrote he would "fight it out on this line if it takes all summer." That heartening message strengthened the will of Northerners and President Lincoln in particular.

Two years earlier, Washburne had pleaded with the President not to remove Grant from his position. Between that low period for Washburne and Grant, April 1862, and the signal victory at Vicksburg, July 1863, the Congressman had been successful in bringing forward Ulysses Grant as a prospective nominee for President on the Republican ticket. Washburne had been thinking, not about the 1864-1865 election and Grant, but the campaign of 1869. Lincoln, concerned that the popular General might aspire to the office in 1864 took the strategic first step, announcing to Grant's spokesman, Elihu, that "a second term would be a great honor and a great labor, which together, perhaps I would not decline, if tendered." To improve the chances of moving Grant forward, Washburne submitted a bill in December 1863, calling for a medal to be struck thanking Grant for victories won with his leadership. The medal was the largest ever struck at the U.S. Mint. One and three quarter pounds of gold costing $600 for the bullion and labor, contains a profile of Grant on one side and on the other side, Liberty. There was a celebration when Elihu, representing the President, presented the medal to the General. Following the presentation, modest Ulysses Grant placed the medallion in the hands of Congressman Washburne to keep for him. At the beginning of the new year, 1864, the Illinois Representative submitted a bill seeking to revive the rank of Lieutenant General of the Army of the United States. Elihu's bill passed both Houses at the end of February and Mr. Lincoln signed the bill on February 29. Lincoln had been assured by Washburne and Elihu's friend and associate, J. Russell Jones, who was also a friend of the General's, that Grant aspired to only one political office, that of Mayor of Galena.

Chapter Twelve

CONTENDING FORCES SEEKING PEACE

"Incidents Concerning Lincoln, Washburne and Grant at War's End"

The last of March 1865 Lincoln left the capital and made his way south into Confederate territory expecting to meet and talk with General Grant about surrender terms. Both the President and the General were confident that the end was near for the rebel army and enemy. Few instructions had to be given by Lincoln to the soon-to-be victorious General. Lincoln would only have to refer Grant to the meeting he and William Seward held with Confederate representatives at Hampton Roads on February 2, 1865.(1) The agreement was simple: Peace could be made with restoration of the Union and the abandonment of slavery.

Gen. Robert E. Lee

Alone among U.S. Congressman, Elihu Washburne was determined to be present when the gruesome carnage of war was brought to an end. Where the final battle was

Gen. Ulysses Grant

to be fought, Washburne of course, did Generals they reasoned it would be the Confederate capital, The object for both Washburne was to be Washburne started for Galena; his destination, at City Point ten miles capital. He arrived there learned that the headquarters to direct the the armies of the James telegram put in Elihu's Grant would not be in days, and before the ten forces would conquer the Virginia. Having failed to headquarters, Washburne at City Point. Lincoln *Queen* at the Point, and Washburne spent the

President Abraham Lincoln

did not know. Neither, Grant or Lee, though within the vicinity of Richmond, Virginia. Lincoln and with Ulysses S. Grant. Washington from Grant's headquarters southeast of the on the 7th of April and commander had left closing movements of and Potomac. A hands announced that Richmond for ten days were up, federal Army of Northern find Grant at his located the President was on the *River* he and Congressman evening together.

Seeing Lincoln jocund, pleased and relieved that the war's end was near, Elihu on that occasion was left with a precious remembrance of his friend of thirty years.
+

Having spent the evening with Old Abe, the Galena Congressman left City Point, hoping to reach Grant's temporary headquarters near Burksville, Virginia. He was bent upon accompanying his friend on his final campaign against Confederate troops. At Petersburg, Elihu sought out Generals who would provide insight about what was likely to transpire. He talked with General Hartsuff, who was to be engaged shortly in the Appomattox Campaign, and with General Warren who was soon to suffer the indignity of a contemptible verbal assault delivered by General Sheridan. Washburne also met and talked with Confederate General Roger Pryor, a rebel prisoner who had been captured at Petersburg. Pryor told the Congressman that the rebel cause was hopeless, and that when he had said as much to Jefferson Davis he was accused of being demoralized. Elihu walked through the devastated part of Petersburg which looked to him like craters of the moon. He then went in pursuit of Grant, passing through town after town, sometimes doubling back, at last exhausted and having to be taken in an ambulance.

Sunday morning, April 10, the Congressman located General Meade's headquarters three miles from Appomattox where at that moment, unbeknownst to Washburne, both Grant and Lee were sitting in the front room of the Wilmer McLean house discussing surrender terms. Grant telegraphed Secretary Stanton at 4:30 in the afternoon,

> General Lee surrendered the Army of Northern Virginia this
> afternoon on terms proposed by myself.

Late that night, E.B. Washburne arrived at General Grant's headquarters, Burksville. He reported that he was greeted by the General's staff "with great cordiality and kindness,"(2) and he stayed the night in Grant's tent.

❖

Early in the morning on Tuesday, Elihu rose intending to go straight to the place where history had been made less than 24 hours earlier, Appomattox. The trip across the miles from Burksville took three hours, and as the sun reached its meridian, the politician from Galena was greeting Generals Custer and Sheridan and other men as he rode his horse among the conquered warriors in the rebel camp. He stopped to talk with the brilliant L.Q.C. Lamar of Mississippi, who earlier had served on Washburne's Committee on Commerce, an ex-member of Congress whose future would not be marred in the slightest by his loyalty to the Confederacy. Lamar served again as representative, and then as U.S. Senator, Secretary of the Interior, and Justice of the Supreme Court. In the camp, Elihu met rebel Generals Lee, Longstreet, Anderson, Ranson, Benning, Alexander, Pickett of Pickett's charge, many of whom were soon to become hero's in children's history books.

Washburne's visit took him through the rebel's camp preparing him for an emotional experience as he watched surrender exercises with the stacking of arms, followed by a march between the stretched out lines of the 5th corps with the band playing Dixie. Washburne went looking for some physical evidence to mark the occasion. He wandered over to the tree where Lee had stood, ready to surrender his sword to the victorious General. Elihu leaned down and gathered up bark from the tree which had shaded the Generals from the sun. When the demonstration was concluded, Washburne joined Union General John Gibbon in his tent where he stayed the night. Three of Gibbon's brothers fought for the Confederacy. John's brigade fought Stonewall Jackson's command at Bull Run, which in itself was enough action to lend fame to his name.

Wednesday morning sitting on the piazza of the MacLean house and writing his exact description of events, Elihu looked up to watch the endless line of rebel soldiers pass in front of the house, "a terrible looking set."(3) A poor, dried up old man climbed up the steps onto the piazza. The wizened, bowed man with white whiskers and long grey hair was Henry Alexander Wise, Virginia Governor at the time John Brown went to the gallows, and who later was diplomatic representative to Brazil. Elihu did not know, but Wise fought at Drewry's Bluff where the rebels gave Sam Washburn's ironsides, the *Galena*, a terrible beating as his ship moved up the James River toward Richmond in 1862.

Washburne looked at his map. An escort was to lead him and the party Elihu formed of Confederate Generals and staffs, first to Farmville, followed by a long rough ride eastward to Burksville, Nottoway, Wellville, Wilson's and finally to City Point. Among those who accompanied Elihu was General John B. Gordon of Georgia. In the several days they rode together on their trek to City Point conversation waxed and waned, and Gordon wrote years later about the warm relations established by the northern Congressman. Washburne assured Gordon "that the South would receive generous treatment at the hands of the general government." The rebel and disbelieving General asked why Washburne thought the

Samuel Washburn fought on this ship, the *Galena*

South would be generously dealt with by the Union government. Washburne's laconic answer was, "Because Abraham Lincoln is at its head." Gordon felt confident about the answer since he knew Elihu to be Lincoln's "intimate friend and counselor." In fact, Elihu had described to the Georgian Mr. Lincoln's character talking about his "genial and philanthropic nature, and entertained the General with anecdotes from the Lincoln genre." Gordon in his book reported that Washburne was emphatic in his declaration that,

> Mr. Lincoln desired only the restoration of the Union--that even
> the abolition of slavery was secondary to this prime object. He
> (Washburne) stated that the President had declared that if he
> could restore the Union without abolition, he would gladly do it;
> if he could save the Union by partial abolition of slavery, he
> would do it that way; but that if it became necessary to abolish
> slavery entirely in order to save the Union, then slavery would be
> abolished.

Elihu added that "it would speedily be known to the Southern people that the President was deeply concerned for their welfare, that there would be no prosecutions and no discriminations, and that the State governments would be promptly recognized . . . "(4) Washburne ended his account of the journey he and rebel Generals made, writing with reference to Georgian General John Gordon in particular,

"[N]o 'Radical' and 'Confederate' ever got along better together."

Thursday morning, April 13, the final few miles found the company of rebels and radicals at Burksville, and thence Elihu went by train to City Point. Four hours later, at 6 p.m., he left the Point for Richmond where he remained all day, leaving at sunset for Point of Rocks Hospital. There he visited with Colonel Francis Washburn who had been wounded in a hand-to-hand combat during the closing hours of the war. Following the visit, Elihu returned by boat down the Appomattox to City Point. When the boat docked, Washburne, exhausted with the arduous trip of several days, was asleep. Captain Atchison came from the telegraph office, awakened Washburne to report shocking news.

The President, Secretary of State, Seward and Seward's son, had been assassinated. --April 14.

ONE NATION - INDIVISIBLE?

April, that "cruelist month,"(5) was redeemed in the achievement of the April victory and with the declaration of peace. But the month regressed to "cruel" in the madness-of-hate with the murder of the greatest soul ever to achieve leadership in a nation-state. The cruel month's events reverted further, throwing into a madness-of-melancholy the wife who believed she had given the light of her life, Abraham, to "the ages." She then began a drift into derangement.

❖

Elihu had wanted to visit relatives while he was in the war zone. One relative, Francis Washburn, he did visit and was gratified to learn that Francis would recover.(6) Elihu wanted also to visit his brother, Sam. Sam was to captain a new ship, the *Gettysburg,* and while it was being put in condition, Sam expressed the hope that Elihu might "make him a visit," as down easterners put it. Before Elihu was able to tarry with Sam, however, word came of the terrible tragedy, President Abraham Lincoln had been murdered! General Edward O.C. Ord put his private boat into Elihu Washburne's hands and the Congressman hastened to Washington. He wrote Adele in despair declaring,

"God only knows what is now in store for our unhappy country."(7)

What was "in store" for the country and for Washburne were sorrowful days during which citizens mourned the loss of their noble leader. Elihu chaired the Special Committee on the Death of President Lincoln. Lincoln's Galena friend accompanied the President's body in a railroad car passing slowly through towns and cities between Washington, D.C., and Springfield, Illinois. What was ahead making for anxiety for Elihu was the business of the country's leadership. Elihu's cousin Hannibal Hamlin, Lincoln's first Vice President, would not now accede to the presidency.(8) Andrew Johnson replaced Hamlin in 1864. What healing would Johnson bring to the grieving nation? Would the modest program Lincoln devised bring the Confederate states back into the Union? Would Johnson adopt his predecessor's program? Would the new President make it his own plan, or would the plan be one moderates and radicals would devise?

Following the passing of the Lincoln led administration, Washburne was anxious about his own future and the future of his friend, General Grant. The turn of events brought unexpected responsibility to the Galena Congressman. He must look after some of Mary Todd Lincoln's vexing headaches and heartaches and worry also about the seance sessions she attended.

There was something unfair about stories developing around the persons of Abraham and Mary, now that Lincoln was dead. Apocryphal stories about the assassinated President made him almost as mythological as George Washington. Would-be biographers lifted Abraham into a fictional realm. Ralph Waldo Emerson said in a eulogy for the President that "in a period of less facility of printing, he would have become mythological in a very few years." Roy Basler(9) writes that facility in printing had made possible the immediate establishment of the myth, adding that Lincoln "is largely a myth." Mrs. Lincoln herself contributed to the idolizing of her husband. She "compared [Lincoln's] life to the Second Coming."(10) On the other hand, with the public's treatment of Mrs. Lincoln as compared with their handling of her husband, it was quite another story. There were exaggerated and fatalistic versions of her unfortunate life experiences. What was said or gossiped about Mary lowered her into an early grave. E.B. Washburne contributed to both happenings, playing a part in lifting Lincoln to the place where he seemed to transcend the human condition, and on the other hand, failing to do Mary's bidding, in her opinion leaving her destitute.

In a speech delivered in the House in May 1860, Congressman Washburne had said Lincoln "was an early advocate of the doctrine of slavery prohibition in the Territories."(11) That was hyperbole. It served Washburne's purpose at the time, which was to make candidate Lincoln appealing by stretching the truth. Elihu knew first-hand that in January of the previous year, Lincoln complained in a letter to him about his brother Israel's speech in which Israel said he wanted freedom for Negroes in the newly created State of Oregon and Lincoln said he wished Israel had not said that. Next, Washburne in his 1860 address again elevated candidate Lincoln, declaring that he gave his great name to the establishment of the Republican party. Washburne conveniently ignored the facts. Lincoln made life onerous for several minor parties attempting to coalesce in order to form a Republican party in Illinois:

> Republican antislavery leaders realized that they would have difficulty in mobilizing a convention that would be truly representative of the whole state unless they could draw the more conservative Whigs and anti-Nebraska Democrats into the coalition. To do that, it would be necessary to win over their leaders, Abraham Lincoln and Lyman Trumbull.(12)

Lincoln made it difficult to organize the new party, resisting for a period of at least two years. Lincoln was fearful of radicalism with reference to Negroes and slavery.

Then there was Mary Todd Lincoln. Failing to act with compassion, Congress left Mrs. Lincoln saying she would pray her Heavenly Father to remove her from the world but for the fact that her boys depended upon her. What was happening to "roving Generals" who have "elegant mansions showered upon them,"(13) created bitterness in her. She had in mind the Lieutenant General whom Washburne was preparing for the presidency, namely Ulysses S. Grant. While Elihu was making way for Grant, Mrs. Lincoln was contacting many of her husband's old friends, lining them up to make the case in Congress on her behalf. The late President's wife wanted one hundred thousand dollars from the government. When she wanted something from Old Abe's long-time friend, Elihu, Mrs. Lincoln's letters to him referred to Washburne's "noble heart." But while requiring that he press her demands in Congress, expecting her cause would be triumphant in his hands, she harbored feelings of resentment. Mary expressed them in a letter to a friend.(14) Washburne, she wrote to Sally Orne, is a self-willed man. She was resentful that the Congressman was "very powerful." In fact, she wrote confidentially to her friend that "W. is the 'rising sun' in America." Elihu had misgivings about Mrs. Lincoln from the time she came to Washington, perhaps at that early period questioning her sanity. At the time he made a judgement he did not care to write in his letter to Adele telling her what were his intimate thought about Mary. He told Adele he would share his impressions when he came home to Galena.

Three letters from Mrs. Lincoln came over the desk of the Galena Congressman within a two-week period. He was about to submit legislation "seeking relief for Mary Lincoln, which was to be President Lincoln's salary in full, $25,000." An amendment was added to Elihu's bill by a Congressman who wanted to provide Mrs. Lincoln with the $100,000 she was hoping to receive. The amendment to the bill did not receive Washburne's support. Before the bill was voted upon, Mary wrote again, expecting to impress Washburne by declaring that, if the bill were not passed, "a fate will meet us which should be truly mortifying to every American who has any respect for my dear husband."(16) She explained that in justice to her husband and his services to the country she should have $50,000 for a house and furniture, and $100,000. to keep up the home. She expressed confidence that whatever figure Elihu named would be adopted. A few days later, Mrs. Lincoln complained that "if a grateful American people only give us . . . $25,000" her portion in life would be to live in a boarding house forever.(17) The sum granted by Congress was $25,000, the amount requested in the House bill by Elihu.

Mrs. Lincoln's life had been uneven and unhappy. In 1875 her son Robert hired Pinkerton detectives to follow her. Doctors declared her insane. That was too much for Mary. She attempted suicide and was institutionalized, but was released to live with her sister Elizabeth Edwards until she left the United States for Europe accompanied by her son, Tad. When Mrs. Lincoln returned to her Springfield family she settled once again in the Ninian Edwards home. There "she lay in her bed, scarcely able to lift her head, lying to one side so as not to disturb 'the President's place' beside her." She died in July of 1882, aged 64.(18)

Mary Lincoln at seance

For Washburne and his problems, he sustained a modern version of Pelion on Ossa. Problems piled up. Difficulties began to mount for the Congressman, accumulating only a few hours after the otherwise happy ending of the war. "I was feeling well and in the highest spirits," Elihu wrote to Adele on the day of the assassination. But think . . .. At the war's beginning in 1861, a worried Elihu had written Adele, saying he feared there was no more happiness "for us or our dear, dear children." Four years later with the war's end he gave voice to the same mood, "God only knows what is now in store for our unhappy country." Either of these times, as well as at times in between, Elihu could have been induced to tell the story of his birth for the purpose of illustrating his fate. His beginnings always suggested to him that he was destined to live in the midst of turmoil:

> Dr. Bradford brought me in the saddle bags to the old house in Livermore. It was . . . [a] frightful evening. I have heard my mother tell it - the rain and the wind and the howling storm sounded through the grand old elms. Perhaps it was all typical of the turbulent and restless life that was to come to me.(19)

The shock of the President's assassination triggered a series of misfortunes from Washburne's perspective. For one thing, he expected to see Lincoln's 10% Plans work for the rebel states, and he even felt he could safely assure former rebel Generals that the Plan would be acceptable to Southerners. Many radicals, however, were suspicious of the 10% Plan. Among other things, the Plan was to pardon and restore rights to all secessionists pledging allegiance to the Union and who accepted abolition. When the number of loyal Southerners amounted to 10% of the votes cast in 1860, a new government could be established. The newly established government would be recognized and represented in Congress, with House and Senate members judging qualifications of those seeking to be seated.

In point of fact, members of Congress thought through more thoroughly than did President Lincoln some of the critical questions regarding postwar relations between the government and the miscreant South. Congressional committees set about designing a Plan permitting Confederate states to be re-united with the Union. The committees asked questions Lincoln seemed not have had in mind:

> --Who should establish the terms, Congress or the President?
> --What kind of system should replace plantation slavery, and how would blacks take their place in the social and political life of the nation and states?
> --How could the federal government provide access to courts by blacks?
> --Was there a way to guarantee the right of blacks to testify in court?
> --Should abandoned land be granted to blacks who for years before had worked to produce the wealth enjoyed by plantation owners?
> --When would there be suffrage for blacks?

Another critical matter might well have been added to the list, though it was not and therefore becomes a commentary on the radicals and their deficiency:

> --When and how would the white man, North and South, be re-educated to accept, and live sensibly with, their fellow black citizens who must be enfranchised?

It was all too clear that there were many in the country who thought like the Indiana Senator who said the same power that had given [the Negro] a black skin, with less weight or volume of brain, had given us a white skin.

❖

A by-play between two New England lawyers focuses attention upon problems which shadowed the last half of the 1860s, with the first portion of the decade leaving a set of nearly insoluble legal problems. The two attorneys representing different ways of tending the issues were Charles Sumner and Elihu's brother Israel Washburn, Jr. Sumner and Washburn looked at the problem of the seceded states and how they were to be treated. The harsher treatment of former enemies was proposed by Senator Sumner. As he reasoned, Confederate states had forfeited their rights by their rebellion, and they should not be permitted to participate in the National Government. Sumner preferred that provisional governments be established in the rebel states. Governor Washburn of Maine on the other hand favored restoration, not reconstruction. He noted that the Constitution required of states that they create laws affecting the security and prosperity of the people. The challenge as he saw it was to determine how Confederate states could again relate positively to the federal government since *those states had never been outside the government*. The Constitution, Washburn declared, reserved to states the power to make laws. Before the war, southern states had perfected their statutes, which were in use and were even obeyed during the war. Such laws should not be considered annulled. Granted, Israel acknowledged, Congress and the President had the authority to provide a republican form of government in each of the states. There was no question for Washburn but what the republican form meant that states were required to respect citizens of all classes and races, and that the national government could not "tolerate . . . doubts as to the perpetual and sacred integrity of the Union." Following victory, said the Maine Governor, the federal government should move to a solution short of continuing to provoke citizens or by destroying infrastructure in the southern states. His solution was:

[To] pass a law prohibiting the coast-wise and inter-State slave trade, and no slaves can be sent from one State or Territory to another; and the result will necessarily be, that in no one of the rebel States can a slave be found or live.

After reading Washburn's essay, Sumner wrote his Maine friend congratulating him. "We are all under obligation to you who has put it so clearly, elaborately and persuasively."(20) It should be pointed out that Israel's proposal prompted some historians to say that "a weary North had relied [too] heavily on law as a panacea," in the hope, said Senator Justin Morrill, "the gristle may harden into the very bones of the Constitution."(21) On the other hand, it was found impossible to put into practice many of the requirements demanded by the more severe and restrictive reconstruction schemes dear to Sumner. Sumner's strictures for example called for "equal access [by blacks] to accommodations in private railroads, steamboats, stagecoaches, streetcars, restaurants, hotels, and theatres, as well as equal entry into public schools, institutions, land-grant colleges, and cemeteries, plus the right to serve on juries."(22) Sumner gave little thought to resistance and a reluctance to accept new modes and new relationships. The consequence of such extraordinary demands resulted in a loss for Republicans in the political arena. Elihu Washburne said that if Sumner's "object could have been . . . to destroy the . . . party, he would have been gratified at his success . . . " There is irony in Washburne's observation in view of the fact that Grant's administration, for which Elihu was laboring, offered the last chance to make the Reconstruction Plan work. The Republican party was not successful during Grant's administration in spite of the fact that Congress and the presidency were controlled by the party. Radical Republicans were unable to sustain the momentum once a second Revolution was put in place.

E.B. Washburne was one of six Congressmen classified as post war radical leaders.(23) Timothy O. Howe, one-time teacher at the Livermore, Maine, school adjacent to the Washburn home, in Congress from Wisconsin, was one of the six. Ben Butler was another. Democrat Butler campaigned for Jefferson Davis in 1860, but fought for the Union once the war began. He was called "Beast Butler" for giving an Order classifying southern women as prostitutes who disabused or insulted federal soldiers by word or gesture. The plan promulgated by these and other radicals initiated that second American Revolution. Robespierre's confiscation program caused many in this country to compare the Radicals' plans of 1866 with the 1789 French Revolution. As in France, so in the U.S. with the Reconstruction Plan, property was confiscated. Military rule re-made some of the state governments. The radical Republicans' policies were compared also with Oliver Cromwell's tyranny. It was said, for example, that Major Generals in this country, as with Cromwell's officers in England, oppressed the people. Elihu Washburne thought differently. His brother, for example, Major General C.C. Washburn, was Commander of Western Tennessee, and after Cadwallader left Memphis, having served as Commander for three years, he was invited to return to be honored by citizens. It was said that,

> By an impartial, just and liberal course in his high official
> capacity, he has endeared himself to all classes and conditions
> of our citizens.

In response to accolades, General Washburn said that under his leadership, "no private interest was ever permitted to stand in the way of the public welfare. . . . Governments," he felt, could "afford to be merciful, magnanimous, and more than just." If all Major Generals were not as scrupulous as C.C. Washburn, most made a serious effort to serve well and to do justly.

Daniel Richards

Nonetheless, the response to the radicals' Reconstruction Plans was one of failure of southerners to accept even minimal demands made of recalcitrant states. Elihu was acutely aware of what was transpiring in that beleaguered part of the country since one of his friends from Illinois, Daniel Richards, himself a radical, had gone to Florida for the Treasury Department, and Richards kept up an extensive correspondence with the Congressman. In addition, while Washburne was learning hard lessons from his Illinois friend in Florida, he was himself learning about extremes of brutality serving as Chairman of the Select Committee on the Memphis riot. He wrote Adele from Memphis saying the country has "no conception of the extent and atrocity of the mob here. . . . And not a single man is held for punishment."(24)

"The Memphis massacre, one of the worst bloody records in the annals of history," is a quotation from an editorial in Elihu's Galena newspaper. The sentence reflects not only the thinking of Galena's Congressman Washburne, but his narrative style. As has been said, Elihu was given to overstatement. The riots in Memphis and New Orleans provided a means by which to display his feelings of abhorrence. *The Galena Gazette* of September 17, 1866, reported the massacre in Memphis said to be "the worst." The editor of the *Gazette,* however, wrote of another riot, "throwing into a shade" even the Memphis riots. The article referred to the "awful butcheries of Union men and colored people of New Orleans." These exclamatory statements led the Galena editor to a predictable conclusion, that Andrew Johnson's policies must account for what happened in those two southern communities. The editorial conclusion was that since "no punishment [was] meted out to red handed murderers," those murderers were "protected and supported by the strong hand of the government." The expression of the editor was tantamount to accusing the President and his policies.

Whether the stories told by Washburne's committee, or by Memphis historians, are true, the events of May, 1866, belong in the history books as butchery, cruel and meaningless. The Memphis Special Congressional Committee tells of an incident where a family of Negroes, including innocent children, was forced to remain in the house as white citizens surrounded the dwelling and watched their fellow humans burn until ashes only were left. Rebels, as Richards referred to many white Floridians, took property which had been purchased by blacks. Washburne's reporter lamented the fact that blacks were deprived of guns and ballots in their possession so as to protect themselves and their interests. "[Blacks] have learned . . . of the fiendish spirit that pursues them . . . and [is] now seeking to take [their life]." "Three times," Richards reports, "[the rebels] *accidentally* ran into a [U]nion mail boat and the last time killed 3 persons and finally compelled her to go north."(25)

> [O]nly yesterday afternoon a colored woman, nearly white, called at a rebel drug store for a dose of medicine and it was given her by the rebel clerk and she sunk down before she got home, only a few rods, and died before dark. He, rumor says, gave her *morphine.*(26)

The political in-fighting between radical and moderate Union men in Florida revealed to Washburne that white citizens were using every device possible to frustrate attempts by black majorities as well as minorities to acquire political power. In a cynical and sarcastic mood, lawyer Richards wrote Elihu, "And such is justice under a Republican government with the great [U]nion party of the country in power, but administered by Andrew Johnson through a *most excellent reconstruction policy*, with Ben C. Truman(27) as confidential advisor and tool, whose mission it is to represent as symmetrical and fair the monstrosities of government, and the provision of law and justice."(28)

Chapter Thirteen

REVOLUTIONARY MOVES BY RADICALS

Sweet little Adele serene in the peaceful valley of Galena was pleased whenever her Elihu was satisfied. He thrived on the frenzied whirl of Washington life. For herself, she preferred living among the extended family of friends and relatives in the lead mining district. She appreciated the interest Elihu demonstrated always asking about the children. Adele kept track of Washington affairs by reading the Galena *Gazette*, along with an eager reading of Elihu's newsy letters. Elly kept her abreast of political goings-on, especially interesting to Adele now that her neighbors, the Grants, were also on the Washington scene and Elihu was spending time, and even sleeping at Grant's house.

In a frank open way, Washburne wrote letters revealing his feelings about each of the family members. On one occasion Pitt was with his father in Washington and ill. "His tongue is coated," Elihu wrote, "and he has that sober, haggard look which has so often made our hearts bleed." Even so, a political note was added at the end of that same letter in which he had disclosed his feelings of anguish. He said he lamented the fact that President Johnson had "gone over to the enemy . . . "(3) He was afraid all was lost that had been gained "in a long and bloody war." He expressed an ardent wish that he was out of unpleasant conflict and "away in some quiet nook surrounded by all [who are] so dear to me." Things were far from peaceful for the new President, however. It was not enough that Johnson had to live with the developing national myth of Abraham--six months dead! --nay, not so much, not six: So excellent a President; that was, to this, hyperion to a satyr . . . In this vein, there were growing numbers who lamented the leadership of the unbending and acerbic Vice President, Lincoln's successor. Adele had reason to believe Johnson's deeds were beginning to turn moderate Senators and Representatives into radical Republicans, though Elihu's latest from the capitol reported that he had just visited President Johnson and found him in good health. "He talked very well indeed," Adele's husband wrote. Elihu even added that he believed there would be no split between Johnson and Congress. Adele was puzzled. She knew that some of the heavies among radical politicians even expressed relief that Lincoln was dead. George Julian was quoted as saying "the . . . feeling among radical men . . . is that his [Lincoln's] death [was] a god-send."(1) It was considered by the fanatic James Ashley that the new President was "rabid and radical." So what was this talk about a split? Elihu only hinted at it in his New Year's letter. What was true was that public discontent was growling beneath the niceties of polite language. The growling would become a roar by the time "the cruelist month," April, came around. April marked one year since the assassination. Beetle-browed Thaddeus Stevens would be persuaded that if suffrage for blacks were not authorized in southern states southern voters would be able to join with Democrats in the North, elect a President, and the blood of Union soldiers would have been shed in vain. The possibility of freedom and security for Negroes in southern communities would be lost--perhaps forever. It was not long before the *Gazette* cleared up what puzzled Adele. Centrist leaders, such as Bingham, Colfax, Banks, Blaine of Maine, and E.B. Washburne, joined with radicals who were intent upon saving the Freedmen's

Bureau. The Freedmen's Bureau was created a month before Lincoln died as an adjunct of the War Department. It's assignment was to distribute rations and medicine among the blacks, establish schools, regulate labor relations between plantation owners and Negroes, to take charge of confiscated lands, and to administer justice. The Bureau was to make arrangements to feed the starving. Homes and acreage were to be purchased with a rent-to-buy arrangement with blacks. Negroes were placed on Bureau committees where decisions were made relating to the affairs of blacks. January 12, 1866, a few days after Adele received Elihu's good tidings about himself in which he spoke of promising relations of the President with Congress, Senator Lyman Trumbull of Illinois submitted Senate Bill 60, the purpose of which was to extend the life of the Freedman's Bureau and a bill to institute Civil Rights. One month and two days later, the President vetoed Trumbull's bills, which among other things would have transferred jurisdiction of civil rights cases from state to federal courts. The veto by the President stirred anger in moderates among whom at that point was Washburne. Moderates or centrists, as

they are called by Michael Les Benedict,(2) began their move into the column of Radical Republicans. Elihu was in the category of moderates according to some historians because after the Christmas recess, when the line had been drawn between the Administration and Congress, Washburne, Fessenden and Reverdy Johnson went to talk with the President on behalf of the controversial Joint Committee on Reconstruction when the three men had assured Andrew Johnson they wanted to avoid controversies. They asked the President to suspend Reconstruction activities, explaining that Congressmen were provoked with Johnson for withdrawing Senator

William Pitt Fessenden

Sumner's provisional governments from several southern states. Washburne and the other two left the White House assured there would be no division. That was the meeting which prompted the New Year's letter pleasing but puzzling to Adele. The President was amicable to Washburne in January and yet Elihu mentioned in January a possible split. In February, with the President's veto of the Freedmens bill, Elihu began to show signs of exasperation, indicated in his vote for a resolution likely to trouble Johnson. The resolution put restrictions on Johnson's home state, Tennessee. Others in the moderate camp were beginning to move in with the radical Republicans. It took four months, but in July of 1866, the House passed the Freedmen's Bureau bill *over Johnson's veto*. The count was 104 to 33.

In addition to being at the center of the wrangling with the Administration when the month of April arrived, Washburne was learning day-by-day the inside story about what was developing in Florida. His friend Daniel Richards, in that state which dangles off the southeastern end of the continent, was holding out almost as though a partisan against a mortal enemy. Washburne knew that the Florida constitution adopted by the new government discriminated against the blacks. He knew that a "black code" had been approved making it possible for authorities to sell any person found wandering or strolling about, or leading an idle course of life. He was well informed also about what was transpiring in Louisiana and Texas. A report from an army officer who had been living in Texas explained that "if the military force were withdrawn [from Texas] there would be neither safety of person nor of property for men who had been loyal during the war, and that there would be no protection whatever for the negro."(4) Elihu was informed about two white men who had taken a black woman into the woods, stripped and beat her to death. The names of the murderers were reported to the Chief Justice. The Chief Justice said no warrant could be issued for their arrest *on the evidence of a Negro*! The Freedmen's Bureau, headed by a friend and neighbor of the Washburns from Leeds, Maine, was being undermined by the President.(5) General O.O. Howard's black beard could not hide the compassion natural to the man. The head of the Bureau was a devout Christian, two of whose brothers were clergymen. General Howard with Secretary of War Stanton sat with the President, appealing to him to protect the freedmen from vindictive whites. The President, it was said, was merely amused by their plea. It was of no importance to him that Negro children were going to have their school taken away. It did not disturb him that there was much to be done to help laborers-- to assist in obtaining black ownership of land--to oversee contracts between blacks and white employers and employees. Howard turned to radical Republicans for help. He knew he could depend on his friend Washburne, who was moving left during the month of February, 1866. In fact, it was Elihu Washburne and one other member of the House who held out for black suffrage to the bitter end.

Gen O.O. Howard

What is clear is that Andrew Johnson, a Tennessean, failed to understand "the principles of the second American revolution."(6) For his fealty to the South, the President was to pay a price as Radical Republicans began to initiate that second Revolution. General Howard's achievement as head of the Bureau saw his name immortalized by a black educational institution, Howard University. As for the Bureau he headed it was the belief of one of the brilliant blacks of this and the last century that the Bureau should have been permanent "with a national system of Negro schools; a carefully supervised employment and labor office; a system of impartial protection before the regular courts; and such institutions for social betterment as savings-banks, land and building associations, and social settlements."(7) For W.E.B. Du Bois, the Freedmen's Bureau was the heart of the Reconstruction effort.

❖

What shot the bolt for E.B. Washburne was the defeat of every radical and centrist Reconstruction measures. Congress did not have a policy. It was what the Chicago *Tribune* wrote in an editorial which exacerbated the northern Illinois politician. The *Tribune* editor noted that, "The fatality of disagreement . . . has been hanging over the majority ever since the opening of the session, preventing all substantial legislative achievements . . . threaten(ing) to become a chronic, insuperable obstacle to the success of Congress in conflict with the President." Elihu in despair wrote home to Galena. The Freedmen's Bureau bill, the cherished child of Washburne's friend from Maine, had been vetoed by Johnson. The Civil Rights bill was before the Cabinet. While only one member opposed the bill, Mealy Potatoes, as the Washburns referred to Gideon Welles, Johnson vetoed the bill. William Seward urged the President to let it be known that he was not opposed to the policy of the bill, only to its detailed provisions. Johnson stubbornly sent an uncompromising veto. Fessenden went again to see Johnson accompanied by Senator Morgan hoping this time the President would consider a compromise bill. No, Johnson would not consider any legislation which acknowledged the black man to be a citizen. The Senate overrode the veto, 33 to 15, and the House overode the veto by a vote of 122 to 41.

"O Gentle Reader, it was good to be there," wrote radical Theodore Tilton from the Senate gallery. "It was a glorious day!" Colfax of the House wrote.

All this in that fated month of April 1866. The angry Congressman from Galena

took the radical stand, joining a few others voting against the admission of Colorado to the Union since Colorado's constitution did not include the enfranchisement of blacks. In fact, Elihu and Senator Jacob Howard of Michigan were the only Republicans who held out for black suffrage to the end. Washburne, Thaddeus Stevens, and Roscoe Conkling voted for disqualification of rebels keeping them from voting and from holding the privileges of office. The man who was to be President in 1880, James A. Garfield, did not insist on black enfranchisement when he had opportunity preferring instead to entrust power to Confederates.

James A. Garfield

The squinty-eyed Tennessee tailor and President of the United States, Andrew Johnson, worked himself into the position where impeachment proceedings were felt to be necessary. The list of predatory acts attributable to the President is long:

--Johnson destroyed the Reconstruction program
enacted by Congress,
--Johnson appointed former rebels provisional
governors,
--Johnson pardoned rebels only upon the
recommendation of his provisional governors,
--Johnson opposed black suffrage,
--Johnson proscribed former Unionists who would not
cooperate,
--Johnson staffed the southern Treasury Department
with former rebels,
--Johnson did nothing when one of the provisional
governors he appointed ordered the U.S.
attorney to halt proceedings for the sale of
confiscated lands,
--Johnson destroyed the capacity of the Freedmen's
Bureau to carry out the mandate of Congress,
--Johnson arranged for 414,652 acres to be returned
to former owners, including almost 15,000
acres that had been turned over to freedmen,

--Johnson used his powers to remove from military
courts the ability to punish wrongdoers when
state courts would not act,
--Johnson removed Generals Sheridan and Sickles
from their posts in Louisiana and the Carolinas,
--Johnson "converted a conquered people, bitter but
ready to accept the consequences of defeat,
into a hostile, aggressive, uncooperative
unit(8).

One history making edict Johnson was unable to nullify with his veto power was the Fourteenth Amendment to the Constitution recognizing that privileges or immunities of citizens could not be abridged by state law; which provided for "due process of law" forbidding states to deny equal protection of the laws to all citizens; and that granted Congress the power (and duty) to pass "appropriate legislation" to guarantee rights . . . "(9) The possibility of using federal force in states abridging such privileges was implicit in the Amendment, and the power to use that force was not invoked until McKinley's time as President when Elihu Washburne's brother was a U.S. Senator.

It is ironic that the radicalism of the older Washburn brothers who sought for twenty years to accord privileges to blacks was voided as swiftly as a man loses his head with a rapier sweep. In 1890, William Drew Washburn, Senator from Minnesota, cast the swing vote denying President McKinley the power to force southern states to honor the Fourteenth Amendment. "Young Rapid,"(10) William, joined mercantile groups in the Republican party who opposed the bill. He and commercial group members believed the party "should ignore the Negro."(11) After W.D. Washburn's betrayal of his brothers, the interest in enforcement on the part of the federal government would not arise again until 1957 when the National Guard was sent to the State of Arkansas.

Washburne was managing Grant's affairs regarding the Johnson impeachment proceedings, and at first advised Grant to say, "it is not proper that a subordinate should criticize the acts of his superior in a public manner."(12) Elihu was persuaded by the editor of the Chicago *Tribune*, Horace White, that it gave people the impression that he was a Johnsonian, and that there was an anti-Grant movement interested in impeachment so as to defeat Grant in his bid for the presidency by replacing Johnson with Benjamin Wade. Washburne encouraged Grant to make his position clear, which he did. Grant said he would not attend Cabinet meetings except to transact business. A cartoon in *Harper's Weekly* shows Washburne holding "baby Grant" in his arms, beard-and-all, talking to Johnson and company in ladies dresses saying, Nurse W----e. "Bless your souls, ladies, the child won't talk for several months yet." Dame A.J. "Say 'My Policy!' that's a little dear."

At the impeachment trial, Washburne's words were as censorious as any pronounced. Duty, he said, required him to take action against "a band of mercenary cohorts and camp followers of a corrupt and treasonable administration." Worse than that, Elihu referred to those who counseled the President as "the worst men that ever crawled, like filthy reptiles, at the footstool of power." Elihu accused Johnson himself of preventing reunion of the States, the restoration of harmony and peace and happiness in the country."

It was this exaggerated stump language recited in the highest court in the land by the Galena Congressman, that evoked harsh criticism of Washburne when Grant appointed him Secretary of State.

The President was not impeached, and ironically escaped with the crucially important vote cast by a Maine man, William Pitt Fessenden after whom Elihu had named his third son, William Pitt Washburne.

WASHBURNE'S WIDER INTERESTS

Elihu's career in the political arena began in 1852. It ended in 1869 when a statesman emerged out of that pugnacious-imperious and (to wife and children) tender-loving E.B. Washburne--the man of whom it was said had wonderful brain power, able to pursue two

Algernon Sidney Washburn

directly antagonistic methods of thought at once--of whom it was said, he was a man of native talent, firmer and more settled in purpose than Lincoln. His political career ended in 1869 when he was sent off to France, a nation, according to Charles Francis Adams, with the only foreign service office worth a whit. It was an office chosen by Washburne and granted by Grant. When Elihu took off from American shores to sail abroad, his brother Sidney quoted their father as saying in jest that "he thought it singular that his smartest boy should leave the country without asking." Sidney added facetiously, "I set down [this] fact as being important to posterity."

How it all happened, and why, and what was transpiring in the ordinary life of Elihu Benjamin Washburne, is recounted in this chapter as in some ways "important to posterity." The story becomes interesting when it is possible to see this busy man making another career quite unselfconsciously.

❖

There is Congressman Elihu B. Washburne, square jawed, steely eyed, not giving a photographer a chance to see more than his severity, now seated in the House beside Thaddeus Stevens, a little to the right flank of the radical forces. He has a high forehead. His hair is iron gray, worn long, half rolled under at the ends, like a man from the rural districts. Those eyes are large and full, deep set, of a bluish-gray color, and they shine like black diamonds. His nose is prominent, of the Roman order. The cheek bones are prominent, square and firmly set. The mouth is large, with thin, tightly compressed lips, forming an almost exact straight line beneath his Roman nose. A deep hollow pouts the underlip slightly, and adds to the decided squareness of the chin. His dress is similar to Thaddeus Stevens', the prominent difference consisting of the fact that he wears a stiff "stock," instead of a "neckerchief." His voice is full and deep. His style of oratory is easy, off-hand and more convincing than that of any other member on the floor of the House. He is earnest in his expressions, and goes into an argument or a debate with honest enthusiasm and thrilling excitement. Socially he is a gem of the rarest price among a thousand. He lives with General Grant, and with his amiable lady Adele to assist him, forms an agreeable addition to the hospitable mansion of that great chieftain. All of this description from a contemporary writer.

We have already seen that child Elihu aspired to be a sea captain; no, not an ordinary seaman, --a Captain! He experienced severe trials and tribulations, physical and mental, at ages seven and fourteen, when hardly more than a waif. A puritan, Elihu advised one of his brothers not to attend the theater, which Washburne believed was "devilish bad business for young men." He selected his model when he was a teenager, Benjamin Franklin, America's first Ambassador to France. Little did the aspiring youngster know that he would sit in the same chair occupied by that Minister to France, and that Washburne would become, as some said, the second greatest Ambassador to that country.

This Washburne worked, studied, craved more learning and went to Harvard Law School, learned alongside men who became as famous as he, -- Governor Alexander Bullock, James Russell Lowell, W.W. Story, William M. Evarts. While still in his 20s, this ambitious downeast lawyer pled cases before the U.S. Supreme Court, and while in Washington presenting cases, chummed around with a man who was to become President of the United States, Abraham Lincoln. As did thousands of New England youth, this Washburne "went west." He settled in Galena, Illinois, a rough, prosperous mining community where Elihu was an instant success as a young Whig politician. On his way west, he had visited with President Martin Van Buren in Washington, and William Henry Harrison in Cincinnati who the following year (1841) became President of the United States. Elected to Congress, Washburne soon earned the rubric, Watchdog of the Treasury, and he became the honored Father of the House. He was father of the house also in Galena where his wife gave birth to seven Gratiot-Washburne children.

Elihu played a part in the election of Lincoln to the presidency, and as well, he was a significant game player in the earned Lieutenant Generalship of Grant, and then was a pivotal figure in the election to the presidency of the enigmatic warrior and fellow townsman, Ulysses S. Grant. During the Civil War the Congressman visited the battlefield and felt the whirr of bullets at the side of Grant. When the war ended and the President was assassinated, Elihu Benjamin Washburne chaired the Special Committee on the Death of President Lincoln. As Chairman of the Committee to Impeach, Washburne worked to unseat another head-of-state, Andrew Johnson.

❖

However much is excerpted from the public life of a man like Washburne, as has been done above, it is only a pinch of time out of a total life span. Elihu had a continuing and vital relationship to six brothers and three sisters, his mother and father as long as they lived, and related caringly to his sons and daughters. He carried on business in the communities of Galena, and in Chicago when he retired. He carried on correspondence with hundreds of people all over the country. Elihu kept up with his ambitious, successful (and the not-so-successful) brothers, advising, supporting, and aiding them in their chosen careers, --supporting one brother when his life was threatened as Minister Resident in Paraguay, --aiding another when he could not pay his employees, loaning money to that hard-up brother, Cadwallader, --always expecting to be paid a good, hefty interest rate.

❖

1866 was not an extraordinary year in the lives of Elihu, his wife, brothers, sisters and friends. Since, however, it is a mid-career year for Elihu, 1866 experiences will serve the purpose of reminding us that the powerful legislator lived and ruled in several spheres, though we know he was able to release his feelings, --able to revive his interest in living, --able to be intimate, soft and tractable, a man who in his public persona was demanding and authoritative. It isn't as though the world of Washburns was occupied with the problems which popped up in Congress - like forget-me-nots in the spring. The Washburn tribe of politically-minded brothers and sisters, while they had strong opinions about issues on the national agenda, yet had their own personal and everyday concerns, including tragedies. When problems were weighty and burdensome, family members were in touch, most of them with Elihu. His comprehension of complex issues, his suggested solutions, even though like pronunciamentos from on high, were yet appreciated.

C. A. Washburn

His domineering and judgmental manner was illustrated when the twin sister of his mother wanted to marry seventy-nine year old Israel, Sr. It was "too utterly outrageous to be tolerated for a moment," Elihu wrote to one of his brothers, instructing him to "nip the affair in the bud."(13)

E.B. Washburne

The brother who was hurting in 1866 was Charles Ames Washburn, U.S. Minister Resident to Paraguay. Charles was troubled, though his troubles in that year do not begin to compare with what was yet to befall him at the end of his term of service in '68. That year, he barely escaped from Asuncion with his life. The big brother with whom Charles shared his worries was Elihu, to whom Charles wrote letters as lengthy and detailed as an essay prepared for publication(14). Charles wrote Elihu, not Sidney, even though Sidney was willing to correspond. Charles felt Sid was "an intolerable nuisance." He told Elihu that Sidney "writes . . . often but never without saying something nasty and insulting."(15) Elihu and Charles, those two "peas in a pod," (Adele's estimate of the two) could not abide the humorous charm and peculiar writing style of Sidney. In 1864, the Minister Resident of Paraguay in a letter to Elihu was more open about his feelings and passions than was usual with the Washburns. Though guarded, he confessed that he needed desperately to leave the single life. "It's no fun . . . living alone," he wrote, "and [it] tends to damage one's morals."(16) With its sexual overtones, his statement is tantamount to an admission one seldom finds in the hundreds of letters written to or by any of the brothers. Charles followed that remark with a demand made of Elihu, "Wherefore I say unto you[,] if you don't do your best to get me leave to go away and get a comforter[,] then be not surprised to hear of a funeral at the American Legation in Paraguay."

This facetious command by Charles had its effect. Elihu and Israel, both able to express their wishes directly to Secretary of State Seward, Seward being a particular friend of Israel's, got from the Secretary the necessary response.

1864 is an election year! Elihu was himself working diligently to raise money for the campaign to re-elect Lincoln, realizing there was a possibility Lincoln might not win. Charles admitted being disheartened with the news, though he too knew that failure to re-elect would mean a Copperhead President would succeed Old Abe. Lost and alone in Paraguay he waited impatiently, in the meantime trying his hand at making love by the use of a quill pen. He made passionate love by mail to a Reading, Pennsylvania, young lady, twenty-two years of age, Sallie Catherine Cleaveland. Charles was more than twice Sallie's age. Bearded and fierce looking, --intense and demanding like his brother Elihu, --even so, the Lothario used his pen with restraint as he communicated by mail. His nearest approach to the forbidden subject of sex, mild as it was, shocked the young lady, herself hardly out of finishing school. Charles in his letter, perhaps innocently, (though I think not) brought up an image for Sallie to visualize, a lovely barefoot belle of Paraguay. Having written of the loveliness of a tempting native girl, hoping thereby to awaken an interest in Sallie in coming to him, he quickly changed his imagery and proceeded to sing praises of the country where she, Sallie, would live. He wrote of its variety of vegetation, its hills, valleys and plains, and its congenial climate. For himself, he could not complain, he said. He had everything; everything but a wife. He had horses, dogs, ducks, turkey and servants, yet he may say like Haman, "all these avail me nothing."

Elihu in Washington loyally did what he could for Charles, working to get Lincoln elected so Lincoln could give Charles his leave-of-absence to get married. Lincoln was elected and Charles got his leave.

❖

In 1866, Elihu no longer felt the need to soothe Sam who had frequently written to him through the war years. Elihu sensed his sailor brother felt isolated. While the Commander, as the brothers referred to him, was alone and lonely sailing the high seas and wondering about life's meaning, Elihu corresponded with him. By the year 1866, Sam had been honorably discharged from the service. He was in Durant, Wisconsin, and soon was to make his way across the Mississippi into Minnesota and to the City of Owatonna, a few miles from his little brother, William, in Minneapolis. In Owatonna, restless Sam put his roots down. He went into the lumber business, became Mayor of the city and worked to settle a Universalist church and minister.

❖

Congressman Washburne was traveling in Europe in the summer of 1866. Committees were still meeting in Washington, and Elihu wrote Israel from Switzerland reporting that a cable had arrived for him at Rogutz in June. The cable, he explained to Israel, notified him that the Judiciary Committee was to censure President Johnson but would not move to impeach. At home in Maine, Representative John Lynch wrote some months earlier reporting to Israel quite a different story. Lynch said in February, four months before Elihu received his June cable, that the President had "thrown himself, body and boots, into the hands of the Copperheads."(17) Lynch assured Israel that Congress would maintain its legitimate powers despite the power of the administration with its patronage, as the administration threatened non-compliant Republicans with loss of jobs.

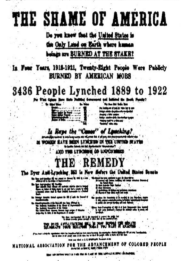

THE SHAME OF AMERICA

Do you know that the United States is the Only Land on Earth where human beings are BURNED AT THE STAKE!

In Four Years, 1918-1921, Twenty-Eight People Were Publicly BURNED BY AMERICAN MOBS

3436 People Lynched 1889 to 1922

Is Rape the "Cause" of Lynching?

THE REMEDY

NATIONAL ASSOCIATION FOR THE ADVANCEMENT OF COLORED PEOPLE

Ordinarily, letters which were passed among three of the brothers, Elihu, Israel and Cadwallader, were not concerned with politics. With Cad, much of the correspondence was about business, banking, bills in Congress, and money exchange. What was interesting about Israel was that he had married a second time, his first wife Mary Maud having died. But Israel's letters to Elihu, to Cad or other brothers made little mention of his new wife, Robina Napier Brown. Come to think of it, even the affectionate Elihu did not write more about Adele than was expected by the standards of the time. Cadwallader seldom mentioned females, his daughters being exceptions. His wife lost her sanity following the birth of her second child and was institutionalized, dying long after the death of her husband.(18) In this medium, Charles was the exception. He always mentioned wife and children, --always asked about Adele when writing Elihu, expressing the wish that he and Adele might correspond. When Elihu failed to write as often as Charles wished, the Paraguayan Minister threatened to forget him and rely upon Adele.

❖

Elihu in Washington in the mid-'60s was the recipient of letters written by men in the South who were loyal to radical Republicanism and the Reconstruction. There was William H. Gibbs, Illinoisan, James L. Alcorn, a successful Southern lawyer and one of Mississippi's wealthiest planters, a Whig who joined the Republican party, and there was the prolific correspondent, Daniel Richards, a great admirer of the Illinois Congressman.

Gibbs knew Washburne was a close friend of Grant's and felt sure complaints would be passed along to the President. As expected, Gibb's grievances were shared with Ulysses. Grant was persuaded to replace General Alvan Gillem, district commander in Mississippi, with General Irwin McDowell. Ex-Confederate Benjamin Humphrey, Governor of the state, was replaced by Adelbert Ames. Gibb's letters to Washburne paid off, and in Washington, continuing reports flowing from Mississippian Gibbs deepened feelings of frustration in Elihu.

The daily harassment of James Alcorn by Ku Klux Klansmen in Mississippi was also reported to the President via Washburne. Though almost a native Southerner, it was Alcorn who said to Elihu, " . . . The poor negroes, (sic) God help them if [the Democratic party] is to rule in the land," adding, "[t]he Republican party has everything staked on the issue; they must play boldly or they are beaten. Has Genl Grant nerve?"(19) With this kind of reporting coming from Alcorn, Elihu's negative feelings were intensified further. Reports such as were mentioned earlier from Daniel Richards were at times a daily affair. Sometimes two of Richards letters arrived on Elihu's desk in Washington on the same day. Washburne probably had a hand in inducing Grant to send a Special Order to Florida at a time when southern whites were determined to take by force properties which had been purchased by Negroes in accordance with U.S. authority. The afternoon of the day rival forces armed with weapons were to come to blows, Grants Special Order arrived. The Order declared that the United States courts must decide tax sale cases.

Having to speak, travel, socialize, read and respond to a long list of requests from constituents, --these kinds of assaults on Washburne's time, together with his Congressional duties associated with reconstruction, found Elihu losing health and strength. One day in June, 1866, he fainted while in the House. He was taken to Grant's home to be cared for. He knew he had to be well again soon since election time presented Washburne with another task, his own re-election.

Back home in Galena, Washburne campaigned for the eighth time to win nomination for Congress. At Elizabeth, Illinois, he was suddenly called upon to speak. He held forth for an hour, lecturing on reconstruction as himself a member of the Joint Committee on Reconstruction, --he explained how he had striven to provide guarantees for the freed men, saying he wanted there to be suffrage for them, --he told his audience about Johnson's plan for the South. The spectacle in Washington, he said, "ought to make angels weep." In descriptive terms he conveyed a picture of what had happened in Memphis with the rioting. It made listeners agree with him that the riot was "the blackest page of American history." All the "right" things were said by Washburne which thrilled the audience at Elizabeth. What he had said represented the thinking of liberal and radical Republicans.

Chapter Fourteen

THE DESTRUCTION OF RECONSTRUCTION

The deceased President Lincoln had insisted that we cannot undertake to run governments in all the Southern states! What impressed Elihu was that Lincoln foresaw southern leaders running governments of the reprobate states as soon as they laid down their arms and "resumed their civil pursuits." The politically minded Lincoln also realized Congressmen were sensitive about their place in the process of reconstructing the South. He said he expected the Administrative branch of government would be the first to grant recognition of *de facto* southern governments, *but only until Congress provided criteria.* Congressman Washburne noted that Lincoln admitted some of [the states] might [govern] badly. Consideration which Lincoln exhibited for the defeated enemy prompted Washburne to say confidently to General John B. Gordon of Georgia that the people of the South would come to love Lincoln. Clearly then, President Lincoln had been aware of the major problems facing the Union with the War's end.

One of two issues centered on the question of the rebel states and how Congress was to relate to the victorious government. That issue brought forth untold turmoil

Alexander Stephens

in Congress, introducing prolonged hostility between Congress and the Executive branch of government. In addition to this first problem was the matter of former slaves and how as freed men and women they would find their place in the political, social, and economic spheres.

Former House member, Representative Alexander Stephens of Georgia, wrote an article in which he granted there were two opposing ideas causing the war. He maintained, however, it was an error to suppose those two ideas were, respectively, slavery on the one hand, and freedom of the slaves on the other. The two opposing views, in Stephens' estimation, "lay in the organic Structure of the Government of the states," the federalist and nationalist approaches to government.(1) Stephens claimed that Jefferson, who wrote in his response to a query from a Maine Senator in 1820 that he could hear a "fire bell in the night"(2) was alluding to the clash between prevailing Whig and Democratic polity, the latter opposing, as Jefferson opposed, the centralizing federalist principles.

Political affairs brought forth a third problem at the war's end. Republican leaders claimed that the foregoing problems would be solved only by the Republican party. In the estimation of Elihu Washburne and other Republican leaders Copperhead Democrats could not be left to determine the correct relations the government must take toward the derelict states, that the party in power *having won the war*, must be the party to deal with the intractable third problem of black Americans.

❖

Two New Englanders without rancor disputed the legal aspects of the problem said to be the most decisive, and which were to breach relations between the U.S. Congress and the then President of the United States, Andrew Johnson. Charles Sumner, brilliant, handsome, aggressive Senator from Massachusetts, stated his understanding of what he considered to be the fundamental issue before Congress. "At this moment," Sumner wrote, "our Domestic Relations all hinge upon one question: *How to treat the Rebel States?*"(3) Congressman Elihu Washburne's brother, Israel, now Maine's Civil War Governor, large headed, small bodied, always gracious, warm and beloved, responded to Sumner's *Atlantic Monthly* essay with a gravamen, complaining that there was "no theoretical or practical objection to considering the rebellious states as being still, strictly and legally speaking, states of the American Union . . . "(4) Sumner insisted that states can commit *suicide*, implying, of course, that the Confederate states on those grounds had ceased to exist. In this, Washburn seemed to concur, admitted that aggression such as the South exhibited, is "a never-wearying suicide." The essential argument for the two men, however, became, (a) "The dogma and delusion of States Rights, which did so much for the Rebellion, [and] must not be allowed to neutralize all that our arms have gained," which also was Sumner's position. (b) But Washburn, invoking the constitution, claimed that "the powers not delegated . . . are reserved to the states respectively, or to the people," contending that laws passed when the state was not

Benjamin Wade

in rebellion were still operative, and that they were not to be considered annulled. With these variations in view noted, Israel was given to understand that Sumner felt that what Washburn wrote in his essay was exactly what he, Sumner, had said. Differences which were played down by Sumner in his letter to Washburn remained a source of irritation, however, between the Executive and Administrative branches--would the Confederate states pick up where they left off, or must they be organized anew?

When Andrew Johnson acceded to the office of President, there was little chaffing between the branches. As has been indicated, even radical Congressmen from House and Senate visiting Johnson came away from appointments satisfied with what the President said he intended to do. "Radical Republicans initially viewed Johnson's accession as a godsend."(5) Radical Benjamin Wade expressed faith in the President who had said to Wade that treason was a crime and crime must be punished. Senator Sumner made daily visits to the White House during April and May, believing fully that the two agreed on the subject of most importance to Sumner, black suffrage.

It was not exactly a subtle difference, but the President got away with making a distinction saying that individual traitors should be punished *but not the states!* On this matter, Andrew Johnson and Israel Washburn were in agreement. And Elihu, perhaps sharing his brother's outlook, visited the President and afterward wrote to Adele expressing feelings of warmth toward Johnson. He wrote, "I hope and believe there will be no split between him and Congress."(6) In 1858, when Johnson was a

Senator from Tennessee, Johnson, a Democrat, had written to Elihu commending him, and reminding him that Republicans must have the post office patronage in their hands.(7) Rumors began to spread that Washburne was going over to Johnson, reinforced by the fact that Washburne's favorite nominee for President, Ulysses S. Grant, was making a trip around the country accompanying the President. A constituent wrote, expressing fear that after all Washburne's endeavors to keep Grant in line, Grant remained a Democrat with sympathies for the South.

The first break between the President and Congress came in May of 1865. The Military Commander in Louisiana, General Nathaniel Banks, countermanded orders of Governor James Madison Wells and the Governor in the absence of Commander Banks, replaced Bank's appointees with members of the old guard. The President confirmed Well's powers. Before the month of May was out, Johnson's reconstruction plan was published bringing shock and anger to those who previously agreed with the radical who said "the Almighty continued Mr. Lincoln in office as long as he was useful, and then substituted a better man to finish the work."(8) Johnson intended to pardon citizens of the southern states who pledged loyalty to the Union and who supported emancipation, *except* owners of taxable property valued at $20,000 or more. The President then took it upon himself to appoint William W. Holden Provisional Governor of North Carolina without consulting Congress. A battle royal then began which was consummated in the month of May, 1868.

Elihu Washburne, while calling himself a radical, yet had held off the radicals when they first began their movement to impeach the President. In January of 1867, Elihu proposed that actual impeachment must be sanctioned by the Judiciary Committee. His motion was approved overwhelmingly, frustrating radical efforts. In the interval between 1866 when so many expressed gratitude for Johnson, and the beginnings of the new year, two respected Senators, John Sherman and Lyman Trumbull, said that the President had deceived them. Next, Sickles and Stanton were removed from office. It was then that Washburne began to sour on the President. The Executive undermined the Freedmen's Bureau by making it impossible for the Bureau to carry out the mandates of Congress. The Bureau was headed, of course, by a friend and a Maine neighbor of the Washburn family, Oliver O. Howard. Washburne was incensed and wrote to his father impugning Johnson as "a bad and faithless man." When a resolution was offered in the House praising General Hancock for conduct as military governor, Washburne sat listening to the resolution read, disapproved, and promptly submitted a substitute utterly "condemning the conduct of Andrew Johnson acting President of the United States."(9) He protested against the appointment of General Hancock by Johnson, contending that by law, Grant, not the President, was supposed to administer the military districts. Still later, Congressman Washburne delivered one of the most painful and sardonic speeches offered by his peers, saying that Johnson's

> . . . [Whole official career as President has been marked by a wicked disregard of all the obligations of public duty and by a degree of perfidy and treachery and turpitude unheard of in the history of the rulers of a free people; his personal and official character has made him the opprobrium of both hemispheres, and brought ineffable disgrace on the American name.

For a time, E.B. Washburne was a member of the Joint Committee on Reconstruction. The committee decided, with Congress affirming, that the southern states would be invited to return to the Union when they could qualify. One of the qualifications for re-admission was endorsement by the rebellious states of the Thirteenth, Fourteenth, and Fifteenth amendments to the Constitution. How to make the new laws operable was a good part of the problem facing the Joint Committee on Reconstruction. The problem was seen as belonging to the conqueror, but as well as to the subdued South. New cultural norms, mores, and legal necessities were seen by the people of the South as impositions *from outside*. In order to grasp the magnitude of the problem facing the victorious party we can look behind the scenes to see what actually happened in one of the southern states as Reconstruction Plans took shape.

Elihu Washburne in Washington was a catalyst in the Florida circumstance. The principle character making Elihu pivotal was Daniel Richards who played out a role as the central character in that political arena. Before leaving Illinois for Florida, Richards had been a functionary in the political arena in Sterling in the early 1860s. He was an attorney, served in the Illinois Senate, and was a radical imitating what he saw as Washburne's radicalism. In 1866, Elihu found a niche for Daniel as an agent of the National Republican Committee while serving as a Tax Commissioner for the Treasury Department with offices located in Tallahassee, Florida.(10) Richards, along with a Colonel William U. Saunders, an articulate black man from Maryland, and Liberty Billings, a Unitarian minister from New Hampshire, attempted to establish a political base in

Daniel Richards

the state. They were charged with writing and arranging for the adoption of a State Constitution acceptable to the United States Congress.

May 7, 1866, Daniel Richards in Tallahassee sat down to write to Elihu Washburne. At the exact time he wrote, atrocities--such as the Floridian feared would break out in Florida-- were already being perpetrated in Memphis, Tennessee. In fact, by the time Daniel's letter reached Washburne's desk it had been decided that Elihu would chair a Congressional Committee to investigate the Memphis Riots. Richards wrote again saying that a war of races could only be prevented by equal suffrage. He reported that the Negroes in Florida were secretly arming themselves since they felt rebels would "shoot them down as they would wild beasts." The letter writer depicted scenes similar to what Washburne would be horrified to learn in chairing the Select Committee Hearings on the riots in Memphis.(11) Richards knew how to arouse the ire and indignation of Congressman Washburne. The Floridian had on his desk a copy of the Report of the Reconstruction Committee. Upon reading that committee's report he commented upon it in his letter to Elihu. He said the Plan would fail, claiming that, with the Plan as written, "the ballot will never be given to the negro [sic]. The inducement," he wrote, "is not sufficient to overcome the prejudices of the *chivalry.*"

"Chivalry" was not a pleasant word in the lexicon of Elihu Washburne. His brother Charles had carried on a running editorial battle with the chivalric in California and he, Charles, was in a duel with one of them. The word "chivalric" was apt to sour in the mouths of all Washburn family members. In Richards estimation, rebels did not care about representation in Congress as much as they did in gaining control of the state government. They knew that, once blacks achieved the right to vote the whites could never deprive them of that privilege. The United States Marshall in Florida, Alexander Magruder, was willing, he said, "to accept every thing [in a constitution], except the doctrine of full and complete equality of the negro with the white race."(12) Richards was sure that in keeping with Washburne's thinking, the solution to the problem created by white men was "to give all parties interested in the laws and their execution a voice in saying who shall make, execute and administer the same."(13)

Five days later, Richards sent off another letter to Washington indicating that trouble was brewing. The rebels were bent upon taking property which had been purchased in accordance with US authority. Guns were readied on the two sides with Union whites and blacks prepared to stand together to shoot it out with rebels. Rebels were being led by the unpardoned General Joseph Finnigan. The issue was attenuated the day southern whites were to advance on Amilia Island. Like the cavalry galloping to the rescue with flags flying, General Ulysses S. Grant's *Special Order to Florida* arrived in the afternoon, saving the day. Richards explained that if the Orders had "arrived but [a] few hours later there would have been . . . a nice little fight . . . " Grant's Order declared that the United States courts must decide tax sale cases.(14) Despite the *Special Orders*, the Circuit Court served up decisions enabling rebels to wrest properties from owners. The series of incidents in Florida involving Washburne was part of President Johnson's "experiment" to return governance to white leadership. Grant's *Special Orders* suggest the possibility that the Illinois Congressman was a factor in enfeebling Johnson's plans. The scenario can depict Washburne receiving Daniel's letter, rising from his chair, exiting angrily from his house to go next door walking into the General's house where he would advise Grant. Strong-willed Elihu was the General's closest advisor. "Elihu is firmer and more settled in purpose than Lincoln," said Charles Francis Adams. "[He is] a man of strong will."(15) Grant was not strong willed and needed to be nudged. A few months later Elihu was interviewed and a report from him was printed in the *New York*

Charles Francis Adams

Times. It was said that the Illinois Congressman "regards General Grant as wholly in sympathy with Congress and its plan of reconstruction . . . .[and] in favor of standing by the blacks in all their civil, social and political rights . . . "(16) In December, 1866, President Johnson replaced General John Pope in Florida at Pope's request since the President had not supported Pope's efforts. General George G. Meade was sent South, a man who was unwilling to use the military to protect blacks and white Union radicals. Meade's political actions mirrored Johnson's in Washington.

Thomas Tullock of the Republican National Committee in Washington withdrew funding for the Union League headed by Daniel Richards, Saunders and Billings. Money was to be sent instead to Harrison Reed, a conservative who was critical of League leaders who, he believed, were "pandering" to Negroes. Richards wrote Elihu striking a sensitive nerve as he explained that Tullock was trying to persuade William Saunders to support Salmon Chase instead of Grant as convention time for the Republicans approached. Washburne, of course, had plans for Grant's future political career.(17) In addition to Tullock, General Conway was in the South, also opposed to Grant and also favoring Salmon Chase. Political machinations of ambitious men in Washington thus were to have an effect upon the adoption of the Florida constitution and upon the election of new political leaders in Florida. Richards sent a letter to Washington telling Washburne that Conway assured Saunders, that if he, Saunders, would support Chase *as against Grant* he would be sustained by the Congressional Committee, and that Saunders, Billing and Richards could have all the money they needed.(18) There was no money for radicals, and later Saunders went over to the conservative Republican nominee for Governor, Harrison Reed.

Republican and Union League members intensified their efforts to gain control of the election of delegates to the convention in Florida called by the Military Commander. Conservative Republicans arranged for a district meeting and overlooked the radicals. The radicals assembled a meeting of their own nominating a slate of delegates. Saunders, Billings and Richards were themselves elected delegates. "God is good," Daniel wrote Elihu, "and the *'radical team'* has triumphed." He claimed that the troika had "literally created the republican party in Florida" and that they had *made* a convention with two thirds if not three fourths of the delegates their friends.(19) The feud between conservatives and radicals began promptly as delegates were called together. At the official convention, January 20, 1868, twenty-nine of forty-six delegates elected a black, Charles H. Pearce, temporary chairman. Richards was made President of the convention. He appointed seventeen committees and set them to work writing the constitution. Conservatives with money from the National Republican Committee moved in and were accused by Richards of buying delegates. "All those of easy virtue soon fall prey to those minions of the devil and A. Johnson who have plenty of money."(20) The President, Richards, tried to keep the delegates by making out requisitions, but General Meade, the Military Commander, would not let the State Treasurer honor the requisitions without his approval, which was not forthcoming. Then came a crafty move by dissident, conservative Republicans.

Unable to gain control of delegates, conservatives left the capital, went to Monticello, a few miles distant leaving the radicals without a quorum. Convention delegates remaining in Tallahassee, however, decided they were a quorum, finished the constitution and dispatched it to General Meade in Atlanta. The radicals then adjourned, though immediately formed themselves into a nominating convention and submitted as a nominee for the office of Governor Liberty Billings. William U. Saunders was nominated Lieutenant Governor, and a black, Jonathan Gibbs, considered the most brilliant and able among delegates, was selected as the candidate for Congress.

The Monticello minority made up of conservatives became a majority as they were successful in lining up more delegates. They wrote their own version of the state constitution, returned to Tallahassee and at midnight on February 10 took possession of the meeting hall. Conservatives were successful in inducing federal soldiers to arrest two members of the Richards group, so that conservatives acceded to the position of the majority. Richards as President of the convention was deposed by vote of the new majority and the Monticello constitution was adopted to be sent off to General Meade. Meade sent the versions to Washington recommending the adoption of the rump group.

Conservatives, including Harrison Reed, took command of the state political machine. He was elected Governor, appointed 173 white county officials and named two former slave holders to his cabinet.

Daniel Richards' career in the latter days had been a three act drama. In the first act he made his journey south to become known as a carpetbagger and subject to diatribes on the part of some historians who misconceived him a "sort of Uriah Heep . . . of moderate ability and elastic conscience."(21) Contrary to those historian's view, Richards was a vigorous political activist, shrewd and calculating, and ready to fulminate against reputed enemies. Like the Republicans in the Whig tradition, however, he was ready to compromise for purposes of advancing a righteous cause, in himself matching historian Kenneth Stampp's description of the heir of the Enlightenment who "believes in the doctrine of natural rights and in the equality of all men before the law, [having] a transcendental faith in the essential goodness of man, [and regarding] slavery as the ultimate abomination."(22)

Andrew Johnson

In the second act there was a classic "gang of three" made villains by poor, dispossessed planters eager to return to political power. The three, Billings, Saunders and Richards, had mixed agendas, all of them striving to achieve goals for the state of Florida as they engaged in drawing civilized constitutional measures giving the dispossessed blacks a lease on life in this happy vale.

The play ended with victory for conservative forces and with sadness for the "righteous." It ended too with bitterness with few antidotes for the sickness of hatred and fear on the part of rebels. The characters in the play, all human, were muddied by politics and greed, and the radicals were blackened with the epithet, "carpetbagger."

The Washburne-Grant team was not yet in the ascendancy in Washington. Johnson equally sincere was flawed by an inherited prejudice and was able easily to frustrate Richards, giving the victory into the hands of conservatives.

In substance, all parties failed despite the fact that they were designated "children of the enlightenment," in that all of them overlooked the extreme need, not merely to educate illiterate blacks who had been held in thralldom, they failed to educate ignorant white men and women whose prejudices fueled the war itself, and at last at war's end almost duplicated the system which had poisoned the South, in all too many instances re-making blacks into serfs.

Chapter Fifteen

TWO GALENA TOWNSMEN CLIMB TO THE TOP

Thaddeus Stevens thought he was aware before others were that Grant was to be an applicant for the office of President. In May of 1866 Stevens let it be known that he was willing to promote Grant, as though this was new knowledge erupting from Stevens' announcement. In truth, Washburne had seen to it that the General started maneuvering for the office in the summer of the previous year. As a starter, the Galena Congressman began to lay plans shortly after Appomattox for his fellow townsman to visit Galena. In May of 1865, when Grant assured Elihu he still considered Galena to be his home town and the place where he would vote, Washburne resolved to arrange for a Grant celebration, an event worthy of being heralded in the media around the country.

In mid-August of 1865 a Reception Committee headed by Washburne and Editor Houghton of the *Galena Gazette*--accompanied by 10,000 people--met the now famous, but former leather salesman, Ulysses Grant, who in earlier times had been called by his brothers, not "Ulysses" but "Useless Grant." Flowers were scattered before the carriage carrying the General onto the Main Street. A welcoming address was delivered by Washburne, and a clergyman responded on behalf of the "silent Cal" of the times, the returning hero. Grant himself delivered a six-sentence greeting to the enthusiastic multitudes. When festivities at Galena ended, the Congressman went to work promptly arranging for the General to visit several cities in the East, West and South,(1) and as the months passed he continued to counsel Grant, particularly with regard to relations with Andrew Johnson.

Given Grant's reluctance to speak, often arranging for Elihu to make pronouncements for him, one does not wonder at a remark made by Cadwallader to Elihu. Cad insisted that, "The public wants to know Grant's opinions," maintaining that Elihu should do something about that.(2) Actually, two of Elihu's brothers did not think highly of their older brother's friend and companion, at least as a potential head of government. Cadwallader expressed his doubt more than once, and Charles, when interviewed in 1879 said he was not "particularly in favor of Grant."(3) In 1864 when Charles was in Paraguay, he conceded that Grant must have a place on the ticket but recommended for President, N.P. Banks, and for vice President, U.S. Grant. Washburne would have to concede the truth of the matter, what a biographer of Hamilton Fish said of Grant, that Grant was "subject to impulsive moods and would need much advice." In itself it suggests the need President Grant had for a person such as Elihu to advise him.(4)

The General testified to his loyalty to Elihu saying he relied on their personal relations which enabled him to speak freely to Elihu upon all important matters.(5) The General was willing to ally himself with Johnson at the time Washburne was attempting to moderate the President's views following a White House visit. Three Congressmen--Washburne, Fessenden and Reverdy Johnson-- disapproved of the effort in January to impeach the President. Soon Washburne saw the anti-Johnson movement as anti-Grant. For a time the two Galeneans, Washburne and Grant, were in accord with the strategy of the obstreperous President Johnson. Grant accompanied Johnson in his "Swing Around the Circle" standing beside him at the several stops made in cities along the way. He accepted the proffered position of

General of the Army, and temporarily, said Grant, the position of Secretary of War. It prompted the New York *Times* to report, however, that the General was Johnson's man.

For his part, the General drew a very different picture of his own expectations. Grant wanted to be seen, not as a compliant member of Johnson's cabinet, but as a man independent of Presidential candidate Johnson. Grant therefore proclaimed that as a soldier he would not be able to assist or promote candidate Johnson. He made his argument palatable to his boss by indicating that he was even unable to support his very good friend, Washburne, who was re-running for his congressional seat. This tactic worked since Grant was able delicately to free himself of an unpleasant expectation that as a member of the President's team, he must back Andrew Johnson. Despite his pronouncement which Grant felt released him from championing the President, he wrote in an August letter to his Galena friend, "Your friendship for me has been such that I should not hesitate to support you for personal reasons, on the ground that there is no one who cannot recognize great acts of friendship."(6) Thus, though Grant refused Johnson, in substance he endorsed candidate Washburne.

Andrew Johnson   **Gen. Philip Sheridan**   **Ulysses S. Grant**

Washburne was in Europe in the summer in 1867. He left the states in April and returned near the end of August. While he was away, the President removed Grant's (and Washburne's) good friend, Philip Sheridan, who was in charge of one of the five military districts in the South. General Winfield S. Hancock was sent to replace Sheridan. Hancock, a Democrat, disapproved of Congresses Reconstruction Act.

A letter received in Europe from O.E. Babcock, Grant's secretary, reported that, "The good Republicans seem to be united on [Grant]," but it was believed by some that the General was being brought out too soon, and, said Babcock, Democrats were saying the whole scheme was worked out by you, Washburne, and your friend J. Russell Jones.

When Elihu arrived back in the U.S. in August his course of action confirms what his brother Charles said of him. "[Elihu] had two qualities which have always been remarked: Boldness and dispatch of business."(7) Washburne promptly urged Grant to re-open the Sheridan case, to protest the selection of Hancock, and to insist that as General of the Army and Secretary of War, it was he, Grant, who should administer the military districts.(8) Elihu counseled the General to confront the President.

At that time Washburne was eager for impeachment proceedings to take place. He was uneasy about Grant's having worked so closely with the President appearing to be a collaborator. There were strong political forces in New England working to undermine Grant claiming that the General had fallen from grace. Washburne hurried to Boston and arranged for a conversation to take place with prominent New England politicians with reporters sitting in.(9) Elihu was anxious to convince New England readers that General Grant was "wholly in sympathy with Congress and its plan of reconstruction." He announced that Grant was "in favor of standing by the blacks in all their civil, social and political rights . . . " and explained why Grant had accepted the cabinet position which had displaced Secretary Stanton. Elihu revealed that Grant had taken the position after consultation with Stanton. Furthermore, said the interviewee, he, Washburne, would deem it "criminal negligence in Grant not to have accepted the place [assigned by Andrew Johnson] under the circumstances."

Soon after Elihu's return to the states, Grant chose to relinquish his office. As *ad interim* Secretary of War Grant did not return his office keys to the President. He left them with a functionary, who put them in the hands of Edwin Stanton, the radicals' choice of Secretary who served in Lincoln's (and Johnson's) cabinet. There was a confrontation such as Washburne had advised. It turned out to be an embarrassment for the General. At a cabinet meeting, Grant was called upon by the President to make a report, despite the fact that Grant had signaled his unhappiness with the administration. In response to the request to report, Grant said simply that he no longer held the office, whereupon the President "tore into him not with a wild tirade, but much more tellingly, with an icy dressing-down."(10)

In February the House of Representatives voted to impeach Andrew Johnson for "high crimes and misdemeanors." Articles of Impeachment contained seventeen charges against the Chief Executive. An Impeachment Committee was appointed by the House with E.B. Washburne as chairman, an angry man. In his testimony before the Senate Committee, flailing his arms, his voice cracking with fury, he said,

[Johnson's] whole official career as President has been marked by a wicked disregard of all the obligations of public duty and by a degree of perfidy and treachery and turpitude unheard of in the history of the rulers of a free people; his personal and official character has made him the opprobrium of both hemispheres, and brought ineffable disgrace on the American name.(11)

These were harsh words delivered in a tenor characteristic of Washburne who frequently spoke in the superlative degree. He was chastised, however, for his uncharitable indictment of the President. Even so, there was an abundance of letters from constituents cheering Elihu on. Despite his critics, Washburne's assaults on President Johnson strengthened his hold on the Republican party.

As for General Grant, he not only testified against Johnson, he called on Senators in their homes wanting to convince them to vote against the President. Further, he lowered himself by arranging for one of his janitors to go through the President's wastepaper basket, and he sent to Washburne's Impeachment Committee papers which the janitor pulled from the crinkly mass. Where earlier, radical Republicans had been suspicious of the person, Grant, who was referred to by the *Times* as "Johnson's man," they now began to swing into the Grant-Washburne orbit, and it appeared that Ulysses S. Grant--not "W" as Mrs. Lincoln predicted--

would be "the rising man."

❖

The Republican Convention was held in Chicago in 1868. It was preceded by a Civil War veterans convention, and there was as expected a carry over from one convention to the other. When the Republicans assembled, there came marching in from the veterans' gathering delegates who treasured the "bloody flag," carrying Old Glory and followed by the war-wounded popular General Sickles. When the assembly was called to order, and at the proper time on the agenda, General John A. Logan submitted Grant's name, delivered an impassioned speech, whereupon a pigeon painted red, white and blue was released in the assembly hall. Curtains parted to show a likeness of the Goddess of Liberty and General Grant.

Governor Fenton of New York, an associate of Washburne's, was considered for the vice presidency, but Schuyler Colfax, twice sworn into office as Speaker of the House by Elihu Washburne, was nominated and elected.

Two months after the May convention, the Grants left Washington for home, Galena. While traveling west, the hero (and sometimes villain) Thaddeus Stevens died and was buried in a pauper's grave in an integrated cemetery. Elihu Washburne succeeded the Pennsylvanian as the powerful leader in the House. Though Elihu admired Stevens and the two voted together frequently on radical measures, two of the Washburnes, Elihu and Cadwallader, were the ones

Thaddeus Stevens

who uncovered sculduggery attributable to Stevens. Stevens, who protested otherwise, was bought off by the Union Pacific Railway Company enabling their bill to pass. That fact was made clear in a letter to the Congressman from a company executive, John D. Perry.

Universalist poets known to Washburne, Alice and Phoebe Cary, wrote a tribute to Stevens following his death. A verse with which the Washburn brothers would have agreed. In part it reads:

> Suppose he swerved from the straightest course--
> That the things he should not do he did--
> That he hid from the eyes of mortals, close,
> Such sins as you and I have hid?

These lyricists and millions more were grateful to Thaddeus Stevens for the contribution he made as a free man and a free mind.

Alice and Phoebe Cary

Ulysses S. Grant on the other hand in the campaign of 1868 did not hold forth for any of the great causes, for some of which the war was fought and for which thousands died. "Let us have peace," was his campaign speech, short enough to be remembered. The candidate always found ways of avoiding speeches for his patient audiences, sometimes saying no more than "I return my sincere thanks." On one occasion he asked his audience to excuse him, for, he said, "I am fatigued, weary, dusty, and unable to address you." He acknowledged in a letter to Elihu that, "a person would not know there was a canvass going on if it were not for the accounts we read in the papers of great gatherings all over the country."(12)

On election day in Galena, however, there was excitement even though the day was rainy and disagreeable. The telegraph company brought a wire into town and directly to Washburne's house. Inclement weather did not keep away guests who crowded into the small petitioned downstairs rooms of Elihu's Greek temple, crowding the two doorways leading into the library where the telegraph operator performed. Ulysses made the five minute walk down the hillside through the meadow between his house and Elihu's, arriving at the Congressman's back door just before dinner. The telegraph keys were not yet clicking away, as Grant may have hoped, but two hours later, news perked up the telegraph operator.

General Rawlins was at the gathering. Rawlins was the man who enthralled Grant in the Call to War meeting which took place in the Galena Town Hall in 1861 at the historic meeting which occurred after the first guns of war had blasted Fort Sumter. Rawlins was the man on Grant's staff who during the war bossed the General and sometimes swore at him for doing things he thought Grant should not do. General and Mrs. Chetlain were at Elihu's on election night. The Lead Mine Band came by to serenade the

Horace Greeley

gathering, and Washburne wrote Adele that everyone felt "pretty foxy." The letter to Adele closed illustrating Elihu's perceptive insight into things political. He wrote, "What a terrific contest we have had! It has come out right, *but what a narrow escape.*" (Emphasis added.) A switch of 29,862 of the 5,717,246 votes cast would have elected Seymour instead of Grant . . . (13)

❖

March 4, 1869. The President-elect refused to ride through the streets to the inaugural exercises with outgoing President Johnson. Johnson had called Grant a liar and Grant never forgave such an affront.

Settled into office, one of the new President's first tasks was to compose his cabinet. The position considered of greatest importance, Secretary of State, was given to Elihu. Elihu's fellow Universalist, Horace Greeley, was present in the room with Washburne and heard the announcement when a young page came with the news meant for the Congressman. Greeley overheard the communiqué and left without so much as a word of congratulation to Elihu. Perhaps Greeley was in accord with the judgment of some who commented upon the appointment, saying Mr. Washburne was half-illiterate, ill-mannered and incredibly undiplomatic.(14) Most historians report that Grant's cabinet selections were made without the knowledge of persons who were to be appointed, including, it was thought, Congressman Washburne. The fact is, Washburne was listed as Minister to France. He wanted to go to Paris, however, with the prestige of having been Secretary of State--or else Grant wanted him to function in France possessed of that status. In which case, Grant and Washburne must have consulted with each other. Contrary to claims to the contrary, Washburne knew he was to be offered the post.

Grant offered Washburne the Interior Department. The Congressman did not want Interior. He would hve accepted the Treasury Department, but Grant had in mind a wealthy businessman, Alexander T. Stewart worth, it was said, forty million dollars. The President sent Stewart's name to the Senate and at the request of fellow Congressmen Washburn went to Grant, sadly to report to him that a law passed in 1784 disallowed any person to be appointed a commissioner of the Treasury who was engaged in any trade or commerce. That did not get Washburne the position, if he still wanted it. It is likely it was too late for a change to be made. By the time the Stewart nomination became a problem, Elihu had settled into the position of Secretary of State temporarily. Grant had it in mind to nominate James F. Wilson of Iowa to succeed the transient Secretary Washburne. Wilson was agreeable that Elihu should serve in the office with the proviso that Elihu not initiate any policies or make any appointments. Lyman Trumbull, no friend of Elihu's (though one of Washburne's sons and Trumbull served together in Trumbull's Chicago law firm) and Trumbull in his biography said Wilson told him specifically that Washburne began immediately to make appointments until, reports Trumbull, Grant called him to order and finally compelled him to resign.(15) Though Trumbull quotes James F. Wilson himself, the procedure reported seems unlikely. A more credible account comes from Roland Frye, Jr., who states that Washburne held office for ten days, five of which were served after his resignation had been laid on the President's desk; that he made no appointments, though applications during the ten-day period may have been routinely sent on their way to the Senate committee. Conveniently, Cadwallader's son-in-law, Charles Payson, was working in the Department of State when Elihu made an attempt to have the claim made by Trumbull confirmed or disconfirmed. Elihu wrote Payson who wrote Elihu April 5, 1880, indicating that after a thorough search of the record with the help of Appointment Clerk, Barble, no list was found, but Barble recalled a list being prepared by Washburne and sent to the Senate. None were confirmed; no appointments were made.

A touching letter from President Grant was written to Washburne and then the Ex-Secretary of State was off to England and France to begin his new career as a diplomat.

It was a mistake for Grant to send Washburne abroad. Grant needed the guidance of an honest, dedicated man such as his fellow townsman, to whom, in addition, Grant was indebted. It was not long before Grant was in trouble and unable to trust his closest advisors. In the end, Grant realized his error. He tried in vain to persuade Washburne to return to Washington and serve in his administration as Secretary of the Treasury. A rift of no great consequence had grown between the two. Charles Washburn explained the breach in an interview saying that after Grant was nominated in 1868 Elihu raised funds for the campaign. One of those approached by Elihu for support was Moses H. Grinnell, a man who had the confidence of businessmen around the country. Charles said Elihu thought Grinnell ought to be appointed Collector of the Port of New York and gave his recommendation to the President. While Grinnell was appointed and served for a short time he was displaced by Tom Murphy. Washburne was disgusted, said Charles, "and I should not wonder if General Grant had come to the conclusion that he had a right to be."

The chicanery and deceit which marked Grant's administration prompted his fellow Galenean, Elihu, to say he was grateful he was out of Washington and out of the country. However, his disagreements with Grant's management of affairs did not alienate the two from each other. Elihu was always ready to come forward and give whatever support he could, short of taking a cabinet position. That inclination to support his old friend included the pre-convention of 1880, though Grant was persuaded, either by John A. Logan or Roscoe Conkling that Elihu was undermining him in his third bid for the presidency. Believing Washburne was his enemy, therefore, Grant to his dying day never forgave the man who "made" him.

❖

Henry Adams writing about the two Galena townsmen, said that Ulysses Grant was awkward in the presence of men of superior knowledge, and that he, Grant, preferred courser politicians. But, Adams added, he was essentially democratic. Elihu was essentially democratic, and doubtless, in Adams' eyes was just such a course politician as he envisioned Grant admiring. Elihu put on no airs, and without the veneer of social elegance and urbanity, Adams and others of his ilk could compliment themselves claiming superiority, not only to General Grant but to Washburne, the farmer's son, the rough frontiersman, with what was considered a defect in his mental vision inasmuch as he was impulsive, headstrong, combative, and unbalanced.(16)

Concerning Grant and Elihu's version of the man, Washburne would have to remind himself of the judgment made of the General by his brother Cadwallader. The Wisconsin Washburn having worked on the General's staff during the war, watching him think, talk and work, wrote to Elihu in March of 1863 saying that he, Elihu, could not "make a silk purse out of a sow's ear." Despite Cadwallader's judgment, it is clear that Washburne had a genuine fondness for the General. When asked what he liked about him, Elihu said, "I admire his simplicity, introspection, sincerity and capacity for every new occasion."

❖

As we verge on learning about Washburne's approaching new career, we need to realize that there were those at home in the United States who referred to the Galena Congressman as low, sordid, and vulgar; a barren, mediocre intelligence, one who raves and rants like a prostitute.(17) Alongside such appalling remarks is the view of Judge William Bradley, a man who had known Washburne for 48 years. The Judge said, "[Mr. Washburne] was a great man, and in some respects he must, I think, be classed as a genius." And yet, Elihu, who, of course, knew himself for 58 years (against Bradley's 48) fitted himself willingly into Henry Adam's portrait. Of himself and wife, he said they were two old fogy country people. That is exactly what some of the crowned heads of Europe--the opinion of certain Bostonians to the contrary notwithstanding--found lovable about Adele, and admirable in Elihu. Since this man off a Maine farm coming to Washington from the wild frontier of the West was soon to be counted preeminent among America's Ambassadors, it is well to read what

Hamilton Fish's biographer, Allan Nevins, wrote about Secretary of State Fish's immediate predecessor, Ambassador E.B. Washburne:

One of the most pleasing discoveries of 1870-71 was the quality of that grizzled veteran of Illinois politics, the Minister to France. Elihu Washburne showed a courage, constancy, and wisdom that did honor to the republic. The last dinner ever given in the Tuileries, June 7, 1870, was for him and his wife--a dinner at which [Washburne] descried 'a cloud of uneasiness' on Napoleon III's brow.(18)

Chapter Sixteen

MOVING INTO NEW ARENAS

Elihu Benjamin Washburne

Only a few words were enough to signal to Adele that her husband had experienced relief following months of anxious campaigning for himself and Grant. Washburne was not surprised with his own victory as he was re-elected for the ninth time. But about Grant's election he had not been sure when election time approached. For one thing, he was anxious about the virtual dismissal of Grant by radicals in Congress. Moderate Elihu had sometimes conveniently referred to himself as a radical, making a slippery move from supporter of Andrew Johnson to becoming one of the most hostile enemies of the President and calling for Johnson's impeachment. He had had to rush off to Boston where, with Vice President Henry Wilson at his side, Elihu explained that Grant before he had stepped into Stanton's shoes at the request of Johnson had arrived at an understanding with Stanton. Stanton, however, had denied talking with Grant before he was fired to be replaced by the General. Elihu had to handle that disagreeable matter, and he had to deal with Cadwallader's complaint, that Grant was not talking to the people during the campaign. Well, said Elihu, the General is not a talker. Campaigning for Grant, he assured audiences that "General Grant is not an indifferent or careless observer of passing events. He is an intelligent, reading man," adding that he consulted the leading journals. The General, Washburne said, carefully noted criticisms upon his movements. Cadwallader had written Elihu in September of 1863 saying Grant was "anything but a statesman" and expressed the hope that some other man might "tower up."

All worries were now over and the Great Commander was soon to fill the seat of Commander-in-Chief.

A NEW RESPONSIBILITY

Following the election, Washburne hurried back to Washington. As Chairman of the Appropriations Committee of the House of Representatives, Elihu must examine for the House the all-important budget. Budget figures would be exceptionally important because as Elihu knew, he would be understood to be spokesman for the new Administration. It was of advantage to Grant that his spokesman, Elihu, had long carried the reputation of Watchdog of the Treasury. The Galenean was himself penurious, doling out in small amounts what his wife, Adele, could have for use by the family. He always made sure that any amount of money he loaned, whether to a friend or his brother, Cadwallader, would be paid back with generous interest. His abstemious ways guided him through committee discussions about the budget and in the writing of his report. He took nearly an entire morning session of reading, discussing and strenuous arguing.

As Committee chairman he noted in his account that the rebellion had been suppressed, slavery abolished, rebellious States reconstructed, and that a loyal administration was secured for the following four years. The people, Washburne said, were turning their attention to questions of finance, taxes, and economy. He had bitter words to say about the railroad and telegraph systems, "monopolies," he called them, "sucking the life-blood of the people." Enough public land had been given to railroads he said, "to make an empire." In a voice suffused with contempt, Elihu referred to "robberies and plunderings of the Treasury by dishonest office-holders," ending that portion of his report with a voice of calm and assurance claiming that the newly elected President was "an honest man and an enlightened statesman." Chairman Washburne had words of warning to fellow Representatives, quoting the Frenchman Buzot as having said what Elihu felt should be engraved in letters of gold over the entrance of every public office, that "No public man can be justified in profiting from the information and advantages of his position."

His committee report called for a return to specie payments with a reduction of interest on the public debt, keeping expenditures at the lowest possible point. He turned his attention to deficiencies with estimated expenses exceeded by millions having to be made up. The chairman felt obliged to "denounce it as one of the most extravagant, unjustifiable and profligate expenditures of the public money ever asked of Congress." For some, Elihu became the villain for having refused to include in the budget a cent for the Columbian Institution for the blind. Washburne then produced the budget submitted to the Appropriation Committee by the Secretary of the Treasury covering anticipated expenses for the several departments of government totaling $158,014,011.74. He indicated what were the sums requested saying what he believed the reductions out of committee would be-- a deduction of $100,000. for the expenses of foreign intercourse, nearly $1,000,000 for the legislative, executive and judicial bills, and he announced that the Military Academy's requests would be reduced, along with the Harbor and River Improvements and public buildings requests. The Naval establishment, Washburne believed, would be reduced from approximately $20,000,000. to $16,000,000.

Secretary of the Navy Gideon Welles was only one of many in Washington who demeaned Washburne at every opportunity for denying funds for the departments of government. Elihu's pruning of budget requests prompted Welles to write in his iary that "Washburne's persistent fight for economy in government has . . . won for him the lasting enmity of the predatory interests,"(9) declaring that Elihu had "the reputation of being 'the meanest man in the House'." The *New York Times*, however, printed glowing tributes acknowledging that Washburne had "made enemies by his relentless opposition to all sorts of jobbery" but that "he [had] always commanded the highest respect of his fellow members for integrity and capacity."(10)

THE SCENE CHANGES -- AN AMERICAN IN PARIS

Elihu's career in the political arena began in 1852. It ended in 1869 when a statesman emerged out of that pugnacious-imperious and (to wife and children) tender-loving E.B. Washburne--the man of whom it was said had wonderful brain power, able to pursue two directly antagonistic methods of thought at once--of whom it was also said that he was a man of native talent, firmer and more settled in purpose than Lincoln. His political career ended when he was sent off to France, a nation, according to Charles Francis Adams, with the only foreign service office worth a whit. It was an office chosen by Washburne and granted to him by Grant. When Elihu took off from American shores to sail abroad, his brother Sidney quoted their father as saying in jest that "he thought it singular that his smartest boy should leave the country without asking." Sidney added facetiously, "I set down [this] fact as being important to posterity."

❖

To say that E.B. Washburne was to change from politician into statesman suggests that the leopard can change its spots. The obstinate, wrathful, bull-like driver, impetuous and irritable, given to shouting in rapid fire sentences of censure from the floor of the House, waving his arms, imposing his will, was hardly a suitable candidate to undertake the duties of suave, polished, polite, even if crafty, diplomat. Washburne knew such a pivotal change was about to take place in his life, and what came to him perhaps as he faced his newest challenge were lessons learned as a young Whig under the tutelage of his father. The Whig, his father might have said, is ideally the archetypal centrist.(1) The centrist-compromiser embodies attributes which approximate the art of diplomacy. Such virtues were counted among the hallowed principles of statesmanship for Whigs. The statesman incarnates ideals of honesty, sincerity, devotion to the good of the country, and dedication to a sense of duty. Stephen Hess writing of Washburne concluded that he was "the personification of the nineteenth-century American ideal."(2) Such an evaluation of the Illinois Congressman would have surprised Gideon Welles. Welles, Secretary of the Navy, considered Washburne "a demagogue without statesmanship." Benjamin Kendricks claimed "Washburne . . . does not deserve to rank as a statesman . . . "(3) Washburne was portrayed as "impulsive, headstrong, combative, and unbalanced," hardly therefore to be recommended for the role of statesman.(4)

Set against these wrathful moods, is the colorful statement published first in the *Chicago Journal*, and reprinted in the *Galena Gazette*.

And so Mr. Illinois Washburne (that is what we used to call him in Congress to distinguish him from his two brothers) is coming to Paris? Well, from what I knew of him in Washington, Louis Napoleon will have a different man to deal with from any American before, if I am not much mistaken. American interests will be . . . taken care of better than they have been for a good many years. My recollections of the American Embassy at Paris go back to poor old Mr. Mason's time and since then, well perhaps the least said the better. The Tuileries will now witness a real American within its walls, and although Mr. Washburne may not dance his legs off at a Court ball, or wear them out driving a velocipede in the Bois, I do not think that the interests of his country [will suffer] in consequence.

Embodying the Whig perspective *a la* Hess, Washburne may have congratulated himself with the left-handed compliment which placed him as the last of the American envoys to the French Empire as one who was "too sincere a Republican to be altogether suitable to the Tuileries." An American Ambassador deceptive, hypocritical? Not in Washburne's judgment, nor in his practice.

The disparaging descriptions of the Illinois Congressman, E.B. Washburne, will prove to be mistaken, including a belief which as a Whig Elihu would have appreciated, namely that he was "too sincere" to fit in with the debauchery of Louis Napoleon's festivities. Elihu and Adele accepted invitations from the wanton Emperor and his Empress--the Empress who, by the way, was proud of her bosom

Louis Napoleon

and introduced to French society the plunging neckline. " . . . The occasional immorality of French literature and art and the superficiality of the French people's 'religion' shocked American puritans," wrote historian Henry Blumenthal.(5) And while the Ambassador is an example of Blumenthal's American puritan, still Elihu and Adele attended their carnivals and jubilees. Washburne traveled to a partying place at Compiegne in company with the Emperor. He danced with Princess Mathilde. And who is to say he was not carousing, having noted himself that there was at the party "one round of pleasure, hunting, shooting, riding, theater, balls, etc."(6)

The last state dinner held before France and North Germany went to war was at St. Cloud in honor of the Ambassador and Mrs. Washburne. If decorum for the occasion was similar to what had taken place when Washburne presented his letters of credence to the Emperor, a designated *Maitre des Ceremonies, Introducteur des Ambassadeurs* appeared at the Washburne residence with two large state carriages, the first to be occupied by the baron who was *Maitre des Ceremonies*, the Ambassador and wife. A second carriage would carry members of Washburne's staff. At the castle Adele was escorted to the head table by Louis Napoleon. On this or another occasion, the Empress Eugenie appeared attired as Marie-Antoinette. Adele knowing about the role, one wonders if she might have mentioned to Eugenie that the mother of a close relative in St. Louis, Missouri, after whom Adele was named, Adele Marie Antoinette de Perdreauville by name, was lady-in-waiting to Queen Marie Antoinette. If so, Mrs. Washburne might have thought also to mention in the same breath that some of her French ancestors were Huguenots. Mention of Huguenots would have ruffled Eugenie, for the Empress was a devout Roman Catholic, and doubtless knew that members of her denomination had slain thousands of Huguenots at the Massacre of St. Bartholomew, August 24, 1572. Elihu would probably have warned his wife not to bring up the subject of religion, or to introduce delicate matters such as Napoleon's attempt to establish a Catholic Latin monarchy in Mexico when the United States was preoccupied with the Civil War, or the sentiment of the Catholic clergy in France which was to support the Confederacy. In any case, no mention was made of those subjects having been discussed as between the Ambassador's sweet, loveable *Petite Cherie*, and Her Majesty Empress Eugenie.

As a first-rate politician very often correct in his predictions about the results in U.S. elections, Washburne was able with that same proficiency to interpret electoral findings almost immediately upon his arrival in France. An election was taking place, and Elihu was able to report and to clarify for Secretary Fish the meaning of the poll. The vote, he wrote, was in opposition to Napoleon's Second Empire, meaning that a Liberal would likely be appointed First Minister by Louis Napoleon. This took place in January of 1870. The Emperor invited republican, Emile Ollivier, to form a new ministry. M. Ollivier was long-headed, had high cheek bones, and a monkish appearance, perhaps having been starved when imprisoned and persecuted by the government he was now to serve. The new executive head, Ollivier, included in his government left-of-center appointees, and he undertook for himself the job of Foreign Minister, meeting often with Washburne. Despite the radical change in administration, the Liberal government performed to the satisfaction of Louis Napoleon until the tenth of July 1870. At that time the performance by Ollivier brought down the government, and without intending to, hastened the downfall of the Second Empire. News arrived in Paris leading overly-sensitive foreign office personnel to believe that Prussian King Wilhelm had insulted the French nation. A telegram was read in parliament which fired the emotions of members. When the reading was completed Emile Ollivier walked to the lectern. It was his intention to express his views in accordance with the expectation of protocol. Unhappily, he spoke too hastily:

"From this day commences for the ministers, my colleagues and myself, a grand responsibility, and we accept it with a light heart."

The Prime Minister was referring, of course, to the acceptance of a state of war. He was saying he and his colleagues approved the challenge of war with a "light heart," *nous l'acceptons d'un coeur léger*.

However cheerfully First Minister Ollivier felt--light hearted- -Emperor Louis Napoleon was unenthusiastic. Napoleon was not ready to go to the battlefield. For one thing, he was growing a stone in his bladder as big as a pigeon's egg. As a Bonaparte he had a reputation to live up to so he prepared to leave Paris, ostensibly to give leadership to his troops. Clearly, the Great Napoleon's nephew was reluctant to face the distinguished Field Marshal Helmuth Carl Bernhard Moltke and his well trained army.

In actual fact, Elihu had gone to France expecting his charge as Envoy Extraordinary and Minister Plenipotentiary to be a sinecure. He arrived in Paris in the spring of 1869, and two months later in July traveled to Carlsbad "to drink the water at one of the health-giving springs." While Washburne's overweight body was soaking in waters housed in the multi-pillared building at the popular resort, his valet came with shocking news. France had declared war against Germany. The Minister's sinecure was at an end. Washburne dried himself, dressed and without delay set out for Paris riding for fifty-two hours without stopping. The motivation to act so promptly was the Whig way of doing things. He explained to his wife in a letter that "duty call[ed]."(7) Similarly, when the French government left Paris along with Ministers from nearly every other country, the American Ambassador explained that he would not think of leaving his post "as long as *it is my duty* to stay here."(8)

He had a fixation on the subject. But duty was not the only Whig value guiding Washburne. He was a compassionate man as became clear when he was charged with providing a way for Germans to depart Paris, often in haste and sometimes with no money. An unwed mother explained to him that she could not return to her family. Elihu went into his pockets to provide means for her to go to Brittany. After working an eighteen hour day, duty meant that he must go to Gare du Nord to make sure Germans to whom he had given *visas* found a place on the train. He arranged during the war for 30,000 people to leave France, and provided financial assistance to over 9,000 people. Elihu even sat by the bedside of people dying, as the account of his life in Paris shows. "Mr. Richards was sick. I found him almost *in extremis* and I remained with him until he died, at 10.40 in the evening. His family had left Paris the Saturday before."

In keeping with his Whig ideals, Elihu announced that he wanted no increase in salary. His salary, he said, was ample for all practical purposes. He intended as an American, a Republican and statesman to heed the rules defined by the rubrics of his father, and dictated by that party which was precursor to the Republican. Also, Elihu's mother had impressed upon her son that a glorious destiny could be achieved "by hard work and education." Work and education were two more virtues included in the catalog of Whig values. While abstinence was another virtue, and Elihu neither smoked nor drank liquor, he imbibed wine, so it could not be said that Elihu was too ingenuous to join the revelry of a carousing Court. Living it up or not, it was said that an imperial dinner without E.B. Washburne was a failure. Only to his wife did he display negative feelings about the way of life of Parisians. In writing Adele he suggested an aversion to the festivities. He wrote about women wearing hideous diamonds; women with low neck dresses and bare arms; women with a reputation for living with "friends" who were really "mistresses," a word he did not care to use when writing his wife.

❖

As a Whig-type centrist, Washburne stood between left-wing Marxists and right-wing Bourbons. In this he played the part of diplomat and statesman. On the one hand, he spoke well of Louis Napoleon and was sincere in saying of Louis that

"the bitterest enemies of the Emperor admit that he . . . acted in entire good faith."
On the other hand, the Ambassador hastened to recognize the Republican
government as soon as it displaced the Bonaparte dynasty. At another time he said
he had no sympathy for the Emperor, believing that "he committed perjury and
destroyed the Republic in 1848." With some notable exceptions the Ambassador
handled with delicacy his relations with the Republican government headed by
Thiers as well as with the National Guard and Commune controlling Paris
independently of the Thiers government in Versailles. These connections may be
said to be examples of statesmanship.

There was the charge to protect Germans within a country invaded by Germany.
He was to help Germans in their effort to flee the city when Paris came under siege
and when the French citizen took expatriates to be traitors assisting the enemy
outside the gates. The siege meant that frightened Germans came to the legation
seeking support. One early morning Elihu counted more than five hundred Germans
waiting for the legation to open. Helping Germans leave was one task, another was
for Washburne to administer relief for the indigent who remained. At one time,
around eight hundred German families depended upon the Ambassador's welfare
program. He wrote Secretary Fish to report frightful conditions he was discovering:

> Cases of terrible suffering are brought to my notice every day. I heard a
> few days ago of a family in the last stage of destitution, absolutely
> perishing of cold and hunger. I immediately sent my messenger with a
> small quantity of wood, some wine, chocolate, sugar, confiture, etc. He
> found a family of seven persons, consisting of the father and mother and
> five children, cooped up in a little seven-by-nine attic, entirely without fire

> and nothing to eat but dry bread. They had
> already burned their last bedstead as a last
> resource. On a little pallet of straw on the floor
> was a little boy, seven years old, so weakened by
> hunger as to be unable to sit up, or scarcely to lift
> his head. I directed some money to be given them,
> and now hope to get them through, unless this
> siege shall last forever.(9)
>
> Living with these pressures required a kind of
> statesmanship not often demanded of Ambassadors.
> Washburne checked the jails and upon finding
> Germans had to go to the Interior Minister, Gambetta,
> asking the Minister to arrange for the Prefect of Police

E.B. Washburne

to release the Germans *en masse*. It was done. Elihu
made a personal visit to St. Lazare prison. Finding
large numbers of German expatriates he immediately arranged for their liberation.
To these delicate problems and pressures a small one was caused by Elihu's friend
back in the states, President Grant. While in France, America's Representative
succeeded in being neutral as between the warring factions, but Grant in the United
States went out of his way to show sympathy for Germany. Actions taken by the
President and his cabinet made it difficult for Washburne to persuade the French that
the United States was friendly, thus making it troublesome for him to continue his
policy of neutrality toward the warring countries. The French Minister in
Washington wrote Jules Favre saying "the Republican Party . . . remains little

sympathetic to us."(10) The sentiments of the American people, Grant's views to the contrary notwithstanding, was changed somewhat after the French defeat and the capture of Louis Napoleon, and with the establishment of a Republican government in France. Money was raised in the U.S. and ships from eastern seaboards carried an enormous amount of produce to the French populace.

At almost the moment Elihu was recognizing the new French Republic, his brother, Israel, was delivering a message in Gloucester, Massachusetts, to an audience of several hundred(11) declaring that the democratic Revolution in America and Governor Washburn's own religion "made their appearance . . . together." Israel was praising the institution of republican government in general while Elihu was being kissed by Frenchmen grateful for America's having recognized their new Republican government.

Complications arose within hours of the Franco-Prussian War's beginning. Problems arose which had no precedent, putting a strain upon the neutrality Washburne intended to observe. Facing the complications, the Ambassador must have thought about similar problems which had confronted his brother, Charles, when Charles was Minister in Paraguay. Charles also had to deal with sensitive issues where there were few precedents to guide. In the case of the Paraguayan Washburn, Charles had been forced to leave the country under threat of death, grateful when he once boarded an American Navy ship that had come for him. And as with Charles, Elihu confronted a corresponding situation where war confounded diplomatic protocol. Charles had aroused the ire of the dictator by refusing to leave Asuncion as Solano demanded when his government retreated to the town of Humaita. Elihu made a similar decision not to vacate Paris when the Thiers government left the city to locate in Versailles along with the French assembly. The two Washburns made their respective government leaders unhappy. For Charles in Paraguay, there were disastrous consequences. The Paraguayan dictator Solano Lopez yearned to be an Emperor like Louis Napoleon. Solano, with his mistress Eliza Lynch, had been received graciously by Napoleon and Empress Eugenie less than twenty years before Elihu Washburne was received at Louis Napoleon's Court. Washburne, however, had considerably more success with his position as Minister to France than Charles had as Minister to the South American nation.

The North Germans put their archives into the care of the American embassy, and, of course, asked the embassy to provide Germans with *visas* permitting them to leave the country. That privilege would have to be given by the French government. The Ambassador called on the French Minister of Foreign Affairs, Duke de Gramont, for purposes of obtaining an official position. The problem was seen by Gramont as too complicated to be solved in a verbal exchange, so Elihu's request was put in writing. In a letter to Gramont Elihu conceded that under the law the Emperor had an absolute right to treat Germans in France as enemies. He tried with a persuasive argument to modify and humanize the law, pleading the case for Germans living in France. No indisputable rule had been laid down to meet such circumstances, and changing the ancient rule of law would mean putting subjects of the North German Confederation under the protection of the American legation, not the French Department of the Interior. Gramont's answer discouraged Germans who wished to return to their native land. Shortly after, the Emperor publicly announced that "German citizens [would] be at liberty to continue their residence in France, and . . . they [would] enjoy the protection of [French] laws . . . "(12) Germans past the age of military service, the Emperor announced, could make application to leave. Those of an age to serve in the military would not be allowed to depart. "No rule of international law obliges a belligerent to allow to depart from his territory subjects of the enemy, who, from the day of their return to their own country, [would] be enrolled in the ranks to take part in the hostilities."(13)

The position taken by the French Foreign Office irked the American, Washburne. In a second statement to Gramont Elihu reminded the Duke that in 1798, when it appeared the U.S. might be at war with France, the American government declared that "subjects of the hostile nation, who might wish to quit the United States . . . should be allowed . . . according to the dictates of humanity and national hospitality . . . "(14) In reference to Washburne's reminder of his government's position in 1758, Gramont simply said that a law which had been made could be changed. Washburne reminded the Frenchman that the 1758 law on the books in the U.S., which Gramont had noted could be changed, had not been changed in seventy years. Soon, the French government was to declare that every German man, woman, and child, was to be expelled. In the meantime, the American Ambassador vetoed Gramont's actions. "He notified Gramont . . . that he could see no reason for refusing the Germans the papers they sought, and . . . he (Washburne) would begin handing . . . out" forms. Gramont reluctantly gave his approval, and Washburne was then besieged by those wishing desperately to leave Paris. There were days when six gendarmes were required to maintain order outside the legation.

❖

There was a climactic moment in French history when the Ambassador and another American, George Eustis, were present at the *Corps Legislatif.* Eustis had been a member of the Confederacy and during the Civil War was secretary to the celebrated Slidell and Mason. Slidell, Mason and Eustis were captured by a U.S. frigate when the three of them were on a British ship bound for Southampton. The ship was on the high seas, consequently the capture of Confederates aboard a British ship became a *cause celebre.* Washburne and Eustis sensed that dramatic changes were about to take placein Paris. The Ambassador was anxious to follow events closely which he felt were to be of monumental importance in the history of the troubled country. A messenger pressed through the throng to reach Elihu to give him a message from the wife of Marshal MacMahon. General MacMahon, Commander of the French army, had been trapped by the German army and was captured along with Emperor Louis Napoleon. MacMahon was wounded. The Marshal's wife was eager to visit her anguished husband. For that she needed a *laissez-passer.* Under the circumstances, with the French government in disarray, the person to whom she could turn was the American Ambassador. The pass was written out and put in the hands of Madame MacMahon.

(Mr. Washburne to the civil and military authorities of the North German Confederation Legation of the United States Paris, September 4, 1870.) This is to request that full permission may be granted to Madame MacMahon, the wife of Marshal MacMahon, and to the Vicomte de Caraman, the brother of Madame MacMahon, and the Sister of Charity Madeleine, to pass all the military lines, in order to visit the Marshal, and to express a hope that all proper facilities may be granted to accomplish this end. In witness whereof I have hereunto set my hand and the seal of this legation at Paris, this 4th day of September, 1870.

Word that the Emperor had been captured stirred the masses in Paris. The populace took over the *Corps Legislatif*, driving legislators from their seats. The people responded to the cry of revolutionaries, "*A l'Hotel de Ville!*" The Hotel de Ville was the seat of the municipal government, and Frenchmen knew in their bones that the government which would succeed the Second Empire must be proclaimed at that place. The revolutionary Municipal Government of Paris had been created at that place in 1789.

60,000 people were mingled in the square in front of the hotel when the Proclamation was made by a young man Washburne predicted earlier had a promising future, Leon Gambetta. At 4:45 in the afternoon, the great headed Gambetta, robust, full rounded beard, appeared in French windows which had been opened out like white wings. Behind him in the hotel room stood the handsome featured, curly headed Jules Favre, he with dark eyebrows and a smile only righteous indignation would erase.

There, standing in the window, Gambetta proclaimed the republic of France!

The slow moving mass of people below drained out of the square through narrow streets toward the Tuileries.

Elihu made his way home, visiting the British Ambassador, Lord Lyons, on the way. At eight o'clock in the evening Washburne left his residence and rode down the avenue to the *Corps Legislatif*. All was quiet. The doors were sealed. He drove through parts of the city where he found that all was quiet. "In a few brief hours of a Sabbath day," wrote Washburne, "I had seen a dynasty fall and a republic proclaimed, and all *without the shedding of one drop of blood.*"(15)

The exultation of Parisians is fully represented in the person of Jules Favre, French Foreign Minister, who sent a message to the Ambassador. Washburne felt that the letter illustrated Favre's mastery of the French language. The long letter is copied in part:

Sir: I look upon it as a happy augury for the French Republic that it has received as its first diplomatic support the recognition of the Government of the United States. For my part I am happy and proud that fortune has permitted me to be the link of union between two peoples bound together by so many glorious memories, and henceforward by so many noble hopes, and I thank you for having, with so great kindness toward myself, expressed all which I feel toward you, as well as my desire to strengthen more and more the relations of affectionate esteem which should united us forever. --Jules Favre

For several days, day-after-day, Washburne was visited by groups of citizens who went through a ritual manner of thanking the Ambassador and expressing gratitude to the United States. The ritual included the *accolade*, --a kiss on both cheeks.

Soon, however, the songs of praise began to sour.

Chapter Seventeen

VOILA! ANOTHER REVOLUTION

A virtual American "Goncourt",(1) Washburne wandered the city under siege, noting changes suspenseful and mundane, some threatening, some appearing humorous to the American spectator. The opening day of the month of November 1871, it being the 44th day of the siege, the Ambassador took note of the fact that members of the newly elected government had been taken hostage in Paris by Red forces in a *coup d'etat.*

"Voila!" Washburne declared, "another revolution."

Before the day was over, however, government hostages were released. On the evening of that 44th day birds with heads under their wing and citizens snuggled in their beds, all having retired into quiet and serenity, prompted the American Goncourt to write, "What a city! One moment revolution, and the next the most profound calm." The amusing side of the uprising--which uprising was so soon flacci--was that soldiers loyal to the national government walked into the Hotel de Ville and walked out with the hostages on their arms. Humorous also, Washburne thought, were orders given by the effete government of Paris demanding fifteen million francs from the Minister of Finance. Just like that! This whole thing Elihu thought was a side-show which existed precariously for twelve hours.

Perhaps the privileged American could not take seriously what the Reds were about to do since he, Elihu, was himself living richly, despite its being the 45th day of the siege by the Germans. He was able to sit down, as he did on that day, to oyster soup, leg of mutton, and roast duck. Only two weeks later, however, the American Goncourt penned in his diary that fresh meat was scarce except for horse, mule, dog, cat and rat meat.

A national election was held and a government was elected by a large majority of citizens, three hundred and twenty-one thousand against fifty-three thousand. Interpreted, these numbers meant that the populace wanted the government to sue for peace with the Germans. For that purpose, Adolphe Thiers was chosen to fill the position of First Minister. With Thiers' insistence the assembly and government moved out of town to Versailles. Washburne now had two offices, one in Paris, one in Versailles. For remaining in Paris where he must do his duty, Elihu became nearly *persona non grata* to Thiers, as had his brother Charles Washburn to the Paraguayan dictator, Francisco Solano. Duty required that the American Ambassador continue his roaming in Paris since Americans, Germans, and even the English needed his assistance. On the 53d day of the siege the English in the city were in trouble, unable to get out of Paris with Lord Lyons in Versailles. The English appealed to Washburne.

"They are all coming to see me and ask if I cannot do something for them," wrote the Ambassador.(2)

Elihu realized the gravity of his position, admitting to himself that in a city of two million, "I am the only man . . . who is permitted to receive anything from outside."(3) Thoughts of that "outside world" on that occasion brought to Elihu's attention on the 60st day of the siege, it being November 18th, that it was the birthday of his father. He put on the page of his diary his tribute to "the glorious, great-hearted, great-headed, noble old man," and expressed the wish for an even simpler epitaph for the gravestone to rest over "the noblest Roman of them all," -- nine words: "He was a kind father and an honest man." Thoughts of home and letters written and received regularly kept his spirit aglow. He was sentimental about family and they could lift his spirits or cast him down. One can easily visualize tears welling from the eyes of this doughty curmudgeon as on Christmas day he sat down to write to "my first daughter," pleading with eleven-year old Susan to "write . . . [your dear little French letter] every week without fail."

Washburne had known suffering and want as a young lad and it is not to be wondered at that words appeared often in his diary, such as, "What misery! what suffering! what desolation!" Some of his sentences remind the reader of Victor Hugo, who, it should be said was one of the socialist dissenters among the leftists in Paris. Elihu was moved to learn that a Prussian woman whom he had helped had given birth to a sixth child and then died. It was reported to him that the fifty-franc note he had given the woman "was found in a little box in a drawer after her death, where she had carefully laid it away." There were problems, some of them personal. Elihu found there was no precedent laid down about living where the government was located, as to whether he must be at Versailles with other Ministers, so many of whom had vacated Paris. He preferred to do what he considered his duty, remain in Paris. In these trying times his old friend, President Grant, was making his life difficult. Grant delivered a pro-German message saying, "the relations of the United States with Germany are intimate and cordial . . . " resulting in a report to Favre from French Ambassador to the U.S., Treilhard, "I have not been able to read without profound regret these praises lavished upon the German union . . . " Grant's favoritism, together with Washburne's failure to move out of Paris, resulted in Minister Thiers making life difficult for the American Ambassador. Premier Thiers found ways of making Washburne wait for weeks before accepting his credentials. Given the burdens of the time, then, Elihu reported in his diary, doubtless with a wry smile, that he had gone one day to have a photograph made of himself. The photographer complained, Washburne said, that he "looked too sober." It was to laugh.

❖

A peace-making government was operating out of Versailles. But, *voila*! In Paris, the mass of "lower class" citizens as they were referred to by Washburne were unhappy with the Versailles government's willingness to bow the neck to the Germans, suing for peace. It was believed the leaders of their nation were betraying France. Soldiers in Paris who had been given guns, artillery and a pittance for a wage had their pittance withdrawn when Thiers took over. That was a mistake. Washburne believed it a mistake. Thousands were left with no work and no income. Starvation became widespread. What happened, Washburne observed, was that thousands of soldiers joined the poverty stricken citizens in the city. The Paris contingent of the National Guard fell in behind those protestors who were, in political terms, leftist. Washburne's friend Gambetta resigned from the new government, writing that his conscience would not permit him to remain a member of the Versailles government.

In his daily-kept diary, the American Goncourt made judgments about the uprising in Paris, about the "better class" of citizens on the one hand, those, of course, who approved of the National Government and on the other hand about those in Paris who were of the "lower class" who had formed their own government. The "lower class" citizens had their critical opinions about Thiers and Favre. Opinions held by the lower class did not move Washburne. If he had listened, he would have heard the claims made by Karl Marx about his friend Jules Favre, and as a New England puritan he would have been deeply troubled about his friend

Karl Marx

Favre, "living in concubinage with the wife of a drunken resident at Algiers, [and who] had, by a most daring concoction of forgeries . . . contrived to grasp, in the name of the children of his adultery, a large succession, which made him a rich man, and that, in a lawsuit undertaken by the legitimate heirs, he only escaped exposure by the connivance of the Bonapartist tribunals?"(4) As for lower class opinions of Thiers, accusations were largely political, personal with only hapless pejorative expressions.

Homely little Thiers was of small stature like Elihu's brother, Israel, also homely as well as short. Governor Israel Washburn, however, did not suffer such jibes as were aimed at Thiers by Communards. The French Minister was called a "monstrous Gnome . . . a little man . . . conscious of withering into nothingness . . . brandishing with his dwarfish arms." Added to these belittling terms Commune intellectuals such as Karl Marx questioned Thiers' integrity, maintaining that "having entered his first ministry under Louis Philippe poor as Job, he left it a millionaire."

The terrors, and there were many wrought by Communards, must be placed beside ghastly deeds of gendarmes acting on behalf of the National Government. Gendarmes surrounded houses into which Communards had fled, poured gasoline on the houses and set fire to them. Communards were shoveled up as charred remains. Less egregious on the part of the government's "better class" was the withdrawal of the modest incomes which sustained soldiers and their families. The "better class" were unable to sympathize with an attempt to form a municipal government for the purpose of equalizing resources. Such action was seen, of course, as a threat to property privately owned by the few at the sufferance of the

many. Blanqui, he of the "lower class," urged the Government to have "all food expropriated and equitably distributed."(5) Frustrated, Communards at the end became brutal, killing easily without trial, often lacking a certainty of guilt. With a touch of irony, Washburne told of an account where "a 'General,' Ganier d'Abain, a dealer in cooking utensils, commanding the National Guard of Montmartre, reported . . . 'nothing new; night calm and without incident,' who then went on to say that 'at five minutes after ten, two sergeants were brought in . . . and immediately shot.' The General [sic] continued, 'At twenty minutes after midnight, a guardian of the peace, accused of having fired a revolver, is shot.' [Ganier] closes his report of that 'calm night without incident'

Auguste Blanqui

by saying that the gendarme brought in by the guards of the twenty-eighth battalion at seven o'clock was shot."

Three lives were fatally entwined as the leftist revolution unfolded in Paris. The three were Auguste Blanqui, Archbishop Darboy and Elihu Washburne. Arch-bishop Darboy, imprisoned by the Commune, was to be visited by the Ambassador much to the disgust of M. Thiers since it was known that the Ambassador in order to secure permission to visit Catholic Paris's leading clergyman must associate with villains. Among the most villainous of the Communards was Raoul Rigault. Thiers knew Elihu must obtain his pass from Rigault. Washburne was perhaps surprised upon meeting the bespectacled Rigault, looking for all the world like a family man with his pince nez glasses, his neatly kept full beard, wearing, if one may say so, an aura of middle-class dignity. Of middle-class origin, Rigault favored sexual promiscuity, and "led the scandalous existence of a spendthrift rake, surrounded by useless persons, and giving up the greater part of his time to debauchery."(6)

Washburne and Darboy

On the day Washburne called he found Rigault in bed at 11 o'clock in the morning. The Frenchman's secretary explained to him what Washburne wanted. He wanted to visit Archbishop Darboy. A permit was provided by Rigault and Elihu made his way directly to Mazas prison. There he found the Archbishop, a slender man, his form somewhat bent and for lack of shaving equipment growing a beard. The clergyman who previously had lived in splendor at his palace was now occupying a cell six by ten feet. Elihu took from his crooked arm a bottle of old Madeira and newspapers, and was soon "charmed by [Darboy's] cheerful spirit . . . " The priest, Elihu said, "had no word of bitterness" and told his visitor that "the world judged [his jailers] to be worse than they really were."

Blanqui, the party of the third part in this trilogy, was known by Washburne as a man with strongly individualistic and anarchist undertones, with ideals which ran counter to the teachings of Marxism. Elihu knew him to be a socialist and the most popular among the Communal leaders. He knew also that Rigault wanted Blanqui back in the Commune for, it was said, without Blanqui nothing could be done. With him, everything.(7) It seemed to Washburne that Darboy's life might be saved if the Thiers government were willing to free Auguste Blanqui. An exchange was offered by Rigault and transmitted to Thiers via the American Ambassador. The Ambassador said to the Premier that the French Government would lose nothing by placing Blanqui at liberty, and by doing so the government would save Darboy's life. After Washburne's suggestion was shared with Thiers, Lord Lyons reported that "they are angry with Mr. Washburne."(8) Thiers was adamant. He did not intend even to recognize the rebels but to treat them as felonious expecting to see them destroyed. Elihu made a sixth and last visit to the clergyman. As he left, Washburne knew he was bidding Darboy a final adieu. At the end of day, the darkness of night came on, leaving against a grey sky only a silhouette of the top of the prison walls of La Roquette. Lanterns sprinkled erratic light on a line of French priests and Chief Justice Bonjean. They all stood as straight as their feeble condition allowed. One of the would-be murderers, having shaken the hand of Monseigneur Darboy, then scratched a cross on the stone wall where the head of Darboy would touch once the fatal shots were fired.

He [Darboy] did not fall at the first volley, but stood erect, calm and immovable, and before the other discharges came which launched him into eternity he crossed himself three times upon his forehead.

He was "afterward mutilated and his abdomen cut open."(9)

❖

As late as March 25th, Washburne visited the assembly in Versailles. He recorded that the "August body [was] fiddling while Paris was burning." The Germans were at the very gates of Paris. The siege continued. Jules Favre confessed to Gambetta that the republican government headed by Thiers and himself was defending Paris, *not against the Prussian soldiers but the working men of Paris.(10)* After the long delay, making Washburne doubt the competence of Thiers, the Versailles government's arm of the National Guard acted. Paris was invaded. Commune members in a frenzy of fear and resentment torched parts of the city. The government's soldiers slaughtered citizens and Paris National Guardsmen without let or hindrance. The Ambassador wrote,

In many cases the National Guard [of the city], refusing to surrender, were hewn down behind the barricades. Nothing could exceed the fury, the courage and the desperation of the insurgents, who fought until their last round of ammunition was exhausted.

CAREER'S END WITH VIOLINS PLAYING

After the tumultuous years of the Franco-Prussian war and the revolutionary uprising in Paris, those terrible months having ended, the Ambassador spent six more years in harness. A continuing and warm relation developed between Washburne and German leaders. The Emperor and Bismarck showed more appreciation of the American in Paris than did Thiers and Favre. Among the citizens on the streets of the city, however, there was appreciation of the Ambassador since thousands remembered his social service system when the poor were fed during the unforgettable days of the siege and the uprising. Even after the Commune was overthrown Elihu's standing enabled him to absolve publicly a man who had been active in the communist movement. He was confident that not all supporters of the Commune were fiends or scoundrels. After all, Darboy spoke gently to him about those who had hauled him off to prison. The priest, standing perhaps shivering in his cold grey brick cell, had said that "the world judged [his jailers] to be worse than they really were." The favorable following Washburne enjoyed in Paris, however, did not deter newspapers from damning him for dealing face-to-face with communist

Paschall Grousset. That was another score against the Ambassador making him rather unacceptable to the government at Versailles. From the government's point of view, Paschal Grousset had appropriated a critical function of the government, presuming to carry on French foreign policy. Actually, both Lord Lyons and Washburne commended the Frenchman, Grousset, for protecting foreign owned properties. The English and American Ministers petitioned in his behalf when the Thiers government proceeded to prosecute Grousset and others who had seized power in Paris.

In Germany, Washburne was entertained by Otto Bismarck and the Emperor, Wilhelm. The Emperor and wife were "full of expressions of gratitude to me," Elihu wrote. Bismarck was almost ingratiating to Washburne, though one must say that, knowing "the great 'I am'," as Elihu characterized Bismarck, makes it difficult to picture the premier as anything other than domineering--certainly never obsequious. During the War he wrote a personal letter to Adele warmly informing her that "relying on your promise to write nothing but family affairs, I shall forward your letter[s], even if sealed, to Mr. Washburne."(11) Mrs. Washburne's was the only mail permitted to enter the besieged city for many months.

French (and American) Roman Catholics were enormously grateful to the Ambassador. Washburne was known in France, Germany and the United States for having saved the lives of French and German nuns, and for having made an energetic attempt also to save the life of the Archbishop.

A TOUCH OF AMERICAN POLITICAL GOINGS ON

Before the 1872 and 1876 elections in the United States, political leaders crossed the waters to talk with Washburne about their interest in having him enter the race as a Presidential nominee on the Liberal party ticket in 1872, and on the Republican ticket in 1876. The Ambassador had no interest in being nominated at the Liberal party convention where his fellow churchman, Horace Greeley, became the nominee. Elihu was loyal to the Republican party his brother had launched, and in good conscience he could not defect to the Liberal party, even though he was unhappy with the Republican administration. Editor Marat Halstead of Cincinnati talked with Elihu in Paris and was told bluntly by the Ambassador that he had made enough enemies when in Congress so that he never would have to worry about being nominated for that high office. "He is entirely sincere," said Halstead in an interview, "in regarding himself as not in the field." The editor said, however, that there were those in America who thought that Morton, Blaine, and Conkling would "use each other up" as candidates, and that then "Washburne would be the man." There were also those who declared that if Washburne would consent to being a candidate, and if Benjamin Bristow would run for the office of Vice President with him, their election would be certain.

Washburne on countless occasions tried to clarify his position on the subject of candidacy. In correspondence with a relative, Ellen Washburn, Elihu wrote, "I should absolutely despair of the country if I [were to discover] that there were a single person . . . fool enough to think of me in the Administration you mention."(12) Doubtless, Ellen had Grant's administration in mind. Proof that Washburne meant what he said comes with his forceful refusal to enter Grant's cabinet as Secretary of the Treasury. He was asked and urged by Hamilton Fish on

Grant's behalf, and by Secretary George Robson, already a member of the cabinet, to return to America and join Grant's team. No, he wrote Ellen, "I cannot be bitten by that maggot."

Word got around that the hitherto minor mutual appreciation society onetime formed by Grant and Washburne was cooling. There had been a series of incidents which soured Elihu. For one thing, there was Grant's deliberate and public show of favoritism for Germany when the United States was otherwise pledged to neutrality. As indicated, the effect was to make Elihu's ambassadorial duties awkward. For another thing, a poor record had been established by the administration as a whiskey fraud was uncovered by Benjamin Bristow, a member of Grant's cabinet. For discovering the fraud and making it public, Bristow was made an enemy of the President. Yet more damning evidence was uncovered indicating that members of Grant's relatives were discovered to be making money from the fraud. Another negative which marked Grant's administration was speculation on the gold market, again undertaken by relatives of the President. It shocked Washburne in France, and Elihu knew Grant was perfectly aware of his scrupulous record as Watchdog of the Treasury, and that he, Elihu, preacher-like in these matters, pounded the pulpit whenever and wherever larceny was exposed. These and other disagreements cooled the relations of the two men. Add to these disappointments that friends of Washburne who had reason to believe Grant would give strong backing to Washburne in the 1876 contest were thwarted. Grant gave no such support. The same was true in 1880 when again it was thought by Elihu's friends that, were Grant to ascertain that he could not be nominated at the convention, he would bring forward his old friend, E.B. Washburne. The Ambassador's son, Gratiot, made life difficult for the one-time Grant-Washburne team. Gratiot signed an anti-Grant advertisement which was widely published. Secretary of State Fish wrote to Paris on Grant's behalf giving Gratiot the benefit of the doubt, saying he and the President believed the advertisement had been a hoax. It was not. Elihu wrote his son telling him not to leave Berlin for St. Petersburg where he had just been assigned a position in the embassy. Washburne probably urged Gratiot to resign. Urged or not, Gratiot did resign. It was thought at first that no hard feelings resulted as between the President and the Ambassador, but what is likely is that the incident strained the relationship.

❖

Ambassador Elihu Washburne, for sixteen years fiery Congressman from Illinois, ended his eight year career as a statesman, "with violins playing." Praise was widespread. Populations in France and Germany, Parliament and the news media in England, along with highly placed individuals in many European countries and the United States, sang the praises of the statesman comparing him with Benjamin Franklin, the first Minister to France from the United States.

The story of representation had come full circle. Benjamin Franklin was an idol for Elihu from his youth onward.

Chapter Eighteen

WEIGHING AND BALANCING

An unalterable personality factor helped Elihu determine the direction his career would take. He was born with the required aptitude for attracting the attention of others. He enjoyed a talent for leading. He was fiercely ambitious. His striving to accomplish can be attributed to teachings in the home, and to a religion which fostered a drive to achieve--these and a third factor, namely, the grinding poverty experienced in his early years. His penurious ways in later life resulted from the ordeal of watching his mother and father struggling to feed and clothe his sisters and brothers, as well as himself while living in impoverishment. Experiences associated with poverty were deeply inbred in Elihu.

A critic of that 19th-Century forgotten man from Livermore, Maine, could well fault Washburne for being too casual about philosophy and ideology. In this, one must remark upon the fact that Elihu Washburne possessed some of the virtues and many of the shortcomings of Whiggery. In keeping with the Whig ethos reinforced with the families' religious emphasis, problems Washburne encountered were always related to persons; evaluations were always of individuals. An illustration of what that means in terms of the Whig outlook brings into focus the fact that corporations did not appear on the scene in America until the latter part of the 19th Century. Before that time "partnerships and the extended kinship group," were controlling factors, as is illustrated by the Washburns.(2) Extensive operations

owned or controlled by Cadwallader and William, were largely a family or kinship matter. Judgments made about flour, lumber, ecology, profiteering, etc., were in terms of individuals, not firms, companies, or institutions.

One of the members of the Reconstruction Committee which submitted to Congress the Fourteenth Amendment was attorney Roscoe Conkling. It was he, Conkling, who gave a different cast to the phrase "due process" in a California case involving a corporation. Corporations thereafter were interpreted to mean that corporations take on the character of *an individual* under the law.

John Q. Adams

During his entire career Elihu Washburne treated social, legal and political matters pretty much as a Protestant critic in the Emersonian tradition. Universalism, in which Elihu was nurtured, was so like the Whig/Republican tradition that it did not seem to jar members of the religious movement when a Universalist minister announced that "Universalism is the same as republicanism, and republicanism is the same as Universalism." Emerson, who reflected the widespread opinion of Protestants including Washburn's Universalism, promoted and elevated the individual. The Whig culture made much of this outlook. " . . . Men in the world of to-day, are bugs, are spawn, and are called 'the mass' and 'the herd.'"(3) Emerson's description and complaint was intended to indicate that for him *collective man.* For him, the individual as person is raised nearly to a place of divinity.

Whig John Quincy Adams did not care for party politics and made little effort to replace the patronage of his predecessor with party subordinates. That attitude is mirrored to a limited extent by Washburne who, as a result, found himself in deep trouble with fellow politicians in Illinois when he adopted an idea expounded by another Universalist, Horace Greeley. Both Washburne and Greeley, along with Charles Ames Washburn in California, wanted Republicans to open their arms to Democrats who wanted to become Republicans. As Daniel Walker Howe indicates, 50,000 Whigs rallied on Bunker Hill in 1840 and adopted a declaration condemning "party spirit."(4)

For the Washburns Whiggery was a culture as well as a party. It is surprising therefore that father Washburn denounced Zachary Taylor for not being sure to which party he belonged. Elihu was not disturbed by Taylor's non-partisanship attitude. Neither was Abraham Lincoln--except where Stephen Douglas was concerned since the popular Douglas as a Republican might frustrate Lincoln's own drive for high office.

It seems an exaggeration to suggest that Whiggery played a part in the evolving American philosophy of pragmatism, particularly that of John Dewey. Howe concludes, however, that the "political ideas of the Whigs derived from their whole experience of life: the attitudes they grew up with, the problems they confronted, the purposes they conceived."(5) Dewey indicated that "experience is experiment," and that approach fits well the way in which Elihu Washburne approached delicate and difficult problems when he became Minister Plenipotentiary to France, having to work through problems peculiar to a war situation and the communist uprising in Paris.

Elihu's brother, Charles, attempted to work through his peculiar problems in Paraguay in the same spirit, except that his righteous indignation got the best of him. He could not, as Elihu did, transcend the personal.

Elihu's self-evaluation in retirement was modest, quite in keeping with his attitude throughout his career. His brothers also, in keeping with that Whig breeding to which Howe alludes, would not let the public get away with using superlative words to describe their brother without making clear that from their vantage point, he was an ordinary mortal, and had his full bag of foibles. Cadwallader once called him a "hairpin."

POLITICS TO THE END OF THE ROAD

Galena, Illinois, continued to have pulling power for Washburne; and the year following his return to the states from the continent, he and Adele re-opened their Galena mansion. They began making preparations for a triumphant return to Galena of the warrior, ex-President Grant. The City had made a gift of a house to President and Mrs. Grant; and Grant had let it be known that it was his wish to return home, never again to seek a public office--except as Mayor of Galena. Grant had tripped around the world with Julia and entourage and tired of traveling he returned to the States earlier than originally anticipated. His arrival was intended to coincide with his reach for the nomination at a Republican convention. So Grant went to his Galena home to be greeted there, not only by the ever-loyal Washburnes but by friends who were brought out of Chicago.

In October when the northern Illinois city was beginning to feel the return of cold winds and freezing nights, Adele busied herself at the Grant home, arranging a dinner to be served to the Grants and friends once the heralded General arrived in town. Governor Shelby M. Cullom, Illinois Senator William B. Allison, Senator-elect John A. Logan were among the guests. The Logans and Washburnes were invited to remain and spend the night. The remaining guests talked their way into the early morning hours before retiring. After six weeks languishing in Galena, Grant decided to take another vacation trip. He invited Elihu to accompany him. Ill health prevented the ex-Congressman from making the trip. Once again, Grant was to return from a trip outside the rim of the States and appear at a strategic moment when the populace was expected to celebrate the arrival of the hero.

The United States needed a new President in 1880 and Republican politicos had laid plans for a convention to be held in Chicago. It was with some reluctance that Grant consented to be a nominee. He would be, he said, if delegates were to vote for him almost unanimously.

Washburne was one of Grant's managers working hard for the campaign leading up to the convention. Two other managers were John A. Logan and Elihu's nemesis, Roscoe Conkling. Logan wanted to extend his control of the Illinois political scene and felt threatened by Washburne. Elihu's friends persisted in promoting Elihu as a potential nominee. Washburne never declared himself, and he made an effort to discourage his friends from championing him. Among others, his supporters were German-Americans, Roman Catholics, with a large bloc of likely voters in New England from whence he came, together with Californians. In California, a San Francisco newspaper published six editorials promoting the Illinoisan. He received hundreds of letters from around the United States urging him to become a candidate. George C. Bates, for example, wrote,

> You are the only man living who can save the Republican Party from defeat in 1880 . . .. From my *heart* of *hearts* I feel that you alone can *save us.* . . . You are *honest,* capable, [and] could bring all the early Republican Germans straight into line.(6)

Suspicious, Logan wrote Elihu telling him it was being said anti-Grant forces were working up matters in anticipation of submitting "another's name," implying Washburne. Next, Logan wrote the retired Ambassador recommending that he run for Governor of Illinois. A decision to run for Governor would remove Elihu from the Presidential contest. The response from Washburne was that he had "no earthly desire for the position" of Governor. Still not relieved of anxiety, Logan asked Washburne to write a strong letter in support of Grant. Logan claimed that word was getting around that Elihu would perhaps be willing to be a tail to the kite of another prospective candidate seeking the nomination, namely James G. Blaine--Blaine-of-Maine.(7) Said Elihu, "every intelligent man knows where I stand," assuring Logan that his name would not be mentioned at the convention. As it was, Washburne was not successful in discouraging Justice John B. Cassoday of Wisconsin who at the convention nominated Elihu, perhaps, it could be said, "using" Washburne. Cassoday's interest seemed to have been in eliminating Grant.

The anti-Grant force was sizeable, made up of delegates who believed Presidents should not serve more than two terms. Elihu, realizing the strength of the anti-Grant movement and wishing to allay fears, suggested in a note to Grant that he make public a letter indicating he, Grant, would not consent to be a candidate should he be re-elected. The Congressman even drew up a statement which Grant could use for that purpose. Grant said it would be improper for him to make such a public statement until he were chosen as a candidate. Then he could assure the public.

Biographer Hunt writes that Washburne had no control of the anti-Grant sentiment, and that Washburne "did not falter in his own refusal to be a candidate."(8) Herman Raster of the *Staats-Zeitung* later wrote about what he believed happened. The German-Americans, he said, took credit for the whole idea of Washburne's being nominated. With the Ambassador nominated on the Republican ticket,

James A. Garfield

> . . . Elihu B. Washburne, as sure as twice two is four, *would* have become President in place of *Garfield* if he had held his tongue, i.e. if he had not on every proper and improper occasion, by speech and writing, declared that *Grant* was his candidate first and last. . .. Like a true Eckardt he remained to the last faithful to his 'friend' Grant and thereby the chance to make him President was lost . .. (9)

From Raster's point of view, "*through exaggerated friendship for Grant* [Washburne] committed *harikari,* i.e., political suicide."

❖

The man from Maine, from a small town lost in the forest, who had taken a hand in electing Abraham Lincoln President, and had played a part in putting Grant into office, chose to work himself out of becoming President of the United States. The most pathetic part of the story, short of the pathos of Elihu's last days, is that Ulysses S. Grant, who owed so much to his fellow townsman, was made to believe Washburne had betrayed him. For the remainder of his life, Grant would not permit Elihu's name to be spoken in his presence. As for Elihu, when Grant was near death he went to Saratoga Springs not far from Grant's cabin in Northern New York. He let it be known he was nearby, hoping Grant would call him to his bedside. Elihu was asked why he did not go directly to the cabin and announce himself. Washburne said, "Because Grant is the greater man."

There are those who disagree with the Man from Maine.

Chapter Nineteen

THE AGONY OF BEING LESS

Charles was the fifth child born to a 30-year-old mother and a 38-year-old father. As son number five, he thought himself less for being left out of the "club" of his four older brothers.(1) We can know with more certainty the psychological effect of being so far down on the age scale as we explore the long-lived life of this fifth brother. Growing up among older brothers, Charles had to be impressed and overwhelmed by the physically sturdy, intensely ambitious, highly intelligent, socially-inclined brothers--Israel, Sidney, Elihu and Cadwallader. When Charles was a pre-pubescent age 12, his brothers were 21, 19, 17, and 15, respectively. Could they have included a 12-year-old in their affairs? Not likely. Having each other, the four older boys hardly needed to consider another intensely ambitious person who, being a Washburn, was vying constantly for their attention, seeking to be recognized and appreciated. The four formed a gang complete in itself. Israel, was the leader of the quartet. Sidney, the humorous member kept his playmates laughing. Elihu was the idea man, and Cadwallader the stabilizer of the club of four. They spurned Charles' pleas for affirmation as he tried to enter their play or join their intimate conferences. He was made to see them only from the outside

Israel Washburn, Jr.

Sidney Washburn

Elihu Washbburne

and as a stranger. The brothers seemed to him to be whole, authentic persons, while in his mind Charles seemed to himself to be "all bits and pieces."(2) There were times when he thought he hated them, one and all. They babied him. Was there a worse punishment than this? The rejective mode eventually made Charles single-minded, self-determined and an angry boy and man. In a determined mood-in-the-making, Charles can be seen as when, "at age fourteen, [he] stayed home from church when all other family members were in attendance." As a small child Charles had

C.C. Washburn

the support of his sister, Martha. She, at least, was protective, noting in a letter to Cadwallader that at school Charles was experiencing rebuffs, "and is not calculated to bear them as well as many. Still he perseveres."(3) He was a loner among siblings and found he must endure the agony of living up to remarkable examples set by the older boys. Later he was languishing on campus at Bowdoin college discouraged because he was not able to foresee a future for himself. His older brother, Israel, had become an important public figure in the Maine legislature. Sid a successful merchant in Boston. Elihu, together with Cadwallader were promising lawyers in Illinois and Wisconsin. As for himself, he was a complete unknown. He was so uncertain about his future that he cared not whether he lived or died.(4)

Brother number five had two younger brothers, Samuel and William. The two coming after him were also of another and "distant" age, as Charles had been distant in relation to his elder brothers. The loner, Charles, had no more warm association with Sam and Willie than the older boys had with him. Sam had little interest in books and learning, while books became a favorite diversion for Charles, driven, as it were, to the cloisters by his isolation where he read all the books in the minister's library. So the last three brothers, Charles, Sam and William, were not close the way the awful four were. As Charles became the recluse among the six brothers, it was like a "kick in the pants" for Israel to complain, saying he was "a poet and dreams, and mystifies, and talks of men, women and books." This was harsh judgment coming from Israel, Jr., who was himself bookish, legalistic, and a literary critic. Charles protested to Elihu about a 60-page story Charles had written and put in the hands of the elder member, the revered Israel, but Israel had not read it. Over the course of their lives, however, Israel turned out to be the brother who was most sympathetic to brother number five, Charles. He wrote Elihu saying, "I devoutly hope you may succeed in lifting Charles over the bar. . ." Israel himself helped Charles to make it "over the bar," when as a Bowdoin student Charles sat under the lawyer brother in Orono, Maine, who persuaded him to "read law." Charles was easily tempted to forgo the law as soon as a teaching position opened up. He must have money, he thought. When Charles later went west Israel supposed he would stop at Galena, and continue to "read law" with Elihu's oversight. Instead, Charles went on to Wisconsin, depending upon attorney Cadwallader to "lift him over the bar." After encouragement from Cad, brother number five became Washburn lawyer number four.

Given Charles' experiences with his older and younger model-making brothers, it is not surprising that he had, as was said, "an unquenching desire to make himself known and respected among men." It was agony for him to realize that with few exceptions in his entire life, whenever he was noticed by the American public at large, it was because of the fame of his brothers. He was once interviewed by a newspaper reporter because his brother, Elihu, was an intimate friend of President Grant. What Charles had to deal with psychologically was Elihu and his drive for power, and the fact that it was said of Charles by Elihu's wife, Adele, that he and Elihu were like two peas in a pod. Charles had to deal also with the fact of Israel's exaggerated desires to go to the United States Senate, or to Russia as Minister Plenipotentiary. Charles' psyche was affected by Cadwallader's aspirations to be elected to the House of Representative, to be Governor of Wisconsin, and, like Israel, Cad's yearning to enter the U.S. Senate. As for Charles' kid brother, William, there seemed no end to the offices to which he aspired--and which he achieved. Striving for status was like a disease for Charles. Despite all he accomplished, sadly there were few kudos for him in youth or old age, a bizarre fact as has been mentioned. He lived a life of high adventure filled with romance and the stuff of which exciting novels are made. His life style was more fascinating than that of any of the celebrated, conformist brothers, Washburn men filled with that 19th-century "go-ahead" spirit. Writing about *The American Family in Past Time,* it was said by John Demos, Brandeis professor of history, that "the vision of worldly gain, the cultivation of the 'go-ahead' spirit, was enormously invigorating . . . but it also raised a specter of chaos; of individual men devouring each other in the struggle for success."(5) Life within the Washburn family burned with that spirit of competition. The inner life of brother number five appeared and re-appeared as "a specter of chaos," and in the family, he was forever attempting to "devour" his brothers, believing they were trying to do the same with him. The competitive spirit brought out harsh critical judgments, pronounced whenever Charles or anyone else appeared to fall below the level of honesty, loyalty or moral rectitude. Elihu told Sidney he had "lost all confidence in [Charles] as he had acted the rascal in roping in his friends for the payment of money . . . with no earthly means of paying them. I consider such conduct," said Elihu, "positively dishonest." Cadwallader, the next oldest to Charles, took it upon himself to restrain Elihu who was forever judging their brother harshly. Cadwallader told Elihu, "you have borne down too hard upon him." Charles had weak points, Cad admitted; but, he said, "in that he is like the rest of us," adding, "for God's sake do not fail to help and encourage him if you can."

The nucleii of the family that sired the loner was, of course, father and mother. At the center of the family was the sentimentalized figure of woman in the person of Martha, mother of the brood. She worked out her personal ambitions through her sons. Father had been a teacher and subsequently a ship builder, farmer and storekeeper, but above all, Father Israel was a political genie. As such, he was a fixed example for all Washburn children, with six of the seven sons entering the political arena as, one might say, professionals. Most of the sons soared far above the father's modest achievements as having represented the district of Maine in the Commonwealth of Massachusetts, and casting a vote in favor of making his district a separate state, Maine.

The admiration in which Henry Clay was hold by the politically-minded Washburns was extraordinary, showing itself in the case of William, the youngest male, when he spent the night in the barn weeping upon learning of the defeat of Clay in 1844. William was then 13 years old. Henry Clay's defeat found Charles writing, "the battle is lost . . . . Our gallant leader is defeated . . . . My political hopes were all centered in Henry Clay . . . the name . . . sweet to my ears." Charles was 22.

When Charles went west, he was no longer in the shadow of his brothers; he did, however, intend to impress them by mail. He wrote long, sometimes fascinating letters, and often complained because his brothers did not respond. When he reached California, Charles wrote Cadwallader explaining that he had worked for six weeks digging, all the while keeping his eyes open to find out how to make money. He said he was ready to demonstrate that money invested could bring 200 percent interest. He was full of proposals. He suggested buying a team for $300, hiring a teamster to drive it, paying him one half the amount raised monthly over and above expenses. Another grandiose plan which enthused Charles was to open a ranch on the Stanislaus river, herd cattle, catch salmon, and open a ferry. "A man . . . can hardly fail to make money hand-over-fist." He told Cadwallader that with

$1,000 and little risk he could buy and sell produce and clear $100 to $150 per week. An average profit, he declared, was 25 percent on goods. None of these options offered by Charles were to be realized, so he went to work for a Sonora newspaper. Next, restless Charles "had a strange desire to go to San Jose." He put a blanket on his back and started across the mountains. As he made the 100 mile trek he said he did a lot of thinking

The agony of living among his talented brothers resulted in Charles'

indecisiveness while he was a young man. He would not be loyal, dependable or hard-working until his work took on the trappings of a kind of religion. He had to find something to which he could commit himself sacrificially. There had been those who over the years had referred to him irreverently as a "work horse" for the Republican cause. His brother, Sidney, and sister, Mary, thought he might be a minister. The family, said Sid, ought to have at least one minister, and Sid was right about Charles' being a minister insofar as he, having found his trade, accepted his work as a vocation--as though "called to serve." It was the Republican cause to which he finally devoted himself. In this, brother number five could be compared favorably with Israel who launched the party in 1854, as well as with fiery Elihu who likewise was devoted to the party; and he could be compared agreeably with committed Cadwallader and dedicated William. All these Washburns were pledged to the cause of Whiggism and subsequently Republicanism.

This was the touchy black-bearded Washburn brother, Charles, with his beautiful light blue eyes, as his adoring daughter Lilian wrote. In a photograph, he looks squarely and sternly at the observer as though presenting a fearful challenge to whoever is looking at him. This Washburn brother had strong shoulders, a scholar's stoop, high forehead, slick brown hair and dark eyebrows. Holding onto his face was a large, slightly hooked nose. With his nose and large ears, Charles looked like his father. He was, according to Lilian, "the student, the dreamer, the inventor, the literary man of the family." The daughter identified her father as one of "the empire makers" who ended his days in the "quiet life of any less prominent man." She called Charles optimistic, as all the Washburn brothers wished to be called, though Lilian granted that her father fell into grisly moods of depression. Such a mood induced Charles to write Elihu, saying,

> I may as well abandon first as last all hope or expectation of ever doing anything more than make a living, and if that is all I can do, I care not how soon this miserable life is at an end.(6)

Republicanism gave him a new lease on life. It became clear to his friends that he was zealous in his devotion, as was illustrated in what R.W. Brush in California wrote to Elihu. Charles, Brush said, had "labored long and under difficulties few would have withstood in the good cause of Republicanism and has done . . . much to bring about the result of the late election [of 1860]."(7)

153

Chapter Twenty

THE VAGABOND PRINCE

Charles Ames Washburn, hiding beneath a bushy black beard, a loner angry with himself for being who he is, feels unhappy that he is not Israel, Elihu or Cadwallader. Hiding himself from himself Charles wanders the earth, going from one place to another, from one task to another bearing out in his career what he

Charles Ames Washburn

considers himself to be--a vagabond. As a young man, Wanderer Washburn leaves his native home in Maine and goes South to teach. At the bidding of his brother Israel, Jr., however, he chooses to settle for a time in Washington, D.C., working for the Treasury Department. Following a stint in the District of Columbia, he moves back to Maine, studies law with Israel, Jr. Leaving Orono, Maine, and his brother, he travels West to Wisconsin continuing his study of law under the patient guidance of his brother, Cadwallader and passes the bar. He heads for the Pacific in 1850 with all the other lemming-like seekers after a fortune, reaching the Golden State at the age of 28, a little more than a quarter of his life. For him, life began at age 28. Joining the swarming hordes descending on the gold mine country of California, the Maine vagabond mines gold, works his way into journalism in Sonora, travels west to

San Francisco, edits and later owned newspapers, publishes novels; and for a time is celebrated in story and print as he makes a life-and-death struggle dueling an excitable Southern Chivalric.(1) In the course of a gun battle between Washburn and Benjamin Franklin Washington, Washburn is wounded but survives. The incident is to be used to frustrate his ambition to serve in Congress with his brothers, Israel, Elihu and Cadwallader.

A vagabond who is trying to escape from himself, Charles A. Washburn nevertheless lives an adventurous life, a prototype for many American men.. For generations American men have striven to achieve, moving from place to place, each new place holding promises of success. The migratory lifestyle becomes part of the mythos of the culture. Typically, Charles is turning out to be something of "a loser." He is losing as four of his enterprising brothers become rich, powerful and popular.

As with so many Americans, Loser Washburn is surrounded by immense natural resources, a virtual *entrepôt* of reserved riches in the land. Despite living as though in an imaginary heaven where streets are paved with gold, many in America are not "making it." They are like Charles. Ordinary persons in every generation recognize their reflection in the mirror of Washburn's frustrating, unsuccessful, however, fascinating life--as exciting as the fiction writers create.

Typically, Charles became preoccupied early in life with a "consciousness of self." His native religion enables him in the words of Owen Barfield to shift "the centre of gravity of consciousness from the cosmos around him into the personal human being himself."(2) Nineteenth-century Americans seek to realize meaning and destiny, satisfied that meaning arises from within individuals, not as revelations passed down from ancient times in the bibles of the world. Self-reliance becomes the watchword. Emerson says the key to the period of history in which Charles lives appears to be that the mind has become aware of itself. Men grow reflective. There is a new consciousness.

With his 19th-century self-centered, ambitious outlook, Washburn as editor of several San Francisco newspapers, has become a player in the political arena. The nomad finds him*self a minor figure in the Republican movement in California in 1859 to 1860, despite the fact that like his brothers Israel, Elihu and Cadwallader, he is instrumental in having organized a new political party.(3) In 1855 Charles called together leading figures in California for the purpose of creating the party. He is involved in making arrangements for a convention to be

Charles Crocker

held in the Congregational church in Sacramento where proto-Republicans expect to formalize their new party. The following year, a California Republican, Charles Fremont, was on the Republican ticket as Presidential nominee and was nearly elected. Present at an organizational meeting in Sacramento, in addition to Charles, are Mark Hopkins, Charles Crocker, Leland Stanford, Edward D. Baker and George Bates. Bates is the principal convention speaker at Sacramento, and he is expected to be critical of Franklin Pierce, Democratic President. In his speech, Bates intends to deplore the passage of the Kansas Act of 1854, the purpose of which is to make a territory into another slave state. Bates is ready as well to condemn Democrat Stephen A. Douglas as an "unworthy and faithless public servant." Gangs of mischief-making Democrats, knowing or suspecting what Bates was to say, started a riot. They hounded delegates out of the church. When convention speaker Bates attempts to address the crowd in a nearby public square, the renegades are making it impossible for him to proceed. To Democrats, these Republicans are abolitionists, dubbed "black Republicans."(4)

Unsuccessful in 1855, a second attempt is made in 1856 to bring Republicans together at the same location--Sacramento. Washburn is present, and his name is before delegates as a candidate for Congress. He aspires to be part of the team of Washburn brothers, three of whom are in the House representing Maine, Illinois and Wisconsin. At the 1856 Sacramento convention Charles thinks that since he has done "the drudgery of the party" in California, he is entitled to "whatever he wants." He is convinced he is "the popular man of the party and popular among the mercantile community. . .. "(5) At the convention, much to his distress, he is not chosen as the nominee on the grounds that he is a dueler, and dueling - everybody knows - has been outlawed in California. Those who do not favor his nomination find an easy way to sabotage his campaign. They cry out, *"Washburn is a duelist!"* When the delegates pass him by, Charles notes that "a regular Presbyterian is nominated."(6)

Suffering his bitter defeat, feeling it is time for another change in his life, peripatetic Washburn leaves California and returns to Wisconsin.(7) Editor Washburn has a new idea and wants to share the idea with the chief entrepreneur of the family--Cadwallader. Charles has already edited that "monument among political institutions," the *Alta California*. He has managed the *Evening Chronicle, Star of Empire*, and is ready to make a move on the Chicago market to establish a new style newspaper. He needs a loan to undertake the project he has in mind and is able to borrow from Cadwallader. Cadwallader is enjoying "strawberries and cream," as Elihu notes, and he, like many in the moneymaking world, is in clover. As noted, Cad, Elihu and Sam have purchased a town in Wisconsin to which they have given the name *Waubeck*. It is thought the town will become the center of a flourishing agricultural area. The Chippewa Boom is located in the town featured as a profitable venture. In addition, C.C. Washburn is credited with playing "the greatest role [of all] in insuring the prosperity of a newly founded city," Minneapolis.

Feeling flush, Cadwallader lent Charles money needed to start his newspaper, not expecting ever again to see the $3,000. Charles takes the loan, goes down to Chicago from Mineral Point, Wisconsin, and in Chicago a few months later produced the *Saturday Evening Chronotype*. Charles produces one issue of the *Chronotype* after which his operation closes. He has printed the first issue just as the panic of 1857 has paralyzed businesses in Chicago and across the country. In August 1857 the Ohio Life Insurance and Trust Company crashes. This was one of the most highly respected financial institutions in New York City.(8) Banks are beginning to fold across America, including the Bank in Hallowell, Maine, managed by Charles' brother, Sidney, and the bank owned by Cadwallader and his partner, Cyrus Woodman, in Mineral Point. Prices are declining on the New York Stock Exchange, railroads face bankruptcy, land values collapse, and factories are shutting down. Robert C. Winthrop, descendant of John Winthrop, writes, "The world never seemed to me a less hopeful place than in this month of September, in the year of our Lord 1857."

The able business tycoon types, Washburns of Wisconsin and Illinois, should have anticipated the trouble that now envelopes the country. As early as 1855, the Bank of Hallowell, was warned it was in trouble. Several reasons were cited by a bank commission charged with examining the bank's records. The report claimed that the bank had commenced business before anything had been paid in, the second installment of $25,000 was never provided as promised, and large loans had been made to persons outside the State without the approval of the Directors. This last is a hit at the Washburns in the West. There were complaints numbering ten in all.

Israel, Jr., forecasts trouble, warning the business community from the floor of the House of Representatives in the early part of the decade, saying, "I should be glad if I could direct the attention of the House to the clouds that are gathering. . .and could impress upon it the necessity of taking measures at once for the safe delivery of the bolts, for disaster and ruin, which are preparing to discharge upon the country." He reminded Congressmen that the famine in Europe had given Americans an extraordinary market, but had ceased to exist. The disturbances and revolutions of 1848 had foreign capitalists investing in the U.S., buying up railroads and other corporations; but Representative Washburn warned that the market for stock would not continue. Israel, Jr., of Maine wanted to see the business community "escape a revulsion such as the country has never known."

The devastating panic brought down upon the Washburns the first of several depressions when they suffer dismaying losses. Charles's experience is like his father's who suffered a similar depression with his little grocery business which had to be forfeited in the 1830s. The depression his father endured splintered the family, nearly putting him and his wife in the poor house. The diaspora began for family members with the onset of that first Washburn experience of depression. Sidney went to Massachusetts, Israel, Jr., to his uncle's home, Elihu ended up in Illinois, and Cadwallader in Wisconsin. Charles, of course, went to California, Samuel was on the high seas, and William went west to Minnesota. Home in Livermore was never the same again. Only the memories only. The brothers and sisters never forgot the devastation wrought by the depression and the effect upon themselves and the Washburn clan of Livermore.

Charles returned to California from Illinois after his failed experiment in Chicago. The records do not show, but it is possible he was able to bring out to San Francisco some of the loan advanced by Cadwallader. At least he had financial means to join with Alvan Flanders and a few merchants in the city to purchase the *San Francisco Daily Times*. His partner, Flanders, like Charles a political activist, later will become Governor of the Washington Territory, but in the late 1850s is a member of the Republican State Committee of California. He must have known that in Charles's absence the Republican party had been falling apart after the convention of 1856. If Flanders did know, he did not work at reconstituting the party. Instead, Charles, when he was back on California soil, sees the party is coming apart, goes to work, as he claimed in a letter to Cadwallader, resurrecting the party. He did in fact become one of the reliable leaders in Republican circles in the west coast city in 1858. In 1859, the two, Washburn and Flanders, established the leading Republican newspaper in California, the *Times*.

Finding Washburn at the outer edges of influence in California Republicanism despite his accomplishments for the cause is something of an enigma. Though as editor Washburn was shrewd and like his brothers endowed with political skills, his skills however were mostly displayed on paper. It must be noted, though, that the best he was able to do at that period of his life was by no means insignificant. His contribution was made as he shared an astute political judgment, providing advice and guidance on the editorial pages of the *Daily Times* in the critical years of 1859 and 1860, leading to the election of the first Republican President, Abraham Lincoln.

The ability to change a political environment is an undertaking which came naturally to each of the politically-minded Washburns. The power the California Washburn possessed was confined within him as heat contained in a raging furnace. His burning ambition was to possess influence such as his brothers commanded in Congress and the business world. Like so many embittered Americans in successive generations, Charles sought to change the political picture both for himself and his caste or class. He intended to alter laws he considered immoral and unjust. He had a lengthy agenda as he endeavored to make changes at the county and state levels, expecting to bring about changes in the wretched Democratic administration program at Washington. His expectations in several areas remained a fantasy.

Charles' daughter, Lilian, remembered her father as "a quiet man with a quill pen in his hand." But in the editorial office of the *Times,* Lilian's "quiet" father laid plans to shape the politics of California. He made known to intimates that he expected to manage patronage in the State once Republicans controlled the government in Washington. With his newspaper he intended to alter the political sentiment of a majority of Californian voters. Prior to 1859 and 1860 the majority of voters favored the Southern cause which included slavery. The change which took place with Washburn's assistance was a transformation of voter attitude. This included what Charles termed "barbaric chivalric sentiments" to endorsement of Lincoln and the Vice Presidential candidate, Hannibal Hamlin. With an excess of pride and ambition, the "quiet man with a quill pen" made suggestions to his brothers. He wrote to Israel, Jr., in Maine, to suggest he "keep Hamlin's seat warm" after Hamlin left the Senate to serve as Vice-President. Editor Washburn then surmised that his Wisconsin brother, Cadwallader, would go into Lincoln's cabinet. For Elihu, he said, there were several openings which Charles thought his Illinois brother deserved, all the way from Speaker of the House to Minister Plenipotentiary to France. The editor's grandiose schemes did not prevent him from pleading with his brother, Cadwallader, already a shining star in the political and financial firmament, urging Cad to write a special letter for him. He explained to the financial wizard of Wisconsin that a letter from him would help his political ventures in California and "might be worth thousands of dollars" to him.

California went Republican in 1860. Washburn went to Washington as an elector. He expected to be rewarded by the administration for his diligence in putting the party together, and for helping in significant ways to elect Republican Congressmen from California as well as persuading voters to vote for Lincoln and Hannibal Hamlin, Charles' cousin. Lincoln was reluctant to reward Charles with the California office he sought, the Custom House. The President considered Charles unstable. Influential California Republicans were in Washington advising Mr. Lincoln to ignore Washburn's request. Charles was aware that dissenters had been sent to Washington to oppose his petition. He referred to them as "sweepings from hell." It was in part his inordinate use of pejorative words that bungled his plans for advancement in the political arena. After three months of waiting with Washburn

cursing the President, Lincoln appointed him Commissioner to Paraguay. Nomad Washburn was sent to serve in a tyrannical Latin American country. It was said by one writer, Gilbert Phelps, that "in 1864, Paraguay was to most Europeans and North Americans a tiny and almost completely unknown republic - somewhere in the middle of the vast South American sub-continent." To this place Charles was virtually banished by Elihu's friend, Lincoln, and Israel's friend, William Seward, Secretary of State. His experiences in the vast world beyond the US began to open up for Charles. His beginning, he

William H. Seward

reminded himself, was in an unimportant rural community in down east Maine, followed by life in perilous San Francisco, and soon he was to be among Paraguayans and have to deal with a paranoid dictator. The succession of tasks continued to test the intellectual and moral caliber of a prototypical 19th-century American.

Failure followed Charles to Paraguay and back to the Golden State. Returning from his post abroad in 1869, Washburn resettled in California. His name was placed in the hat as a nominee for Governor. Israel, Jr., had already served as Governor of Maine. Concurrently, Cadwallader was running for the office of Governor in Wisconsin. Charles' younger brother, William, was to run for

Governor two years later in Minnesota. Elihu was urged to let friends submit his name as candidate for Governor of Illinois, but as we know, Elihu had no interest in the position. Had Elihu chosen to run his election was a certainty after his stint as Plenipotentiary in France. Charles became a contender for the position of Governor in California, but his candidacy did not arouse enough interest to keep him in the running, and he was dropped from consideration --once again "a loser."

Questions arise as to why the bright, able, ambitious Charles, with all his striving, fell so far short of expectations. He made little headway with his surplus of ambition and talent. He wrote and published *Philip Thaxter* which was praised by a critic, who referred to him as "a genius." "...What we have in *Philip Thaxter*," the critic wrote, "[is] to an extent unprecedented in any new novel which has appeared for years, and this gives us a right to see in it, spite of many obvious faults, the presence of many rare qualities of genius." Washburn's book did not win him public plaudits, nor did its publication bring hoped-for additional income. The study of Charles Washburn's life, which follows this opening chapter of his life, unfolding as it has like a drama worthy of the stage, will suggest reasons for his failures. His life involved historic incidents of tragic proportions. So it was a drama played without comedy and with a distinct love interest.

The erratic, troubled life of Washburn did not begin in 1850 when he put a pack on his back and walked from Mariposa to San Jose; nor did his shifting patterns begin with his newspaper career. It did not begin with the duel between himself and B.F. Washington in 1854. None were greatly significant events in his life. What Charles himself took to be the start of the whole unraveling ordeal was his brothers' refusal to provide funds enabling him to finish college without worrying about debt. He had written "had anybody at that time (1848) advanced me two or three hundred dollars I would not have been a wandering vagabond all my life." It is somewhat indicative of a pattern that Charles, when he chose a pseudonym as author of essays written for California magazines, he used the name *Oliver Outcast*. The dramatic turn of events did not begin at any of these turning points. It began when he landed at Asuncion, Paraguay, on November 14, 1861. He was then 39 years of age. The Paraguay adventure began a story which was to turn out to be nearly fictional in character. The weaving of the tale must uncover answers to questions one asks about this brother:

"Why in political history is he not counted among the several distinguished members of the Washburn family?"

Why has he been left in the shadows of history; even of family history? A Washburn scholar, the late L. Robert Hughes, said of Charles that he was a man "who seemed to avoid success like it was a plague." Israel, Jr., the fatherly elder brother in the family of brothers, said Charles seemed "a shade less enterprising than the others . . .. " In spite of these observations and as his daughter, Lilian, believed, it seems heartless for the record to show failure when it can be seen Charles lived the most intriguing, exciting, honest and courageous if inept life of all the brothers. Indeed, his life may be seen finally as greater in its way than the lives of his eminent siblings, those Washburns who were millionaires, Congressmen, Senator, Governors, Ambassadors, lumber moguls, railroad tycoons, and a maker of Presidents.

Chapter Twenty-One

THE FIELD OF BATTLE, SAN FRANCISCO

Editor Washburn chose the enemies he would recognize in the San Francisco *Daily Times*. Some were from the pool of political adversaries. Some were regular readers of his paper. Once enemies were chosen, Charles proceeded to treat them harshly subjecting them to the assaults of an editor's "awful weaponry," pen, ink and the devil's dictionary. To personal antagonists he administered vituperative broadsides cutting deeply. To enemies classified as political, Charles was sarcastic, caustic, satirical. Lilian saw her father's sarcasm as a "shot aimed at a spot where he knew it would hurt the most."(1) She referred to a woman in San Francisco who was said to be robbing men. Her father's criticism forced the woman and her gang to flee the country, and the woman, said Lilian, entered a convent.

William Gwin

Numbered among personal enemies of the editor of the *Daily Times* were Benjamin Franklin Washington, Collector of the Port of San Francisco, and James Simonton,

Stephen A. Douglas

editor of the *San Francisco Bulletin.* As for political adversaries, they were numerous, but in the forefront were Senators William Gwin and Stephen A. Douglas. These were roundly abused by the *Times* editor.

Charles's resentment of B.F. Washington, considered to be a west coast henchman for the Buchanan administration, led to one of the famous challenges resulting in a duel. In an editorial published for his readers two years after the historic affair, Charles put Washington in an ignominious position, explaining what actually happened:

> When the parties . . . took their positions," wrote Charles, "Mr. P.T. Herbert, Washington's second, was to give the word after . . . which the parties were to raise their pieces; but before that word was given, Washington's second . . . saw that his principal was out of time--[he had raised his weapon before the word]; and he cried out 'stop'?

In his nervousness, B.F. Washington made the same mistake five times in succession. The fifth time, Herbert let it pass and Washington saw Washburn's shot strike the ground in front of him, leaving Washington "a dead shot" at his adversary. He took deliberate aim and would have killed Washburn but for the glancing of the bullet. The Washburn-Washington duel took place in 1854. Repeatedly over the following months and years, Charles referred to the Collector deferentially as *Bombastes Furioso*, challenging Washington to come after him again, saying, "We have called [him] liar before, as we do now, but [he] never come[s] after satisfaction."(2) Charles demeaned his opponent in 1860 when "Bombastes" sought the office of U.S. Senator for California. In the *Times*, Washburn announced Washington, "an inflated bladder" with the same intellect.(3) A Southern expatriate with a chivalric outlook, Senator William McKendree Gwin, unlike Collector B.F. Washington, could not be provoked into a duel by Northern expatriate, Washburn. In 1856, Gwin nearly lost his senate seat when David Broderick, possessing sufficient political strength in the California legislature to defeat him, humiliated Gwin. Gwin, acting like the weaker of two animals contesting for a female's favors, submitted to the stronger, slinking away as Broderick demanded the release into his hands of the California patronage. According to Washburn, in the following months Gwin became part of a plot resulting in the murder of Senator Broderick.

Senator Gwin seemed to have not the slightest compunction about lying. His biographer(4) re-tells an account fabricated by the Senator who claimed to have met Abraham Lincoln on February 23, 1861, when the president-elect entered Washington, D.C., for his inauguration. Only one person met Mr. Lincoln at the train station, and that person was Charles A. Washburn's brother, the Hon. Elihu B. Washburne. Gwin, Democrat, cooperating as he did with the administration and voting with the Southern bloc, was a nemesis for Republicans in California.

The railroad was of course a vital issue. Washburn, along with a handful of Republicans, pushed hard to persuade the U.S. government to invest in a railroad line extending to the coast. Democrats had a tradition of discouraging such "internal improvements." Their argument was, that a line to the water's edge in the west would be enormously expensive for tax-payers. Northern and Southern Representatives disagreed as to where the route would be. Should it be a southern route through Texas, or a central or northern route favored by northerners? A typical piece of writing by Washburn tells about the all-important central route and the uselessness of Gwin as an exponent of any plan except the South's:

... California has nothing to hope in the way of a Pacific Railroad from the
Democratic party. From the present administration we have got nothing,
and no one believes we ever could get anything - if Buchanan were to be
President for life, and Gwin Senator til he became honest.(5)

Charles, ready to use Gwin to further the Republican cause in California, added a threat, "The successor of Buchanan" (implying, *if a Republican is not elected!*) "will be a man approved of by Douglas and [Governor] Wise, a cardinal feature with them that the government should not 'be given over to the federal gods of Pacific Railroads'."

A Railroad Convention was held in San Francisco in September 1859. Editor Washburn, eager for an input at the Convention, complained in an editorial about Senator Gwin's wish to have a Central Railroad dip south "through slave country," if indeed the southern route itself could not be chosen, which, of course, Senator Gwin preferred. Charles was pleased with action taken at the Convention, feeling delegates had made clear that people prefer the Central route. Action by delegates prevented Dr. Gwin from opposing it; although, Washburn wrote, the "malignant and pestiferous" Gwin will probably oppose the project covertly.(6)

Senator David C. Broderick ... Charles believed he had in Broderick a lasting friend.(7) There is no way to appraise Washburn's genuine feelings about Broderick after the *Times*' competing newspaper, the *San Francisco Daily Bulletin* published a letter written by Charles A. Sumner, Broderick's official photographer, who wrote:

> Mr. Broderick said to me, within the last month: "Oh, Washburn is the mere tool and mouth-piece of Col. Baker's enemies. He is a dirty dog, sir-- a dirty dog. I never placed the least confidence in him. He use to sniffle and slobber about me last spring; but I understood him, perfectly."(8)

Despite that rendition of Broderick's alleged charge against Washburn, Washburn was one of the Senator's pall-bearers. And the editor, continuing to praise the Senator, suggests that Charles dismissed as scurrilous the photographer's report. Issues of the *Times* following the *Bulletin* article by Sumner quoted several respected men who were close to Broderick, all of whom said substantially what Captain SH. Dubois wrote to Washburn:

> . . . I never heard [Broderick] speak of you but in terms of respect and regard . . . I also know Mr. Broderick's opinion of Sumner. He regarded him with aversion and contempt . . . (9)

The fact is that if one person could be credited with having made Broderick known to hosts outside California, it was editor Washburn. Washburn's newspaper carried the tale of the Broderick-Terry duel eastward to New England, New York and the District of Columbia.

The historic event leading to the duel happened in this manner . . .

David Broderick

A bitter, volatile political campaign came to a close in California on September 7, 1859, when the electorate went to the polls. Many cast their ballot remembering savage attacks made with the use of that "awful weaponry," Washburn's pen and ink. Legislators remembered attacks against Gwin, who, it was declared by the *Times*, "dripp[ed] with corruption."

The day following the election, September 8, a notice appeared in the *Times*:

> RUMORED DUEL. --A rumor was on the wing last evening to the effect that Dr. Gwin had challenged Mr. Broderick, and that the preliminaries were being arranged for a fight today. The rumor was wild. Gwin did not challenge the Senator. The challenge to Broderick came from a California Supreme Justice, David S. Terry.

Two days later, September 10, on a Saturday Morning, the *Daily Times* corrected the rumor regarding a Gwin-Broderick duel.

> THE RUMORED DUEL. --A number of messages passed between Judge Terry, of the State Supreme Court, and Mr. D.C. Broderick . . . Gwin, it seems, is not the antagonist of Mr. Broderick.

Unlike the numerous accounts published in several other San Francisco papers, Charles's report of the death-laden account of the duel, once it took place, was composed with evident feelings of sympathy and affection, at times *poetic*. Washburn's high regard and personal fondness for Broderick can be said to account for disputable claims he was to make after the senator was laid in the grave.

Hundreds were on the *qui vive* Monday evening anxious to witness the proceedings. Nothing had excited San Francisco citizens since the days of the Vigilance Committee as did this contest. Vehicles were chartered and men set out to find the secret location where the duel was to take place. "The instinct . . . which draws the vultures to the feast led each and all to the place." Sixty-seven people found the confined arena located ten miles from San Francisco. The valley where the parties, friends and onlookers gathered, reports the *Times,* was closed in by low hummocks of hills.

The sun rose clear in a bright blue sky, and illuminated the scene with [its] cheerful rays as if in mockery of a bloody work [it] was to witness. Little birds hopped merrily about in the stunted herbage, and, warmed into life by the beauty of the morning, chirped blithely and happily their matin songs. All nature, calm and peaceful, seemed to give the lie to the violence shortly to be enacted. It was six a.m. Duelers with their seconds physicians arrived, neither dueler was anxious. Eight-inch Belgium pistols were brought out and the two solemn men examined the weapons.

Washburn, watching and waiting, observed that "upon the fate of one of the duelers . . . hung the political aspect of the State for years to come . . . the power, influence, and gift of offices, and to it were allied the fierce strife of party, the hates, loves, friendships and enmities of thousands. On the other hand was a man occupying the first judicial position in the State, a man before whose fiat must fall or stand the legal decisions of all other Courts in California, and from whose dictum there could be no appeal."

Space separating the duelers was measured; a mere ten paces. The men will be so near they can whisper to each other. Broderick and Terry stand without coat or collar, watches or coins. Terry throws his articles onto the ground carelessly. Then the *code duello* is read. The referee explains he will count, "Fire, one, two." Broderick pulls his San Jose hat down to eye level, traces the ten paces separating the two "as if drawing a bee-line between them." One newspaper claimed that at that moment Mr. Broderick was nervous and lost his presence of mind. The *Times* declared the claim "utterly false."

7:15! The referee asks, "Are you ready?"

"Ready."

"Ready."

"Fire! --One! Two!"

Senator Broderick raises his pistol with its hair trigger, and before it is fastened upon the Judge the weapon discharges.(10) The bullet creased the dust a few feet in front of Judge Terry, and Terry now had a dead shot at Broderick. He fired. Broderick reeled slowly to the left, and fell to the ground, while the Judge "folded his arms, holding the pistol still smoking in his hand, and did not move from his position." Doctors rushed to tend Broderick. Terry left the field bent for San Francisco, North Beach, and Oakland. At Oakland the Judge took a conveyance to Martinez, was ferried across to Benicia and then went overland to Sacramento. The wounded Senator was placed on a mattress and the pain- racked body was taken over rough roads to the house of Leonidas Haskell at Black Point. Propped up with pillows in his bed Broderick faced the calm of the Bay. Hundred of friends arrived at the Haskell house anxious to learn about his condition. Washburn reported conditions at four, six, eight o'clock onward:

Four, . . . inflammation has set in . . . ;

Six, ... groans are heart-rending, his agony intense ... ;
Eight, ... no hope ... ;
Nine, ... hope ... ;
Eleven, ... slight hopes for recovery ... ;
Eleven-thirty, ... chances of recovery are ... great;
Two o'clock, ... delirium. He will last the night ...

That was Wednesday. Death rattles persisted for two days and then "Governor McDougall closed the eyes that had looked their last ... [,] the signal of desolation to those who surrounded the [Haskell] place, and [men] gave vent to the repressed ... feeling. Heads were bowed down; the deep sobs of strong men, their frames shaking with emotion--the convulsive weeping of women, and long drawn sigh[s] from behind hands which covered agonized faces--these were the features of a scene which will live in memory while life shall remain."(11)

> Tears fell when thou wert dying
> From eyes unused to weep,
> And long where thou art lying
> Shall tears the cold turf steep.

Emblazoned on the masthead Saturday morning, the Daily Times announced the last reported words from the lips of the dead man: "They have killed me because I was opposed to the extension of slavery and a corrupt Administration. --Broderick."

The day before Broderick died, the Times reported that a highly respectable gentleman had arrived at the port of San Francisco saying "it was the common impression among politicians in the Atlantic States [that Broderick] was to be killed off." At that point, Washburn implicated the "audacious villain," Gwin. The editor was certain that the people of the country could not be disabused of the idea that "a plan was deliberately agreed upon and a conspiracy formed."(12) But this "fiendish"(13) idea of Washburn's, that there was a conspiracy, brought another of Washburn's enemies into the melee. The editor of the Daily Evening Bulletin, James Simonton, challenged Charles - without naming him - saying,

William Gwin

> If you *have* *evidence* which proves the
> h o r r i b l e conspiracy which you
> insinuate, or which awakens naturally
> strong suspicions that such exists, MAKE IT
> PUBLIC.

Charles was convinced that Simonton and Gwin were in a conspiracy against the citizens of California, so he took Simonton's broad accusation and his defense of Gwin in stride, satisfied that the senator's San Francisco spokesman, the editor of the Bulletin, was being paid to defend his chief.

James Simonton, Washburn's *bete noire*, was a New York journalist whose most distinguishing achievement as a journalist was the exposure in the *New York Times* of a plot involving Charles' brother, Congressman Elihu Washburne.(14) In the early 1850s, Washburne and Stephen A. Douglas introduced resolutions seeking land grants for the state of Iowa and the territory of Minnesota. A Minnesota Land bill was passed supported by Elihu and his brother, Israel, of Maine. President

Pierce signed the bill.   The result was a crisis fomented when Washburne discovered that a three-letter word "and" had been substituted for a two-letter word, "or," with the change enabling a private company to take into its possession vast lands granted to the railroads by government. Washburne sought the appointment of a special committee to investigate the change. A committee was appointed. Washburne was made chairman, though he resigned after three meetings. Without Elihu, the committee did not make the simple alteration he sought, they defeated the proposal which called for the granting of land to railroads.   That was alright. Washburne by then began to change his opinion about land grants. He was opposed to giving land to the Pacific railways "believing them to be corrupt from scalp to bowels," is the way George Alfred Townsend put it.(15) The fraud, uncovered by Simonton, resulted in the expulsion of four members of the House. The experience was Congressman Washburne's first encounter with private companies with their demands for special privileges. He said to his father in 1856, "Father, those men who are doing so much to open up the northwest and the far west with railway tracks are not all doing it for public benefit. They want to get all sorts of privileges for themselves and their stockholders."(16) James Simonton uncovered the corruption which gave Simonton notoriety for a time. He went West to San Francisco in 1859, became part owner of the *Bulletin*, and immediately found a bothersome antagonist in the brother of Congressman Washburne, Charles, because Simonton appeared to Charles to be Gwin's "man Friday."(17) Washburn could not say enough in criticism of the *Bulletin* editor. Typical sarcasm shows itself in the final paragraph of a Washburn editorial in which Simonton is excoriated:

Do ye hear that, now?   Who shall dare arraign the *Bulletin*! Isn't it everybody's duty to defend the cause of morality? And is not the *Bulletin* morality personified? And if we prove anything against it, is it not an offense against morality? Surely it has said so in its own columns, and who knows so well as its modest and virtuous conductor? Oh, modesty and virtue, how much self-triumphanting are required to sound thy praises?

Despite leaning heavily on "Gwin's man Friday," Simonton's *Bulletin* was seen to have "bore[n] hard upon Gwin for his treachery to the interests of the state, and his complicity in the Lime Point sale to the government, reported to be just consummated, by which $200,000 was paid for a point of barren rock at the Heads, which the state would have sold for $2,000, or whatever price a jury empaneled by the district court should declare it to be worth."(18)

Chapter Twenty-Two

VICTORY

As is indicated in the previous chapter, another of Washburn's political adversaries was no less a Goliath than Senator Stephen A. Douglas of Illinois, the "Little Giant." The editor's brothers in Congress, Israel, Elihu and Cadwallader, carried on a vigorous fight with this Illinois Senator after he submitted a bill allowing slave owners to take their "property" (slaves) into Kansas and Nebraska, the introduction of slaves contingent upon a vote by plebiscite. Israel led Whig forces in the House debate of the Kansas-Nebraska bill. The two Washburns delivered powerful speeches critical of the Douglas-inspired legislation. The House vote went against the Whigs and dissenting Northern Democrats. Elihu was in despair about the voting, as he admitted to a reporter of the *New York Tribune*, James Pike. Israel, however, having suffered the loss of dignity as well as losing the fight, yet would not let himself be defeated. The day following the rout in the House of Representative, Israel invited a dozen congressmen to meet together for the purpose of discussing the virtual impotence of the northern parties, and to plan for a future course of action. This small, influential group headed by Israel historians credit with having launched the Republican party in 1854.

THE REPUBLICAN AND THE WASHBURN VIEW OF SLAVERY

Having introduced the bill permitting citizens to vote on the issue of slavery, Stephen Douglas in effect was read out of the northern Democratic party. The administration's position was that the Dred Scott decision decided the whole matter. The Supreme Court declared that Negroes of slave descent, as an inferior order of beings, were not and could not become citizens of a state. Charles, like Israel and Elihu--and Judge Taney--did not let themselves think the thoughts of blacks and how they

Abraham Lincoln
and
The "Little Giant"

felt. They were not abolitionists who extended themselves to enter empathically the minds of blacks. Israel, for example, was asked later, as Governor of Maine, if free blacks and their families could be settled in the state. He turned down that opportunity saying the cold weather would not suit them. Very likely, Israel did not ask blacks what their wishes were, or whether they could endure cold Maine winters. Washburn's thinking in general coincided with Republican thinking, that blacks should not be slaves, but whether slave or free, they loathed blacks competing with whites. In California, free blacks petitioned the state legislature in 1851, 1852, and 1853 to eradicate a law which prohibited blacks from testifying in court against whites. Republican party members joined Democrats voting to ignore the plea for equal rights. Examples are rampant of the inhumanity of Republicans, Democrats and Chivalrics as they dealt with blacks, Indians, Chinese and "Mongols," which is the term Charles used for the Japanese.

Roger B. Taney

Dred Scott

Senator Douglas broke with the president on Buchanan's contention that slavery could exist in Kansas-Nebraska whether by popular vote or not. Douglas' bill, like the bill introduced by Henry Clay much earlier, inserted the article insisting that slavery must be accepted by citizens. One of Senator Stephen A. Douglas' political associates was David Broderick with whom editor Washburn was friendly. Broderick was the pronounced leader of the Douglas Democrats in California. He also was unhappy with the outcome of the Convention held at Lecompton, Kansas, which had sanctioned slavery and included their position in the Kansas State Constitution.(1) Charles wrote Elihu, explaining with the use of his editorial that "'we' are playing for the Douglas men to come to us." For a time, Senator Douglas' followers in California were David Broderick and his loyal disciples. Neither Douglas nor his California associate wanted to see new states inserting articles in their Constitution making slavery routine, which is what Lecompton legislators had determined was to happen. Elihu and Charles, therefore, were pursuing the task concurrently in Illinois and California, "playing for the Douglas men to come to us," the Republican party. Elihu was mildly rebuked by his friend, Lincoln. Lincoln was under a misapprehension, thinking his Galena associate was trying to persuade Douglas to switch to the Republican party and run as Republican nominee for president. Washburne was a strong Lincoln supporter. He said to Lincoln in no uncertain terms, "When I am for a man, I am for a man all the way!" meaning, of course, that he was 100 percent for Old Abe.

In San Francisco, Charles was aware that "only by winning the support of anti-slavery Democrats could California's Republicans secure office. For that reason, Republicans in 1856 adopted "the doctrine of popular sovereignty,"(2) Douglas' program exactly.

In San Francisco, James Simonton, editor of the *Bulletin*, used his columns to make life miserable for Charles. He accused him of attempting to sell the Republican party to Broderick and Douglas. The *Times* responded hotly saying their paper had never expressed a word of sympathy for Douglas. It was not Douglas that editor Washburn was pursuing. Charles put a line out in hope of catching Democrats who were *anti-Lecompton* and supported Broderick. In the meantime, Douglas reversed his position and reunited with the Buchanan administration. In June, however, a truce had been concluded between the two wings of the Democratic party at the East, and Charles concluded that Douglas was backing "the slave trading Democracy," prompting editor Washburn to ask rhetorically in the columns of the *Times* what the anti-Lecomptonites in California were now going to do. Under the circumstances, he wrote, "The only thing the anti-Lecomptonites can accomplish is the defeat of the Republicans in California."(3) Washburn at that time wanted a mixed ticket of Republicans and anti-Lecompton voters in order, in his words, "to whip out the bastard and corrupt chivalry party that had so long tyrannized over the white man . . . " In characteristic manner, Charles referred to his other nemesis, Douglas, as "that ingrained demagogue . . . who is wrong by instinct; a whiffling, treacherous whiffet, a demagogue destitute of noble or generous impulses."(4) In their effort to persuade anti-Lecompton Democrats to move into their columns, California Republican leaders announced that Republicans had always favored popular sovereignty. That was far from the truth, as Charles knew, since he must have read speeches delivered by his two older brothers, Israel and Elihu.

On April 7, 1854, Israel delivered "the most important and poignant speech that he had thus far made, [and] in the large number of strong speeches made on both sides of the question . . . his was one of the most vital."(5) Israel said, if the Douglas bill were passed, the South and slave holders would say,

. . . Let it be proclaimed everywhere, that the Constitution of the United States, *proprio vigore*, carries slavery wherever the flag of the Union flies." It carries it, we shall be told, into the Territories, and neither Congress nor the local Legislatures, nor both combined, can restrain its march, for the Constitution is above both, is the supreme law of the land. Ay, and carries it into all the States . . . This, sir, is the doctrine with which we shall be vigorously pressed if this bill is carried.(6)

Near the end of July, Douglas in a letter to J.P. Doen of Dubuque, Iowa, announced that he would not let himself be nominated *unless the party re-affirms the Kansas-Nebraska Act of 1854.* Douglas had switched again. Once again he was anti-administration. Charles thought the senator had dismissed the position advanced by Chief Justice Taney, and had shaken himself free of the administration and Southern political leaders.

Charles A. Washburn and Thomas Starr King worked tirelessly, Charles in composing editorials, King in speaking, both intent upon saving California for the Union and for what were considered Eastern values. The two, Washburn and King, had to contend with their Governor John P. Weller, who was saying to legislators in Sacramento that California might found a Pacific republic rather than participate in disunion with the Southern states. Washburn's *Times* between the turn of the year and the 20th of the month of January alone, carried forty editorials related to political issues which he felt Californians must consider in anticipation of the November election. Heavy campaigning continued daily for eleven months. Washburn was instrumental in organizing a Wide-Awakes Club, and in mid-October worked to bring off a mass meeting of 5,000 citizens. A few days before the election, a *Grand Torchlight Procession* of Wide-Awakes brought San Franciscans to the Music Hall for an enthusiastic meeting where orator Edward Baker spoke. Washburn presided, and received the spirited applause of the audience as he read a message from Providence, Rhode Island, women who had made a flag to be used on the occasion. The message from the Rhode Island women read to the vast audience by the *Times* editor is illustrative of the interest East coast people continued to have, as scholars have noted, in impressing West coast people with East coast values.

May it be your highest ambition to extend New England principles, as far as they accord with right.

New Englanders such as Oliver Wendell Holmes and James Russell Lowell, essential Bostonians, illustrate their parochialism, but they also epitomize the interest they have in seeing the West evangelized by the Unitarian mind set. All that Holmes claimed for Boston was that it be seen as "the thinking centre of the continent, and therefore of the planet."(7) James Russell Lowell wanted America to be faithful to what is true, so that whatever is (true) "will rise from one end of the country to the other instinctively to our side . . . " There is irony in the fact that, while the "old" America wanted to influence the growth in the territories and new states, New Englanders and people like Charles from the old colonies, stated clearly that those who had slaves should take care of that problem "without interference from any outside parties." The spirited message was to bring Federalist-Whig-Republican values westward, but not for the purpose of interfering with the barbaric values of the South! Let the South go "without interference . . . "

Charles was feted by "Uncle Abe's Choir" and band as crowds present at the Music Hall marched to his home to serenade him. Two editorials in the *San Francisco Daily Times* published the day before the crucial election turn out to be revealing commentaries on issues and on the author himself with his countless discursive articles poured forth in profusion from the time Charles and Alvan Flanders took over the San Francisco publication . The Saturday editorial summarized the argument made by Chivalrics: Union or disunion to be decided Tuesday. If Mr. Lincoln is elected the South will secede. Sectional pro-slavery candidates must be elected. To that argument the *Times* response was: The Republican cause is just, based on a godlike sentiment, love towards all mankind. Following this preachy statement is the adage of English social philosopher, Jeremy Bentham, invoked to represent the sentiment of the patriot: "The greatest good to the greatest number." The editorial announced that the Republican party would rescue the government from the debauched and profligate crowd who have disgraced the country. And finally, there is the to-be-expected customary assurance, in this case, given by an uncertain advocate, that "we shall win." Another editorial in the same issue declares that Chivalrics are "Hessians." Still ripe in the memory of Americans were the hated soldiers from Germany with "their savage, cowardly and treacherous natures," bought and paid for by the British to fight American patriots. In the editorial, Washburn claims that the modern-day Hessian is also a hireling who will fight for the side which pays. He is a "cross between the puppy dog and the jackass." The modern Hessian "fattens upon the blood of the beautiful and young." As if this character sketch were not enough, almost humorous with its overblown rhetoric, the writer adds that the Hessian is "low, lean and scrawny. He has a shambling, shuffling gate. He is stiff-kneed, spindled-shanked and hunchback," he "hisses with his barbed tongue." Washburn's violent language mirrors the image of a linguist easy with words, who presumed his picturesque language would be a mighty weapon sufficient to put a rod in the backbone of the undecided. But the language suggests his own uncertainty, like a teenager searching the thesaurus for adjectives with which to strangle the adversary. Such language, later placed on the desk and read by the more tolerant Lincoln, might have induced the president to make Washburn wait impatiently in the capital for an appointment. For three months hot-headed Charles was to wait, using strong words and with unfortunate sarcasm never realizing he was "cooking his own goose."

Chapter Twenty-Three

JOBLESS FOR SIX MONTHS

In California in 1861 Republicans won a surprising victory in part due to the

William H. Seward

vigorous campaign undertaken by Charles Ames Washburn. Perhaps, therefore, there was a reward for *Times* editor Washburn? There was instead a turn of events which filled the *Times* editor with bitterness. In the last weeks of his residence in the West, Charles had reason to skim the critical events he would remember when he made his way back East to the nation's capital. In correspondence with one of his brothers, he underscored one of those events. He wrote that he had been fighting the battle on the West Coast and was "among the first to take up the cudgel in defense of free speech and republican ideas."(1)

That was one proud factor. Another was that there were more than a thousand editorials in the *Times* featuring the decisive political issues of 1859-1860:

--Railroads,

--Elections of federal and state senators and representatives,

--The founding of the Republican party in the state,

--Slavery, the Gordian Knot of politics, as Charles named it,

--There had been vigorous consideration of Stephen A. Douglas whose campaign was a threat to the success of the Republican party in 1861,

--There was Washburn's involvement after
the death of his friend, Broderick,

--There was his unsuccessful attempt to join three of his brothers in Congress,

--The discovery of gold and silver,

--The irrepressible conflict.

Charles would have remembered that his candidate for nomination before the Chicago convention was William Seward, not Lincoln, and that his second and third choices were, not Old Abe, but Nathaniel Banks and William Pitt Fessenden. Charles had reason to keep in mind also what he had told his brother, Cadwallader, in a letter dated August 1860, that when he returned to California in 1858 "the Republican party did not exist" and that there would hardly have been an organization if he had not come back.(2) These are a few of the hot issues Washburn had tackled and would not forget as he crossed back over the plains and prairies, heading for Washington. Despite his organizing efforts and his large and generous expenditure of energy, prospects for well-deserved rewards were thwarted. In San Francisco he received a gold watch and a gold headed cane. The cane he gave to his father. As for what he would receive as appointments, these were to be made in quite a different manner. When there was reasonable certainty that the Republicans were in control of the White House there arose in California bitter in-fighting among party members seeking patronage. As Charles indicated there was "petty, nasty jealousy." For a long time Washburn had his eye on one position, the Collectorship at the port of San Francisco. His antagonist, B.F. Washington, held the post and Washington let it be known that if the President appointed Washburn, he would arrive in the capital prepared to fight the appointment in the Senate.

While still in California, Charles had gauged shrewdly the ins-and-outs of the political shenanigans during the crucial two-year period while the Republican party was being re-built. He was subjected to ridicule by purists as he "made a play" for the Douglas men in the state. He knew how powerful the Douglas voting bloc was, confirmed at election time when Lincoln's win over Douglas numbered as few as 737 votes. Washburn's many editorials argued that Douglas' followers in California had no chance of winning, in consequence of which, he declared, Douglasites voting for the Douglas ticket were casting votes for the Democrat-Chivalric party. Washburn's barrage of editorials, if they turned but a few hundred

Stephen Douglas

Douglas followers to join Republicans as fellow anti-Lecomptonites, the *Times* could then be credited with having a hand in saving California for Lincoln.

Back in Washington, Edward Baker, a Washburn critic, was known to be a personal friend of the President-elect. Charles supposed Baker would be the mouthpiece for powerful Golden State Republicans who did not want to see Charles in the Collector's post. J.F. Hoyt wrote Elihu Washburne from California, and in a revealing letter confirmed that there was a concerted plan to defeat "the appointment of your brother . . . to that office."(3) Hoyt also indicated that Charles Fremont was one of Washburn's political antagonists. Later, Editor Washburn pointed out to Elihu that he had satisfactorily blocked that avenue of opposition. He knew Fremont wanted to be appointed Minister to France, and Charles let Fremont know that if he supported his California opponents "there would be hell to pay." He implied, no doubt, that Charles could count on his brothers' opposition in Congress when Fremont set out to obtain the desired post.(4) Hoyt let Elihu know that he had looked over the electorate and he felt that "your brother's appointment will prove generally acceptable."(5)

The witch's brew stirred by Washburn when he left California to report in Washington as an Elector, found him unable to "shape the politics of the State."(6) There were signs of his ineptitude. One was that while still in San Francisco, he had been powerless to gain entrance to the State Central Committee as a member. He accused the committee of having "too much power and influence." An opposition had won a behind-the-scene battle waged from the beginning to keep the *Times* editor off the Central Committee. Arriving in New York in January, Charles wrote in a jubilant mood saying he was in tiptop health, and that he was "in [good] condition to take a hand in the irrepressible conflict." A few weeks later Charles sat in his Fifth Avenue hotel writing again to Elihu. In his lengthy letter he explained in detail the political picture in California as Charles understood it from the inside and historically. He claimed he had things his own way before he left for the East. He insisted that he had been "the popular man of the party." He made it clear in his February letter that he would be willing to accept the post of Governor of the Washington Territory, or an appointment as Minister to Chile, if he could not obtain the Collectorship. Asserting on the one hand that he was in control while still in California, and making concessions on the other hand, suggests Charles' naivete about his own role, or else that in his letter there was a need on his part to impress his older, and certainly more powerful, brother.

In a spring letter written to Elihu, the suppressed anger which lay in Charles

James Watson Webb

came to the surface. He complained that the war took all of Lincoln's attention, and that no attention was paid to office-seekers. He was sure the President had a grudge, not only against him but against the powerful Washburns, including the gracious Israel, loved by so many. Israel told Charles that Lincoln had snubbed him twice. The office-seeking Washburn felt Seward was a friend, but even Seward's friendship was doubted. Soft words by the Secretary of State are cheap, said Charles, and "it costs nothing to profess great respect for the Washburns but unless the acts correspond I shall think they lie."(7) Charles appeared

paranoiac as he waited impatiently for what he considered his well-deserved appointment. He suspected Lincoln had it in mind to put him in the front line to be slain, as David did Uriah. He then added that there was another acceptable post, the Navy Agency, one of the more lucrative positions that was open. The April epistle from Washburn began a verbal bombast which continued in a succession of letters: "Lincoln has . . . sworn against me in his heart." "Old Abe will do nothing for me." "Lincoln . . . yields to the man that bores him the most . . . he will do nothing for me." "It is idle to chase that phantom [an appointment] any farther." "Lincoln hated me," he wrote. For the time being, Charles lost his sense of humor and scuttled his sense of moral equity so conspicuous in his editorials. For the moment, he classed his Republican president as easily as he did General Sherman whom he called "an ass," and General Halleck whom he called "a scoundrel," referring to his political enemies as "the sweepings of hell." And he said of the president that he was "an old fool." There were moody moments of fluff which passed into the air for nought. Charles wrote when in a more congenial attitude of "the great and good Lincoln."

During the five months when he was in Washington after the election, if Charles was not fighting for his life he was certainly fighting for his career. The Washington wait was a marking point in his life. His lively ambition continued to exceed his grasp. After being appointed commissioner to one of the lowliest countries in South America, Paraguay, he still had expectations of being appointed Ambassador to a more important country. The appointment to Paraguay having been made, Gideon Welles wrote in his diary, "Seward repeated a remark heretofore made that the [Paraguay] mission disposed of one of the troublesome family of Washburns who are now all provided for."

It might seem to have taken the onus off Charles by his having claimed that Lincoln had a "grudge against the Washburns." That was not the case. A

Schuyler Colfax

prestigious Washburn appointment was made when William D. Washburn was given the office of Surveyor General for the State of Minnesota. In addition, Lincoln made it known that his interest was in having Elihu made Speaker of the House rather than Schuyler Colfax.

June 13, 1861, Charles Washburn was commissioned.(8) July 27, with diplomatic instructions in hand, he left the United States and by indirect route made his way to the Plata. Before leaving New York Charles posted a letter to Elihu.(9) He wrote about his visit with the Rhode Island Company, a company expecting him to persuade Lopez to pay $500,000 which the American fleet "failed to get."(10)

A few days earlier, on July 21st, the "disgraceful stampede"(11) at Bull Run had turned up a few heroes at least, one of whom was Elihu Washburne. We remember that Washburne had stood in the road at Bull Run trying to turn back fleeing Union soldiers. In his letter of the 27th, Charles wrote he was "glad to see you stood your ground at Manassas."(12) As soon as Charles arrived in Paris, France, he got off another letter to Elihu,(13) explaining that, fortuitously, he had met James Watson Webb who, like Washburn, had been editor and proprietor of a newspaper, and like Washburn, was on his way to be Minister to a South American country. In Webb's case, he was to be Minister to the Empire of Brazil adjacent to Paraguay. Like Washburn, Webb was self-righteous, always certain of what is right and ready to fight. It was General Webb who gave the name of "whig" to the party organized to oppose the Democratic party. Charles wrote deferentially of Webb, referring to him as "the old fellow" who, he wrote, was very cordial appearing to be glad at the prospect of having in Paraguay, himself, Washburn, "the distinguished Minister to the Court of his high mightiness, Commander Lopez."(14) In Paris, Charles met Anson Burlingame whom he admired. Perhaps Burlingame was respected by Charles in part because, like Charles, he had accepted a challenge to duel with a Southerner, Preston Brooks, who had so mercilessly thrashed Senator Charles Sumner. Washburn referred to Burlingame as "a great man, a very great man."(15) He was on his way to China, appointed Minister to that country by Lincoln. In Paris also was an old California friend, Buffum, one time reporter for the *Alta*, a newspaper edited by Washburn. The two felt fortunate to be in Paris on the great fete day of the year when fireworks, unlike any Charles had ever seen, were fired off all over the city. He expected never to see the likes of it again.

The otherwise moody Washburn was feeling cheerful when he wrote his letter from Paris. His writing style and his somewhat forced humor revealed a pleasing temperament and probably gratified Elihu that Charles, about to take off for the wilds more wild than the West in the U.S., was, of course, entirely innocent of what awaited him.

Chapter Twenty-Four

OFF TO PARADISE LOST

After four months of presidential procrastination, Charles Ames Washburn received an appointment. He was "delivered up" to be a victim of one of Latin

President Buchanan

America's hostile dictators in a country where two predecessors held forth for fifty years, José Gaspar Rodriguez Francia and Carlos Antonio Lopez, and where a successor even more brutal, Francisco Solano López, held the office of President during Washburn's entire term. It was not Lincoln's intention to place his Commissioner's life in jeopardy but it seemed to Charles that was the exact design of Lincoln. Charles did not intend that Lincoln should "serve me as David did Uriah, [putting me in] the front ranks."(1) But Lincoln did. After eight years in beautiful, ill-fated Paraguay, Washburn was interviewed by the *Philadelphia Press*. He explained to a reporter that in 1861 he felt the President had a grudge against the Washburns. In that 1879 interview his earlier suspicions were rekindled when a reporter said it seemed strange for Mr. Lincoln to have sent Charles so far away when his brother, Elihu, was a leading Congressman from the president's own state, noting that his brother Elihu had helped put Lincoln in office. Charles said that Elihu was not on good terms with the Commander-in-Chief. The entire Illinois delegation had pressed Lincoln to appoint J. Russell Jones U.S. Marshall, a man preferred by Elihu. Jones, however, was not the President's choice.(2) Charles' memory did not serve him well during the *Philadelphia Press* interview. He forgot he had written Elihu telling Elihu he "must manage" Lincoln.(3) That sentence would not have been written if Charles had known, as he would have known, that the two were mutually antagonistic. The contrary was true with regard to his brother and Lincoln. As has been noted, the President in fact had said he preferred Elihu to Schuyler Colfax as Speaker of the House.

❖

Lowly as was the position of Commissioner, the State Department expected the spurned Washburn to "manifest to the authorities and people of Paraguay, the unaffected friendship and sincere sympathy of this government towards them. "(4) Characteristic of the Washburn brothers, Charles intended to excel at his post. Before leaving the country for the post, he requested of the Department a "minute analysis"(5) of U.S. relations with Paraguay. Secretary Seward excused himself from the task of preparing such a report, pleading lack of time, leaving Washburn to seek out relevant information on his own. Since the Department of State charged Commissioner Washburn with exacting from the Paraguayan government money owed to the Navigation Company, Washburn made a trip to Rhode Island, the headquarters of the American company, thinking this effort would pay off later in Paraguay. In the meantime, the trip to Rhode Island resulted in the State Department docking part of Charles' pay for taking time to make the trip.

As editor of the *Daily Times* in San Francisco Charles had kept himself informed about United States-Paraguayan policies, and in this he was unusual. Gilbert Phelps indicates that to most Europeans and North Americans Paraguay was an unknown republic.(6) Not so for Charles. He had always been ready to find weaknesses in Buchanan policies, and one of the most egregious was sending twenty-three ships to the La Plata region in South America for the purpose of recovering money owed to the American company. Washburn knew about the whole escapade, and knowledgeable editor that he was, he accused Buchanan of "bullying Paraguay."(7) Ironically, with the change of administrations Charles learned from Secretary of State Seward that Lincoln shared Buchanan's views on the touchy issue of the Navigation Company and the Paraguayan government. Had the new Commissioner, Charles, been consistent he would have declared that the Republican president also was "bullying Paraguay."

❖

Washburn left New York for Liverpool on the 27th of July 1861, arriving in London August 9th the day the Mail Packet sailed out of Southampton for Rio de Janeiro. Commissioner Washburn reluctantly remained two days in England, a country for which he bore no great respect. Two months earlier the British government proclaimed the Confederacy in the United States to be a belligerent state knowing the U.S. considered southern states to be insurrectionary. For this performance by the British, John Bull, said Washburn, "must pay."(8) Charles left for France. Antipathy he felt for England he felt for France as well. He made little headway going from one country to another in his aggravation. In France, Emperor Napoleon was making a play for control of Mexico, considered to be within the sphere of U.S. interests. In Paris, Charles roamed the city where his brother, Minister Plenipotentiary E.B. Washburne, would be living following Charles' eight years as Commissioner and Minister to Paraguay. Commissioner Washburn took passage for the La Plata River and in mid-October 1861 he arrived at Buenos Aires. A United States Naval ship took the Commissioner up river to Asunciòn.

❖

Charles hoped to be able at last to take control of events in his life which he was doing as he glided comfortably up river toward Asunciòn aboard the U.S. gunboat *Pulaski*. As reporter and editor, Washburn was a practiced and alert spectator carefully recording his observations. Later he was able to quote from the journal he kept, not needing to edit or change his notes, printing straight from the journal. As the *Pulaski* made its way past riverside communities advancing through parts of Uruguay and Argentina, he recorded what he learned about the lay of the land, the politics of the three countries surrounding land-locked Paraguay, taking notes on the culture, climate, religion, and daily affairs of people in the region. It would be useful for him to know the chief rivers of the country he was to serve, the Paraná and Paraguay. The two rivers hugged the small country between them, the Paraguay on the west, Paraná on the east. He wrote descriptions of the eastern and southern parts of Paraguay's wilderness, its vast jungles, its swamps and lagoons where weeds, swamp-grass, and bamboo grew profusely.

The Naval ship *Pulaski* passed San Antonio, twelve miles below Asuncion. He identified San Antonio as the location of the American Navigation Company whose works had been taken over by Carlos López' government without compensation. As the *Pulaski* plowed the still waters of the Paraguay going north Charles noticed the countryside was so flat that a 300 foot hill, Lambaré, looked like a mountain and was referred to as a mountain. Above Lambaré the Paraguay River turned sharply eastward. The ship passed beneath a bluff and quieted its motors leaving the vessel rocking quietly in a basin of deep water. Straight ahead, the Commissioner gazed upon Asunciòn, the town where his unhappy fate was yet be decided. Asunción was the leading community in Paraguay with a population of less than twenty thousand people. Charles noticed that most of the population in the town seemed to have disappeared as the ship dropped anchor. The dignified Commissioner was lowered into a row boat which moved slowly toward shore. He could see government buildings and what he took to be the Lopez family residences. The church was prominent surrounded by a wide swath of grass where goats were nibbling away keeping the grass short. Unpaved streets wound around the houses, the church, and

The Plaza Or Market-Place of Asuncion

a plaza. The city, stretching eastward into the country, was surrounded by a scattering of humble huts. When he was ashore, Charles a proven Puritan took note of the Guaraní and mestizo females lightly-clothed with their "full bust, roundly-turned arms, small hands, and smaller feet, short petticoat, embroidered tepoi, braided hair, and black eyes . . . "(9) For sale at the plaza the commissioner would learn was chipa, chickens, eggs, mandioca, maize, oranges, melons, wood, molasses and other wares. Donkeys which had hauled carts bringing produce to the plaza were untied and roamed at will through the village.

Asuncion as well as the country was governed by one man, Carlos Antonio López. Weighed atop the enormously corpulent body of López was a large casaba-like head with a few strings of hair patted down across the top, "with chops flapping over his cravat," as Richard Burton wrote. One must think the man lived but to eat. His heavy figure did not detract from skills he possessed as protector of the interests of Paraguay, and in controlling the people in Asuncion and beyond. He had such absolute control of the city and its inhabitants that he could expect at the end of any day to hear about any untoward remarks exchanged at the market-place, and he would know who made the remarks. Dictator Lopez had a cabinet of ministers but cabinet members were mere clerks spying on each other as well as upon folk of the village.

❖

The first official to meet and make himself known to Washburn was Jesuit-trained Vice President Francisco Sánchez, a man in his sixties who had served dictator Francia, and was continuing in the service of the López father and later the son. Sánchez read and wrote letters for the elderly dictator. As minister for foreign relations, he was addressed as *Your Excellency* by Consuls and Ministers. López objected since he as head of State also must be addressed as *Your Excellency*. Sánchez asked an English minister to address him by a less distinguished title. The English minister had to explain protocol to López and the dictator then had to agree,

that Sánchez must indeed be addressed as *Your Excellency*, but, said López to the Minister, "Call him *Excellency*, if you like; he is only a beast."(10)

Another among the notables in Asuncion Washburn would meet was José Berges. Berges' earned a reputation as a Paraguayan Commissioner, highly respected in the United States for work done on the American Navigation Company issue. Six years before Charles' arrival, Señor Berges had been sent to Rio by the elder López for the purpose of negotiating with the Brazilian government on behalf of his country. The sole access to Brazil's Matto Grosso at the northern extreme of Paraguay was by way of the Paraguay river. Brazil was prepared to use force to extract from Carlos López a treaty acknowledging the right of Brazil to traverse the distance past fortified Humaita, past Asunciòn and beyond the cluster of towns to the north. After his successes, Berges was wary about returning to Asuncion. It was feared López might do away with him as a threatening rival.

José Gaspar de Francia

❖

In the Central Square at Asunciòn was the Roman Catholic cathedral. At the center of all the towns rising above the thousand mile Paraguay river were crudely constructed adobe churches where rituals were performed for the benefit of natives. José Francia had set the stage for three generations of unbelievers who were to rule. The church was despised by the dictator though he had himself studied for holy orders and had a Doctor of Theology degree. Francia pronounced his opinion of the ritual of Mass proclaiming, "Pan Pan. Vino Vino; Bread is Bread and Wine is Wine," an entirely humanistic statement which must have impressed the English writer, Thomas Carlyle.(11) The scandalous lives of priests did not turn the dictator against the denomination. He himself fathered children by many women without benefit of clergy. His appreciation of Frenchmen Voltaire and Rousseau explains his abhorrence of organized religion. Francia's successors had little regard for the church, even though, as Washburn discovered, the dictators permitted the churches numerous celebrations and Carlos is said to have attended celebrative ceremonies. As for heretic Francia, he made himself Head of the Church, and treated the denomination's bishop as a subordinate. To keep control of power latent in the church and priesthood, Carlos made his brother León Basilio bishop.

Francia set the example as an inhuman dictator. His successors outstripped him, the thieving Carlos, and the fierce Francisco. José Francia's "Chamber of Truth" held persons in prison, flogging and then starving them until they confessed what Francia wanted to hear, whereupon he allowed his prisoners "a more speedy termination of his sufferings."(12) The United States government did not recognize Paraguayan independence because officials in Washington "were loath to attempt opening relations with Dictator Francia."(13)

It is necessary to grant that Washburn whose views are reflected in this report of Paraguayan personalities was prejudiced due to the treatment he received dating from the period when Lopez moved the capital to Luque, emptying Asuncion of all but a few officers, and Washburn, who absolutely refused to move his legation from the city to the temporary capital. From that period until he left Paraguay under duress the American minister was a subject of continued suspicion.

❖

Fourteen days after Commissioner Washburn disembarked at Asuncion he was granted an audience by Dictator Carlos Antonio López. It was a critical meeting and Charles promptly reported the result to Secretary Seward. He considered it to be of some importance that the President greeted him with his hat off. That was counted "a courtesy not always extended to the representatives of other governments."(14) Following the formalities, López proceeded to rail against the agent of the American Navigation Company, E.A. Hopkins, telling Washburn of Hopkin's personal insults. He said that a native Paraguayan attacked Hopkins' younger brother, Clement, for having frightened his cattle. Hopkins, said the President, rushed to his office angrily demanding redress. Through an interpreter,

Carlos Antonio López

President Lopez told Commissioner Washburn about the subsequent expulsion of agent Hopkins. He reminded Charles of the threats made by the U.S. government at the time. Buchanan had spent a million dollars on a fleet of ships sent off to the La Plata region demanding that restitution be made to the Navigation Company.

Charles had the disagreeable duty of reporting to President Lopez that there was a Buchanan-Lincoln decision nullifying the decision made by a U.S.-Paraguay

Commission which had been charged with determining who had been right, the Paraguayan government or the claims of the Rhode Island company. Lòpez said to Washburn that he wanted from him as Commissioner the latest official instructions from the states so that he could determine "whether my relations with the United States are amicable or otherwise."(15) The parting message of the dictator to Charles was that, unless there was a satisfactory resolution of the Navigation Company's affair, he, Washburn, as representative of the U.S. government, "might be notified that it was time . . . to leave the country."(16) As Charles closed his report to Secretary Seward, Washburn observed that after the encounter with the Paraguayan President he realized he had an opponent "of no ordinary shrewdness and capacity . . . "(17) Washburn was able to report to Seward that President Lòpez feared Paraguay's neighbor to the north, Brazil, where, it should be said, another troublesome representative from the states, J. Watson Webb, was becoming a problem for the Department of State.

Charles expressed it as his private opinion that there was prejudice against Americans in the country. Where the President's possible prejudice was concerned, Washburn may well have mistaken the disgruntlement expressed about him as Commissioner for prejudice toward Americans. The American's manner of presenting himself was also known to be overbearing.

Washburn was confronted with an unfortunate incident involving the American Consul Louis Bamberger. Bamberger was considered even by natives in Paraguay to be a disgrace to his country. Charles was told about an affair involving the Consul's misuse of the American flag. Consul Bamberger had accepted $800. for permitting the American flag's use on a ship plying the river. He was promptly condemned by the Commissioner and returned to the states.

This November narrative from the American legation in Asunción was the first in a series of reports, often of inordinate length, sent by Washburn to Washington. The record of events which unfolded in Paraguay, together with Charles' careful reporting became an important part of the history of diplomatic relations which to this day provoke debate among historians about the wisdom or folly of Charles Ames Washburn as Minister Resident. It is of course wholly coincidental that Charles, following his eight-year stint in war ravaged Paraguay, was matched with an eight-year career of his brother, Elihu, Resident Minister to France during the reign of the war weary and vexatious Napoleon III of France and the Franco-Prussian war.

Chapter Twenty-Five

WORK BEGINS

Paraguay had a remarkable number of passive people in the population. There were few South American nations with such a peace-oriented citizenry. Government functionaries in the country on the other hand were seldom passive. In earlier centuries the natives in Paraguay were said to have been "of exceeding gentleness and hospitality." With the arrival of Jesuits and over a period of a century and a half following, the character of the natives in Paraguay was imperceptibly changed. The prevailing power of the Catholic denomination succeeded in transforming the Guaranis into a submissive population. Washburn likened the dominance of the Jesuits to slave holders in the American South, like Southerners, boasting "of the happiness of their slaves, their piety, and their love toward themselves."(1) Feelings of responsibility and individuality were emasculated in the native population. The people, Washburn writes, eventually "became the willing forgers of their own

José Gaspar de Francia

fetters," having been made serfs by the Jesuits,(2) and ready pickings, therefore, for tyrants José Francia, Carlos Lopez and Carlos' son, Francisco "the monster," as characterized by Ambassador Washburn, all of whom ruled mercilessly. Tyrants Francia, Carlos and Francisco were the virtual history of the nation of Paraguay for more than fifty years.(3) To fifty years of tyranny by the three dictators must be added those one hundred and fifty years of domination by a religious order with the consequent loss of dignity, spirit and initiative on the part of the population. What the country lacked for two hundred years was intelligent, humane leadership.

José Francia, the first of the tyrants and the first El Supremo, so successfully repressed and mesmerized the population that after twenty-six years of rule Francia's own death was doubted. For a time the people remained so fearful of his wizardry that they believed he would magically return from the grave to punish them. Dr. Don Pedro Somellera, author of the revolution in Paraguay, wrote of Francia that he did not appear to be "a man belonging to the human race . . . "(4) Henry Lyon Young wrote that Francia "once having tasted power . . . became voracious for more and would not be satisfied until he had made himself absolute."(5) The Dictator rode through the streets of Asunción dressed in black, on a black horse with black velvet reins. The people prostrated themselves on the ground as he passed. Francia was intent upon abolishing marriage. Not succeeding in that undertaking, he made prostitution a respectable profession, seeing to it that golden combs were worn by ladies of easy virtue to indicate their occupation. Washburn gave his estimate of Francia in a lecture delivered in California in the 1870s, disputing the claims of Thomas Carlyle. Carlyle had made the dictator a Hero of wonderful ability and exalted Patriotism. "Throughout the nations of South America," wrote Charles, "[Francia] is regarded as the worst being who had ever been produced on the American continent *previous to the advent of the younger Lopez."*

Dictator Carlos Lopez, father of "the monster," is referred to by Washburn as "the most absolute despot on the face of the earth."(6) He could, said Washburn, "appoint and remove civil, military, and political employees"; "he could exercise the patronage of the churches, the livings, and ecclesiastical persons according to the laws; he could name the bishops and the members of the ecclesiastical senate . . . "(7) Shortly after Francia's death, Lopez called the congress together and arranged for himself to be elected president for ten years. In ten years he had himself re-elected. In the twenty year period of Lopez' reign, no member of Congress voted contrary to the wish of the dictator.

Carlos Lopez had been in office twenty years when Washburn first appeared before him with his credentials from the Department of State. Following the first session with President Lopez, Washburn in his report to Secretary Seward noted that the portly president had removed his hat in his presence. Lopez had made it a law that all males must own hats so hats might be removed when citizens were in his presence. In this case, the government lifted his own hat, which to Washburn was a promising sign meaning respect for his country. The central issue on the agenda at the first meeting with the second El Supremo was, not trade and good relations, as Secretary of State William Seward had hoped would be the case. Instead, on the agenda was the status of the Paraguay Navigation Company. As explained earlier, President Lopez made clear to Washburn that demands made by the United States regarding what the Company's required must be expunged, or he, Lopez, would ask Washburn to leave the country.

Carlos Antonio Lopez was "a man of extreme corpulency--'with chops flapping over his cravat' Burton says . . ."(8) He married into a wealthy family his young wife carrying another's child. The first of their several children, therefore, Francisco Solano, was not the dictator's blood relative. Nonetheless, in a few years Don Carlos began to see Francisco as his successor. He was, it was thought, educating his son when he sent young Francisco to France to learn the ways of the Napoleons. Francisco returned from France, cleverly positioned himself in office after his father's death and continued the tradition of his cruel predecessors, increasing the terror, and laying upon the Paraguayan population one of the most ruinous wars in the history of South America. Charles wrote his brother Elihu saying President Carlos Lopez was a despot, but added, "he had many good points."(9) The dictator took an interest in the well-being of his people, constructing schools, building a railroad, and opening the country to the outside world. In 1842 he freed the slaves in Paraguay, proclaiming "all men are equal before God and me." Improvements brought about by Lopez at last brought England, France and the United States to recognize Paraguay as an independent state with an exchange of Ministers. It was six years, however, before the U.S. ratified the treaty recognizing the countries' independence, and Washburn became the first official representative from the country to the North.

Don Carlos was not all kindness, nor was he seen in that light by the citizenry of Paraguay. Everyone knew the story of the angry man who tore up and trampled on an official paper with the likeness of Lopez printed on the document. The man was shot and killed for stamping on the president's effigy. On another occasion the president arranged for the arrest of several citizens among whom was an Englishman named Santiago Canstatt. The British Minister at Buenos Aires, Edward Thornton, demanded Canstatt's release. When Lopez refused to free his prisoner, Thornton had Commander-in-Chief Admiral Lushington of the South Atlanta fleet, send two British men-of-war to seize the Paraguayan ship *Tacuari*, carrying Don Carlos' son, Francisco. Thornton held young Lopez hostage for the life of Santiago Canstatt. The Paraguayan government had to pay a heavy fine, but dictator President Lopez arranged for the amount to be kept secret.

Washburn, as he prepared to appear before the President, anticipated Carlos' displeasure. A few years earlier the government, flouting international law, fired upon a United States ship, the Water Witch, killing a U.S. citizen. The result was that the South Atlantic Squadron Commander W.D. Salter was requested to send a warship to Asunción to exact redress and an apology. Unlike British Admiral Lushington, Salter believed his instructions must come from the Navy Department in Washington. The effect of the failure of the Navy to act, provoked Ambassador Washburn to write with a twinge of sarcasm that the U.S. flagship in the South Atlantic Squadron had been turned into a "pleasure yacht."(10) Carlos Lopez had not forgotten the fall-out effects of the affair and the $10,000 he was required to pay.

Charles anticipated difficulties because of the incident involving the Paraguay Navigation Company. That issue was central to a series of meetings and communications carried on between Washburn, Lopez and Foreign Minister Sanchez until the President died. Washburn had the duty of reminding both parties about the details of the events which had placed the Navigation Company issue on . his agenda. A Commission, Charles reminded the Foreign Minister,(11) had been assigned the duty of "agreeing on the amount of the reclamations to which the [Navigation Company] may be entitled," but the Commission assumed the power to decide another question. Now, explained Washburn, both Presidents Buchanan and Lincoln were unwilling to accept the Commission's recommendations, leaving Paraguay still in debt to the American Company. The problem was a canker, continuing to bother Washburn to the point where he told Elihu his having to keep the matter alive had "exposed [Lopez] to war with the U.S. because of the Rhode Island matter."(12)

THE ENCOUNTER

Commissioner Washburn, wanting to be known as a Californian was still a prototypical New Englander; "the placid American of the North" said Henry Lyon Young as he compared a New Englander with "the highly excitable Americans of the South."(13) The tone had long been set for the entrance onto the scene of a man who was representative of the North American culture, staid, righteous, judgmental, protective of self and reputation "the quiet American" of the period, --loyal, patriotic, individualistic, demonstrating the demeanor R.W. Emerson celebrated in the New Man of the New Continent. Washburn was Santayana's *Last Puritan*; last in that there was soon to be a change with the changing of the centuries. In the previous decade of the '50's this Washburn had "become a man" at a late age in his life. As his brother Israel was to say, "he was a little less enterprising than the [other brothers]" until he found his way to California. There, the rough life of the miner, his struggle to find a place in the newspaper profession, and his entrance into the sometimes violent world of American politics, matured Washburn. The ways of men and women in California did not abate his feelings of moral superiority, however.

In his maturity, such as it was, he lost none of the self-righteousness, the imposing dignity, or the annoying declarations of right and wrong. These were very much a part of his make-up as he made his hegira southward to Paraguay.

Being made ready for the confrontation was the representative man of another culture, young General Francisco Solano, small, thickset with bandy legs, not prepossessing, but having a handsome profile reminiscent, it has been said, of the Prince of Wales.(14) In the 1850s he had been sent off to England and the continent. In England he experienced for the first time the shock of being dismissed as vulnerable and inferior. He was to be honored with a visit with the queen. Instead, when he appeared at her residence he was told Queen Victoria was "not at home." After that humiliation Francisco used his influence to punish the British. He canceled the order placed with British industry for the construction of two battleships and put the plans into the hands of U.S. industry. In France, Lopez was sure he would be received by the head of state, Napoleon III. He had two things he was looking forward to, one was an interest in meeting Napoleon. Secondly, he anticipated that Juan Jose Brizuela, his aide, would locate a woman who would be his companion while he was in Paris. Brizuela found for him a beautiful sixteen-year-old, golden haired Irish *femme fatale*, Eliza Lynch, born of a proud family of the landed aristocracy, but an aristocracy lacking land. The family was suffering through the Irish famine of 1845, when for lack of food in the country, there were Irish peasants who had to eat a mixture of their own excrement and cabbage leaves. When fourteen, Eliza was taken with the family to live in France where she was introduced to a veterinary surgeon whom she chose to marry. The French refused to marry an underage child, and the determined Eliza returned to England where she and Dr. Quatrefages were married. She lived in England two years, bored with her marriage to the doctor, returning to France alone. At age sixteen, rather than starve, she sold herself, and was soon living in an opulent apartment. Her chief concern was to find a rich foreigner to care for her. Lopez's Charge d'Affairs brought the fair skinned, golden haired teenager to Gare du Nord for Francisco to meet as he stepped off the train. She welcomed the president's son to Paris.

Elisa Lynch

Francisco López

The emperor and empress were having marriage problems. Napoleon III was carrying on an affair with an English woman, Harriet Howard. The empress went into a deep depression. The imperial Eugénie de Montijo, noted for her beautiful hair and flawless complexion, gave the appearance of thinking herself superior, looking for all the world as if she were wearied of everyone around her. Eugénie may have learned what mistress Howard said of her, that she was "beautiful, boring and barren," enough to bring on, if not depression, melancholia.

General Lopez was to be received by the dazzling if troubled emperor and empress. In preparation for the celebrated meeting, Lopez had himself fitted for a uniform which he designed. His customary attire consisted of a grotesque costume peculiar to savages in Paraguay. In the Parisian design his uniform included gold lace, epaulettes, and royal insignia. He soon came to be known as the first of South American Generals called "Rastaquoéves," --strong men. Young Lopez was conducted through a series of rooms to a chamber where Napoleon stood behind a desk to receive him, accompanied by Eugénie who spoke to the Paraguayan in her native Spanish. Francisco kissed the hand of the empress, proffered gifts from the president of Paraguay, and was himself kissed on both cheeks by Napoleon. Francisco Solano aspired to be the Napoleon of the New World. Commissioner Washburn was going to worry about that ambition of young Lopez.

Two nights after the ecstatic experience of meeting Napoleon, Lopez, attired in his glittering uniform, left an artist's studio where he had been sitting for his portrait.

He went directly to visit the salon where he would meet again the tall, golden haired, blue-eyed teenager, Eliza. This young woman was fully as beautiful as the Empress Eugénie or Napoleon's consort, Miss Harriet. Not known to the Irish teenager, of course, was that this prince-like young officer from Asuncion did not have a good reputation with women. In Paraguay, he had fallen in love with a belle of Asuncion, Carmelita, who was known to be engaged to Don Carlos Decoud. Lopez's proposition to Carmelita was spurned resulting in the arrest and execution of her fiancé, Decoud. The naked body of Carmelita's lover was thrown into the street in front of his mother's house, and Carmelita lost her purchase on sanity, thereafter to be seen

Sallie Washburn

by the public kneeling before a wayside shrine outside the capital.(15)

Eliza was wise to the ways of the male animal, but trusting the future would be good for her she submitted to his blandishments, consented to be his lover and returned with him to Asuncion, already expectant with the prince's child. The reception of the teenage blond by the townspeople at Asuncion, unaccustomed as the natives were to yellow hair, was as though people were looking upon a goddess. Eliza, beautiful in her flowing white attire, was to them an angel, the way the fair-haired English seemed to swarthy Italians when they made their way to the British Isle and first saw those some they straightway called Anglos, angels.

To the Lopez family members, Eliza was an intruder. President Carlos and Francisco's mother were cold to her. His mother declared she would never accept Mrs. Lynch. The English community's wives and others offended her, unwilling to invite her to tea, and refusing to pay obeisance at official parties. When Washburn's wife came to Asuncion, she declined to entertain Eliza at the legation. As for Sallie, Eliza referred to her as a "dull little woman." On one social occasion Mrs. Lynch spurned high society ladies saying,

"It shall be written in my memoirs that I refused to serve cats at my table."

Washburn and Lopez were friendly with one another at the beginning of their relationship, even while the arrogant American and the equally arrogant Paraguayan Chief-of-State sparred. Charles had been prepared for Francisco by having to deal as commissioner with his father, Carlos. In the fashion of the prototypical New Englander, Washburn learned about Carlos' "utter disregard for truth and common honesty."(16) The New Englander had been disturbed to find that Carlos tried to monopolize profitable trade, he taxed the people without justice, and that he kept an immense army. The American learned, of course, that under the reign of Carlos, citizens in Paraguay could not discuss the government. Neither could they leave the country without the president's permission. In a letter to his brother, Elihu, Charles with growing discouragement, expressed his wish to be minister to another country, Argentina, unlike Paraguay, he wrote, "where no one dares speak what he thinks."(17) From childhood days Charles had known about government working for the people. He knew about the freedom to disagree. Though poverty-stricken when the Washburn sons and daughters were youths, Charles knew his father and mother never lied or cheated to put food on the table. His devotion to religion came in the form of respect for persons, with loyalty to community, honoring of his father and mother.

Young Francisco on the other hand took his father's papers the moment his last breathe sighed away his life. He destroyed what plans the president had for the future of his nation, including a possible new constitution. He imprisoned persons who had been close to Carlos, including the chief justice of Paraguay, and his father priest-teacher, Padre Fidel Maiz.(18) "Of those most in his confidence . . . and who were supposed to be his personal friends, nearly all were . . . tortured and put to death by [Lopez'] orders."(19) As time passed, Francisco threatened and finally killed his own brothers, had his sisters and mother flogged. His devotion to religion was a political convenience. Padre Maiz was imprisoned to be freed only when he confessed under torture that he was part of a conspiracy, and was willing to make a public statement that,

> Francisco Solano Lopez is for me more than any other Paraguayan a true
> Father and Saviour; and for the same reason he is also for me very
> especially the only object of the new affections of my converted heart.

Lopez' lack of regard for the people of Paraguay is illustrated in the fact that only a small proportion of men, women and children were alive at the end of the war for which Francisco had been preparing from the time he was inaugurated. It is doubtful that Charles' secretary of state William Seward gave thought to the complications likely to arise in putting together men from two antipodes representing widely diverse personal, social and cultural differences such as existed between Maine's Charles and Paraguay's Francisco. In keeping with state department customs, Charles was instructed to prepare himself for transactions on behalf of business interests. Typically, therefore, his first provoking confrontation with Francisco's father had been about business. It was expected in Washington that Washburn would extract from Lopez $500,000. An increasingly unhappy Charles speculated about the possibility of recommending to Washington that the U.S. minister in residence represent both Paraguay and Uruguay. He tried out that idea on Uruguayans, and reported to Elihu that leaders in Uruguay said it would be pleasing to be represented "by the distinguished diplomat now residing in Paraguay."

❖

Washburn had occasion to disagree with Francisco short of losing his status as minister. He intervened in a dispute concerning the Brazilian minister, Vianna de Lima. In a meeting between Lopez and Washburn shortly after the incident there was a diabolic display of anger. Lopez struck his breast and said it did not matter what other people and other nations might say or think about his decision to send Vianna and his family back to Brazil through the jungle, it was what he said that was important. Charles, at this first serious collision, turned upon Lopez saying he had endeavored to manage it so no Paraguayan interest would be prejudiced, yet, he said, he was distrusted and treated with suspicion. After several more explosive remarks on his part, "not distinguished for amiability," Washburn said he left the presence of the young dictator. A more decisive encounter yet to come was predictable.

THE THRONE.—LOPEZ AND HIS CABINET.

The Throne -- López and his Cabinet

Brazilian Consul Amarro José dos Santos Barboza came to Washburn pleading with him to beg Lopez not to send passengers and the crew of the ship Marquez de Olinda into the interior of the country, but permit them to stay in the Consul's house. Charles was doubtful about obtaining such a concession, but he was able to arrange more pleasant circumstances for the Brazilian prisoners. Despite doubting at times his own abilities, he received from Secretary of State Seward a March 1, 1865, letter saying, "your assiduity, and enterprise, in collecting and preparing the valuable information concerning the disturbances existing in the Oriental Republic of Uruguay, are very satisfactory and meet my approbation."(20)

One of the first activities making for suspicion was a request in March of 1862 for permission to travel in Paraguay. Foreign Minister Sanchez refused to provide passes, prompting Charles to claim that being confined to the capital "makes me a prisoner within the narrow limits of [the] city."(21) In an official communique to the

Foreign Minister, Washburn quoted treaty arrangements regarding travel privileges in the U.S. for Paraguayan diplomats, and for diplomats of other countries who were to be granted the same privileges in Paraguay. Charles threatened to represent to the Department of State in Washington the refusal to provide passes for use by him and his servant. The previous month Charles had asked Elihu to stir the department at Washington to respond to his request to travel in Paraguay, Matto Grosso and Bolivia. In April Seward wrote, "Upon application of your brother, the Hon. E.B. Washburn [sic] . . . permission is hereby granted . . . " Commissioner Washburn was using his considerable writing talent to make an otherwise dull ministry pleasant as he prepared his now classic history of Paraguay. He felt he must travel to obtain material. Sanchez and the president relented, asking Washburn to take back his threatening letter. It was not unusual for government officials, Lopez in particular, to be suspicious, frequently asking themselves if there was an underground movement. All too soon that suspicion would balloon into a fabrication destroying Washburn's ability to function as minister resident. Indeed, if Lopez could have read Charles' correspondence with his brother he would have had reason for misgivings. Charles predicted to Elihu that sooner or later the U.S. would have to give "Lopez a rap over the knuckles" and send a gunboat to La Plata. A casual remark exhibited intense personal feelings about Lopez and conditions in Asuncion. Washburn wrote that "Naples under the Bourbons was a free Paradise compared with this place."(22)

There were rumblings suggesting President Lopez wished to turn the Republic of Paraguay into an Empire, and declare himself Emperor. It was known that Lopez greatly admired the Emperor of France. He knew of course that Napoleon had sent Maximilian to Mexico hoping Mexico might become an Empire and enter the orbit of French interests. Lopez, thought Washburn, had the idea that the creation of an empire would meet with approval in France, Mexico, Argentina and Brazil.(23) He wondered if something more must be done by him, should such a revolutionary change take place. It was customary for diplomats in *pro forma* fashion to grant recognition of *de facto* governments.(24) In line of duty, Washburn shared his apprehension about the designs of Lopez to "substitute monarchies for the Republics of South America under European patronage." Seward's chief ambition as secretary of state was to create an American empire. His vision was of a global "commercial hegemony."(25) He had thought through carefully what was happening in Mexico and in Paraguay, so he responded to Charles' concern with a rather lengthy message:

First, there is not shown anywhere on this continent a popular preparation to return to a monarchical system . . . Secondly, I think the tendency in Europe towards the Republican system is strong . . . Third, the statesmen and rulers of Europe have just now occupations . . . enough . . . (26)

The first serious confrontation between the young dictator and the American minister resident did not occur at the time Francisco had his mind set on being an emperor. And the clash did not come when Lopez began to build a great army. In fact, Charles was complicit as Lopez began his search for military hardware for army and navy. President Lopez let Washburn know he wished to see samples of munitions from the United States. The minister received from him $2400. which was promptly made available to George Woodman, Washburn's financial agent in the U.S. Charles sought advice from the Department of State and received a response approving the undertaking.(27) What would finally bring about the encounter between the two men began when Washburn saw the "'wholesale atrocities' taking place in the middle of 1868."(28) It was that which marked the beginning of the serious encounter between president and minister.

❖

Charles quoted a line of poetry in a forlorn letter written to Elihu from Asuncion.(29) He was lonely. "Far from the trusts of joy and hope, I sit and grieve alone." At age forty-two, far from home and home's companionable females, Charles realized he needed a woman. He wanted a comforter, else his brother would see a funeral at the American legation. The claim was later made that he had found a kind of companionship with an attractive local belle whom he made pregnant.(30)

Even though Charles confessed to Elihu that living alone "tends to damage one's morals," those who knew Washburn found it unlikely he had departed from family values, taking a woman without marrying her and leaving a child of his own without support. Interestingly he did not write to Elihu about prospects of finding a wife. In the heat of the summer of 1863, Charles came as close as he felt he could to inferring he had an interest in the opposite sex. He wrote guardedly that he desired to save money so he could "buy me a farm and take a wife."(31) In January of 1864 he asked his Washington brother to arrange for a leave-of-absence to attend to business "of a private nature" and "of great personal interest."

Anita and Conchita Casal

What gave added zest to Charles' life involved a woman named Sally Cleaveland. Without explaining that he had an inamorata, he had it in mind to court and marry twenty-one year old Sally. Neither in his January or subsequent letters was he candid in revealing his blooming love life. His reluctance to speak of such matters with its overtones of sexuality is reminiscent of the way his younger brother, William Drew, displayed his puritanical virtues when he admitted he had gone a little too far emotionally by commending the joys of marriage.(32) Charles courted Sallie by mail from his remote dwelling. In his long but interesting letters he made no attempt to prepare Sallie for the disjunction she would experience as between life in quiet, suburban New Jersey and life in Asuncion. He created an idyllic image of the country, drawing word-pictures of a beautiful land with hills, valleys and plains and promising a delightful climate. Days would be warm and clear, nights would be cool enough to sleep under blankets.

Wm. D. Washburn

Each day, Charles told his fiancé, he rode horseback assuring her he would teach her to ride Roger d' Coverly, a gentle animal ridden by the

French Consul's wife. The two of them, he claimed, would be taken in a carriage with six horses to visit friends in the city and countryside. The courtier mentioned to her that, as for himself, he lacked nothing in Paraguay, --nothing but a wife. He had horses, dogs, ducks, turkeys, servants and accommodations, but withal, he must say with Haman, "all these avail me nothing." He even teasingly hinted that Sallie had better come soon, wondering on paper if he should tell his love about the graceful barefoot belles of Paraguay. This aficionado may have had in mind the sisters Anita and Conchita. To the 42 year old bachelor, these were two attractive young Spanish women with appealing features and seductive forms. He frequently visited the Casal sisters and their father, Don Mauricio. In fact, he said to Sallie, he made two and three day-long visits to the estancia, hunting in the wilds of the Mauricio plantation. He wanted Sallie to know that Anita and Conchita were not barefoot maids, but well educated and "fit to appear in civilized society."(33) Charles wanted a wife as soon as possible. If he could not have Sallie, he joked, he would take a cup of "cold pizen."

Charles confessed that he was "somewhat given to fanciful creations or . . . building air castles . . . " His confession should have been a forewarning to Sallie, but it was not taken as a warning because like many young girls, Sallie also was a romantic. Her lover's wooing letters from a land far away prompted her to write a school friend saying she believed, "I have yet my happiest days to see."(34) Charles, ill prepared to make a judgment about Sallie's ability to stand the rough life, threatened daily with death by the minions of Francisco Solano Lopez, wrote his father that his wife would prove to be a rugged woman able to endure the primitive life of Paraguay.

Anticipating ecstasy, Washburn sought permission to leave Paraguay, even as the country was preparing for war. His decision to absent himself was criticized, as Elihu's decision to leave his ministerial post in Paris in 1870 was criticized.(35) Lopez expressed disappointment since, as he said, he felt there would soon be negotiations to arrange.(36) The American Minister assured Solano he would return long before steps could be taken regarding the making of peace. The magnet-like attraction of Sally Cleaveland drew the anxious minister northward against odds, and in January of 1865 he left Paraguay for the United States, not to be again in Asuncion until November of 1866. He wrote Sallie saying there is a sailor's proverb that says when the girls at home have got hold of the tow-line a ship moves fast. "I am sure I shall have a speedy voyage for I know you will give a long and a strong pull," he wrote hopefully.(37)

Chapter Twenty-Six

WASHBURN RETURNS

Coming off the stormy Atlantic, the ship with its distinguished passengers, entered the great gaping mouth of the Rio de la Plata sucking in the sea creating tidal waters 1,000 miles into the interior and salting the river as far north as the city of Paraná. Near the further end of the open maw on the south side of Rio de la Plata is Argentina's leading city, Buenos Aires. Charles and his young wife, Sallie, enjoyed a second honeymoon in the Argentine capital until they received sad news; the allies were not going to permit the Ambassador, his wife and staff to pass through the blockade and return to Washburn's post in Asunción. Daily and hourly they had expected the steamer *Shamokin* to arrive to take the entourage up the blockaded river to Asuncion. A month after their return to the region a worried letter from Washburn arrived in the hands of the *Wasp's* Captain, W.A. Kirkland. Charles explained in his letter that he had written Acting Rear Admiral S.W. Godon about his "forlorn condition" abandoned as he and wife were. He impressed upon Kirkland that it was his duty for him to get to his post in Asuncion, expressing the hope that Admiral Godon would come for them and make the thousand mile trip up the river with Charles, wife, and the legation staff.(1) There was no response, Charles explained to Kirkland, saying he wrote again to the Admiral.(2) Washburn write that if he could be in Paraguay before impending battles broke out in the war with the allies he might save the lives of prisoners. What Washburn thought he could

C. A. Washburn   Sallie Washburn

accomplish, however, was not sufficient inducement to persuade the Admiral. More than a month later, Charles wrote Godon once again. He strained to keep his sense of humor, saying he would come to Montevideo to see the Admiral and "take a glass of water strong." In this letter, Charles made a point worthy of the Admiral's careful attention, explaining to Godon that the Brazilian Special Envoy Octaviana had offered to have a Brazilian ship take Charles, his wife and staff through the embattled area to his post. With Brazil at war with Paraguay Charles said it would not be wise for him to accept the offer.(3) If Washburn had felt he could accept Octaviana's invitation he would have disembarked at the port in Asuncion eight months before the U.S. Navy finally put him ashore at the capital of Paraguay.

Further indignity was suffered by the Washburns. The Minister Resident and wife went to Montevideo from Buenos Aires since the Admiral would not come to them. The boat they had intended to take was not available. On the impulse Charles and Sallie took another. Their transport left them off in Montevideo in the evening with no overnight accommodations. Fortunately, a fellow passenger, Dr. Bourse, invited them to his home. Had the doctor not taken in the Minister and his wife, the two Americans would have been on the streets of the city all night. Charles was irritated when he sat down to write explaining to Admiral Godon this latest dilemma. He said he had expected a boat to be sent for him at two p.m. the previous afternoon to take him to the flagship. No crumb of humor was in that brief, curt letter to S.W. Godon written from Dr. Bourse's office in Montevideo. He and Sallie experienced worrisome moments when they went ashore at Montevideo to find they might have to spend the night on a park bench or walking the streets.

❖

Seven months before the return voyage, Argentina, Uruguay and Brazil had declared war against the little interior country of Paraguay. Washburn at that time was still at his post. The Paraguayan Navy ship, the *Tacuari*, had captured a Brazilian ship, thereby performing an Act of War. The ship *Marquiz de Olinda* had arrived at the capital on its way to Matto Grosso loaded with ammunition with an important Brazilian official aboard. The ship signaled the shore and receiving no response continued up the river. Lopez ordered the *Tacuari* to overtake and seize the *Marquez de Olinda*. The President's lame explanation of the unlawful action was that Brazil had invaded Uruguay *against Paraguay's protest*. President Lopez promptly informed the Brazilian Resident Minister that diplomatic relations with his country had ceased. The Resident Minister, Vianna de Lima, asked for his passport. It was placed in his hand with instructions that he and his family must find a way overland to return to Brazil. Such instructions stirred Washburn to vigorous protest. The American minister knew that the prescribed alternative course across a combination of barren country and through jungle would mean death for the Minister and his family. Washburn protested the treatment of Vianna and at the same time objected to the imprisonment of the Matto Grosso Governor, Colonel Federico Carneiro de Campos, who had been taken from the **Marquiz de Olinda**. Critical opinions expressed frankly to Lopez by Washburn caused a rift, worsening relations between the President and himself. Washburn wrote that when he next met Lopez, the man "had a dark and forbidding scowl, and his eyes had a sort of liquid, inflamed, fiendish look such as I had never before seen in the head of a human being . . . "(4) Paraguay, Washburn declared to the President, had not declared war before seizing the *Olinda*. Furthermore, Lopez had added fuel to the fire by sending his brother-in-law Colonel Barrios with an army to Matto Grosso, and that province to the north was ravaged. Cruelties were meted out on all who had been captured. The Paraguayan victory at Matto Grosso provided the Paraguayan military with a rich accumulation of war materiel. The Brazilian province had been made a storage place for materiels in anticipation of war with Paraguay. Before Washburn took his leave-of-absence that day, however, Lopez accommodated himself to the antagonistic mannerisms of the Norte Americano. "[H]is Excellency was . . . all smiles and *condescension*,"(5) said Charles. He even expressed regret that Charles was leaving, wanting the minister present as war was beginning.

On the right, General Bartolomé Mitri with whom Washburn met

A few months later, January 1865, Lopez insisted upon crossing Argentine territory for the purpose of making war on Brazil. Permission was asked of Argentina but not granted, and Lopez's subsequent lawless action in entering the province without the government's approval drove three countries into each other's arms, Argentina, Brazil and Uruguay. A Triple Alliance was signed in May 1865, six months before Washburn arrived back in la Plata region with Sallie, a year after the seizure of the *Marquez de Olinda*, and the invasion of Argentina's Corrientes province by Paraguay.

❖

Eight months of waiting were spent going back and forth from Buenos Aires to Montevideo and Corrientis. In the otherwise merry month of May, Charles admitted in a letter to Elihu, he and Sallie were not merry. They were virtual prisoners. Despair flitted in and out of his letter as he wrote to complain about his failure to hear from Seward. As for the Admiral, Charles said bitterly that Godon had gone up the Uruguay River to hunt and fish. He, Sallie and the servants remained stranded. During the long delay, conscientious Charles went up river to Corrientis to see Argentine President Mitre, the Commander in Chief of the allied forces, about going through the blockade. Mitre agreed, the Ambassador should be put through the lines. Mitri hedged, however, saying all the allies, not just he, must be consulted before he would consent to take Charles to his post. In the letter Washburn said he reminded Mitre that he was within two or three leagues of the seat of government in Paraguay.

Perhaps the Allies had learned that Lopez had purchased military weaponry from the United States with the help of the Minister Resident. Perhaps for that reason the allies were fearful that Lopez, friendly to Washburn at the time, might succeed in implicating the U.S. in the engagement. It is possible that the allies had received through the information sieve intelligence quoting Washburn as having "assured [Lopez] that if he wanted to whip Brazil, or any other of his neighbors, the Yankees would furnish him the tools to do it with greater dispatch, on more reasonable terms, giving at the same time a more efficient article than could other nations or peoples."(6)

It was clear, the allies did not want Washburn back at Asuncion. Mitre was deliberately dragging his heels. The Minister lingered as Mitri waited for a reply from Brazil and Uruguay. At last he said that, yes, perhaps he could help Charles through the lines. Charles was hesitant nonetheless about returning to Buenos Aires and bringing Sallie, servants and the staff so far up the river to Corrientis, a mean army location where, as he wrote, "the people in Corrientes could not understand why the Minister of a great and powerful nation should be thus hanging on in the rear of the allied army like a camp follower, and I heard of numerous discussions whether or not I was an Accredited Minister or an imposter."(7) Corrientis was a community near the allied base. The sick, wounded and dying were hospitalized there and overall conditions in the camp were deplorable. Dead animals lay in the street decaying. Wholesome food was unavailable except at exorbitant prices, and the state department was not paying expenses for the Ambassador's prolonged stay outside Paraguay. But the Argentine President had given Charles confidence that he would be able with his wife and entourage to make their way to the seat of government in Paraguay. So Charles brought Sallie to Corrientis. A month passed, however, and Ambassador Washburn, Sallie and staff were still in Corrientis.

Admiral Godon was sympathetic to the allied position. He displayed feelings of disdain for U.S. representatives abroad. According to Charles, reasons the Admiral gave for refusing to carry Washburn and staff up the river "were garrulously long and monotonous, such as that the muskitoes (sic) were thick, the weather was warm, the men might get sick . . . and more than all[,] it would take from 90 to 100 tons of coal [at] $15.00 a ton."(8)

Washburn embarrassed Minister of Foreign Affairs Elizaldi at Buenos Aires. He arranged for Minister Elizaldi to compose a note to Mitre declaring that the American ambassador was to go through the lines to Asuncion. The ship carrying Charles back to Corrientis from Buenos Aires ran aground and the mishap became another frustrating obstacle. Washburn had to leave his trunks behind, and regrettably one of the trunks contained Elizaldi's message to President Mitre. The message did not arrive for three more weeks. By then, the Argentine Commander-in-Chief Mitre insisted that circumstances had changed since Elizaldi wrote his note. Mitre again asked Charles to be patient. He told the American Ambassador that Special Envoy Octaviana of Brazil was coming to Corrientis and that he might have something to say about getting Washburn on his way to Paraguay. Octaviana came but he did not darken Washburn's door, cruelly disappointing to Charles who on another occasion had reminded Octaviana that he had remained in Paraguay two months after having planned his leave-of-absence in order to assist the Brazilian Minister to leave Paraguay when Lopez had intended to send Minister Vianna, his wife, sister, and children to their death in the jungle on what would have been a 250 mile journey to Corrientis. Since neither Octaviana nor Mitre were willing to yield on the issue of sending Washburn through the lines with his bride, the newly married couple had to remain *six months more* in "the pest haunted disease breeding city of hospitals, Corrientis."(9)

❖

When at last Washburn's ship left Buenos Aires sailing west northwest around the wide curve of the Paraná River and heading north past Entre Rios and Corrientes, the politically astute Charles would likely have reminded himself of events leading up to his return. As the ship made its way slowly against the swift current, Charles looked eastward from the ship into the province of Entre Rios, a province associated with gaucho leader, Venancio Flores. This *caudillo*, Flores, was a famous freebooter whose reputation instilled horror in the hearts of Uruguayans. Gaucho Flores had captured, and then been driven from the presidency of Uruguay in the early 1850s. With his merciless banditti he had fled from Montevideo to Entre Rios. Now in 1865 Flores and his outlaws were attempting to return to power with clandestine help from the government at Buenos Aires. The Paraguayan President had condemned Argentina for interfering in Uruguayan affairs. Lopez, anticipating further trouble with Brazil and Argentina, established a military camp thirty miles east of Asunción at Cerro Leon. He made preparations despite the deathbed warning of his father, Carlos, that Francisco must realize, "there are many problems waiting to be ventilated; but," his father warned, "do not try to solve them by the sword but by the pen, *chiefly with Brazil.*"(10)

William Seward

❖

At last a letter came to the Minister Resident from Secretary of State Seward. Washburn was satisfied upon reading the Secretary's opinion confirming his own, that "the dignity and honor of the United States will not allow a further detention . . ."(11) In a letter written June 27, 1866, Seward wrote that Charles was to return home if the Argentine Republic continued to obstruct his passage. It almost seemed that Seward was ignorant of the fact that a United States Navy ship could have taken Charles to his destination in October of '65; that it was not altogether the fault of the allies that Charles, Sallie and legation members were held up for months now lengthening into a year. Admiral Godon delayed the trip even after the Navy Department instructed him to transport the Ambassador to Paraguay. Seward exasperated complained to Secretary of the Navy Welles, and Welles on April 26, 1866, ordered Godon to take Washburn to his post. The April letter may not have been received by the Admiral until sometime in July, but it was not until October 5 that Seward's and Welles' orders were carried out. J. Watson Webb, U.S. Ambassador to Brazil, like Washburn a former newspaper man who wrote in a bombastic style similar to Washburn, flailed the government of Brazil for failing to permit Washburn and his staff to pass through the blockade. Secretary Seward had given peremptory orders to Webb, as well as to Washburn and the Minister at Argentina, Alexander Asboth, declaring that if Washburn's detention continued, and if within six or eight days satisfactory explanations were not given by the Brazilian and Argentine governments, the ambassadors were "to ask for their passports and return to the United States."

❖

The first great battle of significance between Paraguay and the allies had taken place five months before Washburn returned from the United States. The Paraguayan fleet had been defeated at Riachuelo on the river below the fort at Humaita. It was clear that the allied Navy would be creeping slowly toward the fortified military camp on the river, Lopez's headquarters. The battles on the river became part of the reason Charles was forced to languish in the Rio de la Plata region. Some of the time he spent writing letters. He wrote his father, his brothers, Admiral Godon, the State Department and others. Charles waited impatiently for an American ship he had ordered from the Southern Squadron of U.S. forces to take his entourage past the blockade at Humaita to Asunción. One of his letters was written to a member of the American embassy in Buenos Aires, H.R. Helper. Helper had been a controversial figure in the 1850s in the United States. His book, *The Impending Crisis of the South*, was reputed to have been the most important book ever published in the States. The book by Helper had managed to cause trouble for Representatives Israel, Jr. and Elihu Washburne, who were congressional sponsors of the book. Charles had become acquainted with Helper in San Francisco, and as we shall see, he remained in the orbit of Charles after Charles returned to the United States from Paraguay.

When Charles wrote his father he was feeling jolly, reporting that the voyage from the States was good and that he and Sallie were enjoying a visit to Rio de Janario. In his letter he lamented the loss in lives in the war numbering, he estimated, 40,000, claiming that no more than 500 were killed in battle, the remainder having died of sickness and starvation. So far, he said to his father, the pressures induced by the entente in frustrating his attempt to return home, had not bothered Sallie. She would prove to be, he said, a rugged woman. Little did he know what troubles would soon leave Sallie on the verge of insanity. In the midst of his predicament, Charles dreamed away about the homestead, writing about improvements at the Norlands, and fantasizing his and Sallie's return to the upland, once more to enjoy the quiet and beauty of the Maine countryside.

In March of 1866, Sallie wrote her best friend Sue back in the states. She said to Sue she felt proud that a girl hired to go with the Washburns to Paraguay had refused an offer of marriage in order to accompany her. "I infer from that," she wrote her friend, "she must be fond of me." Sallie and Charles kept farmer's hours, she explained, rising at 5 a.m., taking tea and an egg. Breakfast, she said, was at 11 a.m. A siesta, thought by toiling North Americans to be a waste of good time, was enjoyed from 3 p.m. to dinner at 5 with tea again at 8. Sallie was not pleased or excited about the countries she and Charles were visiting, Argentina, Uruguay and Brazil, and she remarked upon the fact that at Christmas the weather was hot. She anticipated with pleasure, however, the possibility of living in Paraguay where she and Charles expected to be for the next four years. In the letter to her friend, Sallie did not mention the intrigue, the disappointments Charles experienced with the American Admiral, the fruitless struggle with the president of Argentina who was continuing to disobey protocol, disallowing passage through the blockade.

❖

In September Lopez goaded his enemies until Commander in Chief Mitre succeeded in capturing at great loss the battery at Curuzu located midway between the juncture of the Paraná and Paraguay rivers. The defeated Lopez tried another tack. He wrote General Mitre asking for a conference to discuss an armistice. The Marshal, his two brothers, Venancio and Benigno, and his brother-in-law General Barrios, captor of Motto Grosso, rode in an American-made buggy to a conference ground where the overdressed Lopez was to meet the unassuming and victorious General Mitre. Before confronting the general, short fat Lopez, "saddest [sic] with poor teeth,"(12) left the buggy, mounted a white horse to ride the short distance to the grove where Mitre awaited his arrival. The two men talked peace for five hours but to no avail. The Paraguayan president said he would be willing to leave his native land and live in Europe *for two years*. That proposal was turned down. The allies had agreed that Lopez must abdicate and leave the country and General Mitre was in no position to consider a revision.

❖

Once again, Charles turned his hand to letter writing. To Elihu he complained that Corrientes was a disagreeable, expensive place. He expressed bitterness about President Mitre who was, he said, using undiplomatic language, "playing fast and loose" with him. Charles said he could not imagine why the allies considered him in any way helpful to Marshal Lopez. Perhaps, he surmised with tongue in cheek, they think I would be able to offer the dictator the protection of "my house and flag" if his cause were lost. Charles predicted he would be at Corrientes six more months. His guess was one month off. The minister did not need to be sarcastic about that prospect. Charles had said to Admiral Godon that he needed to be in Paraguay so that Lopez, if he were too hard pressed, might be taken out of the country by a U.S. ship.(13) He explained to Elihu that he had written the Secretary of State four months earlier in March asking to be recalled. He had even thought ahead about what he would do if he were relieved of his post. He would return to California where he still had standing and influence. In any case, he said he must have work to keep him busy. He explained that the hot weather had bothered Sallie at Buenos Aries but that she was recovering with cooler weather at Corrientes, and, he boasted, she was "handsomer than ever." He told Elihu he was resentfulness of their brother, Sidney. Sid was writing insolent letters and he had been told by Charles to write no more. His letters would not be opened. Nonetheless, Charles said he had sent Sid $500. to pay for additions to the Livermore home.

Charles kept up his interest in politics, noting that Elihu had "brok[en] ground for the great Ulysses." This observation referred to his brother's sponsorship of Elihu's fellow townsman, Grant, bringing Grant to the public's attention as a nominee for president. As Charles ended his letter to Elihu, he sent love "especially [for] little Pitt," revealing Charles' thoughtfulness when it came to the weak and sick. Pitt was a troubled lad and Charles had a special fondness for him.

❖

In the month of June Seward and President Johnson bore down heavily on the Minister. "The President learns with deep dissatisfaction," Seward wrote concerning Johnson's having learned that Washburn was still being hindered. The President, said Seward, wanted Charles to "at once return to the U.S. States [sic]." The instruction was qualified allowing Charles to continue if the obstructions were removed.(14) This sharp letter from the Department was written in June. The minister to Paraguay had not been returned to Asuncion in July, August, September, or October. In October, despite Washburn's embarrassing situation, a letter from Seward requested of Charles that he attempt to bring peace to the warring parties. In the states, business was being effected. That was disturbing to Seward. As has been indicated, Seward's vision was of an America as a commercial hegemony. War in the Plata region, referred to by Seward as one of the richest regions on the globe, was a hindrance. Five days later, the Secretary wrote another disturbing letter, this time saying he understood Washburn was not being kept out of Asuncion any longer; that the allies had given way. Seward did know, however, that there was personal animosity as between Washburn and the Brazilian special envoy, Señor Octaviana--between Washburn and President Mitre--between Washburn and Admiral Godon. Seward said, "the President expects you to overlook all points of ceremony and of past offense real or imaginary on the part of the allied governments or any of them, and of past neglect real or imaginary on the part of Admiral Godon, and adopt whatever course in your discretion may seem best to reach Asuncion."

Andrew Johnson

There! The lengthy sentence from the Secretary of State had a tone of finality. Charles would have to wait until he was back in the U.S. and in a position to bring injurious personal problems into focus at a Hearing in the House of Representatives.(15) November 1866, Charles, Sallie, their servants and staff were at last settled in the legation at Asuncion. President Mitre and the fire-breathing Brazilian Admiral Baron de Tamandaré, reluctantly submitted to the demands of the Commander of the *U.S. Shamokin*, Pierce Crosby, who was insistent upon sailing up the Paraguay river past naval emplacements to leave the American ambassador on the shore at Asuncion. The ship chosen by the Admiral was difficult to steer. Washburn, paranoid about anything with which Godon was associated, thought the ship was chosen in the hope that the *Shamokin* might not make it to Asuncion.

❖

In July, a long letter had been sent from Charles to J. Watson Webb, resident minister at Brazil. Washburn writing Webb was like writing a letter to himself. The two answered to the same description, if not facially and physically, in manner and mood, in testiness and temperament. Whatever J. Watson may have been as a teenager and however different his experiences in young manhood, Washburn and Webb were alike in having aspired to attend West Point. Webb made it into the military school, being willful enough to have insisted that Secretary of War John C. Calhoun read a statement Webb wrote showing his interest in becoming a soldier. Charles spent a few elated days at the Point and was then given an excuse for being denied a scholarship. Webb became proprietor and editor of the New York *Morning Courier*. Charles was proprietor and editor of the San Francisco *Daily Times*. While Webb named the new political party succeeding the *Federalists, Whig*, Charles' brother, Israel, Jr., named the successor to the *Whig* party, *Republican*. It was said of Webb that in his political career he was "a remarkable example of a brilliant mind governed solely by impulses of right." Another way of stating the foregoing would be to say Webb, like Washburn, was apt to feel strongly on matters of right and wrong. Their editorials and actions bore a sternness which self-righteous people often possess, and which, it might be added, soured men who might otherwise have

James Webb

been admirers of these men. One thinks of striking titles of Washburn editorials in the San Francisco *Daily Times*: "A Monster Anti-Coolie Petition," "The Last Butchery of Indians." Examples of insolence and arrogance on the part of Webb are manifold. Secretary Seward had to reprimand his Brazilian Resident Minister when Webb's blustering and impetuosity almost resulted in a duel between the British Minister in Brazil and himself. Webb's impertinence had earlier lead to a duel between himself and the nephew of Chief Justice John Marshall. Washburn, of course, had dueled with a descendant of President George Washington. In 1861, Charles was appointed Commissioner and later Resident Minister to Paraguay. In 1861, Webb was appointed Envoy Extraordinary and Minister Plenipotentiary to the empire of Brazil. Like Charles, Webb served eight years in the service of the state. Like Charles, he was not averse to intimidating the empire by threatening to resign. He endured a succession of crises of a kind to find him involved, like Washburn, in a series of grave predicaments. Webb had a good relationship with Napoleon III.(16) There was a relationship between the Webb and Washburn families by way of Porter Cornelius Bliss. Charles met Bliss on the Tyne when the two shipped out of England for Brazil. Washburn was impressed by Bliss. They corresponded. Bliss, working for Webb and teaching Webb's children, asked for a release from his position. He traveled to Buenos Aires and thence to Paraguay where he served as Washburn's private secretary.

The two ministers were in agreement concerning their *bete noire*, Admiral Godon, Commander of the South Atlantic Squadron. Godon persistented [sic] in displaying his disapproval of ministers and consuls. The Admiral felt such operatives were useless. Such flunky political appointees as they were, Godon believed, should not pretend to represent the interests of government and business.

In his letter to Webb, Charles likened himself to the way Edward Spangler was treated by the assassin, John Wilkes Booth. Spangler, said Charles, was offered a reward if he would hold Booth's horse, and as a result of his good deed he spent six months in prison. Charles, after having performed his good deed on behalf of the Brazilian minister Vianna de Lima and family, perhaps saving their lives, was "suffering six months imprisonment in the pest haunted disease breeding city of hospitals, [Corrientes]."(17) Despite the agreement between the duo, Webb and Washburn, on the subject of Admiral Godon, there was yet a heated exchange between the two, and Godon was the subject of their dispute. Charles accused the Ambassador to Brazil of defending the Admiral against him. In a report to Secretary Seward, Webb, according to Charles, charged him, "with disobeying instructions and 'consulting my feelings instead of my duties',"(18) in his relations with the Admiral. Webb insisted firmly that he had not intended to dispute Washburn's plans or actions. The two remained friends, even though the Secretary of State rebuked them as a father his child, writing to the two saying "correspondence . . . in relation to [Godon] . . . will end."(19) The humming motors of the *Shamokin* pushed the naval vessel up the Paraguay against the fast moving current, at last to provide Charles and Sallie Washburn a glimpse of the formidable fort at Humaita. The Washburns were relieved to see the fortified emplacement and felt reassured as they entered the safe enclave. The evening of the day of their arrival, the recently wed couple were treated to a grand banquet. Lopez was pleased to have the minister back at his post. He had hoped for months to see some signs of support from the states. So far the most help offered by the U.S. was mediation by Resident Ministers Washburn, Webb and Asboth in Argentina. The day following the evening of good feelings, the Washburn contingent boarded the *Shamokin* once more and continued up the river to the capital. Their food stuffs and supplies of necessities unavailable in wartime Paraguay were placed ashore and the legation staff settled in at the legation. The legation was to be their home for two years only. And while the embassy proved to be a haven for them, for others it would become a virtual prison.

Back at his desk in the legation, Charles gave attention to formal obligations. First he had to make proper contact with the Paraguayan government through its Foreign Minister, Jose Berges. In his letter to Berges Charles referred significantly to the "illegal and discourteous conduct" he had encountered with Paraguay's enemies Brazil, Argentina and Uruguay. That remark encouraged Berges and Lopez. He praised Marshal Lopez and his martial skills. The Marshal, he said, was "surprising enemies and astonishing the world." Intentionally or otherwise, however, Charles pricked the ambitious General ever so slightly as he noted the abandonment by European powers to "force a monarchical form of Government on the . . . Republic of Mexico."(20) The Paraguayan president would likely have felt a twinge of disappointment with that reminder. He had been aspiring since his inauguration to install a monarchy in Paraguay with the approval of European empires, the empire of Brazil, and, he had hoped, Mexico. There were those among the allies as well as the Paraguayans who thought the war which had begun before Washburn left the country would be over in three months. In Buenos Aires, President Mitre said, "The barracks in a day, Corrientes in two weeks, Asuncion in three months!" Charles had felt differently, assuring Lopez he would return in six months, saying that Brazil, in not less than that time would be in a position to begin the war.

Chapter Twenty-Seven

PEACE, NO

At the beginning of a fresh new year 1867 the Resident Minister addressed His Ex'cy Jose Berges, Minister of Foreign Relations, informing him that Secretary Seward had once again instructed Washburn to use his good offices for the purpose of bringing the war to a conclusion. In this singular undertaking Lopez was cooperative. Charles went through the line to the allied camp, met with Commander-in-Chief of the allied forces, the Marquis de Caxias, who stated bluntly there could be no peace nor discussion of peace until President Lopez agreed to leave the country. Washburn returned to Asuncion, reported to Berges, and then wrote to General Caxias objecting to the position he had taken on behalf of the allies. His letter to the General sought a second meeting. The response was curt, with Caxias saying, "I leave Your Excellency's enlightened judgment to appreciate the serious inconveniences which would result, if, as Y(our) E(xcellency) seems to desire, permission were to be granted to Y.E. to come to this encampment whenever it may be desirable . . . " General Asboth had no more success in peace efforts with the Argentines than Washburn with the Brazilians. As for J. Watson Webb in Rio, Webb castigated both Washburn and Asboth for continuing to press for mediation.(1) Seward censured Webb for criticizing his fellow Ministers in their attempts.

Charles in his note to Foreign Affairs Minister Jose Berges wrote warmly of the sympathy the Paraguayan cause had received as a result of the country's willingness to negotiate as against the unyielding position taken by the allies. This congratulatory mood was displayed in a Washburn letter in October. The Resident Minister at that period was attempting to placate the Marshal on the one hand while communicating with Secretary of State Seward about the unfortunate interest Lopez had in converting his Republic to an Empire, making himself Emperor. There was no less sincerity in one communication than the other, though it was thought by some to have been duplicitous. In fact, Washburn continued to support Dictator Lopez until he learned about "wholesale atrocities" being committed in the dictator's name.(2) That was about the period when Washburn began to open the legation doors to Paraguayans, Germans, English, Americans and others. In February of 1868 Charles explained to Berges that it was "necessary for me to take [them] into my service."(3) Coincident with this maneuver which was to cause serious problems was the refusal on the part of the Resident Minister to remove office and staff to the community of Luque, thirty miles from Asuncion. The port city had been emptied by fiat as of February 22nd, except for police and the American Legation. Lopez knew Brazilian iron-clads had been successful in putting the fort at Humaita out of commission. It was expected the capital would soon be shelled, and that the allies would enter the city. In anticipation of this possibility, Asuncion was made a ghost town. More than one hundred people left possessions at the American Legation before fleeing to Luque. Washburn had no difficulty in legitimizing his actions as he took people and possessions into the legation, and refused to follow the government. He quoted liberally from Martens, Wheaton and Vattel, international lawyers whose works were standard and in use in foreign offices of all nations. International law justified the Minister's every action. Washburn refused to move declaring, "if the allies or anybody else choose to blow up the house [legation] they must blow me with it for I shall not leave my post." He meant it. It was thought by the press in Rio, however, that Washburn had "stirred up another storm."(4) Lopez and his advisers also began suspiciously to reflect upon the fact that in the previous month of January, Charles had been with General Caxias at his headquarters. They began to suspect that he had agree with the allied General Caxias about a date when the battle on the river would take place with the iron-clads proceeding through Humaita to Asuncion, and it all suggested to the suspicious Lopez and his lackeys why Washburn insisted on remaining in the capital.

That was one "storm." Another occurred when one of the occupants, an American by the name of James Manlove, found himself in trouble with the police. Manlove had been an officer in the cavalry of the notorious General Nathan Bedford Forrest in the American Civil War. Forrest and his cavalry had been the formidable enemy of Charles's brother, General Cadwallader Washburn. General Washburn was Commander of Western Tennessee charged by General Grant to hunt down and destroy Forrest's marauding cavalry. James Manlove was one of the horsemen. He and another legation occupant, John Watts, one day went on horseback to tend animals in the countryside. The city being empty the two galloped their horses over city streets, a practice disallowed by law. Stopped by local police they were told to appear at the station the following day. Manlove did not know the language well and thought he had been told to go to the station immediately. He went to the station accompanied by officers. Watts returned to the legation and told Washburn what had happened. Charles promptly set out for the station. When he arrived at the *Policia,* as he explained later, he thought Manlove was free and so he had told him to mount his horse and return to the legation. Police surrounded Manlove and Charles said,

"Let him alone, he belongs to me."(5)

This then was the nature of yet another "storm," one which Washburn himself said he regretted. He knew the action he had undertaken at headquarters would enrage Lopez. Men had been shot on the spot for less than such a challenge of authority. Perhaps because Charles was convincing in his refreshing sincerity the matter was dealt with satisfactorily and the subject dropped.

This volatile confrontation occurred in the early part of March. There was a noticeable change in the attitude of the Resident Minister at that fateful Ides of March. Washburn was thought to have learned the truth about Lopez's torturing and killing citizens and non-citizens wholesale. George Thompson in a position to know said after leaving Paraguay that there was "overwhelming corroborations" to justify referring to Lopez as a monster without parallel.(6) It was at this interval that Washburn was believed by the Paraguay administration to have become the leader of a conspiracy against the government. Some scholars concluded that General Resquin and Father Maiz correctly report the American Minister's implication in a scheme to unseat the dictator, with Resquin claiming that Charles "was at the very centre of the web."(7) Historian Harris Gaylord Warren says bluntly that "to the twisted mind of Lopez, a hideous spider sat at the center of the web, a spider named Charles Ames Washburn . . . "(8) Since the Resident Minister was innocent, his utter candor prompted him to prove his integrity by lengthy and detailed recounting *seriatim* endlessly of what had taken place. As one author indicated, "Instead of ignoring the whole business, or merely calling it a stupid fabrication, he increased or created suspicion by replying to the monstrous lies in detail."(9)

The story would perhaps have been heroic if true, that the Livermore lad had gone out into the world to thrash cruel dictators; that his brother Elihu had gone off to France at a critical period of that country's history to play a part in ridding the country of its last Emperor, and to see to the establishment of a Grand Republic.(10) What may have played a part in some scholars' pursuit of the Lopez-Resquin-Maiz thesis was a meeting of Consuls and Resident Ministers held at the American legation in February at the time the iron-clads were scheduled to arrive. Notes taken by Secretary Porter Bliss indicate that at the meeting Washburn advised hoisting the national flags and remaining in town as Asuncion residents left the city for Luque at the bidding of the President. The Portuguese Consul, Leitte Pereira, seconded Washburn's recommendation. The Portuguese Consul was to cause a further rift between the Resident Minister and the Marshal. When the authorities challenged the right of the legation to take in the Consul they were told in substance by the Minister it was none of their business. Bliss records in his legation Minutes that boxes and valuables poured into the American legation on the 23rd of February and that in the evening of the 22nd, "Dr. Carreras and Senor Rodriguez, the former Oriental Minister and Secretary . . . took up their residence under [Washburn's] roof."(11) Adding to these occurrences at about the same time, Paraguayans in positions of authority in Asuncion met together to decide what to do when the iron-clads appeared. At that meeting were Foreign Minister Berges, Acting Foreign Ministers Sanchez, Fernandez and Benitez, joined by Gomez, Sanabria, and Venancio Lopez, brother of the dictator, and brother-in-law Saturnino

Bedoya. Lopez became suspicious, fearful they might have been planning for his ouster. He put Bedoya to torture until Bedoya, his brother-in-law, confessed there was a conspiracy. Lopez's brother Benigno was tortured and forced to give the names of those whom he said were accomplices. Washburn's name was first. In time, all who were at the meeting to decide what to do when the iron-clads appeared were tortured and executed. Since in his official capacity Charles frequented Berges' office, both he and Berges were suspect. Lopez's consort, Mrs. Lynch, approached the Minister Resident to ask if he would take her articles in the legation, and house herself if the allies won.

One of the Washburn's social acquaintances in Asuncion was Doña Carmelita Gill de Corbal. Her brother fought at Humaita. Her husband, a rich man,

Eliza Lynch

was forced into the ranks a barefoot private. Corbal passed away early in the war. It was known that Doña Carmelita hated Lopez. It was known also that she enjoyed talking with Charles about her feelings. The wife of an English doctor, Mrs. William Stewart, not trusting the future would be under Lopez, put a small fortune in the hands of Washburn to keep at the legation. It was clear to all that Washburn would not let himself be intimidated. It was common knowledge that he had defied the dictator. If his writings about Paraguay, were to reach Lopez, it would doubtless result in some form of punishment. Charles hid the pages of his manuscript under the table cloth in the kitchen of his home. These elements were added to the fact of his having been on a peace mission to the camp of the allies where he might have provided information to General Caxias about how to defeat the enemy. Some who examined the life of the Resident Minister confirmed the likelihood when they found that after Washburn escaped he told Caxias everything he knew about military affairs in Paraguay. A novelist, Juan Emiliano O'Leary, writes with certainty that Washburn was "the soul of the movement."(12)

While there is good reason to doubt Washburn's involvement in a conspiracy, what is true about him is that of a certainty he became aware of the terrors inspired by the dictator. Charles quotes the deposition of Alonso Taylor, architect of the palace in Asuncion who was imprisoned and put in chains. At a time when Taylor was being tortured he saw an "Argentine officer chained close beside him taken to the torture-yard. 'When he returned his body was all raw. Next morning when he was loosened (from the chain) I pointed to his back. He did not speak, but let his head fall on his breast and with a stick wrote in the sand "200." In the afternoon he was sent for again, and again wrote "200." The next day he was shot'."(13) As the condition became known more fully, the Ambassador was not skillful in relating to the terror. The want of discretion on Washburn's part, his lack of diplomatic skills attributable to the puritan descendant's evident earnestness, found Washburn bungling his job as Minister and mediator. When Caxias had said to him there would be no peace until Lopez agreed to leave the country, the undiplomatic Washburn said that the charge was comparable to insisting that Emperor Dom Pedro II abdicate his throne in Brazil.

Sallie, Charles' wife, was gravely affected by the series of crises brought about in part by her husband. Threats were made, not only to occupants given asylum, but to Charles. She was keenly aware of Charles' scrupulosity in all things, that he felt he must always be right, giving no quarter when challenged, particularly if morality were in question. She recognized his righteous indignation brought trouble. The newly wed young wife, wilting before her husband's anger and threats made by authorities, together with the presence of the police and sometimes soldiers outside the legation, had but one way to deal with her trials. She became infirm. For months, Sallie Washburn was a semi-invalid after leaving Asuncion.

In mid-morning of mid-July Washburn received a message from Acting Foreign Minister Gumesindo Benitez. The message came to the point without apology. The government, Benitez declared, wanted Dr. Carreras and Senor Rodriguez to leave the legation "by one o'clock today." Carreras in 1864 had been Uruguay's Minister of Foreign Relations, Minister of Finance, and Minister of War and Marines, positions making him what was tantamount to being *the government* of Montevideo. He was later sent to Paraguay for the purpose of inducing Lopez to join Uruguay in opposing Brazil. He returned from his mission and was lauded for having obtained an agreement that Paraguay would resist the encroachments of Brazil at the borders of Uruguay. Ironically, the brilliant Uruguayan diplomat was said to have accountable for the international incident with the capture of the Brazilian ship, *Marquiz de Olinda*. Dr. Carreras was now seen as an enemy by one of the allied powers, Brazil. Anticipating Brazils victory over Paraguay, he appeared at the legation seeking asylum. He needed asylum, not from Paraguay's, but Brazil's, threats. Asylum was granted by Washburn. Rodriguez was considered by Washburn to be "the most earnest, intelligent, sincere, and agreeable man" he had met in his experience in South America. Given the demand by Benitez to send them into the street, these two were about to become captives of "the monstrous" Lopez. Together with Charles, they had been companions and fellow literati at the legation, meeting each morning for five months discussing literature and politics over mate. In response to Benitez's letter demanding the expulsion of Carreras and Rodriguez, Charles wrote, "I am exceedingly anxious that no serious evil shall befall them for then I can have little desire to continue in a diplomatic career but shall have much [desire] to leave it and not expose myself to another so painful experience."(15)

Charles had already refused to release Consul Pereira, drawing another of those lengthy document with quotations from authorities in international law to justify his action. Next, a message from Acting Paraguayan Minister of Foreign Affairs insisted that persons who do not belong to the legation be made to leave "before sunset" on the day the letter arrived. Charles dissented entirely. The occupants, Pereira, Carreras and Rodriguez, said finally if the Paraguayan government insisted, they would leave the legation of their own accord. They did so, leaving the legation which became their last free movement before torture and their execution. Masterman later reported on the last days and hours of Dr. Carreras, "a pitiable object, indeed so changed that I could scarcely believe that the wretched creature before me was really he . . . For two months he had been lying as I saw him, in the open air, with no shelter from the sun or rain but a blanket . . . Dr. Carreras, once the most influential man in Uruguay, an ex-Prime Minister, [was] eagerly gnawing the gristle from a few well-picked bones, contemptuously thrown him by a passer-by."(16)

In his July 14th letter to Benitez, Washburn acknowledged, he seemed "to have lost the confidence and respect of this Government."(17) He did not "see how [he could] be of any service to [his] own Government [or] to that of Paraguay, or to any individual in it by longer remaining . . ."(18)

Porter Bliss and George Masterman did not follow the example of Pereira, Carreras and Rodriguez, putting themselves into the hands of the authorities. And since Washburn did not advise it, once again he had to make the case carefully quoting Marten's *Law of Nations*, Book VII, Chapter IX, noting that Bliss and Masterman could not be tried by the laws of Paraguay, that *"the Minister [Washburn] cannot consent to their extradition or to their being put in judgment . . .."* This challenge of authority on Washburn's part became a *cause celebre*. The Department of State in Washington continued to learn of the burgeoning problem and Seward wrote saying he had "read with painful interest the account which you [Charles] give of the unhappy condition of affairs in Paraguay." At last, the Department of State accepted Charles' resignation. He was given permission to determine himself whether or not he should wait for the arrival of his successor. He certainly would not wait in Asuncion. He would wait in Rio. He had, after all, called for a warship to be sent to take him and his family away from the place of horror. We can suppose that Washburn remembered writing a disparaging editorial in his San Francisco *Daily Times*, accusing the Buchanan administration of "bullying Paraguay." At that time he had fulminated against the administration censuring Buchanan for sending ships to the La Plata region with the intend of anchoring ships off Asuncion and demanding payment for expropriated Navigation Company property. Now the critical editorialist, Washburn, was calling for a warship, and Webb of Brazil was demanding that the whole South Atlantic Squadron sail up the Paraguay to bring Bliss and Masterman to freedom.

THE LAST DAYS FOR MINISTER AND MARSHAL

Twelve famous Washburn letters written in the months of July and August reveal something of the personality and mind set of the farmer's son from Maine. Readers can see that those dozen letters gave satisfaction to Marshal Lopez and his underlings as they realized that Washburn's response to their tactics made a virtual fool out of the American Resident Minister. The letters written by Washburn when put together are of book length, but withal, there are few wasted words. Issues touched upon by Charles were legitimate and his interests were humane, sometimes to the detriment of the institution Washburn was serving, the interests of the United States. In the letters there are unexpected and uncalled for emotional displays. There were more such emotional displays to be seen in Washburn than were to be found in the official letters of the several Acting Foreign Ministers of Paraguay. Washburn expected the letters to exonerate him in the eyes of his accusers. He should not have expected that to happen. Charles did not take into consideration that his accusers knew of his innocence, something he was in a position to know since he was not the monstrous spider in the web conspiracy. As a consequence, his interest in part was to make his accusers confess they were lying. He should not have expected such a conversion to result from his efforts, extensive and correct though his efforts were. The letters can be seen as having been intended by Washburn to be his line of defense if and when a congressional committee began to delve into the quagmire of his eight year term of service.

As letters flew back and forth, Charles was not near winding down his contribution. Indeed, in August he was increasing the length of letters, and Richard Burton referred to them as "windy." They covered each detail raised by Benitez and later by his successor, Luis Camino.(19) Arguments were made point by point. In his August 3 letter he starts by declining further correspondence, then he writes on and on and at great length. It is possible that while Foreign Ministers Benitez and Camino deliberately teased Washburn, once they found how vulnerable he was and how sensitive, he wanting everything to be right and everybody to be honest and sincere--it is possible that he was fooling them, keeping them going, as in *Les Mille et Une Nuit*, so that he might live to leave the city of death, Asuncion. He wrote extensively about Carraras, about Vasconcelles, about the Brazilians who tried, he said, to buy him off. He wrote at length about Berges with whom he had been friendly and indicated he was ready to discard Berges himself saying he, Charles, did not blame the government for being suspicious. Charles complained, saying "it was not showing me the respect which my position and my long known character . . . was entitled, to accept . . . as true the charges . . . of a confessed traitor in the face of my positive denials."(20)

The end came to this possible comedy of errors with the U.S. government instructing Washburn's successor not to present his credentials to the President until grievances had been settled. But grievances settled, Ambassador McMahon, Washburn's successor, became a close, intimate friend of the tyrant and his consort, Eliza.

❖

Before the sun goes down, acting Minister Benitez had demanded, you,

Washburn, will send away persons who do not belong to the U.S. Legation in Asuncion. It is unlikely that many U.S. embassies around the world had ever received such an ultimatum. There was precedent, to be sure. That was why Charles went to his library, pulled books from the shelves and wrote back to Benitez saying the request the Acting Minister had made was impossible; that he, Washburn, dissented entirely from his orders. Charles had a fondness for two of the men wanted by authorities. He made a personal plea saying Carraras and Rodriguez had been part of his household for five months. Charles then began winding the tale, explaining to Benitez the history of the two men's remarkable careers, insisting they were entitled to immunities, and that he would himself be censured by his own government if he sent them away. He refused unequivocally to obey the order. The three, of course, left of their own volition, Pereira having been found guilty of feeding Lopez's Brazilian prisoners, for which he was to die. Marshal Lopez disliked Carraras. He also must die. Rodriguez was tortured until he gave the reason, that he had kept secret that the women servants of Lopez's brother, Benigno, had taken to the legation in big baskets currency amounting to one hundred and forty thousand dollars.

In his response to the ridiculous letter, Charles thought a little reminder might make the Acting Minister think of possible consequences. Without having been asked, Charles added in his letter that a U.S. gunboat was expected hourly. He closed, asking for passports for his "legation family," including Porter Bliss and George Masterman.

Two days later, another letter from Benitez. Send Bliss and Masterman from the embassy! Once again, "No!" Masterman was his medical aide, and had brought his first child into the world. Bliss was serving as Washburn's secretary and was assisting the Minister in writing the history of Paraguay. Furthermore, were Washburn to give these men into the hands of authorities he would be abdicating his functions. The logic used by Benitez, said Washburn, suggests that the government could take away his wife and child. At this point in the literature being shared with the Foreign Minister, Washburn began to be personal. He shared with Benitez his personal unhappiness, presumably, he supposed, because he had taken people into his home, and because the legation was not moved out to Luque. Charles was wrong in his supposition, as he would soon find. Charles was believed by Lopez to be the leader of a conspiracy against the government. Housing people and refusing to move were incidental to the dangerous undertaking yet to be made known to Washburn. Again, he asked for passports.

Before another week passed, another letter arrived from Benitez. Bliss, said the acting Foreign Minister, was under contract with the Paraguayan government. No, Charles echoed back, he was not. What is more, international law does not require that the character of legation personnel be revealed. Bliss was the son of a notable American clergyman and Charles supposed the authorities could not get far with their fictional accounts making Bliss into a diabolic character. Actually, said Washburn, Bliss had not even been sleeping in the legation but in a house adjacent to the embassy. In addition, Bliss had freely walked the streets of the capital and even accompanied Manlove to the police station translating for him. This time, Washburn generously gave the sources of international law, Book VII, Chapter IX, in Martens, Part II, Chapter I, Sections 15 and 16 in Wheaton, and then using a little rhetoric, he impertinently asked, would your honor have Bliss "respect the law or violate it?" That was gratuitous.

The end of writing long letters had not yet come which Charles felt compelled to write. Benitez was beginning to open an hitherto unmentioned subject, that there had been a combination of opponents to the government formed in his Legation. Well, said Charles, he was not surprised to learn that. He had supposed as much because of "unusual measures [which] had recently been taken by the Government." The next sentence put on edge Benitez and Lopez as Washburn adds he had not the remotest idea what persons were involved. In fact, when he thought about it he confessed to have believed there were not enough men in the country to attempt a conspiracy.

"The gunboat," Charles added as he closed, "will eventually force its way past the blockade . . . "

Two days hence, another more serious claim was made. "There is a treasonable combination with the enemy!" Benitez thought that in two more days on the 24th of July certain actions would take place "by persons in the legation." The acting Foreign Minister had Bliss and Masterman in mind, and Charles supposed it must be those two since he had not given a moment's thought to the possibility of being considered guilty of conspiracy. No such hint had been given that Washburn could perceive. So the American Minister said with a whisp of humor that he would "hold Bliss and Masterman 'close prisoners' until they are out of the country."

Twenty-four hours later . . . Benitez instructed Washburn to send him "the sealed package given to him by Foreign Minister Berges. Berges was a man of superior attainment. Washburn in a quick response said Berges had given him no package, and that Berges had provided no message.

Something more than hints were now being slipped in to the Benitez letters "between the lines." The 24th of July had been mentioned by Benitez. Berges had admitted under torture that a revolution had been planned for the 24th, Lopez's birthday. Lopez had told one of his Lieutenants that the allied "iron-clads would force the batteries on that day."(21) On that day, as the iron-clads passed up the river, three men were seen waving a handkerchief and shouted something. Lopez in a message to his Lieutenant asked, "What signal did the first iron-clad make on passing the battery?" The handkerchief men, it was supposed, bore out Lopez's expectation of a revolt. And Charles? Charles, thank you, said Benitez, had mentioned the 24th in an earlier note, in this way intending to make it clear that Benitez knew and now he was asserting that Charles knew about the planned revolt. Charles promptly let Benitez know that the 24th had been mentioned by Benitez in an earlier letter, and he, Charles, was merely responding to what had been said. No, said Washburn, he would not discuss further the question of legal membership in the legation. If Bliss and Masterman were guilty, they must be tried, but Washburn made clear, tried in their own countries. Charles was confident he would be commended around the world for insisting on the rights of legations. As will be seen, however, newspapers in the region and newspapers in the States were unmerciful in their criticism of the American Minister.

Charles closed his letter of the 25th with snide remarks unbecoming a distinguished Foreign Minister, saying with regard to charges made against Bliss that to those charges he would not allude "lest again you should thank me for information that I had only derived from Your Honor," having in mind, of course, what Benitez had done in a previous letter in referring to the date of the 24th as though Charles were the first to use it. The letter to Benitez closed with another inappropriate remark. Washburn had full confidence that his government would administer justice. And the Government of Paraguay? he asked suggestively. Benitez' repeated request for Berges' packages evoked from Charles the remark that the business of packages is not the kind of subject deserving consideration in diplomatic correspondence. He then closed sarcastically, apologizing for not attending Lopez's birthday party. He, Charles, had been preparing a response to Benitez's letter.

In another August 11 letter, which probably should have been written briefly indicating that it must be the last, Washburn went on for eleven pages, single space, apparently twenty-seven foolscap pages written in his own hand. Surprisingly, Charles was apologetic. He was sorry he had not kept a list of names of people to whom he had sent letters. In this tone he asked, "What else could I do . . . ?" "Was it my fault?" "I did only in duty and courtesy [what] I was bound to do."

There were so many falsehoods told by Carraras, Berges and others that it became clear that the parties were deliberately lying, and lying so that it would be abundantly clear to Charles that indeed, they were confessing falsely, suffering the intense pain of *cepo uruguayana.*

❖

September was the fatal month. Like so many foreigners, Charles would be put in chains and left to rot under the sun's rays, or he would "escape," a word the Minister used. He had a difficult series of exchanges with the latest Foreign Minister, Luis Camino, unhappy about Washburn leaving the country and taking money which did not belong to him . After an exchange of notes Washburn was permitted to take the money after paying duty, and after leaving the care of the legation and its possessions in the hands of Italian Consul Señor Chapperon.

In a message written early in the morning a final note was sent off to Camino expressing the hope that Charles and his entourage would leave at 9 o'clock. It had been clear for months that Washburn must be rescued. His friend J. Watson Webb was able to help, threatening to break off relations with Brazil if Brazil would not allow the ship, *Wasp,* to pass the blockade. Admiral Davis finally ordered Commander Kirkland to go through the blockade two hundred miles south of Asuncion. Kirkland was prepared to fight to get to his destination. Brazil gave way. When Kirkland reached the capital and sought out Lopez he told President Lopez frankly that Washburn was a friend of President Grant and that if anything happened to Charles the president would have Lopez's head. Actually, it was Charles' brother Elihu who was Grant's personal friend. Grant appointed Charles' brother Elihu ambassador to France. The difference was slight, that it was not Charles but his brother who was Grant's friend. It would have had the same effect if Commander Kirkland had explained it accurately.

After the confrontation with Kirkland, the Commander's gun strapped to his side, Lopez had no intention of interfering with the departure of Washburn. He did not intend, however, to let Bliss and Masterman escape.

In the cool of the morning, Charles sent his family ahead. He expected violence and did not want Sallie to witness it. The French and Italian Consuls accompanied Washburn with Bliss and Masterman immediately behind. When the embassy party reached the end of the corridor which ran along the side of the estancio, Bliss and Masterman, following Charles, stepped out of the corridor and were surrounded by a half-a-hundred soldiers with swords drawn. They were taken off to prison. Masterman later wrote about the brief escapade, saying Washburn walked so rapidly that the Consuls, Bliss and himself could hardly keep up with him. Masterman said he raised his hat to Charles and said loudly and cheerfully, "Good-by, Mr. Washburn; don't forget us."

Charles had said to the two men that if they were captured they should feel free to make up stories about him if by doing so it would alleviate their sufferings at the hands of Lopez. Lopez would attempt to draw from Bliss and Masterman a record of the Ambassador's supposed conspiratorial activity.

The Washburns were aboard the *Wasp*. Charles knew, however, that despite their safety aboard a warship, Sallie would remain a broken woman. Charles himself was a nervous wreck. Richard Burton saw him in Buenos Aires and described him as "living in a state of nervous excitement, in an atmosphere of terror and suspicion." Burton was under the impression that Charles was not even responsible for his actions.

A small town boy, with religious beliefs which had kept him true to his faith in the ideals of honesty, possessed a distinctive earnestness. Charles had Ralph Waldo Emerson's vision of self-reliance which takes sincerity as a basic human condition. Charles was going through a major crisis in his life.

Chapter Twenty-Eight

THE SINCERE TROUBLEMAKER

"Cherished by both Carlyle and Emerson, sincerity was a popular nineteenth-century ideal that imagined 'a congruence between avowal and actual feeling,' a continuity between persona and inner self. Connecting inner and outer selves, Emerson's vision of self-reliance takes sincerity as one of its basic conditions."

❖

Emerson was an original with his insights, though there are instances in which he was doing hardly more than reporting as a social historian what was to be observed on the streets and in the shopping marts of New England. His description of the "popular nineteenth-century ideal," the sincere man, is a description of what Emerson saw in descendants of the puritan model, and to a considerable extent in what historian Daniel Walker Howe refers to as the culture of Whiggism.(1) Charles Ames Washburn is an instance, as are his six brothers. In living out the ideal, Charles Washburn's experiences as plenipotentiary in Paraguay explain problems as well as promises which followed him during his eight years in that troubled country, in part because of his "sincerity" and related agreeable and disagreeable attitudes. Charles had a self-righteous hold on the kind of social creature who, he was sure, must always be true, honest and forthright, mostly the latter. There is surprising childlikeness and innocence attributable to sincerity as is revealed, even in men like Charles who passed through political, personal and social strife and witnessed manslaughter on a massive scale, yet who did not lose hold on a vision of fairness and virtue. Charles did not hesitate, therefore, to make judgments, sometimes harsh, establishing for himself a personal style characterizing this Washburn during adulthood.

One might think Charles, with his *damned sincerity*, as some were sure to have said, could not be trusted with an office of importance, such as Collector of the Port of San Francisco, or Representative to Congress. It was thought by politicians in California it would be too easy for a person of his ilk to by-pass the "politically deserving," if of questionable honesty, and appoint only "knights in shining armor." Even Lincoln, essentially a politician, struggled with honesty and sincerity. Charles, it seems, could not be trusted, not because he was untrustworthy, but because he was unpredictable. There could be important occasions when Washburn would find it impossible to compromise, as, say, Lincoln was able to do in reference to the despised Simon Cameron of Pennsylvania whom he appointed Secretary of War against the stern advice of Charles' brother, Elihu, another of the sincere type Washburns. The persistent moralist, Charles, wrote in 1885, still clinging to childhood teachings, "It is not in human nature for men to approve what they know to be morally wrong."(2) Lincoln in refusing Washburn number five, Charles, was being his "sagacious" self, "sincere" as the poet has it, but not stupid in his sincerity.(3) Charles belonged among those referred to in a publication about newsmen on the west coast as "serious men, old-fashioned, with very stiff collars." The word-picture is reminiscent of stylized characters from mid-America painted by

Grant Wood.

Charles wrote to Elihu in 1863 from Paraguay,(4) feeling, as he said, some amusement, as a result of his rejection in the political arena in California. In reporting to his brother he revealed a kind of innocence despite an astute awareness of political manners and mores. His typical strong language in the letter disclosed the underside of sincerity. Appointments had been made in Washington by the Lincoln team to include those "deserving" California political leaders, who by the time Charles wrote his letter from Asuncion, were turning out to be villainous. Charles was not surprised. He had expected them to be. But in the course of his recitation of corrupt political personalities, Charles made qualifications. John Conness, who had been elected to the U.S. Senate, had been a Union Democrat. As a Democrat, Conness was a friend of David Broderick, as was Charles. Charles admired Conness though he told Elihu he had broken with him as he had broken with Democrat Broderick when Broderick "undertook to dragoon the Republicans into the support of [Stephen A.] Douglas." Despite the coolness which existed between Charles and Conness, Charles yet said of him that he was "a true man" who "will make more figure in the Senate than any man ever sent from the Pacific."(5) Charles standards were high, but he did not need persons to be Republicans in order to fit his expectations.

Another Lincoln appointee attempted a fraud, Charles wrote. This man, Sargent, wanted to be a U.S. Senator and so supported, not Charles, but another who he knew would use government patronage to elevate Sargent. To that end, Sargent fought "in the war between Rankin and me," wrote Charles. Sargent, said he, will never be a Senator.

Charles listed the names of some of the persons, generally men of considerable eminence in the political picture, whom he fought, including Frank Morrison Pixley, counted by one biographer as "one of the greatest orators and parliamentary debaters of modern times." Ironically, this political enemy, Pixley, succeeded Charles as editor of the San Francisco *Daily Times*. When Pixley announced himself as the new editor no mention was made of his predecessor, Washburn.(6) It seems Charles, almost innocently, took on the leading lights of his time in the political arena, innocently, inasmuch as he was unable to see himself as others saw him. As others saw Washburn they sensed, as Lincoln sensed, they could not trust him to do the *best* thing instead of the *right* thing.

Charles, with his uncompromising attitude made clear in editorials, appeared at the Republican Convention in Sacramento in 1860 as a candidate with the support of a great many Republicans impressed with his downeast honesty and sincerity.(7) The politicians in the new young California Republican party found ways, however, of undermining Washburn's nomination. They were politicians and knew they could not criticize Charles for having praiseworthy attitudes. At the convention they tried to remove him by electing him State Printer. He withdrew his name. The best they could do to help themselves politically was to arrange for him to be an Elector. He garnered the most votes and politicians knew they were then rid of this man with his impressive, if damnable, sincerity. As Elector, he would be off to the other side of the continent.

In 1856, Fremont of California was the first Republican nominee for President of the United States. Charles wrote his inquiring brother Elihu who wanted to know how California stood in the elections. His answer was "typical Charles" with all his seriousness and sincerity. He explained to Elihu that he was publishing a campaign paper for the State Convention. "I write it nearly all myself and endeavor to make it rank 'pison' to the Chivalry." If anyone in California was unfeignedly against Southern principles and the Chivalry, it was Washburn, which was why he supported Fremont and was publishing "pison" to benefit the party. His tactless manners, always sure his ways were "right," won him few plaudits, even from Fremont. Fremont, he was told four years later, did all he could to help the politicians defeat Charles in his bid for office.

It seems that George F. Masterman was nearly right in his opinion about Charles, that it was a mistake for him to reply "*seriatim*" to charges made by Paraguayan Foreign Minister Benitez, arguing points in the most undiplomatic language. Masterman says he watched with great pain the course Charles was adopting, suggesting "a less colloquial style of writing," but to no avail. Charles believed in what he said. He was so sincere about his conclusions that, as Masterman wrote, "it was impossible for me to offer my aid a second time" when his first suggestion to Charles was received so ungraciously.(8) But there were others who knew Washburn intimately who testified to his contributions in Paraguay despite failings. Dr. Frederick Skinner wrote to him, "[Y]our veracity and honor must be thoroughly established and all your conduct vindicated."

Determination fused with self-righteousness can have its dangers, however, as men with such earnestness as was displayed by Charles aspire to positions of power. Their certainty is often persuasive, and, not unusual, hypnotic with mass audiences. One wonders if there were not an incipient mass movement in Charles since he wrote that the "spirit of communism is an expression of revolt against what is conceived to be the injustice which prevails in the distribution of property."(9) In an editorial written in January of 1860, the attitude of Washburn is pronounced. " . . . Commercial interest everywhere is ultra conservative . . . and leaves capital quietly to accumulate, the rich growing richer all the while, and the poor poorer . . . . Any social evils they think must not be seriously interfered with for fear some of the avenues of trade and profit shall be affected." Something in the fundamentals of early Whiggism or Universalism, together with the hard lessons learned about the capitalist economy, flavored the thinking, not only of Charles but of Israel, Jr., and the millionaire brother, Cadwallader. Israel, Jr., "warned of the danger 'that the money-power will be too much centralized, --that the lands and property of the country, in the course of time may come to be held or controlled by a comparatively small number of people."(10) And what arose out of Israel's philosophy to solve that problem was his proposal, "Our eyes must rest occasionally on the statutes of distribution, as well as those of accumulation."(11) Cadwallader as representative and governor worked to make the railroads and telegraph system public utilities. Charles was among the first to advocate the eight-hour working day, and he advocated public ownership of the St. Lawrence. All of the brothers would have been impressed with Whig values as they learned early what Joseph Story had said of a statesman of the Whig movement, that he "must legislate for the future, when it is, as yet, but dimly seen; and he must put aside much, which might now win popular favor, in order to found systems of solid utility, whose results will require ages to develop; but still, whose results are indispensable for the safety, the glory, and the happiness of the country."(12)

An example of the nature of Charles' and Charles' willingness to make judgments accounting for problems he faced because of "sincerity and related attitudes" appear in a press interview held as soon as he set foot on American soil after "escaping" from Paraguay. He said things which were intended for public consumption, that Dictator Lopez hated everyone who was not absolutely loyal to him. He pronounced Lopez by nature "cowardly, cruel and bloody." Such undiplomatic recitations from the lips of the country's official representative to another country! Diplomats are disinclined to vilify nations they have served, or to malign their leaders, leaving that function to reporters and scholarly journals, as in the 20th century the function is left in the hands of the propaganda mills of government.

❖

When Washburn returned to his childhood home following the travail of war and the gruesome massacres in Paraguay one could still hear the echo of a lifelong devotion to attitudes of childlikeness and sincerity as he wrote in the Family Journal:

> The most important event to chronicle in this book, that contains
> so many 'wise saws and modern instances', is to the writer the
> fact that he is here to jot it down.(13)

This jaunty recitation is followed, not with a record of unimagined horrors, but by sentences illustrating a childlike temperament. His report in the Journal reveals a kind of innocence, honesty, and a clear conscience. There is, childlike, an uncalled-for recitation of facts about his wife, "whose name is Sallie," the style to be seen as part of an attempt to recover a manner of sharing family doings. He wrote in the same manner and style about his Paraguay-born daughter, "whose name is Hester." He explained that he was "accompanied by the late Governor of Maine whose visits in this bailiwick being frequent[,] his presence here now is not so signal an event as that of the late Minister to Paraguay." Charles had been through hell, figuratively speaking, but finding himself back in the wilderness and safety of Maine, and conscious of who his Journal Readers would be, he reverted to the Livermore mode of communicating; a dash of humor, and a sprinkle of self-glorification disguised as humor. With his attempted subtlety Charles was instantly identified as the youth known by all Washburn family members. His style is reminiscent of Erik Erikson's view, that adulthood contains a persistent childishness.(14)

❖

Since we are doing an analysis of Minister Resident Washburn, it is necessary for us to consider general ideas and to shake those ideas down into personalities like Charles and his brothers. Of such a general character is a finding of historians, that the Washburns were children of an age in which writers and preachers were sensitive to the uniqueness of the American experience, and of an educational philosophy evolving which can be seen as shades of John Dewey. It was not unusual, therefore, for persons to say in their own words what Orestes Brownson wrote in reviewing an Emerson essay, emphasizing the importance of "belief in which [one] had been brought up, the education which he received, the spirit, habits, beliefs, prejudices, tastes, cravings of the age and the country in which he lived, or for which he sang . . . " Thus, in father Washburn's time, Whiggism and the religion of Universalism, vitally important to Israel, Sr., was thought of as a culture. That "culture" was taught to the children. The culture of New England and of Whigs had decided objectives, many of which were part of the thinking of Israel, Sr.,--universal public education, the development of a native literature, defending freedom of speech, the distribution of public funds for internal improvements, the re-distribution of wealth by way of an increase of the county's wealth. Whigs were aware of the influence of religion. A Universalist church was built, half on Washburn and half on a neighbor's property. Universalist principles were inculcated by the children.

In 1840, 50,000 Whigs gathered at Bunker Hill and adopted a resolution declaring belief "in the benign influence of religious feeling and moral instruction on the social, as well as on the individual, happiness of man."(15)

When Charles was sixty-one years old he delivered an address in Alameda, California, at a reunion of natives of Maine. In his remarks, after paying warm tribute to parents whose "hope and ambition [was] that their children should grow up honored and respected among men," he recalled the broad education received from father and grandfather who helped the Washburns to understand, "almost from our childhood, the fundamental principles of a just government." The community of those days, Charles said, was made up of men interested in public affairs. The spirit of great leaders was diffused among the people, and the Washburn father and mother were filled with this same spirit. For the children they translated the meaning to be seen in exemplary lives of forefathers, and they talked of historic events remembered into their old age. In his Alameda address to natives of Maine, he said 50,000 were summoned to the battlefield.[1]

Father Washburn was a teacher by profession, and the most singular subject "taught" to his children as they were at work in the fields, or when they were gathered at the kitchen table, and at the bedside before they fell to sleep, was the culture of Whiggism. It was those teachings, plus the strong hand and guidance of the mother, that influenced the life and thought processes lived by sons and daughters of Israel and Martha from 1813, when Israel, Jr., was born, until Caroline died in 1920, a total of one hundred and seven years. Apropos of this generalization, consider a fact mentioned at the outset, that in America there is a counterpart to the tradition whereby each Jewish mother-to-be prayed that her child would be "the savior of the nation." In early America, it was not unusual for a mother who began to feel movement in the womb to express the hope that her child might become President of the United States. If there were a more modest dream it was that their child might become Governor, a leader of industry, or a great warrior. Mother Martha possessed such expectations when her children began to arrive. Her hopes had political overtones commensurate with what father Israel was talking about with his political/cultural philosophy. Martha demonstrated her hope for greatness when her first son Israel was born. Upon being instructed by Martha, we remember, the father "took Israel upstairs 'so he may rise'." She predicted when Israel, Jr., was a youngster, that he would be Governor of Maine. He became governor. The mind-set of a Martha Washburn carried her vision for Israel, Jr., extending her hopes for the

---

1. Charles did not say what was true, that those thousands were summoned by his brother, Israel, Jr., Civil War Governor of the State of Maine.

eldest, to the youngest and all in between. All of them felt the near presence of their mother during their entire life. Their father's interest in the body politic also had a marked and measurable influence. Whig culture and philosophy were passed along by the teacher-father to effect the attitudes, to provide techniques for solving problems, and to furnish a sense of identity for the siblings. There was strict adherence to what they interpreted as the Whig, and later Republican, philosophy.(16)

Attitudes with which we are dealing are imprecise. But as we observe the careers of so many of the brothers who became politicians, we are helped to understand what social historians mean when they refer to "Whig attitudes." Six of the seven Washburn brothers were immersed in politics --Charles as an organizer as well as an aspirant for the position of representative in congress, and in later life as a candidate considered for governor of California. As an organizer, his cultivated Whig attitude expecting him to solve problems found him instrumental in organizing the Republican party in the west coast state and in editing what was said to have been the only Republican newspaper in California. The press in that period of American history was often a derivative of political parties and of religious denominations. Charles' experience bears out that claim. He and the Reverend S.D. Simonds, a Methodist minister, edited a religious, anti-slavery newspaper in San Francisco, and of course Charles edited the Republican San Francisco *Daily Times.*

The children were being educated only a few decades after the revolutionary war and the wars with Indians in the district of Maine. Throughout the country, therefore, there was openness to the profession of soldier. Thus, three of the seven sons were involved in, or ambitious to be part of, the military. Cadwallader aspired to a career in the military by attendance at West Point, and while his mother did not encourage his ambition, and he did not remain at West Point, he became a Major General in the Civil War. Charles was anxious to attend the military academy to become an officer in the service, but was eliminated, it is said, when a Maine politician with more influence than the Washburns possessed wanted his son at the Point. Samuel was in the U.S. Navy and Commander of several ships. Elihu had no aversion to the use of force, and threatened himself to use physical coercion, announcing at the time he was a young lawyer that he would throw a certain burly man downstairs from his upstairs office in Galena, Illinois, and he did exactly that. He went to see the battle outside Washington, and was present as a witness to the Battle of Bull Run. When Union soldiers began to retreat Elihu stood in the middle of the road, attempting like an officer to turn back soldiers.

The Washburn children were aware of being descendants of military men. Their mother's father served in the Revolutionary War from the beginning to the end. After the war their grandfather, Lieutenant Samuel Benjamin, settled in Livermore. Living in Livermore during the childhood period of the brothers and sisters were: Thomas Chase who served with John Paul Jones; Thomas Fish, Major in the Continental Army; Elijah Fisher, member of General Washington's Body Guard; Henry Grevy and William Martin, Hessian soldiers; Ebenezer Learned, a General; Daniel Holman, one of the "Minute Men" at Concord; John Walker with Arnold's expedition to Quebec; Josiah Wyer, at the battle of Bunker Hill, and, of course, Samuel Benjamin, their grandfather. The end result of that part of their education was loyalty to country, whether standing in readiness to shed blood, or working for the well-being of the body politic.

The Maine experience with Indians was not immediate as far as Charles and his brothers and sisters were concerned, but there were men alive in Livermore whom they knew personally had fought the Indians, and whose family members had suffered capture and sometimes scalping. David Hinkley, for example, died at the age of 102, born in 1767, and in his lifetime knew about war with the Indians.

The political philosophy of Whigs favored conciliation and compromise. Those principles served Charles, diplomat and lawyer, as he had to justify his positions by invoking international law, and as in fact he attempted to mediate the ongoing war in the Plata region. There were Whig characteristics, however, which argued with the salutary values of conciliation and compromise. Charles in his position as resident minister, for example, suffered as a result of treasured values he was unwilling to compromise. In some instances the unwillingness led to a duel on Washburn's part, and according to his self-analysis, his stubbornness lost him a seat in congress. Whigs like Henry Ward Beecher were preaching that Christians should not elect to office men who engaged in dueling.

Washburn's acquired values as a Whig-Republican were such that, without compunction he became an instrument of policy put in place by Federalist-Whig John Quincy Adams, the policy preached by Jonathan Edwards, and expounded and made the practice of capitalist expansion into the west. That is, he was an agent of the "manifest destiny" pronounced by his government, sent to Paraguay to use techniques acquired as a cultivated Whig on behalf of the business interests of the U.S. He also reacted predictably and negatively without having to be persuaded by William H. Seward, when Napoleon III sent Ferdinand to Mexico to be Emperor of a country belonging within the orbit of supposed United States interests. His response, critical of that move, was similar when he reported to the Department of State that he had on his hands Francisco Solano Lopez who was interested in making Paraguay an empire and himself emperor.

❖

The values distinctive in the Whig tradition fostering attitudes of honesty, sincerity, and openness reveal themselves in Charles' message recorded in the Family Journal on the day he returned home to Livermore, Maine, March 11, 1869. What he recorded amounts to being for us "a few reflections," on his New England attitude, particularly germane if we consider attitudes to be observed among leaders in Paraguay who had a status in society comparable to Washburn's. We cannot conceive Berges or Benitez, and certainly not Dictator Lopez, writing as follows:

Once upon a time Tommy Coolidge met the Senior in front of Water's where the blue-eyed Captain had a young "critter" tied up by its fore legs in a manner that interfered with the beast's locomotion. Says Tommy to the Senior, "Do you see that? What has Waters tied up his steer in that way for?" "Tis breachy"[2] perhaps, responded the Senior. "Breachy! The devil. No, tis fulfilment. The book says "Simeon & Levi; cursed be thine wrath and anger; instruments of cruelty are in thine habitations."

---

[2] Breachy, inclined to break out of fenced-in fields, as, breachy cattle.

Looking out over the hills and valleys averaging five feet of snow leads me to reflect on the philosophy of Tommy and to consider the present snow bound state as fulfilment. Evidently Alfred has this place in his mind's eye when he wrote[,]

> "The long dun wolds are ribbed with snow
> And loud the Norland whirlwinds blow.(17)

And he also must have referred to this place and the Natural C. port in the line, "When Norland winds pipe down the sea." Fulfilment: the poet was a prophet.

I dont [sic] remember all the particulars but I have reason to suppose that 47 years ago today[3] there was some excitement about the house that then stood here, on that day an event occurred of great importance to the writer hereof, for on that day he first bid daylight good morning. Well, tis strange that he should have passed through so many hair breadth escapes and be here to jot it down and still lives good as new and wouldn't change lots with mortal man.

It is 11:45 and 15 minutes since a stranger arrived--it is a boy. His name is Thurlow Washburn. May he live to an age as great, as honored as his grandfather's and may he have " . . . his mother's faith, his father's spirit, without his failin's."

❖

This ends the day's downeast poeticizing by Charles. In what he wrote, there was the ethical note, not lost with eight years of "foreign" learnings about life in the primitive culture of Asuncion and the jungle life of natives. There is humor in his treatment of the biblically astute Tommy Coolidge but respect for the boy's sensitivity. There is appreciation of nature and its beauty, something almost peculiar to the "two Washburn ministers," Charles and Sidney, both of whom broke into lilting phrases moved by the charm of the fields, forests and the distant mountains they often named.(18) There is the solemn recognition of Charles' own birth and the birth of his son, Thurlow, on his, Charles', birthday, along with a tribute to father Washburn, still living, blind, but much admired and loved. Charles modestly acknowledges his wife's "faith" but hopes that the tradition will be handed down from his father.

What is hoped for in these sentences from the Journal, together with commentary, is that the contrast will be felt viscerally as between the trauma of living in Paraguay and the still treasured culture, Whig and otherwise, of downeast New England.

Chapter Twenty-Nine

EXCELLING IN SPITE OF IT ALL

Charles was the consummate writer among the Washburns, --talented, widely read, and a wordsmith of the first order. He wrote more than a thousand editorials and articles of opinion in his newspapers; letters, any two or three of which were lengthy enough to make a small book; ten essays published in the magazines *Hesperian, Pioneer,* and *Overland Monthly*; two novels, and three non-fiction works--put together, these works fill a book shelf--no slight accomplishment. Every book written about Paraguay since the publication of Washburn's "history of hell" includes in its bibliography his two volume *History of Paraguay, with Notes of Personal Observation* and *Reminiscences of Diplomacy under Difficulties*. In the body of any book about Paraguay, the author quotes liberally from Washburn's work. One of Charles' more generous critics was a fellow reporter on the San Francisco *Evening Journal*. As a way of saying goodbye and wishing Washburn well as he left the city for the east in 1856, the admiring fellow reporter wrote his estimate of Washburn's writing skills. "We have met but few that . . . were his equal," concluding that Charles' best efforts had rarely been excelled by any member of the editorial profession. The reporter went on to declare that Washburn belonged in the "front rank in the field of American literature."

On the dark side of the mood, however, an evaluation by a reviewer of *Philip Thaxter* thought Washburn's work was "the veriest twaddle--a dreary waste of puerilities." The critic provided a passage to explain what was meant by puerilities: "Pass on, Philip Thaxter, pass on, nor enter that door . . . The Devil waits for your soul within that house!" *Philip Thaxter* reads like a melodrama intended to elicit laughter from a theater audience. One can easily conjure up 19th century characters on stage with exaggerated gestures, and joshing as the actor recites his lines. The *National Quarterly Review's* critic may, however, have had a hidden moralistic agenda. That is suggested in the closing sentences of his article. The critic preaches that "no respectable parent or guardian would allow [the book] into his house, if he knew its real character, we have thus taken the pains to expose the cheat," referring, of course, to Charles. There is a possibility that Washburn wrote his book intending the work to be what we see, a melodramatic rendering; a making merry with those overly strict, emotionally starved last-century characters caricatured by writers and dramatists.

Washburn's *Gomery of Montgomery* is a gothic novel with a ghoulish, complicated plot. In the style of the genre, his novel is full of sentimentality, and there are instances where the story stirred emotions of pity and fear.(1) The book also reveals some of the author's own prejudices and superstitutions. An Anglophobe, Charles had a character say, "If there is one thing more than another that the people of the U.S. have to be thankful for, it is that so few members of the ruling families of England ever settled in America."

There are instances where Washburn's prose is beneath the skills of a high school freshman, as when Charles says of his hero, "He had not only an unbending will, but a will that never bends."(2)

❖

Charles' writing talents appeared early in his life, and were appreciated by those to whom he wrote letters. He expressed opinions freely, his sentence structure was acceptable, he made a practice of sending valuable information, and in his letters he developed a striking way of relaxing his readers, as when he deliberately used bad grammar, a habit made use of by most of the brothers. At age 16, Charles addressed a letter to Sidney and used a sentence for the purpose of changing subject matter, saying, "But I ain't got nothing to write," proceeding then with more news and opinions.

Ending his letters, there were invariably the invitations, if not pleadings, for recipients to respond. "You must write me by return . . . a letter a mile long." After Charles learned to appreciate the give and take of letter writing, sending and receiving messages to break the monotony of life on the farm, he found that some of his brothers either did not think much of writing letters, or did not care to correspond with him. As a result, Charles spent undue time and space at the beginnings of his letters blasting persons to whom he was writing, chastising them for not responding to earlier letters. "What in thunder is the reason [for not writing]. I never hear from you. You are always blowing me up for not writing. But seriously, I have business of great importance," etc. "As for hearing from home," he wrote in a letter to Sid, "that is entirely out of the question. They never will write me . . . ." Charles started a letter to Elihu in words that became all too familiar to his Galena brother, "Tis a long long time since I have had a word from you." Another began, " . . . You are now in my debt for as many as two letters . . . " In a discouraged mood he noted that everybody was in debt to him for letters he had written. He wrote that he goes to the post office "week after week and month after month, and finding nothing, causes me to exclaim in the language of . . . Harrison Hersey, 'Father I am discouraged.'"

In the content of his teenage letters, he wrote habitually about himself and his health, then about the family and farm, and followed up discoursing at length about politics. In 1841 he was watching Maine become a Whig state. For years Maine had been Democrat. The man elected Whig governor in 1840, Edward Kent, later became an adviser to Israel, Jr., and a friend of the family, visiting the Washburns at their Livermore farm. That letter was exceptionally strong on political matters, which, one might say, led Charles to say to Sid about his politically oriented brother, Israel, that Israel had built "a house that goes before everything on the Penobscot," at a cost of $5,000.

When he was in his late teens he began to write even longer, more newsworthy, opinionated letters,(3) as entertaining to read a century later as they were entertaining to Sidney, Elihu, Cadwallader and others. It became clear to Charles that his brothers were not like him. They did not fancy baring their souls in the written word, and they did not display affection. Charles closed his letters with "yours truly and affectionately . . . " while the others were more formal. Like his brothers, Charles had a pet name. He signed his letters with his nick name, it being some form of "Putt." The signatures represented an inside, if indirect, way of implying devotion as the brothers signed their "special" names. Charles closed his 1838 letter to Sid, "Putnam."

Man and boy, Charles was felt driven to write. If his letters did not give him the outlet he needed, certainly his essays and editorials did. Charles discovered the essayist, Charles Lamb, in all likelihood introduced to him by Israel, Jr., since Lamb was one of Israel's favorite authors. Charles, when he became enamored of the English essayist, copied his style. In one of his published essays, Washburn wrote on the *Ethics of Elia*.(4) It is a touching, well-written piece about the kindness of Lamb who sacrificed to care for his sister, Mary. Mary, in a fit of madness, killed their mother. To Washburn, Lamb was a "domestic hero" and belonged among Carlyle's heroes, though left out of consideration in Carlyle's listing. As an essayist, Washburn showed a talent which could in time have made him into a critic of American literature, politics, and culture, if only he had stayed with the art. He wrote well. In examples we have from his younger years we know he sometimes wrote as well as when he was a grown man. Charles exploited what he knew most intimately, his own negative and pessimistic feelings and experiences. His revealing self-doubt can be seen in his choice of the pseudonym with which he chose to identify himself as essayist, namely, *Oliver Outcast.*

It Might Have Been, was a treatise about a child who, like Oliver was an outcast. A young boy needed work and income to take care of his mother, but, says Charles about himself, he forgot he was to do something for the boy. He forgot once and then forgot again, and by that time the boy's mother was dead, since there was no money for a doctor. The "outcast" youth took his life.

In an 1848 essay, entitled *Imperfect Sympathies*, Charles shares with the reader his thoughts about the uncharitable ways of men whose selfishness "arrays man in hostility against his fellow man." By this, Charles meant to say, we are often mistaken in judging each other. For myself, he wrote, "let me preserve a clear distinction between the wrong and the wrong doer." In this expression, Charles anticipated a similar view expressed later by Mohandas Gandhi, "hate the sin but love the sinner." "Is an act *wrong*," Washburn asks, "and does the wicked *think it right*?" Then, writes the essayist, he is bound in conscience to do it. "Let me not censure him therefore." Furthermore, Charles had noticed in his travels through the world that "different people pass different judgments on the same moral actions." So, in his Lamb-like essay, the author concludes, "In my view a man is guilty just so far as he violates his own conscience."

Mohandas Gandhi

When Charles re-settled in San Francisco following his South American ordeal, he was called upon to deliver orations on special occasions. One was at the Sixth Annual Reunion of Maine People. He delivered what was at least a two-hour speech on the *Political Questions of the Day*, delving deeply into the then long past of his own life and reciting relevant facts taken from his knowledge of American history. His interest, he said, was in "lifting up" some of the country's genuine heroes while "putting down" some who are mistakenly thought to be heroes, such as Ulysses S. Grant,(5) General Sherman, General Sheridan, Admiral Farragut. Some of Washburn's remarks are surprisingly contemporary, even though his address was delivered in 1873. He said,

If for a long time people have been ground under the iron heel of monopolies and corporations, from which there is no escape by means of the Constitution and laws of the country, then it is time for a revolution that shall overturn the Constitution and give us a better government.

On the whole, Washburn's thinking and outlook continued the tradition of Jefferson and Jackson, amounting to repudiation of the Hamiltonian philosophy, economics and foreign policy. Jeffersonians sought to weaken the executive branch of government and favored decentralization, believing that "the protection of democracy at home and the extension of democracy abroad--not commerce--ought to be the central concerns of American foreign policy." Charles reads like Jacksonian journalists suspicious of a strong federal government and of a corporatist world order.(6) The views expressed in his address were to be echoed and expanded by Charles and Mary Beard in the Beards' *Rise of American Civilization*, reflecting a mood of isolationism.

In his lecture Washburn expressed his bitterness about a man he once admired, Leland Stanford. Stanford and his cronies, Charles declared, had created a monopoly of overland business, and had put millions of dollars into his own pocket. The railroad tycoon now expected men to bow down and worship him, a man remembered by Washburn as a once-humble businessman on the streets of Sacramento, California. With Stanford in mind, Charles notes in his address that the "divine right of kings is an exploded doctrine, and is not to be succeeded by the divine right of monopolies."

Like Cadwallader and Elihu, Charles desired the telegraph system to be a self-sustaining institution of government. He wanted more government control of the transportation system at all levels. In his writings as in his speaking Charles commended governments in other lands for having bought up private lines, providing "better service at cheaper rates." Washburn does, however, express concern, as does Israel, Jr., about the dangers of centralization.(7) Like Republicans of the ilk of Teddy Roosevelt, Charles declared "there is no remedy but for the Federal Government to come to the rescue."

His idealism led him to take an impossible utopian view in his speech to the Maine pioneers. He called for the partitioning of the United States into seven divisions led or directed by a board of directors independent of the President, his Cabinet, and Congress. Directors, he proposed, would be ex-Governors. Such a plan, of course, would place two of his brothers, Israel, Jr., and Cadwallader, on the board of directors whose purpose it would be virtually to run the country.

Washburn observed that labor-saving machinery had lifted heavy burdens from "the sons of toil." Labor, he believed, should be able to share the blessings of capital, and working men should refuse to keep the hours of their fathers, who as farmers had labored from before sunrise until after sunset. Workers should labor eight hours a day. In semi-socialist ways of thinking, Charles lamented the inequalities of fortunes. Such inequalities "constitute one of the greatest dangers to a republican form of government.

Excessive luxury," he was convinced, "is always the harbinger of dissolution." These ways of thinking on the part of the west coast brother, and, one should add, on the part of Cadwallader and Elihu, was the reason why in the literature of the day, three and perhaps four Washburns were referred to as "communists."

❖

Much that Charles did was experimental, his trip into the South to teach, his novels, his mining experience of six weeks. His work as editor was solid and lasting, continuing for more than two years leading up to the election of the first Republican President. He displayed unusual skill and even more courage in his treatment of a diversity of subject matter, from the death of David Broderick to the tale about a young man barely saved from suicide. Arguments put forth in editorials about politics, foreign policy, state issues, corruption, education, trade with China and Japan, are like a lawyer's brief, even numbering items as he makes his case in considerable detail. From the pen of this "quiet man," as his daughter Lilian described him, comes forth articles like a blast of heat from a fiery furnace.

Responses from the reading public were mixed, as might be expected. Editor Botts of the *Sacramento Standard,* referring to Washburn's *Times,* wrote "We are sick of the editor of the subject," and Charles responded, "You will be a great deal sicker before we get through with you." A competing newspaper carried letters from a "Rough Rider" who blatantly accused the *Times* of working against the interests of Republicanism by supporting Democrats Stephen A. Douglas and David Broderick. In a series of letters, the San Francisco *Bulletin* treated Washburn roughly, making use of the anonymous correspondence of a "sincere Republican" who was unhappy with the *Times'* constant harping on the "negro question." The editor of the *Times,* together with his brothers, took commendable positions on the question of blacks and Chinese Americans, while given a hard time by the white population of Democrats and Republicans alike. The exception among the brothers was William Drew Washburn, of whom it can be said, in two instances failed the Washburn crusade of 40 years. President Chester A. Arthur called upon Congress to support him in invoking the "Force Bill," so the Southern intransigents could once again be disciplined, as earlier Grant had forced the issue of suffrage with Force Acts passed in 1870 and 1871 at a time when Klansmen were spreading terror. President Arthur wanted power to send federal troops into the South to police the voting to make sure blacks could vote without intimidation. Even with the passage of the Fourteenth and Fifteenth Amendments, and the passage of the Civil Rights Act of 1875, "in the rural

William Drew Washburn

South the basic socioeconomic pattern was not destroyed, for share-cropping replaced the ante-bellum slave-plantation system. . . . Negroes remained a dependent, propertyless peasantry."(9) The Klan was still operating to deny the Negro his rights as a citizen. William, a leader in the U.S. Senate, rationalizing, contended that the Force Bill was an attempt on the part of Republican politicos to hold the South under their banner by once again waving the "bloody flag." Northern businessmen were in sympathy with Southern customers, as was the case with New York City's wholesale grocers, led by Francis B. Thurber, leading businessman and staunch Republican, who campaigned against the Force Bill. William D. Washburn in essence joined the Mugwumps who "opposed measures like the Force Bill because they were willing to accommodate the South in its control of the Black."(10) When voting time came in the Senate, it was William's vote that decided the issue! The bill to assure voting privileges for all citizens of the South was killed by his vote.(11) William himself, in a letter to a constituent, wrote that he felt he had done the right thing "and that [he had] faithfully represented the overwhelming sentiment of the more intelligent and better class of Republicans in Minnesota."(12)

In 1892, the Chinese Exclusion Act went into effect and Senator Washburn delivered a speech on the subject. Cadwallader's valet, William Freeman, a black who had accompanied William Seward on his trip around the world, and was serving Cadwallader in his dying days, wrote,

> I read that speech and must say I think it unworthy of the honored name he [William] bears. I think it quite un-American. It seems to me that it is a retro-grade movement, not only in contravention of solemn treaties with the Chinese nation, but unworthy of the great American nation. I feel keenly the thrust given thus to my people for there is nothing in this measure that does not apply with equal force to us.(13)

Charles' courage, foresight, intelligence shines through in hundreds of editorials he wrote in those trying days before the Civil War. With regularity he wrote about slavery, the first having been to commend Oregon for voting a Republican candidate into Congress to displace the "Know Nothing, Lecompton, slave-extending Democrat."(14) The next day, Charles spread out a lengthy article on the subject of conspiracy. A great leader, honored to this day, was Senator David Broderick, killed in a duel by the Chief Justice of the California Supreme Court, Judge David S. Terry. Charles could have expected nothing but vile hostility as a result of this editorial since, in talking conspiracy, he had to include the other of the two California U.S. Senators, William Gwin. As for Terry, if Charles had a more prominent position in San Francisco, the Judge might have challenged him to a duel. Instead, Terry disappeared after the virtual murder, to re-appear for trial and was exempted from all responsibility. Washburn stayed righteously indignant about this shameless incident and kept the name of Gwin as well as Terry in the headlines of his paper for weeks and months.

The railroad, it was thought, must be extended West to California. Charles' brother, William, had the ambition to make the extension with his rail line, but neither he nor powerful leaders in California were successful for years in obtaining funds for the purpose of uniting East and West. The case in favor of the project was made solidly by Washburn in his editorial, and in doing so was working against the interests of Senator Gwin, assuring investors in England and America that it was safe to buy bonds for the purpose of constructing the Pacific road. He pointed out that bonds of the city of San Francisco were "notoriously above par." And as for foreign capital, foreigners already own a large portion of San Francisco, Washburn wrote.(15)

Charles may not have been wise in passing over Abraham Lincoln as a recommended nominee for President, and failing that touting William Seward. But he was as wise as Israel and Cadwallader, both of whom preferred Seward to Lincoln. Elihu, however, fought hard to assure Old Abe's nomination and election. Charles referred to his preferred candidate as "the ablest living American statesman."(16) The following month, November 9, Washburn felt most assured that Seward was to be the nominee. After the election and Lincoln's appointment of Seward to the office of Secretary of State, Charles was indebted to him later for having persuaded Lincoln to appoint him Commissioner to Paraguay. Support by Seward may have been due to two things, the *Daily Times'* support prior to the Chicago convention, and secondly, the Secretary's regard and affection for Israel, who, along with Charles Francis Adams, was said to have persuaded Seward not to retire from political life.

To illustrate the extensive interests in world affairs, there is an editorial by Washburn entitled, *The European Imbroglio.* As an example of the style of writing and reasoning technique of the *Times* editor, the following paragraph is quoted:

It was natural that Austria should higgle about the boundary between what

The killing of David Broderick by Justice David Terry

she so lately possessed by the power of conquest, and what in Italy she was allowed to retain through the clemency and forbearance of Napoleon. She of course wishes the dividing line between Lombardy and Venitia [sic] to be as far advanced into the former as possible, especially far enough to allow her the complete advantage which the full possession of the historical "quadrilateral" with the Emperor. Secure in that, and in the restoration of the effete dynasties of the Dutchies of Parma, Modena and Tuscany, those satraps of the House of Hapsburg, her power in Italy would still be predominant, especially if allowed a voice, in right of her possession of Venitia in the new Italian Confederation.(17)

The foregoing are precis of writings by Washburn published in the first eleven days of October. Editorials continued to appear, numbering in the hundreds, until the end of August or the early part of September 1860 when Charles was seriously ill and unable to function as editor. Frank M. Pixley, counted one of the greatest orators in California at that period of its history, succeeded Washburn. The discouraged *Daily Times* editor departed the state December 11, 1860, hearing echoes of the grand words said of him in a final goodbye:

> *Mr. Washburn has been one of the earliest and most irrepressible of the little band of Republicans who have never for an instant wavered in their advocacy of the cause from the moment it had birth until it has come out of the conflict with colors flying. No man in California has done more in organizing the party, and in waging the contest to a successful issue.*

There is more written in tribute which might well echo down the centuries were Californian historians more careful in their watch on the times.

Chapter Thirty

INTIMATE GLIMPSES

It is embarrassing to scrutinize from a distance in time intimate phases in the development of a person's id, ego, superego, especially if one's psyche is being misshapen or deformed as one watches the unfolding. It is disconcerting to observe a man, not as he devoutly wishes to be seen, but as he is, gradually losing authenticity. We are witnesses as Charles Ames Washburn constructs a persona, attempting to be a Washburn against the natural inclination to be himself. He wants to be authentic as he believes Israel, Sidney, Elihu and Cadwallader are authentic. Charles' persona becomes misshapen when he reacts not only to what he knows Israel is saying about him, but as he becomes aware that others in the family know what Israel has said, namely that he "is not as ambitious, as imaginative, as energetic as his older brothers," and that he is "a good-for-nothing." Such accusations in the words of Livermore folk are "heavy."

Charles is supposed to be like Elihu. There is a nervous shifting and evolving of persona when Charles has to ask himself if he is supposed to act, speak and think like the correct and precise Elihu. If there is conflict, the super-ego is effected in early stages of growth with a felt diminishment of the authentic person. Even sister Martha, his mentor, friend and protector made fun of him. She thought he was a cry baby, and shared her opinion gaily in a letter to Cadwallader, saying Charles' lower lip was

Martha Stephenson

trembling again. There was also that someone special in the family who believed Charles was lazy. Charles struggled within, not wanting to remind himself what others in the family knew, not only what Israel had said, but knowing that the beloved Cadwallader also thought Charles lazy. So the begetting selfhood of brother number five was pushed further out of shape. It is, as said, embarrassing to look while uncovering facts about Charles' as he tried to be a Washburn with that quartet of brothers who did not include him in their activities. That also was heavy and left psychic scars.

Mother Martha was deferential to Charles. He seemed to her to be childish. She did not exchange views with him the way she did with the older four. In her semi-literate writing style mother wrote to Sid about Charles,

he good boy I think so he seems very happy in his minde. [Charles] sayd that he had ben sick had the doctor see him was getting better I feel great anscity* aboute him I can tel you I fear verry much that he will not be [able] to get throw to his studdes.

In such instances Charles' sensitive and invented persona is getting naked before us. Both the young and the adult Charles had to undress another unfortunate feeling for

---

* "Anscity," meaning "anxiety."

all to see, that his father wrote long, newsy, readable political and personal letters to Elihu and Cadwallader, but never to him. We think of the fact that Charles lived in San Francisco, California, during very dangerous times when men were known to have cut down a hanging carcass-of-a-thief-and eaten him, when vigilantes captured, sentenced and hanged men without trial, and that between the time Charles arrived in California and the year 1854, there were 4200 murders in the city of San Francisco. 1600 died from famine or sickness. This was the setting for Charles of the West coast city. But father and mother Washburn did not write to inquire about his health or well being. Later, Charles lived in Paraguay where his very life was threatened daily at the end of his seven year stay, yet he did not merit the favor of letters of inquiry from his father. The attitude of offishness on the part of parents created psychological scars. Charles sometimes feared within himself that he was not loved by mother and father, at least as much as they loved Israel, Sidney, Elihu and Cadwallader. He "knew the score" even as a young man. Writing Elihu he said,

As to hearing from home that is entirely out of the question. They never will write me and . . . I do not write them . . .(1)

This Washburn brother, Charles, however, had a singular talent or aptitude. It was

Gen Henry W. Halleck

writing. To him, what was seen as a valuable talent, was a mere convenience and was not seen as giving him status. Neither father nor mother took time to praise Charles for his aptitude so that he might feel good about himself. Words were pet things to him. He dashed off long letters with ease. When a teenager he wrote Sid demanding that Sidney write him a letter "a mile long."(2) To Sid, Elihu and Cadwallader, the three with whom brother number five carried on correspondence, Charles's own letters seemed "a mile long" he was so prolix.

Charles's attitude of resentment materialized in expressions of craggy anger about political matters. As has been said, "attitudes are particularly enduring sets formed by past experience."(3) It was socially acceptable in the family to display outrage and hostility toward political figures, including the Chief Executive. A dyspeptic mood prompted him to say that William Tecumseh Sherman was "an ass." He thought Henry Wager Halleck "a scoundrel." He referred to Ambassador James Webb as "a court flunky." John Tyler, Whig President was yet the subject of Charles' wrath in an 1841 letter, Nineteen-year-old Charles had reason to believe his twenty-seven year old brother, Sidney, would appreciate his reference to the "little shitten Tyler." Washburn's anger toward the world at large was being siphoned off in the form of hatred for that "shitten Tyler." He used characteristic sarcasm to make a joke at Tyler's expense, adding,

By the way[,] is this the same Tyler that Lucy Put used to have - or perhaps you don't remember that Lucy Putnam had a little white dog named Tyler. I recollect that she had and I have been thinking whether or not this John Tyler is not the same dog.

Political outrage permitted Charles to be vulgar without guilt, using words customarily left out of the written family record, indicated by "----". Charles would have had no difficulty with a story Sidney once told. When the story was reported in the Journal Israel left a "----" in place of the word which evoked laughter. "Ira Towle," said Sid, "opened up on Goose Howard, threatening to kick Goose so high that the angels could hear him fart." Israel in one version left out the evocative word, and in another he replaced "fart" with "sneeze." Charles would have roared over the story in its original form, and he would have re-told it at every opportunity.

This scourge of anger at age nineteen meant that Charles, like all his brothers and sisters, knew the national as well as local and state political doings. He knew when Henry Clay, the idol of Washburn family members, had been passed over for William Henry Harrison in 1840.(4)

Our gallant leader is defeated and now I care not what they do. My political hopes were all centered in Henry Clay and he is defeated. Henry Clay is a name as dear to his friends now as if success had crowned their efforts. Neither title nor appellation [sic] can make the name of Henry Clay more sweet to my ears. His life as a politician is just, and of all men in this country, even now, he is most to be envied. His words henceforth will be received not as coming from an ambitious aspirant, but as from Henry Clay as he is and always was.

The national Whigs at their Convention rejected Clay as "too southern"(5) then turned around and selected states' right proponent, John Tyler of Virginia, for Vice-President. Tyler's record was clear, even though he had shifted from Democrat to the Opposition party and finally to the Southern Whig faction. It was known that Tyler's intention was "to make Whig Nationalism a states' rights crusade."(6) There was a fear as well that Tyler might do the unforgivable, bring Texas into the Union. So, yes, Charles was angry. He expressed himself in colorful language which was more characteristic of himself than of his brothers.(7) Such picturesque language as Charles vented in writing was seldom put on paper by the other Washburns. Charles sometimes playfully recast his sentences leaving out smutty and offensive language, as when he wrote Elihu to say his preference for candidates in 1852 was for Henry Clay and Horace Mann, ending his letter with the words, "Give Johnny Polk(8) a kick in the -- posteria."

A combination of Editor Washburn's anger and self-righteousness is demonstrated in countless editorials published in his San Francisco *Daily Times*. When referring to President James Buchanan, whom he profoundly disliked he used colorful language to express his feelings without the crudity demonstrated in letters he wrote to his brothers. In the *Times* editorial of June 14, 1859, he said,

Will the depth of Buchanan's degradation never be reached? Is there in the lowest depths a lower deep? Is it bottomless?--Down, down, deep and deeper from the Cincinnati platform through the interposing Constitution, through pledge and promise, through law and through right, deeper and deeper yet, down into the perdition of broken faith and irremediable political damnation? He is going so far that futurity will repeat of him, 'Nine centuries he fell'.

Anger was indeed smoldering in Charles. With all these troubles growing inside him there began to flourish flurries of dyspepsia. Beginning in him was what Henry James called a "fountain of melancholy," depression. Charles' daughter Lilian said that though he was generally cheerful and optimistic, he had a curious turn of superstition and the tendency led to moments of depression. The word superstition may have been the best Lilian could use to describe what was in all likelihood paranoia, a shade of the "misshapen" psyche common among people who have trouble adjusting socially as self evolves. It seems that the most authentic self created out of the social mix was the angry, sometimes depressed Charles. And he worked to hone that self with determination during the years of his editorship and particularly as he was enduring oppression serving his country as representative in Paraguay.

The self myth is the truest part of an individual; by that myth we always seek to live. --Leon Edel.(10)

Social conditioning of Washburn family members is a vital determinant in the evolution of the concept of self, and in the forging of attitudes. The big four, mentioned earlier as a catalyst for Charles, to which must be added the diffidence of father and mother toward Charles and the fact of Charles being born into a household of hardy political proponents, all these were measurable determinants in the evolution of the "myth of the self"(12) by which one seeks to live.

As has been noted previously, the Washburns were Whigs committed religiously to Whig values. The values conditioned Charles and others in the family. Whigs had resolved at a General Convention that there is a "benign influence of *religious* feeling and moral instruction on the social, as well as on the individual, happiness of man." Whig values, social, political and religious, shaped the thinking and attitudes of the Washburn children, suggesting pietism. As good Whigs, for example, the family members learned what party spirit means. And while they learned the meaning of loyalty to party, it was *principle* which was of more importance. Whigs as exemplified by the Washburns spoke for liberty of speech. Charles, along with the "big four," was conditioned by Whig consideration of language and speech, thought to be critical in the movement. One's political party and a religious outlook were dominant influences on the American scene. Whiggism and Universalism represented a combination having a distinct bearing upon Charles

and the evolution of his selfhood. In San Francisco, Charles collaborated with the Reverend S.D. Simonds. These two, with Charles serving as editor of the *Alta California*, turned the paper into a religious, anti-slavery publication. Earlier when Charles bore the entire responsibility of the paper's policy he shifted the established loyalty of the paper from that of a neutral political position to the support of party interests. Charles' actions are consistent with party principles and congruous with the religious impulse fostered by the party.

Another Whig axiom prompted emotional as well as rational commitment while emphasizing the significance of the rational. Harrison in 1840, despite the public display of "Tippicanoe and Tyler too" rhetoric, was systematic in his attack on the known abuses by the Chief Executive. The candidate went on a speaking tour, discussing economic issues argued among voters across the country, not only by Harrison but by Whigs Clay and Webster. While the Democrats

William Ellery Channing

used the closely reasoned writings of Universalist Orestes Brownson's essay on *The Laboring Masses*, the Whigs used William Ellery Channing's analytical essay *On the Elevation of the Laboring Classes.*

Harrison died shortly after the delivery of his inaugural address. He spoke his last words to John Tyler, urging upon him the "true principles of Government." The dying Whig President said he asked nothing more than respect for those principles, in itself a typical Whig stratagem.

Charles as a party member was also impressed, as were Whigs in general, with the emphasis on technology and its improvement on increased wealth which Whigs wished to see distributed widely, even if not equally.

Orestes Brownson

An added feature for Charles and his brothers and sisters was an appreciation of the past. The father and mother exploited for the family's benefit their knowledge of remarkable forebears and contributions made over a period of seven hundred years. Family roots submerged deeply in time back to William the Conqueror when a Washburn was knighted on the field of battle. In the case of Martha, her father was a soldier from the beginning to the end of the Revolutionary War.

The end product of these and other factors were seven sturdy brothers and three intelligent sisters, all possessing attitudes determining, as Gordon W. Allport notes, "what he/she will see and hear, what he/she will think and what [they] will do." Charles possessed the best and worse of the Washburn heritage.

Chapter Thirty-One

DOWNHILL ALL THE WAY

There were to be no more grand successes for Charles Ames Washburn. To the end, however, no matter how dismally life treated him he continued struggling. He had a reputation to sustain and brothers with whom to compete. It was as though he were Oliver Outcast to the end. There were grandiose schemes he wanted to try out, and further adventures of the mind. So he left Livermore, headed west again, glorying in being able to say California was his home state whence he kept returning, like swallows to Capistrano. When Charles reached the Pacific he gave no thought to what worried San Francisco politicians when they learned Washburn was on his way back to their State. Their concern was that he might want an important elective office in the state. The returning old timer was not forgotten in San Francisco. Politicos knew something from personal experience and they knew Washburn's reputation had clung after he left in 1860. They knew the fight that was in him. He was remembered by the elite of the city as one of the old guard who made war with the Democracy "when rotten eggs were showered upon Republican orators." And the politicians knew there was one position left worth fighting for, the governorship.

Gov. Newton Booth

Charles paid attention to the wisdom of shrewd Elihu writing him from Paris. His brother had alerted Charles while he was still in Paraguay not to expect much out in California. He understood the state had sold out to the rebels. Elihu may have had in mind those "rebel feelings" such as often described Chivalric Southerners displaying as they did in an earlier decade their distaste for blacks. But at the time Elihu was writing in 1868, that same mind set was manifesting itself as antipathy toward Chinese Americans. In fact, Newton Booth, who would have been Charles' opponent if Charles had decided to run for the office of governor, ran and won that office on an anti-Chinese platform. In 1872 Charles made no effort to become the third Washburn Governor of the family, even though there was recognition of his availability in a year when Republicans were hurting and needed a "clean" personality to run as candidate. On that basis, Charles should have been their man. Washburn's return to San Francisco was celebrated by 100 old friends who feted the ambassador at a grand banquet.

Immediately after the excitement of the banquet faded, Charles, instead of backing into the traces and making the bid for the governorship, rushed back to Washington. Suspicious reporters asked themselves, why was Washburn going to the capital? "That," one reporter wrote, "is the question which now agitates the politicians." In actual fact, Charles wanted to make sure the federal government was opening its files on the Paraguay Investigation and were preparing to prosecute. He took time to make the trip even though he had yet to finish his "history of hell" about Paraguay. After all, it was Charles who initiated the action against Godon and Davis.

Admiral Davis

So far, the Attorney General from the Department of Justice had only written George M. Robeson, Secretary of the Navy, saying he had been requested by a resolution of the House of Representatives to institute proceedings against S.W. Godon and C.H. Davis. Washburn arrived in Washington in February 1872, "in readiness for any duties that may be required . . . .." No trial took place, but Charles had already had his small victory. A House Committee investigated the Paraguayan-Uruguayan Aragon affront to the U.S. and the poor showing of the American Admirals in refusing to take Washburn to his office at Asuncion. The Committee resolved that the officers had failed to discharge their duty, and made clear that discourtesy to diplomatic officers should be subject to punishment by the Navy Department.

As well as skirting the edge of success during his last years, Charles had to struggle to keep his head above water.(1) He invested what funds were left in his coffers from the sale of the Times and from savings made during his years in Paraguay, by turning his hands and brains to a long-neglected ambition--to invent. He added to his catalog of exploits the typewriter,(2) and a turnstile, the latter registered in the United States Patent Office as an Improvement In Passenger-Registers. He made a pronounced effort to find capitalists to put his typograph on the market, indicating he had improved upon two defects of the Sholes machine. Words, he said, could be read as they were typed on the Washburn machine. Although his perfected machine as manufactured had capital letters, Charles says the typewriter, unlike the Sholes invention, could have capital or small letters as desired. Charles typed a letter for Cadwallader on his "great machine"(3) urging him to invest in the promising venture. Charles granted there were mistakes in his typed letter, but, said he, that is the fault of the operator, not the machine. His humor prevailing, he added a two-line kind of hokku to the letter to Cad:

The pen is mightier than the sword

The typograph beats the pen.

Either of the two millionaires in the family, Cadwallader or William, were in a position to make the investment Charles sought, to put his typograph on the market. Had either Cad or William done so an investment might have tripled their great wealth. Each chose to pass up the offer and opportunity, however, and, as daughter Lilian reported, the patented machine was finally sold to Charles Remington. Lilian thought Remington "must have made millions . . . while the inventor got only a few thousands." Actually, her father did not realize even thousands. He sold the patent for a paltry $500. The original model is said to be on display at the Industrial Arts Museum in Munich, Bavaria, Munich, Germany.(4)

The passing from the scene of brother number five, Ambassador C.A. Washburn, can be appreciated for its bankrupt state representing a kind of tragedy on the order of Death of a Salesman as we see his death from a distance.(5) That is, by remembering that from the beginning Charles was the "odd man out;" that there was a kind of fatalistic consistency in his black swan attitude as a member of the group of seven, Charles had the ambition, the drive, the intelligence, and the devotion which characterized his brothers but he ended up the tragic clown. Charles lacked in some fundamental sense the secret of success, try as he might to "make it," yet experiencing failure repeatedly. Consistent with his reputation, his life closed as a sad confirmation of the pattern.

So now we will take a look at Charles after first considering the last hours of life for Cadwallader (1882), Israel (1883), and Elihu (1887). When time came for the Great Ones to die, their passing moved the citizenry of as many States--Wisconsin, Maine, Illinois, and Minnesota. Cadwallader in Wisconsin was mourned by governors, legislators, generals, business leaders and the humble numbering in the thousands. Hats came off and were held over the heart as the catafalque bearing Washburn's body passed over the Main Street of LaCrosse, Wisconsin, battle flags wrinkling in the wind. The hosts followed the remains to the hilltop cemetery where a cenotaph was to be placed over the grave of the General, the Governor, this son of humble folk from down east Maine. The obelisk marking the burial plot was so immense that it required six horses to pull it through the streets of La Crosse to the cemetery. It dominated the burial ground as Cadwallader in his time had dominated politics and business in his State of Wisconsin, in his community of La Crosse, and almost, it could be said, the great city of Minneapolis, Minnesota, where his flour mill brought fortunes to countless citizens including, of course, himself and his brother, William.

Charles, however, was not numbered among the masses mourning the loss of this great man, Charles' beloved and generous brother, Cad. Charles could not afford the trip.

His brother Israel's funeral turned out from their homes and offices men from all parts of the State of Maine. Crowding the church for the Memorial Service were leaders from the worlds of politics, law, religion, education, railroading, farming, and business until it seemed the state itself must shut down as though it were the Sabbath.

Charles did not hear the soliloquies and tributes paid to Israel, the brother whom he counted his surrogate father after Israel, Sr., died. Money, the lack of same, kept him from the grave side.

World renown brother, Elihu Washburne,(5) died. Observances in Chicago and Galena, Illinois,   found heads of states, foreign dignitaries, generals, congressmen, politicians joined the throng. Business was brought to a close, and, as with Cadwallader, humble folk by the thousands, mourned the passing of another venerated Washburn. The shaft of granite lifting far above the towering trees in the Galena cemetery, its peak lifted high over every other monument, was symbolic of the distinction of the man who had risen to great heights from tending the hen house and cow barn on the farm in Livermore, Maine.

Charles was not present in Chicago or Galena to say goodbye to that closest of all men in all the world, Elihu Benjamin Washburn. Charles could not raise the money to travel so that he might stand by the grave enclosing the body of his distinguished and much loved brother.

The time came for Charles to die. It must be said before he, too, was lowered into the grave that the demiurge remained dominant throughout the life of Washburn brother five: He felt he must succeed, as had Israel, Jr., Sidney, Elihu, Cadwallader and William. He "aimed at the stars" whether he was writing, inventing, or transacting business. ̄ ¡

Charles, walking down the streets of New Jersey and into New York to see his publisher, had some great project on his mind which kept him moving vigorously. Suddenly he was struck and he fell. He had taken the Eighth Avenue

horse car near the Christopher Street ferry, and in a few minutes he was stricken with apoplexy, or Brights disease, the malady which caused his mother's death and the death of four of his brothers. He was removed from the horse car to a drug store nearby where an unavailing effort was made to revive him. On the body of this "nobody" found by strangers was the address of Loring L. Lombard of No. 150 Broadway. Lombard was summoned and he arranged for Mr. Washburn's removal to a hospital. Several institutions were applied to, but there was no room available for Charles' small body, his heart still beating. He was finally "installed," as the news story tells the story, in St. Vincent Hospital. When Sallie arrived at her husband's bedside, Charles was scarcely able to recognize her, and he lapsed into unconsciousness lasting until his death. It must, of course, be reported, and it was reported in the newspapers that "he was one of seven sons," with his brothers, one and all, named. The final blow unfelt in death was that all the others were news. He was not.

A small gathering of relatives and by-way friends attended the simple, unostentatious funeral services. Charles H. Eaton, New York City Universalist minister, conducted the ceremony. It was in this Universalist church that Andrew Carnegie had outlined his philosophy speaking appreciatively of the famous Washburn brothers, meaning Israel, Jr., Cadwallader and William. Carnegie did not include Charles in his praise. Among the pallbearers at the funeral was Charles' financial agent, George Woodman, who had failed Charles when as Ambassador, Charles attempted to line up American companies to trade with President Lopez of Paraguay. With Woodman was H.R. Helper also carrying the casket. Helper was the author made famous by his book published in 1857, The Impending Crisis of the South, said to have been "the most important single book, in terms of its political impact, that [had] ever been published in the United States."(6) The Helper book, signed and promoted by Israel, Jr., Elihu and Cadwallader, generated such intense feelings that every man in both Houses of Congress were said to be "armed with a revolver--some with two--and a bowie knife."(7)

The body of the adventurous romantic, hauled away by a business agent and a renown but forgotten Southern author, Charles Ames Washburn, true to the values he learned in the farmhouse, his life ending without fanfare and with no trumpeted praise, without any of his brothers present, was slowly lowered into the seasonally warm earth, just up the hill from the place of his birth 67 years earlier.

Chapter Thirty-Two

ISOLATES ON A HILLTOP

A rich profusion of events, beliefs, attitudes, and cultural artifacts flourished in America during the decades when Washburn children were growing up in the culturally barren state of Maine where the family was isolated on a hilltop in Livermore. Only indirectly were local citizens swayed by the romantic theories from far off Germany and France which led to the ennoblement of individualism in America. Individualism *sans* scholarly treatises was already widespread in downeast Massachusetts, the district of Maine. Schools of thought thriving in

Norlands at Livermore, a View to the West

Germany left Livermore untouched, though among settlers in town was a Hessian who might be thought to have been a carrier of German culture. Instead, German trends in social thought filtered through to select communities on the eastern seaboard by way of an educated clergy. From Cambridge and Harvard, Unitarian Frederick Henry Hedge settled the church in Bangor, Maine, and Universalist Orestes Brownson of Boston lectured at nearby Orono. Hedge and Brownson had joined Ralph Waldo Emerson as founders of Transcendentalism.(1) The new German inspired religious view made its way slowly into the northern district of Massachusetts. While the Washburns in Livermore knew what their Boston minister Brownson was saying, they did not learn about philosophies coming off the continent and out of England, which is to say, the works of Coleridge, Goethe, Hegel, Carlyle and German idealism. Idealism in religious circles was making post-Calvinist ideas prominent among the more liberal clergy in New England, though the poetry of theology did not appear in the same learned form in village churches. For church people, idealism was translated into personal morality, and a morality citizens expected of the government. Questions regarding right and wrong became pronounced in the major political parties, Democrat and Whig. Different moral equations dominated Know-nothing, the National, Federalist and Abolition parties. Clergy and laity alike insisted that government must be "Christian." It was felt by New York Universalist minister, Edwin Chapin, however, that government, "without assuming any censorship over private opinions," could and should effect a moral influence, breathing "from every institution . . . embodied in every law." Idealism on this continent shaped itself into temperance movements, abolitionism and philanthropy. For Charles' brother Israel, idealism expressed itself in vigorous assertions calling for purification of the American Republic, linking manifest destiny with the Universalist sentiment and belief in "salvation for all mankind."(2)

Israel, Sr., had a vague knowledge of the English school which was developing the economics of acquisition *a la* Adam Smith. There is no indication that he knew about Quesnay, Condorcet, or Du Pont de Nemours, founders of an economy which was social, not limited to industrial or financial concerns. The father of the Washburn family had no way of knowing that the English theories were contra distinct from the equalitarian outlook of the French *philosophes*, whose ideas were conducive to a plantation culture already influential in the South. English economic concepts were pervasive in the North in the United States. Household reading at the Washburns in the early part of the century included *The Yankee*, a newspaper inspired by the writings of Jeremy Bentham. The statement on its masthead read, "The greatest happiness of the greatest number." Washburn read the *Edinburgh Journal and Newspaper*, and in his modest library were the works of William Paley. *The Yankee and Boston Literary Gazette*, and *The Yankee Advertiser* supplied satisfying reading for the father of the family.

In England, Whiggism represented the financial interests of the wealthy middle class, and it was that part of English ideology with its Whig party politics which was readily adopted by the Washburns and by those who had been National, Republican or Federalist. That same political if not economic philosophy was part of the conversation around the families' kitchen table. Henry Clay, John Quincy Adams, Andy Jackson, Henry Carey, which is not to say George Washington, Thomas Jefferson and Alexander Hamilton were names on the lips of old and young alike in the isolated Maine village.(3) If John C. Calhoun of Virginia were on his reading list there is no available evidence to indicate the fact, though clearly, Clay of Kentucky was there for the Washburns. Said by scholars to have lacked a philosophy of his own, the Southern Whig, Clay, on the one hand borrowed from Calhoun who in his systematics had fine-tuned the Southern way of thinking, and on the other borrowed from Jefferson whose outlook, mediated through Clay, was closer to the anecdotal experiences of downeast farmer and small entrepreneur, Israel Washburn, Sr. Democratic freedoms were appreciated by Calhoun and Jefferson, and appreciated as well by Northern Whigs. The departure from the South's principal advocate of plantation economics and States' Rights theories, Calhoun, came with Henry Clay championing centralized government and internal improvements. Southern principles opposed capitalist exploitation. Interestingly enough, Universalist Brownson sympathized with the Southern view, declaring that

there must be no class of our fellow men doomed to toil through life as mere workmen at wages. If wages are tolerated it must be, in the case of the individual operative, only under such conditions that by the time he is of a proper age to settle in life, he shall have accumulated enough to be an independent laborer on his own capital . . .(4)

Whig principles as generalities were accepted by Washburn sons and daughters, though the broad consequences were not to be fully understood until the children were older, and until the English economic system had begun to include them in what Vernon L. Parrington refers to as an "ingenious scheme to milk the cow and divide the milk among those who superintended the milking."(5) Charles, together with Elihu, Cadwallader and Israel, Jr., espoused practices reflecting some of the radical views possessed by the Reverend Orestes Brownson. Charles, for example, promoted the forty-hour week, favored a State University system, demanded a State-run not a privately administered prison system. Unlike his brother William, Charles deplored attempts in California to expel Chinese from the State. The California Washburn was clearly liberal in his religious views, editorializing,

> The staid parson, with his white neck-cloth and long gown must . . . preach to the understanding of his hearers. They will not long receive what he says as gospel truth, when their own reason tells them there is no gospel in it. No, their faith has diminished as their knowledge has increased.(6)

Charles was critical of businessmen, including Leland Stanford. "[Capitalists] wish all to understand that they are responsible to neither God nor man . . ." He criticized "the combinations of capitalists who kept money out of the country in order that interest may be kept at a high rate." Charles called for government control of telegraph and railroads, and felt it would be better for the cities to own their own gas and water works. He wrote, "A privately-owned telegraph system 'is entirely antagonistic to the genius and spirit of Republican institutions . . .'"(7) He proposed a method of taxation similar to those put forward by Henry George, with a single tax on land values.

Country Church Universalist

If the people of Livermore knew little of the grand ideologies sweeping the country beyond their almost vacant village, there was one area about which all of its citizens were well informed, namely, the political. The vital life line to the larger outside political realm was the father. When his sons were members of congress, it is said he could name every member of the House and could name the district from which each man came. Washburn, Sr., was a well informed, committed Whig. In the modest library on the farmhouse shelves were the *Secret Proceedings and Debates of the Convention Assembled in Philadelphia, 1787*, written by Luther Martin (1839), and *Observations of the Writing of Thomas Jefferson* by Charles Carter Lee (1839), and a copy of the *Constitution of the United States*. The *Journal of the Constitutional Convention of the District of Maine With the Articles of Separation and Governor Brooks Proclamation* (1819-20) was added to the library in later years but suggests that the politically astute father of the family knew about such charges as were being made by National Republicans in Maine in 1831, to the effect that "the 'Administration's tariff measures were pro-British'."(8) The father's dissenting prejudices in relation to the British were reflected in Charles and Elihu who on occasion expressed a decided displeasure with the British Islanders. On Mr. Washburn's shelves were the *Annals of Congress* published from 1789-1830. He was a Representative to the General Court of Massachusetts in 1815, 1816, 1818 and 1819.

The wanderings of Israel, Sr., took on a meaning beyond his interest in settling in the country north of Boston. He left a cultured home in Raynham, Massachusetts, choosing primitive living in the district of Maine. With his wanderings he exemplified a generation which was to succeed the "old America," bringing into play a "shifting, restless world, youthfully optimistic, eager to better itself . . ."(9) Five of Israel's sons would take up where their father left off, migrating, going to sea, moving ever farther west with the tidal flow of pioneers. But Israel's sons and daughters had little reason to speculate upon additional subtle meanings of their father's wanderings when he was a young man.

An epidemic widespread in the larger world, leaving dreaded marks on the smallest villages across America, was the economic depression of the 1830s. It was like a contagious disease infecting the population of the most isolated hamlets. The depression so severely damaged the modest business of Father Washburn that he became instantly poor. Poverty brought on by the failure of the American economy devastated the family in Livermore. The eldest Washburn son had to move out of the Livermore home. The next in line, Sidney, went off to Boston to seek his fortune. Samuel went to sea, and in a few years Cadwallader left Maine to settle in Mineral Point, Wisconsin. Elihu followed Cadwallader, settling forty miles from his brother in Galena, Illinois. Charles left Livermore for college in Brunswick, Maine. After graduation instead of returning to the farm Charles wandered South to find work as a teacher. Finding the depression had poisoned the economy of the South as well as the North, he settled restlessly in Washington, D.C., only to leave a safe position in the Land Office for the uncertainty of gold mining in 1850. William, the youngest son, left Maine in 1857, re-settling in Minneapolis, Minnesota. Like father like sons, the brothers suffered severely when the next of the succession of depressions struck the country in the 1850s and 1870s. As noted earlier, Charles folded up his Chicago newspaper the *Chronotype* in the late 1850s, having published but a single issue, and William lost his fortune in the depression of the 1870s.

America in those generative days was in a myth-making mood. Young men and women in the Washburn family were part of new myths-in-the-making as they began their hejira West. Stories surrounding the reputation of Yankees who settled chiefly in Wisconsin, Illinois and Minnesota were on the whole positive. The exception for many was the insistent evangelizing, settling upon the population the practices of New England churches, religion and morality. It kept westernized folk grumbling. Adele Washburne a native Westerner and the first white child to be born in Galena, Illinois, thought it ridiculous to watch the Philoons, recent arrivals from New England, "stop before each meal and cover their faces to say a tremendous long grace."(10) Charles' harsh critique of the churches and religion is an example of the Western mind set. "Of all the cant of this canting age there is none more palpable and absurd than this eternal Picksniffian [sic] lament that some people insist on testing political principles by the standard of religion."(11)

The generosity of Yankees became apocryphal, so that Governor Thomas Ford of Illinois, himself not a Northerner, praised the Yankee who was generous in his contributions benefitting the public,(12) and in serving the public politically. Politically oriented Easterners rose to positions of leadership in the several Northwestern States. "Of Wisconsin's governors the 1st, 3rd, 7th, 11th, 12th and

18th were born in New England," one of whom was Charles' brother, Cadwallader.

Travelers from the East earned the reputation of being inventors. Charles was numbered among those whose inventions were worthy of the myth. He invented a typewriter said to be superior to the machine made by Latham Sholes. Fiction made the Yankee into a teetotaler and temperance man. The Westerner was said to be fond of drinking, betting, horse-trading, stump-speaking, and swearing, so it can be seen that part of the uniqueness which characterized "the West" arose as habits were cultivated which were polar opposites to the habits of the Yankee. The Davy Crockett myth caricatured the West when it was noted that "wastefulness was in the frontier blood, and Davy was a true frontier wastrel. In the course of successive removals he traversed the length of Tennessee, drinking, hunting, talking, speculating, begetting children . . ."(13) Westerner Lester Ward illustrated a current running through the minds of people in his region of the country. Ward encouraged government intervention in the interest of society-at-large. The Western Washburns reflected this well known sociologist's thought about government regulation. Though themselves ardent individualists, the Washburns did not agree with the individualist charges that government management had been disastrous. Cadwallader made a study of the telegraph system in Great Britain and introduced legislation calling for government regulation of telegraphy. Charles and Elihu echoed his sentiments. Israel, Jr., expressed his radicalism in an 1858 article, *Modern Civilization*. "Power," he wrote, "is always stealing from the many to the few . . . Capital is keen-sighted, hard-faced, and close-fisted; it needs to be looked after." And then he warned the business community and politicians that we must consider the importance of "statutes of distribution, as well as those of accumulation."(14) This myth of the West and "Western Mind," however, were hardly more than romantic concepts at the time the Washburn children were growing. What was appealing then were reports made by men who left Livermore earlier traveled west, settled and found farming prosperous, and reported back to friends and relatives about the acquisition of rich lands, describing fortunes made utilizing resources in timber, gold, silver and the building of cities. The allure captivated Yankees including the Washburns. They too in time followed the course of the sun reinforcing aspects of the myth and the mind-set of Westerners.

There was a "New England Mind," though Livermore family members were only vaguely and not self-consciously part of the peculiar mind-set. In itself, that naive quality lacked awareness of who they were in New England. There was a smugness about New England which gets translated into humor belonging uniquely to the region. Martha Washburn was once asked why so many of her sons left Maine. She said wryly, "One State is not large enough for all the Washburn boys." Boston type humor encapsulated a state-of-mind thought to be typical, deserving the appellation "Yankee." Two Boston women were at the World's Fair in San Francisco on a hot summer day in 1815. One said to the other, "Who would have thought San Francisco would be so hot." The other Bostonian reminded the first that they were, after all, 3,000 miles from the ocean." There was a tendency for New Englanders to invent religions of their own, and Universalism, with other religious groups, met that need by adopting a polity which enabled members to define their own religious principles and remain within the church. Their Statements of Faith appended a sentence indicating that the statements were not creedal, nor were they to be used as a test of one's membership.

A myth current in the Washburns' early years was called "the Mind of the South," but in the first quarter of the 19th century a Southern mind could not have been identified in the towns of the North, either by pupils or teachers. The South as a geographic entity and state of mind was solidified in the years when the Washburns were in congress and played a part in bringing on the sectional civil war, having reasons then to regret the Southern mind which had been shaped by a plantation economy, slavery, and the States' Rights political philosophy enunciated by John C. Calhoun. Charles' impressionistic descriptions of the Southern Mind demonized the "chivalric" South, the aristocratic Virginian, the rapier wielding Carolinian who so proudly fought to the death for the sake of Southern "honor." Charles Washburn illustrates a response which many with a New England mind-set would like to have been able to say as explicitly:

> Sectional bigotry was probably never carried to the extremes in any other States in the Union to which it is in this State by the bobbed-tailed politicians, who had been dumped down here in California to live on government patronage and interpret the Democratic policy as it is understood by the overseers and slave-traders in the South.(15) These [Southern] men . . . when they look northward, invariably peer through goggles manufactured in Dahomey, or glasses made from the skin of a Mandingo, and, consequently, everything they see has the negro tint. Like persons looking through stained glass from a steamer's saloon upon the landscape, tree, field and flower taking their tint from the hue of the window pane.(16)

Charles when he was ready to vilify men from the Old Dominion, was able to draw on the frightening experience of being challenged to a duel by a chivalric Southerner. Charles came away from the dueling incident wounded but alive, with the match costing him a possible election as a California congressman. He wrote about modern skulking chivalry's methods, an example of which was a Richmond, Virginia, newspaper having offered one hundred thousand dollars reward for the heads of Charles' brothers, Israel and Elihu. Charles noted that the "miserable sneak who makes the offer does not give his name . . . and the probability is that he never could pay twenty-five cents if the heads . . . were offered to him."(17)

The idea of Progress was, one might say, patented by the people of America. The religion of the Washburn family had a happy mixture of classical Christianity and an almost secularized belief in the "progressive establishment of the kingdom of God." Signs of progress for Americans accompanied their

american universalism

Symbol of Universalism
by Linda Dickinson

treasured liberty and freedom. It was recognized by Universalist William S. Balch who noted that "altho numerous attempts had been made, in all sincerity, to obtain political liberty for men, it was not till the 4th day of July, 1776, that the great truth that 'all men are created equal' was fairly developed and erected into a chief corner stone on which to found a great and growing nation."(18) Israel Washburn, Jr., at a centennial celebration of Universalism in 1870, delivered an address playing on the concept of progress and the future.(19) For Israel, deity's impartial love (universalism), was "destined to become coextensive with humanity."(20) His logic led him to combine his broad Universalist hopes with this country's notion of Manifest Destiny. The U.S. was to "save the world." In a published article in 1850, Israel called attention to "progress in the physical, intellectual, moral and religious worlds."

[At the beginning of the 19th century] we had no steamboats ascending rivers against wind and tide, braving the ocean, and, we may say, bridging it so as to bring countries the most remote into the same neighborhood; no railroads, "modern 'acts of the apostles' of civilization," as they have been called, reticulating nations and continents; and conferring upon the world a new force practically equivalent to half the physical power it possessed before . . .(21) Progress was closely linked with Whig principles and celebrated in speeches and writings, with Democrats equally devoted to the concept. John Quincy Adams wrote on the subject of human progress and the stages of human development. Edmund Burke admired among Whigs was quoted as believing in progress. Henry Clay whose speaking and writing were closely followed by the Washburns also believed in progress, and an official Whig declaration announced that the Whig party was devoted to progress as it sought to establish the equality of political rights leveling upwards, not downwards, by education. The successful embodiment of the notion of progress was seen and experienced in the person of Mother Martha. A superstition co-extensive with the notion of progress was in her instruction to the father when the first born appeared in 1813: "Take Israel upstairs," she said, "*so he may rise!*" Canny sayings by mother Washburn are convincing evidence that European liberalism, having crossed the waters to the new continent, had a decided effect upon the thinking and attitude of people in the Livermores of America. A Washburn family motto quoted for generations was, "Never back, always forward." Charles Ames Washburn's nephew, Cadwallader Lincoln Washburn, a deaf mute, when he drew his last breath, with his arm raised and falling forward, signed to his wife, "Never back, always forward."(22)

❖

Understanding the self is a process one would suppose every author would wrestle with, "committed [as he must be] to understanding and interpreting the self."(23) Charles A. Washburn in his novels draws virtual stick figures for characters who lack vitality and resilience. Charles made hardly more than a superficial analysis of personhood. He was unable to come to grips with a fundamental question to place before the public, as to whether at the center of one's being was the divine, as Emerson supposed, or that at the center was an irrational, divided, uncanny energy, as was concluded by Emerson's contemporaries, Edgar Allen Poe, Nathaniel Hawthorne, and Herman Melville. One of the ministers admired by the Washburns, having two Washburn children named after him,(24) was William Drew. Drew's reflections in his sermons reveal insights into selfhood unusual for country ministers in those days. He extrapolated a theology from views not dissimilar to Emerson's, assuming selfhood and asserting that love of self is an integral part of one's being.(25) He extended the thought of self-love expanding to include the human race.(26)

What seemed to be unclear to the Washburns with the exception of Israel, Jr., was the effect upon organized religion of individualism, with its emphasis upon selfhood, and preoccupation with the myth of "the American self." And yet, as Universalists, the Livermore family did its bit in developing ten strong, self-contained individuals, though not men and women who looked too closely at themselves with an understanding of their own ambitions, and their formidable drive. While Israel might have understood what was happening in the culture, none of the others including Charles reckoned with the fact that authority, which previously belonged to churches and to ministers who had passed judgment on the people, in

R.W. Emerson

the Washburns' time developed into an inward assurance which "lost its religious character . . . [so that] the religious impulse [then] confided to a new temple, the self."(27) Israel and Charles, students of theology, philosophy and literature, would have called the effort to know the self in Emerson's terms solipsistic.

Some of these cultural movements and ideas were reified by the Washburns, whether consciously or not. The strong-willed Elihu, Cadwallader, Charles and William found it to be in their nature to hold forth as private persons whose will should bend the world to their righteous desires. There were during the time of their upbringing few jeremiads being delivered from pulpits or in schools critical of the myth of the self *absent a consciousness of the myth of the collective,* or Emerson's Oversoul, with which to balance the bloated notion of self and its vaunted importance. Under the circumstances, it should not be surprising to learn that Nietzsche, who was familiar with Emerson's writings, is believed by Walter Kaufmann to have developed his concept of the *Ubermensch* or "over-man" from his knowledge of the self-assertive, self-reliant American,(28) and of Emerson's "over-soul." Nietzsche's acquaintance with some of the Washburns might have reinforced what he had to say about the *Ubermensch.*

Chapter Thirty-Three

ISRAEL WASHBURN: THE MAN AND THE PARTY

"Fanatic!" "Black Republican!" "Radical!" "Opportunist!" These were opprobrious labels with which Republicans were tagged in the late 1850s and '60s. It meant that Israel, Elihu and Cadwallader Washburn wore those labels. The terms did not accurately describe Republicans in general, but to a degree they described the Washburns. Israel as a life-long Whig was a prototypical party member, and therefore in no sense fanatical. Nor was he a "Black Republican" or "Opportunist." That he was Radical, however, there was no denying. All three Washburn congressmen are classified as Radical by some historians, and the brothers accepted that definition of themselves.(1) Some historians rank them Moderates.(2) The confusion among historians amplifies a paradox. Republicans tended to be "conservative liberals." Israel, for example, said he expected people to hold on to what they have. He also urged people to institute reforms. In an essay entitled *Secular and Compulsory Education*, the little man from Maine turned to literature when thinking about model Republicans, selecting for his purposes an epigram from Walter Savage Landor. Landor referred to the "King's great" as compared with those he called "God's great." In Israel's perspective, "God's great" were those who from early life onward "hold on to what they have until they see...clearly something better."(3) Such a view illustrates the conservative side of the Maine congressman. But Israel did not appreciate the appellation "conservative." He called conservatives reactionary, hopeless and sour. "God's great," he went on to say, are intellectually active and as they grow older, they are guided by "the polestar of immutable truth." The intellectually active are reformists, and while "truth," immutable or otherwise, is still hobbled as in the time of Pilate, Washburn, feeling he had grasped "truth," intended to be loyal to it. As a reformist, Israel was a liberal. He belonged to the school of Locke and Bentham. Liberalism such as portrays Israel Washburn, is seen in Kenneth Minogue's definition.

> "Out of [an] intellectual foray emerged modern liberal doctrine,
> representing political life as the struggle by which men make their
> society rational, just, and capable of affording opportunities for
> everyone to develop his own potentialities."(4)

"Truth" which gave Israel Washburn his incentive, led him to develop a Whig agenda which was concerned with land tenure, which favored the extension of the franchise, worked for compulsory education, fought for the abolition of slavery, and the reform of prison systems. He labored to introduce progressive measures in government. Washburn's agenda shows him to be a fairly even tempered man, not a fanatic.

That Israel Washburn was not opportunistic is illustrated in the fact that his battles in the political arena did not, in the parlance of the times, "pay off." Israel, like his brothers Elihu, Cadwallader, and William, at different times refused to let themselves be nominated to high offices. They reluctantly submitted to the solicitation of friends who begged them to permit their names to be submitted at conventions. Israel wrote to Dr. Amos Nourse in Maine who had asked if the congressman would let his name be submitted as nominee for governor. Modestly, Israel said he did not want to be a candidate. Elihu likewise said expressly in 1876 he did not want his name submitted as a nominee for governor in Illinois. His election was virtually assured, but he wrote J. Russell Jones, saying, "I would be compelled to decline, absolutely, the nomination for...governor."(5) Elihu also urged friends not to place his name in the lists for nominee on the Presidential ticket in 1880. His old friend, Grant, was in the running and he did not wish to be pitted against him. And Cadwallader had to be pressed into running for governor of Wisconsin. William had a similar experience in Minnesota.

Hesitancy to accept high office was a common trait among the brothers. In that period of history, however, it was a becoming modesty to show reluctance to let one's name be submitted. Playing hard to get was a political ploy. Hannibal Hamlin was a case in point. Having been elected Vice President, he wrote his wife and assured her he neither "expected or desired" the office.(6) In Israel's case, however, he made a sacrifice when deciding to let his name go before the Republican State Convention in Bangor, Maine, in 1860. It would be better for him to be elevated to the U.S. Senate from the House of Representatives than from the governor's chair. He was right, as was his friend, the Reverend E.G. Brooks. Brooks chastised Washburn, saying, "You ought to have staid(sic) in the House till you were elected to the Senate."

Contradictions and Compromises in Israel Washburn

The young, ambitious lawyer from Orono professed uncompromising loyalty to his truth, and would have others believe he was consistent and unbending in his loyalty. But Israel Washburn, like other politicians, compromised with evil. Dealing with the law which required that fugitive slaves be returned to the owners as property, Israel confessed to congressional colleagues, and pointedly to Alexander Stephens of Georgia, that, yes, laws which were an offense to Republican "truth" were yet *laws which must be obeyed.* His radicalism did not suggest civil disobedience, --even though his "truth" saw slavery as an evil. The most Israel could do was to explain, that we *must not make final what is changeable.* And in this, Washburn showed himself to be a doctrinaire liberal in the Bentham tradition. One must acknowledge the political realities, avoid rationalizing, and move to change laws in ways allowed by the Constitution. It did not occur to the congressman that the Constitution might also be wrong. Later, his brother Elihu was aware of the inadequacy of that sacred document and he was a party to adding the fourteenth and fifteenth amendments. Israel, like Abraham Lincoln, felt he must live with an abominable legal system which denied congressmen the right to interfere with slavery in southern states. According to law, slavery must continue. In Israel's eyes, it would not continue with Republican blessings. As he planned it, *the law would be changed!*

Israel also compromised himself when he was governor. In October of 1862, General John A. Dix wrote to the governor in Augusta, explaining that blacks from the South needed asylum. He asked if Maine could provide a place for freed slaves. Israel's answer was prompt, and the answer was no. The governor of Maine rationalized, using the weather as a reason for not welcoming blacks into the State. "...Nothing could be less desirable for these people," Washburn wrote, "than their transportation to Maine at this inclement season."(7) Like southern masters, Israel was willing to make judgments about what was good for the blacks without consulting them on the question as to whether or not they would welcome asylum, even in the frigid northern clime.

Friends and Associates

It is said that a person is known by the friends he keeps. Among the friends of the elder Washburn brother were men like Gamaliel Bailey, Thomas Starr King, Edward Kent, Thomas Eliot. To Bailey, editor of the *National Intelligencer*, Israel generously gave the name, "immediate founder of the Republican party," even though Israel himself was credited with that achievement. Israel realized that many who contribute to the political and cultural life of society are like dark shadows merged with the night. So it was with the editor who was admired by the man from Maine, Gamaliel Bailey. So greatly did the Maine farmer, governor, lawyer, representative appreciate Bailey that he exalted Bailey to the place of founder of the Republican party, even though it was Washburn who took the initiative, bringing together politicians who launched the movement. Explaining in an article published in the *Universalist Quarterly* what occurred in 1854, --after those "Southern Whigs and Democrats and Northern Doughfaces," had won the vote, giving Stephen A. Douglas' bill life and reality, -- Israel said he called together some thirty members of the House, "including anti-Nebraska Whigs and Democrats and 'Free-soil' party men."(8) They took counsel together and Gamaliel Bailey, the only non-congressman present, urged that a new party be formed. He recommended that it be called "Republican...in which all men who thought alike -- on the vital question of the time, that of slavery extension, -- should act together." There is hardly any question but what the bug-a-boo of slavery impelled Israel Washburn to act, speak and write. It was part of his nature to want the public to know the facts. Rather than give credence to the myth which was forming, to the effect that he, Israel, was father of the Republican party, he published the essay which gave credit to the early editor of the *National Intelligenser*, Dr. Gamaliel Bailey. Israel admired him as "a wise and sagacious statesman." Bailey came to see earlier than most anti-slavery men "the necessity and duty of being *practical.* That appealed to the efficient little lawyer from Orono, for Washburn was himself one of the earlier advocates of practical action which would in time free the slaves.

Washburn and Thomas Starr King, California Universalist minister, maintained a friendship through correspondence. It pleased Israel that his brother Charles was a member of the Reverend Mr. King's congregation in San Francisco. King was able to take advantage of their friendship. He requested of Israel that he initiate action to have the government place an observatory on Mt. Washington. In a jocular mood, the minister added that the Washburns should have no difficulty in getting a bill passed, since together they represented a quorum in the House.

Edward Kent and Israel were friends. A fellow Maine lawyer, John Edwards Godfrey, wrote of Kent that he was "a literary man," and "a great lover of fun." Kent, imitated by Israel, was politically ambitious. Kent and Washburn were governors of Maine. Kent was versatile. So was Israel. Both were lovers of fun. The older man, Kent, was Consul to Rio de Janeiro. Israel, like Governor Kent, sought posts abroad. Governor Kent was a moving force in organizing the Republican party in Maine. He delivered the principal address enthusing a large gathering of men from all over the State of Maine and from several parties, including disenchanted Democrats. February 22, the birthday of Washington, became the birthday of the Republican party in 1855. Kent made much of the fact that those present had previously fought and worked against each other, but that they were uniting "in devotion to the interests of humanity." They would stand together "through the great battle, between freedom and slavery..."(9)

Several Universalist clergymen, together with theologian and preacher, Hosea Ballou, were counted among Israel's friends. Ballou was a close acquaintance if not an intimate friend of Israel's, married to a Washburn relative. As the reputed father of Universalism in America, he was responsible for "a great upsurge of liberalism among the lower classes." The class of people to whom Ballou appealed "were mostly untouched by the more literate liberalism of the day," writes Ballou's biographer.(10) Israel was an admirer of this powerful Universalist leader. He joined Ballou in changing the face of religion in America in the nineteenth century.

Amory Battles, Maine Universalist minister, was friend and advisor to Israel. Battles was a man of strong conviction. He would not take an oath to support the constitution. To have done so, the Universalist clergyman felt, would mean he must swear to uphold the Fugitive Slave Act. This fiery and uncompromising Washburn friend advised Israel, writing to him in Washington during the years of Washburn's service in the House. He performed the marriage ceremony for William D. and Elizabeth (nee Muzzy) Washburn.

John L. Stevens, also a Universalist minister, and co-editor with James G. Blaine of the influential *Kennebec Journal*, was a friend and confidant of Washburn's. When Stevens was U.S. Minister to Hawaii, he became a deciding factor in the decision to cede the islands to the United States. He was assisted in that effort by another Washburn friend, Luther Severance of Maine. Severance was founder and editor of the *Kennebec Journal*. Elihu, who had worked for Severance as a lad, once said of him that he was among the finest, most modest of men he ever knew. It was Severance who induced the Maine congressman, Israel, Jr., to submit legislation in 1854 calling for the annexation of the Sandwich Islands.

Bangor lumberman and Mayor of the city of Bangor, Samuel F. Hersey, was a longtime friend of the congressman's. Hersey used his considerable fortune in the way Israel's wealthy brother Cadwallader did, providing institutions benefitting children and youth. He was supportive of Israel in his attempt to reach the U.S. Senate, assuring Washburn in a confidential letter that Hannibal Hamlin would support him should Israel decide to make the run. And for himself, the Bangor lumberman wrote, "if I could make the successor of Mr. Morrill...I would cheerfully part with all changes of personal preferment to place you [in the Senate]."(11)

Elihu, Cadwallader, Sidney, and sister Martha composed a coterie of corresponding friends. They were frequently in touch with each other, asking advice, sharing personal problems, and when desperate for help, they did not hesitate to borrow money from each other. It was expected, however, that money loaned would be paid back with interest.

Israel's dearest friend was the woman he chose for a wife, Mary Maud Webster. Maud was loved by all the Washburns, their wives, husbands and children, as well as by Israel's fellow congressmen. Some of Israel's Washington friends wrote letters to Maud, appending a request that they be remembered to Mr. Washburn. When Maud died, Israel, moaning over her loss, wrote of her as sweet and wise. Revealing starkly the pragmatic side of the man, Israel added as a final tribute that Maud had "good sense." Israel's choice of Miss Webster also tells part of the story of who he was, an ambitious young man who wooed the belle of the town, the daughter of Orono's leading lumberman. She became the wife of the elder Washburn brother who went to Washington.

As this small town small Maine man left for Washington with Mary Maud, he followed in the footsteps of forebears. Six generations of Israels had taken a part in beginning of things and in the creation of the new nation. The nineteenth century Israel from Livermore, Maine, was to play a part in establishing a new American nation.

Chapter Thirty Four

The Center of Israel Washburn's Thinking

The new Maine representative delivered eleven well thought out speeches while he was a member of the House. Only one was related directly to Maine and its interests. That was his *Plan for Shortening the Transit Between New York and London, European and North American Railway and Public Lands,* delivered on March 10, 1852. Representative Washburn knew that Maine, far to the north, suffered economically from being distant from the Boston, New York markets. As a freshman in the House he knew also that control of transportation would be necessary if a State is to prosper. Maine would therefore be helped if the wilds of Washington County in the eastern part of the State could be opened up and tracks laid through the forest of pines from Bangor to Vanceboro, running on into New Brunswick. Goods could be transported thence to Liverpool, England, and the continent. Freshman Congressman Washburn's argument on the floor of the House was that commerce coming through Maine would benefit business in the United States, as well as business in England and on the continent. He contended that a day plus ten and one half hours would be subtracted from the usual time taken to go back and forth between this country and England. He also insisted in his speech before congress that "in this busy and steaming life of ours, this day of competition, enterprise, and unprecedented activity, the saving of half a week's time...determines the whole question."(1) Since the downeasterner was addressing colleagues from all parts of the domain he attempted to assure congressmen that the rail line would benefit every state, north and south, east and west. He buttressed his argument further by invoking a speech delivered in Portland by Navy Lieutenant Maury in 1850. The Lieut. said fortifications were needed in Maine. The Maine congressman added that the road he was proposing would fortify the defense of the whole nation. Washburn and Maury proved correct. Fortifications <u>were</u> needed. Maine, projecting its large nose-like geography into the Atlantic ocean, was susceptible to attack. During the Civil War the Confederate Navy made assaults along the Maine coast.

Continuing in his address on the North American Line, it was clear that Israel had made a *coup.* He had been able to obtain from President Fillmore a letter strengthening his case. The President indicated his pleasure that "another link may be added to the chain which is binding more closely the great commercial interests of this country and Europe." In lawyer-like fashion Israel enumerated the ways people, parties and the nation would benefit from the construction of the European and North American Railway in his home State. He paid attention to the North-South rift in this early period of strife, saying that building the road would "preserve harmony and good feeling between all of the members of the Confederacy." That was a strange, prescient allusion to a dominion which did not yet exist, the Confederacy.

At age thirty-nine, this young, inexperienced congressman had made up his mind about the dangers of centralism in government. He included in his speech on the railroad an opinion about centralism, saying, tendencies toward centralism must be checked by withdrawing "from the central government the disposition of this vast [U.S. Treasury] fund." His argument was intended to justify removing up to

$3,000,000,000 from the treasury. In hoping for decentralization, Israel Washburn could not have anticipated the advent of a President who would, by centralizing, weaken the position of the States, strengthening federal authority, and establishing a bloated treasury. As a result of what was to happen with Abraham Lincoln's initiative, Israel's own position as governor would be diminished, with the power of the executive and congress magnified.

In speeches delivered in the House in mid-nineteenth century, philosophizing was acceptable to members of congress, even though there was sometimes little relevance to the subject under discussion. Washburn took advantage of the opportunity in his hour-long talk, calling up some of his own motivating principles. We are, he said, a special people, "educated and set apart." He thought America's very discovery was providential, as was the settlement of Anglo-Saxons upon its soil. Having introduced his prejudice in favor of Anglo-Saxons, Israel, in extenuation, hurried on, extolling the American "experiment in 'fusion'," where the "blood of all lands and climes" are mixed for the blessings of the country.(2)

With all his efforts, and a well-organized address, Israel's plan to build a railroad through Maine was unsuccessful. Neither Israel nor his associate in Maine, John A. Poor, lost the hope and vision of a great Grand Trunk road, however, and at last, in 1871, the European and North American line was opened. On October 19th of that year the railroad was dedicated with Ulysses S. Grant present, together with James G. Blaine, and Governor Sidney Perham. The rail ran from Bangor in Maine to St. John in New Brunswick. The ground work had been laid nineteen years before as the little man from Orono stood boldly on the floor of the House, himself only a freshman, forcefully delivering an impressive, well-ordered speech. Being new, Israel had no log-rolling leverage with which to move the assembly of men. He had at that time only his logic and powers of persuasion.

❖

Two months later Israel took up the cudgels once again, this time to spar with southern members of his own Whig party. Washburn, a life-long Whig, was fearful of what southern Whigs appeared to be doing to the party. Whiggism could be destroyed, Israel thought, by Johnny-come-lately party members in the South insisting upon a "test of orthodoxy" which was to be administered at the Baltimore Convention of 1852 where a President would be nominated. Southern Whigs wanted a dogma forced upon delegates. The Presidential candidate would then be required to honor the Compromise of 1850 with its hated Fugitive Slave Laws. Israel piqued, reminded listeners that those hated fugitive slave laws were an integral part of that Compromise. For the nominee for President to be forced to make such a pledge would mean that, as President, he would have to be loyal to the prescriptions placed upon Baltimore delegates, loyal, that is, to southern dogma not to the constitution. Israel pointed out, it would be the North only which would be bound to those Compromise measures. That amounted to the ultimate indignity for Washburn and northern Whigs, that the South reserved to itself the right to change Compromise measures. He quoted Senator Benjamin Butler as Butler had chided Mississippi Senator Henry Foote. Butler, in an exchange with Foote, said, "the Senator admits that while he wishes to make the compromise immutable, he is perfectly willing to change it when it suits him. This," said Butler, "is a 'finality of a totality'."(3)

Washburn remembered the instructive letter he had received from his friend Governor Kent. Kent wrote saying the Maine congressman must beware of sectionalism. With Kent in mind, Israel made his uneasiness explicit. There was danger in southern Whigs pressing their orthodox issue. Their course of action could lead to the formation of sectional parties. What is more, Israel warned the legislators that passing the resolution might lead to consequences "we should all deplore." He did not wish to make specific allusion to war, which he had in mind. His brother Cadwallader, however, was not hesitant to recognize the imminence of hostility in his remarks in the House.

The bantam-sized southerner, Alexander Stephens, irked by Israel's having turned to speak to him, interrupted Washburn to say, "I wish to know if the gentleman from Maine alluded to me," when Israel had noted that "...the gentleman from Georgia declared [in 1845] that he was no defender of slavery in the abstract..." Stephens accused the Maine representative of quoting him out of context. He remembered himself as having said also on that occasion that "...the subjection of the African to the white man...bore the impress of the Creator himself..." Washburn got the best of the argument in his rejoinder. "If [Stephens] is opposed to all slavery in the abstract, how can he be in favor of African slavery in the concrete?"

In closing, Israel put the problem in the best light possible, saying, "Come depression, come misrule, come war, come an 'Iliad of woes,' if they must come -- let us bear them as we may -- we can survive...them all."(4)

In the two lengthy floor speeches in 1852, the downeasterner from the town in Maine with a strange Indian name, Orono, was certified, both as a fine speaker and as a promising parliamentarian. His leadership in the House was assured. In an eight-year span, the congressional speeches delivered by Israel Washburn had a substantial listening audience beyond Maine. A Connecticut voter wrote him in 1857 assuring him that "the great body of the people of New England...look upon you as one of *their* representatives..."(5) At the center of that country-wide audience, Washburn sat at his House desk in the half-circle of legislators, "swinging his feet as usual," ready to speak when the occasion demanded.(6) Next, he intended to speak on the subject of foreign policy. The shrewd Maineite had come to realize that the boundaries of the United States were not to stop at the water's edge. He recommended in January of 1854 that Hawaii be included within the American sphere of influence. While the Islands were not to be ceded to the United States until 1898, it was a troika, consisting of the Maine congressman, along with Luther Severance of Maine, and John L. Stephens, who paved the way for Hawaii to be made part of the American empire.(7)

Chapter Thirty-Five

"SPLITTING HISTORY: BEFORE AND AFTER"

"It is an irony of history that slavery was brought to the New World simultaneously with the arrival of those who fled the Old World to seek freedom. Yet the true instincts of America found expression in the Declaration of Independence, which proclaimed that all men were created equal. For that reason the conscience of America could not rest with the paradox of liberty and slavery living side by side."
--Saul Sigelschiffer(1)

Saul Sigelschiffer is not alone is concluding that the Dred Scott decision of the Supreme Court split the country politically into North and South.(2) The importance of that Dred Scott decision escaped the attention of few who were observing events transpiring in Washington in the critical '50s. The Taney Court's decision in 1857 sent Israel Washburn to his desk. Research took place over a period of months and months lengthened into three years. At last, he delivered his speech in the House on May 19, 1860.

The question before the nation as well as the Supreme Court concerned one Dred Scott who believed himself to be a citizen inasmuch as he had been in residence in free territory. The Court was to decide more than what was on the agenda, namely the question of citizenship for Dred Scott. It would decide also if the Compromise law of 1820 was of non-effect. Chief Justice Taney reported out the seven-to-two decision. "We think," he said, [the negroes] are not, and...were not intended to be, included, under the word 'citizens'." Chief Justice of the Maine Supreme Court, John Appleton, a Democrat, wrote Israel, "(Justice Taney) had only to go back to 1812 and he would have found negro voting in his own State from the Revolution to that date."

❖

Using his low desk as a lectern, the Maine lawyer delivered his rebuttal to the Dred Scott case as though to a jury. The people of the North constituted the jury. Carefully, Washburn delineated the case against slavery. He quoted Jefferson on the "execrable commerce" in slave buying and selling. He noted that in wording the Constitution, the fathers "sedulously excluded the idea that men...would be made property." Israel laid blame at the door of the Democratic party for devising a doctrine which prohibited Congress from intervening in the States of the Union with the purpose in mind of excluding slavery. And he lamented above all the fact that nine men could wield power irresponsibly by denying citizenship to black man. He quoted Jefferson once again: "Whatever power in any Government is independent, is absolute also." Jefferson would have none of such absolutism. Nor would Washburn.

Washburn had it as part of his purpose to throw fear into the northerner. So he said that since the courts declared the Negro was property, then, under the Constitution that kind of property "may be taken, held, used, bought and sold, in each and all of the States of the Union." Israel swept in with a flourish what he was certain was legal, that the Constitution of the State of Maine could not stand a moment against the Constitution of the United States in regard to slave property. It was ironic. Property could be regulated within States, except slave property! He enumerated a number of articles which could be included within, or excluded from, the State. But the introduction of slave property into the State could not be regulated."From this examination of the Dred Scott decision, we perceive the startling character and far-reaching consequences of the new claims of the oligarchy. We find that this Constitution of our fathers, in which Madison would not allow the idea of slavery to be seen at all, and which was accepted as a great charter of human rights, under which it was hoped the people of the United States might be able to rid themselves of this acknowledged evil, carries slavery, of its own force, into every State as well as every Territory of the United States, and plants it there so deeply and firmly that no power remains adequate to its expulsion." Israel pointed out that, at the time the Constitution was adopted it was considered that the black man did indeed have "rights which white men were bound to respect;" that the black man may not justly be reduced to slavery for the white man's benefit. He turned to his fellow Universalist, Benjamin Rush, who in 1773 had declared that "the plant of liberty is of so tender a nature, that it cannot thrive long in the neighborhood of slavery." Washburn proceeded to bring before the body of legislators statements of well known people who had proclaimed the error of the slave system. He turned to John Locke who called slavery vile and miserable, and then Israel added a richness to his arguments with quotations from Edmund Burke and Montesquieu.

> "...Slavery is a state so improper, so degrading, and so ruinous to the feelings and capacities of human nature, that it ought not to be suffered to exist." --Edmund Burke

> "It is impossible for us to suppose these creatures to be men; because, allowing them to be men, a suspicion would follow that we ourselves are not Christians." --Montesquieu

Congressmen were reminded on that day by Representative Washburn that President Buchanan and Vice President Breckinridge approved of the Dred Scott decision; that Breckinridge accepted the decision "in all its parts as a sound exposition of the law and constitutional rights of the States." Mr. Washburn then carefully pointed out that there was no difference between Breckinridge's argument and that of Senator Stephen A. Douglas. Douglas had said in New Orleans, December 6, 1858, "The owner of a slave has...[a] right to move into a Territory, and carry his slave property with him..."

Washburn's argument was a bold challenge to the North with its Liberty, Free-Soil and Republican party members who were intent upon excluding slavery from the territories. The Maine Representative was asserting that Dred Scott as precedent would mean that the United States Government was obliged to protect slave property in all the States of the Union, not in the South only.

The arguments about extending the Missouri Compromise Line, or excluding slavery in accordance with the Wilmot Proviso, or the Cass-Douglas argument whereby the decision to allow slaves was to be made by the people of each State, -- all of these were immaterial and irrelevant arguments from Washburn's point of view. The Dred Scott decision, as Israel saw the matter, "covers every claim that the oligarchy sets up; it forbids the prohibition of slavery extension; it declares, in effect, that the Constitution, *ex proprio vigore,* carries slavery into every Territory and every State of the Union.

Reaching the end of an hour-long oration, Israel Washburn said in a firm, steady voice, "Reckless of the noble objects of government, false to the true mission of a political party, deaf to the calls of patriotism and nationality, [slavery] projects the transformation of our political system from a Republic of freemen to an Oligarchy of slave-holders."

"Mr. Chairman," said the lawyer-legislator from the North Country, "it is in this unprecedented and alarming condition of the country, and against combinations and purposes such as I have described, that the Republican party enters upon the campaign of 1860." Addressing his remarks to his peers in the Republican fold, Israel declared that the duty of his party was to resist the extension of slavery. Speaking with an assurance based more on hope than on what history had to teach, he went on to say that when the Republican party was placed in power with its practical beneficence realized, then, said Israel, inimitably optimistic, "another 'era of good feeling' will ensue." Like Pippa, Israel was whistling as he passed the grave yard soon to be filled with the bodies of a half-million men, leaving a legacy, not of "good feeling" but ill will which it would take another century to dissolve. Many, feeling the strength of his irrefutable arguments, and unhappy with his conclusions, were skeptical about there being "a God in Israel."

❖

The Taney Court's decision was followed in a few months by the folly in Kansas. A minority of pro-slavery people, some of whom were brought into Kansas from Missouri, adopted a constitution for a majority of anti-slavery Kansas citizens. It was known as the Lecompton Constitution. Israel had something to say to Congress and the country about that fiasco also.

Given all of Israel's addresses, the single most critical question with which he dealt, next to the war itself, related to what was happening in Nebraska and Kansas in the fatal '50s. Senator Stephen A. Douglas' bill created political turmoil as no other did. Douglas' attempt was to resolve the slave problem in territories seeking to become States. The solution he supplied was legislation which would provide voters living in newly created States the privilege of deciding whether there would be slavery or freedom for blacks.

On April 7, 1854, Washburn delivered one of the finest speeches presented in the House on the subject of Senator Douglas' bill. His speech was entitled, *Bill to Organize Territorial Governments in Nebraska and Kansas.* Gaillard Hunt, author of a book about three of the Washburn brothers, called Israel's April 7th address "one of the most vital" of all the presentations delivered on the subject of Douglas' proposal.(3) With restrained humor, Israel allowed that "the drama of non-intervention after one performance more, will be removed from the stage forever -- as we sometimes read on the play-bills, it is 'positively for one night only'." He continued, troubled that the time might soon come when the South would declare, "The North is sufficiently weakened and humbled...let it be proclaimed everywhere that the Constitution of the United States...carries slavery wherever the flag of the Union flies."(4) Israel's arguments followed, compelling in their logic.

He addressed the question of the legitimacy of the election process, delivering a judicial type opinion worthy of a Supreme Court Justice. He proceeded, putting the Slave Power on trial.

The contending parties in the trial were symbolized, North and South respectively, by two slight, school-boy figures, Israel Washburn of Maine, and Alexander Stephens of Georgia.

The lawyer legislator from the North, addressed his remarks to the Speaker, lamenting the scurrilous record which was indisputable, that armed men from Missouri prevented citizens from electing their representatives. Said Israel,

> "...For the sake of Slavery, solemn compacts of long standing, deliberately entered into, and with mutual considerations, have been destroyed; pledges of faith and honor have been cast like worthless weeds away; the great writ of right, sacred for centuries, wherever the common law has been known, to the protection of mankind -- the *habeas corpus* -- has been struck down; the trial by jury, the palladium of civil right and personal security, born of the conflicts of liberty with despotism, and baptized in the blood of men struggling to be free, consecrated in our hearts as the ancient and indefeasible heritage of the people, guarded by the Constitution, stands against all assaults except those of Slavery..."(5)

The speech took an hour to deliver. At hour's end, the man from Maine sat down, exhausted but excited. He had made that day memorable.

But arguments recited seriatim by Israel were but fodder for rebuttal purposes by representatives from the South. After several days of debate, Douglas' bill passed, resulting in quick action by the Maine Representative who thereupon launched the Republican party, replacing the now shattered Whig party.

Reflections

An appraisal of American politics came from Israel's pen in 1856 when he wrote and then spoke on the *Politics of the Country*.(6) It was in the form of an address about politics and politicians. A politician himself, he was hypercritical of his peers as politicians. He spoke in the voice of preacher. "The powers of right and wrong are face-to-face," he said, pounding the desk as a preacher pounds his pulpit. He was speaking of "the monstrous delusion, that man can...hold property in man." He expressed loathing and unutterable scorn for doughfaces who were timid, easily-influenced politicians of the North. "No, sir, no;" Washburn declared forcefully, "you cannot make this thing of Slavery right. God did not make it right." Israel's wide reading schedule gave to him the use of an unforgettable phrase. "Mr. Chairman," he said in a tone of voice which lifted the eyes of the Speaker from his desk, "as nothing flourished where the foot of the Visigoth had been, so there can be no prosperity beneath the tread of slavery." In his address, Israel did not intend to accentuate sectionalism, at least as coming from his Republican side of the House. Indeed, he accused the Democrats of being the guilty party on that score, since that party, he said, knew "no test but slavery," and the slavery test was an exclusively southern question. Every issue was measured by that rule. How well Washburn knew that. He remembered how that heated subject of slavery was injected into the simple matter of the Hungarian patriot, Ferencz Kossuth, and the possibility of Kossuth speaking in the chambers. He remembered that the congress was aflame with the issue of Kossuth and slavery as Washburn entered the room to attend his first meeting in that majestic room, the House of Representatives, in 1851. So the slavery issue in all its starkness was made a central part of Israel's agenda early in his career.

The first public display of his own gradualist views came in 1854. William Goodell, editor of the *Radical Abolitionist*, acknowledged that Washburn was an early exponent of the constitutional right to exclude slavery from the territories. Washburn's gradualist views were somewhat similar to those held by Abraham Lincoln, though Washburn was more advanced than the Illinois aspirant. Israel's commitment to the issue of freedom versus slavery found him in disagreement also with his friend Charles Francis Adams. Adams advocated the admission of New Mexico to statehood without conditions of slavery. Adams' proposal was followed by one submitted to the senate by another of Israel's friends, William H. Seward, soon to be Secretary of State. Seward recommended an amendment to the Constitution prohibiting congressional interference with slavery. And even Lincoln said at the time that while he had not seen an amendment by Thomas Corwin which was similar in intent to Seward's proposals, Lincoln had no objection to its purpose.

Israel's thinking took him in directions different from Lincoln's, Adams', Corwin's and others. Washburn continued an acquaintance with these men, including his fellow governor, Edwin B. Morgan of New York, despite Morgan's racist attitude. Morgan referred to blacks as "things."(7)

Washburn's Universalist friends among the clergy, and his upbringing in the Universalist movement in Livermore and Orono, contributed to his enlightened views. Washburn sent a copy of his January 10, 1859, speech on *The Republican Party* to the Reverend Amory Battles. Writing to thank Washburn, the Universalist clergyman expressed disappointment with Republicanism as "the White Man's party."(8) He felt equally bitter about the newspaper published by another Universalist layman, Horace Greeley, who, he claimed, had sold out to the nativist American party. In light of Battles' observations about Republicans and Greeley, he told Washburn, "it gives me hearty pleasure to learn that some of you are comprehending the great fact that it is for no transient things that the anti-slavery party is contending[,] but for principles as broad as man and as enduring as God himself." Israel was impressed with the minister's felicitous statement. The concept of universality was widely held among ministers and laity of the Universalist faith. Awareness of what was called "universal salvation" with its correlative ethics lead to arguments against what Universalists called "partialists." The partialist thesis, for many Universalists found politicians wanting when they discriminated, leaving some citizens unjustly or unfairly treated. Charles Buffum from Orono wrote Washburn to express strong feelings about President Franklin Pierce and the despised Nebraska bill which the President supported. Buffum, a Universalist who did not believe in the concept of hell, wrote that "the bill and all who support it, not excepting the President, ought to go to h--l."(9)

The testimony of the Honorable George F. Talbot confirms the idea that Washburn's religious views had an ethical component inspired by his Universalism. Talbot said, "In [Israel], above most of his contemporaries and associates, the ethical and religious element was the dominant influence which fixed his opinions and determined his conduct." Henry Blanchard wrote, "[Washburn's] religion made him the noble politician that he was, and made him think that in America God meant to carry out a large part of his providential drama..." The feeling on Israel's part that God was watching over and guiding America was inherited from his Washburn fathers of six successive generations. This religious view portrays a motivating factor for many who lived in nineteenth century America.

Israel found distasteful, expressions of opinion such as Representative Keitt spoke in the House. On May 4, 1854, Keitt declared that "the federal government can recognize none but whites as people." In an exchange of views, Israel deplored the fact that the country had lived under "this abstract wrong" for thirty-four years." The fugitive slave law troubled Keitt. Incorporated in the compromise measure of 1850, it was a constant source of aggravation, leading Washburn into floor fights with Keitt and other southern representatives. The law meant that blacks escaping North must be returned to owners as property, the way chairs or beds must be returned to property owners if stolen. Israel, as he addressed this question argued that the law, like any other, must not be recognized in "perpetuity." "We cannot by resolutions...make that final which in its nature is changeable," he said. He was a constructionist and argued the position at every opportunity, invoking the constitution.

As a result of the fugitive slave laws, Personal Liberty Laws were written into State statutes. In some cases the laws guaranteed to the fugitive the writ of habeas corpus and trial by jury. An attempt was made in congress to abrogate the Personal Liberty Laws. One of Israel's last desperate acts in congress was to cast a vote along with thirteen others, including two of his brothers, with one hundred and fifty three voting on the other side in favor of a resolution calling for the repeal of those "personal liberty bills, so called, enacted by State Legislatures..." Israel, using a parliamentary tactic, tried to dismiss the resolution. Failing in that, he stubbornly stood with the miserably small minority of thirteen, losing the battle, but expecting eventually to win the proverbial war.

Chapter Thirty-Six

The Washburns, a Quorum

Thomas Starr King, the Universalist Unitarian minister serving the San Francisco Unitarian church, is said to have "saved California for the Union." The San Francisco minister wrote to Israel Washburn from his summer residence in Gorham, New Hampshire. In his letter he explained that he was eager to have an observatory on Mt. Washington. He added that he hoped his Universalist friends, the Washburns, could carry the day in Congress for his cause. "The Washburne's," he joshed, "being at least a quorum...can carry anything."(1)

It was true, the three Washburns in Congress in the 1850s were powerful men, each by himself. When the brothers were counted together it could be said they represented "a sum which is greater than the parts."

In Congress the brothers were movers and shakers. Israel, Elihu and Cadwallader began their congressional careers in the 1850s. A hasty flight over the panorama of that decade of the '50s returns images of half forgotten events and persons who lived in that period of American history. --Lincoln was having a severe struggle with himself after what he considered his ignominious political defeat in 1854. And in the latter part of the decade we see an able ambitious Abraham Lincoln moving toward ultimate victory, with Elihu Washburne part of that landscape.

--The politics of the period of the '50s sees the greying and demise of one party, the Whig, and the birth and almost instant maturity of another, the Republican. The Washburns were there also.

--An intemperate Temperance movement skewed the political picture causing hesitation in the march toward realignment of party politics. The Maine-born family was in that picture. --A new religious emphasis surged forward gaining influence in New England. Universalism, the Washburn family's religion, was thought (by Universalists) to be the religion of the future for America.

--Virtues which were thought to represent the best in the American character were more clearly defined by the '50s. Literature provided examples of paragons. The Washburns epitomized that reputed "American character" with their self-reliance, trust, optimism, openness to new experiences, and tolerance of diversity in a broadening culture.

--Abolitionism, weak and fluttering during the preceding two decades despite Garrisonian dogmatism, became part of the political action of the decision-making masters in the '50s.

The picture began to change decidedly in the 1850s, symbolized in the election of Nathaniel Banks to the Speakership in the House of Representatives in 1854. Washburns were there and were part of the infighting.

--The decade opened with the Washburn's hero, Whig Henry Clay, promoting his 1850 Compromise scheme. With the Compromise, California, the location of another of the Washburns, was admitted as a free state. New Mexico was permitted to bring slaves into the state. Clay's Compromise strengthened the Fugitive Slave Act, which was a part of the measure troubling the Washburn congressmen.

--As Compromiser, Clay was succeeded by Stephen A. Douglas who attempted to re-pattern the Kentuckian's compromising methods with his Nebraska Bill, a bill which extended slavery into the Territories. Senator Douglas's bill moved one Washburn to action resulting in the formation of the Republican party.

--By the late '50s the Southern section of the country had descended to the place where it could produce an editorial in a Richmond, Virginia newspaper admitting, "we have got to hating everything with the prefix free, from free negroes down and up through the whole catalogue -- free farms, free labor, free society, free will, free thinking, free children, and free schools..."(2) This was the newspaper which offered a substantial reward for the heads of three of the Washburns.

--Given President Polk's adventures in the west and southwest and the effort made in the '40s to wrest northwest Oregon from England, by the time the '50s decade opened, the expansionist mood had infected people in the South, North and West. Two western Congressional Representatives, Wick of Indiana and Breeze of Illinois agreed that the West wanted the world's market.(3) William Drew Washburn's political enemy Ignatius Donnelly caught the fever and announced that "[Our] destiny is to grasp the commerce of all the seas and sway the scepter of the world."(4) The Washburns took stands on the subject of expansion, one of the brothers frustrating William Seward's purchase of Alaska, but another urging the inclusion of Hawaii in the Union.

--As Arthur C. Cole notes, "the fifties saw the emerging outlines of a genuinely national system of transportation and communication."(5) Small cities were becoming major metropolises as a result of the improved transportation system. Industries were developing in the 1850s, and agriculture was so successful an enterprise that it was said Illinois alone could feed the world.

During this decade people flooded into the fruited plains of the west. The population grew from twenty-three to thirty-one million people. As an example of that burgeoning west, one Washburn followed three of his brothers who had made the journey west before him. This Washburn, William Drew, settled on the other side of the Mississippi from two of his brother's states of Wisconsin and Illinois. This Washburn soon became a kingpin in the growth of industry, railroading and politicking in his new state of Minnesota. In 1857 he made his home a few blocks from the swiftly moving waters of the Mississippi. He was made Agent of the Minneapolis Mill Company, and within a year was elected to the Minnesota House of Representatives. In 1858 he was instrumental in organizing the Board of Trade and the Minneapolis Commercial Union. In the following year, he organized a church which flourishes today as a leading religious society in Minneapolis.

The '50s had their times of prosperity for some and poverty for many. For the Washburns, the ogre once again of a Depression troubled them. One Washburn blamed the Depression on President Polk's Mexican War costing, he said, $200,000,000.

❖

If ever there was a time in American history when values, institutions, individuals, laws, and even the Constitution of the United States, were to be tested, it was during the 1850s. Slavery and its abolishment were chief among the challengers of the status quo. Citizens and their churches, their homes and very lives, must come to grips with what seemed the insurmountable problem, slavery, the "peculiar institution," as Seward referred to it. Mounting opposition was beginning to have an effect in the 1840s. Like a boil, the problem broke in the 1850s.

A broader time span, inclusive of decades of the '40s and '60s, dilates the high drama of the '50s. It must be granted that seeds were planted in the '40s, and results, good and bad, bore fruit in the '60s. But the '50s was the decade during which a spate of problems cried out to be solved: The drama of Kansas-Nebraska, the organization of the Republican party, slavery, with abolition as a recommended resolution to the appalling slave problem, the coming of railroads, settling a population in the west and the adoption of the Homestead Act. Even the choice of a Speaker of the House provided dramatic days and weeks of wrangling. The Depression of 1857 was another of the burdens of the era. These problems and programs represented turning points in the American economy and in the politics of this republic. In the aggregate, they lead tragically to the Second American Revolution, coinciding interestingly enough with the Second Great Awakening.

The three Washburn brothers in Congress were involved in the enactment of legislation which dealt with these pivotal problems. They had a hand in working out solutions to the problems. The brothers were ever present in the drafting of bills, involved as chairmen, or members of House Committees, they often cast critical votes. And they spoke fearlessly to the House, some of whose members beat each other mercilessly, threatening each other with guns and knives.

--The Homestead Act was guided through the House by Elihu. It became law after a long and bitter battle. Southern Representatives were the chief adversaries. Elihu said to his father that his accomplishment in helping to make the Homestead Act a reality was the single most important achievement of his career.

--An attempt to ban blacks from the benefits of the Homestead Act aroused the Washburns to action. As debaters on the floor evoked reactions, Elihu jumped to his feet, pounding his fist on the desk and shouting, "I want every citizen to have the benefit of this act without regard to the color of his skin!"

--In 1859, the question of the Speakership of the House was crucial for the politics of the House. Among those spoken of as possible Speakers were Israel and Elihu. --Abraham Lincoln's appearance on the national scene as candidate for the office of President on the Republican ticket in 1860 had the support of his long-time friend, Elihu Washburne. Washburne delivered a speech in the House which was made part of Lincoln's official candidating literature.

--Railroading was the bane of existence for farmers and manufacturers in the west. The brothers, Elihu and Cadwdallader, were radical in calling for state control of the roads. Cadwallader was confident that "the constitution gives the legislature absolute control over the question of railroad operation."(6)

Elihu Washburne's demanding, uncompromising attitude, illustrated on the occasion of the debate on the Homestead Act, prompted comments from critics. When the Congressman spoke in Bloomington, Illinois, in 1856 campaigning for Lincoln, the newspapers identified him as "the wildly gesticulating Washburne." He was termed antagonistic by nature very early in his career. Washburne did not restrain himself, or maintain reserve, as he asserted vigorously, "I want no discrimination!"

259

The religious movement important to the Washburns, Universalism, was the first to go on record as being opposed to slavery. William Lloyd Garrison, identified with the abolition movement as its prime mover, grew up in a family of Universalists.(7) The Washburns in Livermore reflected the opinion commonly held among Universalists, which was that belief in the brotherhood of man is one of the distinguishing excellencies of the movement. Elihu, Israel and Cadwallader, as they took their places in Congress, gave evidence of their commitment to the Universalist attitude. Their stands were modified by the felt necessity of compromise, made for the purpose of moving closer to achieving that brotherhood.

When Israel, a Conscience Whig opposed to the extension of slavery, betook himself to Congress in 1851, he and Daniel Webster were not on speaking terms, though they had been friends in Maine. In Washington in 1851, the two men passed each other on the street without speaking. Webster had voted for the Compromise of 1850. The Compromise measure favoring the extension of slavery did not reflect Representative Washburn's sentiments. He said of himself, "I was fiercely liberal and 'conscience'." Neither did Webster's position satisfy New Englanders in general. The Senator was roundly chastised throughout the region. He had "fallen from grace." That American orator, Webster, without peer, felt the brunt of an attack after he delivered his *Seventh of March* speech on the Compromise of 1850. John Greenleaf Whittier penned lines in anger and sorrow which will outlive the memory of Webster himself, except as a traitor and the Judas of his day.

> So fallen! so lost! the light withdrawn
> Which once he wore!
> The glory from his gray hairs gone
> For evermore!

Washburn as a Conscience Whig approximated the sentiment of New Englanders. An admirer wrote to Israel in 1854, claiming he was "the leading man...around New England in this Congress."(8) Tribute was paid to him as one "who has carried into all his political opinions that deep and earnest religious conviction which has distinguished him among our public servants."

A few months into the Maine Representative's congressional career, after he had served his apprenticeship by listening and holding his peace, a heated question arose over the use of a measure which was to be used to test the loyalty of Whigs. An incensed Israel stood on the floor of the House, tall as his pudgy body would stretch, and raised his voice to deliver his first speech. His oration earned the title of *The Compromise As A National Party Test.* In tones indignant, then humorous, with tints of sarcasm and at times bitterness, Israel flailed arrogant men who, professing to be Whigs, though themselves late-comers to the party, questioned the loyalty of old-timers who had been Whigs "from early life to the present hour...never depart[ing] from it the nineteenth part of a hair."

Cadwallader was equally strong in his liberal religious convictions. The Wisconsin Congressman knew about anxieties which prompted the warlike action of John Brown in the state of West Virginia. Cadwallader knew the people of the country severely condemned Brown for the Potawattamie massacre. That widespread negative feeling about John Brown did not, however, deter the

Wisconsin Congressman as he delivered a message on *The Slavery Question.* He declared that "there are many...who admire certain of Brown's traits of character, his bravery, sincerity and truth." It was not easier for him to pay tribute to John Brown than it was for his brother, Charles, to write in the same vein in the Chivalric territory of California.

❖

Abolition was not a subject well received by the American populace, including northerners, in the early 1840s. Slavery was abhorred by men such as the Washburns, but it was accepted as *de facto*, requiring, therefore, the genius of compromising politics in hopes that means and methods would be found to rid the country of the pestilence. Conscience Whigs, Liberty party people, Free-Soil political leaders, and at last Republicans, wrestled with the question of "immediacy." Many who favored abolition did not join Garrison, or even their own religious groups whose members were committed to the immediate freeing of slaves. Universalists, for example, called together an Anti-Slavery Convention in 1840 for the purpose of abolishing slavery. The Washburns were not members of the Society or Convention. They were, as were most Universalists, moderates, believing in degrees of gradualism, "rejecting the militancy, immediatism, and radicalism of William Lloyd Garrison."9 The Washburns followed the course of moderation which marked the approach of Abraham Lincoln, who thought that the cause of freedom and universal suffrage would not succeed, however many in Congress voted for emancipation. The time came, however, when as Maine's Civil War Governor, Israel Washburn was urging the President to be more militant on the slavery issue. In a letter to Hannibal Hamlin in 1862, the Governor importuned Hamlin to impress upon Lincoln the importance of organizing colored Regiments.[10]

Chapter Thirty-Seven

ALGERNON SIDNEY WASHBURN

Sidney Washburn was casual; the kind of man who walked around with his hands in his pockets. He was down-to-earth with people in town. He talked easily and as he spoke he exaggerated the local dialect, enjoying the mis-pronunciations typically used by downeast farmers. "Not much news from Bauston," he would say. He informed his readers that there is "snow news," (no news). Sam was tickled by Sidney's quaint sayings,(1) and his brothers laughed at his raunchy stories. His sisters clucked their tongues. They thought it improper to listen to Sidney repeat what Brother Allen said at a Baptist testimonial when the minister asked Allen how he felt. Brother Allen said he could tell the Lord just how he felt. He felt "just like a dry hossturd trickling down the brook."(2) There was a suggestion of mirth around Sidney's eyes. With the ends of his mouth turned up slightly he wore a permanent smile.

This second oldest Washburn learned to socialize as he grew up among the garrulous Washburns. He became the "kidder" of the family and the family named him that, "Kidder." When Israel was sixty two years old, Sid wrote Cadwallader noting that "...[Israel] is getting boyish and looking about among the girls. Don't it beat White's 'cattale'. 'Tis so." He signed, "John Kidder."(3)

Judgmental Elihu told about Sid's three-week visit with the Ambassador and his family in Paris. "He has been so...gentle...that he has endeared himself more and more to all."(4)

Sidney was dying. Sam was at his bedside. Sam finished the long night watching his brother die. He wrote later in the Family Journal saying that Kidder was "one of the kindest and most genial and best of brothers. How much we shall miss him let these records tell[.] [H]is life seemed to be all sunshine."(5)

As Teller in the bank at Hallowell, Maine, Sidney greeted customers warmly but with sufficient reserve so that they were always aware of his place and power. While affable and informal, Sidney like so many New Englanders was a solitary man. It took him a long time to find a wife. He was forty years old when he married Sarah Moore of Dover, Maine. He once shared his deep and otherwise unmentionable feelings with one of his brothers. He sighed out his loneliness to William with the result that his brother in Minneapolis wrote, "You are sad and forlorn. Come here directly..."(6) William guaranteed he would make him feel light hearted.

In physical appearance, this Washburn dressed formally, wearing his jacket tightly buttoned up inches beneath his chin. He was fastidious in his attire until after he lost his wife in 1866. He then began to lose interest in his clothing, prompting Israel to goad him into getting new clothes so he would not look so seedy.(7) Thin black hair parted in the middle was brushed down smoothly on each side of Sidney's head with a curling of his hair over his ears and around the back of his neck. To balance a receding hair line, he sported a short beard. His eyes were blue under heavy eyelids and dark eyebrows. Being a banker, he wore his closely fitting Sunday clothes all week except Saturday. On Saturday and when he went to the farm he wore an old shirt under overalls.

Kidder enjoyed life. He knew how to be leisurely and not feel guilty. One brother accused him of trifling away his time.(8) Cadwallader once virtually cut himself off from Sidney, addressing a reproachful letter, not to "Dear Brother" but to "Sir," ordering him to return money and pay for damages incurred in what Cadwallader considered a disastrous transaction. That did not bother Sidney. He knew his brother well enough to discount such rebukes. Two months later Cadwallader sent a "Dear Brother" letter full of tenderness at the time Cad's wife lost her sanity and the Wisconsin brother shared with Sidney a detailed and touching account of what had happened.(9) The Hallowell brother was considered the acting minister of the clan. Israel called him priest, sermon, and shrine. Charles wrote Sidney saying he wanted to keep up their "sage-like correspondence."(10) Charles, writing sometimes twice a week, gave him news of family. "We have got our corn and potatoes...weeded..." "We have not heard from Israel." "Elihu has gone to Hallowell to take charge of the post office." "Cad has had the measles."

When Elihu went to Washington and heard Henry Clay speak, he wrote Sidney to tell about the experience. Sister Martha wrote Sidney on behalf of the old folks, acknowledging the arrival of a shawl which Sid had purchased for his mother, adding "I think your taste...very good."(11)

Sidney had his niche in life and was satisfied with place and position. He did well financially, and was scrupulous in his saving habits. He was responsive to Elihu when Elihu wrote from Galena in 1852 asking about organizing a bank in Hallowell. The Galena Washburne said he felt confident that Nathan Corwith, who was a leading banker in his city, would help with the organization of a bank in the east. Elihu saw an article in the Maine *Kennebec Journal* reporting that a bill had passed incorporating the Bank of Hallowell. He asked Sidney to let him know if that was the bank he had been attempting to organize.(12) Sidney became Cashier of the bank, making extensive loans to his brothers in the west.

In the decade when Sidney went down to Maine to work in Hallowell, banks around the country were failing. The bank in Hallowell was among them. Bank Commissioners in 1856 recommended that his bank be put in the hands of a Receiver. The Receiver pointed out that the bank commenced business before money was paid in; that specie was not counted by the Commissioners appointed for the purpose; that the second installment was never paid in. Having been authorized to increase its capital, nothing was paid in. Large loans were made outside the state without the Directors approval and without security, the bonds of the cashier had not been renewed, records were not kept of stockholders, wrongful statements were made to the Commission. If persons such as cashier Washburn were at fault, the Commissioners did not name them. William made reference to a shyster who had been in the Bank of Hallowell. Two years later in 1858, the Commissioners reported that progress had not been made in winding up the affairs of the bank. They listed the assets of the bank which consisted of loans to persons, mostly outside the State of Maine, totalling $42,310.31. They noted that the amount of bills unredeemed was about $40,000. The bank closed.(13)

In 1862, Sidney himself organized the First National Bank of Hallowell. He and William were Directors. Cadwallader was willing to provide substantial sums to enable the bank to open, but he did not want to serve on the Board. Cad told Sidney at the time that Elihu could easily provide $10,000. And Elihu did assist Sidney. He sent $1,000. The total capital of the bank when it opened was $60,000. James H. Leigh was President, and Sidney was Cashier.(14)

In addition to his work as Cashier of the First National Bank, Sidney served as Secretary and Clerk of the Hallowell and Chelsea Bridge Company, Clerk of the Gas Light Company, and, like his father and Samuel, was Justice of the Peace.

When Sidney lived in Boston, he appreciated the city as a cultural center, enjoying the forums and lectures, and attending Universalist and Unitarian services. The great Hosea Ballou, father of Universalism in America, was in the pulpit at the School Street church where a thousand people filled the pews on a Sunday. Sidney was often among the throng. Across the Commons, William Ellery Channing attracted large crowds and Kidder sat in looking into the esthetic features of the distinguished and brilliant Unitarian preacher. In Boston, Sidney was a Unitarian, his wife Sarah, a Universalist.(15)

Had Sidney been ambitious in pursuing a political career along with his brothers, he might have been successful and more popular than they. Thinking about their careers, but spurning the politician's craft, he yet professed self-confidence in himself as a possible legislator. "'Tis a serious thing to be a servant of the people and satisfy them, yet I think I could do it easy."(16) Sidney attended a Whig convention in Boston in 1846. It was the year Whigs in Massachusetts were divided on the question of slavery and were split on the subject of war with Mexico. "Conscience" and "Cotton" Whigs contended for leadership of the party in the Bay State that year. Charles Sumner was brought forward as one of the leaders of the Conscience Whigs. Sidney's Maine brother, Israel, identified himself as a Conscience Whig. Nonetheless, Sidney writing from convention headquarters in Boston, said nothing about the issues being debated. He said nothing about the "Conscience" Whigs and their break with the "Cotton" merchants. It indicated a less than lively interest in the political realm.

While it had been said by Israel that Charles was the lazy one where work and career were concerned, it was Sidney who lacked interest in working to become a public leader. He lacked the enterprise which accounted for his brothers'successes. Though he changed his occupation from Boston merchant to banker in Maine, the move was made, not so much on his own initiative as Elihu's. Both Elihu in Galena and Cadwallader in Mineral Point wanted a bank in the eastern part of the country. Cad and his partner, Cyrus Woodman, had organized their own bank in Mineral Point and they needed a counterpart on the seaboard. In 1850, Elihu tried to find a bank in Maine for Israel to manage. The two Galena and Orono brothers tried to acquire the Charter of the Lumberman's Bank in Old Town. Failing that, Sidney was prevailed upon to return to Maine.

❖

Much was made of Israel's leaving home in 1831, as well as Cadwallader's when he left home in the late '30s to go west. Sid, however, picked up quietly, leaving home during the year Israel went across town to stay with his Uncle Reuel. There was no ritual connected with Sidney's venture when he left, more or less to wander through Maine communities looking for work, ending up in "sin city," Boston. He was seventeen. Whether he received fatherly, motherly or ministerial advice is not known. If he did not receive their tutelage it would have been because he was considered mature for his age, a thoughtful, religious young man, and a son who would be faithful to the values cherished by the Livermore family. There was favoritism in the Washburn clan. Cadwallader was "the chosen" as far as mother Martha was concerned, even though it was Sidney who worked with his mother keeping the house. His mother said he was of more help than the girls. Yet it was a ritual connected with Cad's leaving home which became historic.(17)

The earliest extant letter to Sidney was from his father, written in 1831. As Sidney expected, his father wrote about politics and the weather. Father was glad to hear that the Bay State had not surrendered to the Loco Focos,(18) and he persisted like a preacher, trying to keep politics at the forefront of his son's attention. The politics fronting the father's mind was the Loco Foco movement. A letter written still later by Israel, Sr. reported that the Loco Foco movement was faltering in the Livermore region, and he asked Sidney, "how is it in Massachusetts?"(19)

When mother Martha wrote Sid in 1833, she expressed the hope that he was attending church services. She offered to make shirts and socks for her Boston son. She, like father Israel, reported on political activities. She told him the Whigs were to have a meeting in the church. A revealing letter from mother to son Sid divulges the willingness of Martha to admit faults in herself. She lamented her ignorance in things grammatical. It is noteworthy that Sidney was the one in whom she confided. She wept as she told him that Israel visited near Livermore from Orono and yet failed to visit his father and mother. She wished Israel "cold no how inexpressible is a Mothers love for her offspring."(20)

Many of the Washburns had a flair with words and sentence structure. Sidney was included. As a nature lover, his pen ran over into poetic textures whenever he returned to the house on the hilltop in Livermore.

> The southern slope of Bear [Mountain] is in its best
> attire. The deeper tints of Norton and Chandler and
> rugged Mt. Seer make a picture good to look upon.

He combined his country manner of speaking and writing with his word portraits of Livermore scenes.

> These last items are writ(sic) at 7 1/2 Saturday
> morning, at which time the clouds hang round the
> mountain, the fogs move quickly to the northward
> and the opinions are that it is to be a short storm. If
> the sun does come forth wont(sic) it be splendid,
> shining on the verdure of June.

He remarked upon the fact that the folk in the house all came out in the evening and sat on the piazza facing west "till 11 o'clock, watching the clouds zig zag over the old watery moon..."

William remembered his older brother Sidney had been ready to take him into the business in Boston and make a merchant out of him. But when the younger Washburn was thirty six, he was already a far greater merchant type than Sidney ever was or would be. William was pleased when he visited Livermore from his home in Minneapolis in 1867, and read what Sid had written in the Journal. Using William's nickname, Sidney had said that "Young Rapid" was born in 1831 and was consequently thirty six years old. "It was," Sid wrote, "powerful cold and no snow and 'nusses' (nurses) was 'skerce' (scarce) and Grandsir (Israel, Sr.) had to fly round."

In his quaint and modest way, Sidney had felicitous things to write about all his brothers. One evening when father Israel had gone to bed, Sidney sat up writing in the Journal. He acknowledged that while he was sitting at the table scribbling away, the scholarly members of the house were writing history. Those brothers, Israel and Charles, were not only celebrated for their political accomplishments. They were at that time preparing works for publication. Sidney felt a quiet pride in the two boys, one his senior, one his junior.

When he became the eastern banker for his brothers, Sidney had large responsibilities. Israel thought Sid was accustomed to carrying heavy loads, adding that it gave him opportunity "to let himself out in his letters[,] sweeping the cords now and then of a sweet cynicism."(21) Israel's remark tells something about Sidney, and also reveals Israel's poetic gifts. Israel left for posterity an appealing imagery, hidden between the dusty pages of the family Journal.

The Hallowell banker brother was charged with mediating family problems. Elihu once imposed upon Sidney an unpleasant task. He was told he must break up a proposed marriage. Father Israel at eighty years of age, and widow Polly Ames, nee Benjamin, twin sister of Israel's late wife, Martha, planned to be married. Elihu was horrified at the ridiculous idea. If it were Polly's need to be married, that, said Elihu, can be provided for. But Sidney was instructed to "[block] that game." It was "too utterly outrageous to be tolerated for a moment." Elihu ended his command to Sidney, saying "spare no effort to nip the affair in the bud."(22) Father did not remarry.

Sidney did well financially in his life of sixty-five years. He worked for Jeremiah Fitch, a prominent Boston merchant and importer of English goods. In 1838, only one year before Cadwallader started his journey westward and needed financial assistance, Sidney went to work for Fitch, and was in a position to help both Cadwallader and Elihu when they could not scrape together money to get themselves west. In 1841, Sidney was in partnership with Earl Shaw, and in 1846, Sid and F.K. Nichols opened their own mercantile business. Sidney did well enough financially. He lived in high style at the United States Hotel and the Revere House in Boston. The Revere House had been enlarged the year Sidney took rooms there. The Prince of Wales when he came to Boston, stayed at the Revere, as did the Grand Duke Alexis of Russia. And Ulysses S. Grant was a guest in Sidney's Boston home, named after Colonel Paul Revere.

An attitude peculiar to Sidney was his optimism. He was often quoted as proclaiming after a family misfortune that we should never go backward, but always forward.(23) His words were adopted as more or less a family motto, and the motto is heard repeated by contemporary Washburns.

In 1866, tragedy came to Sidney in a succession of events. His wife of thirty-six years died of rheumatic fever in February. In March his son Cadwallader died.

His son James, died of diabetes in the month of June. Two sons remained, John and Robert. For the bereft Sidney they became his "ivry[sic] idols."(24)

The <u>New York Times</u> of October 2, 1879 announced Algernon Sidney Washburn's death. In Elihu's town of Galena, the <u>Gazette</u> carried a brief announcement indicating Sidney "had never been in political life. He was a merchant and banker, and leaves a handsome fortune..."(25) Thus ended the life of the silent partner of the famed brothers who made history on three continents and in five States of the Union.

Chapter Thirty-Eight

Cadwallader C. Washburn & Minneapolis flour mill

MEET THE MAN

When he spoke, his tone of voice said clearly, "I am Cadwallader Washburn, General [or Congressman or Governor]!"

If asked he would say, "This is my flour mill, the largest and best in the world!"

It was Washburn's way, full of understandable pride. His flour mill in Minneapolis won the gold, silver and bronze medals on the three grades of spring white flour in 1880. After that, his product was on the market as Gold Medal Flour, known throughout the world. Washburn did what he could to have his name known as widely as the flour was known. Boasting by Cadwallader was more modest when talking to his partners John Crosby, William Dunwoody, John Christian. But this Washburn *was* "the greatest" considering his early years, lack of formal education, the obscure location of his home in Maine where poverty was prevalent, and where honesty and ambition were encouraged. If in his late years Washburn, once of Livermore, read *Horatio Alger*, he could have seen himself as something more than a flour merchant, and as something special in the annals of literature. He could have felt himself to be an Alger model. Pre-Horatio Washburn had qualities which made ambitious young men appealing in a *can-do* society of the 1840s.

Appearances were a factor for such models. As a young man, Washburn was handsome, quiet, impressive, and intelligent, and people who met him remembered his appealing qualities. In his 40s Washburn was a sturdy, still handsome, imposing man. Seeing those deep-set azure eyes, his straight ramrod figure dressed in his royal blue uniform with shiny brass-plated buttons fastened to his epaulets, Cadwallader looked for all the world like a poster version of the Civil War soldier. He with his Horatio Alger determined ways won him partnership with an intelligent, ambitious graduate of Bowdoin College, Cyrus, Woodman from Maine. Cyrus, with his monkish look was slim, with receding hairline, a look of confidence in an open face, bearded, but *sans* mustache, possessing a pleasant mouth with a slight, constant philosophic wrinkle of a smile. Woodman provided for Cadwallader Washburn a fitting companion and counter force to partner Washburn, given Washburn's excessive drive, ambition and risk taking.

These two aspiring young men settled in the mining town of Mineral Point, Wisconsin, in the early 1840s. The Point was a community small enough for all Anglo-Saxon Christians to know each other. Anglo-Saxons were a tribe within the town, and were often in each other's homes. They saw to it that those from their number, including such persons as Cadwallader and Cyrus, were appointed to important boards and committees which provided status.

One of the social, legal and political leaders at the Point was Judge Mortimer Melville Jackson, originally from the civilized East, Rensselaerville, New York. He settled at the Point in 1838, four years before Cadwallader came to town. The figure of Judge Jackson in the primitive community of the 1830s and 1840s suggests the fictional James Fenimore Cooper's Judge Temple of *The Pioneers*.

Blanche Tucker

Temple came west to bring civilization to natives, and respect for the law on the part of the Pathfinder who had "gone native." Judge Jackson expected to civilize a disorderly citizenry. He married Catherine Garr, daughter of one of New York's more astute lawyers, Andrew Sheffield Garr, and brought Catherine, a socialite in the east, to uncultured Mineral Point. In Mineral Point, Cadwallader Washburn, of the Anglo-Saxon tribe also, made the acquaintance of Jeannette Garr when Jeannette was visiting her sister, Catherine. Washburn married Jeannette in January 1849. The satisfactions of marriage which followed prompted Cad to write his brother, saying, "She is everything I expected." Cadwallader could not have expected that after the arrival of Fanny, their second child, Jeannette would lose her sanity. The new mother suffered an attack of septic poisoning. The distraught husband explaining her disturbed state and wishing it to be a temporary affliction, wrote friends saying Jeannette seemed to be recovering normality. But Jeannette succumbed finally and was taken east to a home in Brookline, Massachusetts, where the demented were cared for. She remained Cadwallader's responsibility from 1852 until his death in 1882, and his estate saw to it Jeannette was cared for until she died in 1909.

Victor Hugo

Cadwallader, still the handsome, intelligent human being who had courted and won Jeannette, roamed free. From 1852 onward, he was a single man seeking his fortune in law, banking, politics, manufacturing, lumbering--whatever gave promise of financial success. In all the years that followed, Cadwallader was unable to seek female companionship. The law would not permit him to divorce his demented wife, and his upbringing at Livermore discouraged him from trying to find gratification in illicit relations. These considerations can be said to account for his virtual religious devotion to work.

We may only surmise what were Cadwallader's thoughts and feelings about a continuing if irregular, relation with Blanche Tucker. Cad was 54 years old when the beautiful 18-year-old Blanche came to LaCrosse to visit his daughter, Fanny. Blanche confided to her host, Cadwallader, that she wished to study in Europe but did not have money to pursue her ambition. Washburn's response to her plaint was positive. He promised her he would provide means for her to sail to France, live in Paris, study voice and prepare herself for the opera. Cad's brother, Elihu, was in France when Blanche appeared and could be relied upon to assure her well being. Cadwallader was in Europe frequently and did not neglect to visit Blanche. When he was in the States Cad and Blanche corresponded. Cad knew about her growing popularity on the continent where eminent men were among the many who came to admire her. Her beauty was on the lips of men as celebrated as Victor Hugo and Guy de Maupassant. For Hugo, she was "the beauty and genius of the New World." The temptation of intimacy prompted Blanche to say to de Maupassant, "How hard it is for two people to get along well together when they love each other completely--you know what I mean--two people able to give each other the maximum of sensual pleasure. Once that happens, an abyss immediately opens between them." Such suggestive language was not used in correspondence with Cadwallader. Affection and fondness felt by Blanche indicating her impression of Cadwallader came in the way she addressed him in her letters. To her, he was "my beloved." Blanche in one of her letters referred to Washburn and herself enjoying discussions in his hotel on the occasion of one of his visits to the continent. Given Blanche's rejection of unmarried attachments, which, she declared, open an abyss between a man and a woman, and Washburn's Puritan ways made it unlikely that facet of Cad's needs could be usefully explored or exploited.

❖

For Washburn as for others who were brought up in a Puritan culture, the custom of laughing freely, enjoying the intimacies of warm, genuine friendship, running and playing and expressing sentiments concerning the opposite sex, religion or politics were experiences thought to be outlived as teens ran on into their twenties. It was frowned upon for grown men in groups to discuss women, religion or politics,(1) since expressions of opinion on touchy subjects might reveal hidden peculiarities in a defenseless male.

Cadwallader, occupied extensively with the world of commerce, was in love with his wife of three years, Jeannette. But like men in that period of American history, it is unlikely Cad shared his personal anxieties with the woman who bore his children, cooked his meals, and sometimes took off his shoes as he dropped into his evening chair after a hard day's work. In a relaxed state of mind, Cadwallader would only share with himself and with no others his thoughts or sensitive feelings. He would admit only to himself his feelings of anger or uneasiness. Relaxed and ruminating, in reminiscent moods, Washburn remembered happenings from childhood, jokes Sidney told, pranks Elihu and he played on Charles, debates at school or town meetings, and the faces of old friends of childhood days.

With as many memories as could be evoked in moments of musing, it is odd to think that there were not many extravagant moments of happiness for Washburn. If asked, he would have said his happiest time in life was when he was working for David Owens as a surveyor traveling through the wilderness areas of Illinois and Wisconsin. Though it was once said that Cad did not have a drop of despair in his body, there were occasions when he was burdened by weighty depression which came with the onset of physical illness. In 1854 he was seriously ailing and thought to be at death's door. He was taken to Galena and brought back to health and happiness by Adele and Elihu. Elihu wrote his father explaining that he had found his brother immersed in the depths of mental anguish. Elihu brought him out of the melancholia. The same thing happened in 1863 during the Civil War following a period of several weeks of hard labor by the side of soldiers opening the Yazoo River for use by Navy ships. Washburn had hoped and expected to provide General Grant with the means of moving troops south, down the river to the north gate of the impregnable Vicksburg. The effort made to open the river was frustrated at Fort Pemberton in Greenwood, Mississippi. When Grant put an end to the venture, General Washburn, discouraged, returned to Helena, where he became deathly ill. The illness brought on depression once again, and once again Elihu was called to his side. Cadwallader required the earnest optimism of his big brother to bring him back to health and enthusiasm.

❖

With the thousands of letters written by C.C. Washburn, none can be found expressing in depth his personal views of religion. He was known to be a religious man who fulfilled his felt duties to God and country. He attended Universalist churches in communities where he lived and visited, and if there were no Universalist church he attended other denominational services. But for Cadwallader there were no theological "pulls" such as were practiced in his father's house in Livermore. Father Israel and mother Martha were both engrossed in the subject of religion, with a distinctly liberal bias.(2) They encouraged ministers and laity alike to visit the family at the Norlands and to enter into one of Israel's "pulls." General Oliver O. Howard and his ministerial brother, Charles, friends of the Washburns from a nearby village, on an occasion after the Civil War, stopped by to engage in a heated but friendly debate.

Cyrus Woodman

From time to time, Cadwallader received letters from his old friend and former partner, Cyrus Woodman. Cyrus would write him about having heard Theodore Parker, Ralph Waldo Emerson, Cyrus Bartol, or Lyman Beecher. In his letters Cyrus expressed opinions about what the famous preachers had said. If Washburn corresponded with his friend, engaging in extended discussion about the preachers' views, Cyrus makes no mention of it. Woodman himself was somewhat preoccupied with thoughts of death, a subject of concern to most serious church people in New England. He wrote Cad referring to "shadows we pursue," and reminded his former partner that he would soon be "gathered unto the fathers." Remarks about death did not evoke responses from the flour merchant, though it was apparent Cyrus was genuinely interested in having Washburn pursue these abstract, metaphysical subjects. The response of marked silence on this score was characteristic of the new 19th century businessmen in America. As has been noted, "the social sanctions under which businessmen operated changed. . . ." The businessman "was required only to adhere to commonly accepted standards of honesty and morality. . .,"(3) not to the ticklish subject of deity. It became unacceptable for men like Cadwallader to manifest strong opinions about religious subjects.

In letters written by Washburn, there was a failure on his part to express himself on the question of ethics -- why, for example, so many Americans, including himself, wanted black people out of their sight and out of *their* (sic) country. Washburn agreed with Abraham Lincoln and Republicans who favored the emigration of blacks to Liberia or Latin America.(4)

❖

Cadwallader Washburn was an enigma, though not mysterious as an archetype. As archetype he was a well-known New England character, closed, hidden, never doubting his superior worth, ambitious to succeed, stubborn, insisting on "doing it my way," a New Englander with a veneer of honesty, a concern for persons, and possessing a pronounced loyalty to "God and country." Countless studies have been made and books written to describe his type.(5) If this displaced New Englander were in any other sense enigmatic, however, and in some ways he was, it was due to his inability to disclose to anyone including himself the authentic man. There were few among intimate associates, including Cyrus Woodman, who could say they knew Washburn. Cyrus, though himself a typical downeasterner(6) with many of the same qualities which distinguished Washburn, was at least frank about himself *to* himself. He confessed in pathetic tones that in all the years the partners had been together little of their inner "heart feelings" were shared. They had not dared identify feelings with each other.(7) Washburn would not have fathomed the meaning of Woodman's complaint. As Cyrus had occasion to say more than once, probably Cadwallader would have laughed at what Cyrus was admitting.

Despite his inability to *talk feelings*, that did not mean Cadwallader was not himself an empathizing, sympathetic person. It was fully expected on his part that he would leave his fortune to the unfortunate, and that is what happened. He founded a Public Library in LaCrosse, and an orphan asylum in Minneapolis. Generous gifts were made to a long list of people named in his will. Washburn was a compassionate man, even though as a man of his times he was unwilling to discuss ethical principles, morality, or even religion.(8) When tycoon Washburn lay dying, in irrational moments, he became anxious asking about prisoners of War and charging that they be released! In way of further illustration of genuine compassion felt by Cadwallader, he had written Elihu in 1854 explaining that he had visited the family of Levi Sterling when Sterling was in prison. He had seen Levi's darling children. Cad said he wept when he realized they would be denied the love of their father. He wanted Elihu to arrange for Sterling to be released.

❖

Had he lived into the 20th century, Cadwallader would have felt close to the way of thinking and acting of President Herbert Clark Hoover, "the last man to be sent to the White House by the Republicans." Hoover is said by Baltzell to represent "in the highest and best sense, all the virtues of the last Anglo-Saxon-Protestant generation to dominate the American political establishment."(9) It is of interest to realize that Cadwallader's nephew, Stanley Washburn, William's son, was an admirer who corresponded with President Hoover. Stanley, cherishing Hoover's views, can be said to represent the end of the line, for the dynamism of Republican radicals Israel, Elihu and Cadwallader Washburn. Cad's nephew, Stanley, who with Hoover personified "the Protestant-Rural-Republican ethic of self-help and individualism," symbolically puts the period at the end of 100 years of Washburn efforts.

William H. Seward

Cadwallader was either weaker or less interested than Israel and Elihu in open discussion about national and international politics, as illustrated in the result of a face-to-face meeting with Secretary of State William Seward when Seward was a guest in Washburn's LaCrosse home. Charles Francis Adams, who accompanied Seward, was present and in his diary indicated that Washburn was of no great interest to anybody in the colloquy that took place among Seward, Adams, Washburn and a Mr. Goodrich. "Goodrich was great," Adams recorded. But the evening at Washburn's home was a decided bore.

Still it must be said, Washburn would not have been in accord with Hoover's Calvinist faith that financial success was a reward for virtue. Both these men understood that their fortunes must be given back to the people and the country. The two men, Washburn and Hoover, admired by the last of the vigorously ambitious Washburns starting with the John Washburn of 1620, were and are now seen as competent models of Whigs such as have been described by R. McKinley Ormsby in his *History of the Whig Party.* It would have satisfied and pleased father and mother Washburn to have it said of their son, Cad, that he was one who:

[H]as not the gratification of a present passion in view; but crushes out and sacrifices private feelings and interests, and compromises with antagonistic views, to secure the stability of the country, develop its resources, and place its future on a safe and enduring basis. His ideas are not formed on partial views, nor inspired by local interests; but are liberal, enlarged, comprehensive, and are the growth of long-continued and mature reflection.(10)

Chapter Thirty-Nine

THE WANDERER SETTLES

"If one have [sic] a. . .noble ambition to make a resting place for his name, that it may not perish when he is dead, let him connect it as Cadwallader C. Washburn has done, with a public charity which will survive longer than the massive granite monument which stands by his grave." --Judge Bryan.

The inordinate praise offered by Judge Bryan does not explain how the impoverished young "Horatio" from the poor state of Maine and the poorer community of Livermore could have built an industrial empire. Cadwallader Washburn did, however, and his empire made him a wealthy, powerful, charitable man, a striking example of upward mobility popularized by Unitarian minister, Horatio Alger. Following the course of events over the period of Washburn's lifetime will make clear why Judge Bryan said the memory of the man from Livermore would outlast the stone monument towering over his grave.

In the beginning weeks and months of a journey into the West, the resources of the farmer's son were meager. He quarreled with a ship's agent about an overcharge of $12. After lengthy argument by the insistent Cad and the impatient agent, the agent gave Cadwallader a $2 discount on his ticket if he would "say no more. . . .." Arriving in the West with $5.00 in his pocket young Washburn wandered through Iowa and Illinois, exploring possibilities which might guarantee him a prosperous future. He met Mr. C. Gilman of Quincy. Mr. Gilman was willing to use his influence to place schoolmaster Cad in a school. But the school could not be started under eight weeks, so the young teacher wandered over to Davenport, Iowa, and started his own school. With money from 30 pupils, Washburn made his first investment. In a letter to his father, Cad said he would probably "make a claim" on a piece of land outside Davenport. Able to make an investment and keeping in mind what he was learning through hardship, he wrote a letter to folks back east, saying that "the man [who] is well off at the East, to him I would not say come here; but to him that is not, I would say come, if [he] can get here." This advice was a cue for two of his brothers, Sidney and Elihu. Sidney was earning money in a dry goods store in Boston. It was he who "need not come West." As for Elihu, Cad encouraged his older brother to consider the trip after graduating from Harvard, to join him if he could find the money to come. Cadwallader had further advice for Elihu. He recommended that the best place for his brother to settle was St. Louis.

When he was in St. Louis, he went down to the river port and was impressed with the number of boats pulled up on the shore, so in a letter to Elihu he predicted "its destiny [would lead to]. . .greatness. . . .." He predicted St. Louis was going to be the Manchester of the Union. Cadwallader may have learned about Manchester from his younger brother, Samuel. Sailor Sam had been to Manchester and described the city to members of the family. Elihu, when he made the trek West, did not settle at St. Louis. He put his roots down in a town where he met and married a woman whose family was from St. Louis, Adele Gratiot. Adele's parents had gone north to Galena from the predominantly French settlement of the 1840s so as to be out of the slave city on the Mississippi St. Louis.

In 1839 David Owen of New Harmony, Indiana, was appointed by the government to explore the lead district in southwestern Wisconsin, southeastern Iowa, and northeastern Illinois.(1) Cadwallader was hired to work for geologist Dr. Owen, joining the team in September 1839. After surveying some 11,000 square miles in the part of Wisconsin where Washburn later settled, Owen concluded that the district was one of the richest for its size in the world. Cadwallader's contract prompted him to figure carefully what he was to earn. He knew that surveyors received $3 per mile surveyed. There were 60 miles in a township, and it required from one to two weeks to survey a township. He hired five men to assist him, and expected to make $100 a township. The Owen expedition worked around Dubuque and the Turkey River, and in Wisconsin Territory at Prairie du Chien, Madison, and Mineral Point. The surveying afforded opportunity for Washburn to learn about the country and its natural resources. Working for Owen he learned about the potential wealth of resources even before the doctor's views were published. Washburn was interested in lead, and he paid careful attention to timber and the places where sturdy pine was located. After all, Cad was from Maine, the Pine Tree State, and he knew the importance of pine in the west where communities would be springing up and new homes would need to be constructed. He laid up in his mind for future use thoughts about the pine forests of Wisconsin and the possibility of exploiting the wealth of the region.

In the meantime, the ups and downs in Washburn's employment record in 1839 and 1840 prompted Cad to write Sidney saying he was a fellow "bound down by the iron hand of poverty." He explained to Sid that he had worked in a grocery store and the owner had died. He received no pay. His schools were not lucrative. He lost his surveying position when Congress quashed the Owen project. Still optimistic, however, it was like Cad to say he was living in the pleasantest town in the world with pleasant fellows. Much later it was said of Washburn what was largely, but not wholly, true, that in him was "not a drop of despair. . .."

In 1841 Washburn turned over a new leaf as he headed into the new year. But the clean pages were soon smudged. An elective position of County Surveyor opened and Washburn was selected to serve, but the position did not last. He complained to his Boston brother, Sidney, that the contest had cost him $40. He started another school. The best he could report was that in his spare time he studied law, and that he "read some other books occasionally." Even with his thwarted attempts to find jobs, Cad was yet sure he would come out all right. He would come out right, he thought, if he did not become dissipated, "as at least one half of the young men here do."

Washburn's next migration was to the little town of Mineral Point in Wiskonsan. [sic] "What in the name of the 'ten muses' has brought me here. . .?" he asked quizzically in his letter home. He explained that Elihu had inspired Cadwallader to go to the Point and hang out as attorney and counselor at law. E.B., having arrived in the region, had advised his kid brother to leave Stephenson where he was teaching, a town only five years old and with a doubtful future, Elihu thought. With that advice, Cadwallader decided to settle in the seat of Iowa County, Mineral Point, Wiskonsan, as an attorney. He saw his brother as a professional who almost immediately was making a very decent living as a lawyer in Galena. E.B.'s income would be at least $2,000 for the year. He was able to send money home to Maine. Cad, however, was not in a position to help support the Livermore family. Not yet.

In Mineral Point there were the modest beginnings of what was to be a C.C. Washburn empire. While looking at the empire builder, one will discern more than this singular person, Cadwallader Washburn. There were regional types in the West and Northwest, and already Cad and Elihu were exhibiting some of the prototypical regional characteristics. Frederick Jackson Turner defined the Westerner, or what one historian refers to as the American intellect, on the frontier. There is wrote Turner coarseness and strength, acuteness and inquisitiveness, a practical, inventive turn of mind, a masterful grasp of material things, restless, nervous energy, individualism "buoyancy and exuberance which comes with freedom."(2) Richard Henry Dana, classmate of Elihu Washburne's at Harvard, discovered the type in his travels. In *Two Years Before the Mast*,(3) Dana, remembering a man he met in the East, wrote about the same man after he had left Massachusetts for the West. "What a change!" says Dana. Of the Easterner in the West, he wrote,

> Gone was the downcast eye, the bated breath, the solemn, non-natural voice, the watchful gait, stepping as if he felt responsible for the balance of the moral universe! He walked with a stride, an uplifted open countenance, his face covered with beard, whiskers, and mustache, his voice strong and natural, and, in short, he had put off the New England Deacon and become a human being.(4)

These qualities were displayed in the Washburn brothers of Mineral Point and Galena. Cadwallader Washburn's attitude was different from that of the unregenerate Easterner, Cyrus Woodman, Cadwallader's partner. Contrasted, the portraits of Washburn and Woodman sharpen the view of the typical Northwest character. Both Washburn and Woodman were from Maine. For Cyrus, however, entrance into the West was hardly more than an excursion. He went to the Northwest, saw, conquered and returned East to live out his life in Cambridge, Massachusetts. Woodman set Washburn off like a silhouette. Compared with the almost devil-may-care manner of Washburn, who borrowed and bought wildly, burdening himself and his partner with debts, Woodman was the paradigmatic traditionalist. He wrote Cad in 1857,

> . . .[I]f you could cash your lumber this winter you would, before the Mississippi opens next spring, be making your calculations to buy out and cut down all the timber on the Black, Chippewa and Rum rivers, and perhaps be in favor of starting a gigantic joint stock company to cut down all the pine in Oregon the year following.

"He (Cadwallader) must haul in his horns,"(5) Cyrus Woodman's New York brother wrote to him. A friend wrote Cyrus saying he found that westerners "'throw off a good many *customs* which we [in the east] have as *boors*'; for instance, he said, a man might 'kiss in the day time, without being called before the church and kicked to death by the Deacon's wife.'" To Woodman that was a shocking opinion as one who thought women with low-necked dresses were lecherous, "wish[ing] thus to attract the attention of gentlemen."

What appealed to the more conservative of the partners was the prospect of making a fortune. Woodman purchased pine woods for $1.25 an acre and sold for $10 an acre. In one year Cyrus and his partner realized a profit of 50 to 80 percent on their transactions. Cyrus, in a defensive mood, wanted it known that he *did not settle on the_backside of creation*[1] for the pleasure of it. The two were making sizeable profits but their large investments in land meant they must operate on borrowed money. Cyrus was uneasy about being in debt. Not Cadwallader. Israel, Jr., writing in the family journal said his father had been musing. "The Aged goes back in memory to the days of eld," Junior wrote.

> His grandfather, he says, was not afraid to run in debt, and he would predict that his boys would be poor men because they 'were very much afraid of getting into debt.' The Aged says Cad is like his Great Grandfather in this respect.(6)

Woodman spent time thinking about himself, worried because he could not bring himself to write anything in his diary about his feelings. He was self-contained, unlike his fellow easterner, Cadwallader. Cad followed the familiar ways of the West, expressing himself readily, and even using cuss words. He once wrote to Cyrus, "I have been trying all the morning to obtain an interview with that prince of sh--t a---ses. . .." [sic] Washburn persuaded the reluctant Woodman to invest money in a shot tower in Helena, Wisconsin. Cad wanted to buy the tower. The tower, he explained, had a 120-foot shaft blasted through solid rock with a horizontal shaft of 90 feet. Washburn was convinced he could make the shot tower a principle means of income for the partners. He was confident, so Cyrus faced the prospect of indebtedness, knowing both must travel to find resources. Accepting the debt, Woodman still disparaged the new venture. "It is certain," he wrote, "that such an addition to our business would absorb. . .nearly the whole time of one of us." In February 1847, Washburn and Woodman took control of the tower, even with the realization that credit had not been found to carry out the operation once it was in their hands. They needed $50,000. Woodman went to Buffalo to find investors. From there, his hands empty and his heart sad, he went on to Boston. Neither Woodman nor Washburn were successful in any of the several arrangements they offered owners of the tower until Messrs Miller and Cushman agreed to provide them with cash at a high interest rate. By the summer of 1847, the venture began to pay off turning out 150 pounds of shot worth approximately $7,000. The product was superior and orders began to come in from Canada and Boston. The business flourished that year and the next. In 1849, however, so many miners in the region left for the gold country in California that the sale of lead became a problem for Washburn and Woodman. Complications arose when Miller, of Miller and Cushman, went into bankruptcy. The banking firm of Corwith and Company in Galena took most of the shot tower's finished product, providing advances so the tower could continue to turn out shot. Elihu with his power and popularity in Galena was doubtless able to persuade Corwith to support his brother's Helena project.

Partner Woodman was sent off to California in 1850. It was thought that the Washburn and Woodman company might open an office in Sacramento. Management of the shot tower was left in Cadwallader's hands. That year proved to be fruitful with shot going to Milwaukee, Detroit, Cleveland and Buffalo. The operation became so successful, even with the problem of obtaining lead, that it was thought necessary for one of the two firm members to settle in Helena where the mine was located. The hired man on the grounds at Helena and in charge of the

---

[1] Emphasis added.

operation had left. Until 1853 when another employee, John Bradford, was found, there was little activity at the tower. In 1854 the business flourished, and in Helena a store and lumber yard were opened. Helena became a small commercial center with wagons loaded with lead passing over the Main Street of the town on the way to Milwaukee via Madison and Waukesha. Ambitious plans for the town of Helena came to an end, however, when the *Milwaukee and Mississippi* railroad passed through the region on the side of the Wisconsin River opposite the shot tower, leaving the Helena operation without rail accommodations.

Whether Washburn realized it or not, he was responsible for the early development of a Great Lakes oriented manufacturing economy for Wisconsin. During the time he and Cyrus owned the shot tower, the business turned toward the east and to Milwaukee rather than to the nearby Mississippi with its prospective outlets north and south on the river. The *Illinois Central* and *Galena and Chicago Union* brought their rails to nearby Mineral Point. Washburn and Woodman purchased stock in the rail line, and both served as directors. Cyrus was at one time president. Thereafter, Chicago became the principle market for shot from the Washburn-Woodman tower.

From east to west, the country was unsettled where the matter of currency was concerned. Currency was not plentiful, and when a mode of exchange using notes became an accepted method of exchange, banks providing notes sometimes closed when confronted with clients wanting to exchange notes for gold. In Mineral Point, before Washburn and Woodman appeared on the scene, a Mineral Point bank had failed. A member of the bank staff absconded with funds. Hundreds of dollars of unredeemed bills were left. People in the Point as well as elsewhere have a long memory where money is concerned. They were made to realize that corrupt practices could occur even though the U.S. Congress prohibited territorial legislatures from giving licenses to banks. Wily men simply formed companies and found ways of skirting the law. In Wisconsin, a *Marine and Fire Insurance Company* issued certificates of deposit, a custom disapproved by the territorial legislature, but "the company stoutly maintained such action was beyond constitutional rights."(7) At the beginning of the decade, the Washburn-Woodman company began a search for an eastern bank which they could control. In point of fact, it was not difficult to start a bank in the east, so the Washburns went to a friend, J.B. Merrick, in Massachusetts, with a proposal that he obtain a Charter for them. Capital stock could be covered with a promissory note. Merrick tried to purchase a bank for them in Jaffery, Massachusetts, but was unsuccessful. Cadwallader tried to obtain a charter for a bank in a Vermont town. He was not successful. A relative in Winthrop, Maine, offered to assist in establishing a bank in his town. It seemed, however, that eastern business leaders were reluctant to see control pass into the hands of westerners. Cad asked Elihu to talk with their Maine brother, Israel, to seek his assistance in obtaining a Charter in Old Town, Maine. C.C. Washburn visited his parents at Livermore in 1852 and learned of the availability of a bank charter in Hallowell, Maine. He persuaded Elihu to contact banker Henry Corwith in Galena to see if the Galena officers would assist in the purchase of the Hallowell bank. With success at last, Cadwallader asked his Boston brother, Sidney, to leave his merchandising business in the Hub, go to Hallowell and there work as cashier of the new bank. When stock of the Hallowell bank was open to public subscription, Wisconsin's Washburn purchased $31,000 under the names of his brothers, relatives and a friend. The company in Maine was in the control of the Washburn-Woodman Mineral Point establishment. Woodman worried about the Hallowell operation. The bank had been purchased by a "concern without any capital."(8) Partner Washburn, not only was not disturbed, he informed Cyrus that he wanted to organize a chain of banks. Chicago, he thought, was going to be a great trading center and he wanted to establish a bank there. In fact, Cad considered settling in Chicago himself to manage a banking operation. Cyrus would not hear of it, so Washburn turned his attention to opening a banking establishment in Mineral Point.

Wisconsin entered the union, and in 1852 Governor Leonard J. Farwell became engaged in framing banking rules. He requested assistance from Cadwallader in framing the laws of the State. A year later, the legislature created a department and the first Charter of the State Bank of Madison was issued. Laws in Wisconsin then required that a bank sustain a circulation of $25,000. Partner Washburn found the required funds and the Mineral Point bank opened in July 1853. For three years the Hallowell banking operation ran successfully, building a substantial reputation. In 1855 problems began to occur. In Maine at Hallowell, Sidney was careless, failing to live up to standards set by the State of Maine, requiring among other things a specie ratio of one to three. The Maine Bank Commissioners examined the Hallowell bank and in 1856 took action against the operation. One of the complaints made by commissioners was that large loans were made to persons outside the state without the approval of the Directors. The out-of-state persons examiners had in mind, of course, were Washburn and Woodman. Sixteen major and minor infractions were listed by the examiners, and in 1858, the Bank of Hallowell was closed. In Mineral Point, with Cyrus Woodman as Cashier, the Washburn-Woodman enterprise remained solvent with never a suspended specie payment.(9)

"Marriage At Mineral Point"

The spacious and beautiful house at St. Mark's Place in New York was the home of a prosperous attorney, Andrew Sheffield Garr, and Elizabeth Garr née Sinclair, the latter descended from an English Earl, a fact of importance to the Garr family. One daughter, Catherine, married Judge Mortimer Jackson and went west to live in Mineral Point, Wisconsin. Catherine's sister, Jeannette, married Cadwallader Washburn, also of Mineral Point. The sisters, of course, had to leave their palatial home where they grew up in high society. Neither of the two girls ever experienced poverty and may not have known it existed as they grew up. Upbringing did not prepare Jeannette for life in a community which, though it did not have sod houses, yet accommodated the poor in wretched homes where living conditions were primitive. Frightening to the eastern young woman, the lead mine town had its criminal elements. Some miners had escaped from their native land, coming to this continent to find work in the lead mines where they lived raucous, rough lives within the community of 600.

Cadwallader Washburn, different from his new young wife, was from a town in Maine where he grew up poor. His farmer father lost his emporium and had to farm out his sons. Young Washburn, unlike Jeannette, knew poverty and hunger. He settled in the town of Mineral Point in 1842 at the age of 26, hanging out his shingle and offering his services as an attorney. Cadwallader met Jeannette in November of 1848 while she was visiting her sister Catherine. For the two months of courtship and leading up to the wedding, Jeannette lived in the Bracken House on Davis Street, a home hardly large enough to accommodate a guest without embarrassment if the guest were a female from New York high society. The home of a Judge, the Bracken House constructed of field stone, was hardly cozy. November and December in Wisconsin in 1848, even in the home of a leading citizen, was difficult to endure.   Two days after the wedding ceremony for Cadwallader and Jeannette, Cad's sister Martha, and his brother Charles, wrote to their brother, Elihu in Galena.(10) They wrote that they had "something of importance to tell. . .." "What think you, can it be? [T]is no less than the marriage of our brother Cad."

Martha suppressed slight resentment, observing in assumed indifference, that "[Jeannette] had only been here two months when she was lawfully pronounced Mrs. Washburne [sic]." Martha added a description of "our new sister." Jeannette, she said, was pleasant, lively, agreeable and of a good disposition. She was taller than Martha and had dark hair and dark eyes. As to the new bride's age, it was said by Martha it would take a lawyer to find out one's age in the West. "Cad will be happier," said his sister, and Cadwallader himself announced to Elihu that he found his wife "all and more than my fancy."

Two years straight, of business dealings more than husbanding, turned Washburn from lawyer into speculator in timber, scheming to monopolize the Wisconsin pineries, purchasing a shot tower, intending to extend his and his partner's business further west to Sacramento, California, opening banks in Maine and Wisconsin, attempting to open three more in New England and one in Chicago, working to keep the Land Office open in Mineral Point, and searching in New England to find a medical doctor for the Point. Cad, in his attempt to keep the federal government from adding Land Offices, wrote Congressman Washburne telling Elihu if he could block the wheels and prevent new legislation he would pay him $500, "but if unsuccessful - then you are to have nothing." The Washburn-Woodman firm was considered to be second only to the Rothschilds in importance and responsibility. Washburn had it in mind to get $25,000, buy railroad bonds, and obtain bills which would buy $25,000 more bills until the firm reached $100,000. When Wisconsin announced the sale of $50,000 bonds at 30 percent interest, the firm applied for the entire amount. To make payments they arranged for another loan.

If these tasks were stressful to Washburn, there was a far more serious affect on Cad's black eyed and pregnant wife who had been expecting since July 1849. Their first child, Jeannette, was born April 25, 1850. In May, Cad wrote his brother Sidney in Boston reporting the birth "of the finest specimen of humanity."(11)

A letter exposing the emotional desperation of Cadwallader Washburn arrived at Cyrus' residence in Sacramento. Five months after Jeannette's birth, Cadwallader explained to Cyrus, he left Mineral Point to meet Jeannette, the mother and child, in Milwaukee. He found his wife insane.(12) Insane was the word used by the Milwaukee doctor who informed Washburn he had no other choice but to place Jeannette in an asylum. Cadwallader took her back to New York to be with her family and brought in a doctor who was experienced in treating cases of insanity. The New York doctor said her treatment at Milwaukee had been improper, that Jeannette would recover. Washburn in his letter then explained to his partner, Cyrus, that he was anxious and needed to get back to Mineral Point. As soon as it appeared Jeannette was on the way to recovery he returned to his business interests at the

Point. Jeannette was still ill in December.

Two years more of intense work on the part of Washburn, and in June of 1851, five or six months after his wife's return to reasonable normality, she was pregnant once again, and the last of March, 1852, Fanny was born. The second birth experience brought the black-eyed beauty to the end of normality. She became truly insane with the birth of the second child. She was overcome by a disease which in that period of history formed 40 percent of the total maternal mortality in childbearing. Beautiful Jeannette was taken to a place in Brookline, Massachusetts, where she was to be cared for as an invalid for the rest of her days, dying after nearly all members of Cadwallader's generation of the Washburn family were dead. Her death occurred March 12, 1909, and she was buried at Walnut Hills Cemetery in Brookline.

"Now for Politics"

Twelve years after settling in Western Wisconsin, the farmer's son received a letter dated August 5, 1854, from prominent citizens of Rock County, and signed by a representative of the Republican State Convention, J.A. Sleeper; Louis Powell Harvey, later Governor of Wisconsin; and J. Baker, editor of the Janesville *Free Press*. A four-sentence letter asked if Washburn would accept "nomination. . .for Congress," and inquired if he would "cordially endorse the principles. . .set forth in the Resolutions adopted . . . at Madison. . . " The reputation of young Washburn had spread. He was known to be an excellent real estate lawyer, and in addition, it was common knowledge that Cadwallader had two brothers in Congress, Israel, Jr., and Elihu. Cadwallader, unlike his brothers, Israel, Elihu, and later, William, expressed no interest in political life. Nevertheless, four days after the receipt of the August 5 letter, Cadwallader sent a letter to Mr. Sleeper, *et al*, saying "if the tender (for the office) came with unanimity," he would consider accepting. He gave assurance that he endorsed the principles of the party.

Thomas Starr King

In August also, the Democratic party, wishing to replace their incumbent congressional representative, Ben Eastman, invited Cad's partner, Cyrus, to succeed Eastman. Democrat Eastman had voted against the Nebraska bill, and Cyrus, turning down the invitation from party leaders said he took the same position as Mr. Eastman. The leaders still insisted they be able to nominated him. Woodman was not interested in running for an office against his partner, and he declined the offer.

During the political campaign, the Democrats tried to capitalize on the bank problems in Hallowell, Maine, hoping, of course, to discourage voters who favored candidate Washburn. The *Daily Argus and Democrat* printed an error which the editor was forced to correct. The editor claimed that the Bank of Hallowell had been suspended. Suffolk Bank of Boston, a Clearinghouse for Massachusetts banks, had merely refused to accept Hallowell notes at par for one day. The editor of the democratic paper recanted, adding that the bank "is now as good as ever."(13)

The voting district in Wisconsin where Washburn was campaigning was the largest and most populace in the United States. Cad was elected with votes from 25 counties. He was reelected in 1856 and 1858. He joined his brothers, Israel and Elihu, in Washington in December 1855. As indicated earlier, the three Washburns became a force in the capital, to the point where Thomas Starr King, Universalist minister serving the Unitarian church in San Francisco, wrote Israel suggesting he "call a caucus of the Washburns" to pass legislation. It was said that the Washburns "at one time were spoken of as one might speak of a distinct party, so great were their influence and fame."(14) Elihu gave teasing credence to that idea, saying to Israel and Cadwallader, "I guess among us we can make Congress listen." To loyal followers and admirers there were times when gargantuan feats could be performed by the three in combination.

❖

The Washburn-Woodman partnership broke up in 1855. Washburn drew up the article of dissolution which stated:

Whereas, we have for upwards of ten years been doing business as partners under the name of Washburn and Woodman, during which time our intercourse, interrupted by no untoward circumstances, has been marked by a constant feeling of kindness and good will, coupled with an unusual degree of unanimity of sentiment in relation to our business transactions.

With Washburn in Congress and in Washington, Cyrus found the burden of carrying on the business too heavy. Furthermore, profits were not large. Profits realized from the Hallowell and Mineral Point banks amounted to no more than $20,000. The benefit to the partners was indirect since advertising the firm in the East made it possible for them to borrow more freely. Cadwallader, having instigated the banking enterprise, the task of liquidating was turned over to Washburn. The bank was offered for sale free of debt for $5,000. The dissolution of the Washburn-Woodman company left the available money with Woodman, and Cadwallader's compensation was the business and the Lacrosse mill and pine on Rum River and the upper Mississippi. There were pine holdings on the Black and Chippewa river valleys running over into Minnesota. One year later Washburn's lumber business was valued at half a million dollars. Cadwallader and two of his brothers, Elihu and Samuel, built the largest mill of pre-Civil War days in a town they owned, Waubec, in Dunn county. Washburn then moved from Mineral Point to La Crosse, Wisconsin, to be near his operation on the Chippewa.

In the 1850s, Washburn stood on the west bank of the Mississippi at St. Anthony Falls, remembering perhaps the manufacturing he had seen at Wiscasett, Maine, when he was a school teacher in town. "He saw the possibilities of the water power,"(15) and sought out Robert Smith, the owner of properties at St. Anthony and bought stocks from Smith in cooperation with Dorilus Morrison, a Livermore, Maine, relative then living in Minneapolis. The purchase marked a new beginning for Washburn. Following the Civil War, his substantial wealth was to come from the Minneapolis property on the Mississippi. His brother, William, was also to thrive in Minneapolis as Cadwallader did. Severe financial problems faced Washburn in the late 1850s, however, and the struggle to survive continued.

Chapter Forty

ON THE SEESAW OF MINERAL POINT AND WASHINGTON, D.C.

Cadwallader C. Washburn, hard-working entrepreneur, was unhappy unless "in water up to his mouth." So said his partner referring to Washburn's willingness to borrow and gamble investment funds.(1) He gambled on many fronts. In 1855 he took a chance on a fresh new life style. He left the hamlet of 2,000 souls where he was "chief man of business," broke out of a lucrative partnership with Cyrus Woodman, interrupting his scheme for digging himself out of poverty. He left the business of business, departing Mineral Point where he had enjoyed a few years of married bliss with his handsome, but now insane wife, Jeannette, and was going to return East to settle in Washington, D.C., as a Congressman. As a Congressman Cad would be joining two of his older brothers, Israel and Elihu. The brothers from Maine and Illinois, joined by Cadwallader from Wisconsin, were then to become that "quorum in the House," as referred to facetiously by the Reverend Thomas Starr King.(2) And since he was to be in politics, the gamble in Cad's life would become even more capricious.

Washburn and his well-educated, upper-class wife, Jeannette, had lived uneasily in the small Wisconsin town. Jeannette felt she was living among a backward people--people who were shocked to hear the unbiblical scientific explanation of the earth's development. Backward views did not disturb Cadwallader. His devotion, even though a churchman, was to business and ethics in business, not biblical studies. The year Washburn settled on Shakerag Alley, "Mineral Point was still a blustering frontier town often plagued with violence."(3) When a man murdered another, Jeannette Washburn's brother-in-law, Judge Mortimer Jackson, sentenced the culprit to hang. The murderer died with a sort of 'terrific grandeur' in front of an audience of four to five thousand who sat comfortably with their picnic baskets on the hillsides.(4)

What historian Frederick Jackson Turner concluded about frontier life and frontier personalities was illustrated by Cadwallader and the Washburns of Illinois and Minnesota--Elihu and William, the latter the youngest of the seven Washburn boys. These men fused their "coarseness and strength combined with acuteness and inquisitiveness; that practical, inventive turn of mind, quick to find expedients; that masterful grasp of material things, lacking in the artistic, but powerful to effect great ends; that restless, nervous energy; that dominant individualism; working for good and for evil, and withal that buoyancy and exuberance which comes with freedom-- these are traits of the frontier."(5) These were traits of the Wisconsin Washburn who was to betake himself with his typical western ways to the capital of the country. There, making the gamble, he would take a long step up the ladder of success.

Mineral Point

It was eight years before Washburn's arrival in Mineral Point that the land where the community was to spring up was cleared of the "dark and silent forest."(6) It was eight years after Cadwallader settled there that Wisconsin became a state--16 years from the time the land was traversed by Indians only--that the territory joined the Union as a state. In 1849 the town began to lose many of its citizens to mining in California. In one season townspeople witnessed more than 60 wagons with 200 passengers drive their wagons down High Street and out of town heading West. Even Cadwallader's partner left Mineral Point for the West to explore business opportunities in Sacramento, California, for the enterprising company. Washburn's younger brother, Charles, arrived in Mineral Point, stayed long enough to pass the bar to become the fifth attorney among the brothers then he, too, passed on to gold country.

While living at the Point, Washburn and Woodman saw the arrival of what they called modernism. Iron bands tied the Point to seaboard communities of the East, prompting Cyrus to remark that with the rails having reached southern Wisconsin, he no longer considered Mineral Point as "the West."(7) In the 1850s, trains puffed their way into town. It was 13 years after the partners made their homes in primitive Mineral Point.

"Up One Rung"

Politics intervened in the Washburn-Woodman partnership in the month of September 1854. The political party which had been launched that same year by Cadwallader's older brother, Israel, nominated and elected Cadwallader. In the previous month of August, a letter arrived on Washburn's desk signed by J.A. Sleeper, Republican Representative of the State Convention; Louis P. Harvey, later governor of Wisconsin; Charles Holt and J. Baker, newspaper editors; and William Tallman, perfume manufacturer and owner of an Italian villa in Janesville, Wisconsin. These political leaders asked Washburn if a nomination for Congress would "accord with [his] feelings and wishes"?(9) Four days later, Washburn

Stephen A. Douglas

responded to the letter. He would consider the matter, he wrote, "if the tender came with unanimity on the part of the Convention."(10) If elected, Cad would represent the second district, "the largest and most populace . . . in the United States."(11) A Republican convention was held at Mineral Point. On that day, the local newspaper featured Washburn as the party's anti-Nebraskan candidate, maintaining that, "If our friends. . .want an honorable true and substantial man in Congress as their agent who is not afraid to take his stand on right measures and see that 'justice be done though the heavens fall' and represent their wants as though they were his own, let them elect C.C. Washburn. . ."(12)

Come election time in 1855, Cadwallader broke the Democratic party's hold in his Wisconsin district. His brother, Israel, in 1850 had broken the steady cycle of Democratic elections in his District in Maine. In 1852 Elihu had done the same in Illinois, following a string of Democratic victories.

Dr. Otis Hoyt was the Democratic candidate in the Second District of Wisconsin. He declared himself and his party in support of the Kansas-Nebraska bill, vigorously opposed by Cadwallader and the Republicans. The Kansas-Nebraska bill was the creature of Illinois' popular Democrat, Senator Stephen A. Douglas, Chairman of the Senate Committee on the Territories of Kansas and Nebraska.

Douglas was a man who wanted the presidency for himself. He submitted a bill he knew would endear him to southern leaders. The bill would permit the territories to be open to slaves and slave owners. If it were favorably voted, the bill would invalidate the Missouri Compromise. The Missouri Compromise of 1850 had pledged that the Kansas-Nebraska regions would never be open to the slave population. Democratic leaders in the Second District of Wisconsin had earlier implored Cadwallader's partner, Cyrus, to let them place his name in nomination

Horatio Alger

even though Woodman had made it clear he, too, like Washburn, was anti-Nebraska. The Democratic leaders switched back again to support of the Douglas bill after Cyrus refused to let his name be placed in nomination.

During the campaign, a tactic of the Democrats was to slip word to newspapers accusing Washburn of being a "nativist" American, critical of foreigners. The opposition also declared that Washburn's Maine bank had been suspended. The partners, Washburn and Woodman, promptly announced that the report was unqualifiedly false. "The notes of that bank are, and will always hereafter be, received by this bank as other currency."(13) The *Madison Journal* carried a story reinforcing the partner's protest against the claim of insolvency, saying that "the bills [from the Hallowell bank] never have fallen in disfavor," noting that the State Bank of Madison accepted paper from Hallowell. The editor of the newspaper in Washburn's district which carried the indictment was forced to publish an apology. Washburn won handily with a vote of 11,930 to Dr. Hoyt.

"Up and Down, Cadwallader and Cyrus"

Change of location from Mineral Point to Washington, D.C., would represent a fresh new beginning for the adventurous and risky Wisconsin Washburn. Cadwallader was off to the capital of the country and in a few years would play a role in the War then only a cloud on the horizon. After serving in the House and engagement in the Civil War, Washburn would make further progress toward realizing the Horatio Alger goal of success against insurmountable odds.

The "gambler," Cadwallader was to make a change. For Cyrus, Cad's partner of ten years, the separation date represented the beginning of a long, unadventurous, lonely life, almost pathetic in its yearning to revitalize his decennary friendship with his former partner. In Mineral Point, the two had enjoyed intimacies that came from years of enjoyment, struggle, and the exchange of views about politics, business, women and religion--all perennially interesting topics. They had attended church services together, Cyrus always keeping in mind that his partner appreciated "the stated preaching of the gospel." The gospel was a Universalist interpretation of Old and New Testaments. Nostalgically, Cyrus remembered that he and his wife with Cadwallader without wife visited homes of friends in Mineral Point. Socializing in the evenings, they enjoyed singing the old songs, with Washburn expected always to sing his favorite ballad, *Auld Robin Gray*--a ballad of hopeless love.(14)

Unusual for a westernized Yankee, Cad's partner let his feelings show, posting his lament in his diary or commonplace book. The two had socialized and yet had not dared, Cyrus confessed, to "name to each other" their inner "heart feelings." As far as Washburn was concerned, he would manifest his intimacy only going so far as to deviate from the use of polite language in talking with or writing to Cyrus. In a letter, he referred to someone as "a lying son of a b---." That was a startling expression of passion.

Cyrus urged his partner to retire, hoping the two families might settle as neighbors in Helena, Wisconsin. When it was clear that was not going to happen, and after Cad resettled farther to the north in LaCrosse, Cyrus thought he also would settle in Cad's new home town. The former partner continued a vital relationship in an informal, advisory capacity. As a kind of unofficial advisor, he warned his former partner to beware of an excessive interest in making money and in making it too fast. In 1855, the year the partnership came apart, Cyrus noted that Cadwallader had made $40,000 in 60 days from lumber sales. He advised Cad to cooperate with him in establishing a Washburn-Woodman library in Madison. He advised the construction of an Agricultural School in Helena Valley, and then counseled his old partner to retire from business and become a statesman.

When Cyrus finally retired, he wandered off to Europe, hoping at first to have Cadwallader as a traveling companion. The theme of loneliness frequently appeared in Woodman's carefully kept diary. The period of Cyrus's life which was filled with its greatest joy were the years lived in the primitive little mining town of Mineral Point when the partnership kept them in close, intimate relationship.

While Cyrus lamented what he took to be an absence of sentimentality on the part of his former partner, it is clear that there was a side of Cadwallader willing to wear his heart upon his sleeve; but for his brother, Elihu. Cad once wrote heart-rending letters to Elihu pleading with him to arrange for his friend, William Sterling, to be released from prison. He had written as well to Governor Dodge seeking a pardon for Sterling, the son of an old and dear friend. Cadwallader explained to Elihu that he had been at the home of his imprisoned friend, and confessed that he had wept upon seeing the lovely Sterling children deprived of their father.(15) "As you hope for yourself now or hereafter," he wrote Elihu, "I charge you not to let this man die in prison and indelible shame be attached upon his innocent and interesting family for any effort on your part to prevent it."(16) There are ample evidences of compassion on Washburn's part as will be indicated, even though there was little display of sentimentality. As for displays of love for another woman, that is a matter not easily treated, but . . .

"A Woman and a Washburn"

There was Blanche Tucker who appeared years after Jeannette, unbalanced, was committed to a home outside Boston, Massachusetts, as noted, beautiful, popular, and intelligent. In her teens, Miss Tucker became a promising singer who needed voice training. A visit to the continent for the purpose of studying voice was made possible by "bachelor"" Washburn. When Blanche was on the continent, and in the years before her marriage to an Italian Count, she and her patron corresponded; and when Cadwallader was in Europe, the two saw each other. Blanche, in her letters to him, addressed Cad in affectionate terms, referring to "my dear benefactor," and ended letters with "much love," counseling Cad to "believe in love." It is not known whether Cadwallader was as phlegmatic and frosty in evaluating Blanche Tucker as Elihu was. Elihu sent a letter off to his Wisconsin brother telling him that, "It was a great pity that you ever sent Blanche Tucker out here. She is a talented and brilliant girl, very pretty, [with] a fair voice, but she is light and wants stability and seriousness of character."

"The Wisconsin Washburn Sent to Washington"

Wisconsin's Washburn was returned East to the capital by vote of citizens of District Two. He was soon perceived by fellow Congressmen as an archetype possessed of what is described as "an American character,"--self-reliant, trusting, optimistic, open to new experience, and tolerant of diversity.

As for tolerance of diversity, his not untypical Wisconsin village, was an example of early multiculturalism with inhabitants including Cornish, German, Italian, and Irish. Historians inform us that a characteristic of the typical American is hard working and pleasure seeking. Hard work described Washburn from his teens to the time of his death. It must be said, however, that he was seldom pleasure-seeking. It is believed he was celibate following the loss of his wife to derangement when he was 36. He did not indulge in excessive drinking, nor was he given to traveling for sheer pleasure. Europeans of the period, reporting their impressions of Americans, noted that they were consumers. Cadwallader and all the Washburn brothers lived up to that portrayal of Americans. They bought or built large, expensive houses, brought furniture and other appliances from the American East and from the continent, put books on their shelves, traveled widely, and ate well. The same Europeans also had it that Americans are "always borrowing," which can be said of archetypal Cadwallader. Father Israel Washburn noted that his own grandfather "was not afraid to run in debt," adding that "Cad is like his Great Grandfather."(18) Confirming that view is what Elihu wrote half in jest, that his Wisconsin brother would never get out of debt. "You would be unhappy," he added, "if you could not buy the whole world and give your note for it."(19)

"Preconceptions"

During the Washburns' time in Congress, and long before President Monroe fabricated his theory about expansionism, Americans were deepening their belief in this country's manifest destiny. Popular Attorney General Caleb Cushing had asked rhetorically, "Is not the occupation of any portion of the earth by those competent to hold and till it, a providential law of national life?" William Seward was bent upon preparing Americans for their mission abroad, and to that end he believed the people "would have to be politically united, economically strong, morally upright, and dedicated to democratic principles."(20) The thinking of Seward, with whom the Washburns were well acquainted, was in accord with the outlook of Cadwallader when Seward said,

> The nation that draws the most materials and provisions from the earth, fabricates the most, and sells the most of productions and fabrics to foreign nations, must be, and will be, the great power of the earth.(21)

Representative C.C. Washburn reflected the Seward sentiment in a statement he made to Congress that in the march of time, Mexico and Central America would be annexed by the United States because of the character of this country's citizens. The cultural milieu of the period included a mind set accepting of the idea of empire, when all countries of the world must become democracies. Americans resonated to the picturesque language of John Quincy Adams expressing in Quincy's words his (and Henry Clay's) vision of the future for this nation.(22) Adams declared vehemently that he had no desire to have the United States a "cock-boat in the wake of a British man-of-war." Adams' expression possessed implications beyond mere reference to the British. Cadwallader reminded Congressmen however that, "Men talk about 'manifest destiny,' and assure us that we are destined to absorb this entire continent, and the ideas seem so grand that no one feels inclined to count the cost or inquire into consequences."(23)

This was one of the partialities brought to the attention of Congressmen recurrently by one or another Washburn. Cadwallader and his brothers played a part, moralizing and challenging as government kept reaching beyond its grasp, driving Indians ahead of its encroachment onto their lands.

Distaste for the American Indian from whom land was taken in large gobs was pervasive during the time of the Washburns, Cadwallader, Elihu and Israel. At worst, the Indian population was decimated, and at best tribes were herded onto reservations. Where the first was concerned, Benjamin Franklin believed in "the design of Providence to extirpate those savages in order to make room for the cultivators of the earth." The Washburns were not untouched by the prevailing attitude as can be illustrated by Charles Ames Washburn's fictional representation of the Indian as primitive and brutal, and by Cadwallader's interest in improving the fate of the Indian--*but on reservations*. Israel and Elihu were more sympathetic to the Indians. Elihu's mother-in-law felt she owed her life and the life of Elihu's wife, Adele, to the thoughtfulness of an Indian woman. In fact, Indians came annually to Elihu's and Adele's Galena home, camping on the property for the purpose of acknowledging in several days' celebration their indebtedness to the Washburne-Gratiot family.

Another partiality coloring the outlook of Americans was the subject of individualism. Individualism as part of the cultural surrounding was so natural to Americans that it was hardly necessary for political philosophers to factor it out of the philosophy of John Locke for popular audiences. Locke in his *Letter Concerning Toleration* (1666) indicated that,

The only narrow way which leads to heaven is not better known to the
magistrate than to private persons. . . The care, therefore, of every man's
soul belongs unto himself, and is to be left unto himself.

There is no question but what this pervasive notion concerning individualism affected members of the Washburn clan. Their written, political, and religious works bristle with proof of their enchantment with the concept. Their Universalism bore out an appreciation of the virtues detailed by Locke when he wrote that "a Church [is] a voluntary society of men joining themselves of their own accord."(24)

The Whig movement also fitted itself into the Washburn religious persuasion which at some points is to talk of culture more than religion. "There is. . .appropriateness," writes Daniel Walker Howe, "in treating Whiggery as a culture rather than merely as a party. . ."(25) The Washburns were prototypes as Whigs. Acquaintance with the upbringing of children in the Washburn home explains why so many in the family moved into politics. " . . .[P]olitical ideas of the Whigs." says Howe, "derived from their whole experience of life: the attitudes they grew up with, the problems they confronted, the purposes they conceived."(26)

Religion was pervasive, certainly in the Washburn household. However much or little the populace deliberated on theological matters, the residue of their thinking was a generalized ethic called Christian. The ethic could be invoked to justify slavery as well as abolition. It provided a reason for making war on the South by the North, and justified the protection of the homeland and the southern culture--a culture which it was declared the bible itself championed. While evangelical religion is frequently credited with providing a religious base for the Whig culture, there were additional religious traditions in which Whig principles were accepted and promoted. Universalism was one such religious movement, along with Unitarianism. Washburns were strong Universalists and the Whig-Universalist influence was a potent factor in their lives and thought.

Involved as the Washburns were in the beginnings of the Republican movement, they embodied a carry-over of Whiggism into Republican party convictions demonstrating the division which deepened the chasm separating South and North. Washburn of Wisconsin displayed his Whig-Republican convictions and culture in a speech full of foreboding. As he ended a moving speech to the House, Cadwallader asked,

Will [the North] pass their . . . necks beneath the southern yoke? Let us

have disunion, and, if need be, Civil War, rather than dishonor.(27)

Speeches delivered by the Washburn brothers provide a rounded picture of events and ideas, hopes, partialities and prejudices which led to the fateful date of April 12, 1861. From the April date through the period of the Civil War and the interval of postwar fever, the Washburns were representative figures. What happened in the country to large numbers of people--with America's changing economics, politics, the growth of cities, the effect of war upon marriage and family, the radical shift in political ideologies, the evolution of and American Foreign Policy, manufacturing, and much more--all had their effect in Congress, affected in turn by the Washburns. Aspects of the American culture were unmistakably part of the thinking of political leaders, as was illustrated by the mind-set of Israel, Elihu and Cadwallader, and later by their younger brother, William.

When Cadwallader settled in Washington in 1855, cultural and religious values came to mean for him strict observance of moral principles. As with Israel and Elihu, it meant devotion to the needs of constituents and conformity with Whig-Republican ideas concerning the issues of the day. It meant temperance, sensitivity to the problem of slavery, the adoption of Henry Clay centrism, economic well-being, distrust of government, and the promotion of tariff.

"Freshman in Congress"

We may wonder how easy or hard it was for the younger Washburn brother to enter the lists alongside his senior siblings, Israel and Elihu. Israel and Elihu were fast becoming distinguished in the House of Representatives. Israel had become prominent during the lengthy contest with Southerners as he favored the despised Kansas-Nebraska bill. American party members, Free-soilers, Northern Democrats and other minority representatives faced a solid bloc of southern voters, Democrats and Whigs. Floor manager, Israel Washburn, drew derisive laughter when he was the first person to rise and speak when the infamous (from the Northern point of view) bill was placed before the House. The little man from Maine stood to submit the motion "to lay aside that bill." Everyone knew the Kansas-Nebraska bill was like a giant wheel now in motion and that anyone attempting to obstruct its passage was a fool. The motion which elicited laughter actually gave the bill's managers, both *pro* and *con*, what they sought--namely an approximation of the size of the adversary. Managers could better understand the task confronting them when the vote on Israel's motion turned out to be 85 in favor of laying aside the bill and 105 favoring discussion. Once the debate began, it was deliberately dragged out by the designing of managers of northern force, and it was a full month before Kansas-Nebraska was given final consideration and the Northern forces lost. Before the final vote was cast, Cad's brother, Israel, delivered what biographer Gaillard Hunt wrote was one of the most vital of the many speeches delivered on the agitated question.(28) Senator Henry Wilson of Massachusetts had written urging Israel to "create a North," calling for the dissolution of the Whig party. The Maine Whig Washburn had indicated two years earlier in May 1852 that he would be willing to leave his party if another party could be formed.

As a result of the victory by the South on the Kansas-Nebraska issue, Israel if interested could be sure his name would go down in history. On May 9 he arranged with Gamaliel Bailey, editor of a Washington newspaper, the *National Era*, to meet with about 30 Whigs, northern Democrats, and Free-Soilers. They discussed and evaluated what had transpired. Israel and Bailey addressed the group urging formation of a Republican party, the result of which was the launching of a new party. The convoking of leaders who had important constituencies meant that Israel Washburn of Maine would be invoked as one of the founders of the new party and therefore one of the politicians who, in Henry Wilson's terms, did indeed create a North.

Elihu was one brother to whom Cadwallader would be compared. His next oldest brother would be held up as a man to be emulated by the Wisconsin Washburn. The Illinois brother was coming to be known as the Representative who would succeed Thaddeus Stevens as Leader of the House. He was Watchdog of the Treasury and eventually Father of the House. Entering Congress to begin his duties, with two such celebrated brothers putting him the shadow, might have put the quietus on Cadwallader. He indeed became singularly silent-- for a Washburn.

Thaddeus Stevens

He came east from Wisconsin in mid-winter, signing in on December 3, 1855. He acted like a freshman. For two months he made no objections to bills, produced none himself, until the end of February. Then he submitted a simple request dealing with the Court of Claims, requesting that bills which had been forwarded to the Court be returned to the House. There were polite challenges to his request by

Representatives from New York and Arkansas. Neither Israel nor Elihu involved themselves in the minor fracas. Cadwallader Washburn backed away, withdrawing his resolution, but in a few days the Wisconsin delegate proved to have had the correct position and got his way. In April there were motions made by Cadwallader without a ripple of dissent. His first substantial involvement was the end of May 1856, five months after being seated. He challenged the Indiana Representative, Mr. Miller, because Washburn had not seen the bill requesting a continuance of the land office at Vincennes, Indiana. The following day, however, Washburne (sic)(29) of Wisconsin took up the bill in support of Mr. Miller. He explained that on the previous day he had not read the bill. He then went on to make the case more persuasively than did Mr. Miller, asking that the President be authorized to continue land offices for other states, including Wisconsin in addition to Indiana. Other bills were submitted and Washburn succeeded in having federal land in Wisconsin turned over to the State to aid in the improvement of navigation on the Wisconsin River, and successfully eked out bounty land for officers and soldiers who had not been compensated by the government. Tennessee Representative Jones carried on a disagreeable argument aided by McMullin of Virginia, but Cadwallader walked off the victor. Joining others who wanted land to be provided for public schools, Washburn called for the resolution to include the Territories of Kansas as well as Nebraska and Minnesota. It was done.

One bill submitted by Cadwallader had no opposition from Southern Representatives. It had the approval of the Secretary of War, the Honorable Jefferson Davis.

While serving in Congress, Cadwallader carried on business ventures in Wisconsin and Minneapolis. He had bought into a company having river rights at St. Anthony Falls and was in competition with a company on the opposite bank of the river. He and his cousin, Dorilus Morrison, also from Livermore, Maine, and Robert Smith of Illinois--aggressive businessmen all--owned land strategically placed where the city's center was to be developed. Mills and factories were built on the river only to be hurt during the *Panic* of 1857. Cadwallader, with the help of Elihu, managed to have internal improvements undertaken by the federal government when the Mississippi River needed improvements. In January 1858 the Wisconsin Representative--with vested interest in the Minneapolis venture--submitted a resolution instructing the Committee on Commerce, chaired by brother Elihu, to "inquire into the practicality of improving the Des Moines and Rock Island rapids, *and the navigation generally of the upper Mississippi river*, by means of dams and reservoirs upon the head waters of the Wisconsin, Black, Chippewa and St. Croix rivers, and other tributaries of said Mississippi river. . ." Elihu's political interests would be met with the passage of such a bill, since the Galena river was one of the Mississippi's important tributaries.

❖

A challenge to President James Buchanan came in January 1858 when the Wisconsin legislator was unhappy with the President's analysis of onerous economic conditions. He lamented that no course of action had been recommended in the Chief Executive's report to mitigate the effects of the depression. The handsome Wisconsin Washburn, eyes burning in a fashion reminiscent of Daniel Webster, stood in the well of the House to denounce the President. To appreciate the force and intensity with which Washburn delivered his criticism, it should be remembered that the year following Cadwallader's entry into the House, the United States experienced a depression more ruinous than the fateful economic slump remembered by all the Washburns, namely the set-back in 1837 which resulted in the break-up of the family. A factor partly responsible for the 1857 disaster was the ending of the Crimean War (1853-1856). For years, the War fueled the American economy. The exact date of the onset of the *Panic* was August 24, 1857, when one of New York's largest financial institutions failed--the Ohio Life Insurance and Trust Company. A domino falling followed. One Galena, Illinois, banker lost $80,000 in the Ohio Life. The price of a share of Illinois Central Railroad stock fell from $113 to $92. Wheat flour prices fell from an average of $6.35 to $4.55 in three months. Employees were laid off. Stocks everywhere dropped dramatically. Companies went bankrupt. Banks closed. In fact, so frequent were the closures that the *Cleveland Plain Dealer* listed the names of banks under the caption of "List of Late Bustified Banks. (Corrected Hourly)."(30)

Conditions grew increasingly worse. Responsibility for the economic downturn was laid at the doors of western farmers, the eastern bankers, and even demonic forces. Westerners refused to sell their produce. The unfair distribution of wealth was listed as provocation. Low tariffs in the year of the *Panic* were also believed to have been a factor in bringing on the depression, along with wildcat banking and government-backed railroad expansion. As might be expected, the vices of selfishness, dishonesty, and speculation, were claimed as causes as well.(31) It was, of course, the calamity provoked by the *Panic* that prompted Washburn's powerful speech. Part of the speech probably prompted someone to remark, for the first time, but not the last, that Washburn was a communist--a communist, it was thought, because he said that to restore public confidence, government must "give employment to the millions. . .in idleness." Mr. Washburn, wrote the *New York Times*, thought President Buchanan mistaken in having concluded that monetary evils were due solely to bank suspensions. The *Times'* page one story announced that the Congressman from Wisconsin

disapproved of the government's asking Congress to issue 20 millions of "red-dog and wild-cat money."(32) In his speech on the *President's Message*,(33) Representative Washburn regretted that no program had been recommended by the President or Cabinet members, so that "while the country is crushed" the administration is doing "literally nothing." Differing with Buchanan, Washburn insisted that the problem was not the system of bank credits, but rather "the corrupting

President Buchanan practices of the government itself during the previous twelve years."(34) This was a hit at Democratic party leadership going back to Polk's provoking the Mexican War. That War, debated in a school session at Livermore by Cadwallader, still rankled the now Representatives and the Whigs in general.(35) The expenditure of $200,000,000 and the loss of 80,000 lives in that War had unsettled the public mind, and it was then, said Washburn, that "The Halls of Montezumas" prompted our otherwise staid population to become "revelers." Before the revelry, he remarked, customs in the country had required "frugality and economy." But no more. A new attitude about money, brought about by Democrats, was in Cad's mind a factor accounting for the depression. Drawn mostly from abroad, the $200,000,000 raised upon the credit of the government, was put in circulation. It amounted to almost the total sum of paper money in circulation. That increase created inflation and the "steady habits of our people were. . .destroyed." Importation of goods from abroad nearly doubled between the years 1847 and 1851 and would have created havoc with the economy but for the discovery of gold in California.

Washburn went on to analyze the report of the President's Secretary of the Treasury. Revenues, the Representative claimed, were $8.3 millions short of the amount needed. In addition, a mistake in computing income to be realized on sugar and molasses, Washburn, said would leave government with a short-fall. $9.1million. With further addition and subtraction, Washburn concluded that the deficiency for the government would be $25.1 million at the end of the year. He then complained to House members about the lack of representation on the Ways and Means Committee. Regrettably, he said, New England had no representation on that most important House committee.

It was being said in 1858 that few Americans anticipated the 1857 disaster.(36) Cadwallader's elder brother, Israel Washburn, Jr., of Maine, in an address delivered December 21, 1852, was seen as one of those occasional "prophets" who foresaw the coming of the storm. Cadwallader in an 1858 speech, picked up on his brother's metaphor, predicting more storms to come, and that "balmy breezes and pleasant sunshine would soon be followed by an equinoctial storm producing a great upheaval in the ocean of business." As did Israel in 1852, Cadwallader in 1857 noted that there was a surplus in the Treasury. And Cad in his speech reminded the House and those who had wanted to distribute the surplus in the Treasury to the States that he had voted against that move.

Algernon Washburn

"The Pain of the *Panic*"

Robert Smith of Alton, Illinois, wrote to Cadwallader in September 1858 saying, "I have never seen such times. . .." He wrote Elihu Washburne saying he "never wanted to live to see another such time."

Washburn and Woodman had opened a bank in Mineral Point referred to by Cadwallader as "a redemption agency." The Mineral Point bank had been able earlier to help the Hallowell bank stay in operation. Help from Mineral Point made it possible for Sidney to offer gold for notes. Cad arranged for Sidney to maintain a large reserve in case the Suffolk Bank system in Boston were to test the Hallowell bank. The Boston bank did exactly that, testing the Hallowell operation, presenting $15,000 in Hallowell paper. Sidney paid up in gold coin. Without intending to hurt Washburn's political campaign, the Suffolk Bank made an egregious error. Anticipating that the Maine bank would not be able to make payment on the notes, they announced publicly that the Hallowell bank was bankrupt. There was a hasty and embarrassed retraction on the part of the Boston bank and the Democratic paper in Mineral Point which had announced what they had been led to believe was the failure of the Hallowell bank. The Maine public thereafter considered the Hallowell operation one of their strongest. George Smith came to this country from Scotland for the purpose of capturing and controlling the banking system. Smith was successful in lining up banks across the country. Among others, he threatened the Hallowell and Mineral Point banks. He got nowhere with the Washburns, however. The Washburns were unwilling to join Smith's wildcat scheme. Cadwallader and Elihu faced down Smith, taking as many notes as they could gather to the Georgia bank demanding gold. As a result of that Washburn victory, Smith gave up his banking business in the U.S. and returned to Great Britain where he lived out the remainder of his years. The Washburn success virtually came to nought once the *Panic* quickly spread like a virus across the country. While Cad was in Washington, the clerk left in charge of the Mineral Point bank, Luther Whittlesey, did not carry out the instructions of his boss. As a result Cad's Mineral Point bank became insolvent. With the *Panic* it closed. The banking institutions in Hallowell and the Point, though they brought little by way of profit,(37) paid off by having brought needed capital to the Wisconsin Washburn enterprises. The available money enabled Cadwallader to develop several projects, one of which was at St. Anthony Falls in Minneapolis. Lumbering, another Washburn undertaking with an accumulation of 60,000 acres in Wisconsin and Minnesota, made possible in part by the success of the banking business, fell on bad times in 1857. That year, the value of pine stumpage hit a new low. Cad's lumber enterprises did not recover from the economic crisis until after the Civil War. "Production fell off to about three million feet from an estimate of twelve million, and remained approximately at that figure throughout the next five years."(38) A steam mill had been constructed in the town of Waubeek, Wisconsin, owned by C.C. Washburn, Elihu and their younger brother, Samuel. The mill went into operation just prior to the onset of the 1857 *Panic*. Cad suffered losses steadily in the later years of the 1850s. There are those who believe he entered the military so he could not be taxed out of ownership while away at War, in consequence of which he did not recover from the *Panic* until 1864 when he sold the lumbering business to Knapp, Stout and Company--reputed to be the largest lumbering corporation in the world.

There were many in Wisconsin and Minneapolis who thought Cadwallader had come to the end of his career. The depression having set in, "an enormous amount of logs and lumber, mostly from Saint Anthony, lay in the river at the Mississippi ports of Lyons, Keokuk, Muscatine, and Clinton, and Washburn was unable to 'raise a dime'."(39) The load, said Cadwallader, was worse than the pack of Bunyan's Pilgrim. Cad gave credence to what Elihu had once said of him. He wrote in 1858 that he must make up his mind to wade with the water up to his mouth and ears for months to come.

Chapter Forty-One

WARRIORS WASHBURN

Henry Wilson of Massachusetts wrote Cadwallader's brother, Israel, in May 1854, praising the Maine Congressman for an impressive speech on the North-South crisis. Wilson, Senator and Vice-President to be, urged Israel to "act now and act boldly [to] *'make a North.'*" He had in mind the possibility of Washburn's launching a new political party. Cad's brother, Israel, did exactly that; and it was perhaps the first giant step taken among the Washburns in the direction of a sectionalism which would lead to War.

Wm Lloyd Garrison

Six years after the Republican party had been organized, with the North and South having become further estranged, Henry Wilson was among Northerners who sought a *peaceful* separation of the South from the North. In this, he stood with William Lloyd Garrison, Wendall Phillips, Henry Ward Beecher, and the gentle Quaker, John Greenleaf Whittier. These men feared War would bring anarchy. Unitarian minister Henry W. Bellows feared disunion would bring "a new adult individualism [where] the private man feels that he is the State."

The War came. Henry Wilson changed his tune, whereupon he promptly attributed the honor of having "made a North," not to Washburn, but to the attack on Fort Sumter. "Fort Sumter made a north," said he. Wilson then became a vigorous supporter of the War. Bellows revised his pulpit messages preaching that disunion would call forth obedience to law and order. The gentle Quaker, Whittier, accepted the War, concluding that strife represented the chastisement of Divine Providence. Universalist ministers who were heeded by the Washburns joined energetically in the Call to Arms. The Reverend Elbridge Gerry Brooks declared, "At last the crisis has come. . . ..War has begun [and] we. . .are summoned to be heroes. . .to make history fragrant with the aroma of sacrifice."(1) Editor George Emerson, wrote in the *Universalist Quarterly* that "we cannot be Christians unless we fight. . . .. It is God's war; and we, the subjects of his government, have but to obey his will."(2)

Henry Wilson

As for Cadwallader and his brothers, all may have listened to what their ministers championed, namely War with the South; but their initial response to the disloyal action taken at 4:30 a.m., April 12, at Charleston, South Carolina, makes clear that the Washburns needed no goading by clergy or by the conforming news media. With no delay, the Washburns were solidly and inescapably involved. Elihu particularly was at the center of the emerging conflict.

After Abraham Lincoln was elected but before he

was inaugurated, he needed to know if the Chief of the Army, General Winfield Scott, would be ready for action if the recalcitrant South were to take the federal forts by force. Lincoln called on Cadwallader's elder brother, Elihu, asking him to visit General Scott, and to say to Scott that the President-elect would be obliged to him to be as well prepared as he could be, either to hold or re-take forts after the inauguration. Washburne eased the mind of the President-elect, assuring him that General Scott was prepared to perform as requested.

The fated April 12 day arrived. In Galena Washburne at once took the initiative. Citizens were assembled so they could react to the militancy of the rebellious South.(3)

Near the end of 1859 an urgent appeal came to Israel in Washington from "down in Maine." Dr. Amos Nourse wrote begging the Congressman to let Republicans in Maine place his name before delegates as their candidate for governor. Reluctantly and strictly out of loyalty, Washburn acceded. He aspired to become a United States Senator not Governor. After an easy campaign, he was elected in 1860. With the outrage committed by South Carolina in April 1861, the Maine Governor became one of Lincoln's staunchest heads of state. He was one of the first governors to call a special session of the legislature to prepare for War. Cadwallader and Israel ended their service as Congressmen the month before the outbreak of War. Before the March date, Cadwallader had rendered exceptional service to benefit the newly-elected President. As a member of the ill-reputed Committee of Thirty-three, the Wisconsin Representative submitted to the House a Minority Report on behalf of himself and Mason Tappan of New Hampshire. The majority of the Committee of Thirty-three were prepared to submit to Congress their recommendations which included an agreement that slavery be recognized by Congress, that jurisdiction over slavery in the District of Columbia should "never be interfered with. . ." There were six propositions totally, each one objectionable to members in the North, including Washburn of Wisconsin and Tappan of New Hampshire. Thirty-one members of the Committee of Thirty-three voted to submit the offensive proposals to the House. Cadwallader Washburn delivered the riposte to the sizeable majority's case. In his history, James G. Blaine recorded for posterity that "the only bold words spoken [in opposition to the Committee's proposals] were in the able report by Cadwallader C. Washburn of Wisconsin. . . Wrote Blaine, "[He] made an exhaustive analysis of the situation in plain language," vindicating the conduct of the General Government. . ..(4)

Cadwallader's former partner, Cyrus Woodman, favored the position taken by the majority of the Committee of Thirty-three. For his part, he "should be willing to give part of the country south of 36.30 to slavery. . ." Woodman reflected more accurately than his partner the mood of the country.

While preparing the Minority Report, Wisconsin's Representative was making his first bid for the U.S. Senate. When the Legislators in Wisconsin cast their first ballots for Senator on January 18, Cadwallader polled the largest vote. It was not a majority, however, and at that point, a third man entered the race, having the effect of determining Washburn's defeat. Timothy Howe, one-time teacher at the little schoolhouse a few yards from the Washburn farmhouse in Livermore, "slender, handsome, sprightly, [a] former judge" also sought the office of U.S. senator.(5) When it became clear to the third contestant for the office, Governor Randall, that the contest was to be between the two former

Benjamin Wade

Livermore men, Washburn and Howe, Randall gave his support to Howe and withdrew.(6)

Cadwallader did not seem to be much disappointed in defeat. He wrote W.C. Rogers saying that "if anybody supposes that I shall break my heart in case I am defeated they mistake me greatly He was confident he retained power, and when Rogers indicated an interest in becoming postmaster at La Crosse, Washburn wrote, "Let not your heart be troubled. You shall be the next P.M. at La Crosse. The Congressman assured Rogers that he would wield authority in Washington even if he should lose in the bid for the Senate seat. In the letter to the aspiring postmaster, he said to Rogers that the prospect of War was likely. Washburn had reason to know. He had thrown down the gauntlet in his speech of January 24, 1861, saying to gloomy listeners,

If this Union must be dissolved, whether by peaceable secession or through fire and blood and Civil War, we shall have the consolation of knowing that when the conflict is over, those who survive it will be, what they never have been, inhabitants of a free country.(7)

He was referring, of course, to blacks, declaring they would at last live in a free country.

It seemed clear to politicians North and South that War was imminent. Some of the language spoken in the House and Senate was so heated that the irascible Benjamin F. Wade of Ohio carried a brace of horse pistols into the senate, and laid them on the lid of his desk. . ..(8) The mood in Washington was tense. At social gatherings it was forbidden to discuss politics. Cad's former partner, Cyrus Woodman, wrote that he had been expecting War, and predicted it would be "a long and bloody one. "Governor Andrew in Massachusetts wrote Woodman in February saying he was "as quiet and calm as a philosopher, but I stand surprised. . .at the content with which others received the efforts of traitors to break up the Government." (9)

In the capital, Lincoln's friends, including the Washburns, were anxious about the trip the President-elect would make from Illinois. Assassination was in the minds of southern sympathizers and Elihu with William Seward were charged by House and Senate to look into the claims which had been made to assassinate Mr. Lincoln. The exact hour when Lincoln would arrive in the capital was a secret, known only to Washburne and Seward It was a dramatic moment when the President's train arrived in the station Elihu who had been waiting patiently started toward his friend, Lincoln The President's bodyguard was ready to strike the Congressman until Lincoln halted his bodyguard, saying, "That's Washburne!"

❖

The Wisconsin Washburn brother had not given up easily when his aspiration to be a Senator was frustrated. Defeated in January, he picked himself up and a few months later ran for another office, that of governor. Politicking went on during August and September. A pre-convention rump party was set up for the purpose of defeating Washburn. When the Republicans met at their convention they accepted the recommendation of the rump group and elected L.P. Harvey Governor.

Cad's time had not come. Nonetheless, the businessman-politician, in profile looking as handsome as a Greek god, had before him an unusually promising career. He busied himself with business transactions both before and after the fated Fort Sumter cannonading. He purchased water rights at Minneapolis on the Mississippi which gave promise of a breakthrough for him in the business world. Part of the excess of activity was taken up in planning for the construction of a great flour mill in Minneapolis. The panic or depression of the late 1850s distracted him from fulfilling his monumental plans for St Anthony Falls. In the meantime he assembled a team including his younger brother, William Drew Washburn, whom he had encouraged to move west from Maine The two, Cadwallader and William, together with Dorilus Morrison, a cousin from Livermore, Maine, gained complete control of the Minneapolis Mill in the decade of the 1860s. Despite his tireless activities in the political arena as well as in the domain of business, Washburn took time out to move from Mineral Point to La Crosse.

If Mineral Point was the place where Wisconsin began, and which was already in decline,(10) Washburn may have expected La Crosse to become the community of the future. Cad was the largest lumber operator on the Black River a few miles north of La Crosse. Status in the new location permitted him to begin changing the landscape. He wrote an associate in La Crosse telling him he was going to put a steam ferry on the Mississippi to compete with the McRoberts ferry. He would reduce the rate of ferrage [sic] 50 percent below McRobert's prices. In other words, Washburn took action with regard to the ferry in March, month he moved to La Crosse.

William Seward

A year before the attack on Sumter, the Wisconsin Representative had stood on the floor of the House defending the South's unregenerate Northerner, William Seward, for having used the menacing term, "irresistible conflict." In that House speech, Cad, in defending Seward, made known his own position, referring to the Fugitive Slave law as a disgrace on the statute books of a Christian country. He regarded slavery "as a great social and political evil." But given his strong stands on the race issue, it is eerie to note that when Washburn spoke of "the deliverance of our brethren" he meant deliverance from slavery, not for *acceptance as a citizen*. His speech, a virtual challenge to the South to put 'em up and fight, can be seen as part of the politics which anticipated War. As we have seen, the Washburn brothers played a measurable part in the onset of the bloodshed and slaughter.

Washburn's Political Opponent Appoints Him Colonel

After Governor Randall threw his weight behind Timothy Howe, and Washburn had lost in the race for the U.S. Senate, it was the War Department in Washington, not Governor Randall in Madison, that took the initiative authorizing the organization of a Second Cavalry in Wisconsin. The acting Secretary of War, Thomas A. Scott, wrote Governor Alexander Randall instructing the Governor to organize an additional regiment of cavalry "of which the Honorable C.C. Washburn shall be Colonel." In October 1861, 900 of the Colonel's men were brought together at Camp Washburn in Milwaukee. By March 1862 a fully organized and well-trained regiment was ready for the battlefield. The regiment was mustered into service on March 24. Led by Colonel Washburn, the men marched to Springfield, Illinois, arriving on June 9.Six days later, two battalions of the Wisconsin cavalry, and one battalion of the 10th Illinois were ordered to join General Samuel Curtis in Arkansas. With cliff-like eyebrows, mottled side-burns and disporting a hefty belly and a stern look befitting a Brigadier General, Curtis was marching through Missouri. He was chasing Confederates south and eastward like fall leaves before a north wind.

A sheer outline of the block of Confederate states shows a likeness of a dog's head with Florida the front paws, and the border state, Missouri, the stiff tail of an Airedale. Starting in the West with the "tail", Missouri received the full force of Federal Army activities. The broad interest of the Union government was to perform a giant pincer movement. West of the Mississippi River and moving eastward was the Department of the West. General Nathaniel Lyons was first charged with driving the Confederates from Missouri. His successor, General Curtis, was expected to propel his army through Missouri into Arkansas, take Little Rock and push on toward the "father of waters," as Lincoln referred to the Mississippi. The pincer movement in the east consisted of George B. McClellan's Army of the Potomac, charged with the task of moving out of Washington, marching to the capital of the Confederacy, Richmond, capturing Jefferson Davis and bringing the rebellion to a quick close. The eastern battle plan expanded and the Army of the Potomac pushed South out of Washington, terminating at last in Sherman's march through Georgia, and then moving westward to the Mississippi with the conquest of the Gibraltar of the Mississippi-Vicksburg. As an example of the pincer movement initiated at the beginning of the War, a seesaw of battles between contenders on the fronts east and west took place between May and August 1861.On May 10 Union forces in the west captured Camp Jackson in Missouri, and in the east on the 24th the Army of the Potomac seized Alexandria, Virginia. In June in the eastern theater, there were the battles of Fairfax Courthouse and Big Bethel, and the battle of Boonville in the western theater. In July there were several battles in Virginia in the east, and one in Carthage in Missouri. A fateful fight in August at Wilson's Creek in Missouri took the life of Brigadier General Nathaniel Lyons who, Congress later declared, saved Missouri for the Union. Curtis was made Commander of the Department of Missouri and the armies east and west, like a turtle moving its head out and back again defensively, still moved slowly toward each other.

❖

As noted, Washburn and his men joined Curtis in July 1862. Curtis' 11,000 man army was headed for Arkansas. On the way the army cleared Missouri of Confederate forces. The Missouri-Arkansas experience introduced Cadwallader to some of the grief soldiers expect to confront at a cost in human lives. At the Cache River an engagement was fought and the enemy routed. The excitement of that battle won by the federals did not assuage hunger pangs of the men who marched on to Clarendon, fully expecting to find waiting for them a shipload of food and needed supplies. The boat at Clarendon had chugged away leaving General Curtis and his army in enemy territory stranded and starving. Curtis turned to Colonel Washburn, and as Cadwallader explained in a letter to the Assistant Adjutant General, directed the Colonel to lead a column of 2500 cavalry from Clarendon to Helena, Arkansas, where Helena was to be liberated and the army fed. If supplies had been in Clarendon, it is expected Curtis' forces would proceed through Arkansas to take Little Rock--a Confederate manufacturing center. Instead, Helena needing to be guarded as an important federal post on the Mississippi, and Washburn was assigned command of the city. From July to November, the Colonel and his regiment remained on the bluffs overlooking the Mississippi, a location about which Mark Twain said was "one of the prettiest situations on the river."(11)

❖

In the opening weeks of 1862, Washburn had been whiling away his time at Camp Washburn in Milwaukee, anxious to enter the contest against rebellious Confederates." This holiday soldiering I do not fancy," he wrote his brother. It is "not profitable to the country."(12) In March he wrote again to his Washington brother declaring that he deserved to be a Brigadier General. By July he was moved up in the echelon of officers, thanks to Elihu and Congressmen who had fraternized with Cadwallader when he was in the House. Eleven months after complaining of being a "holiday soldier," and thinking his military career was withering away on the bluffs of Helena, Washburn was gratified when General Grant ordered him to make an incursion into the interior of enemy country. The aggression meant the newly-appointed Brigadier General was going to play a part in the pincer plans.

Another Washburn in the War

While Cadwallader thought he was wasting time at Helena, his brother, Samuel, sat on board the Flag Ship *U.S.* Galena, wistfully recalling his proposal of marriage to Lorette Thompson one year earlier to the day--May 12, 1861. That day in May the Monitor came into the James River and anchored at the stern of the Mother Flag Ship, the *Galena*, nursing its wounds following its hard fought victory over the Merrimac. The next day the little fleet of ships, including the Flag Ship, anchored temporarily at City Point on the James, and in mid-afternoon continued farther up the river to within 25 miles of the capital of the Confederacy.

300

The *Galena* was a ship visited frequently by dignitaries from Washington. Several highly-placed officials, including "Old Blair," as Sam referred to him, President Lincoln and Secretaries Chase and Stanton, together with several Generals, boarded Sam's ship. General McClellan came on board one day to report that his army was within eight miles of Richmond.   On May 15, the *Galena* sailed up river to within seven miles of Richmond. A tempestuous battle was fought at Drewry Bluff. Sam and the men on board his flag ship must have felt themselves fortunate to be afloat. Stubbornly doing battle until its ammunition was used up, the ship at last withdrew, backing down the river to City Point. The ship, wrote Sam, looked as though it had smallpox. In his journal he expressed the wish that he had been Flag Officer of the fleet. Like his Washburn brothers, Sam was confident he knew what had gone wrong and wrote his opinion in high Washburn style enumerating errors. The position of the ship, he said, should not have been 700 yards from the bluff but two miles off shore. The ship should not have remained still. As soon as the rebels found the range, they were able to pepper the *Galena*, hitting whatever they aimed at. Even if the ship had silenced the guns at the Bluff, sailor Sam thought, enemy territory could not have been taken since there were sharpshooters up and down the shore making it impossible for boats to land. In his judgment, however, Sam thought "the battle was a gallant one and worthy of better result." Samuel got hold of a copy of the *New York Herald*, which he referred to as "a d---d lying nuisance. "The newspaper unhappily reported that the *Galena* took only a small part in the battle at Drewry's Bluff. What he knew, of course, was that the *Galena* was the only ship engaged in the fight. Other ships in the small fleet had not been exposed to the withering bombardment. If they have been they would have been utterly destroyed.

Sam, in control of one of the ship's guns during a day of rifle practice put live shells through the center of two houses at City Point. That shooting, he said, was considered "the best shots that were ever made on the *Galena*." Forever judgmental, another Washburn characteristic of the brothers, Sam, having caught glimpses of rebel soldiers on shore, likened them to "Falstaff's company that marched through Coventry." He wrote also in his diary about "Old Goldsborough," saying Goldsborough was not fit to be in the U.S. Navy "or in

Salmon Chase

any place but Hell." The Admiral had informed the Captain of Sam's ship that the men had no time to read letters. "Damn him," scribbled sailor Sam.

On June 3 Sam's diary notation made it clear that he tried to keep track of what his brothers were doing. He took note of the evacuation at Corinth, Mississippi--Cadwallader's territory. In his notation, however, he made no mention of the humiliating Union victory which was "tantamount to a defeat," as the *Chicago Tribune* asserted.(13) On that day, June 3, his brother, Cad, was leading four companies out of Helena, Arkansas, marching toward Cuscumbia and Lebanon. Sam wished he could receive a letter from Cad and his other brothers.

An astronaut sliding over the United States could take a clear, revealing snapshot of the states of Mississippi and Tennessee. The snapshot would include a piece of geography where some of the toughest battles of the Civil War were fought, at Donelson, Shiloh, Corinth, Tupelo, Vicksburg and other strategic locations. The photograph from space would show at a glance the distance from Corinth, but a few miles south of the Tennessee border in northern Mississippi, to Fort Hudson south of Vicksburg, 400 miles away. It would expose the winding Mississippi river looking like a rope thrown randomly across the landscape from north to south. It would include the capital of Mississippi, Jackson, and of course, the snapshot would show the Gibraltar on the Mississippi--Vicksburg. The panorama with its god-like view from the heavens could lay out scenes where battles were fought beginning November 2, 1862, the date, according to Lieutenant General Grant, when the contest to take Vicksburg began. Eight months later, Grant and General John Pemberton sat on a rock between the antagonists respective lines, shook hands and agreed upon surrender terms.

❖

November 2, General Ulysses S. Grant was south of the border of Tennessee. The beginning of his effort to take Vicksburg was to move down through the state. He would lead his army to Grenada, and thence farther south to the state capital, and finally to Vicksburg. Confederate Lieutenant General John C. Pemberton's forces intended to frustrate Grant's grand strategy. In the northern part of the state of Mississippi, Union forces had stabilized Holly Springs, Grant's supply base. The Springs was thought to be a safe distance from Pemberton's forces. Given assurance of food, clothing and ammunition, the General planned to march almost straight downstate, following the line of the Mississippi Central Railroad, moving first into Grenada, then beyond into Jackson. He expected Grenada to be the federals first important victory.

As for Pemberton, his army was stretched along the Tallahatchie River in a strongly-fortified position where he expected Grant to "waste [his armies] strength in fruitless attacks."(14) Grant turned to the, by then *General* Washburn, who was at Helena directing Washburn to ford the Mississippi with a substantial force, move across the delta region to a position between Pemberton and Union lines. The two lines were stretched for miles across the narrow width of the state, moving up and down like great synchronized flapping wings. In his expedition into Mississippi with his cavalry and foot soldiers Washburn obliged Pemberton to relinquish his defense on the Tallahatchie. Union leaders surmised that if a column of Union soldiers crossed the Mississippi at Helena and was able to reach Grenada, the

John C. Pemberton

Confederate military would be embarrassed. The Southerners would probably

break contact with Grant's military and back the Army south of the Yalobusha river. The invading force between the armies was headed by Generals Washburn and Charles E. Hovey.

When Cadwallader knew he was to set out on a dangerous expedition into the battle zone between the Union army moving south, and Confederate forces fixed and ready to fight at the Tallahatchie, he understood he might be killed. He did not want to die owing money, so he placed $1,000 in the hands of a gentleman who, if warrior Washburn did not return, was to put the money in his brother, Elihu's, hands.(15) Before starting the journey into "no man's land," Cadwallader wrote his daughters, aged ten and twelve. He wanted them to know that nine months had passed since he had gone off to War."It seemed," he wrote, that "the War would never end." It had hardly begun. Like a typical New Englander to whom education was important, he admonished Fanny and Jeannette to "improve [their] time." Music lessons were emphasized. He wanted them to know their geography and told them to look on a map and trace the journey their father had made from Milwaukee, where he started on March 24 from Camp Washburn. Cadwallader gave the girls the names of towns he passed through-- Ozark, Forsyth, Jacksonport, and Clarendon. As they marched across enemy territory, the Colonel took great care of his battalions. His trainload of 1,000 men filled ten miles of passenger cars, and he saw to it they were well guarded. The Wisconsin contingent marched 400 miles, finally to join General Samuel R. Curtis at Augusta, Arkansas. He remarked in his letter to the girls back home that he had done battle at the Cache River, told about the long march to Clarendon, and then mentioned the place where he was sitting as he wrote--Helena, Arkansas.

At Clarendon, he explained to the girls, General Curtis "ordered Gen. Washburn to take 2,500 cavalry and by a forced march reach Helena and order supplies to that place from Memphis, 90 miles above."(16) After capturing the Arkansas city on the Mississippi, Washburn explained that he was placed in command at Helena.(17) Colonel Washburn's residence in the captured city had been the home of General Thomas C. Hindman, who years earlier had been a member of Congress with Washburn.

In November, Washburn wrote a goodbye letter to Elihu two days before starting east, telling his brother he was about to leave on a 40 mile journey into enemy territory. Washburn and Hovey collaborated in making the hazardous journey. They located on their map a point ten miles down the Mississippi river where there was a town on the east side called Friar's Point. Hovey's 7000 infantrymen and Washburn's 2000 cavalry went south from Helena on the west side of the river crossing at the Point. Washburn marked the location where Grant and the Union Army were quartered 60 miles from the Confederate Army under Pemberton. The map showed a cluster of towns scattered through the no-man's land between Grant and Pemberton, Senatobia, Abbeville, Panola, Charleston, Coffeeville. On the one hand, Cadwallader had reason to believe Confederate soldiers were patrolling those towns. On the other hand, he knew those patrolling were aware that the federal juggernaut would soon heave south passing through to conquer, and that the federals were heading straight for those towns and beyond them to Grenada. These scattered villages were invaded by Washburn's cavalry, sometimes in company with Hovey's infantry, and at times with Washburn's contingent of 2,000 men on horseback. He drove the enemy out of

Panola. Seeing Abbeville on his map 25 miles northwest, Cadwallader with his cavalry raced off toward that town. From Abbeville, men and horses headed directly south 40 miles to Coffeeville. The cavalry destroyed the railroad in the rear of the rebel army at Grenada, and as predicted, compelled Confederates to retreat, abandoning their railroad facilities. After the destructive raids, Washburn returned to Charleston where Hovey's supporting forces were located. On the way to Charleston the invaders from Helena met, fought and defeated a Texas brigade. Pemberton had called in the Texas Cavalry led by Lieutenant Colonel John S. Griffith. The report from Washburn was that his cavalry went to Oakland where the Texans were located, confronted and drove them away toward Coffeeville. Griffith, however, reported to his headquarters that the Texans drove the federal forces back to Charleston. Griffith declared in his report that he was determined to fight Washburn "at the junction of the road upon which he was traveling with the Charleston road and a half a mile beyond Oakland." General Washburn moved up through a long lane, the Texan wrote; and when he arrived within 200 yards of us, his men opened his batteries upon us, pouring the grape and canister at a fearful rate and with a rapidity that excelled anything I ever saw before. Griffith with his 60 Texas cavalry says he took the battering, but finally withdrew. To sweeten the report, he added that six-shooters, coats, blankets, hats, etc., dropped in such rich profusion by General Washburn's bodyguard, were picked up and borne away in triumph by my boys. The Texan also wrote that, having fought them a spirited battle of some 50 minutes, I ordered my command "to horse." The safety of the command, he said, demanded an immediate withdrawal, which was done in good order. The Texans departed for Oakland where they reformed.

❖

General Curtis in his report to H.W. Halleck wrote that he especially approved "the energy and spirit manifested by Brigadier Generals Hovey and Washburn." General Hovey recounted events saying, "It gives me great pleasure to say that Brig. General Washburn's conduct during our expedition was dashing, bold, fearless and effective and could not have been excelled." General Sherman with information he had of the expedition, declared, "the enemy is shaken by their being outwitted at the Tallahatchie." It was clearly a victory because of Washburn's and Hovey's successes. Washburn said of himself and his regiment that the entire rebel army was stampeded by him--hyperbole perhaps for the benefit of his admiring brother, Elihu. John E. Phillips, Assistant Adjutant-General, wrote that the Hovey-Washburn thrust into no-man's land "accomplished one of the most remarkable marches made during the War, penetrating to the very heart of the enemy's country. . .."

❖

Pemberton was not the only threat to the Union Army of 32,000 men. Two Generals, Van Dorn and Nathan Bedford Forrest, the latter of whom was to be Washburn's *bete noir* for as long as he was commander of western Tennessee, devised plans to frustrate the federals scheme. The cavalries of the two

Confederate Generals moved into Holly Springs. From their point of view, they liberated the Springs with its $400,000 cache of supplies. The Van Dorn-Forrest team then split. Forrest's horses galloped north into Tennessee, cutting railroads and telegraph lines, throwing federal forces into confusion. The December victory at Holly Springs was probably seen by Southerners to be a perverse Christmas present to invaders from the north.

In mid-December, following the successful expedition into central Mississippi, Washburn was encouraged by General Sherman to pursue a course

Nathan B. Forrest

which Cadwallader had proposed to him. Cad wanted to take his cavalry on a foray into central Mississippi to the city of Yazoo. He felt confident he and his force could destroy the nest of Confederate and privately-owned ships floating quietly on the Yazoo River at that location. Cadwallader was frustrated in his attempt, however, by the indecisive of General W.A. Gorman, Cadwallader's superior. Gorman waited to decide until it was too late to make the journey into the swamp of the delta.

Washburn devised another plan, one that would prove more promising, he thought, than either the raid into no-man's land, or than the proposed journey to Yazoo city. He wanted to open the entire Coldwater, Tallahatchie and Yazoo rivers system enabling federal forces to ship south to within three miles of Vicksburg. This, Washburn thought, was the most sensible route to Vicksburg in accompaniment with the Army's trip down the Central Mississippi Railroad. His plan won the approval of General Grant. Cadwallader, together with Colonel James H. Wilson, began the arduous task of opening the river system. The rebels, anticipating the effort of the federals to open the Pass holding back the mighty waters of the Mississippi from the delta and the river system, plugged the Coldwater the way Washburn's logs back in Wisconsin had corked up the Black River or the Chippewa. The rebels felled timber which Washburn-Wilson and their crew had to remove. The undertaking took weeks of laborious work finally landing Washburn in sick bay. The General was so ill he implored his brother, Elihu, to leave Washington and come and help nurse him back to health.

Grant in the meantime continued his turtle-like progress down along the Mississippi Central, bulldozing Confederates, calling in General Sherman to join in the forward movement. It was at this moment in the engagement that General Grant became mystified by what was happening in Washington. George Brinton McClernand of Illinois and President Lincoln were designing a blueprint permitting McClernand to raise troops on his own in the West with the promise that he could lead newly-formed divisions down the Mississippi River to Vicksburg coincidental with Grant's movement through the state. The perplexity arose for Grant because General Halleck and the President did not advise Grant of the plans. In mid-December, Halleck in an almost incidental manner mentioned to General Curtis, "I have been informed that the President has selected a special commander." When it became clear to Grant that McClernand, once he had put together his forces, was to take an army south on the Mississippi River to Vicksburg, the commanding General decided to change his plans for taking

Vicksburg. He ordered Sherman and his divisions to retrace their journey to Memphis, proceed by steamboat down the Mississippi from Memphis, attack, and hopefully take Vicksburg. In the meantime Pemberton with his Confederate forces moved south from the Grenada region, entering the shelter of Vicksburg with his forces. The rebels under Pemberton were then entrenched and ready to meet Sherman's assault. The day after Christmas 1862, Sherman with his 32,000-man army fought and failed to take the City. South and North there were bitter defeats for the Union.

Cadwallader wrote Elihu noting that Sherman had unexpectedly returned to Memphis and explained that the General was to find more troops to accompany him south to "take Vicksburg." To his brother, Cad reported optimistically that he was coincidentally to land 100 miles above Vicksburg at Yazoo Pass with 5,000 men, charged with opening the Pass.

Despite vanquishment of Sherman's force, Washburn was not discouraged. He was confident Vicksburg could be reached as soon as the river system in northern Mississippi was opened and boats could carry all the military and supplies needed to enable Union forces with certainty to conquer Vicksburg. At the end of December and at the request of Grant, Washburn and his cavalry were to re-cross the Mississippi below Helena to strike out for the Coldwater River and join Grant. The bottom-lands, however, were impassable and Washburn and his troops had to return to Helena. It was fortunate for the entourage that it was stopped at the Coldwater since Van Dorn and Forrest were at that time making their successful raid on Holly Springs.

For the federal armies and for President Lincoln, a discouraging 1862 turned into a challenging new year. The country's attention focused on Grant and his plans for victory in the West. Memphis was in Union hands as the new year began. In April Washburn was placed in command of all of Western Tennessee with headquarters at Memphis. He was visited by Grant in January, and Grant disclosed that Vicksburg would be taken only by a land force "in the rear." As Grant saw it, it would be necessary for him to make his way down river past Vicksburg, cross the Mississippi at Grand Gulf, travel northwest to Jackson, turn

west to the half-circle of ramparts protecting the front entrance (called the rear as Grant made plans) to Vicksburg. For Washburn, the way to that front door of the Gibraltar of the West was for Union forces to make the trip down the center of the state, assisted by naval power traversing the spider-web of streams and rivers to Vicksburg.

J.P. Benjamin, Secretary of the Confederate War Department, contended that the Yazoo Pass Expedition was "from its inception as stupid and impossible as was ever made by incompetent commanders." Also, the Wisconsin General

William T. Sherman

apparently overlooked predicaments which induced Grant to make his (to Washburn) far-fetched trip down the Mississippi and up around Vicksburg. Why did Grant not travel 100 miles east of the Mississippi, instead of 300 miles, making it necessary for naval ships to pass under bristling guns at Vicksburg, and for Union forces to march eastward without supplies, at last to park himself with his army at the front door of the impregnable city? Washburn reminded himself that Grant had even written to Cadwallader's brother, Elihu, saying, "The Yazoo Pass expedition is going to prove a perfect success." General Prentiss wrote Grant in February saying he had no doubt that the plan favored by Washburn would be successful. When Cadwallader felt assured that the Yazoo plan was certain and ready to be exploited, he thought it would be wise to throw the enemy off guard. He wrote Grant asking that the Associated Press be notified that the "attempt to open the Yazoo Pass is likely to prove an entire failure."(18) Vicksburg, Cadwallader said to his General, would learn this news and perhaps not besiege President Davis to send help. In addition to others who anticipated success on the Yazoo, General James McPherson was anxious to have the project succeed. He was, as he reported to Grant, eager to get into the Yazoo "as soon as possible with re-enforcements."(19) Washburn was so convinced of the scheme's success that he wrote Elihu, declaring that,

> Grant with the means he has had should have taken V[icksburg] long ago. There is but one way to take it. . .You [Elihu] are responsible for Grant. You must go to see him and talk with him. . .

In his letter Cadwallader explained sadly that the fleet had to back out of the Yazoo Pass, the route Washburn was still sure could provide the means of taking Vicksburg. That [Yazoo plan], wrote Cadwallader, should have been an overwhelming success, and I am mortified and humiliated at its miscarriage.(20)

The provoked Wisconsin General sent off angry letters to Grant and to Grant's aide, Rawlins, saying a magnificent chance had been thrown away. He blamed it on the inexcusable slowness and timidity of the Naval Commander. No boats of the right size had been sent to the delta. Washburn said he could not disguise his impatience at the delays, "fatal to the success of this undertaking." As he maintained in his letter to General Grant, with Yazoo City in the possession of Union forces, "Vicksburg is at our mercy." Washburn hoped to be given a command as a result of what he and Col. Wilson had achieved in the river system reaching Greenwood. The achievement opening the rivers made logical an assignment to a command since the feat was made in the face of obloquy by officers who grandly "pronounced [it] an impracticable and foolish undertaking. . .." C.A. Dana, reporting to Secretary Stanton and the President, wondered why Cadwallader had not been given greater responsibility. He wrote about Cadwallader that he had good qualities for the military--"better qualities for the military than for politics," he added wryly. He acts, said Dana, with independence. While the Wisconsinite was felt to be an above-average General, Dana was sorry to have to report that Washburn had no ambition to learn the military art "which every commander ought to exhibit."(21) Also, Grant had not placed him in command of armies because Washburn was, Dana reported, one of the very youngest in rank of Major Generals. Grant did not want to give older soldiers a reason to complain that Washburn was "promoted without regard to his merits."(22)

❖

Washburn did not participate in the naval maneuver down the Coldwater and Tallahatchie to Greenwood and Fort Pemberton. He did not appreciate the circumstances faced by the Navy. Historian Alan Whitehead has explained that at Greenwood the rebels made the area impregnable.(23) The narrow Tallahatchie River virtually runs into Fort Pemberton at Greenwood, so that the artillery at the fort was able to stop ships a half mile away and almost destroy those attempting to move close to the flat land where the fort was located. Making conquest of the area impossible was the lay of the land. On the right flank of the fort was the Tallahatchie River, and on the left a bayou. Militating against the plan as well was the feeling that if successful at Greenwood, the Yazoo River still would not be ready for use by the military *until after the siege of Vicksburg had begun.*

Sherman in his assignment to take Vicksburg had settled himself and his army at the lower end of the Yazoo River, and he with his attempt was unsuccessful. Federal forces had to withdraw from the region. The rebels made the bluffs north of Vicksburg invincible. Washburn would learn how safe the Confederate forces had been at that location when he was given command of those same bluffs during the siege of Vicksburg. He reported that he could readily see how 13,000 men could defend the bluffs against 30,000.Historian Whitehead observed that approaching the well-fortified city from the

Gen. C.C. Washburn

northern end of Vicksburg would have been "like marching across a plain and up a mountain."(24)

There is a touch of irony in the fact that two prominent newspapers reported the success of the Yazoo Expedition. One paper claimed that 26 rebel steamers had been captured. Vicksburg was said to have been evacuated. That, of course, had been the dream of the Wisconsin General. He continued to think Grant was at fault thinking the Yazoo venture could not succeed.

Snyder's Bluff

In June 1863, Major General Washburn arrived at Snyder's Bluff. He was put in command of the Sixteenth Army Corps, and was instructed to fortify the area against rebel attempts to enter Vicksburg by way of the Mechanicsburg Corridor. The Corridor was a stretch of land lying between the Yazoo and Big Black rivers extending north to the east of Yazoo City. His pickets reported large reinforcements of rebel forces; and as a result Grant created an Army of Observation out of Washburn's Sixteenth, General John Clark's Ninth Army Corps, and a few divisions from his own Fifteenth as well as from the Seventeenth Army Corps, amounting to 30,000 troops. The Army of Observation was commanded by General Sherman whose purpose it was to assure Grant that General Joe Johnston in the Big Black River area was not going to be able to slip into Vicksburg to relieve General Pemberton.

The Snyder's Bluff operation, now only partially under the control of Washburn, was instrumental in enabling Grant finally to capture Vicksburg lying on the shores of what Sherman referred to as "the spinal cord of America," the Mississippi river. Union troops received food, clothing, medicine and munitions, as well as reinforcement of men by way of the Mississippi, the lower end of the Yazoo River, and the bluffs where ships were unloaded. General Johnston was a constant threat. He put on edge commander Washburn as well as General Sherman. Washburn and Sherman were both concerned that Johnston might cross the Big Black and attack the bluffs at Snyder's and Haines, or that he might turn south, enter Vicksburg, and help General Pemberton defend the city. Johnston was under pressure from the Confederate President to save Vicksburg. President Davis did not appreciate General Johnston who realized the impossibility of crossing the river to get at the bluffs. He finally tried to move south to Vicksburg down through the Mechanicsburg Corridor. It was then he learned Pemberton had surrendered. To preserve his army Johnston promptly retreated east to Jackson. Part of Washburn's Corps participated in Sherman's march to Jackson to fight Johnston. Cadwallader was not involved in the sweep.

❖

In Grant's *Memoirs* it is made clear that the spongy land, the bayous and countless streams, rivers and rivulets made it difficult for a large army to make their way from the Mississippi river eastward, whether from Helena or other locations south to Vicksburg. It was surmised, however, that Washburn, at the time he made his way across the delta to Grenada in December 1862, could have entered that city. Washburn admitted as much, and later expressed regret that he had not invaded the Confederate stronghold, Yazoo City. If he had he might then have made possible the isolation of Pemberton's forces making it easier for Sherman to take Vicksburg.(25)

When Washburn was in command at Synder's Bluff, he set men to work constructing defensive works, felling oak trees and digging rifle pits. The work enabled Sherman to move his regiments two to three miles nearer to Vicksburg, camping at the foot of the bluff. The shore at the foot of the hills was so narrow that Union soldiers were strewn along the bottom of the hills for miles. While in Benton due east of Yazoo City, Johnson telegraphed Pemberton saying he was ready to move but was uncertain of the route he should follow. One route was at the bluffs controlled by the Yankees. Washburn had seen to it that there were massive abatis on the north end of the slopes. When he saw them, Sherman was prompted to say that Washburn's troops could "hold any force from north and northeast." Nonetheless, the Confederate General headed toward Haines' Bluff due west of Brownsville and east of the Big Black River. His men encamped between Brownsville and Big Black expecting on the following day to make the attempt to conquer those

Joseph Johnson

Yankees forced to spread themselves thin along the lower edge of the bluffs. But following a reconnaissance, Johnston became convinced after all that an attack was unwise.

Military-Political Command at Memphis

Major General Cadwallader Washburn's outlook was optimistic when the year 1863 began. He fully expected victory in relatively short order after the capture of Vicksburg, foreseeing Vicksburg captured with his plan operating. The January beginnings of 1864, however, were not as promising. With his army Washburn was stranded on an island at Pass Cavello on the Gulf of Mexico where a constant gale blew day and night, and the weather was cold. On the island there was one house. All others had been burned 12 months before. It was a barren waste with not a tree or shrub for 50 miles. General Washburn thought being holed up on a god-forsaken island in the Gulf of Mexico served no purpose, and he wanted to push on with his army. A ship bound for Santiago docked off the island with 100,000 rations. The General confiscated 35,000 rations from the ship since his army had been without food for days. His mood was foul, and it set him to thinking about how pleasant it was in New Orleans where the quartermaster shamelessly occupied a magnificently-furnished house. A pleading letter was sent off to the Chief of Staff in which it was reported by Washburn that he had two brigades having not a mouthful of anything but fresh beef for days, and colored troops with rations which would last one day more. Washburn's style of writing in this faultfinding mood was reminiscent of biblical literature. After descrying the sight of officers in New Orleans living high on the hog, he wrote to Elihu, saying, "Tell this to Nottingham. N.O. should crimson the cheek of every true man with shame."(26)

The General had asked the Commander of Union forces in the Gulf, N.P. Banks, for a leave-of-absence. On the eighth, Banks sent a letter to Abraham Lincoln on behalf of Washburn explaining that his leader at Pass Cavello was to be in Washington. Could he see the President? Banks also expressed the wish that Cadwallader return to his department, for "he is a valuable officer." Further trouble for the Washburn who was isolated at the Pass was a shameless attack on him in the columns of the *New York* Herald. The Coteau disaster in Louisiana was reputed to be his personal responsibility. Washburn explained in his inimitable military mode of reporting that he had responded to an urgent request from General Burbridge which brought into play the First Division of the Thirteenth Army Corps resulting in defeat of the rebel force. The reporter's unfortunate narrative caused a flurry of excitement among generals and civilians who took time out to try to correct the error. A letter from Colonel Bunghurst, an actor in the Coteau contest, assured Washburn that the reporter was in error, and that he, the Colonel, had written the *Herald* suggesting that "justice requires a correction of the correspondent's unfavorable story." A correction was not forthcoming from the New York paper, but the *Cincinnati Gazette* published a story prompted by General Ord's report of the affair in which Ord and the *Gazette* story made abundantly clear that Washburn not only had no responsibility for the disaster at Coteau, but "so far from being in fault, [was] promptly on the battlefield as soon as notified of the attack and had reinforcements up as soon as practicable. . ."

A bubble appeared on the surface of things in February 1864, which was to determine a signal change in the General's future career once he had been freed from service in the U.S. Volunteer Army. To explain the "bubble," it is well to remember that Cadwallader, like all men serving in the armed forces, had enjoyed an active life before the War. He was an enterprising lumberman, banker, attorney and adviser to the Wisconsin State government. In 1858 he had added to his large holdings in pine on the Black and Chippewa rivers a steam-run saw mill in the town of Waubeek--a town owned by three Washburns. Cad's brother, Sam, ran the Waubeek operation, and, in Cadwallader's judgment failed to make a success of the project. In 1863 the Waubeek operation had been rented to Knapp, Stout and Company.

There was a poor market for lumber during the War; but in the month of July 1863, a few days before Pemberton surrendered at Vicksburg, lumber prices went up. Prices jumped from $6 a thousand feet to $15. The market looked promising for Knapp and Stout, a company aspiring to become the largest lumber operation in the world. On the other hand, things continuing to look dismal for Washburn, he made the decision to sell off all his holdings to Knapp and Stout, retaining 25,000 acres. The company agreed to pay Washburn in lumber and cash.

At the time the transaction was taking place, Cad, bowed by the weight of problems, militarily, of course, and economically as well, displayed his despair in a letter to Elihu. Referring to his rich holdings in pine in Wisconsin, he said despondently that he had to "give the thing away. . .there was no help."

Sheer chance, however, made Washburn a rich man for having accepted the arrangement with Knapp, Stout and Company. The price of lumber rose dramatically at the War's end and payments by the company unexpectedly made him a very wealthy man. A new career opportunity rose out of this "bubble" of fateful experience. The unexpected fortune from Knapp and Stout enabled him to invest in the flour business at St. Anthony Falls in Minneapolis. It was as a flour merchant that Washburn was to acquire fame and eventually to accumulate his millions, not by way of his achievements as Major-General in the U.S. Army of Volunteers.

Reluctantly, Cadwallader expected to return to the flourish of battles in the Gulf region. He wrote Elihu protesting that he did not wish to be restored to Banks' department, despite Banks' regard for him. Washburn was discouraged with what he termed the "imbecility and profligacy" of Banks' department. Banks gave a masquerade ball in New Orleans which Cadwallader called shameless. General Dana had replaced Washburn at the Gulf and Washburn was sure Dana likewise was corrupt. He urged his brother to "get [Dana] ordered to Washington and before [a] committee."

As usual, Elihu was able to pull strings. General Washburn's order were changed. He was told to take command of a division of the Ninth Army Corps reporting to General Burnside. When the instructions came, Cadwallader was at Annapolis where he was staying in the hotel in which George Washington had lived, and he occupied the first President's room, sleeping in the same bed. Humorously, referring to Washington and Washburn, he added wryly, "Very striking resemblance." Cadwallader remembered that Washington had taken note of "very fine ladies" at Annapolis which Washington's descendants said "were no better than they should be."(27) Plans changed in mid-stream, as it were, and on April 16, before Washburn embarked on his journey to join Burnside, Sherman recommended to Grant that he "send Washburn to Memphis" as Commander of West Tennessee. With droll humor Sherman noted that General Hurlbut had 10,000 men at Memphis, "but if he had a million he would be on the defensive." Washburn replaced Hurlbut and was told he was to command all U.S. forces at and in the vicinity of Memphis, controlling forces at Cairo, Illinois, and all Western Tennessee. The first of August, Washburn's control was extended to cover Vicksburg. Sherman said the river "could be controlled by one mind." In fact, Sherman reported to the Memphis commander, "you have the whole of [the State of] Mississippi to manage." The specific charge to Washburn was that he keep General Nathan Bedford Forrest out of Sherman's war. The instructions prompted Washburn to tally up the numbers of his troops, amounting to 1,800 mounted cavalry, 2,000 weak infantry and 3,500 weak colored troops. He knew Forrest had 8,000 men galloping around Mississippi and Tennessee.

Nathan Bedford Forrest is said by historian, Shelby Foote, to be "a natural genius. . .born to be a soldier the way John Keats was born to be a poet."(28) By the time Washburn was settled in Memphis, Forrest's reputation as cavalry General was well known throughout the Union. He had thrown a "skeer" into Generals from Washburn to Grant. Sherman more than others was sensitive to the threat represented by Forrest when Sherman was "marching through Georgia." Between April and August, Washburn continued to warn of an imminent raid on Memphis by Forrest's cavalry.

❖

A regular Paul Revere, Colonel Starr first awakened General Washburn, warning him that Jesse Forrest, Nathan's brother, was at the front door of the Williams house intent upon capturing him. Starr then awakened Brigadier

General Dustan who fired a gun used as a signal of alarm. This was the raid predicted with frequency by Washburn, prompting one historian to refer to him as "the highly agitated Memphis commander."(29) For weeks Washburn had been responding to calls from Generals Smith, Steele, Andrew, Sherman, Canby and others to supply them with infantry and cavalry out of the Tennessee post. The requests honored had all but emptied Memphis itself. The *Memphis Review* report concerning Sunday was that as the day was dawning and all were resting in the folds of Morpheus, about one thousand rebels, stealing through the deep fog, fell upon our soldiers and the roar of musketry startled our citizens from oblivion.. . .(30) General Washburn in the dark at three a.m. left his bedroom in haste, exiting at the back of his Union Street house--dressed in his

E. B. Washburne

night gown.(31) He made his way to Fort Pickering, a half-mile distant. The invader's troops made no attempt to capture the armory and Washburn was soon back at his post. He tried immediately to communicate with General A.J. Smith, instructing him to intercept Forrest as he would return to Mississippi via Hernando and Panola. One of his four messages confused General Smith, however. Washburn was nonetheless critical of Smith for not obeying his commands. In the raid, one officer was killed, six wounded, four captured. Among enlisted men, 14 were killed, 59 wounded, and 112 were missing.

A bitter General Stephen A. Hurlbut, Washburn's predecessor, not captured because absent from his room at the Gayoso Hotel, wrote, "They removed me from command [in Memphis] because I couldn't keep Forrest out of West Tennessee, and now Washburn can't keep him out of his own bedroom!"

The Paul Revere of the affair, Colonel Matthew H. Starr of the Sixth Illinois Cavalry, who had alerted Washburn and others, set out after the fleeing rebels at 9 a.m., overtook them south of town with Starr confronting Forrest. A saber duel followed. Starr was wounded.

Southern hospitality induced Forrest to return Washburn's uniform, which he learned had been taken from the Williams residence. Some time later, Washburn sent Forrest a fresh, new Confederate uniform made in Memphis by Forrest's own tailor. Perhaps a note accompanied the uniform as Washburn passed on sentiments expressed by General Sherman. Sherman wrote Washburn asking him to send word to Forrest telling him that he, Sherman, "admired [Forrest's] dash but not his judgment" in "running his head against Memphis."

When Cadwallader got around to telling Elihu about the affair, he said, "we had a big thing here on Sunday morning, and ran a very narrow escape, indeed it was almost a miracle that I was not either killed or captured. One main drive of the Expedition was to catch me."

Chapter Forty-Two

STARTING NEW AT AGE FORTY-NINE

In 1865 General Cadwallader Washburn walked away from a blighted South. The Commander left the South having fought back and forth over the region for four years. He knew exactly what General Sherman meant when he said the land was so

completely denuded that "a crow could not fly over it without carrying his rations with him." Despite the blight and the hostility toward Northerners responsible for the widespread devastation, General Washburn was pleased as he listened to nine complimentary toasts delivered at a banquet held in his honor. Memphis praised his record as Commander of Western Tennessee, commending him as a statesman, and for having endeared himself to all classes and conditions of citizens. He was even applauded as an anti-slavery man. This in Memphis! According to General Augustus Chetlain, one of many who lifted the cup to Cadwallader, he had "been weighed in the balances and not found wanting."

William Tecumseh
Sherman

While still in Western Tennessee in 1864, Washburn gave attention to the career he would pursue once he departed the South. With a leave of absence in January, he returned to Lacrosse. While on leave he sold his timberland on the Chippewa, marketed his sawmill at Waubec to lighten his financial load, and in his mind he fashioned the gigantic flour mill he would build in Minneapolis. He had his

heart and pocketbook set on building a mill which would be six stories high, with 12 pairs of millstones, costing $100,000, and able to produce more flour than it was supposed the market could absorb. When constructed, it would be without comparison for size anywhere west of Buffalo.(1)

Millers Refer to His Project as Folly

Washburn's Folly

William C. Edgar observed that miller Washburn "anticipated the future and built accordingly."(2) Historians writing about successful leaders in early America's business community describe entrepreneurs as "risk takers," men who are creative. . .J.B. Say, a 19th century economist, might have been describing C.C. Washburn when he wrote that the business leader is one who unites "all means of production--the labor of one, the capital or land of the others, and who finds in the value of the products and who finds in the value of the products which result from their employment the reconstitution of the entire capital that he utilizes, and the value of the wages, the interest, and the rent which he pays, as well as the profits belonging to himself."(3) That was Cadwallader Washburn.

Lumbering had been Washburn's trade before the War; he returned to it with renewed vigor. The lumbering industry tied together the time-span which began before, and continued after, the War. He spent a total of 30 years in the lumbering industry, purchasing land, locating pineries near streams and rivers, and strategically constructing what the natives called "Big Mill" at Lacrosse. From Washburn's Big Mill more than a million feet of lumber was retailed locally and in Minnesota. He placed his brother-in-law, Gustavus Buffum, in charge of a yard at Iowa City and Lyons, Iowa; and in 1873 he placed Gustavus at Louisiana, Missouri. At the Missouri yard he constructed a large planing mill, and with it prospered through hard times.

There was a period, however, when Washburn had to struggle to remain in business in face of competition. In 1857 there was the devastating depression, one of the series that settled like a plague upon the nation. Competition came from Chicago lumbermen willing to sell lumber in nearby Missouri at wholesale prices. What saved the Missouri venture was Cad's fortunate ownership of pineries purchased 30 years earlier at paltry federal prices. In addition he was able to obtain cheap transportation using his own railroad, the Minneapolis and St. Louis. But the depression almost destroyed Washburn as a lumberman. He persevered, freeing himself of debt only at the end of ten years of struggle. Washburn was sensitive about the 1857 fiasco. He wrote his former partner, Cyrus Woodman, in 1863, recalling the difficult times.(4) He said to his old friend, if he ever again got caught as in 1857, "you may kick me high nor a kite," using a peculiar downeast expression. Woodman on the other hand, knowing about the fierce ambition which fired Cadwallader, penned a note which when read by Cad must have brought forth a hearty chuckle. His old partner wrote, "Though you talk of drawing your business to a close. . . I have no doubt that if you could cash your lumber this winter you would, before the Mississippi opens next spring, be making your calculations to buy out and cut down all the timber off the Black, Chippewa and Rum rivers, and. . .be in favor of starting a gigantic joint stock company to cut down all the pine in Oregon the year following.

❖

In his youth Cadwallader Washburn favored Thomas Jefferson's idea of economic democracy. In the third phase of his life following the War Cadwallader's thinking no longer coincided with Jefferson's, nor was he in agreement with Whig hopes to keep America a nation of farmers and small towns. To be sure, Washburn favored a cheap land policy which encouraged small farmers to settle the west. The policy of the government was to attract the mobile population to the farm front. the east, in most instances were made through large land-owners, making the Washburn-Woodman partners beneficiaries of the federal plan, voiding early Whig interest in benefitting the individual. Cadwallader was among the moneyed men who could afford to buy large plots of land. At the same time, many who wished to settle in the west could not afford to purchase plots from land rich men like Washburn.(5)

Cadwallader Washburn's first giant step was taken when he and two of his brothers, Elihu and Sam, purchased a Wisconsin town on the Chippewa River-- Waubec.(6) Elihu invested $10,000 in the daring Cadwallader project. Sam hired himself out as Cad's foreman on the Chippewa operation. Years later, Elihu took off from Congressional duties to travel north from Galena to Reed's Landing, 25 miles from Waubek, to a "remote and desolate region" where he owned a piece of Cad's town in Dunn County. He went to work at Reed's Landing helping his crew put logs into the stream and down river to Cadwallader's steam saw mill and boom at the nine-mile slough on the Chippewa. From the Landing, Elihu wrote his wife, Adele, in a lightsome mood saying he was getting to be the philosopher-Frenchman, adapting himself to circumstances such as the severe March winds darkening his skin so one could not tell whether he was white or Indian. Complimentary references to the French were for Adele's benefit. Adele came from French stock. Elihu explained to his wife that he hoped to put more logs into the water to add to supplies which in the previous year could not be sent down river because of low water.

Elihu joined Cadwallader at Waubec in 1857. The year had been characterized by one of the Washburns as an "evil hour"--evil because of the severity of the depression. It was as consequential in its effect upon Cadwallader, Elihu and William Drew Washburn as the depression of the 1830s had been to the Livermore family. That ghastly experience of childhood in Maine was a factor accounting for the penurious ways of both Elihu and Cadwallader. Elihu, looking after every scrid of property and every cent that belonged to him, wrote a troubling letter to his Wisconsin brother. Cad responded with bitterness and sarcasm, saying it was remarkable that Elihu was suddenly worked up thinking about what belonged to him at Waubec. Where had Elihu been, he wanted to know, when Cadwallader needed counsel and advice? Cad wrote with vitriol, saying Elihu had only been anxious to save himself from ruin, adding bitterly that he was left with a $150,000 debt. Cadwallader added that nonetheless, he intended to "ride out the storm." He said harshly that in his case he was "determined to struggle while. . .life remained." In his letter Cad kept at Elihu, goading him further by explaining he had given him "the cream on which no stick had been cut," and that what Elihu received was "worth not less than $20,000." Then, to make Elihu suffer, Cad said, as for himself, he had to sell 10,000 acres of his best pine lands at $3 an acre. It was likely that Elihu's bitter brother had obtained the pine lands for $1.25 an acre or less.

A few years later, the matter once again aggravated Cadwallader as he thought about the Waubec property. He declared in a letter to Elihu that the property belonged to himself. He had, however, deeded Waubec to Sam, who was in turn to pay him for the property. Then, descending upon Elihu in his letter, Cad disclosed it was just now, in 1872, that he learned Sam had deeded half of the property to Elihu *without telling him*! In his letter Cad confessed amazement that Elihu had not told him and furthermore that he had not paid Cad for his half. With biting sarcasm, a means used habitually by Washburn family members, Cadwallader concluded, well, he was of no account anyway; he was nothing but a "perfect cipher." He arrived at the end of his letter claiming that Sidney also, even ministerial-type Sidney, had once left him in the lurch.

The miller-lumberman Cadwallader Washburn, prosperous in 1872 and counted among the first millionaires whose fortune was founded on pine lumber in Wisconsin, yet felt put upon by his brothers. For the moment he had forgotten that his next oldest brother, Elihu, truly beloved by Cadwallader, had come to Cad's rescue countless times when the miller-lumberman was in desperate need of cash,

sometimes to pay laborers, at times to pay the mortgage on his railroads. Cadwallader continued to be troubled by business arrangements he had made with Elihu and Sam. He was worrying about his uncertain status financially even back while he was fighting at Vermillion Bridge in Louisiana. He wrote Elihu from the battlefield commenting on his partnership with Sam at Waubec. The partnership, Cad felt, was "the most unproductive act of my life." Sam, Cad said to Elihu, "was perfect sneak," incompetent to make a dollar on his own. Full of righteousness, Cad came down hard on Sam because his little brother had said he was going to bring a woman to

Thaddeus Stevens

Waubec. Two virtues were emerging in the Civil War General. One virtue was in the integrity of work, honoring the work ethic. The second was the righteousness demanded of every man and woman, virginity before marriage and faithfulness toward each other by the contracting parties.

All said and done, however, the LaCrosse Washburn was always generous to members of the family, only needing to complain, perhaps to convince himself he was a worthwhile person in the eyes of his peers, and that he was doing the right thing.

Elihu, who possessed decidedly prideful feelings about his younger brother, Cad, and whose love he would never have revealed in words, gave way to overwhelming emotional feelings only when Cad died. In the meantime, unlike Blanche in *Streetcar Named Desire*, Cadwallader had to depend upon women, not men--women such as Elihu's Adele, for Adele did not hesitate to speak of her admiration and affection, providing the millionaire brother with needed words of comfort and assurance.

❖

Cadwallader returned to his home and children in the North. This was the new beginning of a 34-year interval, having already achieved what ten men might with difficulty accomplish, ending with his death in May 1882. On that fateful date, the city of LaCrosse would be made virtually lifeless in honor of their famous citizen. While Washburn was being eulogized, the community would be quiet as a graveyard. Tears were shed by those who lined the street as the

Adele Washburne

remains of the pioneer from the East passed between rows of saddened citizens. The once little lad from Maine now a worn, lifeless form, was taken to the hilltop cemetery.

Ironically, beloved and admired as Cadwallader was to be, his death would bring forth extraordinary "judicial fireworks [with] injunctions, mandamuses, posse comitatuses, habeas corpuses and riot acts."

During his life up to the year 1865 Cadwallader had fitted nicely into the decades of a 49-year period of history at a time when in America remarkable changes were taking place economically, commercially, culturally, socially, and in the many facets of government, federal and state. For 49 of his years Washburn could be numbered among pioneers who "on. . .arrival on the soil of an unfamiliar, even hostile, world. . .had transformed it into an ordered, if not always orderly, society. By act of will [the pioneer] had created a vivid new version of the civilization [he had] left behind." Illustrating a transformation which would take place in the commercial life of the country, Cadwallader purchased water rights on the Mississippi River in 1855. In that decade farmers in Minnesota could not provide enough wheat to meet the needs of its own people, and the production of wheat supplying Minneapolis amounted to 30,000 bushels. Ten years later 2,500,000 bushels were wheeled into the City to be processed primarily at a Washburn mill. When Cadwallader bought into the Mississippi River project, there were only occasional transportation facilities going east, west, north or south in and out of Minneapolis. He arranged for rail lines to be constructed saving Minneapolis from becoming an adjunct of the Chicago market. In these and other ways, Washburn played an important part in the settlement and growth of Frederick Jackson Turner's "real America."

❖

C.C. Washburn was almost a stranger moving into a strange land as he turned his face North in the month of May 1865. If he had his eyes open he would have realized that:

> ✔ The North which he reentered displayed an immense manufacturing system, nearly 252,000 establishments compared with 140,000 in the late 1850s,
>
> ✔ Like a mighty tsunami pouring in over the land, people had swept in upon these shores from the continent, England, and the Far East,
>
> ✔ American trade had expanded. War such as his brother, Charles, was striving to settle in Paraguay benefitted trade for U.S. firms,
>
> ✔ Steel was invented and used extensively in the mid-West.
>
> ✔ Petroleum was discovered, and by the time Cadwallader came onto the scene in 1865, extensive pipe-lines had been laid to carry oil over stretches of land,
>
> ✔ Goods were being manufactured by large corporations and sold in quantity,
>
> ✔ Washburn himself introduced extensive flour milling, putting Minneapolis on the map as one of the country's principle cities.

William Seward had foreseen a shift of political power as the Civil War came to an end. "When the next census shall reveal your power," he said to a Madison, Wisconsin, audience, "you will be found to be the masters of the United States of

America. . ." The beneficiary was the northern half of the Mississippi Valley, including, of course, Cadwallader's and Elihu's domain--Illinois and Wisconsin. A succession of six presidents, skipping two, came from the region benefitting from a massive shift of population with the growth of its vast agricultural empire and the expansion of cities and manufacturing as in Chicago, Cincinnati, Milwaukee, Minneapolis. Growth in Chicago provides an example of what was happening and would continue happening to the end of the century. The Chicago *Tribune* reported that in a single week, 9000 foreigners came to the city, most destined for settlements in the West. Robert Louis Stevenson settled for a time in the West, and with a show of surprise noted that his daily companions at a restaurant were, respectively, a "Frenchman, an Italian, a Mexican and two Portuguese, who were occasionally joined by a Middle Westerner, an Indian, a Chinese, a Switzer and a German." The shifts taking place affected the power positions of three Washburns--Cadwallader, Elihu and Israel. As Governor of Maine, Israel's power relationship to the federal government diminished during the period of his incumbency. Given the shift, the status of the Illinois and Wisconsin brothers was augmented, particularly Elihu's. Elihu became leader of the House when Thaddeus Stevens passed from the scene.

General Grant had it right. "Whatever power holds. . .[the Mississippi] river," he said, "can govern this continent." When Cadwallader left the South and succeeded in playing his part in bringing Minneapolis forward, he joined with other leaders who worked to control the mode of transportation to the east coast and across the waters to foreign markets. We will learn of Cadwallader's and William's efforts to construct the Soo Line to Canada, freeing merchants and farmers in the mid-west from the clutches of Chicago which strove to control rail rates making transportation costs prohibitive.

The way was being prepared for the ambitious Washburns. When the largest sawmills in the mid-west were built by Cadwallader, and when the enormous six-story flour mill, "Washburn's Folly," went up, the market was there to absorb the enormous outpouring of produce. Natives in the region were not yet aware of the possibilities, though Washburn was among the handful of men who listened to the words of wisdom spoken by the prescient Secretary of State, William Seward, old friend of Israel Washburns. Seward had observed that "the line of civilization [moved] westward thirty miles each year."

❖

The ex-General had to start almost fresh in his home state, with a somewhat diminished reputation. For him it may have seemed that his successes had meant little. From 1848 onward, he had worked at becoming "the chief man of business in his part of Wisconsin" at the age of 35. He had been one of the principal loggers in the young state, along with his partner, the sad, straight-laced conservative from Buxton, Maine--Cyrus Woodman. Returning home, he found he was rich in land but poor at tax time. Sales of land had been brisk in 1855--the year Cadwallader moved to LaCrosse from Mineral Point. More than 1,000,000 acres of federal timber land had been sold in 1855. But sales decreased during the following five years, and in 1860, only 36,882 acres were on the market. In the 1860s, Cadwallader sought loans in vain needing money to pay taxes. The load of debt weighing on his back, he wrote, was "worse than the pack of Bunyan's Pilgrim." He foresaw prosperity in the

Minneapolis undertaking, but not with lumber. He closed his lumbering enterprise at Minneapolis, and continued to log on the Black River in Wisconsin.

In LaCrosse, Washburn arranged for five businessmen to join him in constructing the largest, best, and most modern lumber mill in the West at a cost of approximately $100,000.

The population had increased and farmers prospered bringing an increase of sales in housing construction. Lumberman Washburn took full advantage of the burgeoning market. His LaCrosse location on the Mississippi made Washburn's Big Mill ideal. His immense pinery property north of the City was able to keep the mill and its men busy. Logs were sawed into lumber and floated down the Mississippi to such places as Fulton City and Clinton. The Big Mill's capacity was approximately 200,000 feet of lumber a day, including 60,000 thousand shingles, and 50,000 laths.

Six partners had undertaken the manufacturing enterprise, the Big Mill at the north end of LaCrosse. In 1875 Washburn bought up the stock held by the five partners. He then began to harvest his pine logs on the Black River, and in 1877 the Big Mill turned out 20 million board feet of lumber.

It was this project at LaCrosse, not the vast mills at Minneapolis, which required Washburn's over-anxious attention. The day before he was taken ill for the last time, he was in Chicago with Elihu. Against the advice of his brother, Cadwallader took the night train to LaCrosse, arriving home Saturday morning. After a hastily-consumed breakfast, he went to the Big Mill to check up on repairs. He had barely returned to his office when he was "stricken down with paralysis followed by long and violent vomiting." The paralysis marked the beginning of the end for Cadwallader, though he continued to wield power and give advice to his several managers and partners from April 28, 1881 to May 1882.

Chapter Forty-Three

THE BEGINNING OF CAREER THREE

Give him a river with falls and he will grow a mighty city on its banks, Minneapolis, Minnesota. He will produce a manufacturing center on the Mississippi,

with dams, canals, railroads, elevators, and the largest flour mills in the world. Give him natural resources and he will enlarge upon them. Add to these resources personal ingredients of imagination, determination, and honesty as pure as a clear whistle; see in him a genius self-contained, blunt, distant, not a politician, yet Governor and Congressman. Let the land he chooses be occupied by American Indians. Let bad luck start him on a milling career during the devastating depression of 1857 followed by five years of war. In this man you will see a revolutionary who was often called a communist,

The Mississippi at Minneapolis

declaring, as he did, that legislation which favors none but the capitalist should be changed, and himself working during his legislative career for government control of railroads and the telegraph. This is the man who was to be numbered among the ten greatest men who ever lived in the State of Wisconsin. He would reach the time in his career when he could boast of being "the greatest miller in the world."

This man, however, Cadwallader Colden Washburn, was something of a prototype. Nineteenth century America grew many such men of genius, all of whom played their part in bringing power, privilege, wealth and robust nationhood to this European offshoot, the United States of America. The long list includes such men as Abraham Lincoln, the Pillsburys, Jay Cooke, James J. Hill, John D. Rockefeller. Another of the types, Andrew Carnegie, said of Cadwallader Washburn and

Andrew Carnegie

his six remarkable brothers that, "their career is typically American. Seven sons and all of them men of mark. . .[becoming] part of their country's history."

❖

"The spinal cord of America," the Mississippi River, has falls which drop 16 feet at one place only in over 2,000 miles, St. Anthony-Minneapolis. This place by the side of the Falls gives promise of becoming a city of power and wealth. The river, backbone of the American continent, flows southward 2,350 miles to the birdfoot-like delta on the Gulf of Mexico, a river navigable by ocean-going vessels to Baton Rouge, Louisiana, and by barges north to Minneapolis. As for flour being part of Cadwallader Washburn's vision of the great city, a n d how long he might have had the manufacture of flour in mind, it can only be said that in 1839, Washburn, moving by boat past Rochester, New York, on his way West, sat down to write home that "here [in Rochester] perhaps are the most extensive flour mills in the U.S."(1) Flour was certainly on his mind.

James J. Hill

In early stages of their lives it seems there were latent aptitudes and temperaments hinting directions yet to be pursued by Cadwallader and his brother, Elihu. An illustration for Cadwallader is seen in a transaction which took place during his journey west when a ship's agent demanded money Cad had not intended to have to pay. Before a squabble between the agent and Washburn was over, the agent gave him $2 to keep quiet. It is clear that commerce was constantly in Cadwallader's thinking. By contrast, when Cad's older brother, Elihu, made the trek westward a year later, he paid no attention to commercial affairs. Instead, Elihu made it a point to visit political personages--in Washington, President Van Buren; in Cincinnati, General Harrison, a future President; at Burlington, Iowa, James W. Grimes, future Governor and Senator,

Chas A. Pillsbury

and Joseph Wells, afterwards Lieutenant Governor of Illinois. Elihu himself in time became one of the country's foremost political leaders. In autobiographical notes, the talented, if then only potential, politician, Elihu confessed that "there was great political excitement. . .in 1837 and my studies suffered by the attention I gave to politics."(2)

❖

When General Cadwallader Washburn left Tennessee in 1865 he was part owner of property in the recently-named community--Minneapolis. Purchase had been made in 1856. Stock was owned by himself, his brother William, his cousin Dorilus Morrison, and Congressman

Dorilus Morrison

Robert Smith of Alton, Illinois--Congressional acquaintance of Cad's brother, Elihu. The year after Cad's original outlay of funds, Cad encouraged his brother, William, to move west to Minnesota from Maine. In Orono, William had been apprenticing under his lawyer brother, Israel. The year the General returned home from the war, Smith transferred his stock to his brother, and Cadwallader as major stockholder became president. Two years later, he purchased the Smith share. In the frightening depression years beginning in 1857, stockholders accrued debts resulting from investments made in water-power improvements. Improvements were made at Minneapolis, however, because Cadwallader was thinking in long time terms--the kind of thinking shared by William and Dorilus Morrison who were confident in the City's potential as a manufacturing center. The three Maine expatriates believed their own future lay in building mills at the falls as well as in selling water power.(3)   William was placed in the strategic office of agent for the company. This was the second Washburn exhibiting astute executive ability who was in at the beginning of Minneapolis' phenomenal growth yet to take place. Under William's management a dam and raceway were built providing water power and making possible the creation of Cad's immense flour mills. William's leadership led to the construction of the Minneapolis and St. Louis railroad. His struggles during the panic period paid off when in the mid 1860s the corporation distributed cash dividends amounting to $19,872.

The Washburns were giants from the East possessing a surplus of aggressive energy. William was dogmatic and arrogant, illustrated by his Napoleonic pose for photographers, hand under his jacket, seeming in his facial expression to own whoever looked at his likeness. Cadwallader was the more likeable of the two, handsome as was William, but decidedly more friendly than his younger brother.

In managing the Minneapolis Mill Company, the Washburns and Morrison had the good sense to draw on the experience of eastern companies, such as Hadley Falls in Holyoke, Massachusetts, carefully delineating policies which eventually enriched the west-side company. St. Anthony on the east side of the Mississippi, dissipated its energies resulting in a decrease in the town's population. The population in Minneapolis when William arrived in 1857 was about 2,500. By 1870, over 13,000 people had settled on the west side of the river. There were citizens of St. Anthony who considered consolidating with Minneapolis, which took place in 1872. The worth of manufactured commodities in Minneapolis increased from $357,900 to $6,810,970 by 1870.(4)

A deciding factor giving promise of success was the construction in 1866 of Cadwallader's large and imposing six-story mill.

"You Can Go Home Again"

In December 1866 a contented Cadwallader, happy with his flour mill which was open and operating, took his two daughters, Nettie and Fanny, and traveled east to the old home in Livermore, Maine. The wifeless, motherless family was to spend Christmas with some of Cad's sisters, brothers and father.

When the three were near the end of the long journey from LaCrosse, the sleigh taking them to the Norlands,(5) rolled over unloading occupants into the snow, including dignified daddy. The teenage daughters thought it great fun.

Unhurt, the three Washburns continued on, arriving at the hilltop farmhouse in the evening. Mary, screaming explosions of delight, reached with open arms to embrace her nieces and brother. First thing the following morning Cad went to the room where the Washburn Family Journal rested, like the bible on a pulpit. He was ready to record incidents of the previous day, and to announce for history's sake the arrival of the three Washburns. The Family Journal kept a continuing chronicle of the seven sons. To readers, the Journal reveals a style of writing used to different advantages by the brothers providing readers a keen awareness of downeast humor.(6) It shows also that the more serious among members of the clan copied the style-setter, Algernon Sidney, the humorist of the family.

Cad's first record, penned the morning after his arrival, adopted Sid's method of spelling. He referred to U. John, U meaning you, and John being one of Sidney's many nicknames. At different times, Sidney was addressed as Uncle John, Kidder, J.K., John of Hallowell, or by one of several other pseudonyms. The father of the tribe was Grandsir or the Venerable. Israel, Jr., was Gabe or G. Beans, Gov, or Collector of Customs. Elihu was Cibber or Gentle Elihu. The Gentle Elihu label was understood by all family members to be used or spoken with tongue in cheek. Except for his treatment of wife, women, and his children. Cad was addressed as Mr. Fish, Muckle, Mucklebacket and, of course, Cad.

The practice of recording one's thoughts in the Journal provided opportunity for knocking down a peg or two some of the up-tight brothers. On that day Cad referred to "some foolish people" who use the name "croft" to designate an upper room in the house. With a touch of sarcasm, but lightheartedly, he referred to Israel's failure to meet him at the train. It was "the bad faith of the sons of men." "O! Tempera! O! Mores!" he wrote, doubtless eliciting chuckles from Gabe, Cibber, as well as Mr. Fish for having written it. For Cadwallader and for the irascible Cibber, the enjoyment of coming home was in the opportunity to be what most of the brothers thought was *being himself* at all times: Genuine and with the guard down. Exploits of childhood were confessed in the Journal if not verbally. Elihu confessed that once when father, desperately opposed to horse racing was in Boston he sought permission from mother to go to the races. Our good and indulgent mother, said Gentle Elihu, said yes we might go. When Cad took his turn at the Journal he recalled Sally Coffin perhaps an early love interest for him. Sally, he said, crossed a brook on a log and fell down. She declared, Cad wrote, that she was injured "by the sticking of a knot hole in that part of her person which was the most vulnerable part of the *Dragon of Wartley*."(7) Such reminiscing was expected and acceptable.

In his notations on December 24, Mr. Fish (Cadwallader) recalled humorous incidents and waxed eloquent in the manner of John of Hallowell (Sidney). Cad wrote, "I cannot go out to view the landscape o'er so, like John of Patmos [Sid] I will write. . ." Sid's flowery prose was sprinkled throughout the Journals. He wrote,

> The sun has gone over the heavens today
> --Without observation.
> And is about hiding
> --Behind the Hartford hills.

The Washburn boys loved to recall their father's recitations, some of which were his own remembered words and stories, and some of which came from the classics. Sidney happened to announce one day in the presence of the Venerable: "An April Day!" The Venerable responded,

A little rule, a little sway,
A sunbeam on an April day,
Is all the proud and mighty have
Between the cradle and the grave.(8)

Israel, Jr., left many poetic lines in the Journal: "The wind at night has a melancholy, moaning sound as it comes from the western slope of Vinegar Hill or the summit of Sier."

Sidney sadly announced a disaster for the family, written in an inimitable style. He said he reached the Norlands after the Washburn home had burned to the ground.(9)

In less than two brief hours
Like a pageant faded
And left not a wreck behind.
Crumbling granite
Naked and tumbling chimneys.
Desolation now marks the spot
Cherished with memories of happy hours
And a few of sadness or pain.

Cadwallader, one-time President of the Wisconsin Historical Society, wanted history to be prized by Washburn descendants. He wrote on that same December day,(10) "In these records some notice should be taken of Dr. Cyrus Hamlin(11) who built the old house where the tribe of Israel were born. The house stood where this house stands and was torn down in 1843. . . .. I have the old House in my minds eye and if I had any gifts at drawing I would make a draft of it right here. Dr. Hamlin, who built it, came into town about 1794 or 5. When he came it was said he rode a very poor horse and looked very seedy himself. As there was no doctor in town the inhabitants offered to board him and keep his horse for one year gratuitously if he would settle in the town. He accepted

Sidney Washburn

C.C. Washburn, daughters, son-in-law and grandson

the offer and as he was to board round he went first to Mr. Tho. Coolidges, one of the earliest settlers, and as they were somewhat short of lodging room he was turned in with their son "Tommy" whose astonishment when the Dr. came to undress was as great as that of Tam O'shanter when he saw Nannie in her "cutty Sack" in Alloways Auld Haunted Kirl." The Dr. came from Massachusetts, as did his brothers Hannibal, Europe, Asia, Africa, America, and Eleazer and his half brother Isaac. The record of important historical events never ends, even with the story told of cousin Cyrus' son, Vice President Hannibal Hamlin. Maine politician Hannibal fought it out with Israel, Jr., who yearned to be the first United States Senator among the brothers. He wanted to follow cousin Hannibal in that office, but it was not to be.

❖

Journal writers expected children to read what the brothers wrote. With that expectation, Cadwallader wrote that the 12-year old son of Elihu, William Pitt, intended to fire off a *feu de joie* when the Wisconsinites arrived, but regrettably did not, since arrival time was not as planned. William Pitt 12 years of age on this occasion found uncle Cad writing family history, so he said to his uncle that he had "some poetry in his mind" and wished to record it. Of the 21 lines of his poetry, four are

> I love the grand Old Eagle
> As it soars on high
> The king of all the birds
> And ruler of the sky.

Cuss words were used but not spelled out. Reference was made to the "d---l." "Devilish" was acceptable, as when Sam wrote, "Maine is a devilish place for oats." "D--n" was considered the correct spelling of damn in the Washburn Journal.

On December 27, Cadwallader completed his visit home. As he prepared to leave there were tears. Blind father Israel could not see mother Martha's favorite son, but he surely would have listened attentively, probably able to repeat every word spoken by his wealthy, powerful son from Wisconsin. As Mary had screamed in delight when brother and nieces arrived, she would likely have wept profusely as they left.

Sidney noted the same day in the Family Journal that Cad took with him "his two dautr.[,] Mrs. Adele Gratiot Washburne with an 'E', her two daughters and maid. . .." The boys never ceased plaguing Elihu for being the only brother who used the English spelling, so Sidney in a few words took him down a peg closing the Journal report of that December day, implying that because Elihu was with the Cadwallader party they all walked across the Androscoggin River.

"An Independent City"

Cadwallader C. Washburn did not let grass grow under his feet. There was always something he must do to stay ahead in the highly-charged atmosphere of

Hannibal Hamlin

buying, selling and brutal competition. He was going to put down a railroad line in Wisconsin from Hudson to Bayfield on Lake Superior. When the land offered to him for the railroad was of poor quality, and because he was preoccupied with the B Mill at Minneapolis he abandoned that Wisconsin railroad project. Cad realized, though, that his manufacturing schemes were virtually locked in at Minneapolis. He had no way to deliver his lumber and flour except as he depended upon rails owned and controlled by parties who could punish him with exorbitant prices. Jealous of St. Paul, Chicago was seeking the loyalty of Minneapolis millers. St. Paul merchants were attempting to make their city the terminal point with the flour city, Minneapolis, depending upon a spur line from Mendota. William began complaining to Cadwallader that their mill company cars were being backed-tailed into Minneapolis.(12)

William, who was Cad's agent, kept track of his milling activities and wrote anxiously to his brother, pressing upon him what course he should take. He explained that the North Packet Line from Duluth could move their boats from St. Paul to Minneapolis three times weekly, making use of the transport system on Lake Superior. This, William knew, would be seen as competition with the railroads. Consequently, William saw that using the waterway was a way to get the greedy railroad managers to reduce tariffs.

He-devil, Merrill,(13) William explained to Cadwallader, had increased the price of wheat ten cents a bushel. Merrill regulates "freight on his road to suit himself." Agent Washburn exclaimed indignantly that Merrill had made a half million dollars in the past three years setting the prices. This was possible, he explained, because the Milwaukee line has no competition.

Another urgent letter arrived three weeks later full of advice. Cad, he said, should attend a meeting of the board of the Milwaukee railroad and confront the he-devil, Merrill. In June a week later, William insisted that the Washburns "get control. . .of the Valley Road." He told Cad about a prosperous Minneapolis attorney, Alexander Harrison, who had invested $120,000 in the Milwaukee line, saying Harrison was "sore at the management of the road" because the road was being managed in the interest of St. Paul, not Minneapolis.(14) William felt confident that Harrison would enter a movement to get control of the line, and he added that Cadwallader should turn to Oake Ames(15) for help in solving the transportation problem. A few years earlier, Congressman Cadwallader Washburn had alerted congress to the chicanery of Congressman Ames who was said to be bribing fellow Congressmen.(16) William closed his letter offering to invest $25,000 if that amount would be helpful in gaining control of the road.

In 1870 the Minneapolis and St. Louis Railroad was controlled by Cadwallader. That road linked with wheat-growing regions in the southern and northern parts of the state. Cad purchased valuable property in the mill area to be used exclusively by the Minneapolis and St. Louis. That move by Cad proved to be "one of the wisest moves of his career." It provided the millers leverage and rate reduction on trans-Wisconsin lines.

Flour merchant Washburn added a 28-mile branch from Minneapolis to the junction of the Hastings and Dakota lines, confident that revenues from use of the road once built would pay for the construction. He had plans for extending roads which were to serve the city. Another railroad magnet, President J.W. Brooks of the Burlington and Missouri River Railroad in Nebraska, considered Washburn's plans visionary. Brooks insisted to Cyrus Woodman that St. Paul, not Minneapolis, was to become the center of industry. Historian Clare Marquette, on the other hand, has said that the belief that Minneapolis would grow was hardly a distant vision to Washburn. "[Washburn] had long envisaged a city which would one day be the metropolis of the northwest.' But it needed rail connections," Marquette added, saying that "the Washburn investments stood well to face bankruptcy without them."(17)

Control of the Minneapolis, St. Louis road lay in the hands of five people, two of whom were Washburns--William and Cadwallader. Cad was a Wisconsin citizen. He arranged for the incorporation of the Northwestern Construction Company which was to build the roads, but he became a silent partner, putting William and his cousin, Dorilus Morrison, and an associate, W.W. Eastman on the construction company board. Washburn continued to build roads north and south, and with every mileage added, he provoked the Chicago roads. The flour merchants and lumber dealers in Minneapolis and vicinity were understandably grateful and praised Washburn.

An extensive program directed by the Washburn brothers took roads into the great wheat empire in Iowa and Minnesota. The program as envisioned was expected to supply mills at the Falls with all the raw material required for the making of flour. The Millers' Association at Minneapolis came to think of their state as tributary to their mills. New towns were built along the railroad lines, and lumber was supplied by William's large lumber mill at Anoka. Even Sam the sailor man, who came West after the Civil War, settled in Minnesota and became owner of a lumber yard. Sam proved to be so generous with his customers that he went bankrupt as debtors were unable to pay for goods delivered.

Minneapolis was at last prepared to accept its place as the market center of the West. It was even thought that Missouri cotton could be manufactured at the Falls more cheaply than by New England mills.(18) One of Washburn's lines reached coal mines in Iowa and began to deliver tonnage to Minneapolis, 13,902 tons in 1879, 15,946 in 1881. These achievements during the decade of the 1870s succeeded in making unhappy the "he-devil" S.S. Merrill and his Milwaukee and St. Paul Line.

It had taken Washburn less than 15 years from the start of his third career to put Minneapolis on the map. A final great railroad had yet to be constructed. It was to be a road recommended by Cadwallader's brother from Maine, Governor Israel Washburn. That story, however, remains yet to be told, for construction does not begin until the 1880s.

❖

Like a cook preparing for a grand banquet, Cadwallader Washburn had been readying so many dishes that one wonders how one man could perform with such skill and so successfully. While building flour and lumber mills and buying stock to control railroads, C.C. Washburn was candidating for Congress, and attempting to get himself elected U.S. Senator from Wisconsin. Cad yearned as much as Israel did to become the first Washburn brother to serve in the Senate.

Chapter Forty-Four

THE WASHBURN REGIME

With so many Washburns in seats of power, one wonders to which "Washburn's regime" does this chapter refer? The elder brother, Israel, had his regime in the State of Maine when he was Governor. Elihu was a ruler among rulers in Illinois politics and wielded substantial power in Washington. Charles in California made an attempt to build a regime. He insisted he was a puissant force in California politics when the Republican party was formed in 1854-55, and that he carried weight as editor of his own San Francisco newspaper in 1859-60. William was more powerful than any of his brothers, and the term *regime* could be used to fit his uses of power in Minneapolis and Minnesota as well as in the U.S. House and Senate.

Cadwallader, the more admired among his brothers, is credited with exercising the most imposing power. The term *the Washburn Regime* fits Cadwallader more brilliantly and in actual fact than it does Elihu or William with all their awesome political power.

❖

In 1861 Congressman Washburn was not going to let his name go before the people of his district for a third time. He did not want to return to the House because his ambitious eye caught sight of Charles Durkee over in the Senate. Durkee's term was about to end. At the age of 43 Cad thought the time had come for him to join that exclusive Washington Club.

James Doolittle

With the help of many of his politicals allies constituting an incipient regime Washburn made overtures to Wisconsin House and Senate members. Despite his interest in serving in the Senate Washburn delivered a controversial if historic address in the House of Representatives. His Minority Report as a member of the Committee of Thirty Three could thwart his efforts to attain, not only the position of Senator but *any* office in the public domain. The Committee had voted by a sizable majority to make concessions to the South, and of course by doing so hoped to avoid fratricide. But Cadwallader, representing one other Congressman, Mason W. Tappan of New Hampshire, presented the Minority Report asking rhetorically if Northerners were going to "pass . . . obedient necks beneath [the] southern yoke?" Washburn preferred that the North assert its manhood; that it not "purchase" union or "peace at any price." In

Elisha Keyes

no uncertain terms, the Wisconsin Congressman declared that secession threatened by southern leaders was revolution. It was war against the government which he pronounced *treason*. Washburn said he preferred disunion and if need be "Civil War, rather than dishonor."(3) As a member of the Special Committee charged with divining how war might be avoided, Washburn delivered his virtual Declaration of War. He still hoped, however, that he might become Senator Durkee's successor.

It was the Washburn style to give little thought to the possibility of undermining his chances to win by delivering such a fighting speech. His headstrong views give credence to the opinion of the Republican Boss of Wisconsin, E.W. Keyes. Keyes in his analysis of the career of the Congressman wrote that "[Washburn] was . . .*one of the poorest politicians . . . the state ever produced.*"(4) He entered the lists and on the first ballot polled the largest vote. But he lacked a majority. His attempt to enter the exclusive Senate Club was foiled when one of the remaining two contenders withdrew inviting his backers to vote for Timothy Howe, native of Maine and family friend of the Washburns. Cadwallader lost and joined the army.

❖

Cad made a bid for the Senate once again while in the service attempting to wrest from James R. Doolittle his seat in the Senate. In his encounter with Doolittle, Washburn received six votes. His opponent received 48. So the Wisconsin General continued in the Army. He left the service two years later ready to conquer the world. He had it in mind to build gigantic mills in Lacrosse, Wisconsin, and Minneapolis on the Mississippi. In the interregnum, between 1863 when he experienced humiliating failure politically, and 1868-69 Washburn had became a well-defined, respected, if not revered, public figure and had reason to think he had earned a good name for himself. It was known that he assisted in the writing of banking laws for the State, that he had served as a congressman in the 1850s, was honored for his generalship in the war, and was one of a handful of prominent lumber barons in the State.

Elisha Keyes, boss of the Republican party's Madison Regency, had never been enthusiastic about the powerful and ambitious Wisconsin lumber baron. A superficial friendship was cracked open like sun-dried soil when Washburn in his next try for the Senate found he was going to be fighting against Keyes' chosen candidate, Matthew Hale Carpenter. Cadwallader was the leading candidate but saw on the horizon a cloud the size of a clenched fist. Carpenter, a former Democrat and an engaging public speaker was also the man Secretary of War Edward M. Stanton urged to come to Washington as Senator from Wisconsin. Attorney Carpenter's political skills were soon demonstrated. First, he visited "the very Gibraltar of republicanism in Wisconsin," Alexander Thomson, editor of the Janesville *Gazette*.(1) Cadwallader too had expected to have Thomson's support, but he delayed making the trip to Janesville and Carpenter won the day and the man. One of the first political ploys managed by Cadwallader in his engagement with Matthew was reactive and demeaning except by standards which were acceptable in the game of politics. Cad's opponent had written a letter several years earlier in which he stated that Lincoln's Emancipation Proclamation was "an unpardonable sin," that "it breaks a democratic's heart to think a Negro may be free." Carpenter wrote then that the Democratic party was "the last and only hope of our country." Parts of the letter appeared in C.C. Washburn's Lacrosse newspaper, the *Republican*. Severely edited, it was printed also in the Republican party's *Wisconsin State Journal*, edited by David Atwood and Horace Rublee. Rublee in 1868 was a third candidate along with a fourth, Edward Salomon and a fifth, O.H. Waldo.

Carpenter's advisor, Keyes, had a hand in arranging 46 of the 66 Wisconsin newspapers to support the Milwaukee attorney. The influence of Keyes accounted for the fact that when the Wisconsin legislators met in January, Carpenter's sponsor, Thomson, was chosen Speaker of the Assembly. The selection represented Carpenter's first triumph. The test came for the five candidates in a set-up arranged by Speaker Thomson. The editor-speaker suggested that all the candidates make a presentation at a publicly-called competition. Carpenter, of course, was ready and willing to participate. None of the others welcomed the opportunity. Cad knew he did not excel in declamation and he was well aware of Carpenter's reputation as an orator. At the evening encounter, a large crowd of excited people appeared anticipating an animated evening of debate. Carpenter spoke first, impressing the audience. He knew the line as though an old hand at campaigning, good to this day. The handsome mustachioed lawyer stood before the large audience and said,

> There are a few leading ideas that must always be borne in mind. Strict economy; no more subsidies; such appropriations only as are strictly within the provisions, the letter and spirit of the constitution; necessary improvement of our harbors and rivers; an equal and honest adjustment of the burthens of national taxation; a firm resolution to keep the public faith inviolable; and all will be well.

After a straightforward presentation, brief as Lincoln's Gettysburg address, Carpenter was seated to loud cries of approval. Next, Washburn in an obstinate frame of mind stood to speak, unhappy to be there and less happy to be following Matt. He was forced to deliver a truncated speech. His first words when he spoke were critical of Matt. Audience members practically growled at Cadwallader for excoriating the candidate they had just wildly applauded. Cad, recognizing his mistake and trying to change his tone, said Carpenter had declared that if he were defeated, he, Carpenter, would "never dare again appear before the people. . ."(2) That had not been said by Carpenter and the audience knew it. Coming at Cad from the audience were disagreeable remarks. "He did not say that . . ." "You speak an untruth . . ." The clack among members of the sizeable audience drowned out Washburn's attempt to apologize. He backed away from the podium and sat down. It resulted in a clear victory for the late intruder, Matthew Carpenter, Esq. For Washburn, as Matthew expressed it much later, the weight which pulled Cadwallader down on that occasion was "vanity, pomposity and self-sufficiency."

After the official balloting was disclosed, one wonders if Washburn might not have determined before the dark fell that day that he would beat Carpenter seven years hence. In any case, there was a final attempt to win the brass ring in the merry-go-round of Wisconnsin politics. Despite the 1868 upset for Washburn, the Washington contingent of the states Republican congressmen agreed that Cadwallader should have the governorship in 1872. There was a *quid pro quo* accompanying the congressmen's pledge to support him. Washburn must agree never again to run for the Senate against Timothy Howe or Matthew Carpenter. In what form this unusual requirement was passed along to Washburn is not ours to know. It was probably through Senator Howe, frequently a go-between for Washburn and Carpenter. But that this arrangement was laid on Cadwallader as an obligation became clear when a letter written by him and in the hands of Cad's friend, General Jeremiah Rusk, came to light. A sentence in the letter to Rusk reads,

As to the senatorship, you can say I shall never contest for that position against either Howe or Carpenter.(3)

A possi ble interpretation is that Washburn wrote in the mood of one who had been through a trying experience saying, "Well, I've had enough of *that*!" It is not like sturdy, obstinate Washburn to sell his soul for a mess of pottage--even for a position in the Senate. What needs to be noted now is that with the alleged understanding in writing that Washburn would not compete later, the powers-that-be stumped the State for Cadwallader for governor.

Editor Thomson in his appraisal of Washburn's stint as administrative head of Wisconsin's government reports that "Governor Washburn's administration was. . .clean and economical." That judgment might be taken to mean Washburn played it safe, did nothing and reaped the reward of nomination for a second term. He was chosen as candidate for a second term, not however because he avoided controversy, but because he was, said Keyes, a factor in engendering humiliation for the Republican organization. The administration of the new Wisconsin leader began January 1, 1872. Eleven days later the governor entered the chamber with a throughly prepared address and in chamber faced the elected representatives. His opening words could not have displeased even Democrats, since he indicated that despite recession in other parts of the country, manufacturing industries in Wisconsin increased, education was progressive, public charity had brought relief to the deaf and sightless, and only 95 persons had entered state prison the previous year, with 99 having been released. Totally, he reported, there were 202 prisoners, and only two were women. Washburn also was able happily to announce the completion of the State Capitol at a cost of $550,000 placing it as one of the charming buildings among the capitols of the country. Washburn was especially pleased as well to report that women were attending the State University. In this one area, it is known that Washburn differed with his father. Israel, Sr., exploded a "No!" when asked if he favored women's suffrage. On that occasion, father Cadwallader's daughter, Fanny, had vigorously debated the matter with her grandfather.

Included in Governor Washburn's Report to the assembled Representatives were recommendations to meet critical needs he knew must be maneuvered through the Senate and Assembly.

> ✔ The Governor found State property undervalued, requesting that new laws be drawn defining new duties of Assessors,
>
> ✔ The Governor asked for $20,000 to enlarge buildings to benefit the deaf and dumb,
>
> ✔ "The duty of the State to kindly care for her insane is so clear that it may not be neglected. . ." Many of those listening may have been ignorant of the fact that Washburn's wife had been mentally deficient since the Governor was a young man. He knew whereof he spoke about the needs of the insane,

✔ Children of veterans brought into the state Washburn declared must be allowed to enter the Soldiers' Orphan Home,

✔ An unsightly fence surrounded the attractive new capitol, with enormous mounds of coal piled on the lawn in winter. These he announced had to be taken care of by legislative fiat, as they were for a total of $15,000.

More consequential as one of the factors accounting for the humiliation Keyes mentioned about Washburn as politician. Washburn referred publically to "the intemperate use of intoxicating liquors, an evil. . .to be deprecated." Washburn realized there could not be a complete remedy to meet the problems caused by intoxicants, but it was like him to say that he deemed it his *duty* to call the subject to the attention of legislators. Governor Washburn had every reason to know what the entry of this touchy subject would do. His brother in Maine had to sustain attacks from teetotalers and imbibers alike. Portland, Maine citizen, Neal Dow, had become nationally prominent for inducing Maine to outlaw the sale of liquor. That contest occurred in the 1850s when Israel, Jr., was in Congress. Democrats fared well in Maine in the voting that year, and Orr of South Carolina questioned Washburn about the victory. Israel explained that Democrats were elected because Whigs were responsible for the Maine Liquor Law. Orr asked Israel,

"Then do I understand that the people of Maine like whiskey better than they do freedom?" (Shouts of laughter..) Israel responded,

"Not exactly that; they like a little of the former and a good deal of the latter." (Renewed laughter.)(4)

Governor Washburn of Maine did not feel as strongly as his Wisconsin brother about the liquor question, and he was unhappy that Neal Dow's prohibition laws obscured the slavery issue. In Wisconsin, Republican Alexander Graham presented a bill requiring a $2,000 bond from liquor licensees, and dealers in liquor were to pay for damages caused by customer intoxication. The Graham Law passed and imposed penalties on persons convicted of drunkenness. The legislation aroused the ire of German-Americans which was to effect the outcome of the coming 1873 elections. Many German-American Republicans were sure to be indecisive about voting for Republican party candidates. They were in agreement with brewers Blatz and Schlitz who accused the legislature of making Wisconsin into a police state.

A factor more cataclysmic than the liquor question in upsetting the political balance in Wisconsin was the relation of the state and its people to the railroads. Washburn, it was known, was himself a builder of rail lines; and in his address to the legislature he spoke appreciatively of the accomplishments of railroad managers in Wisconsin, noting that railroads had spent $100,000,000 in the State. The governor added a warning, however. There was no branch of industry not dependent upon rail facilities which, he said, by unfriendly action on the part of managers, "may not at any time [be] crush[ed] out." That pronouncement by Washburn must have jerked the listeners to attention, particularly when he went on to say that railroad managers seem to think "their will is the supreme law." In these words, Governor Washburn was throwing down the proverbial gauntlet. He made his case, declaring that roads are public corporations, authorized by the State to take private property, and that railroads are public highways. The Constitution, he believed, gave the legislature absolute control over railroad operations. He lamented that towns, in encouraging roads to come through their area, sometimes borrowed money beyond their ability to pay. He recommended the passage of a law prohibiting any incorporated area from creating debt in excess of 5 percent of assessed value of the town's property. Finally, Washburn recommended that a Board of Railroad Commissioners be organized. He outlined the functions of such a Commission. It would have power to inquire into complaints and abuses, it would exercise general supervision of the railroads within the state, and it would be charged with recommending legislative action, reporting annually to the Governor.

Historian Richard Current indicates that "the railroad men feared manufacturer Washburn more than they did farmer Taylor,"(5) the latter of whom was nominated by a Reform party to succeed Cadwallader. In his 1872 Report, radical Governor Cadwallader Washburn had proposed that a new means of communication be made so cheap that it would be within reach of the populace, not available just to business institutions. He was referring to the postal telegraph system, and pointed out to the legislators that there is "hardly any civilized country on the globe where telegraph is used so little by the masses as in the United States." The case was made for postal telegraphy being a public utility. He had an accumulation of information from the postal telegraph bill he had submitted earlier to Congress. His bill had been shunted aside even though it had the support of powerful allies including the President. Action was undertaken by the Wisconsin Legislature memorializing Congress to consider the postal telegraph legislation. Chairman James A. Garfield wrote the Governor saying that the postal telegraph question had been referred to his Committee. "I hope before many weeks we may be able to do something," Garfield wrote, "the appearances are rather unfavorable."(6) The bill did not get out of Committee.

The Most Exciting Campaign

Senator Timothy Howe was a pivotal figure in the 1875 battle between warhorse Washburn and Matt Carpenter, Esq. Howe made an announcement which

succeeded in spiking Washburn's guns. Cadwallader had intended to strengthen his own crusade against the popular orator Senator Carpenter by agreeing fully with the Republicans who felt Carpenter's vote for a "back-pay steal" was offensive. Carpenter himself said to Washburn that he, Cadwallader, could be held responsible for the passage of the back-pay bill for which he voted in 1856, since the bill passed by only one vote and if Washburn had voted any other way the bill would have been defeated. Howe released a letter with shock value in it, saying if people cannot forgive a mistake, then they cannot consent to Senator Carpenter's re-election. But, they cannot consent either "to the election of Gov. Washburn." Howe questioned if the people would crucify one (Carpenter) and crown the other

James A. Garfield

(Washburn).

The back-pay bill was not the only issue troubling voters about Senator Carpenter. The senator had scoffed at the Crédit Mobilier issue.(7) Voters in

Wisconsin were aware that it was Cad who had brought that *cause célèbre* into public view with his bill to regulate the rates of transportation over the Pacific Railroad. In fact, a newspaper article accused Carpenter of having frightened Oakes Ames, himself a Congressman and one of a coterie of men building the line to the West, the article claiming that Carpenter had reported to Ames that Washburn might win the senatorship, thus persuading Ames who was fearful of Cad to pay Carpenter $10,000 as counselor to the Pacific line.(8) Matt Carpenter's Republican friends made a point of asserting that, should Matt win the caucus vote, and should Washburn fail to support their candidate, then Cad's dereliction might give the Democrats the victory in Wisconsin. Carpenter was quoted as saying, however, "[Washburn] is not the man to pull down the house which he has built up." Timothy Howe, pleading with his old friend and fellow Maineite, reminded Washburn that in 1880 his brother Elihu might be a nominee for President of the United States, in which case, wrote Howe, "I should be sorry not to have Wisconsin. . .there"(9) to vote for Elihu.

A factor some thought might strengthen Washburn's chances were 18 Republican dissidents who were not, however, encouraged by Cadwallader. If Washburn were not to win in the caucus, there was a compact among these 18 Republicans who were absolutely unwilling to vote for Carpenter. They organized themselves into a solid bloc referred to as *bolters*, and waited for the strategic moment to send their message to fellow Republican legislators. They had constituents, they insisted, who had been nearly unanimous in their opposition to Carpenter. The 18 reminded Republicans who were ready to support Carpenter about the resolution passed at the recent convention denouncing "all official frauds and corrupt legislation, whether in Land Grants and subsidies to Railroads, in Crédit Mobiliers, or in the management of the Revenues," noting that the resolution practically pledged the party *not to indorse Mr. Carpenter*.(10) This was the message the "bolters" planned to release if after the informal caucus Carpenter prevailed. The caucus votes numbered 40 for Carpenter, 12 for Washburn. Three days later, therefore, and before the official votes were to be cast, the *bolters* released their message, proceeding to frustrate the attempt to re-elect Carpenter. They consulted with Democrats, and the two groups agreed to submit to the legislature the name of Angus Cameron of Lacrosse. Cameron was elected, which was no great misfortune to Washburn, for in 1867, Cadwallader had a hand in getting a judgeship for Cameron. The new Senator was indebted to his fellow Lacrosse Republican leader. As might be expected, Senator Cameron voted consistently with Republicans during the years of his term.

The lack of harmony among Republicans prompted a prophetic observation by Carpenter in a letter written to Elisha Keyes. "If," he wrote Elisha, "a handful of sore-heads can bolt. . .it does not require a prophet to predict the fate of such a party."(11)

"Prophecy Realized"

Predictably, the Graham bill had a devastating effect on the election in Wisconsin. If German-Americans, so many of whom were bitterly opposed to the Graham bill, did not leave the party, or slipped over into the Liberal Republican faction, they stayed home in droves when the polls opened. The Liberal

Republicans, running their own candidate in 1872, found sympathizers among German-Americans in part because it was said the administration in Washington had been providing arms for the French in the Franco-Prussian war. The charge was circulated by Liberal Republicans, even though a loyal member of the administration, Elihu Washburne, Ambassador to France, had been approached and asked to let his name be submitted as nominee for president on the Liberal Republican party ticket. The administration in Washington could not have helped the French without Elihu's knowledge, or, for that matter, without the consent of Washburne. In 1870, the Republicans had made it appear that the Germans, not the French, were benefitting from the administration's largess. The propaganda ploy was different in 1873. In that year, the leading German-American newspaper, the Milwaukee *Herald*, switched from the Republican to the Liberal Republican party.

A further complication in the political contest came from the fact that the nominee for president on the Liberal Republican ticket was Horace Greeley, a friend of the Washburns. He was a handicap to the party, looked upon by German-Americans as a "water-bibber" discouraging some German-Americans from going over to the Liberal Republicans. But those were likely the Republicans who stayed home at election time.

C.C. Washburn's nemesis, Elisha Keyes remained party boss and many of his appointments were said to have been from the Whiskey Ring. The whiskey issue was kept alive throughout the campaign, and its importance put Governor Washburn to work researching in earnest the national Whiskey Ring. He wrote to Secretary of the Treasury B.H. Bristow. Prosecution of the Ring in Wisconsin would result in justice being done if, wrote Washburn, the case were left in the hands of a Mr. McKinney who had been in charge of the case. Washburn explained in his letter to Bristow that he had received a report to the effect that Gerry W. Hazelton had been appointed to take the case in hand, in which instance, said Cadwallader, "you may just as well have the case dismissed at once. Hazelton is about a fifth rate lawyer." On the Whiskey Ring deal, Washburn expected "politics" were being played from Washington. The exchange of letters initiated by Cadwallader and dealing with the Ring continued beyond the time when the issue could affect his re-election, and it serves to illustrate Washburn's conscientious devotion to what he frequently referred to as his *duty*. The involvement of the temperance issue in the campaign of 1873 was extensive and deadly for Republicans who had held power in Wisconsin, almost without exception, since the Civil War--in fact, since Cad's brother, Israel, launched the Republican party and after its first president was elected in 1860.

Edward Ryan

The hostile reaction affecting Republican politics widened to include businessmen and farmers. They resented the power of big corporations and the railroads. For the Republicans to lose the business community was comparable to the rout of German-Americans resulting from the Graham bill. The Milwaukee Chamber of Commerce President, Francis H. West, was a harsh critic of Alexander Mitchell, President of Milwaukee and St. Paul Line and a Democrat. The loss of loyalty by commerce was unnatural, because the Washburn regime had a reputation for being critical of corporations, and as Governor he had taken a forceful stand against the railroads. Washburn had on several occasions warned against the power of monopolies. He sought legislation to regulate the roads, starting when he was in Congress. His attempt in Congress resulted in making public the infamous Crédit Mobilier case. Two years hence, in the 1875 contest with Senator Carpenter, the Mobilier case should have represented a plus for Washburn among farmers and the business community. But knowledge of the Mobilier case was not enough for Cadwallader to win. Driving business and farmers into the arms of the Reform party was a decision made to raise prices on the part of the railroad companies just before the election. Then, coincident with that politically devastating maneuver, and but three days following the rise in prices, came the Panic of 1873. The farmers were hurt by the price rise and by the Panic of 1873. Wisconsin had just recovered from the Panic of 1867, and the 1873 depression was the worst the country had experienced. In Wisconsin the Panic was a catalyst leading to a demand for reform between business and state government. The demand resulted in the virtual overthrow of the Republican party which had dominated Wisconsin politics since the decade of the 60s. The reform effort, directed by Governor Taylor, was not as well managed as it likely would have been by the efficient Washburn.(12) The laws devised by Taylor's administration for the purpose of regulating the railroads was soon repealed.

The most significant and lasting statement to come from the reform effort in Wisconsin was an address by Chief Justice Edward G. Ryan. Justice Ryan recognized that a "new and dark power" was "looming up." He was referring to corporations, including railroads, which, he warned, were threatening the sovereignty of the state. The Justice would have perceived as an illustration the fact that the railroad corporations in Wisconsin challenged the newly-devised legislative acts until the State backed down. Ryan's rhetoric, addressed to students of the University of Wisconsin, asked, "which shall rule--wealth or man; which shall lead--money or intellect; who shall fill public stations--educated and patriotic freemen, or the feudal serfs of corporate capital?" One student listening to Ryan was 18-year-old Robert M. La Follette.(13) The influence of Ryan's insights were carried over the edge of the 19th century into the 20th. Ryan's opinion echoed views expressed by Cadwallader Washburn. In the Governor's second message to the Wisconsin legislature he also warned of the "vast and overshadowing corporations" he considered, as he said, a "source of alarm."(13) Washburn's views looked toward the generating of public utilities, prompting another Wisconsin judge to conclude that legislation Governor Washburn sought embodied "the spirit of communism."

Lucius Fairchild

In the election, William R. Taylor was chosen over Washburn, who lost the governorship by 15,000 votes. Former Governor Fairchild, now Consul at Liverpool, wrote Cadwallader remarking upon "the terrible news of the defeat of the Republicans in Wisconsin," adding that he was "especially sorry to lose you from the Executive Chair. . ."(14) A reinforcement of Cadwallader's discouragement came from W.B. Allison of Iowa, the diplomatic Congressman, about whom Iowans boasted "could walk on eggs from Des Moines to Washington without breaking one of them."(15) Allison wrote, "if you cannot succeed what will become of the rest of us?"(16) Washburn's old and trusted friend, Horace Rublee, editor of the *State Journal* and one of the Wisconsin founders of the Republican party in 1854, wrote from the legation in Berne. He perhaps had a quieting and comforting effect on the defeated and conscientious Washburn, saying, "it is not for mortals to command success, but that the most they can do is to deserve it." He told the Governor "there is no disgrace in such a defeat."(17) Rublee had a long view of the party, having been an active participant from the year 1854. His analysis, while kind to Washburn, was yet implicitly critical. Mentioning the German-Americans discontent with the Graham bill, Rublee wrote, "but for this question, I think, we should have carried the State in spite of a disadvantage." Rublee knew Washburn played a significant part in the passage of the bill. He saw Cadwallader's adversary as an unfortunate alliance of Democrats, Republican *bolters*, Grangers, railroad men, saloon keepers, but did not think the new alignment would last long. He expressed the hope that the party would reorganize on a sound basis and recover lost ground. That point of view coming from one of the more powerful politicos in the state, Rublee, encouraged Washburn.

❖

It is difficult to discern the genuine feelings of a politician no matter how genuine and impressive his words. The politician is always conscious of at least two audiences, himself and everybody else. Cadwallader, though single-minded and sincere, kept in mind that larger audience, as he impressed a visiting body of pro-Carpenter, anti-Washburn Republicans. The visitors themselves were aware of the power to damage the Republican party which lay in Washburn's hands. They wanted to feel Carpenter must be right when he had said Washburn would not pull down the house he had built up.

The informal caucus vote had been cast and carried a clear message to the losing candidate. Cadwallader did not have to think twice; it was the first stage of what was to be a clear victory, unless, he thought, the bolters would frustrate the legislature when time came to cast the official votes.

Before the critical votes were cast, Washburn opened his door to visitors who had been obstructing his attempts to grasp the ring. The men from the Carpenter camp were aware that, as one of them wrote, Cadwallader had just lost what was "more desiring than the piles of gold and clusters of diamonds."(18) What Washburn said in response to questions they asked in their interview impressed upon them that he was a generous, manly, dignified man, and honorable. Tribute was paid as the writer of a news story maintained,

. . .Never did General Washburn appear so worthy to be a Senator from Wisconsin. . . There was a feeling of regret among those present that there were not two offices to be conferred upon two such men as Matt H. Carpenter and General Washburn.

The ex-Governor should not have felt badly anyway. He had said continuously that he had been "forced" to run for the office. But his brother, Israel, did not take Cad's claim seriously, partly because over the years Cad had continued to say that. Israel wrote, "Do they continue to *force* you, the rascals? They never undertake that with me. If anything the reverse is the order here. . ."(19) Israel was popular, well-loved, and an able administrator who also aspired to be a United States Senator. But he was not a rich man. Cadwallader was a wealthy Republican who was in on the ground floor when the party was organized in Wisconsin. That became one of the reasons why Carpenter supporters spoke in glowing terms in their post-election session. From their point of view, they wanted assurance that he would not hurt the Republican movement, and secondly, his contributions must not be lost.

Timothy Howe had appealed to the humane side of his fellow Maineite. His appeals did not move Washburn. He pled with Cad to consider that "Carpenter can't go to the House now. That is death to him. . . Your withdrawal would lose you no friends and (would). . .remove your last enemy. . . Trust me now as your 40-year [friend] I have been. You owe something. He struggled hard for you three years ago."(20) Moving over into the political realm from Washburn's customary business domain seems to have hardened the otherwise fair-minded manufacturer. And yet Cadwallader was not like "the tough-minded empiricist, materialistic, pessimistic, irreligious, pluralistic, skeptical" businessman described by John Tipple in his book, *The Capitalist Revolution.*(21) He was sharp enough, however, to play politics, and knew that while Carpenter partisans pretended to be visiting him in order to report his great good will and generosity, Cad, with his political hat on and aware of his larger audience, was in every moment hoping that the bolters would make a difference, that he might yet have a chance.

Cadwallader thought to make the Wisconsin Republican party part of his "regime." He was successful in persuading Philetus Sawyer, a contemporary political power in the state, along with his 40-year old friend, Howe, to join in dumping Elisha Keyes, boss of the Madison Regency. There is no other satisfactory way of gauging Washburn's typically political way of acting than to suppose he at all times saw what he did as his *duty* to the people. Perhaps an example of Cadwallader's devotion to *duty* was his response to the demolition of his great mill in Minneapolis. The explosion and destruction occurred after the "forced" candidate, Cad, agreed to lead the charge against the ex-Democrat. He walked out the measurements of the new mill which would replace the one which were now stones beneath his feet. Washburn had to spend inordinate time fighting the insurance companies. Nonetheless, he continued to "do his duty" where the campaign was concerned.

❖

Cadwallader had four more years to live and he made them count, continuing to do his duty when paralysis misshaped his fine soldier's physique. Isolated in the wilderness of Arkansas, sick and dying, he administered his mills, and conferred with his partners and employees.

The remarkable life and presence of C.C. Washburn was abbreviated once again for admirers to see and feel as the inert body was returned to Wisconsin from Arkansas and the day long ceremonials brought him "alive" again in haunting expressions of respect and affection.

Chapter Forty-Five

AN INTIMATE LOOK BEFORE CLOSING THE LID

Cadwallader Washburn

Exposing Cadwallader and Elihu Washburn to an X-ray sketch, we catch a glimpse of 19th-century Americana. That is our interest, though when examining their lives and personae the Washburns seem impervious. That fact in itself is part of the 19th century tale. American studies scholars have demonstrated something mysterious about American men of that period. Unlike contemporaries in that same century in France or Ireland, such as Proust or Sean O'Casey, autobiographies in America were not revealing of the self. In typical American life stories, we are permitted to see only outward manifestations.

In the case of one Washburn, outward manifestation is what is impressive in the non-fiction genre. It is as though the story were indeed fiction, describing a young Major General, standing now a stone statue in the Memorial Park at Vicksburg. In the park is the statue of a well-built man, broad-chested, with a body kept slim by the hardships of the cavalry officer. The statue's metal-made jutting chin breaks into an evenly trimmed beard, betokening a commanding personality. Portraits of the subject tell even more than a statue can reveal about a handsome, stern, determined, unsmiling Union officer, where a straight line could measure from hairline to the end of a classic Greek nose. Dark eyebrows frame the General's eyes which have the capacity to convey messages of kindness or anger, sympathy or lordship, changing with the subject's mood.

Contemporaries were aware of an opaque persona in their friend, Washburn. They knew his affectation of dignity denied them an intimate look into the weaknesses as well as the strengths of "the boss," "the General," "the Governor," "the Congressman," any one of which positions, gave to them the appearance of a lesser god. The affectation of formality was a left-over from a New England upbringing. Assuming a role as dignified officer, Congressman or Governor was Cad's way of demonstrating that he felt, even if he would not admit it to himself, that he was once removed from most of his acquaintances. General Stephen Hurlbut felt the force of Washburn's lonely watch during the war and correctly described him, saying the General "considers himself a sort of independent command." Cyrus Woodman, long-time colleague of his wifeless partner, Cad, sensed the reality of the inner Washburn. He knew from long acquaintance the meaning behind behavioral characteristics of his partner and insisted on describing traits for Cad himself to see. After Cyrus learned his former partner had suffered a loss with the explosion of his great flour mill at Minneapolis, he wrote Cad telling him, "You like the excitement of [being in] hot water This kind of happiness, having become second nature, you will revel in it to the end of your days."(1)

Hot water or not, Washburn expressed his opinion regarding financial and political matters. He stated his opinion about greenbacks, imperialism, the railroads, the American Indian. His opinion about slavery he made clear, regarding slavery "as a great social and political evil."(2) But Cadwallader seldom addressed subjects which might reveal deeply-felt personal idiosyncracies. Self is not exposed in announcements which convey only outward manifestations. Even Elihu, without intending to, revealed more of himself than did Cadwallader. Cadwallader was cautious, letting only that part of himself show which appeared to serve his purpose. If he came across as severe, as at times he did, it was because he wanted to be seen in that light at that moment.

Cyrus Woodman

Cadwallader exuded the power of his personality, though his naturalness in wielding power was a source of puzzlement for men who knew him, for it was common knowledge Washburn did not possess magnetic power over men. It was acknowledged, however, that he had an "acute and powerful mind."(3)

His brothers, and we suppose his mother, knew him on intimate terms. They knew him in childhood when he brooded, bawled, climbed trees, worried his parents, or had temper tantrums. Elihu knew the child, Cad, inside and out and he knew equally well the adult millionaire. There were no secrets between the two brothers. Cad and Elihu became bosom pals in childhood, and remained intimate to their lives' end. A revealing insight into the life and trials of the next youngest in line, Charles, derives from the fact that Elihu and Cadwallader were so closely attached. Whether intentional or otherwise, Charles was on the outside looking in where the two older and stronger Washburns were concerned. Crude Elihu never hesitated to lay into Charles, to criticize and humiliate him. Cadwallader, of a softer nature, was protective of his kid brother, though that did not mean he shared himself with Charles. The exclusion from their company and the intimacies shared by the two close companions left Charles with an identifiable neurosis, troubling him to the unhappy end, dying like a ne'er-do-well as he fell dead on the streets of a New Jersey city, unidentified and unknown.

A vital part of Cadwallader's make-up had to do with his self-conscious, self-centered outlook. The self-centered aspect did not translate into selfishness. It was necessary and not unnatural for Washburn to keep himself at the center of power and attention, illustrated in a humorous incident mentioned by his partner, John Crosby. A design for a new brand of flour to be painted on a barrel head was brought to Crosby. Crosby observed that the first letter of Washburn, "w", was smaller than the rest of the label. Cad's partner glanced at it, shook his head, and said to the sign painter, "It's no use, William. No use at all. It will never do. You might as well spell God with a small 'g', as "washburn" with a small 'w'."

While self-centeredness was conspicuous it was not Washburn's intention that anyone should know about all his praiseworthy accomplishments. He was modest about expenditures made to benefit others. An exception which proves the rule was what he once wrote Woodman, boasting that his policies as Commander in

Tennessee were "working like a charm." Even while he was accounted "the severest commander they [had], ever had," still, he was, he wrote, "universally popular." He hastened to add, "This I [can] say to you . . . because you know that I do not say it for the purpose of self-glorification." Humility is a word which d o e s   n o t   d e s c r i b e Cadwallader; certainly not Elihu. Nonetheless, their bluster shrouds an understanding they had of themselves as sons of a humble downeast farmer; humble as they were put into positions of power by admirers. Cad and Elihu felt deep inside themselves that they did not deserve authority they knew they possessed. This was

Elihu B. Washburne

particularly true of Elihu. In 1872 Elihu's name was bandied about as a nominee for president on the Republican ticket. Writing about himself at the time, Elihu said to Cadwallader that anyone who was serious about the prospects for him was "a natural fool." Cadwallader responded, agreeing. Having known Elihu as long as he had, he wrote, it all seemed rather funny to think of ol' Elly as Commander-in-Chief of the nation. This attitude on the part of the Washburns can take on the character of humility, though neither Elihu nor Cadwallader would have welcomed that judgment for public usage.

Non-politician Washburn, as Keyes and others judged him to be, Cadwallader believed he could be, and he wanted to be, a United States Senator. In 1873, Washburn suffered defeat giving up the governorship to farmer and virtually unknown, William R. Taylor. By working to win a second term as Governor, and attempting a third time in 1875 to become U.S. Senator, it seems hard to think of Washburn as a humble man. The struggling can be seen as that of a downeasterner who in typical fashion committed himself in earnest, only endeavoring *dutifully* to achieve. It does not necessarily mean that he judged himself to be superior or to have special powers. Indeed, Cadwallader told Elihu he was practically pushed into running for Congressman and Governor. Elihu, more than once, said the same thing as he stood for an elected political office. Israel, Jr., repeated the same line, as did William. By the time the protest technique was picked up and used by William, however, it had become a mere political ploy. The older brothers were surprised when they found themselves possessors of power in the political arena. If humility is not a suitable word to describe partisan politicians, another word can be found to describe the Washburns more accurately. The word "diffidence" will suffice.

❖

The Wisconsin-Minnesota businessman belongs at the teetering edge of the capitalist revolution which began in the last quarter of the 19th century.(4) Washburn was an axial figure, active in what is said to be the first stage of the development of American businesses, carrying over into a revolutionary second stage. As a businessman, he was able early in his career to turn to a powerful politician in Washington, his brother Elihu, to further the interests and control of the political world by business. Cadwallader wrote Elihu in 1850 complaining that the Mineral Point Land office was to be moved to another place. He informed Elihu, saying, "If you can . . . block the wheels so as to prevent it from becoming law, those of us interested here will pay you $500.00." Within a period of ten short years Washburn was acknowledged the chief man of business in the western half of Wisconsin. His interests were in banking, land development, lumbering, mining, railroading, and the practice of law. In 1850 he entered the political arena himself and began to represent the interests of commerce. As a Whig, however, Washburn hardly appreciated Adam Smith's *laissez faire* economy which disapproved of endeavoring to get federal and state governments to finance railroad systems and internal improvements--in a word, business interests. Cadwallader, as he developed his businesses, moved in the direction of the second stage of the business world in America, namely, the era of specialization, combination and integration. Charles Francis Adams, whom Washburn had met before when Adams, chair of the Committee of Thirty-three, led his committee to adopt a proposal which would engraft slavery upon the American culture forever. The Committee recommendations were vigorously opposed by Cadwallader. Adams popped up again 20 years later. In the 1880s, Adams was siding with business interests promoting consolidation as a necessity and natural law of growth. That was a direction Washburn did not adopt, nor was it the interest of Cad's younger brother, William Drew Washburn.

We have come to know Cadwallader through knowing his elder brother. The flour merchant, lumber tycoon and politician can be even better known and understood by knowing the youngest of the brothers, William, or "W.D." When William was born, Cadwallader was a teenager. When W.D. was a teenager, his brother was 26, teaching school in Wiscasset and thinking about leaving Maine to go west. After William's elders, Israel, Elihu and Cadwallader, had fought in the legislature and on the battlefield, respectively, during a distinct period of American history, William appeared as the scene was changing culturally, economically and politically. Walter Prescott Webb

C. F. Adams

claims that in the 1890s, when W.D. was at the apex of his power, the three centuries' frontier process came to an end. The effects, reflected in the thought and action of William Drew, "were present everywhere, in democratic government, in boisterous politics, in explosive agriculture, in mobility of population, in disregard for conventions, in rude manners, and in unbridled optimism."(5) Cadwallader, though wealthy, would not have appreciated an observation made by Carl Russell Fish; but William would. "The fortunes of the rich . . . were beyond anything previously dreamed of in America."(6) Like Cad and while Cad was living and for a time after Cad's death, William fought trusts and combinations which represented that new, revolutionary era, thought to be the second stage of capitalist growth. In an interview with John Crosby, son of Cadwallader Washburn's partner, the author of *The Waterfall That Built A City,*(7) Lucille M. Kane, asked why Washburn and Crosby continued a partnership rather than incorporate. Mr. Crosby said, "I think perhaps in those days partnerships were more common and incorporations were fewer than today." It was only after the elder John Crosby's death in 1887 that Washburn's flour business was incorporated. It was an unyielding Washburn attitude regarding relationships which explains Cadwallader's continuation of partnerships in the milling and lumber enterprises. He was pragmatic, a distinct sign of the first stage of the capitalist era, so that when something worked, as the fact of trust in one's fellowman did, Cad made a ritual of annual partnership meetings. There was a shaking of hands and a sharing of stories and jokes.(8) This proved to be a satisfactory method of guaranteeing continued successes in Washburn's several concerns. The ritual, passé in the 1880s, showed a side of the man which marked him as determined and forceful. The story of the singular course followed by the youngest Washburn, William, disassociating him more in kind than degree from the economic, political and cultural attitude of Israel, Elihu and Cadwallader, is another story. For present purposes, W.D. becomes a bench mark with which to measure distance from Cad and other brothers.

Cadwallader had a sentimental side.(9) As a sentimentalist he was perhaps to be numbered among the last man of the age leading to the *Capitalist Revolution.* The American ethos, strong on individualism and the self-confident man, was already soaring when Washburn was in his 60s and William in his late 40s. Expectations on the part of persons of Washburn's breed, to the effect that "Americans would arrive at a better society and become in general worthier men,"(10) had led to disenchantment of the system in the final decade of the century. Sentimentalism was hardly *au courant* in the circle of policy makers, general managers and "robber baron" types from Rockefeller to Vanderbilt. Cadwallader wept over the failures of men and fretted over children who underwent the sickening effects of debauchery. Levi Sterling, son of a dear friend, was imprisoned. Cadwallader wrote Elihu, virtually demanding that Elihu find a release for Sterling. He wrote in a touching letter, "A few weeks ago I was moved . . . to tears on meeting two of the children . . .."(11) Or can one imagine a tough old pragmatic millionaire wishing to sing a sentimental Scottish song about *Auld Robin Gray*, Washburn's favorite melody and lyrics? What was the song about but young Jamie who went to sea, leaving his bride to be for lack of lucre. Leaving, Jamie did not know that the heroine who had sent him off to sea, was left with a poor father who broke his arm, a mother fallen ill, and a stolen cow. Cad may have been touched by the story of the composer, Lady Anne Lindsay, who modestly would not reveal her authorship though her song became popular throughout

Scotland, and was carried to India and America where it was sung mournfully or with mock sorrow in towns east and west. In any case, the song was a favorite for C.C. Washburn, and in his younger days, when an aspiring young man seeking a lover, and finding one in Jeannette, he would visit friends and neighbors in Mineral Point, ready to respond to eager requests for him to sing the song of hopeless love.(12) Strict and stern, there was yet room for songs patriotic and religious which at times moved him to tears. When Lincoln was assassinated a public meeting was called in Memphis. Several officers and others delivered orations or eulogies. General Washburn begged off, overcome with grief. For the 19th-century American man, tears were not permitted as outward manifestations, even at funerals.

It was said by Cyrus that Cadwallader liked the "stated preaching of the gospel."(13) If so, it was the version of the "gospel" preached in Universalist churches where stories of Jesus were told with a humanistic flavor. Ministers downplayed the conventional view of Jesus as the Christ. The man was seen as a human figure, suffering and in anguish on a cross because of the weaknesses of persons who did not know what they were doing. Blood was being shed by a man who saw weak people as the Creator's children and therefore his "brothers" and "sisters."

The feeling side of Cadwallader Washburn is demonstrated in occasional breaks from the well-planned presentation of self. Cadwallader felt so strongly about honesty that he used vile language damning a man for not paying his bills. It surprises us, unless we are acquainted with Jungian psychology, to hear a magnate such as Washburn refer to a person who does not honor his pledge to pay a debt, as a "sh-t a-s." [sic] It was not beyond Cadwallader to explode a phrase accusing a person of being a "lying son of a b----."[sic]

A warm feeling belonging to Cadwallader affects us emotionally when we read about his response to the man who became his chief engineer, William de la Barre, a German expatriate who was a learned man, but who knew little about flour milling. Washburn yet invited him to become his adviser. One can imagine a person like de la Barre, humble in the presence of the Minneapolis magnate, knowing he was ignorant about milling, confessing his ignorance and yet hearing Governor Washburn say, "No one knows where this thing will lead. We will grow up in it together." In this incident is an example of implicit trust which Washburn preferred in his relations with associates. The betrayal of trust would have turned Cadwallader into what for a German like de la Barre would have been a heartless *gauleiter*. Rather, Cadwallader said softly to the modest de la Barre, "We will grow together."

Satisfying Work and Acceptance of Death

In this exordium leading to the sickness and death of C.C. Washburn, we examine his personal anxiety concerning control of his Minneapolis and St. Louis Railroad. He was anxious about the possible sale of the road to James Hill's Northwestern line, a course of action vigorously opposed by Cadwallader's friends in the flour city. Next, we will look at the illness which overtook Washburn leading to the last months of his life. We are looking at events beginning in February 1881, ending in May 1882 when the doctor standing by his bedside finally pronounced the fatal words, "He breathes no more."(14)

❖

The "puny," "weak sister"(15) Minneapolis and St. Louis Railroad troubled Cadwallader in the months prior to the fatal February date in 1881. It gave him qualms the way a possible loss of the line agitated Minneapolis merchants. The anxious in Minneapolis included the president of the road, W.D. Washburn. William's anxiety over the possibility of the sale doubtless added to his brother Cad's uneasy feelings. Both Washburns knew the Minneapolis and St. Louis line, if sold, might go into the hands of persons friendly to the cities of Chicago and Milwaukee. Minneapolis merchants claimed "the sale [would be] a violation of the faith of the city . . . .which had given $350,000 in aid to the construction of the line 'on the distinct understanding that the road was to be kept, if possible, under the control of citizens of Minneapolis . . ..'"(16) Leaders in the city communicated to Cadwallader their belief that sale of the rail line would make their city a way station out of Chicago.

What was happening? The Washburn brothers had themselves believed 20 years earlier that by the year 1880 rail lines and water power would make the city "second only to Chicago" as the leading mid-west metropolis, and indeed, by 1880 these two factors could explain the remarkable growth pattern which had occurred. The population of the city increased from 18,079 to 46,887 in a decade. In that same year, 1880, William borrowed funds to build six dams for the purpose of supplying water for the mills of the city.(17) The younger Washburn was continuing the Washburn tradition. He was one of those responsible for the salutary fact that at the beginning of the decade, Minnesota led the country in lumbering. W.D. constructed a lumber mill in nearby Anoka while continuing to collaborate with Cadwallader and others of his brothers who had an interest in the lumbering trade. Beginning in 1880 the promising "Young Rapid," as William was called in imitation of Elihu, was instrumental in laying down the "Soo" line, starting at Minneapolis and ending at Sault Ste. Marie, Michigan, connecting across the bay with the Canadian Pacific. It was a remarkable feat put through by William, the idea having been recommended to the people of Minneapolis in 1873 by another Washburn--Israel. Israel had recognized what merchants were sorely afraid of, that they might become an adjunct of Chicago. The Maine Collector at Portland had a vested interest in the line. His state, and Portland in particular, would benefit. In his 1873 lecture Israel delineated the route out of Minneapolis, a route, he said, enabling the mid-western city to reach an Atlantic seaport. Perhaps "old C.C." anticipated the completion of the Soo line and felt that he and other Minneapolis millers would have a secure way out of the mid-west by rail, and therefore would not have to depend upon lines into Chicago.

A substantial number of stockholders favored the sale of the Minneapolis and St. Louis knowing ample profit would be realized. One Minneapolitan predicted that under those circumstances, "old C.C. [would] sell and decide the matter." Final papers were drawn up for the sale of the road to Hill's Northwestern company. But through efforts of William D., the sale did not take place. This fierce competition between brothers was not unusual for the Washburns.

They had lived with disagreement from childhood but had always remained close, mutually admiring one another. While Cadwallader was drawing a contract with Marvin Hughitt of the Chicago line, William was urging Minneapolis stockholders not to sell. He began a campaign to win the public to his position and made a trip to New York to persuade Cadwallader to reconsider. Cad agreed at least to sell only to people favorable to Minneapolis. He accommodated both William and Minneapolis merchants by adding reservations to the contract drawn for Hughitt. Hughitt was unwilling to purchase the line with Washburn's exceptions attached. William returned to Minneapolis where he succeeded in obtaining financial assistance and he purchased the road. That effort also was in vain, however. Stockholders outside Minneapolis had the power to replace officers, putting the line in the hands of persons from Chicago and other locations where there was

little symphathy for the flour city. The new officers made the final decisions and the sale was completed. With the sale, C.C. Washburn was relieved of one of his tiresome burdens. He then had money needed to modernize his lumber mill at LaCrosse. The Minneapolis observer was thus correct who said, "If there were profit in the transaction, old C.C. will sell and decide the matter."(18)

❖

William D. Washburn

Cadwallader, as Woodman noted, always in hot water would at last suffer the consequences of living continuously under tension injurious to one's health. Undue stress finally brought on the ailments which had already taken his mother and Sidney--Bright's disease.(19)

During his working life, Cad, Elihu reported, had remarkable strength and vigor. The record confirms Elihu's observation. Cad's powers of endurance were excellent, and "few men could perform a larger amount of mental and physical labor."(20) Elihu in his biographical record does not speculate as others have about reasons why Cadwallader worked so hard all his life; engaging himself in so many enterprises; involving himself in politics nationally, locally, in Wisconsin and Minneapolis; why he spent five years of his life fighting for the Union. It was supposed that Washburn was compensating for lack of a love life, sublimating sexual needs with overindulgence in work.

In January 1881 Washburn was in Washington visiting his daughter, Jeannette Kelsey. Jeannette and her father had been at odds since 1876, with money the source of difficulty between them. Mrs. Kelsey's altercation with her father found its way into the public press. As a result Cadwallader gave Jeannette an annuity of $2500. The elder daughter's apparent resentment on the occasion of her father's visit that year may have produced emotional distress in Cadwallader.(21) In any case, Washburn left Jeannette's home resolving to make his way to LaCrosse by way of Chicago as quickly as he could. During his visit with Elihu and family in Chicago Cad, complained of feeling ill. His brother tried to persuade him to remain and rest. Business required his presence at LaCrosse, Cad insisted; and he left Chicago by train during the night so he would arrive on Saturday morning, February 3. He ate a hasty breakfast at his hotel and took the horse car in the cold

Louis Napoleon

February weather, arriving at his sawmill to give instructions about needed repairs. He returned to his office, "stepped into the adjoining office of his friend, Hon. G.C. Hickson and it was at that moment he was stricken down with paralysis . . . "(22) Physicians who tended Cadwallader knew instantly the nature of his ailment, declaring that paralysis had been brought about by kidney disorder.

Washburn was bent upon regaining health. It was as though he were commanding wellness. He went promptly to Hot Springs, Arkansas, an area fought over, incidentally, by General Washburn in 1862. The governor's condition improved slightly, though Charles Martin, visiting from Minneapolis, reported in February that his friend was experiencing vertigo. Physicians and friends advised Cadwallader to hire a valet and travel to Europe where healing waters and rest would improve his chances of recovery. The attendant Cadwallader took with him was William Freeman. Freeman, an impressive, highly intelligent man "born a slave but . . . a man all the same," said Washburn, had accompanied Secretary of State Seward in a tour around the world. The last of May, the paralytic Cadwallader went first to Washington. Writing to his chief engineer he made clear that he expected to keep in touch with business in Minneapolis while abroad. There had been a small fire in one of his mills, and he charged his engineer, de la Barre, to fix the problem so that "it can never happen again."

Washburn arrived in Ems, the community where years earlier Chancellor Bismarck had commenced the Franco-Prussian war with a mere telegram. As ambassador to France, Cad's brother, Elihu, had suffered the fallout effects of that war begun at Ems with a message aimed at insulting Louis Napoleon, like a glove striking across the face of an adversary. At Ems, Cadwallader once again wrote de la Barre and in this instance exhibited humor as well as firmness about business matters. He closed his letter saying that Kaiser William and the King of Sweden were both at Ems; "but," he wrote in droll fashion, "they do not worry me, nor I them." Two weeks later he wrote from a hotel in Würtemberg that he would be in Germany until he went to Switzerland. He was going to remain in Europe longer than planned, returning to the States only if it were necessary. He ended his letter to Barre with a statement which may have been the principle reason for writing, saying his engineer must perfect the fire alarm system, and he gruffly announced that Henry Douglass must lower the bed of the Mississippi river before adding a turbine.

That there was still vitality in "old C.C." is illustrated in what happened in August when Washburn wrote de la Barre about one of his employees--McMillan. "McMillan ought to be church mauled," he wrote, as though about an erring child.

McMillan had put weak piers in place, failing to go down to the ledge with the feet of the piers. Cadwallader even threatened to dissolve partnership with someone if McMillan did not rectify the problem. He wrote with feeling, that he intended to bring all railroads to his mills "in spite of opposition."

Vitality or not, there is no indication that, while in Europe Cadwallader visited the bewitching beauty-- Blanche Tucker. Blanche was the young woman who wrote letters to Cad addressing him as her "beloved." She, at age 22 in 1881, was married. Cad would have been mortified, given his unfailing dignity, holding his paralyzed arm against his body and having to drag his foot over the sill of some fine d'Alligri home in Italy to visit the vivacious Blanche.

Governor Washburn had a hope and vision in mind during his convalescence. He was making plans to construct a new mill. It would be, he claimed, his <u>beau ideal</u> the most perfect ever built.

In September Cad was still filled with apprehension about conditions at his mill, expressing himself as suffering a "monstrous outrage" which had been laid upon him, and assuring de la Barre that he felt "perfectly competent to direct [his] business." The not so subtle observation he then made in that letter about a Mr. Bailey confirmed his declaration that he could handle his affairs. Like "the boss" he continued to be, he expressed the hope that de la Barre and Bailey were getting along smoothly, saying of Bailey that "he [was] a smart and capable fellow if you can bear his self-conceit."

In November Washburn was back in the country. In New York he wrote explaining in a letter that he was on his way to Philadelphia; and he summoned de la Barre to Philadelphia where the two were to talk over the building of the mill he was going to build "without interference from any quarter."

He had continued through the period of illness and recovery to keep careful check on finances. He wrote his banker, General G. Van Steenwyk, complaining about the amount of money his brother-in-law, S.L. Nevins, was spending on himself and family. Washburn suspected that Nevins' son, Alex, who was editing an opposition newspaper in LaCrosse, had been receiving support from Nevins with Washburn money. That, said Steenwyk, galled the Governor. Charles J. Martin, one of Washburn's partners, visited Cadwallader and reported to Elihu that he tried to think the situation was not hopeless, but feared the worse. This was in October 1881. The fighting flour merchant was able to keep himself alive until May 1882.

When Washburn knew he would return from Europe, he made it known that he wanted very much to see Cyrus. Woodman had an engagement, but he told Elihu he would break the engagement if he could be of service to Cad. Cyrus feared that too much company would harm his former partner. When Woodman went to see Cad, he found his popular friend at breakfast with Israel, Charles Martin, General Van Steenwyk, Henry Douglas, and Mr. Copeland of LaCrosse. Cyrus, of course, became the sixth man at the breakfast table.

❖

Elihu, expecting the passing of Cadwallader, sought information from those who knew Cad as a young man. He wrote S.W. McMaster and received from him his recollection, saying "Cad [had been] a sedate, quiet young man."(23) Israel was thinking also of the coming death of Cadwallader and announced that he was having a portrait made of his brother. Elihu made a record of a letter from Steenwyk in which the banker says "the death of Elihu's brother would be a loss he would feel more than the death of any other mortal man."(24) Elihu treasured the letter from William Freeman in which he was told that in December, Washburn "got up singing as gay as a lark . . .. The words of the refrain . . . ran thus, Sing ging-a, sing ging-a cha so rah." It pleased Elihu to learn from Freeman that when Cad read what Elihu had written about "dear old Galena," Freeman "thought Cadwallader would die laughing." An expression of opinion unusual for the Governor indicates his graduated feelings changing day by day and soon changing hourly, so that, as he said to Cyrus, he was ready "to 'leave the warm precincts of the cheerful day' when the Master calls." Still the mood was not always somber as is clear upon reading a lengthy letter from C.C. to Elihu which brought back memories for the writer and recipient.(25) Cad recalled a childhood democrat friend of Elihu's, Timberly, who was a Jackson man. When grown, Timberly's wife was pregnant and brought to bed with father and mother hoping for a boy so he could be named Andrew Jackson. It was a girl. Seeking to console the parents, Mucletom Bryant's wife said, "Law me. Call the child after Mrs. Jackson. I understand she was a clever woman." In his letter Cadwallader then extolled the virtues of Rachel Jackson, saying he carried in his wallet a tribute to Rachel written by Andy, the president. Cad then quoted to Elihu the lengthy epitaph which showed Rachel to be something of a model for Cadwallader:

> . . . Her face was fair, her person pleasing, her temper amiable, her heart kind! She delighted in relieving the wants of her fellow creatures, and cultivated that divine pleasure by the most liberal and unpretending methods! To the poor she was a benefactor! To the rich an example! To the wretched a comforter! . . . A being so gentle and so virtuous, slander might wound, but could not dishonor, even death when he took her from the hands of her husband, could but transport her to the bosom of her god!

In a long, extended letter to Elihu, Cadwallader joshed his brother, saying he must come and stay a while. He had found a suitable room for his brother, Cad said, at an "Old Man's Home." That announcement brought a chuckling reply from Elihu. In his letter, Cadwallader then went on as Washburn-the-Historian, dictating facts in his letter about the Mississippi River, its discoverer, Marquette, and about La Salle who discovered the mouth of the river. Cadwallader said he and Lyman Draper, Secretary of the Wisconsin Historical Society, had tried to add "body and soul" to the river story but, said Cad, "we failed to start the ripple. Few people heard of Marquette and less cared for him and we had to abandon [the project]."

❖

Eureka Springs waters in Arkansas were said to cure Bright's disease. Cadwallader, together with Israel and his wife, made their way, traveling night and day in a stagecoach "over the worst road ever traveled by that kind of conveyance." Drinking the Springs' water at the Springs exacerbated Cad's condition, though he was informed that the first effect of drinking was to make the patient worse and better afterwards. It did, his appetite improved and he gained strength, and, said Elihu, he slept soundly. Washburn called to come visit him friends from their distant homes, partners and his chief engineer, for at that time Washburn "commenced taking up the threads of his business interests." People were astonished at the sharpness of his memory. The tone of many letters, dictated to anyone who would write for him, was cheerful and even hopeful.

On Thursday, the 4th of May, desirous to test his strength and without the knowledge of anyone but his valet, whose arms he took, he walked to the bathhouse some distance from the hotel. On his return he seemed greatly fatigued.

The next morning "[speaking] in a voice firm and natural, he said, 'I feel that my end is near'." Elihu read to him from a newspaper and Cad asked Freeman to assist him. He rose from his chair, walked to the balcony to see for the last time the beautiful forest of trees and the land over which he had galloped energetically, seeking the enemy 20 years before. He was assisted back to his room, removed his coat, lay down, never to rise again. His mind began to wander. Doctors remained at his bedside through the night. His daughter Fanny, and husband, Charles Payson, arrived and Cadwallader roused to say he was sorry they had traveled so far to see him. Two days later his brother-in-law, Gustavus Buffum, arrived and the two talked rationally. He spoke of his flouring mills and lumber interests, and his mind wandered over his military service. "At one time [he] aroused the attention of his attendants by exclaiming, 'Where are the prisoners, are they still held? Let them all be paroled.'" Physicians declared they had never before witnessed such tenacity of life.

Saturday morning, the 14th of May, the curtain was raised and the sun suffused his massive features as he suffered the throes of death. Elihu wrote,

At five o'clock and thirty minutes on the afternoon of May 14, 1882, the doctor, standing pensively at the side of the bed, pronounced the fatal words, "He breathes no more." The soul of C.C. Washburn had winged its flight to the world beyond.

❖

Cad's and Elihu's brother, Charles, was in San Francisco. Charles had been given financial help from his brother through the years. He borrowed money from Cad to establish a short-lived newspaper in Chicago, and he wanted Cadwallader's financial backing to market a typewriter Charles invented. When the end came, Charles indicated to Elihu that Cadwallader had been providing Charles' family with $100 a month. Elihu sent a telegram to the San Francisco brother announcing Cad's passing. The west coast Washburn noted in a letter to Elihu that Cadwallader had made the gift of an orphanage "as a tribute to our good and noble mother . . . A mother and son each worthy of the other."

❖

A not unusual reverence appeared immediately in a LaCrosse newspaper:
Few men have exercised a greater or more beneficent influence
over the destinies of the Great Northwest than did the Hon. C.C.
Washburn . . ..
His death was counted "a public calamity." "The slave found in him an able

advocate and staunch friend." He was "a lion-hearted man." "He had no halting opinions; he had a judgment, and a decided judgment on every question that was ever presented to him." His physical stature, his mind, his manner, his address--gave the impression of massiveness." "Mr. Washburn was liberal minded and full of charity." His Minneapolis Universalist minister said, "There was not a drop of despair in his mind." At the funeral nearly every town in the State of Wisconsin was represented; "the farmer left the plow; the mechanic the shop; the merchant the counting room. In Minneapolis, the wheels of the manufacturing establishments ceased to move."(26)

The obsequies began with a poetic flourish as acquaintances expressed genuine feelings of loss. The heralded remains were taken from Eureka Springs over rough roads to railroad cars and on to Chicago where Governor Rusk of Wisconsin and distinguished guests met the sorrowing party. Railroad cars were placed at the disposal of a committee by Alexander Mitchell, president of the Chicago, Milwaukee and St. Paul, and a sleeping car was made available for relatives and friends. Free trains accommodated friends from Minnesota who would attend services at LaCrosse. Two hundred and fifty persons attended from Minnesota. Members of the light horse squadron came up from Milwaukee. "The elegant private car of Hon. W.D. Washburn of the Minneapolis and St. Louis Road which was heavily draped in mourning inside and out, contained the catafalque upon which rested the casket."

Touching for Minneapolis attendees was "the most elaborate tribute of all" from the employees of the Washburn mill. Designed in floral decorations was a broken wheel of white and salmon roses, reminding employees and mill owners in attendance that in 1878 one of Washburn's great mills had been totally destroyed in an explosion. Sixteen men were killed. Cadwallader had a broken wheel designed to symbolize the loss of the working man, and the symbol was placed over the grave of the those who died.

Governors, ex-governors, judges, generals, mayors, politicians, soldiers and hundreds who only knew the sight of a figure walking to work on Main Street, or a man talking and no more, made up the audience of mourners. Singular among guests was a proud black man from Washington, D.C., William Freeman, who tended Cadwallader in sickness and health until death. The tribute of Freeman's very presence was for some as meaningful as the eloquent words spoken by renown clergy and orators. Ten thousand persons trailed the catafalque through the streets and to the hilltop.

A massive monument was yet to be raised over the site where Washburn's body would lie. Thirty-two work horses were required to haul the massive Washburn monument to cemetery hill. On the obelisk were to be carved words of Henry Wadsworth Longfellow,

> Lives of great men all remind us
> We can make our lives sublime,
> And, departing, leave behind us
> Footprints on the sands of time.

Eulogistic remarks seemed endless, printed in journals across the country. The LaCrosse newspaper filled over four pages with information about the elaborate plans made for the Memorial Service, including the names of people in attendance from communities across Wisconsin, Minnesota, Illinois, Maine, Washington,

D.C., and other places across the world.

Perhaps the most touching tribute, expressing fully the sorrow of a beloved brother, was what Charles wrote in response to Elihu's telegram. The vagabond brother penned these words,

"A great light has gone out."

BIBLIOGRAPHY

(An attempt has not been made with this brief bibliography to provide titles of all books and journal article used. The reader, however, can find from the mixture that follows many interesting studies having a bearing on the subject of this book.)

Craven, Avery O., "Civil War In the Making 1815-1860" (Louisiana State University Press, Baton Rouge, 1959).

Speech of Hon. E.K. Smart, of Maine, in "Defense of the North Against the Charge of Aggression Upon the South," delivered in the House of Representatives, April 23, 1852. This speech includes considerable information comparing south and north, economically and politically.

Theodore Parker delivered a speech, May 7, 1856, entitled, "The Present Aspect of the Antislavery Enterprise." It is an eloquent speech in which Parker said 2/3 of the population are at the North. 3/4 of the property is at the North. 4/5 of the education at the North, and, he supposed, 6/7 of the Christianity.

Woodward, C. Van, "The Populist Heritage and the Intellectual" (The American Scholar, XXIX Winter, 1959-1960), 55-72.

House Executive Document No. 9, 46th Congress, 1st Session Misc., 1879. Contested Election of Donnelly vs. Washburn.

Roosevelt, Blanche Tucker, "Marked In Haste," or "A Story of Today," Published in 1883 Charles Washburn (Fordham Monthly 4/10, #7), p. 452.

Washburn, Charles, "Paraguay and the Present War" (North American Review, October, 1869), page 510

Beedy, Helen Coffin, "Mothers of Maine" published 1895

Coffin, Charles Carleton, "The Seat of Empire" (James R. Osgood & Co., Boston, 1871).

Ross, Earle Dudley, "The Liberal Republican Movement" (Henry Holt & Co., N.Y., 1919).

Holmes, Frank R., "Minnesota in Three Centuries" (The Publishing Society of Minnesota, 1908, Vo. I-IV).

Halbo, Paul, "Wheat or What? Populism and American Fascism" (The Western Political Quarterly, XIV, September, 1961), pages 727-736.)

Warren, Harris Gaylord, "Paraguay An Informal History" (University of Oklahoma Press, Norman, 1949).

Atlantic Monthly, article by Charles Sumner, "Our Domestic Relations; Or, How to Treat the Rebel States," Vol. 12, 1863.

Peterson, Harold F., "Efforts of the United States to Mediate in the Paraguayan War" (Hispanic American Historical Review, XII, February 1932).

MacMahon, Martin T., "Paraguay and Her Enemies" (Harper's Monthly Magazine, XL, 239, April 1870).

Loubere, Leo A., "Louis Blanc" (Northwestern University Press, 1961).

Marx, Karl, "Notebook on the Paris Commune" (Independent Socialist Press, 1971).

Blanc, Louis, "1848 Historical Revelations" by Howard Fertig, N.Y., 1971.

Concourt Journal, "Paris Under Siege, 1870-1871" edited by George J. Becker (Cornell University Press, Ithaca and London, 1969).

Bury, J.P.T., "Gambetta and the Making of the Third Republic" (Longman 1973).

"The American Journalism of Marx and Engels," edited by Henry M. Christman (New American Library, 1966).

Phelps, Alonzo, "Contemporary Biography of California Representative Men." (At California State University Sacramento on microfilm F 868 A15 C3, reel 26:2.)

Donald, David H., "Liberty and Union." Records of A California Family: Journals and Letters of Lewis C. Gunn and Elizabeth LeBreton Gunn, ed. Anna Lee Marsteon, San Diego, 1928.

Plumb, Ralph B., "Wisconsin At Washington" (Maresch Printing Co., Manitowae, Wisconsin, 1961).

Sanford, Eleanor Roberts, "The Public Career of Governor Cadwallader Colden Washburn" (M.A. thesis, University of Wisconsin, 1923).

Stuart, Graham H., "American Diplomatic and Consular Practice" (D. Appleton-Century Co., Inc., N.Y. 1936).

Hanneman, Richard Lee, "The First Republican Campaign in Wisconsin 1854" (M.A. thesis at the University of Wisconsin, 1966).

Wright, John S., "Lincoln and the Politics of Slavery" (University of Nevada Press, Reno, Nevada, 1970). Page 71 concerns fusionist backing of E.B. Washburne

Curry, Leonard P., "Blueprint for Modern America" (Vanderbilt University Press, Nashville, 1968). Curry called E.B. Washburne an "advanced moderate."

Bartlett, Ruhl Jacob, "John C. Fremont and the Republican Party" (The Ohio State University, Columbus, Ohio 1930).

Benedict, Michael Les, "A Compromise of Principle" (W.W. Norton & Company, Inc., N.Y. 1974).

Berger, Raoul, "Impeachment: The Constitutional Problem" (Harvard University Press, Cambridge, Massachusetts, 1973).

Blumenthal, Henry, "France and the United States: Their Diplomatic Relations 1789-1914 (Chapel Hill: University of North Carolina Press, 1970).

Chetlain, Augustus, "Recollections of Seventy Years," (Galena, Illinois: Gazette Publishing Co., 1909).

Clifford, Dale, "Elihu Benjamin Washburne: An American Diplomat in Paris 1870-71" (Prologue, the Journal of the National Archives, II, Winter 1970, 161-174).

Douglass, Elisha P., "The Coming of Age of American Business" (The University of North Carolina Press, Chapel Hill, 1971).

Frye, Roland M., "The Relationship Between Elihu B. Washburne and Ulysses S. Grant (Senior Thesis to the History Department of Princeton University in partial fulfillment of the requirements for the degree of Bachelor of Arts, 1972).

Hanson, J.W., "Universalism the Prevailing Doctrine of the Christian Church During Its First Five Hundred Years" (Universalist Publishing House, Boston and Chicago, 1899).

Hatch, Louis Clinton, "Maine" (New Hampshire Publishing Company, Somersworth, 1919).

Hesseltine, William B., "Lincoln and the War Governors" (Alfred A. Knopf, New York, 1948).

Howe, Daniel Walker, "The Political Culture of American Whigs" (The University of Chicago Press, Chicago and London, 1979).

Hunt, Gaillard, "Israel, Elihu and Cadwallader Washburn" (Da Capo Press, New York, 1969).

Kane, Lucile M., "The Waterfall That Built a City" (Minnesota Historical Society, St. Paul, 1966).

Mohr, James C., "The Radical Republicans and Reform in New York during Reconstruction" (Cornell University Press, Ithaca and London, 1973).

DeNovo, John A., Editor, "The Gilded Age and After," Selected Readings in American History (Charles Scribner's Sons, New York, 1972).

Washburn, Charles Ames, "History of Paraguay, With Notes of Personal Observations and Reminiscences of Diplomacy Under Difficulties" (New York and Boston, 1871).

Washburn, Charles Ames, "Philip Thaxter" (Books for Libraries Press, Freeport, New York, 1971).

Washburn, Israel Papers, Library of Congress.

Washburn, Julia Chase, "Genealogical Notes of the Washburn Family" (Press of Journal Company, Lewiston, Maine, 1898).

Washburn, Lilian, "My Seven Sons" (Falmouth Publishing, Portland, Maine, 1940).

Washburne, Elihu B. Papers, Library of Congress.

Washburne, Elihu Benjamin, "Recollections of a Minister to France, 1869-1877," Vols. I-II (Charles Scribner's Sons, New York, 1887).

Williams, George Hunston, "American Universalism," A Bicentennial Historical Essay (Universalist Historical Society, 1971).

Willson, Beckles, "America's Ambassadors to France" (J. Murray, London, 1928).

Wold, Frances, "The Washburn Lignite Coal Company: A History of Mining At Wilton, North Dakota" (North Dakota History Journal of the Northern Plains, Vol. 43, Fall, 1976, No. 4), pages 4-20

Brooks, Noah, "Washington in Lincoln's Time," Edited by Herbert Mitgang (Rinehart & Company, Inc., New York, 1958).

Cole, Arthur Charles, "The Whig Party in the South" (Peter Smith Publisher, Gloucester, Mass., 1962).

Samuels, Ernest, "Henry Adams," The Major Phase (The Belknap Press of Harvard University Press, Cambridge, Massachusetts, 1964).

Wilson, James Grant, "General Grant's Letters to a Friend" (T.Y. Crowell & Co., N.Y. and Boston, 1897).

Van Deusen, Glyndon G., "William Henry Seward" (Oxford University Press, N.Y., 1967).

Russell, Charles Edward, "Blaine of Maine" (Cosmopolitan Book Corp., N.Y. 1931).

Nevins, Allan, "The War for the Union" (Charles Scribner's Sons, N.Y. 1971). Vol. IV.

Riddleberger, Patrick W., "George Washington Julian, Radical Republican" (Indiana Historical Bureau, 1966).

Johnnsen, Robert W., "Stephen A. Douglas" (Oxford University Press, 1973).

Fessenden, Francis, "Life and Public Services of William Pitt Fessenden" (Dacapo Press, New York, 1970), Vol. I and II.

"The Sherman Letters," edited by Rachel Sherman Thorndike (Da Capo Press, N.Y. 1969).

Speech of Hon. E.K. Smart, of Maine, in "Defense of the North Against the Charge of Aggression Upon the South," delivered in the House of Representatives, April 23, 1852. This speech includes considerable information comparing south and north, economically and politically.

Angle, Paul M., "Tragic Years 1860-1865" (Simon and Schuster, N.Y., 1960), vols. I and II. In volume II, Medill's letter to E.B. Washburne concerning Lincoln's "copperhead" cabinet member, Blair, page 824; and Henry J. Raymond to Lincoln, 1864, indicating that Lincoln could not be elected, quoting Washburne in a letter.

Longacre, Edward G., "From Union Stars to Top Hat" (Stackpole Books, 1972). See Chapter 3 on the Yazoo Pass Expedition.

Wilson, James Harrison, "The Life of John A. Rawlins" (The Neale Publishing Co., N.Y., 1916). See pages 184-185 for Rawlins on Washburne and his feelings regarding Lincoln and Grant, etc., and page 302 concerning Elihu's work for the generals at Rawlin's urging.

Gillette, William, "Retreat from Reconstruction, 1869-1879" (Louisiana State University Press, Baton Rouge, 1979). Of the civil rights bill by Sumner, Washburne said, "If his (Sumner's) object could have been, in thrusting it forward, to destroy the Republican party, he would have been gratified at his success, had he lived." Page 256.

Kolko, Gabriel, "Railroads and Regulation 1877-1916" (Princeton University Press, Princeton, New Jersey, 1965).

Davis, John P., "The Union Pacific Railway" (S.G. Griggs and Company, Chicago, 1894).

Trottman, Nelson, "History of the Union Pacific" (Augustus M. Kelley, Publishers, New York, 1966).

Hess, Stephen, "America's Political Dynasties from Adam to Kennedy" (Doubleday, Garden City, N.Y. 1966).

Badeau, Adam, "Grant In Peace from Appomattox to Mount McGregor" (S.S. Scranton & Company, Hartford, Connecticut 1887).

"Saturday Evening Chronograph," 1857: Edited by Charles A. Washburn. (The paper was published for three months. Copies are in the "Collection of the Illinois State Historical Library), vol. VI.

Arnold, Isaac N., "The History of Abraham Lincoln and the Overthrow of Slavery" (Clarke and Col, Publishers, Chicago, 1866).

Bemis, Samuel Flagg, "The American Secretaries of State" (Alfred A. Knopf, N.Y., 1928).

"U.S. Diplomatic and Consular Service," Our Representatives Abroad: Biographical Sketches, edited by Augustus C. Rogers (Atlantic Publishing Co., N.Y., 1874).

"The Edwards Papers," Being a Portion of the Collection of the Letters, Papers and Mss. of Ninian Edwards, Edited by E.B. Washburn (Chicago; Fergus Printing Co., 1884).

"Sketch of Edward Coles," by E.B. Washburne (Chicago: Jansen, McClurg & Co., 1882).

"History of Chicago," Vol. I, by A.T. Andreas, Chicago (A.T. Andreas, Publisher, 1884).

Simon, John Y., "From Galena to Appomattox: Grant and Washburne" (Journal of the Illinois State Historical Society, LVIII, Summer, 1965).

Gammon, Billie & Richards, Glenda, "Rural Reflections, Life at Norlands," 1840-1880, Printed 1976.

Thorp, Curti, and Baker, "American Issues," Vol. I (The Social Record, Lippincott Co., 1941).

Beard, Charles A. and William, "The American Leviathan" (The Republic in the Machine Age, MacMillan, 1931).

Robertson, James Oliver, "American Myth, American Reality" (Hill & Wang, N.Y., 1980).

Mumford, Lewis, "The Myth of the Machine" (the Pentagon of Power, Harcourt Brace Jovanovich, Inc., New York, 1970).

Jones, George, "Joseph Russell Jones" (Printed by George Jones, 1964).

Caughey, John W., "California" (Prentice-Hall, 1961).

Thomas, Emory, "The Confederate Nation 1861-1865" (Harper & Row, 1979).

Young, Henry Lyon, "Eliza Lynch, Regent of Paraguay" (Anthony Blond, Ltd., Great Britain, 1956).

Martin, Albro, "James J. Hill" (Oxford University Press, 1976).

O`Connor, Thomas, "The Disunited States" (Dodd, Mead & Co., 1972).

Pletcher, David, "Reciprocity & Latin America in the Early 1890s: A Foretaste of Dollar Diplomacy" (Pacific Historical Review, February 1978, Vol. XLVII, No. 1), pages 53-89.

Sturtevant, Reginald, "A History of Livermore" (Twin City Printery, Lewiston, Maine, 1970).

May, Henry F., "The Enlightenment in America" (Oxford University Press, 1976).

Hicks, John D., "A Short History of American Democracy" (The Riverside Press, 1943).

Nelson, Truman, "The Surveyor" (Doubleday & Co., 1960).

Mazlish, Bruce, "The Idea of Progress" (Daedalus, Summer 1963), pages 447-461

"American Thought, Civil War to World War I," edited by Miller, Perry, Holt, Rinehart & Winston, 1962.

Jones, Howard Mumford, "Revolution & Romanticism" (Harvard University Press, 1974).

Corwin, Edward S., "The `Higher Law` Background of American Constitutional Law" (Cornell University Press, 1929).

Rosenberg, John S., "Toward a New Civil War Revisionism" (American Scholar, Spring 1969, Vol. 38, No. 2), pages 250-272.

"Essays in American History & Culture," Vol. II, edited by Joseph M.Collier (American Studies Publishing Company, 1983).

Welter, Rush, "The Mind of America, 1820-1860" (Columbia University Press, 1975).

Paolino, Ernest N., "The Foundations of the American Empire, William Henry Seward and U.S. Foreign Policy" (Cornell University Press, 1973).

Degler, Carl, "Out of Our Past" (Harper & Row, 1962).

David, William, "Duel Between the First Ironclads" (Louisiana State University, 1975).

Matthiessen, F.O., "American Renaissance, Art and Expression in the Age of Emerson and Whitman" (Oxford University Press, N.Y., 1941).

Bowen, Catherine Drinker, "Family Portrait" (Little, Brown & Co., Boston, 1970).

Leech, Margaret, "In the Days of the McKinley" (Harper & Brothers, N.Y. 1959).

ENDNOTES
Chapter One
"A Family Without Equal in America"

(1) Bruce Mazlish, James and John Stuart Mill (Transaction Books, New Brunswick, 1975), xv.

(2) Elihu Washburne early in life chose the English spelling and used it throughout his life.

(3) Julia Chase Washburn, Genealogical Notes of the Washburn Family (Press of Journal Company, Lewiston, Maine, 1898).

(4) Leon Edel, Writing Lives (W.W. Norton and Company, New York, 1984).

(5)Reginald H. Sturtevant, A History of Livermore, Maine (Twin City Printery, Lewiston, Maine, 1970).

(6) Charles Ames Washburn, Philip Thaxter (Books for Libraries Press, Freeport, New York, 1970, first published in 1861).

(7) Washburn Journal, vol. I, September 24, 1866 to May 25, 1868, edited by Ethel Wilson Gammon. Israel Washburn, Jr., November 30, 1866, page 18.

(8) Gordon Shipman, Handbook for Family Analysis (Lexington Books, D.C., Heath and Company, Lexington, Massachusetts 1982), page 136.

(9) Ethel Wilson Gammon, The Three Daughters of Israel and Patty Washburn (Personal copy, 1973).

(10) Carl Russell Fish, The Rise of the Common Man (Quadrangle Books, Chicago 1927), page 6.

(11) Bernard Farber, Family and Community Structure: Salem in 1800, in The American Family in Social-Historical Perspective, Michael Gordon, Editor (St. Martin's Press, New York 1973), page 107.

(12) Alice S. Rossi in A Biosocial Perspective on Parenting (Daedalus, Spring 1977), page 8.

(13) Daniel Walker Howe, The Political Culture of the American Whigs (University of Chicago Press, Chicago and London 1979), Introduction pages 1-10.

(14) George Santayana, Character and Opinion in the United States (London: Constable, 1920), page 3.

(15) "Dear Sir: I am obliged to you for a copy of your speech. It reads like one of Webster's old speeches." --Letter to Israel Washburn, Jr., from Duncan McGaw, Bangor, Maine, June 29, 1852 (Washburn Memorial Library, Livermore, Maine).

(16) Charles Sumner to Israel Washburn, Jr., July 13, 1865 (Washburn Memorial Library, Livermore, Maine).

(17) Charles Sumner, Our Domestic Relations (Atlantic Monthly, Ticknor and Fields, Washington St., Boston), vol. XII 1863

(18) Israel Washburn, Jr., The Logic and the End of Rebellion (Universalist Quarterly and General Review, Thomas B. Thayer, Editor, Boston: Tompkins and Company, 1864).

(19) Lilian Washburn, My Seven Sons (Printed privately. Washburn Memorial Library, Livermore, Maine).

(20) Elihu Benjamin Washburne, Recollections of a Minister to France 1869-1877, two volumes (New York: Charles Scribner's Sons 1887).

(21) Henry Steele Commager, The American Mind (Yale University Press, New Haven 1950), page 16.

(22) Sam was Samuel Benjamin, Elihu's younger brother. Addie was Sam's second wife, and Ben was the child of Sam and Addie.

(23) Commager, The American Mind, page 163.

(24) Russell Miller, The Larger Hope, (Unitarian Universalist Association, Boston, 1979), 212-222; Journal of the Universalist Historical Society, Jerry V. Caswell, A New Civilization Radically Higher Than the Old (Vol. VII, 1967-68. Copyright 1969 by the Universalist Historical Society) pages 70-97.

(25) Ibid, Miller, page 212.

(26) J.W. Hanson, Universalism the Prevailing Doctrine of the Christian Church During Its

First Five Hundred Years (Universalist Publishing House, Boston, 1899).

(27) Quoted from Fellowship of Religious Humanists (Issue No. 15, March 1972), page 4. Caspar Schwenkfeld von Ossig, founder of sect called "Schwenkfelders." He lived in Germany from 1489 to 1561.

(28) The Washburn Journal, volume IV, page 35.

Chapter Two
"Father Israel and Mother Martha"

(1) Ibid, volume I, page 135.

(2) Ibid, volume III, page 103.

(3) Ibid, volume II, page 5

(4) Ibid, volume II, page 7.

(5) Ibid, volume I, page 18.

(6) Dedicatory Exercises of the Washburn Memorial library (Fergus Printing Company, Chicago 1885) page 32.

(7) Lilian Washburn, My Seven Sons.

(8) Mrs. J.H. Hanson of Chicago, wife of a one-time minister in Livermore, declared that Martha's character impressed itself by a quiet yet irresistible influence on all who knew her.

(9) Author's interview with Margaret Washburn, wife of Cadwallader Lincoln Washburn, nephew of Algernon Sidney Washburn.

(10) W.D. Washburn to Major W.D. Hale, March 9, 1889 (W.D. Washburn Collection, Minnesota Historical Archives, St. Paul, Minnesota).

(11) Ibid, Margaret Washburn interview.

(12) Augustus Chetlain, Recollections of Seventh Years (Galena Gazette Publishers, 1899).

(13) Tribute paid by an acquaintance who added, "these qualities she transmitted to her sons."

(14) In Memoriam Israel Washburn, Jr., (Privately Printed, 1884), page 126.

(15) Ibid, Hunt, page 158.

Chapter Three
"Religion and the Washburns"

(1) Richard Eddy, Universalism in America (Universalist Publishing House, Boston 1886), page 19.

(2) Ibid, page 118.

(3) Henry Steele Commager, The American Mind (Yale University Press, New Haven 1950), pages 165-166.

(4) Ibid, page 332. "It would not be just, perhaps, to claim George Washington as a Universalist--at least, not as a professed Universalist; but the following remark, attributed to him by Weems, in his 'Life of Washington,' may properly be cited as showing his Christian conviction and hope. Having witnessed the results of an Indian massacre of a mother and her children, Weems says that Washington used these words: 'To see these poor innocents . . . just entering upon life, and instead of fondest sympathy and tenderness, meeting their hideous deaths--and from brothers, too!--filled my soul with the deepest horror of sin, but at the same time inspired a most abiding sense of that religion which announces the Redeemer, who shall one day do away man's malignant passions, and restore the children of God to primeval love and bliss. Without this hope, what man of feeling but would wish he had never been born'."

(5) Israel Washburn, Jr., to Dr. A. St. John Cambre, July 24, 1880. Israel Washburn, Jr., Collection, Library of Congress.

(6) Emerson Hugh Lalone, And Thy Neighbor As Thyself (The Universalist Publishing House, Boston, Massachusetts 1959), page 2.

(7) Ibid, Lalone, page 33.

(8) The Rose of Sharon, edited by Miss S.C. Edgarton, A. Thompkins and B.B. Mussey, Boston 1846, article by E.H. Chapin, Mystery and Faith, pages 273-274.

(9) Ibid.

(10) <u>Fifteen Sermons from Fifteen Universalist Clergymen Of Maine</u>, the Reverend G.W. Quinby, Editor (S.H. Colesworthy, Publisher, Portland and Saco: 1845).

(11) Frederick Henry Hedge, "Ecclesiastical Christendom," <u>Christian Examiner</u> 51 (1851): 129.

(12) Ibid, W.A. Drew.

(13) George Bates, <u>Experience and Doctrine</u>.

(14) Ibid.

(15) D.T. Stevens, <u>The True Light</u>.

(16) The Reverend L.C. Todd, " . . . Every Universalist is a Republican, and every Republican should be a Universalist," <u>Orthodoxy and Despotism, Compared with Universalism and Republicanism</u> in <u>The Universalist Miscellany, A Monthly Magazine</u>, Volume I, 1844.

(17) Stephen Hess, <u>An American in Paris</u> in <u>American Heritage</u>, February 1967, Volume XVIII, Number 2, pages 18-28.

(18) J.H. Tuttle, <u>Human Nature, Its Capabilities</u>, pages 23-45, from <u>The Latest Word of Universalism</u>, Universalist Publishing House, Boston 1892.

(19) <u>A Half Century of Minneapolis</u>.

(20) George H. Emerson, <u>Christianity and the War</u> (<u>The Universalist Quarterly</u>), October 1861.

(21) Ibid, page 387.

(22) Elbridge Gerry Brooks, <u>Our Civil War</u> (<u>The Universalist Quarterly</u>), July 1861.

(23) Ibid, page 253.

(24) <u>Centennial</u>, pages 59-61, esp. page 59A. For his wartime mood, see his "The Logic and the end of the Rebellion" (<u>The Universalist Quarterly and General Review</u>), n.s. 1864, pages 1-25. Quoted in <u>The Journal of the Universalist Historical Society</u>, Volume IX, 1971, page 26.

(25) The Reverend A.J. Patterson, <u>Centennial Anniversary of the Planting of Universalism in Portsmouth, N.H., November 16 & 17, 1873</u>, Portsmouth 1873, page 70 (<u>Universalist Quarterly</u>), XI.

(26) Ibid, L.C. Todd, page 374.

(27) Historian Henry Steele Commager commented on the subject in "<u>The American Mind,</u>" writing "Logically, perhaps [Americans] should have abandoned a religion which, in flagrant contradiction to all experience, taught the depravity of man and the corruption of society and subordinated this life to the next, but Americans were not a logical people. . .. The revolt, in short, was moral and social, not intellectual. Americans rejected the application of Calvinism rather than the philosophy, the conclusions rather than the premises or the logic. There were . . . scattered revolts against the logic. Deism had its day, and Unitarianism Universalism commanded, for a time, the allegiance of a distinguished if not a numereous body. Yet the only well-established churches whose membership declined, absolutely, during the twentieth century were the Unitarian, Universalist, and Quaker." Pages 162-163. (Yale University Press, New Haven 1950).

(28) First Universalist Church (Church of the Redeemer) Records, Minnesota Historical Society, St. Paul, Minnesota.

(29) The Reverend Dr. A.C. Smith, oration at the funeral of E.B. Washburne (The Galena *Gazette*) October 28, 1887).

(30) E.B. Washburne to C.C. Washburn, May 24, 1847. "You will recollect the conversation we had in relation to our Unitarian clergyman, the Reverend Mr. Woodward, preaching occasionally at our place. Galena can't keep him and if your people desire it, he could preach for you one Sabbath in four." The Mineral Point brother would, said E.B. Washburne, make arrangements for Mr. W. [Woodward] to preach, $10. Plus expenses. "I think when you have heard him once you will want to hear more of him. $100.00 a year, plus expenses. Mr. W. is an educated N.E. gentleman . . .."

(31) Ibid.

(32) In the San Francisco *Daily Times*, May 12, 1860, Charles A. Washburn, editor, writes

of a lecture by Thomas Starr King being "more beautiful than we can repeat." May 3, 1860, an editorial announced the arrival of King in the city and mentioned that he spoke on Sunday at the Unitarian church. Washburn quoted Horace Greeley as saying that Mr. King is the third most popular lecturer in the world. May 15, 1860, the *Daily Times* announced the Reverend T. Starr King's second lecture. The editorial stated, "The last lecture of Mr. King was pronounced by all to be one of the finest efforts ever listened to by the large audience in attendance."

(33) C.A. Washburn, Political Evolution; or, From Poverty to Competence (J.B. Lippincott Company, Philadelphia 1885). The method of taxation proposed by Washburn in his book was similar to the scheme devised by Henry George. Both proposed a single tax on land values only. One difference between their proposals was that Mr. Washburn recommended the land tax be graduated so that those owners with large acreages would pay a higher tax rate than those with small acreages. Henry George proposed no graduation.

(34) Washburn Journal, July 18, 1869, Volume II, page 101.

(35) Washburn Journal, page 35, September 25, 1877, Volume IV.

(36) Ibid, Volume I, page 86.

(37) Russell E. Miller, The Larger Hope (Unitarian Universalist Association), page 406.

Chapter Four
"A Forward Look"

(1) Thomas Jefferson to John Holmes, April 22, 1820 (Ford, X, 157-158, quoted from Jefferson and His Time, volume six, The Sage of Monticello by Dumas Malone (Little, Brown and Company, Boston 1981), page 335.

(2) Hinton Rowan Helper, The Impending Crisis of the South by George M. Fredrickson (the Belknap Press of Harvard University Press, Cambridge, Massachusetts 1968), ix.

(3) In point of fact, the threat of secession first came, not from South Carolina, Arkansas or Texas, but from Massachusetts. In the Commonwealth, New England Federalists saw nullification as their defense against what they declared was the tyranny of Jefferson democracy.

(4) The World's Great Speeches edited by Lewis Copeland (Garden City Publishing Company, Inc., Garden City, N.Y. 1942), page 293

(5) William and Bruce Catton, Two Roads to Sumter (McGraw-Hill Book Company, Inc., New York 1963), page 121.

(6) Calhoun, John C., Slavery, in The World's Great Speeches, edited by Lewis Copeland (Garden City Publishing Company, Inc., Garden City, N.Y. 1942).

(7) Ibid.

(8) R.D. Hitchcock to Israel Washburn, Jr., June 10, 1852 (Washburn Memorial Library, Livermore, Maine).

(9) Israel Washburn, Jr., Washburn Journal, volume IV, July 10, 1876, to August 14, 1882, page 102 (Washburn Memorial Library, Livermore, Maine).

(10) Martha Washburn to E.B. Washburne, 1846. It is not clear to whom Mrs. Washburn is referring but Henry Clay is a likely person (Washburn Memorial Library, Livermore, Maine).

(11) Emphasis added. Sermons by E.G. Brooks, The Fugitive Slave Law, Our Duty, the Union (The Universalist Quarterly and General Review, vol. VII 1850. Harvard Divinity School archives).

(12) Speech entitled Compromise As A National Party Test delivered in the House of Representatives, May 24, 1852 (Washington: Printed by Congressional Globe Office), 1852, 8vo. Pp. 12).

(13) Ibid.

(14) John D. Hicks, A Short History of American Democracy (Houghton Mifflin Company, Boston 1943), page 322. William Gienapp, The Whig Party, the Compromise of 1850, and the Nomination of Winfield Scott (printed in Presidential Studies Quarterly).

(15) E.B. Washburne to Israel Washburn, Sr., Mineral Point, Wisconsin, September 6, 1852 (Washburn Memorial Library, Livermore, Maine).

(16) E.B. Washburne predicted there would be 300 votes more for him than for Thomas Campbell. Washburne's record for predicting votes remained remarkable throughout his career, not only in the United States but in France where as ambassador he took an interest in French politics.

(17) Philip Greven, Jr., The Protestant Temperament (New York: Knopf 1977).

(18) Quoted from Daniel Walker Howe, The Political Culture of the American Whigs (The University of Chicago Press, Chicago 1979), page 149.

(19) E.B. Washburne to Adele G. Washburne, July 19, 1870 (Washburn Memorial Library, Livermore, Maine).

(20) Speech of Hon. Israel Washburn, Jun., of Maine, delivered in the House of Representatives, May 19, 1860 (Harvard College Library).

(21) Israel Washburn, Jr., July 4, 1874 at Cherryfield, Maine (Washburn Memorial Library, Livermore, Maine).

(22) Howe, Ibid, page 6.

(23) Ibid, page 33.

(24) Letter of Lieber, Thomas Sergeant Perry, The Life and Letters of Francis Lieber (Boston 1882), page 315.

(25) "There was no doubt in Emerson's mind that the war, clearly 'God's doing' and therefore 'marvelous in our eyes,' would be the final and most dramatic stage of this corrective process." Len Gougeon, Emerson, Carlyle, and the Civil War. (New England Quarterly, September 1989), page 404.

(26) Dedication of the Soldier's Monument at Cherryfield, Maine, July 4, 1874 by Hon. I. Washburn, Jr.

(27) Israel Washburn, Jr's., speech on the Plan for Shortening the Transit Between New York and London, European & North American Railway and Public Lands, March 10, 1852.

(28) Politics and the Crisis of 1860, edited by Norman A. Graebner (University of Illinois Press, Urbana 1961), pages 33, 34.

(29) C.C. Washburn to E.B. Washburne, LaCrosse, August 20, 1859 (Washburn Memorial Library, Livermore, Maine).

(30) This takes into account the view expressed by Gordon S. Wood who reviewed James MacGregor Burns' volume one of The American Experiment, in which Wood notes that Burns was aware of uncontrollable power of impersonal forces that are, wrote Burns, "the product of millions of tiny decisions by countless individuals." (New York Review of Books, February 18, 1982), page 3.

(31) E.B. Washburne to Adele Washburne, September 7, 1862 (Washburn Memorial Library, Livermore, Maine).

Chapter Five
"The Child, Father to the Man

(1) Timothy Howe graduated, taught school in Livermore and later moved to Wisconsin where he became United States Senator at a time when Elihu Washburne was a prominent member of the House of Representatives.

(2) Seton, "a twist of silk or similar material passed under the skin . . . in order to cause . . . a discharge." Websters New Twentieth Century Dictionary (the World Publishing Company, New York 1868).

(3) Gaillard Hunt, Israel, Elihu and Cadwallader Washburn (Da Capo Press, New York 1969), page 167.

(4) Ibid, Hunt, page 168.

(5) E.H. Derby to E.B. Washburne, March 8, 1869, Boston, Massachusetts (Washburn Memorial Library, Livermore, Maine).

(6) E.B. Washburne to Hon. Lemuel Shaw, Law School, Cambridge, Massachusetts, December 3, 1839 (Letters from the Massachusetts Historical Society, Boston).

(7) E.B. Washburne to Martha Washburn, Law School, Cambridge, No. 11 Divinity Hall, May 22, 1839 (Washburn Memorial Library, Livermore, Maine).

(8) A.C. Buffum, Orono, Maine, April 6, 1854, to Israel Washburn, Jr. (Washburn Memorial Library).

Chapter Six
Cosmopolitan Galena

(1) Kenneth N.Owens, Galena, Grant, and the Fortunes of War (Northern Illinois University, 1963), page 3.

(2) Tacie N. Campbell, Historic Illinois (Vol. 6, No. 1, June 1983).

(3) E.B. Washburne to Adele Washburne from Paris (Washburn Memorial Library, Livermore, Maine).

(4) Adele Washburne to E.B. Washburne, Gratiot's Grove, January 12, 1848 (Washburn Memorial Library, Livermore, Maine).

(5) E.B. Washburne to C.C. Washburn, Washington, D.C., December 12, 1848 (Washburn Memorial Library, Livermore, Maine).

(6) Ibid.

(7) A. Lincoln to E.B. Washburne, April 30, 1848 (Washburne Memorial Library, Livermore, Maine).

(8) The Congressional Globe, June 19, 1854, reports Congressman E.B. Washburne saying to members of the House that he "helped to nominate Henry Clay in 1844." There is no other evidence that he delivered a nominating speech or submitted Clay's name since he wrote a letter to his brother Cadwallader, dated May 4, 1844, indicating that he was deathly ill on the day nominations were made at the convention in session at the Universalist church of Baltimore, Maryland. Congressional Globe, page 1444.

(9) Cyrus Woodman to C.C. Washburn, August 14, 1848 (Washburn Memorial Library, Livermore, Maine).

(10) There is much that can be said about the Whig party, but a paragraph from a book by Daniel Walker Howe, The Political Culture of the American Whigs (The University of Chicago Press, Chicago, 1979), will be helpful for the Reader: "The Whigs' responses to social problems often mirrored their responses to personal problems. Their devotion to productivity, equanimity, discipline, and improvement can be traced on a psychic as well as a social or political level. There was a personal, as there was a social, ideal toward which Whigs strove, and these two were broadly congruent. Looking back on their striving, we become conscious of a great irony: dedicated as they were to the idea that an individual could and should reshape himself and the world around him through the exercise of willpower, the Whigs themselves were, in fact, profoundly conditioned by the situation into which they were born."

(11) Israel Washburn, Sr., to E.B. Washburne, Livermore, January 23, 1848 (Washburn Memorial Library, Livermore, Maine).

(12) Ibid.

(13) E.B. Washburne to C.C. Washburn, Washington, D.C., Jany [sic] 30, 1848 (Washburn Memorial Library, Livermore, Maine).

(14) Ibid.

(15) Ibid.

(16) James G. Blaine, Twenty Years of Congress: from Lincoln to Garfield (Henry Bill Publishing Company, Norwich, Connecticut 1884, Volume I), page 41.

(17) Ibid.

(18) The Free-soil party was hostile toward slavery, believed in individual freedom, and gave strong support to the Republican party after its formation following the Kansas-Nebraska vote opening those states to the introduction of slavery.

(19) E.B. Washburne to Zebina Eastman, from Paris, February 3, 1874 (Washburn Memorial Library, Livermore, Maine).

Chapter Seven
"The End and the Beginning"

(1) Elihu B. Washburne to Israel Washburn, Jr., November 21, 1842 (Washburn Memorial Library, Livermore, Maine).

(2) Israel Washburn, Jr., The Logic and The end of the Rebellion. The Universalist Quarterly and General Review, 1864, page 13.

(3) William E. Gienapp, The Whig Party, the Compromise of 1850, and the Nomination of Winfield Scott (Presidential Studies Quarterly).

(4) Ibid, Gienapp, page 402.

(5) College Recollections, Fordham in the Fifties, by C.B. Connery 1953 (The Fordham Monthly), page 459.

(6) In 1860 Israel Washburn, Jr., chaired a select committee to revise the rules of the House. His committee submitted "its famous report" embracing 38 amendments. George B. Galloway, History of the House of Representatives (Thomas Y. Crowell Co., New York 1961) page 50.

(7) The Nebraska and Kansas Bill, Mr. Washburne of Illinois (Appendix to the Congressional Globe, 33d Cong., 1st Sess., April 5, 1854), page 460.

(8) Ibid.

(9) Ibid, Hunt, page 30.

(10) Kansas-Nebraska Speech of Mr. I. Washburn, Jr., of Maine in the House of Representatives (Congressional Globe, April 7, 1854).

(11) Ibid.

(12) Ibid.

(13) Ibid.

(14) Henry Wilson to Israel Washburn, Jr., May 28, 1854 (Washburn Memorial Library, Livermore, Maine).

(15) Notes in the possession of the author of an interview with Barbara Hitchner or Orono, Maine.

(16) E.B. Washburne to James Pike, Washington, D.C., May 8, 1854 (Washburn Memorial Library, Livermore, Maine).

(17) E.B. Washburne to James Pike, Washington, D.C., May 13, 1854 (Washburn Memorial Library, Livermore, Maine).

(18) A.C. Buffum, Orono, April 6, 1854 (Washburn Memorial Library, Livermore, Maine).

(19) Ibid.

(20) Louis Clinton Hatch, Maine A History (American Historical Society, New York 1919, page 381).

(21) Speech of Hon. I. Washburn, Jr., in the House of Representatives, March 14, 1856 (Harvard College Library).

(22) C.G. Holbrook to E.B. Washburne, December 30, 1854 (Washburn Memorial Library, Livermore, Maine).

(23) William B. Dodge to E.B. Washburn e, January 20, 1855 (Washburn Memorial Library, Livermore, Maine).

(24) General George W. Smith in Early Chicago and Illinois claimed that in 1856 E.B. Washburne was "instrumental in bringing Illinois as a State into Republican control," even saying "he was in advance of Lincoln."

(25) Richard N. Current, The History of Wisconsin, Volume II (State Historical Society of Wisconsin, Madison 1976), page 220.

(26) The Crawford County Courier (Washburn Memorial Library, Livermore, Maine) No date.

(27) Anna C. Lee Marston (ed), Records of a California Family, Journals and Letters of Lewis G. Gunn and Elizabeth Le Baron Gunn, San Diego, 1928).

(28) Robert W. Johannsen Stephen A. Douglas (Oxford University Press, N.Y. 1973), page 635. "Congressman Washburne urged that 'the door of our party' be kept wide open so that all who wished could come in. He saw no policy in abusing the Douglas men now. 'They are certainly not dangerous to us'."

(29) Lloyd Wendt Chicago Tribune (Rand McNally & Co., Chicago 1972), page 84. "Horace

Greeley sent Congressman Elihu Washburne, friend of [Charles A.] Ray from Galena days, and a long time correspondent of [Joseph] Medill's, to urge Senator Douglas be taken into the Republican fold. Ray did not agree with the somewhat Machiavellian strategy. Medill favored, which consisted of showing some friendship to the little Giant . . . to further the split of Buchanan." There is some confusion about Lloyd Wendt's understanding, that Medill favored inviting Douglas to join with the Republicans. In a letter Abraham Lincoln wrote E.B. Washburne dated May 27, 1858, Lincoln says, ". . . This morning my partner Mr. Herndon, receives a letter from Mr. Medill of the Chicago Tribune showing the writer to be in great alarm at the prospect North of Republicans going over to Douglas, on the idea that Douglas is going to assume steep free soil ground, and furiously assail the administration on the stump when he comes home."

(30) Abraham Lincoln to E.B. Washburne, Urbana, Illinois, April 26, 1858 (Lincoln's letters to Washburne, private collection of author).

(31) In the Weekly Northwestern Gazette of March 1, 1859, the following: "Elihu Washburne's brother, Charles A. Washburn, is preparing to start a Republican paper in San Francisco." (Washburn Memorial Library, Livermore, Maine).

(32) J.F. Hoyt to E.B. Washburne, January 19, 1861 (Washburn Memorial Library, Livermore, Maine).

Chapter Eight
"The New Administration an War"

(1) Abraham Lincoln to Truman Smith, Springfield, Illinois, November 10, 1860, The Life and Writings of Abraham Lincoln, edited by Philip Van Doren Stern (The Modern Library, New York 1940), page 623.

(2) Abraham Lincoln to E.B. Washburne, Springfield, Illinois, December 13, 1860 (Washburn Memorial Library, Livermore, Maine).

(3) Editorial in the San Francisco Daily Times, May 17, 1869 (State Library, Sacramento, California).

(4) The North American Review, edited by Allen Thorndike Rice, vol. CXLLI (No. 30 Lafayette Place, N.Y. 1885).

(5) Van Densen, Glydon G., William Henry Seward (Oxford University Press, New York 1967), pages 230-231.

(6) Abraham Lincoln to William H. Seward, Springfield, Illinois, December 8, 1860.

(7) Inside Lincoln's Cabinet, edited by David Donald (Longmans, Green and Company, New York, 1954, Kraus Reprint Co., N.Y. 1970) page 11.

(8) Riddle, Donald W., Congressman Abraham Lincoln (Greenwood Press, Publishers, Westport, Connecticut).

(9) E.B. Washburne to F.R. Bennett, Rock Island, December 4, 1850 (Washburn Memorial Library, Livermore, Maine).

(10) The Congressional Globe, 40th Congress, 2nd Session.

(11) The Congressional Globe, Thursday, January 24, 1861, remarks of Representative C.C. Washburn of Wisconsin.

(12) Within minutes after the inauguration Abraham Lincoln visited briefly with James Buchanan's cabinet members, and then left to call on General Scott, indicating the importance to Mr. Lincoln of having an ally in the Commander-in-Chief of the Army.

(13) Washburne had seen a great deal of the general prior to his nomination in 1852 and he was a strong Scott supporter at the Baltimore Convention. The two had kept up acquaintances over the years. . .. From The Lincoln Papers, edited by David C. Means, Doubleday and Company, Inc., Garden City, N.Y. 1948.

(14) A. Lincoln, Springfield, Confidential, to E.B. Washburne, December 21, 1860. Forts in Charleston Harbor, including, of course, Fort Sumter.

(15) Isaac N. Arnold to Susan Washburne, February 1882 (Washburn Memorial Library, Livermore, Maine).

(16) W.D. Washburn interview with a reporter of the Minneapolis Tribune (Minnesota

Historical Society).

(17) Ibid.

(18) Ibid.

(19) Ibid.

(20) Ibid.

(21) John Y. Simon, From Galena to Appomattox: Grant and Washburne, (Journal of the Illinois State Historical Society, vol. LVIII, No. 2, Summer 1965, printed by authority of the State of Illinois), pages 165-189.

(22) Ibid, Owens, page 35.

(23) George W. Emerson, Christianity and the War (The Universalist Quarterly 1861).

(24) William B. Dodge, Millburn, December 22, 1860 (Washburn Memorial Library, Livermore, Maine).

Chapter Nine
"The Countdown to April 1861"

(1) C.H. Ray to E.B. Washburne, December 16, 1854 (Washburn Memorial Library, Livermore, Maine).

(2) Abraham Lincoln to E.B. Washburne, Springfield, February 9, 1856 (Washburn Memorial Library, Livermore, Maine).

(3) Daily Illinois State Journal (Springfield), July 17, 1855, page 2, quoted from Journal of the Illinois State Historical Society, Vol. LXIV, Number 3, Autumn 1971.

(4) Owens, Kenneth N., Galena, Grant, and the Fortunes of War (Northern Illinois University, 1963), page 28.

(5) C.G. Holbrook to E.B. Washburne mentioned in Journal of the Illinois State Historical Society, vol. LXIV 1971, page 286.

(6) Cyrus Woodman to E.B. Washburne, October 6, 1855 (Washburn Memorial Library, Livermore, Maine).

(7) John A. Clark to E.B. Washburne, October 30, 1855 (Washburn Memorial Library, Livermore, Maine).

(8) Ibid, 297.

(9) Ibid, 299.

(10) Ibid, 303.

(11) C.H. Ray, Norwich, New York, to E.B. Washburne, December 24, 1854 (Washburn Memorial Library, Livermore, Maine).

(12) Ibid, 304.

(13) Leonard Swett of Maine and Illinois taught school at Livermore where the Washburns attended. In 1864 Swett and Washburne collaborated raising large funds for the purpose of re-electing Abraham Lincoln President.

(14) Howard, 305.

(15) Ibid, 306.

(16) C.A. Washburn to E.B. Washburne, April 16, 1861 (Washburn Memorial Library, Livermore, Maine).

(17) Hale, John B., America in 1857 by Kenneth M. Stampp (Oxford University Press, New York 1990), page 12.

(18) E.B. Washburne to Adele Washburne, from Reed's Landing, March 24, 1857 (Washburn Memorial Library, Livermore, Maine).

(19) Joseph Schafer, The Wisconsin Lead Region (State Historical Society of Wisconsin, Madison 1932).

(20) Israel Washburn, Jr., The Congressional Globe, December 21, 1852, page 116, related to the Annual Message of the President regarding tariff.

(21) Ibid.

(22) Ibid.

(23) Ibid.

(24) James L. Huston, The Panic of 1857 and the Coming of the Civil War (Louisiana State

University Press, Baton Rouge 1987), page 79.

(25) Orestes A. Brownson, <u>The Laboring Classes</u>, quoted from <u>The Transcendentalists</u> by Perry Miller (Harvard University Press, Cambridge, Massachusetts 1950), page 439.

(26) From the Introduction by George M. Frederickson to <u>The Impending Crisis of the South</u> by Hinton Rowan Helper (The Belknap Press of Harvard University Press, Cambridge, Massachusetts 1968).

(27) Ibid, xii.

(28) Ibid.

(29) <u>Speech of Hon. Israel Washburn, Jun., of Maine</u>, delivered in the House of Representatives, May 19, 1860 (<u>Congressional Globe</u>).

(30) Ibid.

(31) Ibid.

(32) Ibid.

(33) Ibid.

(34) Russel B. Nye, <u>Fettered Freedom</u> (East Lansing, Michigan: Michigan State University Press 1949) in Kenneth M. Stampp's <u>The Causes of the Civil War</u> (Prentice Hall, Inc., Englewood Cliffs, New Jersey 1965), page 6.

(35) Ibid, Stampp, page 7. The list includes the following: The fugitive slave law of 1793; the Creek and Negro troubles in Fl,orida in 1815; the Seminole War; the maintenance of slavery in the District of Columbia; the refusal to recognize Haiti; the attempts to recapture fugitive slaves from Canada; the suppression of petitions in the House after 1836; the attacks on free speech and press . . ..

Chapter Ten
"The Washburn Brothers When the War Began"

(1) Lilian Washburn, <u>My Seven Sons</u> (Falmouth Publishing House, Portland, Maine, 1940).

(2) Ibid.

(3) <u>Samuel Benjamin Washburn Diary</u>, March 16, 1861 (Washburn Memorial Library, Livermore, Maine).

(4) Washburn, Julia Chase, <u>Genealogical Notes of the Washburn Family</u> (Press of Journal Company, Lewiston, Maine) and Washburn, Brenton P., <u>The Washburn Family in America</u> (Privately printed, 1983).

(5) Author's interview of Barbara Dunn Hitchner, Orono, Maine.

(6) Shipman, Gordon, <u>Handbook for Family Analysis</u> (Lexington Books, D.C. Heath and Company, Lexington, Massachusetts 1982), page 136.

(7) W.D. Washburn to Sidney Washburn, Bangor, Maine, April 12, 1859 (Washburn Memorial Library, Livermore, Maine).

(8) Ibid, April 22, 1859 (Washburn Memorial Library, Livermore, Maine).

(9) E.B. Washburne <u>Diary Collection</u> (Harvard University Archives).

(10) Israel Washburn, Sr., to E.B. Washburne, Livermore, July 2, 1852 (Washburn Memorial Library, Livermore, Maine).

(11) Bayley, John, <u>Sons and Brothers</u>. Article in the <u>New York Review of Books</u>, volume XLI, Number 3, February 3, 1994), page 22.

Chapter Eleven
"The Washburns At War"

(1) Dwight G. Anderson, <u>Abraham Lincoln, the Quest for Immortality</u> (Alfred A. Knopf, New York 1982), page 170.

(2) "Grant's First Newspaper Controversy," <u>Ulysses S. Grant Association Newsletter 6</u> , no. 2 (January 1969): 14, quoted from <u>U.S. Grant: The Man and the Image</u> by James G. Barber (published by the National Portrait Gallery, Smithsonian Institution, Washington City in association with Southern Illinois University Press, Carbondale and Edwardsville, 1985), page 14.

(3) Israel Washburn to Hannibal Hamlin, December 20, 1862 (Washburn Memorial Library, Livermore, Maine).

(4) <u>Maine</u>, edited by Louis Clinton Hatch (New Hampshire Publishing Company, Somersworth, 1974), pages 473-474.

(5) Abraham Lincoln to E.B. Washburne, January 29, 1859. "His (Washburn's) objection to the Oregon constitution because it excludes free Negroes, is the only [statement] I wish he had omitted." The reference is to Israel Washburn's speech on the Republican Party in the House of Representatives delivered January 10, 1859. <u>The Collected Works of Abraham Lincoln</u>, volume III, Roy P. Basler, Editor (Rutgers University Press, New Brunswick, New Jersey, 1953).

(6) Israel Washburn to Hannibal Hamlin, December 20, 1862 (Washburn Memorial Library, Livermore, Maine).

Chapter Twelve
"Contending Forces Seeking Peace"

(1) February 2, 1864, President Lincoln and William Seward, Secretary of State, met with Alexander H. Stephens, Vice President of the Confederacy, R.M.T. Hunter, and J.A. Campbell on the Union transport *River Queen* in Hampton Roads.

(2) Ibid, Hunt, pages 221-223.

(3) Ibid, Hunt, page 223.

(4) General John B. Gordon, <u>Reminiscences of the Civil War</u> (Charles Scribners' Sons, N.Y., 1904), pages 451-452.

(5) From T.S. Eliot poem <u>The Waste Land</u>:
> April is the cruellest month, breeding
> Lilacs out of dead land, mixing
> Memory and desire, stirring
> Dull roots with spring rain.

(6) Francis Washburn did not recover.

(7) E.B. Washburne to Adele Washburne, Sunday April 16, 1865 (Washburn Memorial Library, Livermore, Maine).

(8) Johnson was President. Hannibal Hamlin might have been but for the disappointing victory of the Tennessee Senator. Charles Hamlin, son of Lincoln's first vice president, wrote W.D. Washburn saying it was an established fact "that Lincoln desired my father's renomination in '64 and was disappointed at the nomination of Johnson." Hamlin wrote in the same letter that "the Radical Republicans offered him the nomination for president against Lincoln in '64." Hannibal Hamlin of course declined. Charles Hamlin to Senator Washburn from Bangor, Maine, April 4, 1896 (Washburn Memorial Library, Livermore, Maine).

(9) Roy P. Basler, <u>The Lincoln Legend</u> (Octagon Press, N.Y. 1935), page 296.

(10) Ibid, Turner, page 291.

(11) Speech of Hon. E.B. Washburne, Illinois, in the House of Representatives May 29, 1860 (<u>Appendix to the Congressional Globe</u>).

(12) Victor B. Howard, <u>The Illinois Republican Party</u>, Part II, <u>The Party Becomes Conservative, 1855-1856</u> (<u>Journal of the Illinois State Historical Society</u>, vol. LXIV/Number 3/Autumn 1971), page 293.

(13) Justin G. Turner and Linda Levitt, <u>Mary Todd Lincoln</u> (Alfred A. Knopf, New York 1972), page 245.

(14) Ibid, Turner. Mrs. James (Sally) H. Orne of Philadelphia. Her husband was a heavy contributor to the Republican party and to the war effort. Page 549.

(15) Ibid, Turner, page 528.

(16) Mary Lincoln to E.B. Washburne, December 9, 1865 (Washburn Memorial Library, Livermore, Maine).

(17) Mary Lincoln to E.B. Washburne, December 15, 1865 (Washburn Memorial Library, Livermore, Maine).

(18) Ibid, Turner, page 716.

(19) Family Letters, volume 37 (Washburn Memorial Library, Livermore, Maine).

(20) When the number of loyal Southerners amount to 10 percent of the votes cast in 1860, this minority could establish a state government.

(21) Charles Sumner to Israel Washburn, Jr., Boston, July 13, 1865 (Washburn Memorial Library, Livermore, Maine).

(22) William Gillette, Retreat from Reconstruction (Louisiana State University Press, Baton Rouge 1979.) Page 364.

(23) Ibid, page 197.

(24) Michael Les Benedict classifies E.B. Washburne as a "consistent conservative," while Hans L. Trefousse classifies Washburne a radical. The three brothers, Israel, Elihu and Cadwallader rank themselves radical; Israel as a "conscience Whig." Michael Les Benedict, A Compromise Principle, W.W. Norton and Company, New York 1974. Hans L. Trefousse, The Radical Republicans (Louisiana State University Press, Baton Rouge 1968).

(25) E.B. Washburne to Adele Washburne, Memphis, Wednesday morning, May 24, 1866 (Washburn Memorial Library, Livermore, Maine).

(26) Letterbook 49, Letter No. 9824. D. Richards, Florida, May 7, 1866, to E.B. Washburne (Washburn Memorial Library, Livermore, Maine).

(27) Letterbook 49, Letter No. 9848. D. Richards, Florida, to E.B. Washburne, May 12, 1866 (Washburn Memorial Library, Livermore, Maine).

(28) Ben C. Truman, private secretary of President Johnson, had been sent into the South to "examine into the doings of the commissioners" and report. Richards said Truman was present for three days and "did not see a *sober* day," --that he did not spend time with Union men, --and that he was fond of "good wine, champagne suppers and the women." Letterbook 49, Letter No. 9451. D. Richards, Fernandina, Fla., to E.B. Washburne, June 7, 1866 (Washburn Memorial Library, Livermore, Maine).

Chapter Thirteen
"Revolutionary Moves by Radicals"

(1) Trefousse, Hans L., The Radical Republicans (Louisiana State University Press, Baton Rouge 1968).

(2) Ibid, Benedict.

(3) E.B. Washburne to Adele Washburne, March 11, 1866 (Washburn Memorial Library, Livermore, Maine).

(4) Nelson, Russell K., The Early Life and Congressional Career of Elihu B. Washburne, Ph..D. thesis, 1954, the University of North Dakota.

(5) See Chapter Two of this work for reference to O.O.D. Howard and Israel Washburn, Sr.

(6) Pall Mall Gazette, February 22, 1866, copied from William S. McFeeley's Yankee Stepfather.

(7) W.E.B. DuBois, quoted from Staughton Lynd is Reconstruction (Harper and Row, Publishers, New York 1967), page 8.

(8) Benedict, Michael Les, A Compromise of Principle, W.W. Norton and Company, New York 1974. Benedict has been used to list the egregious actions taken by President Johnson which led to the effort to impeach him.

(9) Meyer, Howard N., The Amendment That Refused to Die (Beacon Press, Boston 1973).

(10) "Young Rapid" is the nickname given to William D. Washburn by the brothers, inferring that he was like Elihu who advanced "rapidly."

(11) Stanley P. Hirshson, Farewell to the Bloody Shirt (Indiana University Press, Bloomington 1962), page 223.

(12) Ulysses S. Grant to E.B. Washburne (Library of Congress).

(13) E.B. Washburne, Galena, June 10, 1863, to "Dear Bro" (Washburn Memorial Library, Livermore, Maine).

(14) It is regrettable that only a few letters written to Charles Ames Washburn from E.B.

Washburne are extant.

(15) Charles Ames Washburn to E.G. Washburne from Corrientis, June 1, 1866 (Washburn Memorial Library, Livermore, Maine).

(16) Charles Ames Washburn to E.B. Washburne, June 3, 1864, from Asuncion (Washburn Memorial Library, Livermore, Maine).

(17) Representative John Lynch to Israel Washburn, Jr., February 12, 1866 (Washburn Memorial Library, Livermore, Maine).

(18) Jeannette Garr married C.C. Washburn on January 1, 1849. Puerperal fever followed the birth of the second child. Mrs. Washburn died at Brookline, Massachusetts, March 12, 1909.

(19) Richard Nelson Current, Those Terrible Carpetbaggers (Oxford University Press, New York 1988).

Chapter Fourteen
"The Destruction of Reconstruction"

(1) Stephens, Alexander H., A Constitutional View, quoted from The Causes of the Civil War, Kenneth M. Stampp, Editor (Prentice-Hall, Inc., Englewood Cliffs, New Jersey 1965), page 38.

(2) See the current work, Chapter Four, page 56.

(3) Sumner, Charles, Our Domestic Relations, or, How to Treat the Rebel States (The Atlantic Monthly, Ticknor and Fields, Boston, Massachusetts, volume XII, 1863).

(4) Washburn, Israel, Jr., The Logic and the End of the Rebellion (Universalist Quarterly and General Review, Thomas B. Thayer, Editor, Boston: Tompkins and Company, Volume I, 1864), page 16.

(5) Foner, Eric, Reconstruction, America's Unfinished Revolution (Harper and Row, Publishers, New York 1988). Page 177.

(6) E.B. Washburne to Adele Washburne, January 7, 1866 (Washburn Memorial Library, Livermore, Maine).

(7) Andrew Johnson to E.B. Washburne, January 15, 1858 (Washburn Memorial Library, Livermore, Maine).

(8) Ibid, Foner, page 178.

(9) Ibid, Hunt, page 237.

(10) Letterbook 49, Letter No. 9935, Library of Congress, William E. Chandler to E.B. Washburne.

(11) Memphis Riots and Massacres, 1866 (Reprinted by Mnemosyne Publishing Co., Inc., Miami, Florida, 1969), 394 pages.

(12) Shofner, Jerrell H., Nor Is It Over Yet (The University Presses of Florida, Gainesville 1974), page 177.

(13) Letterbook 49, Letter No. 9824, E.B. Washburne Collection, Library of Congress.

(14) Ibid, Letterbook 49, Letter No. 4898.

(15) Galena Gazette, May 10, 1876.

(16) New York Times, Monday, September 16, 1867, page one, column two, A Conversation with Hon. E.B. Washburn [sic].

(17) Ibid, Letterbook 53, Letter No. 10786.

(18) Ibid, Letterbook 53, Letter No. 10786.

(19) Ibid, Letterbook 53, Letter No. 10825.

(20) D. Richards to E.B. Washburne, February 2, 1868, quoted from Jerrell H. Shofner, Nor Is It Over Yet (University Presses of Florida, Gainsville 1974).

(21) Davis, William Watson, The Civil War and Reconstruction in Florida, page 496.

(22) Litwack, North of Slavery, page 99.

Chapter Fifteen
"Two Galena Townsmen Climb to the Top"

(1) Washburne arranged for U.S. Grant to visit Boston, Massachusetts; Dubuque, Iowa; St.

Louis, Missouri; New York City; and the South.

(2) C.C. Washburn to E.B. Washburne, September 5, 1867 (Washburn Memorial Library, Livermore, Maine).

(3) *Galena Weekly Gazette*, February 7, 1879, page 4, column 6. Taken from an interview with Charles A. Washburn in the *Philadelphia Press*.

(4) Nevins, Allan, Hamilton Fish, the Inner History of the Grant Administration (Frederick Ungar Publishing Co., New York 1936, volume I), page 129.

(5) Ibid, Letters, U.S. Grant to E.B. Washburne, March 4, 1867.

(6) General Grant's Letters to a Friend, edited by James Grant Wilson (T.Y. Crowell and Company, New York and Boston 1897).

(7) General Grant and E.B. Washburne, interview with Charles A. Washburn in Philadelphia Press, reprinted in the Galena Weekly Gazette, February 7, 1879, page 4, column 6.

(8) It appears that Washburne forgot that when the Reconstruction Act included a section indicating that the general commanding the army should name commanders of the five districts in the South, General Grant indicated he preferred to have the designation left to the President. Despite his deference to the office of president in this matter, Congress passed a bill forbidding the commander-in-chief to issue orders to the army except through the general in command.

(9) *New York Times*, Monday, September 16, 1867, page 1, column 2, A Conversation with Hon. E.B. Washburn [sic]. Copied from the Boston Commonwealth.

(10) Ibid, McFeely, page 270.

(11) Ibid, Hunt, page 237.

(12) U.S. Grant to E.B. Washburne, Galena, Illinois, September 23, 1868, Ibid, Letters.

(13) Ibid, McFeely, page 284.

(14) Ibid, Woodward, page 399.

(15) White, Horace, The Life of Lyman Trumbull (Houghton Mifflin Co. 1913), page. 334.

(16) These statements were attributed to Henry Adams and George Julian.

(17) Ridge, Martin, Ignatius Donnelly (the University of Chicago Press 1962), page 112.

(18) Nevins, Allan, The Inner History of the Grant Administration (Dodd, Mead and Company, New York 1936), page 404.

Chapter Sixteen
"Moving Into New Arenas"

(1) Howe, Daniel Walker, The Political Culture of the American Whigs (the University of Chicago Press, Chicago and London 1979).

(2) Hess, Stephen, An American in Paris (American Heritage, February 1967, Volume XVIII, Number 2). Emphasis added.

(3) Kendrick, Benjamin B., The Journal of the Joint Committee of Fifteen on Reconstruction, submitted in partial fulfilment of the requirements for the degree of Doctor of Philosophy, New York 1914.

(4) Horace White, The Life of Lyman Trumbull (Houghton Mifflin, Boston 1913).

(5) Blumenthal, France and the United States (University of North Carolina Press, Chapel Hill 1970), page ix.

(6) E.B. Washburne, Palace of Compiègne, to Ellen Washburn, November 14, 1869 (Washburn Memorial Library, Livermore, Maine).

(7) E.B. Washburne to Adele Washburne, Paris, July 19, 1870 (Washburn Memorial Library, Livermore, Maine).

(8) E.B. Washburne to Adele Washburne, Paris, evening, October 16, 1870 (Washburn Memorial Library, Livermore, Maine).

(9) Ibid.

(10) Treilhard to Favre, December 1870.

(11) Williams, George Huntston, American Universalism Journal of the Universalist Historical Society, Volume IX, 1971.

(12) Ibid, Washburne, page 44.

(13) Ibid, pages 44-45.

(14) Ibid, page 46.

(15) It is interesting to note that Jules Favre, a legislator admired by Washburne, blamed the government for contributing to spy scares by prohibiting departure of Germans owing military service, thus retaining large numbers of Germans to alarm the populace. John Ezekiel Lancaster, France and the United States, 1870-71: Diplomatic Relations During the Franco-Prussian War and the Insurrection of the Commune. Requirement for the Degree of Doctor of Philosophy, Athens, Georgia 1972, footnote page 240.

Chapter Seventeen
"Voila! Another Revolution"

(1) Goncourt, Edmond and Jules, brothers to whom "humanity is as pictorial a thing as the world it moves; they do not search further than 'the physical basis of life'; and they find everything that can be known of that unknown force written visibly upon the sudden faces of little incidents, little expressive moments" (Encyclopedia Britannica, Vol. 10, the University of Chicago, 1910, page 513) Wandering through the city streets of Paris day-by-day, they recorded such "incidents [and] little expressive moments."

(2) Ibid, page 219.

(3) Ibid, page 224.

(4) Karl Marx and V.I. Lenin, The Civil War in France: The Paris Commune (International Publishers, New York 1940).

(5) Ibid, Horne, page 92.

(6) Alistair Horne, The Fall of Paris (Penguin Books, 1965).

(7) Ibid, Horne, page 406.

(8) Ibid, Horne, 423.

(9) Ibid, Washburne, Vol. II, pages 184-185.

(10) Emphasis added.

(11) Otto Bismarck to Adele Washburne, January 3, 1871 (Washburn Memorial Library, Livermore, Maine).

(12) E.B. Washburne to Ellen Washburn, March 4, 1874 (Washburn Memorial Library, Livermore, Maine).

Chapter Eighteen
"Weighing and Balancing"

(1) Obid, Howe, Introduction, page 5.

(2) Elisha P. Douglass, The Coming of Age of American Business (The University of North Carolina Press, Chapel Hill, 1971), page 288.

(3) Ralph Waldo Emerson, The Complete Essays and Other Writings of Ralph Waldo Emerson (The Modern Library, New York, published 1940). The quotation is from Emerson's essay on The American Scholar, page 58.

(4) Ibid, page 2.

(5) Ibid, page 3.

(6) George C. Bates to E.B. Washburne, June 21, 1878. Washburne Collection Library of Congress. Quoted from Frye, page 66.

(7) Blaine of Maine had been Governor Israel Washburn, Jr's., aide in Washington during the Civil War.

(8) Ibid, Hunt, page 278.

(9) Ibid, Hunt, pages 280-281.

Chapter Nineteen
"The Agony of Being Less"

(1) "The entrance of a third party into the boundaries of a dyad produces the phenomenon of

triangulation, with the third entity often reducing the feelings of intimacy for which the original members of the dyad continue to yearn." Quoted from Unmasking Another Villain in Conrad Aiken's Autobiographical Dream by Kenneth Womack in Biography, Vol. 19, Number 2, Spring 1996. The reference is to Charles P. Bernard and Ramon Garrido Corrales, The Theory and Technique of Family Therapy, Springfield, Illinois: Charles C. Thomas, 1979.

(2) Anna Makolkin, Probing the Origins of Literary Biography, page 87.

(3) Martha Washburn to C.C. Washburn, December 7, 1848 (Washburn Memorial Library, Livermore, Maine).

(4) C.A. Washburn to E.B. Washburne, Orono, Maine, January 9, 1847, "I care not how soon this miserable life is at an end" (Washburn Memorial Library, Livermore, Maine).

(5) John Demos, The American Family in Past Time in The American Scholar, Summer 1974, Vol. 43, No. 3, pages 422-446.

(6) C.A. Washburn to E.B. Washburne, January 9, 1847 (Washburn Memorial Library, Livermore, Maine).

(7) R.W. Brush to E.B. Washburne, December 15, 1860 (Washburn Memorial Library, Livermore, Maine).

Chapter Twenty
"The Vagabond Prince"

(1) Chivalric was a term used with sarcasm by northerners. Southerners had the reputation of being generous, honorable, knightly, and chivalrous. Republicans, with the kind of sarcasm for which Charles Ames Washburn was notable, made it a swear word.

(2) Owen Barfield, History in English Words (London 1954), page 166.

(3) Charles Washburn's brother, Israel Washburn, Jr., launched the Republican party in 1854. His brother, Elihu Washburne, was a party organizing the Republican party in Illinois.

(4) Republicans at that period in our history favored "free men and free labor," indicating Republican opposition to the introduction of slaves outside the bloc of Southern states. The sentiment of the majority of voters in California at the time Washburn was editing San Francisco newspapers favored slavery and championed segregation.

(5) C.A. Washburn to E.B. Washburne, February 22, 1861 (Washburn Memorial Library, Livermore, Maine).

(6) C.A. Washburn to E.B. Washburne, October 5, 1856 (Washburn Memorial Library, Livermore, Maine).

(7) Washburn left San Francisco on Monday evening, May 5, 1856.

(8) Ibid, Stampp, page 221.

Chapter Twenty-One
"The Field of Battle, San Francisco"

(1) Lilian Washburn, My Seven Sons (privately published).

(2) In the San Francisco Daily Times, December 16, 1859, Modern Chivalry (California State Library, Sacramento, California).

(3) In the San Francisco Daily Times, January 7, 1860, The Senatorship (California State Library, Sacramento, California).

(4) Lately Thomas, Between Two Empires, the Life Story of California's First Senator, William McKendree Gwin (Houghton, Mifflin Co., Boston, 1969), page 236.

(5) San Francisco Daily Times, Thursday Morning, May 26, 1859.

(6) Ibid, Friday Morning, September 23, 1859.

(7) Charles, friendly with the now dead Senator, was nonetheless critical of him. Broderick, Charles believed, made terms with his unholy nemesis, William McKendree Gwin, enabling Gwin to continue in the office of United States Senator. After Broderick's life had been taken, Charles wrote that he had now "atoned for that error with his blood."

(8) Daily Evening Bulletin, Friday Evening, September 16, 1859. The letter was signed by

"Vindex," but a later letter to the Bulletin explained in greater detail what purports to be Broderick's feelings about Washburn was signed by Charles A. Sumner.

(9) Captain SH[sic] Dubois, to Mr. C.A. Washburn, San Francisco, September 21, San Francisco *Daily Times*, Thursday Morning, September 22, 1859.

(10) The same thing happened in the duel between Washburn and Washington. Washburn's bullet struck the ground in front of his opponent.

(11) Ibid, Saturday Morning, September 17, 1859.

(12) Ibid, Friday Morning, September 16, 1859.

(13) The *Daily Evening Bulletin*, Wednesday Evening, September 14, 1859, editor James Simonson.

(14) Among the seven Washburn brothers, Elihu was the one who always added the "e".

(15) Quoted in Gaillard Hunt's Israel, Elihu and Cadwallader Washburn (Da Capo Press, New York, page 191. 1969 reprint.

(16) Washburn Memorial Library, Livermore, Maine.

(17) San Francisco *Daily Times,* Friday Morning, February 10, 1860.

(18) Hubert Howe Bancroft, The Works of Hubert Howe Bancroft, Vol. XXIV, History of California, Vol. VI (Published at Santa Barbara by Wallace Hebbert, 1970).

Chapter Twenty-Two
"Victory"

(1) Charles felt Broderick, had he lived, would have switched his loyalty to the Republican party bringing many of his followers with him.

(2) The Republican Party in California, 1856-1868, by Gerald Stanley 1973.

(3) Ibid, June 2, 1859.

(4) Ibid.

(5) Gaillard Hunt, Israel, Elihu and Cadwallader Washburn (Da Capo Press, New York 1969), page 30.

(6) Israel Washburn, Jr., Nebraska-Kansas Speech in the House of Representatives (Congressional Globe, April 7, 1854).

(7) Oliver Wendell Holmes, The Professor at the Breakfast Table, page 104.

Chapter Twenty-Three
"Jobless for Six Months"

(1) C.A. Washburn to E.B. Washburne, January 3, 1861 (Washburn Memorial Library, Livermore, Maine).

(2) C.A. Washburn to C.C. Washburn, August 1860 (Washburn Memorial Library, Livermore, Maine).

(3) J.F. Hoyt to E.B. Washburne, January 19, 1861 (Washburn Memorial Library, Livermore, Maine).

(4) The post of ambassador to France which Charles' brother, Elihu, was later assigned by Ulysses S. Grant.

(5) Ibid.

(6) Ibid, C.A. Washburn to C.C. Washburn.

(7) C.A. Washburn to E.B. Washburne, April 28, 1861 (Washburn Memorial Library, Livermore, Maine),

(8) Although the letter offering Washburn the post in Paraguay is dated June 13, the Register of the Department of State (Washington: Government Printing Office, 1874) gives the date of Washburn's commission as June 8, 1861. From a letter to T.A. Webb from L. Robert Hughess, February 8, 1974.

(9) C.A. Washburn to E.B. Washburne, New York, July 27, 1861 (Washburn Memorial Library, Livermore, Maine).

(10) Ibid.

(11) Ibid.

(12) Ibid.

(13) C.A. Washburn to E.B. Washburne, Hotel du Louvre, Paris, August 11, 1861 (Washburn Memorial Library, Livermore, Maine).

(14) Ibid.

(15) Ibid.

Chapter Twenty-Four
"Off to Paradise"

(1) C.A. Washburn to E.B. Washburne, February 22, 1861 (Washburn Memorial Library, Livermore, Maine).

(2) C.A. Washburn's memory was not correct. E.B. Washburne was considered to be the President's right hand, and he preferred Washburne as Speaker of the House over Schuyler Colfax who was elected.

(3) C.A. Washburn to E.B. Washburne, June 6, 1861 (Washburn Memorial Library, Livermore, Maine).

(4) Department of State, Washington, D.C., 9 July, 1861, to Charles A. Washburn.

(5) Ibid.

(6) Gilbert Phelps, Tragedy of Paraguay (St. Martin's Press, New York 1975). "In 1864, Paraguay was to most Europeans and North Americans a tiny and almost completely unknown republic--somewhere in the middle of the vast South American sub-continent," page xii.

(7) The San Francisco Daily Times, Monday Morning, August 6, 1859, editorial entitled, Neither Native-born nor Naturalized Protected.

(8) C.A. Washburn to E.B. Washburne, March 3, 1862 (Library of Congress, Washington, D.C.).

(9) Harris Gaylord Warren, Paraguay An Informal History (University of Oklahoma Press, Norman 1949), page 151.

(10) Ibid, Washburn, volume II, page 229.

(11) Thomas Carlyle praised Dictator Francia, for which C.A. Washburn excoriated Carlyle. The record is replete of the dictator's inhumanity.

(12) Ibid, Washburn, volume I, page 287.

(13) The Diplomatic Career of Charles Ames Washburn, United States Minister to Paraguay, 1861-1868, by Henry Stanley Kolakowski, Jr., St. Bonaventure, New York, 1956.

(14) No. 2, Legation of the United States, Asuncion, Paraguay, November 30, 1861, C.A. Washburn to William H. Seward.

(15) Ibid.

(16) Ibid.

(17) Ibid.

Chapter Twenty-Five
"Work Begins"

(1) Ibid, page 130.

(2) Ibid, page 66.

(3) R.W. Emerson, "there is properly no History; only biography." In this sense I have suggested that the dictators are the history of Paraguay before and during the time Charles A. Washburn was the U.S. Representative to the country. Anna Makolkin expressed a similar opinion in regard to Plutarch, who insisted he "was not writing histories but lives."

(4) Ibid, page 184.

(5) Henry Lyon Young, Regent of Paraguay (Anthony Blond, publisher, 1966) page 9.

(6) C.A. Washburn to E.B. Washburne, October 5, 1862 (Washburn Memorial Library, Livermore, Maine).

(7) Ibid, Washburn, volume I, page 468.

(8) Gilbert Phelps, Tragedy of Paraguay (St. Martin's Press, NY 1975), page 34.

(9) Ibid, Charles to Elihu, October 5, 1862.

(10) Washburn, volume I, page 375.

(11) C.A. Washburn to His Excellency Francisco Sanchez, Minister for Foreign Affairs, Legation of United States, Asuncion, January 11, 1862 (Washburn Memorial Library, Livermore, Maine).

(12) C.A. Washburn to E.B. Washburne, October 5, 1862 (Washburn Memorial Library, Livermore, Maine).

(13) Ibid, Young, page 24.

(14) Ibid, page 29.

(15) Harris Gaylord Warren, Paraguay (University of Oklahoma Press, Norman, Oklahoma), page 200.

(16) Washburn, volume I, page 479.

(17) C.A. Washburn to E.B. Washburne, February 5, 1862. Charles had been in Paraguay fewer than four months when he made this observation.

(18) Harris Gaylord Warren reported that Carlos Lopez' first choice of his sons to call Congress together after his death was Benigno, not Francisco, but that the latter forced the old man to name him. Paraguay (University of Oklahoma Press, Norman 1949), page 198.

(19) Ibid, Washburn, vol. II, pages 51-52.

(20) Washburn had been able also to interest the administration in American business, as a result of which the Department of State wrote to assure Charles and Lopez that railroad cars could be procured and expressed pleasure in "an increase of commerce beneficial to both countries." --Department of State, Washington, 6 July 1863, to Charles A. Washburn, Esq.

(21) C.A. Washburn to His Excellency Francisco Sanchez, Foreign Minister, March 29, 1862 (Washburn Memorial Library, Livermore, Maine).

(22) C.A. Washburn to E.B. Washburne, February 6, 1864 (Washburn Memorial Library, Livermore, Maine).

(23) As soon as Lopez was inaugurated he set about changing his government from a Republic to an Empire. He changed his name from Excellentissimo President to Francisco Primero. The Emperor of Brazil, Don Pedro II, encouraged Lopez to make the change, according to what Washburn says Lopez told him.

(24) It is interesting to realize that a turn-over was indeed realized in France. Charles' brother, Elihu, was Ambassador in 1870 when France became a republic and Elihu was feted by the French in Paris for having been the first foreign representative to recognize the new Republic.

(25) Ernest N. Paolino, The Foundations of the American Empire (Cornell University Press, Ithaca 1973).

(26) Department of State, Washington, January 29, 1864, to Charles A. Washburn, Esq., from William H. Seward.

(27) William H. Seward, Washington, to C.A. Washburn, March 1, 1865.

(28) Phelps, Tragedy of Paraguay, page 185.

(29) C.A. Washburn to E.B. Washburne, Asuncion, June 3, 1864 (Washburn Memorial Library, Livermore, Maine).

(30) Washburn's successor as Minister Resident, M.T. McMahon, published a letter in the New York Evening Post, dated January 14, 1871, in which he wrote "a little one of two or three years . . . was brought to my house . . . almost naked, and presented as the child of Mr. Charles A. Washburn."

(31) C.A. Washburn to E.B. Washburne, Asuncion, July 4, 1863 (Washburn Memorial Library, Livermore, Maine).

(32) W.D. Washburn to A.S. Washburn, April 22, 1859 (Washburn Memorial Library, Livermore, Maine).

(33) Washburn, volume I, page 444.

(34) Sallie Cleaveland to "Sue," Boston, May 16, 1865 (Washburn Memorial Library, Livermore, Maine).

(35) Though Ambassador Washburne rushed back to France from Carlsbad, Henry Blumenthal, A Reappraisal of Franco-American Relations, 1830-1871, page 201, calls the minister's failure to return immediately to Paris "inexcusable;" and Francis X. Gannon, A Study of Elihu Benjamin Washburne: American Minister to France During the Franco-Prussian War and the Commune, pages 68-71, is critical of Washburne for having failed to report on foreign affairs prior to his departure for Carlsbad.

(36) Ibid, vol. II, page 8, and Gilbert Phelps' Tragedy of Paraguay, page 183, "[Washburn] had left Asuncion early in 1865 . . . an odd time to choose for it, perhaps, with Paraguay already at war . . . ."

(37) C.A. Washburn to Sallie Cleaveland, Asuncion, May 21, 1864 (Washburn Memorial Library, Livermore, Maine).

Chapter Twenty-Six
"Washburn Returns"

(1) C.A. Washburn to Captain W.A. Kirkland, U.S. Steamer Wasp, Buenos Aires, December 23, 1865 (Washburn Memorial Library, Livermore, Maine).

(2) C.A. Washburn to Admiral S.W. Godon, Buenos Aires, December 30, 1865 (Washburn Memorial Library, Livermore, Maine).

(3) Later, Seward wrote to say that accepting the invitation would have been quite proper.

(4) Ibid, volume II, page 4.

(5) Ibid, volume II, page 6.

(6) Ibid, Phelps, pages 65-66.

(7) Ibid, Washburn, vol. II, page 120.

(8) C.A. Washburn to James Watson Webb, from Corrientis, July 5, 1866 (Washburn Memorial Library, Livermore, Maine).

(9) C.A. Washburn to J. Watson Webb, October 1, 1866 (Washburn Memorial Library, Livermore, Maine).

(10) Gilbert Phelps, Tragedy of Paraguay (St. Martin's Press, New York 1975, page 65.

(11) " . . . the dignity and honor of the United States will not allow a further detention on the way to your mission under any conceivable circumstances. If, therefore, the obstructions which have been placed in your way by the authorities of the Argentine Republic and Brazil, shall have continued until the arrival of this communication, you will at once return to the United States . . .." --Department of State, Washington, June 27, 1866, Charles A. Washburn, Esq., Asuncion, from William H. Seward.

(12) Ben Macintyre, Forgotten Fatherland (Farrar Straus Giroux, New York, 1992), page 9.

(13) S.W. Godon to Gideon Welles, October 27, 1866. Godon in his letter indicates that Washburn wants to be in Asuncion to assist Lopez in escaping when the allies press him too hard.

(14) Department of State, Washington, June 27, 1866, C.A. Washburn, Esq., Asuncion, from William H. Seward.

(15) A May 20, 1867, letter from the Secretary of State acknowledged that C.A. Washburn had continually called for the investigation of Admiral Godon, and that both Asboth and Webb had filed similar complaints. Four days later, May 24, 1867, Seward in a follow-up letter wrote that Godon could not be condemned "save after due inquiry, which would have to stand in formal charges by you."

(16) While Charles did not have an association with the Emperor, his brother, Elihu, enjoyed a special and similar tie with Napoleon when he became Minister Plenipotentiary to France.

(17) C.A. Washburn to J. Watson Webb, July 5, 1866 (Washburn Memorial Library, Livermore, Maine).

(18) C.A. Washburn to J. Watson Webb, September 5, 1867 (Washburn Memorial Library, Livermore, Maine).

(19) William H. Seward to C.A. Washburn, July 13, 1867.

(20) C.A. Washburn to His Excellency Jose Berges, Minister of Foreign Affairs, November

Chapter Twenty-Seven
"Peace, No"

1) Ibid, J. Watson Webb, page 186.

(2) Ibid, Phelps, page 185

(3) In August 1868 Washburn wrote the Acting Foreign Minister Benitez protesting the use of the word "asylum," but the Resident Minister had written Secretary Seward in October 1867 indicating the likelihood of giving asylum in the legation had the approval of Seward. --No. 75, Department of State, Washington, January 14, 1868, Charles A. Washburn, Esq., from W.H. Seward.

(4) Ibid, Webb, page 186. Of some interest is the fact that Charles' brother, Elihu, when he was Ambassador during the Franco-Prussian War, remained in Paris when the government moved to Versailles. There was no problem with his decision on the part of the French government.

(5) James Manlove was executed the following August 22nd along with 36 other men according to the official register of General Resquin.

(6) Ibid, Phelps, page 211.

(7) Ibid, page 215.

(8) Ibid, page 202.

(9) Ibid, page 252.

(10) Elihu Washburne was the Ambassador to France when Louis Napoleon lost his throne. Washburne was acclaimed when, representing the U.S., he recognized the Republic on September 7, 1870.

(11) Reports to the State Department and letters of exchange between Washburn and Paraguayan ministers.

(12) Quoted from Warren, page 252.

(13) Ibid, Graham, page 239. The quotation is from Graham but the story is included in Washburn's works.

(14) Legation of the United States, Asuncion, July 13, 1868, His Honor Gumesinda Benitez, Acting Minister for Foreign Affairs (Washburn Memorial Library, Livermore, Maine).

(15) Ibid, Washburn, volume II, pages 456-457.

(16) The reader may wonder when the Acting Foreign Minister also lost confidence in his government inasmuch as Benitez, who drew up the charge against Washburn, was arrested and shot as a ringleader.

(17) Legation of the United States, Asuncion, July 14, 1868, His Honor Gumesindo Benitez, Acting Minister for Foreign Affairs (Washburn Memorial Library, Livermore, Maine).

(18) The imprisoned Masterman reported later that he saw "Don Gumesindo Benitez, bareheaded and with naked fettered feet."

(19) C.A. Washburn to Gumesindo Benitez, August 3, 1868.

(20) Ibid, Phelps, page 214.

(21) Alonso Taylor, a British subject in the service of Lopez described his torture in the Cepo Uruguayano. "I sat on the ground with my knees up, my legs were first tightly together, and then my hands behind me with the palms outwards. A musket was then fastened under my knees; six more of them tied in a bunch were then put upon my shoulders and were looped together with a hide rope at one end; they then made a running loop on the other side, from the lower musket to the other, and two soldiers hauling on the end of it forced my face down to my knees and secured it so. The effect was as follows: first the feet went to sleep, and then a tingling commenced in the toes, gradually extending to the knees, and the same in the hands and arms till the agony was unbearable. My tongue swelled up and I thought my jaws would have been displaced. I lost all feeling in one side of my face, for a fortnight afterwards. The suffering was dreadful."

Chapter Twenty-Eight

Chapter Twenty-Eight
"The Sincere Troublemaker"

(1) It is of some interest to know that Orestes Brownson, the brilliant if erratic Universalist, Unitarian turned Roman Catholic, expressed as his opinion that this model of Americans he regarded as "compatible with Catholicism, the Old America, 'republican to the backbone . . .'" --Quoted from Carl F. Krummel, Catholicism, Americanism, Democracy, and Orestes Brownson (American Quarterly, vol. VI, Spring 1954, No. 1), page 23.

(2) C.A. Washburn, Political Evolution (J.B. Lippincott Co., Phila. 1885) page 62.

(3) Abraham Lincoln had done much for Israel, Jr., Elihu, and Cadwallader.

(4) C.A. Washburn to E.B. Washburne, Asuncion, July 4, 1863.

(5) Later, John Conness became a Republican and even nominated Elihu for Vice President at the Republican Convention in Chicago in 1880.

(6) San Francisco Daily Times, Monday Morning, April 29, 1861.

(7) Something which was equally true with Israel, Jr., Elihu and Cadwallader Washburn when they were being considered as nominees for high office.

(8) George Frederick Masterman, Seven Eventful Years In Paraguay (Sampson Low, Son and Marston, London 1870).

(9) Ibid, pages 62-63.

(10) R. Howard Lake, Israel Washburn: A Radical Republican, history paper for course at Colby College, December 5, 1974.

(11) Israel Washburn, Jr., Modern Civilization (Universalist Quarterly, General Review, January 1858), page 25.

(12) E.B. Washburne studied under Joseph Story when at the Harvard Law School.

(13) Washburn Family Journal, January 1, 1869, page 56 (Washburn Memorial Library, Livermore, Maine).

(14) Erik H. Erikson, Young Man Luther: A Study in Psychoanalysis and History (W.W. Norton & Co., N.Y., 1858).

(15) "A Declaration of Principles and Purposes, Adopted by a General Convention of the Whigs in New England," published in Writings and Speeches of Daniel Webster (Boston: Little, Brown, 1903), 3:42. --Quoted from Daniel Walker Howe, The Political Culture of the American Whigs, page 149.

(16) R. McKinley Ormsby in 1859 described what he took to be the ideal Whig personality type. A Whig is "one who has not the gratification of a present passion in view; but crushes out and sacrifices private feelings and interests, and compromises with antagonistic views, to secure the stability of the country, develop its resources, and place its future on a safe and enduring basis. His ideas are not formed on partial views, nor inspired by local interests; but are liberal, enlarged, comprehensive, and are the growth of long-continued and mature reflection." --Quoted from Howe, ibid.

(17) This quotation from Alfred Lord Tennyson from Ballad of Oriana, gave a kind of official name to the Livermore home. From 1869 until the present, the home at Livermore has been referred to as "The Norlands."

(18) Members of the Washburn family at different times refer to Sidney and Charles as the family's "ministers," though neither, of course, became professionals.

Chapter Twenty-Nine
"Excelling In Spite Of It All"

(1) Edith Birkhead, The Tale of Terror, A Study of the Gothic Romance (London, Constable & Co., 1921).

(2) C.A. Washburn, Gomery of Montgomery, page 53.

(3) Charles continued to piece together articles, letters and essays throughout his life expressing his opinion. Sidney once wrote in Volume II of the Family Journal that Charles is "great on conclusions," meaning to say Charles is opinionated.

(4) The Pioneer or California Monthly Magazine, edited by F.C. Ewer, Volume. III, July to

December, 1854 (Published by Le Count and Strong, San Francisco, Cal. 1854).

(5) Charles' brother, Elihu, had for years been an intimate friend of Grant's, but there was a falling out which was intensified in 1880 when both Grant and Elihu Washburne were nominees for president on the Republican ticket.

(6) Walter Russell Mead, Hamilton's Way, World Policy Journal, volume XIII, No. 3, Fall 1996.

(7) "Centralization, with its hundreds of millions for yearly disbursement, must breed carelessness and prodigality, while vast and loose expenditures feed and strengthen centralization." --Hon. Israel Washburn, Jr., Dedication of the Soldier's Monument," at Cherryfield, Maine, July 4, 1874.

(8) Kenneth M. Stampp, The Era of Reconstruction (Indiana University Press, Bloomington 1962), page 220.

(9) Stanley P. Hirshson, Farewell to the Bloody Shirt (Indiana University Press, Bloomington 1962), page 220.

(10) William Washburn's son, Stanley, reported that "the President was so indignant at my father's action in killing this bill that he cut off his patronage for two years. But before he retired as president he congratulated my father on his courage and restored his patronage."

(11) W.D. Washburn to John Brown, February 7, 1891 (Washburn Memorial Library, Livermore, Maine).

(12) W.L. Freeman to De La Barre, Eureka Springs, Arkansas, April 1, 1882.

(13) Daily Times, Saturday Morning, October 1, 1859.

(14) Ibid, October 1, 1859.

(15) Ibid, October 1, 1859.

(16) Ibid, October 11, 1859.

(17) Ibid, December 11, 1860.

Chapter Thirty
"Intimate Glimpses"

(1) C.A. Washburn to Algernon Sidney Washburn, September 6, 1841 (Washburn Memorial Library, Livermore, Maine).

(2) C.A. Washburn to Algernon Sidney Washburn, April 30, 1838 (Washburn Memorial Library, Livermore, Maine).

(3) Solomon E. Asch, in Attitudes edited by Marie Jahoda and Neil Warren (Penquin Books 1966).

(4) Charles' brother Elihu met add talked at length with William Henry Harrison when he was crossing the country on his way to Illinois, and wrote a glowing report about the old warrior.

(5) William W. Freehling, The Road to Disunion (Oxford University Press, New York 1990).

(6) Ibid, page 357.

(7) Although Cadwallader Washburn once used the word "shitten" in one of his letters.

(8) James Knox Polk, 11th President, Democrat, born in North Carolina. As a candidate he demanded control o Oregon and annexation of Texas, and after his election sent Zachary Taylor to the border of Mexico and declared war.

(9) Leon Edel, Writing Lives (W.W. Norton & Company, New York 1984).

Chapter Thirty-One
"Downhill All the Way"

(1) Charles could not hold his family together. Cadwallader, realizing the poor circumstances, provided a modest income for Sallie.

(2) Washburn referred to his machine as a typograph. The first crude typewriter was constructed by Charles C. Sholes in 1867 in Milwaukee, Wisconsin, and was patented in June of 1868.

(3) C.A. Washburn to C.C. Washburn, from Colt's Armory, Hartford, Connecticut, October

6, 1866. In his letter, Charles referred to his typograph as the "great machine."

(4) An attempt was made by correspondence to confirm the claim made about the location of the original model but without success.

(5) Elihu, unlike his brothers and sisters, added the "e" to the family name using the English spelling.

(6) Hinton Rowan Helper, The Impending Crisis of the South, edited by George M. Frederickson (The Belknap Press of Harvard University Press, Cambridge, Massachusetts, 1968), originally published, 1857.

(7) Quoted from John D. Hicks, A Short History of American Democracy (Houghton Mifflin Company 1943), page 357.

Chapter Thirty-Two
"Isolates On A Hilltop"

(1) Perry Miller, The Transcendentalist (Harvard University Press, Cambridge, Massachusetts 1950), page 106.

(2) George Hunston Williams, American Universalism, in The Journal of the Universalist Historical Society (Universalist Historical Society 1971) page 27.

(3) It is a matter of historical interest that Alexander Hamilton's wife traveled to Galena, Illinois, the location of E.B. Washburne's second home. Mrs. Hamilton came to Galena for the purpose of visiting her son, William, who lived in very humble circumstances. Mrs. Hamilton while in Galena stayed at the home of Elihu's wife's family, the Gratiots.

(4) The Works of Orestes Brownson, edited by Henry F. Brownson, 20 volumes, Detroit, 1882-1902.

(5) Ibid, page xii.

(6) The San Francisco Daily Times, March 20, 1860, Free Thought.

(7) The Political Question of the Day, an address delivered by C.A. Washburn at the Broadway Hall, Oakland, 1873.

(8) Rush Welter, The Mind of America 1820-1860 (Columbia University Press, New York 1975), page 34.

(9) Vernon Louis Parrington, Main Currents in American Thought, vol. II (A Harvest Book, Harcourt, Brace and Company, New York 1927), page viii.

(10) Adele Washburne to E.B. Washburne, January 12, 1848 (Washburn Memorial Library, Livermore, Maine).

(11) C.A. Washburn, San Francisco Daily Times, June 15, 1860, Religion and Politics (California State Library, Sacramento, California).

(12) Stewart H. Holbrook, The Yankee Exodus (University of Washington Press, Seattle 1950), page 64.

(13) Ibid, Parrington, page 171.

(14) Israel Washburn, Jr., Modern Civilization (Universalist Quarterly General Review 1858), page 24.

(15) C.A. Washburn, San Francisco Daily Times, October 24, 1859, Plantation Insolence.

(16) Ibid, January 19, 1860, Sectional Prejudices.

(17) Ibid, January 12, 1860, Virginia's Courage.

(18) Quoted from Rush Welter, Ibid, page 5.

(19) Unitarians were even more pronounced using words "onward and upward forever" in their official declarations.

(20) Ibid, Williams, page 27.

(21) Israel Washburn, Jr., Modern Civilization (Universalist Quarterly and General Review, volume I, 1850).

(22) Related to the author by Cadwallader Lincoln Washburn's wife.

(23) Jeffrey Steele, The Representation of the Self in the American Renaissance (The University of North Carolina Press, Chapel Hill 1987), page 25.

(24) The first child to be named after William Drew died, and the last of the Washburn boys

was given the name.

(25) For purposes of clarity I have used "being" while William Drew used the term "God."

(26) W.A. Drew, <u>The Life After Death, from Fifteen Universalist Clergymen</u>, C.W. Quinby, Editor (S.H. Colesworthy, publisher, Portland and Saco 1845).

(27) Quentin Anderson, <u>Practical and Visionary Americans</u> (The American Scholar, Summer 1976), page 407.

(28) Ibid, Steele, page 178.

Chapter Thirty-Three
"Israel Washburn, the Man and the Party"

(1) Hans L. Trefousse, <u>The Radical Republicans</u> (Louisiana State University Press, Baton Rouge), page 74.

(2) Michael Les Benedict, <u>A Compromise of Principle</u> (W.W. Norton and Company, Inc., New York 1974).

(3) Israel Washburn, Jr., <u>Secular and Compulsory Education</u> (The Universalist Quarterly, January 1877).

(4) Kenneth R. Minogue, <u>The Liberal Mind</u> (Vintage Books, New York 1968), page 2.

(5) E.B. Washburne to J. Russell Jones, April 25, 1876 (E.B. Washburne Collection, Library of Congress).

(6) Hannibal Hamlin to Ellen Hamlin, May 20, 1860 (Hamlin Papers, University of Maine Library).

(7) Governor Israel Washburn, Jr., to Major General John A. Dix, October 24, 1862 (Israel Washburn, Jr., Collection, Library of Congress).

(8) Israel Washburn, Jr., <u>Gamaliel Bailey</u> (Universalist Quarterly, July 1868).

(9) Kennebec Journal, March 2, 1855 (Norlands Library).

(10) Ernest Cassara, <u>Hosea Ballou</u> (Universalist Historical Society, Boston and Beacon Press, Boston 1961) page vii.

(11) Samuel F. Hersey to Israel Washburn, Jr., February 5, 1870 (Israel Washburn, Jr., Collection, Library of Congress).

Chapter Thirty-Four
"The Center of Israel Washburn's Thinking"

(1) Israel Washburn, Jr., <u>The Plan for Shortening the Transit</u> (Congressional Globe for the First Session, 32nd Congress: Speeches and Important State Papers, by John C. Rives. New series, vol. 25, City of Washington, printed at the office of John C. Rives, 1852).

(2) Ibid.

(3) Israel Washburn, Jr., <u>On the Compromise As A National Party Test</u>, House of Representatives, May 24, 1852 (Printed at the Congressional Globe office, Washington: 1852).

(4) Ibid.

(5) James Dixon to Israel Washburn, Jr., Hartford, Connecticut, August 5, 1857.

(6) Charles L. Stephenson to E.B. Washburne, March 9, 1864. "The little Gov. is swinging his feet as usual." (E.B. Washburne Collection, Library of Congress).

(7) Ralph Kuykendall, <u>The Hawaiian Kingdom</u> (University of Hawaii Press, Honolulu, 1967), Vol. II.

Chapter Thirty-Five
"Splitting History: Before and After"

(1) Saul Sigelschiffer, <u>The American Conscience, the Drama of the Lincoln-Douglas Debates</u> (Horizon Press, New York 1973).

(2) Ibid, page 29.

(3) Ibid, Hunt, page 30.

(4) <u>Biographical Encyclopedia of Maine of the Nineteenth Century</u> (Metropolitan Publishing

and Engraving Company, Boston 1885).

(5) Speech of Hon. I. Washburn, Jr., of Maine, in the House of Representatives, March 14, 1856, on the Resolution reported by the Committee of Elections, in the <u>Contested Election Case from the Territory of Kansas.</u>

(6) Israel Washburn, Jr., <u>Politics of the Country</u>, House of Representatives, June 21, 1856.

(7) Edwin B. Morgan to Israel Washburn, Jr., November 29, 1859. "Give the brave Virginians 'Hail Columbia' . . . who have been able with the aid of Uncle Sam to capture 17 men and 5 things [meaning 'darkies']" (Israel Washburn, Jr., Collection, Library of Congress).

(8) The Reverend Amory Battles to Israel Washburn, Jr., February 8, 1859 (Israel Washburn Collection, Library of Congress).

(9) A.C. Buffum, April 6, 1854 (Israel Washburn Collection, Library of Congress).

Chapter Thirty-Six
"The Washburns, A Quorum"

(1) Thomas Starr King to Israel Washburn, Jr., July 17, 1856 (Israel Washburn, Jr., Collection, Library of Congress).

(2) Arthur Cole, <u>The Irrepressible Conflict</u> (Quadrangle Books, Chicago, 1934, page 51).

(3) William Appleman Williams, <u>The Roots of the Modern American Empire</u> (Vintage Books, 1970), page 91.

(4) Ibid, Williams, page 130.

(5) Ibid, Cole, page 3.

(6) James Gray, <u>Pine, Stream and Prairie</u> (Alfred A. Knopf, New York 1946) page 65.

(7) George N. Marshall, <u>Challenge of a Liberal Faith</u> (published by Church of the Larger Fellowship, Boston 1975) page 106.

(8) James Dixon, Hartford, Connecticut, to Israel Washburn, Jr., August 5, 1857 (Israel Washburn, Jr., Collection, Library of Congress).

Chapter Thirty-Seven
"Sidney Algernon Washburn"

(1) Samuel Washburn in the Washburn Journal, Vol. III, June 30, 1876, page 134.

(2) Ibid, A.S. Washburn, Vol. I, January 13, 1867, pages 41-42.

(3) A.S. Washburn to C.C. Washburn, October 20, 1875.

(4) E.B. Washburne to C.C. Washburn, June 16, 1876 (E.B. Washburne Collection, Library of Congress).

(5) Ibid, Vol. IV, September 18, 1879, page 116.

(6) W.D. Washburn to A.S. Washburn, December 20, 1869. Sidney Washburn's wife had died three years earlier.

(7) Israel Washburn, Jr., to A.S. Washburn, August 26, 1867 (A.S. Washburn Collection, Duke University).

(8) Ibid, Duke University, C.C. Washburn to A.S. Washburn, April 18, 1850.

(9) Ibid, Duke University, C.C. Washburn to A.S. Washburn, September 11, 1850.

(10) C.A. Washburn to E.B. Washburne, December 29, 1844 (E.B. Washburne Collection, Library of Congress).

(11) Ibid, Duke University, Martha Washburn to A.S. Washburn, October 26, 1839.

(12) E.B. Washburne to C.C. Washburn, April 14, 1852. This letter has a fuller explanation than the letter to Sidney (E.B. Washburne Collection, Library of Congress).

(13) Walter Chadbourne, <u>A History of Banking in Maine</u> (University Press, Orono, Maine 1936).

(14) Lilian Washburn in her book, <u>My Seven Sons</u>, reported that Sidney was President of the First National Bank, but no further evidence has been located to confirm Ms. Washburn's claim.

(15) Private interview of author with Sidney Young, granddaughter of Algernon Sidney

385

Washburn, author's notes.

(16) Ibid, Duke University, Martha Washburn to A.S. Washburn, October 26, 1839.

(17) A.S. Washburn to E.B. Washburne, November 10, 1874 (A.S. Washburn Collection, William R. Perkins Library, Duke University).

(18) Ibid, Duke University, A.S. Washburn to E.B. Washburne, September 22, 1846.

(19) Father, mother and the minister sat down with Cadwallader to pray, at which time a wedding ring was placed on the young boy's finger as an emblem of the family's affection.

(20) Locofocos worked in behalf of hard money and the abolition of monopolies. They felt the depression was caused by fluctuations of paper currency. They sought the separation of government and banking, and wanted a return of gold and silver coins as the ordinary circulating medium.

(21) Ibid, Duke University, Israel Washburn, Sr., to A.S. Washburn, April 11, 1840.

(22) E.B. Washburne to A.S. Washburn, June 10, 1863 (E.B. Washburne Collection, Library of Congress).

(23) Washburn Journal, Vol. I, July 3, 1867. The Washburn home burned to the ground.

(24) Ibid, Journal, Vol. I, June 2, 1867, page 64.

(25) *Galena Gazette*, October 2, 1879.

Chapter Thirty-Eight
"Meet the Man"

(1) A Haverhill, Massachusetts, Men's Club over 100 years old stated such a rule in its original by-laws and illustrates the custom that women, religion and politics are not to be discussed.

(2) The Universalist religion did not demand consent to a creedal stance, and the Universalists tended to desire open discussion of dissimilar religious views.

(3) Elisha P. Douglass, The Coming of Age of American Business (The University of North Carolina Press, Chapel Hill 1971).

(4) Leon F. Litwack, North of Slavery (The University of Chicago Press, Chicago, 1961), page 29.

(5) A classic study revealing of the Washburn type is the work of F.O. Matthiessen, American Renaissance (Oxford University Press, New York, 1941). Even the photograph of Donald McKay as the frontispiece reminds one of the strengths and innate intelligence and the suggested firmness of the business mogul. E. Digby Baltzell, The Protestant Establishment (Random House, New York 1964).

(6) Illustrating how typical Woodman's and Washburn's view of the female was is the following notation by Cyrus: "Had a talk with Lucy this morning about low-necked dresses. She substantially agrees with me. At parties and balls, the majority of them do not like to wear them but follow the fashions set by a few lecherous women who wish thus to attract the attention of gentlemen." Cadwallader's brother, Elihu, made a similar judgment.

(7) Larry Gara, Westernized Yankee, the Story of Cyrus Woodman (the State Historical Society of Wisconsin, Madison: 1956).

(8) In this, Cadwallader was different from his brother. Israel had a close relationship with the church and in correspondence brought up the subject of religion frequently.

(9) Ibid, Baltzell, page 227.

(10) R. McKinley Ormsby, History of the Whig Party (Boston, 1859), pages 372-373.

Chapter Thirty-Nine
"The Wanderer Settles"

(1) Dictionary of Scientific Biography (Charles Scribner's Sons, N.Y. 1974, volume X), page 258.

(2) Frederick Jackson Turner, The Significance of the Frontier in American History, copied from The American Experience, edited by Hennig Cohen (Houghton Mifflin Company,

Boston 1968), Everett S. Lee, The Turner Thesis Re-examined, page 65.

(3) R.H. Dana, Jr., <u>Two Years Before the Mast</u> (P.F. Collier & Son Corporation, New York 1947).

(4) Ibid.

(5) George Woodman to Cyrus Woodman, September 3, 1857 (Cyrus Woodman's Papers, Maine Historical Society, Portland, Maine).

(6) Israel Washburn, Jr., in the Family Journal, February 6, 1869 (Washburn Memorial Library, Livermore, Maine).

(7) <u>The Business Activities of C.C. Washburn</u>, thesis by Clare Leslie Marquette (University of Wisconsin, Madison, Wisconsin).

(8) Ibid, page 115.

(9) <u>Galliard Hunt, Israel, Elihu and Cadwallader Washburn</u> (Da Capo Press, New York 1969).

(10) Martha and Charles Washburn to E.B. Washburne, January 3, 1849 (Washburn Memorial Library, Livermore, Maine).

(11) C. Washburn to Sidney Washburn, Esq., Boston, Massachusetts, May 9, 1850 (Washburn Memorial Library, Livermore, Maine).

(12) C. Washburn to Cyrus Woodman, New York, September 12, 1850 (Washburn Memorial Library, Livermore, Maine).

(13) *Daily Argus and Democrat*, November 11, 1854 (Washburn Memorial Library, Livermore, Maine).

(14) The Fordham Monthly (<u>College Recollections, Fordham in the Fifties</u>, by C.B. Connery, 1953), page 459.

(15) Ibid, Clare Marquette.

Chapter Forty
"On the Seesaw of Mineral Point and Washington D.C."

(1) Cyrus Woodman to C.C. Washburn, March 8, 1856 (Washburn Memorial Library, Livermore, Maine).

(2) Thomas Starr King to Israel Washburn, Jr., Gorham, N.H., July 17, 1856 (Washburn Memorial Library, Livermore, Maine).

(3) Frank Humberstone, Jr., and Anne D. Jenkin, <u>The Homes of Mineral Point</u> (Fountain Press, Mineral Point, Wisconsin 1976).

(4) Ibid.

(5) Frederick Jackson Turner, <u>The Significance of the Frontier in American History</u> (American Historical Association Annual Reports, Washington, D.C., pages 199-227.

(6) Quoted from Richard N. Current, <u>The History of Wisconsin</u>, vol. II (State Historical Society of Wisconsin, Madison, 1976), page 113.

(7) Ibid, vol. II, page 113.

(8) Messrs. Sleeper. Harvey, Baker, Holt, Tallman to C.C. Washburn, Janesville, August 5, 1854 (Washburn Memorial Library, Livermore, Maine).

(9) C.C. Washburn to J.A. Sleeper, August 9, 1854 (Washburn Memorial Library, Livermore, Maine).

(10) E.B. Washburne in his biographical sketch of the life of C.C. Washburn (Washburn Memorial Library, Livermore, Maine).

(11) *The Mineral Point Tribute*, September 13, 1854.

(12) C.C. Washburn, President; C. Woodman, Cashier, October 30, 1854, in The Mineral Point Tribune.

(13) Clare Leslie Marquette, <u>The Business Activities of C.C. Washburn</u>, Ph.D. thesis, University of Wisconsin, June 1, 1940. Also, from The Mineral Point Tribune, November 1, 1854, the following: "The disgraceful attempt of the Nebraska swindlers to throw discredit upon a New England bank because the cashier is a brother of the Republican candidate for Congress has been nipped in the bud . . .."

(14) <u>Our Familiar Songs and Those Who Made Them</u>, by Helen Kendrick Johnson (Arno Press, a New York Times Company, N.Y. 1974).

(15) "A few weeks ago I was moved even to tears on meeting two of the children at Old Squire, one a little, bright black eyed girl . . . and the other a very spright boy about 8 years old." --C.C. Washburne [sic] to E.B. Washburne, December 9, 1854 (Washburn Memorial Library, Livermore, Maine).

(16) Ibid.

(17) Her grave at Brompton Cemetery in London is marked by a life-size marble statue of Pandora, in remembrance of the role she performed in 1881.

(18) Israel Washburn, Sr., to Israel Washburn, Jr., February 6, 1869 (Washburn Memorial Library, Livermore, Maine).

(19) E.B. Washburne to C.C. Washburn, from Paris, October 5, 1876 (Washburn Memorial Library, Livermore, Maine).

(20) Ernest N. Paolino, <u>The Foundations of the American Empire</u> (Cornell University Press, Ithaca and London 1973), page 4.

(21) Ibid, page 27.

(22) John D. Hicks, <u>A Short History of American Democracy</u> (Houghton Mifflin Company, Boston 1943), page 211.

(23) Speech of Hon. C.C. Washburn, of Wisconsin, in the House of Representatives, July 1, 1868.

(24) F.S.C. Northrop, <u>The Meeting of East and West</u> (Collier Books, New York 1946), page 88.

(25) Daniel Walker Howe, <u>The Political Culture of the American Whigs</u> (The University of Chicago Press, Chicago and London, 1979), page 3.

(26) Ibid, page 3.

(27) The Congressional Globe, Thursday, January 24, 1861.

(28) Ibid.

(29) For a time C.C. Washburn permitted the House to add the "e" to his name, but in a few months the "e" was left off and Washburn did not take up the practice again.

(30) James L. Huston, <u>The Panic of 1857 and the Coming of the Civil War</u> (Louisiana State University Press, Baton Rouge 1987).

(31) Ibid, Huston and Kenneth M. Stampp, America in 1857 (Oxford University Press, N.Y. 1990).

(32) "Red-dog" refers to gambling, a betting game. "Wild-cat" is explained by C.C. Washburn as banks issuing money payable at some remote and difficult point of access.

(33) The Financial Embarrassments of the Government of the Country, speech by Hon. C.C. Washburn, of Wisconsin, delivered in the House of Representatives, January 25, 1858.

(34) Washburn had himself been fighting strenuously the "vicious system of bank credits," and he earned the praise of men and institutions for success in fighting George Smith's wildcat banking scheme.

(35) "Whigs generally regarded [the Mexican War] as an unjust war of aggression provoked by our side." <u>Thomas Corwin on The Mexican War</u>, from Howe, Ibid.

(36) Ibid, Huston, page 6.

(37) It is reported that their profits in the banking scheme amounted to between $15,000 and $20,000.

(38) Ibid, Marquette.

(39) Ibid, Marquette, page 217.

Chapter Forty-One
"Warriors Washburn"

(1) The Reverend Elbridge Gerry Brooks, <u>Our Civil War</u> (The Universalist Quarterly 1861).

(2) Ibid, George Emerson.

(3) It was at the Galena town meetings that Congressman Washburne "discovered" Ulysses

S. Grant. Washburne arranged for him to preside at a second town meeting.

(4) James G. Blaine, Twenty Years of Congress: from Lincoln to Garfield (The Henry Bill Publishing Company, Norwich, Connecticut 1884), volume I, page 265.

(5) Earlier, Timothy Howe lost in a bid for the office due to his unwillingness to vote in favor of states' rights. Times and issues changed.

(6) Ibid, Current, page 292.

(7) Representative C.C. Washburn, The Congressional Globe, Thursday, January 24, 1861.

(8) Margaret Leech, Reveille in Washington (Time Incorporated, N.Y.), page 22.

(9) Governor John A. Andrew to Cyrus Woodman, February 16 (Woodman's Diary, Historical Society, Portland, Maine).

(10) Ibid, Current, volume II.

(11) In the meantime, the hand of Elihu Washburne was seen in moving his brother, Cadwallader, upward in the military hierarchy from Colonel to Brigadier General.

(12) C.C. Washburn to E.B. Washburne, Camp Washburn, January 22, 1862 (Washburn Memorial Library, Livermore, Maine).

(13) Shelby Foote, The Civil War (Random House, New York 1958), volume I, page 385.

(14) Edwin C. Bearss, Decision in Mississippi (Published by Mississippi Commission on the War Between the States, Jackson, Mississippi).

(15) C.C. Washburn to E.B. Washburne from Helena [December] (Washburn Memorial Library, Livermore, Maine).

(16) History and Reminiscences of the Second Wisconsin Cavalry Regiment.

(17) Ibid.

(18) C.C. Washburn to U.S. Grant from Yazoo Pass, February 16, 1863.

(19) James B. McPherson to U.S. Grant, Lake Providence, LA, Mar 13, 1863.

(20) Ibid, Hunt, page 342.

(21) Recollections of the Civil War, Some Contemporary Portraits.

(22) Alan White, historian, Greenwood, Mississippi, to the author.

(23) Ibid.

(24) Author's interview with Terry Winschel at Vicksburg.

(25) C.C. Washburn to E.B. Washburne, January 11, 1864 (Washburn Memorial Library, Livermore, Maine).

(26) C.C. Washburn to E.B. Washburne, April 8, 1864 ((Washburn Memorial Library, Livermore, Maine).

(27) The Civil War.

(28) Bearss, Edwin C., Decisions in Mississippi (Mississippi Commission on the War Between the States, Jackson, Mississippi) page 141.

(29) Robert Selph, First With the Most, Forrest (The Bobbs-Merrill Co., Indianapolis, IN 1944), page 336.

(30) One account states that Washburn left "his wife, uniform, hat, boots, saber and private papers behind" (Jack D.L. Holmes, Forrest's 1864 Raid on Memphis, from Civil War Times). General Washburn's wife was in a care home in Massachusetts.

(31) A.J. Smith explained to Major General Washburne that his message led him to believe Forrest would retreat through Holly Springs. Washburn had said in one communication, "I am at a loss to know whether he [Forrest] means to cross at Panola, or go via Holly Springs." In another message it was said brigade leaders "think the enemy will retire via Holly Springs." But Washburn had been more specific in his last message received by General Smith, saying "Forrest left Hernando this morning and will cross the Tallahatchie at Panola. . . . If not intercepted at Panola he should be caught between Yocona and Tallahatchie."

Chapter Forty-Two
"Starting New At Age Forty-Nine"

(1) Clare Leslie Marquette, The Business Activities of C.C. Washburn, thesis, University of Wisconsin 1940.

(2) William C. Edgar, A Story of Industrial Achievement (Publisher not known), page 12.

(3) Elisha P. Douglass, The Coming of Age of American Business (The University of North Carolina Press, Chapel Hill 1971), page 7.

(4) C.C. Washburn to Cyrus Woodman, May 21, 1863 (Woodman Papers).

(5) Ellis B. Usher, Cyrus Woodman: A Character Sketch (Wisconsin Magazine of History, 1918-1919), pages 393-413.

(6) Waubec, sometimes called Waubeek, meaning "metal" or "stone."

Chapter Forty-Three
"The Beginning of Career Three"

(1) C.C. Washburn to Israel Washburn, Jr., June 16, 1839 (Washburn Memorial Library, Livermore, Maine).

(2) E.B. Washburne autobiography, 1874 (Washburn Memorial Library, Livermore, Maine).

(3) Lucile M. Kane, The Waterfall That Built a City (Minnesota Historical Society, St. Paul, 1966), page 51.

(4) Ibid, Marquette, page 234.

(5) "Norlands" was the name given to the Livermore home by Charles Ames Washburn. The word comes from a poem by Tennyson.

(6) The Washburn sisters did not adopt the practice of recording events or thoughts about life. It was the province of the brothers.

(7) Washburn Family Journal, December 23, 1866 (Washburn Memorial Library, Livermore, Maine).

(8) Lines of an obscure English poet, John Dyer (1700-1758), Epistle to a Famous Painter.

(9) Algernon Sidney Washburn in the Washburn Family Journal, July 3, 1867, page 68.

(10) Washburn Family Journal, December 24, 1866 (Washburn Memorial Library, Livermore, Maine).

(11) W.D. Washburn to C.S. Washburn, May 6, 1869 (Washburn Memorial Library, Livermore, Maine).

(12) S.S. Merrill, General Manager the Chicago, Milwaukee & St. Paul R.R.

(13) Ibid, May 6.

Chapter Forty-Four
"The Washburn Regime"

(1) Washburn's protest against serving started with the first invitation in 1854 when asked to permit his name to be entered as a nominee of the new party. As one newspaper account reported it, "In November, 1854, Mr. Washburn against his will, was elected to Congress by the republicans, then just organized." (The clipping does not indicate the source).

(2) Elisha Keyes, The Rise and Fall of Washburn, in an unmarked newspaper article.

(3) Frank A. Flower, The Life of Matthew Hale Carpenter (David Atwood and Company, Madison, Wisconsin 1883), page 254. The Gazette under another editor was the Janesville newspaper which put Washburn's name in nomination when Cadwallader was a candidate for Congress in 1855.

(4) Ibid, page 263.

(5) Horace Rublee to Washburn, December 4, 1873 (Cadwallader C. Washburn Papers, Madison, Wisconsin).

(6) R. Howard Lake, Israel Washburn: A Radical Republican, a paper prepared for a course at Colby College 1974.

(7) Ibid, Current, page 594.

(8) JA Garfield to C.C. Washburn, Washington, D.C., February 12, 1872 (Washburn Memorial Library, Livermore, Maine).

(9) "The men entrusted with the management of the Pacific Road made a bargain with themselves to build the road for a sum equal to about twice its actual cost, and pocketed the profits, which have been estimated at about thirty millions of dollars--this immense sum

coming out of the pockets of the tax payers of the United States." --Edward Winslow Martin, Behind the Scenes in Washington (The Continental Publishing Co. And National Publishing Co. 1873).

(10) "One of the current rumors is to the effect that another of the men concealed in Oake Ames capacious jacket is the Senator from Wisconsin, Mr. Matthew H. Carpenter. . . . At the time of the senatorial election in Wisconsin which was trembling in the balance and the changes seemed to be rather in favor of General Cadwallader C. Washburn, Butler or some other acute person went to Oake Ames saying, 'In case General Washburn is elected to the Senate you have there a persistent and untiring opponent of your Union Pacific Railroad schemes; in case Mr. Carpenter is elected to the Senate you have an untiring persistent friend. $10,000 will settle it but why don't you instantly retain Mr. Carpenter as counselor in the Pacific Railroad and pay him a fee of $10,000?'" (The news source of the article is not known.)

(11) T.O. Howe to C.C. Washburn, November 26, 1874. Actually, Elihu Washburne was nominated for President at the Chicago Republican convention in 1880. The one steady voting group to support Elihu was the Wisconsin contingent. When at last it was seen as impossible for Washburne to be selected, it was the chairman of the Wisconsin committee who cast the Wisconsin votes for James A. Garfield, thereby starting a stampede resulting in Garfield's election.

(12) Matthew Hale Carpenter to Elisha Keyes, Washington, March 3, 1875, ibid, Frank Flower, page 304.

(13) Even the Madison Democrat acknowledged that Governor Washburn had served faithfully. Herman J. Deutsch (Wisconsin Politics of the Early Seventies, the Wisconsin Magazine of History, March 1932, volume 15, No. 3), page 291.

(14) Ibid, Current, pages 595-596. Senator La Follette never forgot Ryan's words and he is said to have repeated them in speeches of his own.

(15) Ibid, Current, page 591.

(16) Horace Rublee, U.S. Legation, Berne, December 4, 1873 (Washburn Memorial Library, Livermore, Maine).

(17) General Washburn and the Republican Party of Wisconsin. The date is February 3, 1879, the newspaper from Milwaukee is not known.

(18) Israel Washburn, Jr., Hallowell, December 22, 1874, to C.C. Washburn (Washburn Memorial Library, Livermore, Maine).

(19) T.O. Howe, November 26, 1874, Washington (Washburn Memorial Library, Livermore, Maine).

(20) John Tipple, The Capitalist Revolution, a History of American Social Thought 1890-1919 (Pegasus, N.Y. 1970).

Chapter Forty-Five
"An Intimate Look Before Closing the Lid"

(1) Cyrus Woodman to C.C. Washburn, May 16, 1878 (Washburn Memorial Library, Livermore, Maine.)

(2) Speech by C.C. Washburn of Wisconsin, U.S. House of Representatives, April 26, 1860 (Widener Library, Harvard University).

(3) W.H.C. Folsom, Fifty Years in the Northwest (Pioneer Press Co., 1888). "Hon. C.C. Washburn was a man of rare nobility of character and possessed of an acute and powerful mind."

(4) John Tipple, The Capitalist Revolution (Pegasus, N.Y., 1970.

(5) Walter Prescott Webb, The Great Frontier (The University of Texas Press, Austin 1951) page 5...

(6) Carl Russell Fish, The Rise of the Common Man (Quadrangle Paperbacks, Chicago 1927) page 328.

(7) Lucile M. Kane, The Waterfall That Built A City (Minnesota Historical Society, St. Paul

391

1966).

(8) In the Kane-Crosby interview, Mr. Crosby said that each year when partners met they told some of the same stories and jokes and laughed at the same places, which I deem ritual activity.

(9) Ibid, Tipple, page 81.

(10) C.C. Washburn to E.B. Washburne, December 9, 1854. (Washburn Memorial Library, Livermore, Maine).

(11) Our Familiar Songs and Those Who Made Them, Helen Kendrick Johnson (Arno Press, a New York Times Company 1974).

(12) Cyrus Woodman to C.C. Washburn, February 8, 1862 (Maine Historical Society, Portland, Maine).

(13) Sketch of Governor C.W. Washburn by E.B. Washburne, 1882 (Wisconsin Miscellaneous Pamphlets, vol. 23, Wisconsin Historical Society).

(14) Albro Martin, James J. Hill and the Opening of the Northwest (Oxford University Press, N.Y. 1976).

(15) Clare Leslie Marquette, The Business Activities of C.C. Washburn, thesis, University of Wisconsin, June 1, 1940).

(16) "I am almost entirely responsible for the conception and building [of] this system of Reservoirs, as all the early appropriations were secured by me when in the House of Reps. In the early 80s." --William Drew Washburn in The Waterfall That Built A City by Lucile M. Kane (Minnesota Historical Society, St. Paul, 1966) page 129.

(17) Pioneer Press, January 25, 1881.

(18) Any of several diseases of the kidney marked by the presence of albumin in the urine.

(19) Ibid.

(20) It was to be Jeannette, the first-born, who would challenge the will after her father died. In an anonymous newspaper article, she claimed her father was deranged when he made out his will. She and her lawyer indicated that when the will was drawn his heirs-in-law were absent, that the will, drawn up with the assistance of Cadwallader's friend, Cyrus Woodman, was understood to be temporary. Jeannette maintained that Washburn had notified Woodman that he, Cadwallader, intended to draw up a new will. Woodman categorically denied the assertion.

(21) Ibid.

(22) W. McMaster to E.B. Washburne, May 26, 1882 (Washburn Memorial Library, Livermore, Maine).

(23) General Steenwyk to E.B. Washburne, October 22, 1881(Washburn Memorial Library, Livermore, Maine).

(24) C.C. Washburn to E.B. Washburne, January 10, 1882, Philadelphia (Washburn Memorial Library, Livermore, Maine).

(25) Remarks taken from In Memoriam, Cadwallader C. Washburn, LL.D. (Report and Collections of the State Historical Society of Wisconsin, vol. IX, David Atwood, State Printer, Madison 1882).

(26) "This monument located just north of the mausoleum at Oak Grove Cemetery was so huge it took 32 horses to draw the rig taking it to the cemetery." (*LaCrosse Morning Chronicle*, May 18, 1882).

ISBN 155212255-7

9 781552 122556